PLAY
CRICKET A

71st

EDITED BY

All statistics by the Ed

D0318287

FOREWORD

A recent article by the unmissable Mike Atherton (Cambridge University, 115 Test caps, 54 as captain, and SJA Cricket Writer of the Year for the last four years) began with the words: 'Cricket. Go figure.' One is tempted to say that if *he* can't work out what is going on, then how can anyone else? And that applies especially to the beleaguered cricket fan. As *Playfair* is now 70 years old, we could chunter on the sidelines and grumble about how things aren't as they should be and once were, but actually the real problem comes when you try to define what cricket *should* be today.

Is it about the longer format? The red-ball game seems everywhere to be under pressure, despite record-breaking Ashes crowds. If a one-sided series can generate that much interest, then surely there is hope. But it needs nurturing, and this summer sees no Test match cricket between 5 June and 1 August. The rhythm of the sporting calendar is something people grow used to. Around the time of publication of this annual, there is always the US Masters, the Grand National and the Boat Race. By the same logic, the first half of July is for Wimbledon, the Open and a Test match, preferably at Lord's. Don't break that rhythm or you lose people.

Test cricket does have two new hopes, in Afghanistan and Ireland. For the first time, *Playfair* contains a players' register for the Irish squad and it can only be a good thing that the game's most challenging format has two new nations. They need to be given plenty of opportunities to make their way. A two-division league format would enable this to happen, as well as ensuring that each series had real meaning. If you split the divisions with six teams in each, according to the ICC rankings Pakistan would slip into Division Two. Would a series between them and Sri Lanka (ranked sixth) not be more compelling to fans if the threat of relegation, or the prospect of promotion, hung over it?

If its long history, and the importance attached to it by the players, preserves red-ball cricket, what does the future hold for the 50-over game? Domestically, the Royal London One-Day Cup doesn't always get much attention, though at least the schedulers have moved it slightly later in the season this year, which should help. At the same time, Eoin Morgan's limited-overs side is England's top-ranked team across all three formats. This has been a case where a clear strategy to build up to the 2019 World Cup is bearing fruit. But how much of this is down to a strong domestic supply line, and how much due to the England team operating as a separate entity?

Meanwhile, T20 is taking over the world. It's instant, it pulls in the crowds, and the TV companies love it, because it is quick and provides lots of wickets and sixes – or should that be maximums? This year, *Playfair* gives more space to this format than ever before, with three new features: an England T20 career records section, plus coverage of the Big Bash and the Kia Super League. The latter competition, with attendance up 44% on the year before, highlights one area of undoubted progress in the game: women's cricket is growing and improving fast. While participation in men's sport – not just cricket, but rugby and even football – declines, women's cricket is thriving. A full house at Lord's last summer saw Heather Knight's England side crowned world champions, and match-winner Anya Shrubsole rewarded with a place on the cover of *Wisden*.

Playfair hasn't gone down the same route. Instead, we celebrate another history-maker: James Anderson, who somehow got to the age of 35 without ever appearing on the front. But in a year when he reached the top of the ICC rankings, achieved his career-best Test figures (7-42 v West Indies at Lord's) and became the first England bowler to take more than 500 Test wickets, his claim couldn't be overlooked any longer.

As ever, during the season there will be regular updates on www.playfaircricket.co.uk which will highlight career bests as they happen and provide mini biographies of any newcomers not already featured in the players' register. Pakistan and India will be the main focus of the summer, but I urge readers to go and watch some cricket when they can. If more people did so, then perhaps we would realise that there isn't so much to figure out after all, as the game will do its own talking.

Ian Marshall
Eastbourne, 14 March 2018

GUIDE TO USING PLAYFAIR

The basic layout of *Playfair* has remained the same for this edition. The Annual is divided into five sections, as follows: Test match cricket, county cricket, international limited-overs cricket (including Twenty20), other cricket (Ireland, universities, IPL, Big Bash, Kia Super League and women's international cricket), and fixtures for the coming season. Each section, where applicable, begins with a preview of forthcoming events, followed by events during the previous year, then come the player records, and finally the records sections.

Within the players' register, there has been some debate with the county scorers over those who are defined as 'Released/Retired', as some players are drafted in for a game or two, and may re-appear in the current season, despite not having a contract as the book goes to press. What I try to do is to ensure that everyone who appeared in last season's games is included somewhere – this way, at least, if they do play in 2018 their details are available to readers. Players' Second XI Championship debuts and their England Under-19 Test appearances are given for those under the age of 25.

In the county limited-overs records in the Register, those records denoted by '50ov' cover any limited-overs game of 50 or more overs – in the early days, each team could have as many as 65 overs per innings. The '40ov' section refers to games of 40 or 45 overs per innings.

Records are provided for all three formats of the women's game – Test, limited-overs and T20 – and there is an England women's register. Fixtures for the Kia Super League are provided.

ACKNOWLEDGEMENTS AND THANKS

As I say every year, this book could not have been compiled without the assistance of many people giving so generously of their time and expertise, so I must thank the following for all they have done to help ensure this edition of *Playfair Cricket Annual* could be written:

At the counties, I would like to thank the following for their help over the last year: Derbyshire – Chris Airey, Tom Skinner and John Brown; Durham – Luke Bidwell and William Dobson; Essex – Alastair Cliffe and Tony Choat; Glamorgan – Andrew Hignell; Gloucestershire – Lizzie Allen and Adrian Bull; Hampshire – Tim Tremlett and Kevin Baker; Kent – Thomas Brown and Lorne Hart; Lancashire – Diana Lloyd and Chris Rimmer; Leicestershire – Jen Wilks and Paul Rogers; Middlesex – Steven Fletcher and Don Shelley; Northamptonshire – Tony Kingston; Nottinghamshire – Helen Palmer and Roger Marshall; Somerset – Spencer Bishop and Gerald Stickley; Surrey – Steve Howes and Keith Booth; Sussex – Colin Bowley and Mike Charman; Warwickshire – Keith Cook and Mel Smith; Worcestershire – Carrie Lloyd and Sue Drinkwater; Yorkshire – Janet Bairstow and John Potter.

Thanks to Alan Fordham for the Principal and Second XI Fixtures, and Philip August for the Minor Counties. Philip Bailey once again provided the first-class and List A career records, and he continues to be a huge help in compiling the book, with an eagle eye for detail.

At Headline, my thanks as always go to Jonathan Taylor for his support and encouragement; Louise Rothwell continues to oversee the production process with huge efficiency; Robert Chilver took charge of the *Playfair* website and ensured it was kept as up-to-date as possible. John Skermer is another long-established member of the team, and did another excellent and speedy job checking the proofs. At Letterpart, the *Playfair* typesetter since 1994 (so this must be their 25th edition), Chris Leggett and Caroline Leggett ensured the book was laid out superbly.

But my biggest thanks go to my family for their help and patience. Computer and Wi-Fi problems drove me indoors from my office for the final push, which meant that daughters Kiri and Sophia had to be quieter than usual when they got back from school – I think we just about made it work! That we did so was especially thanks to my wife Sugra, who made sure that all was calm. Thank you all.

ENGLAND v PAKISTAN

SERIES RECORDS 1954 to 2016
HIGHEST INNINGS TOTALS

England				
England	in England	589-8d	Manchester	2016
	in Pakistan	546-8d	Faisalabad	1983-84
	in UAE	598-9d	Abu Dhabi	2015-16
Pakistan	in England	708	The Oval	1987
	in Pakistan	636-8d	Lahore	2005-06
	in UAE	523-8d	Abu Dhabi	2015-16

LOWEST INNINGS TOTALS

England	in England	130	The Oval	1954
	in Pakistan	130	Lahore	1987-88
	in UAE	72	Abu Dhabi	2011-12
Pakistan	in England	72	Birmingham	2010
	in Pakistan	158	Karachi	2000-01
	in UAE	99	Dubai	2011-12

HIGHEST INDIVIDUAL INNINGS

England	in England	278	D.C.S.Compton	Nottingham	1954
	in Pakistan	205	E.R.Dexter	Karachi	1961-62
	in UAE	263	A.N.Cook	Abu Dhabi	2015-16
Pakistan	in England	274	Zaheer Abbas	Birmingham	1971
	in Pakistan	223	Mohammad Yousuf	Lahore	2005-06
	in UAE	245	Shoaib Malik	Abu Dhabi	2015-16

HIGHEST AGGREGATE OF RUNS IN A SERIES

England	in England	512	(av 73.14)	J.E.Root	2016
	in Pakistan	449	(av 112.25)	D.I.Gower	1983-84
	in UAE	450	(av 90.00)	A.N.Cook	2015-16
Pakistan	in England	631	(av 90.14)	Mohammad Yousuf	2006
	in Pakistan	431	(av 107.75)	Inzamam-ul-Haq	2005-06
	in UAE	380	(av 63.33)	Mohammad Hafeez	2015-16

RECORD WICKET PARTNERSHIPS – ENGLAND

1st	198	G.Pullar (165)/R.W.Barber (86)	Dacca	1961-62
2nd	248	M.C.Cowdrey (182)/E.R.Dexter (172)	The Oval	1962
3rd	267	M.P.Vaughan (120)/G.P.Thorpe (138)	Manchester	2001
4th	233	A.N.Cook (105)/P.D.Collingwood (186)	Lord's	2006
5th	219	P.D.Collingwood (82)/E.J.G.Morgan (130)	Nottingham	2010
6th	166	G.P.Thorpe (118)/C.White (93)	Lahore	2000-01
7th	167	D.I.Gower (152)/V.J.Marks (83)	Faisalabad	1983-84
8th	332	I.J.L.Trott (184)/S.C.J.Broad (169)	Lord's	2010
9th	76	T.W.Graveney (153)/F.S.Trueman (29)	Lord's	1962
10th	79	R.W.Taylor (54)/R.G.D.Willis (28*)	Birmingham	1982

RECORD WICKET PARTNERSHIPS – PAKISTAN

1st	173	Mohsin Khan (104)/Shoaib Mohammad (80)	Lahore	1983-84
2nd	291	Zaheer Abbas (274)/Mushtaq Mohammad (100)	Birmingham	1971
3rd	363	Younus Khan (173)/Mohammad Yousuf (192)	Leeds	2006
4th	322	Javed Miandad (153*)/Salim Malik (165)	Birmingham	1992
5th	248	Shoaib Malik (245)/Asad Shafiq (107)	Abu Dhabi	2015-16
6th	269	Mohammad Yousuf (223)/Kamran Akmal (154)	Lahore	2005-06
7th	112	Asif Mujtaba (51)/Moin Khan (105)	Leeds	1996
8th	130	Hanif Mohammad (187*)/Asif Iqbal (76)	Lord's	1967
9th	190	Asif Iqbal (146)/Intikhab Alam (51)	The Oval	1967
10th	62	Sarfraz Nawaz (53)/Asif Mahmood (4*)	Leeds	1974

BEST INNINGS BOWLING ANALYSIS

England	in England	8-34	I.T.Botham	Lord's	1978
	in Pakistan	7-66	P.H.Edmonds	Karachi	1977-78
	in UAE	6-62	M.S.Panesar	Abu Dhabi	2011-12
Pakistan	in England	7-40	Imran Khan	Leeds	1987
	in Pakistan	9-56	Abdul Qadir	Lahore	1987-88
	in UAE	7-55	Saeed Ajmal	Dubai	2011-12

BEST MATCH BOWLING ANALYSIS

England	in England	13- 71	D.L.Underwood	Lord's	1974
	in Pakistan	11- 83	N.G.B.Cook	Karachi	1983-84
	in UAE	7-149	M.S.Panesar	Dubai	2011-12
Pakistan	in England	12- 99	Fazal Mahmood	The Oval	1954
	in Pakistan	13-101	Abdul Qadir	Lahore	1987-88
	in UAE	10- 97	Saeed Ajmal	Dubai	2011-12

HIGHEST AGGREGATE OF WICKETS IN A SERIES

England	in England	26	(av 16.73)	C.R.Woakes	2016
	in Pakistan	17	(av 24.11)	A.F.Giles	2000-01
	in UAE	14	(av 21.57)	M.S.Panesar	2011-12
Pakistan	in England	22	(av 25.31)	Waqar Younis	1992
	in Pakistan	30	(av 14.56)	Abdul Qadir	1987-88
	in UAE	24	(av 14.70)	Saeed Ajmal	2011-12

RESULTS SUMMARY – ENGLAND v PAKISTAN – IN ENGLAND

	Tests	Series			Lord's			Nottingham			Manchester			The Oval			Birmingham			Leeds		
		E	P	D	E	P	D	E	P	D	E	P	D	E	P	D	E	P	D	E	P	D
1954	4	1	1	2	–	–	1	1	–	–	–	–	1	–	1	–	–	–	–	–	–	–
1962	5	4	–	1	1	–	–	1	–	–	–	–	1	1	–	–	–	–	–	1	–	–
1967	3	2	–	1	1	–	–	1	–	–	–	–	–	–	–	–	–	–	–	1	–	–
1971	3	1	–	2	–	–	1	–	–	1	1	–	–	–	–	–	–	1	1	–	–	–
1974	3	–	–	3	–	–	1	–	–	–	–	–	1	–	–	1	–	–	–	–	–	1
1978	3	2	–	1	1	–	–	–	–	–	–	–	–	–	–	–	1	–	–	1	–	–
1982	3	2	1	–	1	–	–	–	–	–	–	1	–	–	–	–	1	–	–	–	–	–
1987	5	–	1	4	–	–	1	–	–	1	–	–	1	–	–	1	–	–	1	–	1	–
1992	5	1	2	2	–	1	–	–	–	1	–	1	–	–	1	–	1	1	–	1	–	–
1996	3	–	2	1	–	1	–	–	–	–	–	–	1	–	1	–	–	–	–	–	–	1
2001	2	1	1	–	1	–	–	–	1	–	–	–	–	–	–	–	–	–	–	–	–	–
2006	4	3	–	1	–	–	1	–	–	–	1	–	–	1	–	–	1	–	–	–	–	–
2010	4	3	1	–	1	–	–	–	–	–	–	–	–	–	1	–	1	–	–	1	–	–
2016	4	2	2	–	–	1	–	–	–	–	1	–	–	–	–	1	1	–	–	–	1	–
	51	22	11	18	4	4	6	3	–	1	2	1	3	2	3	2	5	–	3	5	1	3

ENGLAND v PAKISTAN – IN PAKISTAN

	Tests	Series			Lahore			Dacca			Karachi			Hyderabad			Faisalabad			Multan		
		E	P	D	E	P	D	E	P	D	E	P	D	E	P	D	E	P	D	E	P	D
1961-62	3	1	–	2	1	–	–	–	–	1	–	–	1									
1968-69	3	–	–	3	–	–	1	–	–	1	–	–	1									
1972-73	3	–	–	3	–	–	1				–	–	1	–	–	1						
1977-78	3	–	–	3	–	–	1				–	–	1	–	–	1						
1983-84	3	–	1	2	–	–	1				–	–	1				–	1	–			
1987-88	3	–	1	2	–	1	–				–	–	1				–	–	1			
2000-01	3	1	–	2	–	1	–				1	–	–				–	–	1			
2005-06	3	–	2	1	1	–	–				–	1	–							–	1	–
	24	2	4	18	1	2	5	–	–	2	1	1	5	–	–	2	–	2	–	–	4	–	1	–

ENGLAND v PAKISTAN – IN UNITED ARAB EMIRATES

	Tests	Series			Dubai			Abu Dhabi (SZ)			Sharjah		
		E	P	D	E	P	D	E	P	D	E	P	D
2011-12	3	–	3	–	–	2	–	–	1	–	–	–	–
2015-16	3	–	2	1	–	1	–	–	–	1	–	1	–
	6	–	5	1	–	3	–	–	1	1	–	1	–

Totals	81	24	20	37

ENGLAND v INDIA

SERIES RECORDS 1932 to 2016-17
HIGHEST INNINGS TOTALS

England	in England	710-7d	Birmingham	2011
	in India	652-7d	Madras	1984-85
India	in England	664	The Oval	2007
	in India	759-7d	Chennai	2016-17

LOWEST INNINGS TOTALS

England	in England	101	The Oval	1971
	in India	102	Bombay	1981-82
India	in England	42	Lord's	1974
	in India	83	Madras	1976-77
HIGHEST MATCH AGGREGATE		1614 for 30 wickets	Manchester	1990
LOWEST MATCH AGGREGATE		482 for 31 wickets	Lord's	1936

HIGHEST INDIVIDUAL INNINGS

England	in England	333	G.A.Gooch	Lord's	1990
	in India	207	M.W.Gatting	Madras	1984-85
India	in England	221	S.M.Gavaskar	The Oval	1979
	in India	303*	K.K.Nair	Chennai	2016-17

HIGHEST AGGREGATE OF RUNS IN A SERIES

England	in England	752	(av 125.33)	G.A.Gooch	1990
	in India	594	(av 99.00)	K.F.Barrington	1961-62
India	in England	602	(av 100.33)	R.S.Dravid	2002
	in India	655	(av 109.16)	V.Kohli	2016-17

RECORD WICKET PARTNERSHIPS – ENGLAND

1st	225	G.A.Gooch (116)/M.A.Atherton (131)	Manchester	1990
2nd	241	G.Fowler (201)/M.W.Gatting (207)	Madras	1984-85
3rd	350	I.R.Bell (235)/K.P.Pietersen (175)	The Oval	2011
4th	266	W.R.Hammond (217)/T.S.Worthington (128)	The Oval	1936
5th	254	K.W.R.Fletcher (113)/A.W.Greig (148)	Bombay	1972-73
6th	171	I.T.Botham (114)/R.W.Taylor (43)	Bombay	1979-80
7th	162*	M.J.Prior (103*)/S.C.J.Broad (74*)	Lord's	2011
8th	168	R.Illingworth (107)/P.Lever (88*)	Manchester	1971
9th	103	C.White (94*)/M.J.Hoggard (32)	Nottingham	2002
10th	70	P.J.W.Allott (41*)/R.G.D.Willis (28)	Lord's	1982

RECORD WICKET PARTNERSHIPS – INDIA

1st	213	S.M.Gavaskar (221)/C.P.S.Chauhan (80)	The Oval	1979
2nd	314	G.Gambhir (179)/R.S.Dravid (136)	Chandigarh	2008-09
3rd	316	G.R.Viswanath (222)/Yashpal Sharma (140)	Madras	1981-82
4th	249	S.R.Tendulkar (193)/S.C.Ganguly (128)	Leeds	2002
5th	214	M.Azharuddin (110)/R.J.Shastri (111)	Calcutta	1984-85
6th	181	K.K.Nair (303*)/R.Ashwin (67)	Chennai	2016-17
7th	235	R.J.Shastri (142)/S.M.H.Kirmani (102)	Bombay	1984-85
8th	241	V.Kohli (235)/J.Yadav (104)	Mumbai	2016-17
9th	104	R.J.Shastri (93)/Madan Lal (44)	Delhi	1981-82
10th	73	A.Kumble (110*)/S.Sreesanth (35)	The Oval	2007

BEST INNINGS BOWLING ANALYSIS

England	in England	8-31	F.S.Trueman	Manchester	1952
	in India	7-46	J.K.Lever	Delhi	1976-77
India	in England	7-74	I.Sharma	Lord's	2014
	in India	8-55	M.H.Mankad	Madras	1951-52

BEST MATCH BOWLING ANALYSIS

England	in England	11- 93 A.V.Bedser	Manchester	1946
	in India	13-106 I.T.Botham	Bombay	1979-80
India	in England	10-188 C.Sharma	Birmingham	1986
	in India	12-108 M.H.Mankad	Madras	1951-52

HIGHEST AGGREGATE OF WICKETS IN A SERIES

England	in England	29	(av 13.31)	F.S.Trueman 1952
	in India	29	(av 17.55)	D.L.Underwood 1976-77
India	in England	19	(av 26.63)	B.Kumar 2014
	in India	35	(av 18.91)	B.S.Chandrasekhar 1972-73

RESULTS SUMMARY – ENGLAND v INDIA – IN ENGLAND

	Tests	Series			Lord's			Manchester			The Oval			Leeds			Nottingham			Birmingham			Southampton		
		E	I	D	E	I	D	E	I	D	E	I	D	E	I	D	E	I	D	E	I	D	E	I	D
1932	1	1	-	-	1	-	-	-	-	-	-	-	-	-	-	-	-	-	-	-	-	-	-	-	-
1936	3	2	-	1	1	-	-	-	-	1	1	-	-	-	-	-	-	-	-	-	-	-	-	-	-
1946	3	1	-	2	1	-	-	-	-	1	-	-	1	-	-	-	-	-	-	-	-	-	-	-	-
1952	4	3	-	1	1	-	-	1	-	-	-	-	1	1	-	-	-	-	-	-	-	-	-	-	-
1959	5	5	-	-	1	-	-	1	-	-	1	-	-	1	-	-	1	-	-	-	-	-	-	-	-
1967	3	3	-	-	1	-	-	-	-	-	-	-	-	1	-	-	-	-	-	1	-	-	-	-	-
1971	3	-	1	2	-	-	1	-	-	1	-	1	-	-	-	-	-	-	-	-	-	-	-	-	-
1974	3	3	-	-	1	-	-	1	-	-	-	-	-	-	-	-	-	-	-	1	-	-	-	-	-
1979	4	1	-	3	-	-	1	-	-	-	-	-	1	-	-	1	-	-	-	1	-	-	-	-	-
1982	3	1	-	2	1	-	-	-	-	1	-	-	1	-	-	-	-	-	-	-	-	-	-	-	-
1986	3	-	2	1	-	1	-	-	-	-	-	-	-	-	1	-	-	-	-	-	-	1	-	-	-
1990	3	1	-	2	1	-	-	-	-	1	-	-	1	-	-	-	-	-	-	-	-	-	-	-	-
1996	3	1	-	2	-	-	1	-	-	-	-	-	-	-	-	-	-	-	1	1	-	-	-	-	-
2002	4	1	1	2	1	-	-	-	-	-	-	-	1	-	1	-	-	-	1	-	-	-	-	-	-
2007	3	-	1	2	-	-	1	-	-	-	-	-	1	-	-	-	-	1	-	-	-	-	-	-	-
2011	4	4	-	-	1	-	-	-	-	-	1	-	-	-	-	-	1	-	-	1	-	-	-	-	-
2014	5	3	1	1	-	1	-	1	-	-	1	-	-	-	-	-	-	-	1	-	-	-	1	-	-
	57	30	6	21	11	2	4	4	-	5	4	1	7	3	2	1	2	1	3	5	-	1	1	-	-

ENGLAND v INDIA – IN INDIA

	Tests	Series			Mumbai			Kolkata			Chennai			Delhi			Kanpur			Bangalore		
		E	I	D	E	I	D	E	I	D	E	I	D	E	I	D	E	I	D	E	I	D
1933-34	3	2	-	1	1	-	-	-	-	1	1	-	-	-	-	-	-	-	-	-	-	-
1951-52	5	1	1	3	-	-	1	-	-	1	-	1	-	-	-	1	1	-	-	-	-	-
1961-62	5	-	2	3	-	-	1	-	1	-	-	1	-	-	-	1	-	-	1	-	-	-
1963-64	5	-	-	5	-	-	1	-	-	1	-	-	1	-	-	1	-	-	1	-	-	-
1972-73	5	1	2	2	-	-	1	-	1	-	-	1	-	1	-	-	-	-	1	-	-	-
1976-77	5	3	1	1	-	-	1	1	-	-	1	-	-	1	-	-	-	-	-	-	1	-
1979-80	1	1	-	-	1	-	-	-	-	-	-	-	-	-	-	-	-	-	-	-	-	-
1981-82	6	-	1	5	-	1	-	-	-	1	-	-	1	-	-	1	-	-	1	-	-	1
1984-85	5	2	1	2	-	1	-	-	-	1	1	-	-	1	-	-	-	-	1	-	-	-
1992-93	3	-	3	-	-	1	-	-	1	-	-	1	-	-	-	-	-	-	-	-	-	-
2001-02	3	-	1	2	-	-	-	-	-	-	-	-	-	-	-	-	-	-	-	-	-	1
2005-06	3	1	1	1	1	-	-	-	-	-	-	-	-	-	-	-	-	-	-	-	-	-
2008-09	2	-	1	1	-	-	-	-	-	-	-	1	-	-	-	-	-	-	-	-	-	-
2011-12	4	2	1	1	1	-	-	1	-	-	-	-	-	-	-	-	-	-	-	-	-	-
2016-17	5	-	4	1	-	1	-	-	-	-	-	1	-	-	-	-	-	-	-	-	1	-
	60	13	19	28	4	4	5	2	3	5	3	6	2	3	-	4	1	-	5	-	1	2

	Tests	Chandigarh			Ahmedabad			Nagpur			Rajkot			Visakhapatnam		
		E	I	D	E	I	D	E	I	D	E	I	D	E	I	D
2001-02		-	1	-	-	-	1	-	-	-	-	-	-	-	-	-
2005-06		-	1	-	-	-	-	-	-	1	-	-	-	-	-	-
2008-09		-	-	1	-	-	-	-	-	-	-	-	-	-	-	-
2011-12		-	-	-	-	1	-	-	-	1	-	-	-	-	-	-
2016-17		-	1	-	-	-	-	-	-	-	-	-	1	-	1	-
		-	3	1	-	1	1	-	-	2	-	-	1	-	1	-

	Tests			
Totals	117	43	25	49

TOURING TEAMS REGISTER 2018

Neither Pakistan nor India had selected their 2018 touring teams at the time of going to press. The following players, who had represented those teams in Test matches since 1 December 2016, were still available for selection:

PAKISTAN

Full Names	Birthdate	Birthplace	Team	Type	F-C Debut
AHMED SHEHZAD	23.11.91	Lahore	Habib Bank	RHB/LB	2006-07
ASAD SHAFIQ	28.01.86	Karachi	Sui Northern	RHB/LB	2007-08
AZHAR ALI	19.02.85	Lahore	Sui Northern	RHB/LB	2001-02
BABAR AZAM	15.10.94	Lahore	Sui Northern	RHB/OB	2010-11
HARIS SOHAIL	09.01.89	Sialkot	ZT Bank	LHB/LM	2007-08
HASAN ALI	07.02.94	Punjab	Islamabad	RHB/RMF	2013-14
IMRAN KHAN, Mohammad	15.07.87	Lower Dir	Peshawar	RHB/RMF	2007-08
MOHAMMAD ABBAS	10.03.90	Sialkot	Sui Northern	RHB/RMF	2008-09
MOHAMMAD AMIR	13.04.92	Gujar Khan	Sui Southern	LHB/LFM	2008-09
RAHAT ALI	12.09.88	Multan	Khan Research	RHB/LFM	2007-08
SAMI ASLAM	12.12.95	Lahore	Sui Southern	LHB/OB	2012-13
SARFRAZ AHMED	22.05.87	Karachi	PIA	RHB/WK	2005-06
SHADAB KHAN	04.10.98	Mianwali	Sui Northern	RHB/LBG	2016-17
SHAN MASOOD	14.10.89	Kuwait	United Bank	LHB/RM	2007-08
SHARJEEL KHAN	14.09.89	Hyderabad	United Bank	LHB/LB	2009-10
SOHAIL KHAN	06.03.84	Malakand	United Bank	RHB/RFM	2007-08
WAHAB RIAZ	28.06.85	Lahore	WAPDA	RHB/LF	2001-02
YASIR SHAH	02.05.86	Swabi	Faisalabad	RHB/LB	2001-02

INDIA

Full Names	Birthdate	Birthplace	Team	Type	F-C Debut
ASHWIN, Ravichandran	17.09.86	Madras	Tamil Nadu	RHB/OB	2006-07
BUMRAH, Jasprit Jasbirsingh	06.12.93	Ahmedabad	Gujarat	RHB/RFM	2013-14
DHAWAN, Shikhar	05.12.85	Delhi	Delhi	LHB/OB	2004-05
JADEJA, Ravindrasinh Anirudsinh	06.12.88	Navagam-Khed	Saurashtra	LHB/SLA	2006-07
KOHLI, Virat	05.11.88	Delhi	Delhi	RHB/RM	2006-07
KULDEEP YADAV	14.12.94	Kanpur	Uttar Pradesh	LHB/SLC	2014-15
KUMAR, Bhuvneshwar	05.02.90	Meerut	Uttar Pradesh	RHB/RFM	2007-08
MISHRA, Amit	24.11.82	Delhi	Haryana	RHB/LB	2000-01
MOHAMMED SHAMI	03.09.90	Jonagar	Bengal	RHB/RFM	2010-11
MUKUND, Abhinav	06.01.90	Madras	Tamil Nadu	LHB/LBG	2007-08
NAIR, Karun Kaladharan	06.12.91	Jodhpur	Karnataka	RHB/OB	2013-14
PANDYA, Hardik Himanshu	11.10.93	Choryasi	Baroda	RHB/RMF	2013-14
PATEL, Parthiv Ajaybhai	09.03.85	Ahmedabad	Gujarat	LHB/WK	2004-05
PUJARA, Cheteshwar Arvindbhai	25.01.88	Rajkot	Saurashtra	RHB/LB	2005-06
RAHANE, Ajinkya Madhukar	06.06.88	Ashwi Khurd	Mumbai	RHB/RM	2007-08
RAHUL, Kannur Lokesh	18.04.92	Bangalore	Karnataka	RHB/OB	2010-11
SAHA, Wriddhaman Prasanta	24.10.84	Siliguri	Bengal	RHB/WK	2007-08
SHARMA, Ishant	02.09.88	Delhi	Delhi	RHB/RFM	2006-07
SHARMA, Rohit Gurunath	30.04.87	Bansod	Mumbai	RHB/OB	2006-07
VIJAY, Murali	01.04.84	Madras	Tamil Nadu	RHB/OB	2006-07
YADAV, Jayant	22.01.90	Delhi	Haryana	RHB/OB	2011-12
YADAV, Umesh Tilak	25.10.87	Nagpur	Vidarbha	RHB/RFM	2008-09

STATISTICAL HIGHLIGHTS IN 2017 TESTS

Including Tests from No. 2242 (Australia v Pakistan, 3rd Test) and No. 2244 (South Africa v Sri Lanka, 2nd Test) to No. 2286 (Australia v England, 4th Test) and No. 2290 (South Africa v Zimbabwe, Only Test).

† = National record

TEAM HIGHLIGHTS
HIGHEST INNINGS TOTALS

687-6d	India v Bangladesh	Hyderabad
662-9d	Australia v England	Perth
622-9d	India v Sri Lanka	Colombo (SSC)
610-6d	India v Sri Lanka	Nagpur
603-9d	India v Australia	Ranchi
600	India v Sri Lanka	Galle

HIGHEST FOURTH INNINGS TOTAL

391-6	Sri Lanka (set 388) v Zimbabwe	Colombo (RPS)

LOWEST INNINGS TOTALS

68	Zimbabwe v South Africa	Port Elizabeth
81	Pakistan v West Indies	Bridgetown
90	Bangladesh v South Africa	Potchefstroom
96	Sri Lanka v Pakistan	Dubai (DSC)

HIGHEST MATCH AGGREGATE

1511-30	Bangladesh (595-8d & 160) v New Zealand (539 & 217-3)	Wellington

Bangladesh one man short in second innings.

LARGE MARGINS OF VICTORY

Inns & 254 runs	South Africa (573-4d) beat Bangladesh (147 & 172)	Bloemfontein
Inns & 239 runs	India (610-6d) beat Sri Lanka (205 & 166)	Nagpur
Inns & 209 runs	England (514-8d) beat West Indies (168 & 137)	Birmingham
340 runs	South Africa (335 & 343-9d) beat England (205 & 133)	Nottingham
333 runs	Australia (260 & 285) beat India (105 & 107)	Pune
333 runs	South Africa (496-3d & 247-6d) beat Bangladesh (320 & 90)	Potchefstroom
304 runs	India (600 & 240-3d) beat Sri Lanka (291 & 245)	Galle

NARROW MARGINS OF VICTORY

20 runs	Bangladesh (260 & 221) beat Australia (217 & 244)	Mirpur

FOUR HUNDREDS IN AN INNINGS

South Africa (573-4d) v Bangladesh	Bloemfontein
India (610-6d) v Sri Lanka	Nagpur

SIX FIFTIES IN AN INNINGS

England (490-8d) v West Indies	Leeds

BATTING HIGHLIGHTS
DOUBLE HUNDREDS

A.N.Cook (2)	243	England v West Indies	Birmingham
	244*	England v Australia	Melbourne
V.Kohli (3)	204	India v Bangladesh	Hyderabad
	213	India v Sri Lanka	Nagpur
	243	India v Sri Lanka	Delhi
C.A.Pujara	202	India v Australia	Ranchi
Shakib Al Hasan	217	Bangladesh v New Zealand	Wellington
S.P.D.Smith	239	Australia v England	Perth

HUNDRED IN EACH INNINGS OF A MATCH

| S.D.Hope | 147 | 118* | West Indies v England | Leeds |

FASTEST HUNDRED

C.de Grandhomme (105) 71 balls   New Zealand v West Indies   Wellington

HUNDRED RUNS SCORED BEFORE LUNCH

| H.H.Pandya | (1*-108*) | India v Sri Lanka | Kandy |
| D.A.Warner | (0-100*) | Australia v Pakistan | Sydney |

On Day 1; only fifth batsman to score century before lunch on first day in Tests.

MOST SIXES IN AN INNINGS

| 7 | H.H.Pandya (108) | India v Sri Lanka | Kandy |

HUNDRED ON TEST DEBUT

| T.A.Blundell | (107*) | New Zealand v West Indies | Wellington |

CARRYING BAT THROUGH COMPLETED INNINGS

| A.N.Cook | (244*) | England (491) v Australia | Melbourne |

The highest score made by anyone carrying their bat in Test cricket.

LONG INNINGS (Qualification: 600 mins and/or 400 balls)

Mins	Balls			
588	407	A.N.Cook (243)	England v West Indies	Birmingham
634	409	A.N.Cook (244*)	England v Australia	Melbourne
556	405	F.D.M.Karunaratne (196)	Sri Lanka v Pakistan	Dubai (DSC)
672	525	C.A.Pujara (202)	India v Australia	Ranchi

NOTABLE PARTNERSHIPS

Qualifications: 1st-4th wkts: 250 runs; 5th-6th: 225; 7th: 200; 8th: 175; 9th: 150; 10th: 100.

Second Wicket

| 253 | S.Dhawan/C.A.Pujara | India v Sri Lanka | Galle |

Third Wicket

| 292 | H.M.Amla/J.P.Duminy | South Africa v Sri Lanka | Johannesburg |
| 283 | M.Vijay/V.Kohli | India v Sri Lanka | Delhi |

Fifth Wicket

| 359† | Shakib Al Hasan/Mushfiqur Rahim | Bangladesh v New Zealand | Wellington |

A record partnership for any wicket for Bangladesh.

| 301 | S.P.D.Smith/M.R.Marsh | Australia v England | Perth |
| 237 | D.J.Malan/J.M.Bairstow | England v Australia | Perth |

Eighth Wicket

| 212† | S.O.Dowrich/J.O.Holder | West Indies v Zimbabwe | Bulawayo |

BOWLING HIGHLIGHTS
EIGHT WICKETS IN AN INNINGS

N.M.Lyon	8-50	Australia v India	Bangalore

TEN WICKETS IN A MATCH

M.M.Ali	10-112	England v South Africa	Lord's
H.M.R.K.B.Herath (2)	11-249	Sri Lanka v Zimbabwe	Colombo (RPS)
	11-136	Sri Lanka v Pakistan	Abu Dhabi
N.M.Lyon	13-154	Australia v Bangladesh	Chittagong
S.N.J.O'Keefe	12- 70	Australia v India	Pune
K.Rabada (2)	10- 92	South Africa v Sri Lanka	Cape Town
	10- 63	South Africa v Bangladesh	Bloemfontein
Shakib Al Hasan	10-153	Bangladesh v Australia	Mirpur

FIVE WICKETS IN AN INNINGS ON DEBUT

T.S.Roland-Jones	5-57	England v South Africa	The Oval

HAT-TRICK

M.M.Ali	England v South Africa	The Oval

60 OVERS IN AN INNINGS

S.N.J.O'Keefe	77-17-199-3	Australia v India	Ranchi

200 RUNS CONCEDED IN AN INNINGS

M.D.K.Perera	45-2-202-3	Sri Lanka v India	Nagpur

WICKET-KEEPING HIGHLIGHTS
FIVE WICKET-KEEPING DISMISSALS IN AN INNINGS

Imrul Kayes	5ct	Bangladesh v New Zealand	Wellington
Q.de Kock	5ct	South Africa v New Zealand	Hamilton

EIGHT WICKET-KEEPING DISMISSALS IN A MATCH

A.B.de Villiers	8ct	South Africa v Zimbabwe	Port Elizabeth

NO BYES CONCEDED IN AN INNINGS OF 600

687-6d	Mushfiqur Rahim	Bangladesh v India	Hyderabad

FIELDING HIGHLIGHTS
FOUR CATCHES IN AN INNINGS IN THE FIELD

T.B.de Bruyn	4ct	South Africa v England	Manchester
C.R.Ervine	4ct	Zimbabwe v West Indies	Bulawayo
A.M.Rahane	4ct	India v Sri Lanka	Colombo (SSC)
S.P.D.Smith	4ct	Australia v England	Brisbane
Soumya Sarkar	4ct	Bangladesh v Sri Lanka	Colombo (PSS)

LEADING TEST AGGREGATES IN 2017

1000 RUNS IN 2017

	M	I	NO	HS	Runs	Avge	100	50
S.P.D.Smith (A)	11	20	3	239	**1305**	76.76	6	3
C.A.Pujara (I)	11	18	1	202	**1140**	67.05	4	5
D.Elgar (SA)	12	21	–	199	**1128**	53.71	5	4
V.Kohli (I)	10	16	2	243	**1059**	75.64	5	1
F.D.M.Karunaratne (SL)	13	26	–	196	**1031**	39.65	3	4
L.D.Chandimal (SL)	12	24	2	164	**1003**	45.59	3	5

RECORD CALENDAR YEAR RUNS AGGREGATE

	M	I	NO	HS	Runs	Avge	100	50
M.Yousuf (P) (2006)	11	19	1	202	**1788**	99.33	9	3

RECORD CALENDAR YEAR RUNS AVERAGE

	M	I	NO	HS	Runs	Avge	100	50
G.St A.Sobers (WI) (1958)	7	12	3	365*	**1193**	132.55	5	3

1000 RUNS IN DEBUT CALENDAR YEAR

	M	I	NO	HS	Runs	Avge	100	50
M.A.Taylor (A) (1989)	11	20	1	219	**1219**	64.15	4	5
A.C.Voges (A) (2015)	12	18	6	269*	**1028**	85.66	4	3
A.N.Cook (E) (2006)	13	24	2	127	**1013**	46.04	4	3

50 WICKETS IN 2017

	M	O	R	W	Avge	Best	5wI	10wM
N.M.Lyon (A)	11	548.2	1484	63	**23.55**	8-50	5	1
K.Rabada (SA)	11	360.0	1156	57	**20.28**	6-55	3	2
R.Ashwin (I)	11	554.0	1545	56	**27.58**	6-41	2	–
J.M.Anderson (E)	11	426.0	967	55	**17.58**	7-42	4	–
R.A.Jadeja (I)	10	508.3	1245	54	**23.05**	6-63	3	–
H.M.R.K.B.Herath (SL)	11	465.1	1432	52	**27.53**	6-43	5	2

RECORD CALENDAR YEAR WICKETS AGGREGATE

	M	O	R	W	Avge	Best	5wI	10wM
M.Muralitharan (SL) (2006)	11	588.4	1521	90	**16.90**	8-70	9	5
S.K.Warne (A) (2005)	14	691.4	2043	90	**22.70**	6-46	6	2

50 WICKET-KEEPING DISMISSALS IN 2017

	M	Dis	Ct	St
Q.de Kock (SA)	12	50	45	5

RECORD CALENDAR YEAR DISMISSALS AGGREGATE

	M	Dis	Ct	St
J.M.Bairstow (E) (2016)	17	70	66	4

20 CATCHES BY FIELDERS IN 2017

	M	Ct
S.P.D.Smith (A)	11	21
A.M.Rahane (I)	11	20

RECORD CALENDAR YEAR FIELDER'S AGGREGATE

	M	Ct
G.C.Smith (SA) (2008)	15	30

TEST MATCH SCORES
INDIA v AUSTRALIA (1st Test)

At Maharashtra C.A. Stadium, Pune, on 23, 24, 25 February 2017.
Toss: Australia. Result: **AUSTRALIA** won by 333 runs.
Debuts: None.

AUSTRALIA

M.T.Renshaw	c Vijay b Ashwin	68	(5)	c Sharma b J.Yadav		31
D.A.Warner	b U.T.Yadav	38	(1)	lbw b Ashwin		10
*S.P.D.Smith	c Kohli b Ashwin	27		lbw b Jadeja		109
S.E.Marsh	c Kohli b J.Yadav	16	(2)	lbw b Ashwin		0
P.S.P.Handscomb	lbw b Jadeja	22	(4)	c Vijay b Ashwin		19
M.R.Marsh	lbw b Jadeja	4		c Saha b Jadeja		31
†M.S.Wade	lbw b U.T.Yadav	8		c Saha b U.T.Yadav		20
M.A.Starc	c Jadeja b Ashwin	61		c Rahul b Ashwin		30
S.N.J.O'Keefe	c Saha b U.T.Yadav	0		c Saha b Jadeja		6
N.M.Lyon	lbw b U.T.Yadav	0		lbw b U.T.Yadav		13
J.R.Hazlewood	not out	1		not out		2
Extras	(LB 6, NB 9)	15		(B 4, LB 9, NB 1)		14
Total	**(94.5 overs; 366 mins)**	**260**		**(87 overs; 299 mins)**		**285**

INDIA

M.Vijay	c Wade b Hazlewood	10		lbw b O'Keefe		2
K.L.Rahul	c Warner b O'Keefe	64		lbw b Lyon		10
C.A.Pujara	c Wade b Starc	6		lbw b O'Keefe		31
*V.Kohli	c Handscomb b Starc	0		b O'Keefe		13
A.M.Rahane	c Handscomb b O'Keefe	13		c Lyon b O'Keefe		18
R.Ashwin	c Handscomb b Lyon	1		lbw b O'Keefe		8
†W.P.Saha	c Smith b O'Keefe	0		lbw b O'Keefe		5
R.A.Jadeja	c Starc b O'Keefe	2		b Lyon		3
J.Yadav	st Wade b O'Keefe	2		c Wade b Lyon		5
U.T.Yadav	c Smith b O'Keefe	4	(11)	not out		0
I.Sharma	not out	2	(10)	c Warner b Lyon		0
Extras	(NB 1)	1		(B 8, LB 4)		12
Total	**(40.1 overs; 173 mins)**	**105**		**(33.5 overs; 124 mins)**		**107**

INDIA	O	M	R	W		O	M	R	W	FALL OF WICKETS
Sharma	11	0	27	0	(5)	3	0	6	0		A	I	A	I
Ashwin	34.5	10	63	3	(1)	28	3	119	4	Wkt	1st	1st	2nd	2nd
J.Yadav	13	1	58	1	(4)	10	1	43	1	1st	82	26	10	10
Jadeja	24	4	74	2	(2)	33	10	65	3	2nd	119	44	23	16
U.T.Yadav	12	3	32	4	(3)	13	1	39	2	3rd	149	44	61	47
										4th	149	94	113	77
AUSTRALIA										5th	166	95	169	89
Starc	9	2	38	2		2	2	0	0	6th	190	95	204	99
O'Keefe	13.1	2	35	6	(3)	15	4	35	6	7th	196	95	246	100
Hazlewood	7	3	11	1	(4)	2	0	7	0	8th	205	98	258	102
Lyon	11	2	21	1	(2)	14.5	2	53	4	9th	205	101	279	102
										10th	260	105	285	107

Umpires: R.A.Kettleborough (*England*) (42) and N.J.Llong (*England*) (41).
Referee: B.C.Broad (*England*) (83).   **Test No. 2249/91 (I509/A798)**
M.T.Renshaw retired hurt at 82-1 and resumed at 149-3.

INDIA v AUSTRALIA (2nd Test)

At M.Chinnaswamy Stadium, Bangalore, on 4, 5, 6, 7 March 2017.
Toss: India. Result: **INDIA** won by 75 runs.
Debuts: None.

INDIA

K.L.Rahul	c Renshaw b Lyon	90		c Smith b O'Keefe	51
A.Mukund	lbw b Starc	0		b Hazlewood	16
C.A.Pujara	c Handscomb b Lyon	17		c M.R.Marsh b Hazlewood	92
*V.Kohli	lbw b Lyon	12		lbw b Hazlewood	15
A.M.Rahane	st Wade b Lyon	17	(6)	lbw b Starc	52
K.K.Nair	st Wade b O'Keefe	26	(7)	b Starc	0
R.Ashwin	c Warner b Lyon	7	(9)	b Hazlewood	4
†W.P.Saha	c Smith b Lyon	1		not out	20
R.A.Jadeja	c Smith b Lyon	3	(5)	b Hazlewood	0
U.T.Yadav	not out	0		c Warner b Hazlewood	1
I.Sharma	c Handscomb b Lyon	0		c S.E.Marsh b O'Keefe	6
Extras	(B 12, LB 4)	16		(B 11, W 4)	15
Total	**(71.2 overs; 291 mins)**	**189**		**(97.1 overs; 401 mins)**	**274**

AUSTRALIA

D.A.Warner	b Ashwin	33		lbw b Ashwin	17
M.T.Renshaw	st Saha b Jadeja	60		c Saha b Sharma	5
*S.P.D.Smith	c Saha b Jadeja	8		lbw b Yadav	28
S.E.Marsh	c Nair b Yadav	66		lbw b Yadav	9
P.S.P.Handscomb	c Ashwin b Jadeja	16		c Saha b Ashwin	24
M.R.Marsh	lbw b Sharma	0		c Nair b Ashwin	13
†M.S.Wade	lbw b Jadeja	40		c Saha b Ashwin	0
M.A.Starc	c Jadeja b Ashwin	26		b Ashwin	1
S.N.J.O'Keefe	not out	4		b Jadeja	2
N.M.Lyon	lbw b Jadeja	0		c and b Ashwin	2
J.R.Hazlewood	c Rahul b Jadeja	1		not out	0
Extras	(B 14, LB 3, NB 5)	22		(B 8, LB 2, W 1)	11
Total	**(122.4 overs; 493 mins)**	**276**		**(35.4 overs; 158 mins)**	**112**

AUSTRALIA	O	M	R	W		O	M	R	W
Starc	15	5	39	1		16	1	74	2
Hazlewood	11	2	42	0		24	5	67	6
O'Keefe	21	5	40	1	(4)	21.1	3	36	2
M.R.Marsh	2	0	2	0	(5)	3	0	4	0
Lyon	22.2	4	50	8	(3)	33	4	82	0

INDIA	O	M	R	W		O	M	R	W
Sharma	27	8	48	1		6	1	28	1
Yadav	24	7	57	1	(3)	9	2	30	2
Ashwin	49	13	84	2	(2)	12.4	4	41	6
Jadeja	21.4	1	63	6		8	5	3	1
Nair	1	0	7	0					

FALL OF WICKETS				
	I	A	I	A
Wkt	1st	1st	2nd	2nd
1st	11	52	39	22
2nd	72	82	84	42
3rd	88	134	112	67
4th	118	160	120	74
5th	156	163	238	101
6th	174	220	238	101
7th	178	269	242	103
8th	188	274	246	110
9th	189	274	258	110
10th	189	276	274	112

Umpires: R.K.Illingworth (*England*) (26) and N.J.Llong (*England*) (42).
Referee: B.C.Broad (*England*) (84).   **Test No. 2250/92 (I510/A799)**

14

INDIA v AUSTRALIA (3rd Test)

At JSCA International Stadium Complex, Ranchi, on 16, 17, 18, 19, 20 March 2017.
Toss: Australia. Result: **MATCH DRAWN**.
Debuts: None.

AUSTRALIA

M.T.Renshaw	c Kohli b Yadav	44	(2) lbw b Sharma		15
D.A.Warner	c and b Jadeja	19	(1) b Jadeja		14
*S.P.D.Smith	not out	178	(4) b Jadeja		21
S.E.Marsh	c Pujara b Ashwin	2	(5) c Vijay b Jadeja		53
P.S.P.Handscomb	lbw b Yadav	19	(6) not out		72
G.J.Maxwell	c Saha b Jadeja	104	(7) c Vijay b Ashwin		2
†M.S.Wade	c Saha b Jadeja	37	(8) not out		9
P.J.Cummins	b Jadeja	0			
S.N.J.O'Keefe	c Vijay b Yadav	25			
N.M.Lyon	c Nair b Jadeja	1	(3) b Jadeja		2
J.R.Hazlewood	run out	0			
Extras	(B 9, LB 11, NB 2)	22	(B 9, LB 4, NB 3)		16
Total	**(137.3 overs; 558 mins)**	**451**	**(6 wkts; 100 overs; 377 mins)**		**204**

INDIA

K.L.Rahul	c Wade b Cummins	67
M.Vijay	st Wade b O'Keefe	82
C.A.Pujara	c Maxwell b Lyon	202
*V.Kohli	c Smith b Cummins	6
A.M.Rahane	c Wade b Cummins	14
K.K.Nair	b Hazlewood	23
R.Ashwin	c Wade b Cummins	3
†W.P.Saha	c Maxwell b O'Keefe	117
R.A.Jadeja	not out	54
U.T.Yadav	c Warner b O'Keefe	16
I.Sharma	not out	0
Extras	(B 14, LB 5)	19
Total	**(9 wkts dec; 210 overs; 869 mins)**	**603**

INDIA	O	M	R	W		O	M	R	W
Sharma	20	2	70	0	(4)	11	0	30	1
Yadav	31	3	106	3	(3)	15	2	36	0
Ashwin	34	2	114	1	(1)	30	10	71	0
Jadeja	49.3	8	124	5	(2)	44	18	54	4
Vijay	3	0	17	0					

AUSTRALIA	O	M	R	W
Hazlewood	44	10	103	1
Cummins	39	10	106	4
O'Keefe	77	17	199	3
Lyon	46	2	163	1
Maxwell	4	0	13	0

FALL OF WICKETS

	A	I	A
Wkt	1st	1st	2nd
1st	50	91	17
2nd	80	193	23
3rd	89	225	59
4th	140	276	63
5th	331	320	187
6th	395	328	190
7th	395	527	–
8th	448	541	–
9th	449	595	–
10th	451	–	–

Umpires: C.B.Gaffaney (*New Zealand*) (13) and I.J.Gould (*England*) (59).
Referee: Sir R.B.Richardson (*West Indies*) (7).   Test No. 2251/93 (I511/A800)

INDIA v AUSTRALIA (4th Test)

At Himachal Pradesh C.A. Stadium, Dharamsala, on 25, 26, 27, 28 March 2017.
Toss: Australia. Result: **INDIA** won by eight wickets.
Debut: India – Kuldeep Yadav.

AUSTRALIA

D.A.Warner	c Rahane b Kuldeep	56	(2) c Saha b Yadav		6
M.T.Renshaw	b Yadav	1	(1) c Saha b Yadav		8
*S.P.D.Smith	c Rahane b Ashwin	111	b Kumar		17
S.E.Marsh	c Saha b Yadav	4	(6) c Pujara b Jadeja		1
P.S.P.Handscomb	b Kuldeep	8	(4) c Rahane b Ashwin		18
G.J.Maxwell	b Kuldeep	8	(5) lbw b Ashwin		45
†M.S.Wade	b Jadeja	57	not out		25
P.J.Cummins	c and b Kuldeep	21	c Rahane b Jadeja		12
S.N.J.O'Keefe	run out	8	c Pujara b Jadeja		0
N.M.Lyon	c Pujara b Kumar	13	c Vijay b Yadav		0
J.R.Hazlewood	not out	2	lbw b Ashwin		0
Extras	(B 1, LB 10)	11	(B 4, LB 1)		5
Total	**(88.3 overs; 347 mins)**	**300**	**(53.5 overs; 213 mins)**		**137**

INDIA

K.L.Rahul	c Warner b Cummins	60	not out	51
M.Vijay	c Wade b Hazlewood	11	c Wade b Cummins	8
C.A.Pujara	c Handscomb b Lyon	57	run out	0
*A.M.Rahane	c Smith b Lyon	46	not out	38
K.K.Nair	c Wade b Lyon	5		
R.Ashwin	lbw b Lyon	30		
†W.P.Saha	c Smith b Cummins	31		
R.A.Jadeja	b Cummins	63		
B.Kumar	c Smith b O'Keefe	0		
Kuldeep Yadav	c Hazlewood b Lyon	7		
U.T.Yadav	not out	2		
Extras	(B 4, LB 11, W 5)	20	(B 4, LB 5)	9
Total	**(118.1 overs; 500 mins)**	**332**	**(2 wkts; 23.5 overs; 111 mins)**	**106**

INDIA	O	M	R	W		O	M	R	W	FALL OF WICKETS				
Kumar	12.3	2	41	1		7		27	1		A	I	A	I
Yadav	15	1	69	2		10	3	29	3	Wkt	1st	1st	2nd	2nd
Ashwin	23	5	54	1	(5)	13.5	4	29	3	1st	10	21	10	46
Jadeja	15	1	57	1		18	7	24	3	2nd	144	108	31	46
Kuldeep Yadav	23	3	68	4	(3)	5	0	23	0	3rd	153	157	31	–
										4th	168	167	87	–
AUSTRALIA										5th	178	216	92	–
Hazlewood	25	8	51	1	(2)	6	2	14	0	6th	208	221	106	–
Cummins	30	8	94	3	(1)	8	2	42	1	7th	245	317	121	–
Lyon	34.1	5	92	5	(4)	5	0	19	0	8th	269	318	121	–
O'Keefe	27	4	75	1	(3)	4.5	1	22	0	9th	298	318	122	–
Maxwell	2	0	5	0						10th	300	332	137	–

Umpires: M.Erasmus (*South Africa*) (43) and I.J.Gould (*England*) (60).
Referee: Sir R.B.Richardson (*West Indies*) (8).   **Test No. 2252/94 (I512/A801)**

SRI LANKA v BANGLADESH (1st Test)

At Galle International Stadium, on 7, 8, 9, 10, 11 March 2017.
Toss: Sri Lanka. Result: **SRI LANKA** won by 259 runs.
Debuts: None.

SRI LANKA

F.D.M.Karunaratne	b Mehedi	30	c Mahmudullah b Taskin		32
W.U.Tharanga	b Subashis	4	b Mehedi		115
B.K.G.Mendis	c Tamim b Mehedi	194	c Taskin b Shakib		19
L.D.Chandimal	c Mehedi b Mustafizur	5	not out		50
D.A.S.Gunaratne	b Taskin	85	b Shakib		0
†D.P.D.N.Dickwella	c Mahmudullah b Mehedi	75	c Liton b Mehedi		15
M.D.K.Perera	lbw b Mehedi	51	c Liton b Mustafizur		33
*H.M.R.K.B.Herath	c Soumya b Mustafizur	14			
R.A.S.Lakmal	run out	8			
P.A.D.L.R.Sandakan	c Mehedi b Shakib	5			
C.B.R.L.S.Kumara	not out	0			
Extras	(B 4, LB 10, NB 5, W 4)	23	(B 2, LB 1, NB 1, W 6)		10
Total	**(129.1 overs; 575 mins)**	**494**	**(6 wkts dec; 69 overs; 291 mins)**		**274**

BANGLADESH

Tamim Iqbal	run out	57	c Gunaratne b Perera		19
Soumya Sarkar	c Kumara b Lakmal	71	b Gunaratne		53
Mominul Haque	lbw b Perera	7	lbw b Perera		5
*Mushfiqur Rahim	b Herath	85	c Dickwella b Sandakan		34
Shakib Al Hasan	c Dickwella b Sandakan	23	c Karunaratne b Herath		8
Mahmudullah	b Kumara	8	lbw b Herath		0
†Liton Das	c Gunaratne b Herath	5	c Tharanga b Herath		35
Mehedi Hasan	lbw b Perera	41	c Kumara b Herath		28
Taskin Ahmed	lbw b Perera	0	c Mendis b Herath		5
Subashis Roy	not out	0	(11) not out		0
Mustafizur Rahman	c Mendis b Herath	4	(10) lbw b Herath		0
Extras	(LB 6, NB 2, W 4)	11	(B 1, LB 4, NB 4, W 1)		10
Total	**(97.2 overs; 414 mins)**	**312**	**(60.2 overs; 251 mins)**		**197**

BANGLADESH	O	M	R	W		O	M	R	W		FALL OF WICKETS			
Mustafizur Rahman	25	5	68	2	(3)	9	4	24	1			SL	B	SL	B
Taskin Ahmed	21	3	77	1	(5)	8	0	32	1		*Wkt*	*1st*	*1st*	*2nd*	*2nd*
Subashis Roy	24	4	103	1	(1)	7	0	34	0		1st	15	118	69	67
Mehedi Hasan	22	1	113	4	(2)	20	1	77	2		2nd	60	127	134	80
Shakib Al Hasan	32.1	5	100	1	(4)	25	2	104	2		3rd	92	142	198	83
Soumya Sarkar	3	0	9	0							4th	288	170	199	104
Mahmudullah	2	0	10	0							5th	398	184	222	104
											6th	432	192	274	158
SRI LANKA											7th	457	298	–	166
Lakmal	14	0	42	1		7	3	12	0		8th	480	298	–	180
Kumara	16	1	70	1	(6)	3	0	10	0		9th	494	308	–	194
Perera	19	4	53	3	(2)	15	0	66	2		10th	494	312	–	197
Herath	26.2	4	72	3	(3)	20.2	5	59	6						
Sandakan	22	5	69	1		9	0	29	1						
Gunaratne					(4)	6	1	16	1						

Umpires: Alim Dar (*Pakistan*) (110) and M.Erasmus (*South Africa*) (42).
Referee: A.J.Pycroft (*Zimbabwe*) (53).   Test No. 2253/17 (SL257/B99)

SRI LANKA v BANGLADESH (2nd Test)

At P.Sara Oval, Colombo, on 15, 16, 17, 18, 19 March 2017.
Toss: Sri Lanka. Result: **BANGLADESH** won by four wickets.
Debut: Bangladesh – Mosaddek Hossain.

SRI LANKA

F.D.M.Karunaratne	c Mehedi b Mustafizur	7	c Soumya b Shakib	126
W.U.Tharanga	c Soumya b Mehedi	11	b Mehedi	26
B.K.G.Mendis	st Mushfiqur b Mehedi	5	c Mushfiqur b Mustafizur	36
L.D.Chandimal	c Mosaddek b Mehedi	138	c Mushfiqur b Mustafizur	5
D.A.S.Gunaratne	lbw b Subashis	13	lbw b Shakib	7
D.M.de Silva	b Taijul	34	c Mushfiqur b Mustafizur	0
†D.P.D.N.Dickwella	b Shakib	34	c Mushfiqur b Shakib	5
M.D.K.Perera	c Soumya b Mustafizur	9	run out	50
*H.M.R.K.B.Herath	c Soumya b Shakib	25	lbw b Taijul	9
R.A.S.Lakmal	c Soumya b Subashis	35	c Mosaddek b Shakib	42
P.A.D.L.R.Sandakan	not out	5	not out	0
Extras	(B 1, LB 13, NB 2, W 6)	22	(B 4, LB 8, W 1)	13
Total	**(113.3 overs; 504 mins)**	**338**	**(113.2 overs; 503 mins)**	**319**

BANGLADESH

Tamim Iqbal	lbw b Herath	49	c Chandimal b Perera	82
Soumya Sarkar	b Sandakan	61	c Tharanga b Herath	10
Imrul Kayes	lbw b Sandakan	34	c Gunaratne b Herath	0
Sabbir Rahman	c de Silva b Lakmal	42	lbw b Perera	41
Taijul Islam	lbw b Sandakan	0		
Shakib Al Hasan	c Chandimal b Sandakan	116	(5) b Perera	15
†*Mushfiqur Rahim	b Lakmal	52	(6) not out	22
Mosaddek Hossain	st Dickwella b Herath	75	(7) c Dickwella b Herath	13
Mehedi Hasan	lbw b Herath	24	(8) not out	2
Mustafizur Rahman	lbw b Herath	0		
Subashis Roy	not out	0		
Extras	(B 4, LB 8, W 2)	14	(B 4, LB 1, W 1)	6
Total	**(134.1 overs; 560 mins)**	**467**	**(6 wkts; 57.5 overs; 215 mins)**	**191**

BANGLADESH	O	M	R	W		O	M	R	W			FALL OF WICKETS			
Mustafizur Rahman	21	6	50	2	(3)	23	3	78	3			SL	B	SL	B
Subashis Roy	17.3	2	53	2	(1)	16	4	36	0		Wkt	1st	1st	2nd	2nd
Mehedi Hasan	21	2	90	3	(2)	24	0	71	1		1st	13	95	57	22
Taijul Islam	17	2	40	1	(6)	11	1	38	1		2nd	24	130	143	22
Shakib Al Hasan	33	4	80	2	(4)	36.2	9	74	4		3rd	35	192	165	131
Mosaddek Hossain	4	0	11	0	(5)	3	0	10	0		4th	70	192	176	143
											5th	136	198	177	162
SRI LANKA											6th	180	290	190	189
Lakmal	25	3	90	2	(5)	2	0	7	0		7th	195	421	217	—
Perera	33	5	100	0	(1)	22	1	59	3		8th	250	454	238	—
Herath	34.1	6	82	4	(2)	24.5	2	75	3		9th	305	454	318	—
Gunaratne	7	0	38	0	(6)	1	0	4	0		10th	338	467	319	—
Sandakan	33	2	140	4	(4)	6	1	34	0						
De Silva	2	0	5	0	(3)	2	0	7	0						

Umpires: Alim Dar (*Pakistan*) (111) and S.Ravi (*India*) (20).
Referee: A.J.Pycroft (*Zimbabwe*) (54).　　　　Test No. 2254/18 (SL258/B100)

NEW ZEALAND v SOUTH AFRICA (1st Test)

At University Oval, Dunedin, on 8, 9, 10, 11, 12 (*no play*) March 2017.
Toss: South Africa. Result: **MATCH DRAWN**.
Debuts: None.

SOUTH AFRICA

S.C.Cook	lbw b Boult	3	c Watling b Boult		0
D.Elgar	c Watling b Wagner	140	c Williamson b Patel		89
H.M.Amla	b Wagner	1	c sub (T.G.Southee) b Wagner		24
J.P.Duminy	c Taylor b Wagner	1	lbw b Wagner		39
*F.du Plessis	c Boult b Neesham	52	not out		56
T.Bavuma	c Watling b Boult	64	b Santner		6
†Q.de Kock	c Wagner b Patel	10	b Patel		4
V.D.Philander	b Boult	21	not out		1
K.A.Maharaj	c Neesham b Boult	5			
K.Rabada	b Patel	4			
M.Morkel	not out	0			
Extras	(B 4, LB 1, W 2)	7	(B 1, LB 3, W 1)		5
Total	**(122.4 overs; 496 mins)**	**308**	**(6 wkts; 102 overs; 428 mins)**		**224**

NEW ZEALAND

T.W.M.Latham	c de Kock b Philander	10
J.A.Raval	c Elgar b Maharaj	52
*K.S.Williamson	c de Kock b Rabada	130
L.R.P.L.Taylor	not out	15
H.M.Nicholls	c Amla b Maharaj	12
J.S.Patel	c du Plessis b Philander	16
J.D.S.Neesham	c de Kock b Morkel	7
†B.J.Watling	b Maharaj	50
M.J.Santner	c Maharaj b Morkel	4
N.Wagner	c Duminy b Maharaj	32
T.A.Boult	b Maharaj	2
Extras	(LB 8, NB 2, W 1)	11
Total	**(114.3 overs; 510 mins)**	**341**

NEW ZEALAND	O	M	R	W		O	M	R	W		FALL OF WICKETS		
											SA	NZ	SA
Boult	32.4	12	64	4		15	4	34	1	Wkt	1st	1st	2nd
Wagner	31	8	88	3		27	7	57	2	1st	10	15	0
Patel	33	12	85	2	(4)	36	15	72	2	2nd	20	117	39
Santner	18	5	32	0	(3)	19	6	37	1	3rd	22	165	113
Neesham	8	2	34	1		5	0	20	0	4th	148	184	193
										5th	252	193	206
SOUTH AFRICA										6th	265	277	218
Rabada	30	7	92	1						7th	279	297	–
Philander	27	11	67	2						8th	298	304	–
Morkel	24	6	62	2						9th	308	324	–
Maharaj	28.3	7	94	5						10th	308	341	–
Duminy	5	0	18	0									

Umpires: H.D.P.K.Dharmasena (*Sri Lanka*) (44) and B.N.J.Oxenford (*Australia*) (38).
Referee: D.C.Boon (*Australia*) (39). **Test No. 2255/43 (NZ420/SA409)**
L.R.P.L.Taylor retired hurt on 8* at 148-2 and resumed at 324-9.

NEW ZEALAND v SOUTH AFRICA (2nd Test)

At Basin Reserve, Wellington, on 16, 17, 18 March 2017.
Toss: South Africa. Result: **SOUTH AFRICA** won by eight wickets.
Debut: New Zealand – N.T.Broom.

NEW ZEALAND

J.A.Raval	c Amla b Maharaj	36	(2) st de Kock b Maharaj		80
T.W.M.Latham	c Elgar b Morkel	8	(1) c Duminy b Morkel		6
*K.S.Williamson	lbw b Rabada	2	c de Kock b Morkel		1
N.T.Broom	c de Kock b Rabada	0	c de Kock b Morkel		20
H.M.Nicholls	b Duminy	118	b Maharaj		7
J.D.S.Neesham	st de Kock b Maharaj	15	c du Plessis b Maharaj		4
†B.J.Watling	c de Kock b Duminy	34	c Duminy b Maharaj		29
C.de Grandhomme	c Amla b Duminy	4	b Maharaj		0
T.G.Southee	c Philander b Morkel	27	c Duminy b Maharaj		4
J.S.Patel	not out	17	c de Kock b Rabada		0
N.Wagner	lbw b Duminy	2	not out		4
Extras	(LB 4, W 1)	5	(B 10, LB 1, W 5)		16
Total	**(79.3 overs; 349 mins)**	**268**	**(63.2 overs; 281 mins)**		**171**

SOUTH AFRICA

S.C.Cook	c Neesham b Southee	3	c Neesham b Southee		11
D.Elgar	c Neesham b de Grandhomme	9	c Watling b Wagner		17
K.Rabada	b Southee	9			
H.M.Amla	c Nicholls b de Grandhomme	21	(3) not out		38
J.P.Duminy	c Nicholls b Wagner	16	(4) not out		15
*F.du Plessis	c Watling b de Grandhomme	22			
T.Bavuma	c Neesham b Wagner	89			
†Q.de Kock	c Watling b Neesham	91			
V.D.Philander	not out	37			
K.A.Maharaj	c Williamson b Wagner	1			
M.Morkel	b Patel	40			
Extras	(B 4, LB 5, W 12)	21	(W 2)		2
Total	**(98 overs; 433 mins)**	**359**	**(2 wkts; 24.3 overs; 112 mins)**		**83**

SOUTH AFRICA	O	M	R	W		O	M	R	W	FALL OF WICKETS				
Morkel	18	3	82	2		11	0	50	3		NZ	SA	NZ	SA
Philander	15	7	29	0		12	3	28	0	*Wkt*	*1st*	*1st*	*2nd*	*2nd*
Rabada	19	6	59	2		17	5	38	1	1st	11	12	16	18
Duminy	11.3	2	47	4	(5)	3	1	4	0	2nd	13	12	26	48
Maharaj	16	4	47	2	(4)	20.2	7	40	6	3rd	21	26	64	–
										4th	73	59	86	–
										5th	101	79	90	–
NEW ZEALAND										6th	217	94	155	–
Southee	27	7	98	2		6	2	17	1	7th	221	254	161	–
De Grandhomme	23	7	52	3		8	1	20	0	8th	222	290	167	–
Wagner	22	1	102	3		8	2	18	1	9th	266	302	167	–
Patel	14	1	57	1						10th	268	359	171	–
Neesham	12	2	41	1	(4)	2.3	0	28	0					

Umpires: H.D.P.K.Dharmasena (*Sri Lanka*) (45) and R.J.Tucker (*Australia*) (52).
Referee: D.C.Boon (*Australia*) (40).   **Test No. 2256/44 (NZ421/SA410)**

NEW ZEALAND v SOUTH AFRICA (3rd Test)

At Seddon Park, Hamilton, on 25, 26, 27, 28, 29 (*no play*) March 2017.
Toss: South Africa. Result: **MATCH DRAWN**.
Debut: South Africa – T.B.de Bruyn.

SOUTH AFRICA

D.Elgar	b de Grandhomme	5	c Watling b de Grandhomme	5
T.B.de Bruyn	c Latham b Henry	0	run out	12
H.M.Amla	b de Grandhomme	50	c de Grandhomme b Patel	19
J.P.Duminy	c Patel b Henry	20	b Patel	13
*F.du Plessis	c Latham b Santner	53	not out	15
T.Bavuma	c Raval b Henry	29	c Watling b Henry	1
†Q.de Kock	lbw b Wagner	90	not out	15
V.D.Philander	c Latham b Henry	11		
K.A.Maharaj	c Watling b Wagner	9		
K.Rabada	c Watling b Wagner	34		
M.Morkel	not out	9		
Extras	(LB 1, W 3)	4		
Total	**(89.2 overs; 379 mins)**	**314**	**(5 wkts; 39 overs; 166 mins)**	**80**

NEW ZEALAND

T.W.M.Latham	c de Kock b Morkel	50
J.A.Raval	c de Kock b Morkel	88
*K.S.Williamson	c Philander b Morkel	176
N.T.Broom	lbw b Rabada	12
H.M.Nicholls	c de Kock b Rabada	0
M.J.Santner	c Duminy b Rabada	41
†B.J.Watling	b Maharaj	24
C.de Grandhomme	c de Kock b Morkel	57
M.J.Henry	c Elgar b Maharaj	12
J.S.Patel	c de Kock b Rabada	5
N.Wagner	not out	0
Extras	(LB 12, NB 7, W 5)	24
Total	**(162.1 overs; 716 mins)**	**489**

NEW ZEALAND	O	M	R	W	O	M	R	W
Henry	24	2	93	4	11	4	20	1
De Grandhomme	24	4	62	2	8	5	15	1
Wagner	25.2	2	104	3	5	0	16	0
Patel	7	0	30	0	12	2	22	2
Santner	9	3	24	1	3	0	7	0

SOUTH AFRICA	O	M	R	W
Philander	33	7	79	0
Morkel	36.1	7	100	4
Rabada	34	3	122	4
Maharaj	50	8	118	2
Duminy	6	0	38	0
Elgar	1	0	13	0
Bavuma	2	0	7	0

FALL OF WICKETS

	SA	NZ	SA
Wkt	1st	1st	2nd
1st	5	83	13
2nd	5	273	25
3rd	64	293	49
4th	97	293	50
5th	148	381	59
6th	190	397	–
7th	219	443	–
8th	249	477	–
9th	295	489	–
10th	314	489	–

Umpires: B.N.J.Oxenford (*Australia*) (39) and R.J.Tucker (*Australia*) (53).
Referee: D.C.Boon (*Australia*) (41).   Test No. 2257/45 (NZ422/SA411)

WEST INDIES v PAKISTAN (1st Test)

At Sabina Park, Kingston, Jamaica, on 21, 22, 23, 24, 25 April 2017.
Toss:.Pakistan. Result: **PAKISTAN** won by seven wickets.
Debuts: West Indies – S.O.Hetmyer, V.A.Singh; Pakistan – Mohammad Abbas.

WEST INDIES

K.C.Brathwaite	c Younus b Abbas	0	b Shah		14
K.O.A.Powell	c Younus b Amir	33	c Younus b Shah		49
S.O.Hetmyer	b Amir	11	b Shah		20
S.D.Hope	b Amir	2	lbw b Shah		6
V.A.Singh	c Azhar b Riaz	9	(6) b Amir		9
R.L.Chase	c Riaz b Shah	63	(7) not out		16
†S.O.Dowrich	b Shah	56	(8) lbw b Abbas		0
*J.O.Holder	not out	57	(9) c Sarfraz b Riaz		14
D.Bishoo	c Sarfraz b Amir	28	(5) c Younus b Abbas		18
A.S.Joseph	b Amir	0	lbw b Shah		1
S.T.Gabriel	b Amir	5	c Abbas b Shah		0
Extras	(B 4, LB 18)	22	(LB 5)		5
Total	**(95 overs; 429 mins)**	**286**	**(52.4 overs; 237 mins)**		**152**

PAKISTAN

Azhar Ali	c Dowrich b Joseph	15	b Joseph		1
Ahmed Shehzad	lbw b Holder	31	c Dowrich b Gabriel		6
Babar Azam	b Gabriel	72	not out		9
Younus Khan	c Brathwaite b Gabriel	58	lbw b Bishoo		6
*Misbah-ul-Haq	not out	99	not out		12
Asad Shafiq	c Dowrich b Gabriel	22			
†Sarfraz Ahmed	b Bishoo	54			
Mohammad Amir	c Dowrich b Joseph	11			
Wahab Riaz	b Joseph	9			
Yasir Shah	run out	8			
Mohammad Abbas	lbw b Chase	1			
Extras	(B 4, LB 10, NB 12, W 1)	27	(LB 2)		2
Total	**(138.4 overs; 634 mins)**	**407**	**(3 wkts; 10.5 overs; 48 mins)**		**36**

PAKISTAN	O	M	R	W	O	M	R	W
Mohammad Amir	26	11	44	6	14	4	20	1
Mohammad Abbas	22	4	63	1	11	1	35	2
Wahab Riaz	23	6	66	1	6	0	29	1
Yasir Shah	24	5	91	2	(3) 21.4	4	63	6

WEST INDIES	O	M	R	W	O	M	R	W
Gabriel	29	6	92	3	3	1	7	1
Joseph	31	8	71	3	3	1	6	1
Holder	30	6	65	1	(4) 2	1	2	0
Bishoo	33	2	106	1	(3) 2.5	0	19	1
Chase	8.4	1	37	1				
Brathwaite	7	1	22	0				

FALL OF WICKETS

Wkt	WI 1st	P 1st	WI 2nd	P 2nd
1st	1	23	22	7
2nd	24	54	72	7
3rd	32	185	84	24
4th	53	186	89	–
5th	71	236	110	–
6th	189	324	129	–
7th	189	341	129	–
8th	264	355	151	–
9th	274	373	152	–
10th	286	407	152	–

Umpires: R.K.Illingworth (*England*) (27) and R.A.Kettleborough (*England*) (43).
Referee: B.C.Broad (*England*) (85).   **Test No. 2258/50 (WI521/P408)**

WEST INDIES v PAKISTAN (2nd Test)

At Kensington Oval, Bridgetown, Barbados, on 30 April, 1, 2, 3, 4 May 2017.
Toss: West Indies. Result: **WEST INDIES** won by 106 runs.
Debut: Pakistan – Shadab Khan.

WEST INDIES

K.C.Brathwaite	c Sarfraz b Amir	9	c Younus b Shah	43
K.O.A.Powell	lbw b Amir	38	c Sarfraz b Abbas	6
S.O.Hetmyer	c Azhar b Abbas	1	b Amir	22
S.D.Hope	c Sarfraz b Shah	5	c Azhar b Shah	90
R.L.Chase	c Younus b Amir	131	c and b Shah	23
V.A.Singh	c Younus b Abbas	3	b Abbas	32
†S.O.Dowrich	c Younus b Shadab	29	c Shafiq b Shah	2
*J.O.Holder	c Sarfraz b Abbas	58	c Younus b Shah	1
D.Bishoo	c Shah b Abbas	14	c Azhar b Shah	20
A.S.Joseph	b Shah	8	c Amir b Shah	7
S.T.Gabriel	not out	0	not out	0
Extras	(B 4, LB 10, W 2)	16	(B 16, LB 2, NB 1, W 3)	22
Total	**(98.5 overs; 444 mins)**	**312**	**(102.5 overs; 458 mins)**	**268**

PAKISTAN

Azhar Ali	c Dowrich b Bishoo	105	c Hetmyer b Gabriel	10
Ahmed Shehzad	c Hope b Bishoo	70	lbw b Joseph	14
Babar Azam	c and b Gabriel	0	c Dowrich b Joseph	0
Younus Khan	c Gabriel b Bishoo	0	lbw b Holder	5
*Misbah-ul-Haq	c Hope b Holder	99	c Hope b Gabriel	0
Asad Shafiq	lbw b Holder	15	c Powell b Gabriel	0
†Sarfraz Ahmed	c Powell b Gabriel	9	c Chase b Holder	23
Shadab Khan	c Chase b Gabriel	16	c Dowrich b Holder	1
Mohammad Amir	c Hope b Holder	10	c Singh b Gabriel	20
Yasir Shah	c Dowrich b Gabriel	24	b Gabriel	0
Mohammad Abbas	not out	1	not out	0
Extras	(B 16, LB 16, NB 12)	44	(B 4, LB 1, NB 3)	8
Total	**(140 overs; 631 mins)**	**393**	**(34.4 overs; 191 mins)**	**81**

PAKISTAN	O	M	R	W	O	M	R	W		FALL OF WICKETS			
Mohammad Amir	26	5	65	3	21	8	44	1		WI	P	WI	P
Mohammad Abbas	23	6	56	4	25	6	57	2	Wkt	1st	1st	2nd	2nd
Yasir Shah	25.5	2	83	2	39.5	12	94	7	1st	12	155	8	10
Shadab Khan	23	3	90	1	17	0	55	0	2nd	13	156	41	11
Azhar Ali	1	0	4	0					3rd	37	161	97	27
									4th	102	259	155	30
WEST INDIES									5th	107	316	235	30
Gabriel	32	6	81	4	11	4	11	5	6th	154	325	235	35
Joseph	19	5	48	0	12	1	42	2	7th	286	329	236	36
Chase	19	2	74	0					8th	286	354	252	78
Holder	29	11	42	3	(3) 11.4	4	23	3	9th	312	384	261	81
Bishoo	41	11	116	3					10th	312	393	268	81

Umpires: R.A.Kettleborough (*England*) (44) and B.N.J.Oxenford (*Australia*) (40).
Referee: B.C.Broad (*England*) (86). **Test No. 2259/51 (WI522/P409)**

WEST INDIES v PAKISTAN (3rd Test)

At Windsor Park, Roseau, Dominica, on 10, 11, 12, 13, 14 May 2017.
Toss: West Indies. Result: **PAKISTAN** won by 101 runs.
Debut: Pakistan – Hasan Ali.

‡ (J.Blackwood)

PAKISTAN

Azhar Ali	b Chase	127	c sub‡ b Gabriel		3
Shan Masood	c Holder b Chase	9	lbw b Gabriel		21
Babar Azam	c Powell b Joseph	55	c Hetmyer b Chase		0
Younus Khan	lbw b Holder	18	c Powell b Bishoo		35
*Misbah-ul-Haq	c Dowrich b Chase	59	c Dowrich b Bishoo		2
Asad Shafiq	c Singh b Chase	17	c and b Joseph		13
†Sarfraz Ahmed	c Hope b Bishoo	51	c Dowrich b Joseph		4
Mohammad Amir	b Holder	7	c Bishoo b Joseph		27
Yasir Shah	c Powell b Holder	0	not out		38
Mohammad Abbas	st Dowrich b Bishoo	4			
Hasan Ali	not out	8	(10) not out		15
Extras	(B 4, LB 6, NB 8, W 3)	21	(LB 5, NB 4, W 7)		16
Total	**(146.3 overs; 672 mins)**	**376**	**(8 wkts dec; 57 overs; 270 mins)**		**174**

WEST INDIES

K.C.Brathwaite	c Sarfraz b Shah	29	c Hasan b Shah		6
K.O.A.Powell	c Azhar b Shah	31	c Masood b Shah		4
S.O.Hetmyer	c Sarfraz b Shah	17	b Amir		25
S.D.Hope	c Misbah b Azhar	29	lbw b Hasan		17
R.L.Chase	b Abbas	69	not out		101
V.A.Singh	lbw b Abbas	8	c Azam b Shah		2
†S.O.Dowrich	b Amir	20	c Azam b Shah		2
*J.O.Holder	not out	30	lbw b Hasan		22
D.Bishoo	c Younus b Abbas	0	c Masood b Abbas		3
A.S.Joseph	b Abbas	0	c Sarfraz b Hasan		5
S.T.Gabriel	c Azam b Abbas	0	b Shah		4
Extras	(B 4, LB 2, NB 3, W 5)	14	(B 6, NB 3, W 2)		11
Total	**(115 overs; 537 mins)**	**247**	**(96 overs; 447 mins)**		**202**

WEST INDIES	O	M	R	W		O	M	R	W	FALL OF WICKETS				
											P	WI	P	WI
Gabriel	32	9	67	0		10	1	24	2	*Wkt*	*1st*	*1st*	*2nd*	*2nd*
Joseph	27	9	64	1		15	3	53	3	1st	19	43	6	7
Chase	32	5	103	4		9	0	31	1	2nd	139	69	8	22
Holder	32	9	71	3		9	4	7	0	3rd	177	97	57	47
Bishoo	23.3	3	61	2		14	2	54	2	4th	241	152	65	66
										5th	274	189	72	76
PAKISTAN										6th	311	218	82	93
Mohammad Amir	27	12	32	1		15	8	22	1	7th	322	239	90	151
Mohammad Abbas	25	7	46	5		20	9	31	1	8th	322	239	151	181
Yasir Shah	40	4	126	3		37	13	92	5	9th	367	241	–	197
Hasan Ali	17	4	22	0		20	7	33	3	10th	376	247	–	202
Azhar Ali	6	1	15	1		2	0	3	0					
Asad Shafiq						2	0	15	0					

Umpires: R.K.Illingworth (*England*) (28) and B.N.J.Oxenford (*Australia*) (41).
Referee: B.C.Broad (*England*) (87).   **Test No. 2260/52 (WI523/P410)**
R.L.Chase retired hurt on 60* at 183-4 and resumed at 218-6.

ENGLAND v SOUTH AFRICA (1st Test)

At Lord's, London, on 6, 7, 8, 9 July 2017.
Toss: England. Result: **ENGLAND** won by 211 runs.
Debut: South Africa – H.G.Kuhn.

ENGLAND

A.N.Cook	c de Kock b Philander	3	c Bavuma b Morkel		69
K.K.Jennings	lbw b Philander	8	c de Kock b Morkel		33
G.S.Ballance	lbw b Morkel	20	c de Kock b Morkel		34
*J.E.Root	c de Kock b Morkel	190	b Maharaj		5
†J.M.Bairstow	lbw b Philander	10	st de Kock b Maharaj		51
B.A.Stokes	c de Kock b Rabada	56	lbw b Rabada		1
M.M.Ali	b Rabada	87	b Maharaj		7
L.A.Dawson	lbw b Morkel	0	b Rabada		0
S.C.J.Broad	not out	57	c de Bruyn b Maharaj		0
M.A.Wood	lbw b Rabada	0	b Rabada		28
J.M.Anderson	c de Kock b Morkel	12	not out		0
Extras	(LB 2, NB 13)	15	(LB 4, NB 1)		5
Total	**(105.3 overs)**	**458**	**(87.1 overs)**		**233**

SOUTH AFRICA

*D.Elgar	c Ballance b Ali	54	(2) c and b Ali	2
H.G.Kuhn	c Cook b Broad	1	(1) c Bairstow b Anderson	9
H.M.Amla	lbw b Ali	29	lbw b Dawson	11
J.P.Duminy	lbw b Broad	15	c Ali b Wood	2
T.Bavuma	c Stokes b Ali	59	(6) b Ali	21
T.B.de Bruyn	c Bairstow b Anderson	48	(7) c Stokes b Ali	1
K.Rabada	c Bairstow b Dawson	27	(10) c Bairstow b Ali	4
†Q.de Kock	c Stokes b Anderson	51	(5) b Ali	18
V.D.Philander	b Ali	52	(8) not out	19
K.A.Maharaj	lbw b Dawson	9	(9) b Ali	10
M.Morkel	not out	2	c Jennings b Dawson	14
Extras	(B 4, LB 7, NB3)	14	(B 7, LB 1)	8
Total	**(105 overs)**	**361**	**(36.4 overs)**	**119**

SOUTH AFRICA	O	M	R	W		O	M	R	W		FALL OF WICKETS			
												E	SA	E	SA
Morkel	25.3	2	115	4		21	6	64	3		*Wkt*	*1st*	*1st*	*2nd*	*2nd*
Philander	20	3	67	3	(5)	5	1	9	0		1st	14	10	80	12
Rabada	28	4	123	3	(2)	20	5	50	3		2nd	17	82	139	12
Maharaj	22	1	107	0	(3)	32.1	8	85	4		3rd	49	98	142	25
De Bruyn	5	1	30	0							4th	76	104	146	28
Bavuma	5	0	14	0							5th	190	203	149	64
Duminy					(4)	9	2	21	0		6th	367	244	180	67
ENGLAND											7th	367	248	181	72
Anderson	19	6	44	2		6	2	16	1		8th	413	314	182	82
Broad	18	5	62	2	(3)	1	5	0			9th	413	337	227	94
Wood	20	5	65	0	(4)	1	0	3	1		10th	458	361	233	119
Dawson	15	2	67	2	(5)	11.4	4	34	2						
Ali	20	7	59	4	(3)	15	4	53	6						
Stokes	13	2	53	0											

Umpires: S.Ravi (*India*) (21) and P.R.Reiffel (*Australia*) (31).
Referee: J.J.Crowe (*New Zealand*) (82).   Test No. 2261/146 (E984/SA412)

ENGLAND v SOUTH AFRICA (2nd Test)

At Trent Bridge, Nottingham, on 14, 15, 16, 17 July 2017.
Toss: South Africa. Result: **SOUTH AFRICA** won by 340 runs.
Debuts: None.

SOUTH AFRICA

D.Elgar	c Dawson b Anderson	6	(2) c Anderson b Stokes		80
H.G.Kuhn	b Broad	34	(1) c Root b Anderson		8
H.M.Amla	c Wood b Broad	78	lbw b Dawson		87
†Q.de Kock	c Cook b Broad	68	c Bairstow b Anderson		1
*F.du Plessis	c Bairstow b Stokes	19	lbw b Stokes		63
T.Bavuma	c Bairstow b Stokes	20	c Root b Ali		15
V.D.Philander	c Dawson b Anderson	54	c and b Ali		42
C.H.Morris	c and b Anderson	36	c Ballance b Ali		13
K.A.Maharaj	c Root b Anderson	0	c Broad b Ali		1
M.Morkel	c Bairstow b Anderson	8	not out		17
D.Olivier	not out	0			
Extras	(LB 12)	12	(B 8, LB 8)		16
Total	**(96.2 overs)**	**335**	**(9 wkts dec)(104 overs)**		**343**

ENGLAND

A.N.Cook	c de Kock b Philander	3	c de Kock b Morris		42
K.K.Jennings	c de Kock b Morkel	0	b Philander		3
G.S.Ballance	b Philander	27	lbw b Philander		4
*J.E.Root	c de Kock b Morkel	78	b Morris		8
†J.M.Bairstow	b Maharaj	45	c Morris b Maharaj		16
B.A.Stokes	c de Kock b Maharaj	0	c and b Philander		18
M.M.Ali	c du Plessis b Morris	18	c Kuhn b Maharaj		27
L.A.Dawson	c Amla b Maharaj	13	not out		5
S.C.J.Broad	lbw b Morris	0	c Morkel b Maharaj		5
M.A.Wood	c du Plessis b Morris	6	c Morris b Olivier		0
J.M.Anderson	not out	0	c de Kock b Olivier		0
Extras	(B 4, LB 10, W 1)	15	(LB 5)		5
Total	**(51.5 overs)**	**205**	**(44.2 overs)**		**133**

ENGLAND	O	M	R	W		O	M	R	W	FALL OF WICKETS
Anderson	23.2	6	72	5		20	4	45	2	
Broad	22	4	64	3		19	4	60	0	
Wood	17	3	61	0		5	68	0		
Stokes	18	3	77	2	(5)	20	4	34	2	
Dawson	7	1	26	0	(6)	11	1	42	1	
Ali	8	1	21	0	(4)	16	2	78	4	
Jennings	1	0	2	0						

SOUTH AFRICA										
Morkel	13	2	45	2		13	4	30	0	
Philander	13	2	48	2		10	3	24	3	
Morris	8.5	1	38	3	(4)	6	3	7	2	
Olivier	7	0	39	0	(3)	3.2	0	25	2	
Maharaj	10	1	21	3		12	2	42	3	

	SA	E	SA	E
Wkt	1st	1st	2nd	2nd
1st	18	3	18	4
2nd	66	3	153	28
3rd	179	86	154	55
4th	194	143	216	72
5th	220	168	253	84
6th	235	177	275	122
7th	309	199	304	126
8th	317	199	307	133
9th	330	199	343	133
10th	335	205	–	133

Umpires: S.D.Fry (*Australia*) (6) and P.R.Reiffel (*Australia*) (32).
Referee: J.J.Crowe (*New Zealand*) (83).   Test No. 2262/147 (E985/SA413)

ENGLAND v SOUTH AFRICA (3rd Test)

At The Oval, London, on 27, 28, 29, 30, 31 July 2017.
Toss: England. Result: **ENGLAND** won by 239 runs.
Debuts: England – D.J.Malan, T.S.Roland-Jones, T.Westley.

ENGLAND

Batsman	1st innings		2nd innings	
A.N.Cook	lbw b Morkel	88	b Morkel	7
K.K.Jennings	c Elgar b Philander	0	c Morris b Rabada	48
T.Westley	c du Plessis b Morris	25	st de Kock b Maharaj	59
*J.E.Root	c de Kock b Philander	29	c Morkel b Maharaj	50
D.J.Malan	b Rabada	1	lbw b Morris	10
B.A.Stokes	c Rabada b Morkel	112	b Morris	31
†J.M.Bairstow	c du Plessis b Rabada	36	c Rabada b Maharaj	63
M.M.Ali	c de Kock b Morris	16	run out	8
T.S.Roland-Jones	lbw b Maharaj	25	not out	23
S.C.J.Broad	c Amla b Rabada	3		
J.M.Anderson	not out	1		
Extras	(B 7, LB 7, W 3)	17	(LB 11, W 3)	14
Total	**(103.2 overs)**	**353**	**(8 wkts dec; 79.5 overs)**	**313**

SOUTH AFRICA

Batsman	1st innings		2nd innings	
D.Elgar	c Bairstow b Roland-Jones	8	(2) c Stokes b Ali	136
H.G.Kuhn	lbw b Roland-Jones	15	(1) b Broad	11
H.M.Amla	c Bairstow b Roland-Jones	6	c Root b Roland-Jones	5
†Q.de Kock	c Stokes b Roland-Jones	5	b Stokes	5
*F.du Plessis	lbw b Anderson	1	lbw b Stokes	0
T.Bavuma	c Bairstow b Roland-Jones	52	lbw b Roland-Jones	32
C.H.Morris	c and b Anderson	2	(8) c Stokes b Ali	24
K.A.Maharaj	c Cook b Stokes	5	(9) not out	24
K.Rabada	b Broad	30	(10) c Stokes b Ali	0
M.Morkel	c Cook b Anderson	17	(11) lbw b Ali	0
V.D.Philander	not out	10	(7) lbw b Roland-Jones	0
Extras	(B 4, LB 5, NB 3)	12	(B 4, LB 7, NB 4)	15
Total	**(58.4 overs)**	**175**	**(77.1 overs)**	**252**

SOUTH AFRICA	O	M	R	W		O	M	R	W
Morkel	28.2	7	70	3		19	6	44	1
Philander	17	6	32	2		15	3	54	0
Rabada	26	4	85	3		18	4	56	1
Maharaj	15	1	61	1	(5)	13.5	2	50	3
Morris	17	1	91	1	(4)	11	0	70	2
Elgar						3	0	28	0

ENGLAND	O	M	R	W		O	M	R	W
Anderson	13	6	25	3		13	3	26	0
Broad	15	5	44	1		16	4	47	1
Roland-Jones	16.4	4	57	5		18	4	72	3
Stokes	7	1	26	1		14	1	51	2
Root	2	0	5	0					
Ali	5	1	9	0	(5)	16.1	5	45	4

FALL OF WICKETS

Wkt	E 1st	SA 1st	E 2nd	SA 2nd
1st	12	18	30	21
2nd	64	23	92	47
3rd	113	30	170	52
4th	120	47	180	52
5th	183	47	202	160
6th	258	51	251	160
7th	279	61	265	205
8th	316	114	313	252
9th	331	161	–	252
10th	353	175	–	252

Umpires: Alim Dar (*Pakistan*) (112) and J.S.Wilson (*West Indies*) (5).
Referee: R.S.Madugalle (*Sri Lanka*) (176).   **Test No. 2263/148 (E986/SA414)**

ENGLAND v SOUTH AFRICA (4th Test)

At Old Trafford, Manchester, on 4, 5, 6, 7 August 2017.
Toss: England. Result: **ENGLAND** won by 177 runs.
Debuts: None.

ENGLAND

A.N.Cook	c de Kock b Maharaj	46	c de Bruyn b Morkel		10
K.K.Jennings	c de Kock b Olivier	17	c Amla b Rabada		18
T.Westley	c de Kock b Rabada	29	c sub (A.K.Markram) b Morkel		9
*J.E.Root	lbw b Olivier	52	b Olivier		49
D.J.Malan	c du Plessis b Morkel	18	c de Bruyn b Maharaj		6
B.A.Stokes	b Rabada	58	c du Plessis b Olivier		23
†J.M.Bairstow	lbw b Maharaj	99	c Rabada b Olivier		10
T.S.Roland-Jones	c Bavuma b Rabada	4	(9) c Maharaj b Rabada		11
M.M.Ali	c du Plessis b Rabada	14	(8) not out		75
S.C.J.Broad	b Morkel	7	c de Bruyn b Morkel		5
J.M.Anderson	not out	4	c de Bruyn b Morkel		2
Extras	(B 6, LB 6, NB 2)	14	(B 9, LB 13, NB 1, W 2)		25
Total	**(108.4 overs)**	**362**	**(69.1 overs)**		**243**

SOUTH AFRICA

D.Elgar	lbw b Anderson	0	(2) c Bairstow b Broad		5
H.G.Kuhn	c Stokes b Ali	24	(1) c Cook b Anderson		11
H.M.Amla	c Bairstow b Roland-Jones	30	lbw b Ali		83
T.Bavuma	b Anderson	46	c Bairstow b Roland-Jones		12
*F.du Plessis	b Anderson	27	c Bairstow b Anderson		61
†Q.de Kock	c Bairstow b Broad	24	c Cook b Ali		1
T.B.de Bruyn	c Root b Anderson	11	c Stokes b Ali		0
K.A.Maharaj	lbw b Ali	13	not out		21
K.Rabada	c Stokes b Broad	23	c Westley b Anderson		1
M.Morkel	not out	20	c Root b Ali		0
D.Olivier	c Bairstow b Broad	4	c Stokes b Ali		0
Extras	(B 3, NB 1)	4	(B 4, LB 3)		7
Total	**(72.1 overs)**	**226**	**(62.5 overs)**		**202**

SOUTH AFRICA	O	M	R	W	O	M	R	W		FALL OF WICKETS			
Morkel	26	5	92	2	13.1	2	41	4			E	SA	E	SA
Rabada	26	7	91	4	17	4	50	2		*Wkt*	*1st*	*1st*	*2nd*	*2nd*
Olivier	21	3	91	2	(4) 12	5	38	3		1st	35	2	16	10
Maharaj	30.4	9	58	2	(3) 27	5	92	1		2nd	92	47	30	18
De Bruyn	5	0	18	0						3rd	92	84	55	40
ENGLAND										4th	144	131	72	163
Anderson	17	5	38	4	14	7	16	3		5th	187	132	129	173
Broad	16.1	4	46	3	12	5	24	1		6th	252	146	134	173
Roland-Jones	11	3	41	1	9	1	52	1		7th	271	167	153	183
Ali	21	5	57	2	19.5	1	69	5		8th	303	189	211	195
Stokes	6	0	34	0	6	1	26	0		9th	312	220	237	202
Malan	1	0	7	0						10th	362	226	243	202
Root					(6) 2	0	8	0						

Umpires: Alim Dar (*Pakistan*) (113) and H.D.P.K.Dharmasena (*Sri Lanka*) (46).
Referee: R.S.Madugalle (*Sri Lanka*) (177).   **Test No. 2264/149 (E987/SA415)**

SRI LANKA v ZIMBABWE (Only Test)

At R.Premadasa Stadium, Colombo, on 14, 15, 16, 17, 18 July 2017.
Toss: Zimbabwe. Result: **SRI LANKA** won by four wickets.
Debut: Zimbabwe – T.K.Musakanda.   ‡ (M.D.Gunathilleke)

ZIMBABWE

H.Masakadza	c Mendis b Herath	19	lbw b Herath		7
†R.W.Chakabva	b Herath	12	b Herath		6
T.K.Musakanda	c Dickwella b Kumara	6	c Karunaratne b Herath		0
C.R.Ervine	c Perera b Kumara	160	c Karunaratne b Perera		5
S.C.Williams	c Gunaratne b Perera	22	b Herath		22
Sikandar Raza	lbw b Herath	36	b Herath		127
P.J.Moor	c Kumara b Gunaratne	19	c sub‡ b Kumara		40
M.N.Waller	b Herath	36	c Tharanga b Perera		68
*A.G.Cremer	b Gunaratne	13	c Karunaratne b Herath		48
D.T.Tiripano	c Karunaratne b Herath	27	lbw b Perera		19
C.B.Mpofu	not out	0	not out		9
Extras	(NB 5, W 1)	6	(B 4, LB 14, NB 1, W 7)		26
Total	**(94.4 overs; 401 mins)**	**356**	**(107.1 overs; 477 mins)**		**377**

SRI LANKA

F.D.M.Karunaratne	c Masakadza b Tiripano	25	b Williams		49
W.U.Tharanga	run out	71	c Moor b Cremer		27
B.K.G.Mendis	c Chakabva b Cremer	11	c Williams b Cremer		66
*L.D.Chandimal	c Chakabva b Cremer	55	c Masakadza b Cremer		15
A.D.Mathews	c Masakadza b Williams	41	c and b Cremer		25
†D.P.D.N.Dickwella	b Cremer	6	c Chakabva b Williams		81
M.D.K.Perera	run out	33	(8) not out		29
D.A.S.Gunaratne	c Masakadza b Williams	45	(7) not out		80
H.M.R.K.B.Herath	st Chakabva b Williams	22			
R.A.S.Lakmal	c and b Cremer	14			
C.B.R.L.S.Kumara	not out	1			
Extras	(B 8, LB 10, NB 3, W 1)	22	(B 9, LB 8, W 2)		19
Total	**(102.3 overs; 401 mins)**	**346**	**(6 wkts; 114.5 overs; 441 mins)**		**391**

SRI LANKA	O	M	R	W		O	M	R	W
Lakmal	14	1	58	0		14	0	43	0
Kumara	17.4	2	68	2	(4)	20	3	72	1
Herath	32	4	116	5	(2)	39.1	5	133	6
Perera	24	0	86	1	(3)	30	2	95	2
Gunaratne	7	0	28	2					
Mendis					(5)	4	0	16	0

ZIMBABWE	O	M	R	W		O	M	R	W
Mpofu	11	2	41	0	(5)	6	3	10	0
Tiripano	10	1	38	1					
Sikandar Raza	18	2	60	0	(1)	13	1	58	0
Cremer	39.3	4	125	5	(3)	48	6	150	4
Waller	1	0	2	0	(4)	4	0	10	0
Williams	23	3	62	2	(2)	43.5	2	146	2

FALL OF WICKETS

	Z	SL	Z	SL
Wkt	1st	1st	2nd	2nd
1st	23	84	14	58
2nd	38	107	16	108
3rd	38	116	17	133
4th	70	212	23	178
5th	154	226	59	203
6th	195	238	145	324
7th	260	274	289	–
8th	282	322	306	–
9th	356	343	361	–
10th	356	346	377	–

Umpires: I.J.Gould (*England*) (61) and N.J.Llong (*England*) (43).
Referee: B.C.Broad (*England*) (88).   **Test No. 2265/18 (SL259/Z102)**

SRI LANKA v INDIA (1st Test)

At Galle International Stadium, 26, 27, 28, 29 July 2017.
Toss: India. Result: **INDIA** won by 304 runs.
Debuts: Sri Lanka – M.D.Gunathilleke; India – H.H.Pandya.   ‡ (D.M.de Silva)

INDIA

Batsman	1st innings		2nd innings	
S.Dhawan	c Mathews b Fernando	190	c Gunathilleke b Perera	14
A.Mukund	c Dickwella b Fernando	12	lbw b Gunathilleke	81
C.A.Pujara	c Dickwella b Fernando	153	c Mendis b Kumara	15
*V.Kohli	c Dickwella b Fernando	3	not out	103
A.M.Rahane	c Karunaratne b Kumara	57	not out	23
R.Ashwin	c Dickwella b Fernando	47		
†W.P.Saha	c Perera b Herath	16		
H.H.Pandya	c sub‡ b Kumara	50		
R.A.Jadeja	b Fernando	15		
Mohammed Shami	c Tharanga b Kumara	30		
U.T.Yadav	not out	11		
Extras	(B 2, LB 5, NB 3, W 6)	16	(LB 1, NB 1, W 2)	4
Total	**(133.1 overs; 584 mins)**	**600**	**(3 wkts dec; 53 overs; 228 mins)**	**240**

SRI LANKA

Batsman	1st innings		2nd innings	
F.D.M.Karunaratne	lbw b Yadav	2	b Ashwin	97
W.U.Tharanga	run out	64	b Shami	10
M.D.Gunathilleke	c Dhawan b Shami	16	c Pujara b Yadav	2
B.K.G.Mendis	c Dhawan b Shami	0	c Saha b Jadeja	36
A.D.Mathews	c Kohli b Jadeja	83	c Pandya b Jadeja	2
†D.P.D.N.Dickwella	c Mukund b Ashwin	8	c Saha b Ashwin	67
M.D.K.Perera	not out	92	not out	21
*H.M.R.K.B.Herath	c Rahane b Jadeja	9	absent hurt	
A.N.P.R.Fernando	b Pandya	10	(8) c Kohli b Ashwin	0
C.B.R.L.S.Kumara	b Jadeja	2	(9) c Shami b Jadeja	0
D.A.S.Gunaratne	absent hurt		absent hurt	
Extras	(LB 4, W 1)	5	(LB 3, W 7)	10
Total	**(78.3 overs; 258 mins)**	**291**	**(76.5 overs; xxx mins)**	**245**

SRI LANKA	O	M	R	W		O	M	R	W
Fernando	31	2	132	6		12	2	63	0
Kumara	25.1	3	131	3	(3)	12	1	59	1
Perera	30	1	130	0	(2)	15	0	67	1
Herath	40	6	159	1		9	0	34	0
Gunathilleke	7	0	41	0		5	0	16	1

INDIA	O	M	R	W		O	M	R	W
Mohammed Shami	12	2	45	2		9	0	43	1
Yadav	14	1	78	1		9	0	42	1
Ashwin	27	5	84	1	(4)	27	4	65	3
Jadeja	22.3	3	67	3	(3)	24.5	4	71	3
Pandya	3	0	13	1		7	0	21	0

FALL OF WICKETS

Wkt	I 1st	SL 1st	I 2nd	SL 2nd
1st	27	7	19	22
2nd	280	68	56	29
3rd	286	68	189	108
4th	423	125	–	116
5th	432	143	–	217
6th	491	205	–	240
7th	495	241	–	240
8th	517	280	–	245
9th	579	291	–	–
10th	600	–	–	–

Umpires: R.K.Illingworth (*England*) (29) and B.N.J.Oxenford (*Australia*) (42).
Referee: Sir R.B.Richardson (*West Indies*) (9).   **Test No. 2266/39 (SL260/I513)**

SRI LANKA v INDIA (2nd Test)

At Sinhalese Sports Club, Colombo, 3, 4, 5, 6 August 2017.
Toss: India. Result: **INDIA** won by an innings and 53 runs.
Debut: Sri Lanka – P.M.Pushpakumara.

INDIA

S.Dhawan	lbw b Perera	35
K.L.Rahul	run out	57
C.A.Pujara	lbw b Karunaratne	133
*V.Kohli	c Mathews b Herath	13
A.M.Rahane	st Dickwella b Pushpakumara	132
R.Ashwin	b Herath	54
†W.P.Saha	st Dickwella b Herath	67
H.H.Pandya	c Mathews b Pushpakumara	20
R.A.Jadeja	not out	70
Mohammed Shami	c Tharanga b Herath	19
U.T.Yadav	not out	8
Extras	(B 8, LB 4, NB 2)	14
Total	**(9 wkts dec; 158 overs; 640 mins)**	**622**

SRI LANKA

F.D.M.Karunaratne	c Rahane b Ashwin	25		c Rahane b Jadeja	141
W.U.Tharanga	c Rahul b Ashwin	0		b Yadav	2
B.K.G.Mendis	c Kohli b Yadav	24		c Saha b Pandya	110
*L.D.Chandimal	c Pandya b Jadeja	10	(5)	c Rahane b Jadeja	2
A.D.Mathews	c Pujara b Ashwin	26	(6)	c Saha b Jadeja	36
†D.P.D.N.Dickwella	b Shami	51	(7)	c Rahane b Pandya	31
D.M.de Silva	b Jadeja	0	(9)	c Rahane b Jadeja	17
M.D.K.Perera	b Ashwin	25		st Saha b Jadeja	4
H.M.R.K.B.Herath	b Shami	2	(10)	not out	17
P.M.Pushpakumara	not out	15	(4)	b Ashwin	16
A.N.P.R.Fernando	b Ashwin	0		c Dhawan b Ashwin	1
Extras	(B 4, LB 1)	5		(LB 5, NB 2, W 2)	9
Total	**(49.4 overs; 195 mins)**	**183**		**(116.5 overs; 472 mins)**	**386**

SRI LANKA	O	M	R	W		O	M	R	W
Fernando	17.4	2	63	0					
Herath	42	7	154	4					
Karunaratne	8	0	31	1					
Perera	40	3	147	1					
Pushpakumara	38.2	2	156	2					
De Silva	12	0	59	0					

INDIA	O	M	R	W		O	M	R	W
Mohammed Shami	6	1	13	2	(3)	12	3	27	0
Ashwin	16.4	3	69	5		37.5	7	132	2
Jadeja	22	6	84	2	(4)	39	5	152	5
Yadav	5	1	12	1	(1)	13	2	39	1
Pandya						15	2	31	2

FALL OF WICKETS			
	I	SL	SL
Wkt	1st	1st	2nd
1st	56	0	7
2nd	109	33	198
3rd	133	60	238
4th	350	64	241
5th	413	117	310
6th	451	122	315
7th	496	150	321
8th	568	152	343
9th	598	171	384
10th	–	183	386

Umpires: B.N.J.Oxenford (*Australia*) (43) and R.J.Tucker (*Australia*) (54).
Referee: Sir R.B.Richardson (*West Indies*) (10). **Test No. 2267/40 (SL261/I514)**

SRI LANKA v INDIA (3rd Test)

At Pallekele International Cricket Stadium, Kandy, 12, 13, 14 August 2017.
Toss: India. Result: **INDIA** won by an innings and 171 runs.
Debuts: None.

INDIA

S.Dhawan	c Chandimal b Pushpakumara	119
K.L.Rahul	c Karunaratne b Pushpakumara	85
C.A.Pujara	c Mathews b Sandakan	8
*V.Kohli	c Karunaratne b Sandakan	42
A.M.Rahane	b Pushpakumara	17
R.Ashwin	c Dickwella b Fernando	31
†W.P.Saha	c Perera b Fernando	16
H.H.Pandya	c Perera b Sandakan	108
Kuldeep Yadav	c Dickwella b Sandakan	26
Mohammed Shami	c and b Sandakan	8
U.T.Yadav	not out	3
Extras	(B 10, LB 6, NB 2, W 6)	24
Total	**(122.3 overs; 534 mins)**	**487**

SRI LANKA

F.D.M.Karunaratne	c Saha b Shami	4		c Rahane b Ashwin	16
W.U.Tharanga	c Saha b Shami	5		b Yadav	7
B.K.G.Mendis	run out	18	(4)	lbw b Shami	12
*L.D.Chandimal	c Rahul b Ashwin	48	(5)	c Pujara b Kuldeep	36
A.D.Mathews	lbw b Pandya ·	0	(6)	lbw b Ashwin	35
†D.P.D.N.Dickwella	st Saha b Kuldeep	29	(7)	c Rahane b Yadav	41
M.D.K.Perera	c Pandya b Kuldeep	0	(8)	c Pandya b Ashwin	8
P.M.Pushpakumara	b Kuldeep	10	(3)	c Saha b Shami	1
P.A.D.L.R.Sandakan	c Dhawan b Ashwin	10		c Saha b Shami	8
M.V.T.Fernando	b Kuldeep	0		not out	4
C.B.R.L.S.Kumara	not out	0		b Ashwin	10
Extras	(B 4, LB 1, W 6)	11		(B 2, NB 1)	3
Total	**(37.4 overs; 171 mins)**	**135**		**(74.3 overs; 290 mins)**	**181**

SRI LANKA	O	M	R	W		O	M	R	W		FALL OF WICKETS
Fernando	26	3	87	2							
Kumara	23	1	104	0							
Karunaratne	7	0	30	0							
Perera	8	1	36	0							
Sandakan	35.3	4	132	5							
Pushpakumara	23	2	82	3							

	I	SL	SL
Wkt	1st	1st	2nd
1st	188	14	15
2nd	219	23	26
3rd	229	38	34
4th	264	38	39
5th	296	101	104
6th	322	107	118
7th	339	125	138
8th	401	125	166
9th	421	135	168
10th	487	135	181

INDIA	O	M	R	W		O	M	R	W
Mohammed Shami	6.5	1	17	2		15	6	32	3
Yadav	3.1	0	23	0	(3)	13	5	21	2
Pandya	6	1	28	1	(5)	1	0	2	0
Kuldeep Yadav	13	2	40	4		17	4	56	1
Ashwin	8.4	2	22	2	(2)	28.3	6	68	4

Umpires: R.K.Illingworth (*England*) (30) and R.J.Tucker (*Australia*) (55).
Referee: Sir R.B.Richardson (*West Indies*) (11).   **Test No. 2268/41 (SL262/I515)**

ENGLAND v WEST INDIES (1st Test)

At Edgbaston, Birmingham, on 17, 18, 19 August 2017 (day/night).
Toss: England. Result: **ENGLAND** won by an innings and 209 runs.
Debuts: England – M.D.Stoneman; West Indies – K.A.Hope.

ENGLAND

A.N.Cook	lbw b Chase	243
M.D.Stoneman	b Roach	8
T.Westley	lbw b Cummins	8
*J.E.Root	b Roach	136
D.J.Malan	c Blackwood b Chase	65
B.A.Stokes	c Blackwood b Chase	10
†J.M.Bairstow	b Holder	18
M.M.Ali	c Brathwaite b Chase	0
T.S.Roland-Jones	not out	6
S.C.J.Broad		
J.M.Anderson		
Extras	(LB 10, NB 7, W 3)	20
Total	(8 wkts dec; 135.5 overs; 588 mins)	514

WEST INDIES

K.C.Brathwaite	c Bairstow b Anderson	0	lbw b Ali	40
K.O.A.Powell	run out	20	c Cook b Anderson	10
K.A.Hope	c Stokes b Anderson	25	lbw b Roland-Jones	12
S.D.Hope	b Roland-Jones	15	c Root b Stokes	4
R.L.Chase	b Anderson	0	lbw b Broad	24
J.Blackwood	not out	79	st Bairstow b Ali	12
†S.O.Dowrich	lbw b Roland-Jones	4	b Broad	5
*J.O.Holder	c Bairstow b Ali	11	c Cook b Broad	5
K.A.J.Roach	b Broad	5	b Anderson	12
A.S.Joseph	lbw b Broad	6	c Stokes b Roland-Jones	8
M.L.Cummins	run out	0	not out	0
Extras	(LB 1, W 2)	3	(B 9, LB 1)	10
Total	(47 overs)	168	(45.4 overs)	137

WEST INDIES	O	M	R	W	O	M	R	W
Roach	28	8	86	2				
Joseph	22	3	109	0				
Cummins	24	3	87	1				
Holder	29.3	4	103	1				
Chase	26.2	2	113	4				
Brathwaite	6	0	6	0				
ENGLAND								
Anderson	15	6	34	3	7	2	12	2
Broad	16	3	47	2	10	4	34	3
Roland-Jones	6	0	31	2	6.4	3	18	2
Stokes	7	0	40	0	9	4	9	1
Ali	3	1	15	1	13	2	54	2

FALL OF WICKETS			
	E	WI	WI
Wkt	1st	1st	2nd
1st	14	0	15
2nd	39	45	41
3rd	287	47	60
4th	449	47	76
5th	466	89	102
6th	505	101	104
7th	506	129	104
8th	514	134	115
9th	–	162	137
10th	–	168	137

Umpires: M.Erasmus (*South Africa*) (44) and S.Ravi (*India*) (22).
Referee: D.C.Boon (*Australia*) (42).   **Test No. 2269/152 (E988/WI524)**

ENGLAND v WEST INDIES (2nd Test)

At Headingley, Leeds, on 25, 26, 27, 28, 29 August 2017.
Toss: England. Result: **WEST INDIES** won by five wickets.
Debuts: None.

ENGLAND

A.N.Cook	c K.A.Hope b Gabriel	11	c Dowrich b Holder	23
M.D.Stoneman	c Dowrich b Roach	19	b Gabriel	52
T.Westley	lbw b Roach	3	c Dowrich b Holder	8
*J.E.Root	c Blackwood b Bishoo	59	c S.D.Hope b Gabriel	72
D.J.Malan	b Holder	8	b Chase	61
B.A.Stokes	c Dowrich b Gabriel	100	c Brathwaite b Chase	58
†J.M.Bairstow	c Holder b Gabriel	2	b Chase	18
M.M.Ali	c Chase b Roach	22	c Brathwaite b Bishoo	84
C.R.Woakes	c Dowrich b Roach	23	not out	61
S.C.J.Broad	b Gabriel	0	not out	14
J.M.Anderson	not out	0		
Extras	(B 2, LB 3, NB 2, W 4)	11	(B 13, LB 5, NB 12, W 9)	39
Total	**(70.5 overs)**	**258**	**(8 wkts dec; 141 overs)**	**490**

WEST INDIES

K.C.Brathwaite	b Broad	134	c Stokes b Ali	95
K.O.A.Powell	c Cook b Anderson	5	c Stokes b Broad	23
D.Bishoo	c Bairstow b Anderson	1		
K.A.Hope	c Root b Anderson	3	(3) run out	0
S.D.Hope	c Bairstow b Anderson	147	(4) not out	118
R.L.Chase	c Cook b Stokes	5	(5) c sub (M.S.Crane) b Woakes	30
J.Blackwood	run out	49	(6) st Bairstow b Ali	41
†S.O.Dowrich	c Root b Anderson	0	(7) not out	0
*J.O.Holder	c Ali b Woakes	43		
K.A.J.Roach	not out	6		
S.T.Gabriel	lbw b Stokes	10		
Extras	(B 8, LB 11, W 5)	24	(B 4, LB 9, NB 1, W 1)	15
Total	**(127 overs)**	**427**	**(5 wkts; 91.2 overs)**	**322**

WEST INDIES	O	M	R	W	O	M	R	W
Roach	19.5	4	71	4	(2) 24	8	95	0
Gabriel	17	4	51	4	(1) 26	3	125	2
Holder	16	5	45	1	33	10	95	2
Chase	12	1	59	0	32	5	86	3
Bishoo	6	0	27	1	25	1	67	1
Brathwaite					1	0	4	0

ENGLAND	O	M	R	W	O	M	R	W
Anderson	29	7	76	5	24	6	73	0
Broad	24	2	95	1	25	4	91	1
Woakes	21	4	78	1	(4) 12.2	2	44	1
Stokes	25	9	63	2	(5) 5	0	25	0
Ali	24	4	84	0	(3) 25	3	76	2
Westley	4	0	12	0				

FALL OF WICKETS				
	E	WI	E	WI
Wkt	1st	1st	2nd	2nd
1st	19	11	58	46
2nd	26	31	81	53
3rd	37	35	94	197
4th	71	281	212	246
5th	140	296	303	320
6th	152	329	312	–
7th	220	329	327	–
8th	258	404	444	–
9th	258	406	–	–
10th	258	427	–	–

Umpires: C.B.Gaffaney (*New Zealand*) (14) and S.Ravi (*India*) (23).
Referee: D.C.Boon (*Australia*) (43). **Test No. 2270/153 (E989/WI525)**

ENGLAND v WEST INDIES (3rd Test)

At Lord's, London, on 7, 8, 9 September 2017.
Toss: West Indies. Result: **ENGLAND** won by nine wickets.
Debuts: None.

WEST INDIES

K.C.Brathwaite	c Bairstow b Anderson	10	b Anderson	4
K.O.A.Powell	c and b Anderson	39	b Anderson	45
K.A.Hope	c Bairstow b Anderson	0	lbw b Broad	1
S.D.Hope	c Cook b Roland-Jones	29	c Bairstow b Anderson	62
R.L.Chase	b Stokes	18	c Bairstow b Anderson	3
J.Blackwood	b Roland-Jones	1	c Bairstow b Anderson	5
†S.O.Dowrich	c Cook b Stokes	1	c Broad b Roland-Jones	14
*J.O.Holder	b Stokes	9	c Anderson b Broad	23
D.Bishoo	not out	13	b Anderson	0
K.A.J.Roach	c Anderson b Stokes	0	b Anderson	3
S.T.Gabriel	b Stokes	0	not out	0
Extras	(LB 1, NB 2)	3	(LB 17)	17
Total	**(57.3 overs)**	**123**	**(65.1 overs)**	**177**

ENGLAND

A.N.Cook	c Dowrich b Roach	10	lbw b Bishoo	17
M.D.Stoneman	c Dowrich b Roach	1	not out	40
T.Westley	lbw b Holder	8	not out	44
*J.E.Root	c Powell b Holder	1		
D.J.Malan	c Dowrich b Roach	20		
B.A.Stokes	b Gabriel	60		
†J.M.Bairstow	lbw b Roach	21		
M.M.Ali	c K.A.Hope b Roach	3		
T.S.Roland-Jones	c S.D.Hope b Holder	13		
S.C.J.Broad	c Dowrich b Holder	38		
J.M.Anderson	not out	8		
Extras	(LB 4, NB 7)	11	(B 4, LB 1, W 1)	6
Total	**(52.5 overs)**	**194**	**(1 wkt; 28 overs; 100 mins)**	**107**

ENGLAND	O	M	R	W		O	M	R	W
Anderson	16	7	31	2		20.1	5	42	7
Broad	12	5	24	0		19	9	35	2
Roland-Jones	11	4	32	2		11	4	31	1
Stokes	14.3	6	22	6		12	3	41	0
Ali	4	0	13	0		2	0	6	0
Root						1	0	5	0

WEST INDIES	O	M	R	W		O	M	R	W
Roach	24	8	72	5	(2)	1	0	4	0
Gabriel	15	1	64	1	(1)	5	0	22	0
Holder	13.5	1	54	4		6	1	16	0
Bishoo						11	2	35	1
Chase						5	1	25	0

FALL OF WICKETS

	WI	E	WI	E
Wkt	1st	1st	2nd	2nd
1st	18	1	6	35
2nd	22	15	21	–
3rd	78	19	69	–
4th	78	24	94	
5th	87	63	100	
6th	100	119	123	
7th	101	128	155	
8th	119	134	155	
9th	123	163	177	
10th	123	194	177	

Umpires: M.Erasmus (*South Africa*) (45) and C.B.Gaffaney (*New Zealand*) (15).
Referee: D.C.Boon (*Australia*) (44).   **Test No. 2271/154 (E990/WI526)**

BANGLADESH v AUSTRALIA (1st Test)

At Shere Bangla National Stadium, Mirpur, on 27, 28, 29, 30 August 2017.
Toss: Bangladesh. Result: **BANGLADESH** won by 20 runs.
Debuts: None.

BANGLADESH

Tamim Iqbal	c Warner b Maxwell	71		c Wade b Cummins	78
Soumya Sarkar	c Handscomb b Cummins	8		c Khawaja b Agar	15
Imrul Kayes	c Wade b Cummins	0	(4)	c Warner b Lyon	2
Sabbir Rahman	c Wade b Cummins	0	(7)	c Handscomb b Lyon	22
Shakib Al Hasan	c Smith b Lyon	84	(6)	c Cummins b Lyon	5
*†Mushfiqur Rahim	lbw b Agar	18	(5)	run out	41
Nasir Hossain	lbw b Agar	23	(8)	c Wade b Agar	0
Mehedi Hasan	c Handscomb b Lyon	18	(9)	c Khawaja b Lyon	26
Taijul Islam	lbw b Lyon	4	(3)	lbw b Lyon	4
Shafiul Islam	c Hazlewood b Agar	13		c Handscomb b Lyon	9
Mustafizur Rahman	not out	0		not out	0
Extras	(B 15, LB 3, NB 2, W 1)	21		(B 15, LB 3, W 1)	19
Total	(78.5 overs; 322 mins)	**260**		(79.3 overs; 343 mins)	**221**

AUSTRALIA

D.A.Warner	lbw b Mehedi	8	lbw b Shakib	112
M.T.Renshaw	c Soumya b Shakib	45	lbw b Mehedi	5
U.T.Khawaja	run out	1	c Taijul b Shakib	1
N.M.Lyon	lbw b Shakib	0	(10) c Soumya b Mehedi	12
*S.P.D.Smith	b Mehedi	8	(4) c Mushfiqur b Shakib	37
P.S.P.Handscomb	lbw b Taijul	33	(5) c Soumya b Taijul	15
G.J.Maxwell	st Mushfiqur b Shakib	23	(6) b Shakib	14
†M.S.Wade	lbw b Mehedi	5	(7) lbw b Shakib	4
A.C.Agar	not out	41	(8) c and b Taijul	2
P.J.Cummins	b Shakib	25	(9) not out	33
J.R.Hazlewood	c Imrul b Shakib	5	lbw b Taijul	0
Extras	(B 15, LB 3, W 5)	23	(B 7, LB 2)	9
Total	(74.5 overs; 303 mins)	**217**	(70.5 overs; 286 mins)	**244**

AUSTRALIA	O	M	R	W		O	M	R	W
Hazlewood	15	5	39	0		4.1	2	3	0
Cummins	16	1	63	3		14	3	38	1
Lyon	30	6	79	3		34.3	10	82	6
Agar	12.5	2	46	3	(5)	20.5	2	55	2
Maxwell	5	0	15	1	(4)	5	0	24	0
Khawaja						1	0	1	0

BANGLADESH	O	M	R	W		O	M	R	W
Shafiul Islam	6	0	21	0					
Mehedi Hasan	26	6	62	3	(1)	19	3	80	2
Shakib Al Hasan	25.5	7	68	5		28	7	85	5
Taijul Islam	8	1	32	1		19.5	2	60	3
Mustafizur Rahman	8	3	13	0		1	0	8	0
Nasir Hossain	1	0	3	0	(2)	3	2	2	0

FALL OF WICKETS

Wkt	B 1st	A 1st	B 2nd	A 2nd
1st	10	9	43	27
2nd	10	14	61	28
3rd	10	14	67	158
4th	165	33	135	171
5th	188	102	143	187
6th	198	117	186	192
7th	240	124	186	195
8th	246	144	186	199
9th	246	193	214	228
10th	260	217	221	244

Umpires: Alim Dar (*Pakistan*) (114) and N.J.Llong (*England*) (44).
Referee: J.J.Crowe (*New Zealand*) (84). Test No. 2272/5 (B101/A802)

BANGLADESH v AUSTRALIA (2nd Test)

At Zahur Ahmed Chowdhury Stadium, Chittagong, on 4, 5, 6, 7 September 2017.
Toss: Bangladesh. Result: **AUSTRALIA** won by seven wickets.
Debuts: None.

BANGLADESH

Tamim Iqbal	lbw b Lyon	9	st Wade b Lyon		12
Soumya Sarkar	lbw b Lyon	33	c Renshaw b Cummins		9
Imrul Kayes	lbw b Lyon	4	c Maxwell b Lyon		15
Mominul Haque	lbw b Lyon	31	(8) c Cummins b Lyon		29
Shakib Al Hasan	c Wade b Agar	24	c Warner b Lyon		2
*†Mushfiqur Rahim	b Lyon	68	c Wade b Cummins		31
Sabbir Rahman	st Wade b Lyon	66	st Wade b Lyon		24
Nasir Hossain	c Wade b Agar	45	(4) c Smith b O'Keefe		5
Mehedi Hasan	run out	11	not out		14
Taijul Islam	c Smith b Lyon	9	b Lyon		4
Mustafizur Rahman	not out	0	b O'Keefe		0
Extras	(B 5)	5	(B 12)		12
Total	**(113.2 overs; 458 mins)**	**305**	**(71.2 overs; 283 mins)**		**157**

AUSTRALIA

M.T.Renshaw	c Mushfiqur b Mustafizur	4	c Mushfiqur b Shakib		22
D.A.Warner	c Imrul b Mustafizur	123	c Soumya b Mustafizur		8
*S.P.D.Smith	b Taijul	58	c Mushfiqur b Taijul		16
P.S.P.Handscomb	run out	82	not out		16
G.J.Maxwell	c Mushfiqur b Mehedi	38	not out		25
H.W.R.Cartwright	c Soumya b Mehedi	18			
†M.S.Wade	lbw b Mustafizur	8			
A.C.Agar	b Shakib	22			
P.J.Cummins	lbw b Mehedi	4			
S.N.J.O'Keefe	not out	8			
N.M.Lyon	c Imrul b Mustafizur	0			
Extras	(B 8, LB 3, W 1)	12			—
Total	**(119.5 overs; 519 mins)**	**377**	**(3 wkts; 15.3 overs; 74 mins)**		**87**

AUSTRALIA	O	M	R	W		O	M	R	W
Cummins	22	5	46	0		11	3	27	2
Lyon	36.2	7	94	7		33	11	60	6
O'Keefe	23	0	79	0		22.2	6	49	2
Agar	23	9	52	2		5	1	9	0
Maxwell	4	0	13	0					
Cartwright	5	1	16	0					

BANGLADESH	O	M	R	W		O	M	R	W
Mehedi Hasan	38	6	93	3					
Mustafizur Rahman	20.5	2	84	4	(1)	5	1	16	1
Shakib Al Hasan	31	3	82	1	(2)	6	1	35	1
Taijul Islam	21	1	78	1	(3)	4	0	26	1
Nasir Hossain	6	2	14	0	(4)	0.3	0	10	0
Mominul Haque	2	0	6	0					
Sabbir Rahman	1	0	9	0					

FALL OF WICKETS

	B	A	B	A
Wkt	1st	1st	2nd	2nd
1st	13	5	11	13
2nd	21	98	32	44
3rd	70	250	37	48
4th	85	298	39	–
5th	117	321	43	–
6th	222	342	97	–
7th	265	346	129	–
8th	293	364	149	–
9th	296	376	156	–
10th	305	377	157	–

Umpires: I.J.Gould (*England*) (62) and N.J.Llong (*England*) (45).
Referee: J.J.Crowe (*New Zealand*) (85).   Test No. 2273/6 (B102/A803)

SOUTH AFRICA v BANGLADESH (1st Test)

At Senwes Park, Potchefstroom, on 28, 29, 30 September, 1, 2 October 2017.
Toss: Bangladesh. Result: **SOUTH AFRICA** won by 333 runs.
Debuts: South Africa – A.K.Markram, A.L.Phehlukwayo.

SOUTH AFRICA

D.Elgar	c Mominul b Mustafizur	199	(2)	lbw b Shafiul	18
A.K.Markram	run out	97	(1)	c Liton b Mustafizur	15
H.M.Amla	c Mehedi b Shafiul	137		c Liton b Mustafizur	28
T.Bavuma	not out	31		c Liton b Mominul	71
*F.du Plessis	not out	26		lbw b Mominul	81
†Q.de Kock				st Liton b Mominul	8
A.L.Phehlukwayo				not out	6
K.A.Maharaj				not out	19
K.Rabada					
M.Morkel					
D.Olivier					
Extras	(LB 4, W 2)	6		(NB 1)	1
Total	**(3 wkts dec; 146 overs)**	**496**		**(6 wkts dec; 56 overs)**	**247**

BANGLADESH

†Liton Das	c Amla b Morkel	25	(6)	lbw b Rabada	4
Imrul Kayes	c Markram b Rabada	7		c de Kock b Maharaj	32
Mominul Haque	c Markram b Maharaj	77		lbw b Morkel	0
*Mushfiqur Rahim	c Markram b Maharaj	44		c Amla b Rabada	16
Tamim Iqbal	c de Kock b Phehlukwayo	39	(1)	b Morkel	0
Mahmudullah	b Morkel	66	(5)	b Rabada	9
Sabbir Rahman	b Olivier	30		lbw b Maharaj	4
Mehedi Hasan	c Elgar b Rabada	8		not out	15
Taskin Ahmed	run out	1		lbw b Maharaj	4
Shafiul Islam	c Amla b Maharaj	2		run out	2
Mustafizur Rahman	not out	10		c and b Maharaj	1
Extras	(B 1, LB 9, NB 1)	11		(B 1, NB 2)	3
Total	**(89.1 overs)**	**320**		**(32.4 overs)**	**90**

BANGLADESH	O	M	R	W	O	M	R	W
Mustafizur Rahman	27	2	98	1	(3) 11	2	30	2
Shafiul Islam	25	5	74	1	13	1	46	1
Mehedi Hasan	56	4	178	0	(1) 11	0	69	0
Taskin Ahmed	26	5	88	0	6	0	29	0
Mahmudullah	5	0	24	0	(6) 4	0	21	0
Mominul Haque	2	0	15	0	(7) 6	0	27	3
Sabbir Rahman	5	1	15	0	(5) 5	0	25	0

SOUTH AFRICA	O	M	R	W	O	M	R	W
Morkel	19	7	51	2	5.2	2	19	2
Rabada	24	5	84	2	10	3	33	3
Maharaj	27.1	8	92	3	(4) 10.4	1	25	4
Olivier	11	1	52	1	(3) 5.4	1	12	0
Phehlukwayo	6	2	18	1	1	1	0	0
Markram	2	0	13	0				

FALL OF WICKETS

Wkt	SA 1st	B 1st	SA 2nd	B 2nd
1st	196	16	30	0
2nd	411	36	38	0
3rd	445	103	70	49
4th	–	158	212	55
5th	–	227	217	62
6th	–	292	222	67
7th	–	304	–	67
8th	–	305	–	71
9th	–	308	–	75
10th	–	320	–	90

Umpires: C.B.Gaffaney (*New Zealand*) (16) and B.N.J.Oxenford (*Australia*) (44).
Referee: R.S.Madugalle (*Sri Lanka*) (178).　　　　Test No. 2274/11 (SA416/B103)

SOUTH AFRICA v BANGLADESH (2nd Test)

At Mangaung Oval, Bloemfontein, on 6, 7, 8 October 2017.
Toss: Bangladesh. Result: **SOUTH AFRICA** won by an innings and 254 runs.
Debuts: None.

SOUTH AFRICA

D.Elgar	c Mustafizur b Subashis	113
A.K.Markram	b Rubel	143
H.M.Amla	b Subashis	132
T.Bavuma	c Liton b Subashis	7
*F.du Plessis	not out	135
†Q.de Kock	not out	28
A.L.Phehlukwayo		
W.D.Parnell		
K.A.Maharaj		
K.Rabada		
D.Olivier		
Extras	(B 4, LB 2, NB 1, W 8)	15
Total	**(4 wkts dec; 120 overs; 508 mins)**	**573**

BANGLADESH

Imrul Kayes	c de Kock b Rabada	26	c de Kock b Olivier		32
Soumya Sarkar	b Rabada	9	c du Plessis b Rabada		3
Mominul Haque	c de Kock b Olivier	4	c Maharaj b Rabada		11
*Mushfiqur Rahim	c Bavuma b Olivier	7	lbw b Rabada		26
Mahmudullah	c de Kock b Parnell	4	c Elgar b Rabada		43
†Liton Das	c du Plessis b Rabada	70	b Phehlukwayo		18
Sabbir Rahman	c Parnell b Rabada	0	c du Plessis b Phehlukwayo		4
Taijul Islam	b Olivier	12	b Rabada		2
Rubel Hossain	b Rabada	10	b Rabada		7
Mustafizur Rahman	c Markram b Maharaj	0	(11) b Phehlukwayo		7
Subashis Roy	not out	2	(10) not out		12
Extras	(LB 3)	3	(LB 6, NB 1)		7
Total	**(42.5 overs; 207 mins)**	**147**	**(42.4 overs; 221 mins)**		**172**

BANGLADESH	O	M	R	W	O	M	R	W
Mustafizur Rahman	25	3	113	0				
Subashis Roy	29	3	118	3				
Rubel Hossain	22	1	113	1				
Soumya Sarkar	5	0	21	0				
Taijul Islam	27	0	145	0				
Mahmudullah	9	2	35	0				
Mominul Haque	1	0	6	0				
Sabbir Rahman	2	0	16	0				

SOUTH AFRICA	O	M	R	W	O	M	R	W
Rabada	13.5	4	33	5	11	1	30	5
Olivier	12	3	40	3	11	1	39	1
Parnell	7	1	36	1	(4) 5	0	31	1
Maharaj	5	2	7	1	(3) 6	1	30	0
Phehlukwayo	5	1	28	0	9.4	2	36	3

FALL OF WICKETS

	SA	B	B
Wkt	1st	1st	2nd
1st	243	13	13
2nd	276	26	29
3rd	288	36	63
4th	535	49	92
5th	–	61	135
6th	–	65	139
7th	–	115	145
8th	–	143	145
9th	–	143	156
10th	–	147	172

Umpires: H.D.P.K.Dharmasena (*Sri Lanka*) (47) and B.N.J.Oxenford (*Australia*) (45).
Referee: R.S.Madugalle (*Sri Lanka*) (179).   **Test No. 2275/12 (SA417/B104)**

PAKISTAN v SRI LANKA (1st Test)

At Sheikh Zayed Stadium, Abu Dhabi, 28, 29, 30 September, 1, 2 October 2017.
Toss: Sri Lanka. Result: **SRI LANKA** won by 21 runs.
Debut: Pakistan – Haris Sohail.   ‡ (W.S.R.Samarawickrama)

SRI LANKA

Batsman	1st innings		2nd innings	
F.D.M.Karunaratne	run out	93	c Masood b Shah	10
J.K.Silva	b Hasan	12	lbw b Sohail	25
H.D.R.L.Thirimanne	lbw b Shah	0	c Sarfraz b Shafiq	7
B.K.G.Mendis	c Sarfraz b Shah	10	lbw b Abbas	18
*L.D.Chandimal	not out	155	c Shafiq b Shah	7
†D.P.D.N.Dickwella	b Hasan	83	(7) not out	40
M.D.K.Perera	b Sohail	33	(8) lbw b Shah	6
H.M.R.K.B.Herath	c Azam b Shah	4	(9) c Masood b Shah	0
R.A.S.Lakmal	lbw b Abbas	7	(6) c Azam b Abbas	13
P.A.D.L.R.Sandakan	lbw b Abbas	8	c Amir b Shah	8
A.N.P.R.Fernando	b Abbas	0	b Hasan	0
Extras	(LB 11, NB 3)	14	(LB 3, NB 1)	4
Total	**(154.5 overs)**	**419**	**(66.5 overs)**	**138**

PAKISTAN

Batsman	1st innings		2nd innings	
Shan Masood	b Herath	59	c Silva b Perera	7
Sami Aslam	lbw b Perera	51	c Karunaratne b Herath	2
Azhar Ali	c sub‡ b Herath	85	c Dickwella b Lakmal	0
Asad Shafiq	c Thirimanne b Herath	39	c Karunaratne b Herath	20
Babar Azam	c Dickwella b Fernando	28	c Dickwella b Perera	3
Haris Sohail	c Lakmal b Fernando	76	lbw b Perera	34
*†Sarfraz Ahmed	b Lakmal	18	st Dickwella b Herath	19
Mohammad Amir	lbw b Lakmal	4	(9) b Herath	9
Yasir Shah	c Thirimanne b Herath	8	(10) not out	6
Hasan Ali	st Dickwella b Herath	29	(8) b Herath	8
Mohammad Abbas	not out	1	lbw b Herath	0
Extras	(B 5, LB 9, NB 8, W 2)	24	(B 1, LB 4, NB 1)	6
Total	**(162.3 overs)**	**422**	**(47.4 overs)**	**114**

PAKISTAN	O	M	R	W	O	M	R	W
Mohammad Amir	27	5	63	0	12	4	27	0
Mohammad Abbas	26.5	0	75	3	12	3	22	2
Yasir Shah	57	11	120	3	27	5	51	5
Hasan Ali	27	6	88	2	7.1	0	21	1
Shan Masood	1	1	0	0				
Haris Sohail	13	0	51	1	5	2	7	1
Asad Shafiq	3	0	11	0	(5) 3.4	0	7	1

SRI LANKA	O	M	R	W	O	M	R	W
Lakmal	22	5	42	2	5	1	12	1
Fernando	25.3	1	77	2	(4) 2	1	4	0
Perera	37	10	92	1	18	4	46	3
Sandakan	35	7	98	0	(5) 1	0	4	0
Herath	40	12	93	5	(2) 21.4	4	43	6
Karunaratne	3	1	6	0				

FALL OF WICKETS

	SL	P	SL	P
Wkt	1st	1st	2nd	2nd
1st	34	114	20	4
2nd	35	116	33	7
3rd	61	195	51	16
4th	161	266	65	32
5th	295	294	73	36
6th	387	316	86	78
7th	396	326	101	98
8th	408	340	101	100
9th	419	390	135	111
10th	419	422	138	114

Umpires: R.A.Kettleborough (*England*) (45) and N.J.Llong (*England*) (46).
Referee: A.J.Pycroft (*Zimbabwe*) (55).   **Test No. 2276/52 (P411/SL263)**
I.J.Gould (*England*) was the nominated umpire, but was unwell and unable to take the field.

PAKISTAN v SRI LANKA (2nd Test)

At Dubai Sports City Stadium, 6, 7, 8, 9, 10 October 2017 (day/night).
Toss: Sri Lanka. Result: **SRI LANKA** won by 68 runs.
Debuts: Sri Lanka – P.L.S.Gamage, W.S.R.Samarawickrama.

SRI LANKA

F.D.M.Karunaratne	b Riaz	196		b Riaz	7
J.K.Silva	c Sarfraz b Shah	27		c Sarfraz b Abbas	3
W.S.R.Samarawickrama	c and b Amir	38		c Sarfraz b Riaz	13
B.K.G.Mendis	c Shafiq b Shah	1		c Sarfraz b Sohail	29
*L.D.Chandimal	lbw b Shah	62	(6)	lbw b Riaz	0
†D.P.D.N.Dickwella	c Sarfraz b Abbas	52	(7)	c Sarfraz b Riaz	21
M.D.K.Perera	b Shah	58	(8)	lbw b Shah	0
H.M.R.K.B.Herath	not out	27	(9)	c Azam b Sohail	17
R.A.S.Lakmal	b Abbas	8	(5)	lbw b Shah	1
P.L.S.Gamage	st Sarfraz b Shah	1		not out	1
A.N.P.R.Fernando	c Shafiq b Shah	0		lbw b Sohail	0
Extras	(B 1, LB 3, NB 5, W 3)	12		(LB 1, NB 3)	4
Total	**(159.2 overs)**	**482**		**(26 overs)**	**96**

PAKISTAN

Shan Masood	b Gamage	16		c Dickwella b Perera	21
Sami Aslam	lbw b Perera	39		c Mendis b Gamage	1
Azhar Ali	lbw b Herath	59		c Silva b Fernando	17
Asad Shafiq	c Mendis b Lakmal	13	(5)	c Mendis b Lakmal	112
Babar Azam	c Samarawickrama b Herath	8	(6)	c Silva b Perera	0
Haris Sohail	lbw b Perera	56	(4)	c Dickwella b Perera	10
*†Sarfraz Ahmed	c Mendis b Perera	14		c Fernando b Perera	68
Mohammad Amir	lbw b Herath	7		lbw b Perera	4
Yasir Shah	b Lakmal	24		st Dickwella b Herath	5
Wahab Riaz	c Samarawickrama b Gamage	16		c Chandimal b Herath	1
Mohammad Abbas	not out	1		not out	3
Extras	(B 4, LB 2, NB 4)	10		(LB 1, NB 5)	6
Total	**(90.3 overs)**	**262**		**(90.2 overs)**	**248**

PAKISTAN	O	M	R	W		O	M	R	W		FALL OF WICKETS			
												SL	P	SL	P
Mohammad Amir	19.3	5	74	1							*Wkt*	*1st*	*1st*	*2nd*	*2nd*
Mohammad Abbas	33	9	100	2	(1)	4	2	6	1		1st	63	61	3	5
Wahab Riaz	26	6	62	1		9	0	41	4		2nd	131	65	22	36
Yasir Shah	55.5	9	184	6	(2)	12	2	47	2		3rd	136	92	26	49
Asad Shafiq	11	1	24	0							4th	282	109	33	52
Haris Sohail	14	3	34	0	(4)	1	0	1	3		5th	370	180	34	52
											6th	429	199	59	225
SRI LANKA											7th	454	214	60	230
Lakmal	17.3	5	41	2		14	4	35	1		8th	469	220	95	244
Fernando	9	2	21	0	(4)	11	3	21	1		9th	474	250	96	244
Gamage	15	2	38	2	(2)	16	5	29	1		10th	482	262	96	248
Perera	26	3	72	3	(5)	26	1	98	5						
Herath	23	3	84	3	(3)	22.2	3	57	2						
Mendis						1	0	7	0						

Umpires: R.A.Kettleborough (*England*) (46) and N.J.Llong (*England*) (47).
Referee: A.J.Pycroft (*Zimbabwe*) (56).   Test No. 2277/53 (P412/SL264)

ZIMBABWE v WEST INDIES (1st Test)

At Queens Sports Club, Bulawayo, on 21, 22, 23, 24 October 2017.
Toss: West Indies. Result: **WEST INDIES** won by 117 runs.
Debut: Zimbabwe – S.F.Mire.

WEST INDIES

Batsman	1st innings		2nd innings	
K.C.Brathwaite	c Chakabva b Jarvis	3	lbw b Sikandar Raza	86
K.O.A.Powell	c Ervine b Cremer	56	b Cremer	17
K.A.Hope	c Chakabva b Mire	16	lbw b Jarvis	43
S.D.Hope	not out	90	lbw b Jarvis	44
R.L.Chase	c Ervine b Sikandar Raza	31	b Williams	95
J.Blackwood	st Chakabva b Cremer	1	st Chakabva b Williams	3
†S.O.Dowrich	c Masakadza b Williams	11	c Masakadza b Williams	12
*J.O.Holder	lbw b Williams	8	c Mpofu b Cremer	24
D.Bishoo	c Ervine b Williams	0	c Williams b Cremer	44
K.A.J.Roach	lbw b Cremer	0	b Cremer	0
S.T.Gabriel	c Ervine b Cremer	0	not out	0
Extras	(B 3)	3	(B 3, LB 2)	5
Total	**(82.5 overs)**	**219**	**(126 overs)**	**373**

ZIMBABWE

Batsman	1st innings		2nd innings	
H.Masakadza	c Dowrich b Bishoo	42	c S.D.Hope b Brathwaite	57
S.F.Mire	c Brathwaite b Roach	27	b Roach	47
C.R.Ervine	lbw b Bishoo	39	lbw b Bishoo	18
B.R.M.Taylor	c Blackwood b Bishoo	1	run out	73
S.C.Williams	c Dowrich b Roach	7	st Dowrich b Bishoo	6
Sikandar Raza	c Gabriel b Bishoo	6	c Chase b Bishoo	30
M.N.Waller	b Holder	11	run out	11
†R.W.Chakabva	c Chase b Bishoo	12	c and b Chase	1
*A.G.Cremer	b Holder	0	c and b Bishoo	9
K.M.Jarvis	not out	2	not out	23
C.B.Mpofu	c Dowrich b Gabriel	10	c Powell b Chase	33
Extras	(LB 2)	2	(B 5, LB 1, NB 2)	8
Total	**(61.3 overs)**	**159**	**(90.4 overs)**	**316**

ZIMBABWE	O	M	R	W		O	M	R	W
Jarvis	14	2	40	1		24	1	66	2
Mpofu	14	4	28	0		10	3	30	0
Mire	7	0	22	1	(6) 2	0	5	0
Cremer	23.5	3	64	4		34	5	114	4
Sikandar Raza	11	1	42	1		19	4	53	1
Williams	13	4	20	3	(3) 35	8	91	0
Waller						2	0	9	0

WEST INDIES	O	M	R	W		O	M	R	W
Gabriel	11.3	4	24	1	(2) 10	2	50	0
Holder	14	5	25	2	(3) 4	0	30	0
Bishoo	24	4	79	5	(4) 32	8	105	4
Chase	1	0	6	0	(5) 13.4	2	61	2
Roach	11	5	23	2	(1) 13	3	34	1
Brathwaite						10	1	30	1

FALL OF WICKETS

	WI	Z	WI	Z
Wkt	1st	1st	2nd	2nd
1st	14	44	25	99
2nd	35	91	107	109
3rd	110	93	174	141
4th	174	110	211	155
5th	179	123	224	219
6th	202	133	244	246
7th	212	139	277	249
8th	218	147	369	253
9th	219	147	369	263
10th	219	159	373	316

Umpires: H.D.P.K.Dharmasena (*Sri Lanka*) (48) and P.R.Reiffel (*Australia*) (33).
Referee: J.Srinath (*India*) (36).   **Test No. 2278/9 (Z103/WI527)**

ZIMBABWE v WEST INDIES (2nd Test)

At Queens Sports Club, Bulawayo, on 29, 30, 31 October, 1, 2 November 2017.
Toss: Zimbabwe. Result: **MATCH DRAWN**.
Debut: Zimbabwe – T.S.Chisoro.

ZIMBABWE

H.Masakadza	c Dowrich b Bishoo	147	b Roach		5
S.F.Mire	c Dowrich b Roach	4	lbw b Roach		0
C.R.Ervine	b Gabriel	0	b Bishoo		22
B.R.M.Taylor	b Roach	1	lbw b Gabriel		10
P.J.Moor	b Chase	52	c S.D.Hope b Gabriel		42
Sikandar Raza	c K.A.Hope b Gabriel	80	b Holder		89
M.N.Waller	b Brathwaite	0	c Blackwood b Bishoo		15
†R.W.Chakabva	b Bishoo	10	not out		71
*A.G.Cremer	run out	11	not out		28
T.S.Chisoro	lbw b Roach	9			
C.B.Mpofu	not out	4			
Extras	(LB 6, NB 2)	8	(B 10, LB 8, NB 1)		19
Total	**(109.1 overs)**	**326**	**(7 wkts; 144 overs)**		**301**

WEST INDIES

K.C.Brathwaite	c Masakadza b Cremer	32
K.O.A.Powell	c Ervine b Mpofu	90
D.Bishoo	c and b Sikandar Raza	23
K.A.Hope	lbw b Sikandar Raza	1
S.D.Hope	b Sikandar Raza	40
R.L.Chase	lbw b Sikandar Raza	32
J.Blackwood	c Cremer b Sikandar Raza	5
†S.O.Dowrich	lbw b Chisoro	103
*J.O.Holder	b Chisoro	110
K.A.J.Roach	lbw b Chisoro	0
S.T.Gabriel	not out	5
Extras	(B 3, LB 3, NB 1)	7
Total	**(178.2 overs)**	**448**

WEST INDIES	O	M	R	W		O	M	R	W
Gabriel	22	4	64	2		21	7	34	2
Roach	18.1	5	44	3		22	10	37	2
Blackwood	4	1	8	0	(7)	10	4	21	0
Holder	16	2	49	0		22	7	42	1
Bishoo	25	2	82	2		34	7	74	2
Chase	14	1	50	1		17	3	31	0
Brathwaite	10	0	23	1	(3)	17	2	44	0
Powell						1	1	0	0

ZIMBABWE	O	M	R	W
Mpofu	28	10	55	1
Mire	5	2	5	0
Cremer	52	8	161	1
Sikandar Raza	48	12	99	5
Chisoro	41.2	9	113	3
Masakadza	4	1	9	0

FALL OF WICKETS			
	Z	WI	Z
Wkt	1st	1st	2nd
1st	4	76	5
2nd	11	131	8
3rd	14	135	23
4th	156	163	46
5th	246	219	144
6th	248	225	172
7th	267	230	210
8th	310	442	–
9th	319	443	–
10th	326	448	–

Umpires: H.D.P.K.Dharmasena (*Sri Lanka*) (49) and S.D.Fry (*Australia*) (7).
Referee: J.Srinath (*India*) (37).   **Test No. 2279/10 (Z104/WI528)**

INDIA v SRI LANKA (1st Test)

At Eden Gardens, Kolkata, on 16, 17, 18, 19, 20 November 2017.
Toss: Sri Lanka. Result: **MATCH DRAWN**.
Debuts: None.

INDIA

K.L.Rahul	c Dickwella b Lakmal	0	b Lakmal		79
S.Dhawan	b Lakmal	8	c Dickwella b Shanaka		94
C.A.Pujara	b Gamage	52	c Perera b Lakmal		22
*V.Kohli	lbw b Lakmal	0	not out		104
A.M.Rahane	c Dickwella b Shanaka	4	lbw b Lakmal		0
R.Ashwin	c Karunaratne b Shanaka	4	(7) b Shanaka		7
†W.P.Saha	c Mathews b Perera	29	(8) c Samarawickrama b Shanaka		5
R.A.Jadeja	lbw b Perera	22	(6) c Thirimanne b Lakmal		9
B.Kumar	c Dickwella b Lakmal	13	c Perera b Gamage		8
Mohammed Shami	c Shanaka b Gamage	24	not out		12
U.T.Yadav	not out	6			
Extras	(B 6, LB 4)	10	(B 7, LB 1, NB 1, W 3)		12
Total	**(59.3 overs; 294 mins)**	**172**	**(8 wkts dec; 88.4 overs; 418 mins)**		**352**

SRI LANKA

W.S.R.Samarawickrama	c Saha b Kumar	23	b Kumar		0
F.D.M.Karunaratne	lbw b Kumar	8	b Shami		1
H.D.R.L.Thirimanne	c Kohli b Yadav	51	c Rahane b Kumar		7
A.D.Mathews	c Rahul b Yadav	52	lbw b Yadav		12
*L.D.Chandimal	c Saha b Shami	28	b Shami		20
†D.P.D.N.Dickwella	c Kohli b Shami	35	lbw b Kumar		27
M.D.Shanaka	lbw b Kumar	0	not out		6
M.D.K.Perera	c Saha b Shami	5	b Kumar		0
H.M.R.K.B.Herath	c Shami b Kumar	67	not out		0
R.A.S.Lakmal	b Shami	16			
P.L.S.Gamage	not out	0			
Extras	(B 4, LB 4, W 1)	9	(LB 1, NB 1)		2
Total	**(83.4 overs; 397 mins)**	**294**	**(7 wkts; 26.3 overs; 132 mins)**		**75**

SRI LANKA	O	M	R	W		O	M	R	W		FALL OF WICKETS				
Lakmal	19	12	26	4		24.4	4	93	3			I	SL	I	SL
Gamage	17.3	5	59	2		23	2	97	1		Wkt	1st	1st	2nd	2nd
Shanaka	12	4	36	2		22	1	76	3		1st	0	29	166	0
Karunaratne	2	0	17	0							2nd	13	34	192	2
Herath	2	0	5	0		6	1	29	0		3rd	17	133	213	14
Perera	7	1	19	2	(4)	13	2	49	1		4th	30	138	213	22
											5th	50	200	249	69
INDIA											6th	79	201	269	69
Kumar	27	5	88	4		11	8	8	4		7th	127	201	281	75
Mohammed Shami	26.3	5	100	4		9.3	4	34	2		8th	128	244	321	–
Yadav	20	1	79	2		5	0	25	1		9th	146	290	–	–
Ashwin	8	2	13	0							10th	172	294	–	–
Kohli	1.1	0	5	0											
Jadeja	1	0	1	0	(4)	1	0	7	0						

Umpires: R.A.Kettleborough (*England*) (47), N.J.Llong (*England*) (48) and J.S.Wilson (*West Indies*) (6).
Referee: D.C.Boon (*Australia*) (45).

Test No. 2280/42 (I516/SL265)

INDIA v SRI LANKA (2nd Test)

At Vidarbha C.A. Stadium, Nagpur, on 24, 25, 26, 27 November 2017.
Toss: Sri Lanka. Result: **INDIA** won by an innings and 239 runs.
Debuts: None.

SRI LANKA

W.S.R.Samarawickrama	c Pujara b I.Sharma	13	b I.Sharma		0
F.D.M.Karunaratne	lbw b I.Sharma	51	c Vijay b Jadeja		18
H.D.R.L.Thirimanne	b Ashwin	9	c Jadeja b Yadav		23
A.D.Mathews	lbw b Jadeja	10	c R.G.Sharma b Jadeja		10
*L.D.Chandimal	lbw b Ashwin	57	c Ashwin b Yadav		61
†D.P.D.N.Dickwella	c I.Sharma b Jadeja	24	c Kohli b I.Sharma		4
M.D.Shanaka	b Ashwin	2	c Rahul b Ashwin		17
M.D.K.Perera	lbw b Jadeja	15	lbw b Ashwin		0
H.M.R.K.B.Herath	c Rahane b Ashwin	4	c Rahane b Ashwin		0
R.A.S.Lakmal	c Saha b I.Sharma	17	not out		31
P.L.S.Gamage	not out	0	b Ashwin		0
Extras	(LB 2, NB 1)	3	(LB 2)		2
Total	**(79.1 overs; 319 mins)**	**205**	**(49.3 overs; 204 mins)**		**166**

INDIA

K.L.Rahul	b Gamage	7
M.Vijay	c Perera b Herath	128
C.A.Pujara	b Shanaka	143
*V.Kohli	c Thirimanne b Perera	213
A.M.Rahane	c Karunaratne b Perera	2
R.G.Sharma	not out	102
R.Ashwin	b Perera	5
†W.P.Saha	not out	1
R.A.Jadeja		
U.T.Yadav		
I.Sharma		
Extras	(B 4, LB 4, W 1)	9
Total	**(6 wkts dec; 176.1 overs; 731 mins)**	**610**

INDIA	O	M	R	W		O	M	R	W		FALL OF WICKETS		
I.Sharma	14	3	37	3		12	4	43	2			SL	I	SL
Yadav	16	4	43	0	(4)	9	2	30	2		*Wkt*	*1st*	*1st*	*2nd*
Ashwin	28.1	7	67	4	(2)	17.3	4	63	4		1st	20	7	0
Jadeja	21	4	56	3	(3)	11	5	28	2		2nd	44	216	34
											3rd	60	399	48
SRI LANKA											4th	122	410	68
Lakmal	29	2	111	0							5th	160	583	75
Gamage	35	8	97	1							6th	165	597	102
Herath	39	11	81	1							7th	184	–	107
Shanaka	26.1	4	103	1							8th	184	–	107
Perera	45	2	202	3							9th	205	–	165
Karunaratne	2	0	8	0							10th	205	–	166

Umpires: R.A.Kettleborough (*England*) (48), J.S.Wilson (*West Indies*) (7).
Referee: D.C.Boon (*Australia*) (46).   **Test No. 2281/43 (I517/SL266)**

INDIA v SRI LANKA (3rd Test)

At Feroz Shah Kotla, Delhi, on 2, 3, 4, 5, 6 December 2017.
Toss: India. Result: **MATCH DRAWN**.
Debut: Sri Lanka – A.R.S.Silva.

INDIA

M.Vijay	st Dickwella b Sandakan	155		c Dickwella b Lakmal	9
S.Dhawan	c Lakmal b Perera	23		st Dickwella b Sandakan	67
C.A.Pujara	c Samarawickrama b Gamage	23	(4)	c Mathews b de Silva	49
*V.Kohli	lbw b Sandakan	243	(5)	c Lakmal b Gamage	50
A.M.Rahane	st Dickwella b Sandakan	1	(3)	c Sandakan b Perera	10
R.G.Sharma	c Dickwella b Sandakan	65		not out	50
R.Ashwin	c Perera b Gamage	4			
†W.P.Saha	not out	9			
R.A.Jadeja	not out	5	(7)	not out	4
I.Sharma					
Mohammed Shami					
Extras	(LB 1, NB 7)	8		(B 1, LB 2, NB 3, W 1)	7
Total	(7 wkts dec; 127.5 overs; 564 mins)	536		(5 wkts dec; 52.2 overs; 254 mins)	246

SRI LANKA

F.D.M.Karunaratne	c Saha b Shami	0		c Saha b Jadeja	13
M.D.K.Perera	lbw b Jadeja	42			
D.M.de Silva	lbw b I.Sharma	1		retired hurt	119
A.D.Mathews	c Saha b Ashwin	111	(5)	c Rahane b Jadeja	1
*L.D.Chandimal	c Dhawan b I.Sharma	164	(6)	b Ashwin	36
W.S.R.Samarawickrama	c Saha b I.Sharma	33	(2)	c Rahane b Shami	5
A.R.S.Silva	c Dhawan b Ashwin	0		not out	74
†D.P.D.N.Dickwella	b Ashwin	0		not out	44
R.A.S.Lakmal	c Saha b Shami	5	(4)	b Jadeja	0
P.L.S.Gamage	lbw b Jadeja	1			
P.A.D.L.R.Sandakan	not out	0			
Extras	(B 4, LB 5, NB 2, Pen 5)	16		(B 5, LB 1, NB 1)	7
Total	(135.3 overs; 562 mins)	373		(5 wkts; 103 overs; 398 mins)	299

SRI LANKA	O	M	R	W		O	M	R	W	FALL OF WICKETS
Lakmal	21.2	4	80	0		14	3	60	1			I	SL	I	SL
Gamage	25.3	7	95	2		12.2	1	48	1		Wkt	1st	1st	2nd	2nd
Perera	31.1	0	145	1		11	0	54	1		1st	42	0	10	14
Sandakan	33.5	1	167	4	(5)	10	0	50	1		2nd	78	14	29	31
De Silva	16	0	48	0	(4)	5	0	31	1		3rd	361	75	106	31
											4th	365	256	144	35
INDIA											5th	500	317	234	147
Mohammed Shami	26	6	85	2	(2)	15	6	50	1		6th	519	318	–	–
I.Sharma	29.3	7	98	3	(1)	13	2	32	0		7th	523	322	–	–
Jadeja	45	13	86	2	(4)	38	13	81	3		8th	–	331	–	–
Ashwin	35	8	90	3	(3)	35	3	126	1		9th	–	343	–	–
Vijay						1	0	3	0		10th	–	373	–	–
Kohli						1	0	1	0						

Umpires: N.J.Llong (*England*) (49), J.S.Wilson (*West Indies*) (8).
Referee: D.C.Boon (*Australia*) (47).   **Test No. 2282/44 (I518/SL267)**
D.M.de Silva retired hurt at 205-5.

AUSTRALIA v ENGLAND (1st Test)

At Woolloongabba, Brisbane, on 23, 24, 25, 26, 27 November 2017.
Toss: England. Result: **AUSTRALIA** won by ten wickets.
Debut: Australia – C.T.Bancroft.

ENGLAND

A.N.Cook	c Handscomb b Starc	2	c Starc b Hazlewood	7
M.D.Stoneman	b Cummins	53	c Smith b Lyon	27
J.M.Vince	run out	83	c Smith b Hazlewood	2
*J.E.Root	lbw b Cummins	15	lbw b Hazlewood	51
D.J.Malan	c Marsh b Starc	56	c Smith b Lyon	4
M.M.Ali	lbw b Lyon	38	st Paine b Lyon	40
†J.M.Bairstow	c Paine b Cummins	9	c Handscomb b Starc	42
C.R.Woakes	b Lyon	0	c Smith b Starc	17
S.C.J.Broad	c Handscomb b Hazlewood	20	c Paine b Starc	2
J.T.Ball	c Warner b Starc	14	c Handscomb b Cummins	1
J.M.Anderson	not out	5	not out	0
Extras	(B 5, NB 1, W 1)	7	(NB 2)	2
Total	**(116.4 overs; 509 mins)**	**302**	**(71.4 overs; 325 mins)**	**195**

AUSTRALIA

C.T.Bancroft	c Bairstow b Broad	5	not out	82
D.A.Warner	c Malan b Ball	26	not out	87
U.T.Khawaja	lbw b Ali	11		
*S.P.D.Smith	not out	141		
P.S.P.Handscomb	lbw b Anderson	14		
S.E.Marsh	c Anderson b Broad	51		
†T.D.Paine	c Bairstow b Anderson	13		
M.A.Starc	c and b Broad	6		
P.J.Cummins	c Cook b Woakes	42		
J.R.Hazlewood	b Ali	6		
N.M.Lyon	c Cook b Root	9		
Extras	(LB 1, NB 1, W 2)	4	(LB 2, NB 1, W 1)	4
Total	**(130.3 overs; 561 mins)**	**328**	**(0 wkts; 50 overs; 212 mins)**	**173**

AUSTRALIA	O	M	R	W	O	M	R	W
Starc	28	4	77	3	16	1	51	3
Hazlewood	22.4	6	57	1	16	3	46	3
Cummins	30	8	85	3	12.4	4	23	1
Lyon	36	12	78	2	24	4	67	3
Smith					3	0	8	0
ENGLAND								
Anderson	29	10	50	2	11	2	27	0
Broad	25	10	49	3	10	2	20	0
Ali	30	8	74	2	4	0	23	0
Woakes	24	5	67	1	11	1	46	0
Ball	18	3	77	1	8	1	38	0
Root	4.3	0	10	1	6	1	17	0

FALL OF WICKETS

Wkt	E 1st	A 1st	E 2nd	A 2nd
1st	2	7	11	–
2nd	127	30	17	
3rd	145	59	62	
4th	163	76	74	
5th	246	175	113	
6th	249	202	155	
7th	250	209	185	
8th	270	275	194	
9th	286	298	195	
10th	302	328	195	

Umpires: Alim Dar (*Pakistan*) (115) and M.Erasmus (*South Africa*) (46).
Referee: Sir R.B.Richardson (*West Indies*) (12).   Test No. 2283/342 (A804/E991)

AUSTRALIA v ENGLAND (2nd Test)

At Adelaide Oval, on 2, 3, 4, 5, 6 December 2017 (day/night).
Toss: England. Result: **AUSTRALIA** won by 120 runs.
Debut: England – C.Overton.

AUSTRALIA

Batsman	1st innings		2nd innings	
C.T.Bancroft	run out	10	c Bairstow b Anderson	4
D.A.Warner	c Bairstow b Woakes	47	c Root b Woakes	14
U.T.Khawaja	c Vince b Anderson	53	lbw b Anderson	20
*S.P.D.Smith	b Overton	40	lbw b Woakes	6
P.S.P.Handscomb	lbw b Broad	36	c Malan b Anderson	12
S.E.Marsh	not out	126	(7) b Woakes	19
†T.D.Paine	c Ali b Overton	57	(8) c Overton b Woakes	11
M.A.Starc	c Anderson b Broad	6	(9) c Ali b Anderson	20
P.J.Cummins	c Malan b Overton	44	(10) not out	11
N.M.Lyon	not out	10	(6) c Broad b Anderson	14
J.R.Hazlewood			c Malan b Overton	3
Extras	(B 6, LB 6, W 1)	13	(LB 2, W 2)	4
Total	(8 wkts dec; 149 overs; 615 mins)	**442**	(58 overs; 271 mins)	**138**

ENGLAND

Batsman	1st innings		2nd innings	
A.N.Cook	c Smith b Lyon	37	lbw b Lyon	16
M.D.Stoneman	lbw b Starc	18	c Khawaja b Starc	36
J.M.Vince	c Paine b Hazlewood	2	c Handscomb b Starc	15
*J.E.Root	c Bancroft b Cummins	9	c Paine b Hazlewood	67
D.J.Malan	c Paine b Cummins	19	b Cummins	29
M.M.Ali	c and b Lyon	25	(7) lbw b Lyon	2
†J.M.Bairstow	c and b Starc	21	(8) b Starc	36
C.R.Woakes	c and b Starc	36	(6) c Paine b Hazlewood	5
C.Overton	not out	41	lbw b Root	7
S.C.J.Broad	c Paine b Lyon	3	c Paine b Starc	8
J.M.Anderson	lbw b Lyon	0	not out	0
Extras	(LB 15, W 1)	16	(B 7, LB 5)	12
Total	(76.1 overs; 331 mins)	**227**	(84.2 overs; 379 mins)	**233**

ENGLAND	O	M	R	W		O	M	R	W
Anderson	31	5	74	1		22	7	43	5
Broad	30	11	72	2		13	6	26	0
Woakes	27	4	84	1	(4)	16	3	36	4
Overton	33	3	105	3	(3)	2	0	11	1
Ali	24	3	79	0		5	0	20	0
Root	4	0	16	0					
AUSTRALIA									
Starc	20	4	49	3		19.2	3	88	5
Hazlewood	16	3	56	1		20	7	49	2
Cummins	16	3	47	2		20	6	39	1
Lyon	24.1	5	60	4		25	6	45	2

FALL OF WICKETS

Wkt	A 1st	E 1st	A 2nd	E 2nd
1st	33	29	5	53
2nd	86	31	39	54
3rd	139	50	41	91
4th	161	80	50	169
5th	209	102	71	176
6th	294	132	75	177
7th	311	142	90	188
8th	410	208	122	206
9th	–	227	128	224
10th	–	227	138	233

Umpires: Alim Dar (*Pakistan*) (116) and C.B.Gaffaney (*New Zealand*) (17).
Referee: Sir R.B.Richardson (*West Indies*) (13). Test No. 2284/343 (A805/E992)

AUSTRALIA v ENGLAND (3rd Test)

At W.A.C.A.Ground, Perth, on 14, 15, 16, 17, 18 December 2017.
Toss: England. Result: **AUSTRALIA** won by an innings and 41 runs.
Debuts: None.

ENGLAND

A.N.Cook	lbw b Starc	7	c and b Hazlewood	14
M.D.Stoneman	c Paine b Starc	56	c Paine b Hazlewood	3
J.M.Vince	c Paine b Hazlewood	25	b Starc	55
*J.E.Root	c Paine b Cummins	20	c Smith b Lyon	14
D.J.Malan	c sub (P.S.P.Handscomb) b Lyon	140	c Paine b Hazlewood	54
†J.M.Bairstow	b Starc	119	b Hazlewood	14
M.M.Ali	c Smith b Cummins	0	lbw b Lyon	11
C.R.Woakes	c Cummins b Hazlewood	8	c Paine b Cummins	22
C.Overton	c Bancroft b Hazlewood	2	c Khawaja b Hazlewood	12
S.C.J.Broad	c Bancroft b Starc	12	c Paine b Cummins	0
J.M.Anderson	not out	0	not out	1
Extras	(B 10, LB 2, NB 1, W 1)	14	(B 6, LB 11, NB 1)	18
Total	**(115.1 overs; 523 mins)**	**403**	**(72.5 overs; 332 mins)**	**218**

AUSTRALIA

C.T.Bancroft	lbw b Overton	25
D.A.Warner	c Bairstow b Overton	22
U.T.Khawaja	lbw b Woakes	50
*S.P.D.Smith	lbw b Anderson	239
S.E.Marsh	c Root b Ali	28
M.R.Marsh	lbw b Anderson	181
†T.D.Paine	not out	49
M.A.Starc	run out	1
P.J.Cummins	lbw b Anderson	41
N.M.Lyon	c Ali b Anderson	4
J.R.Hazlewood		
Extras	(B 4, LB 16, NB 1, W 1)	22
Total	**(9 wkts dec; 179.3 overs; 776 mins)**	**662**

AUSTRALIA	O	M	R	W	O	M	R	W	FALL OF WICKETS			
										E	A	E
Starc	25.1	5	91	4	17	5	44	1	Wkt	1st	1st	2nd
Hazlewood	28	9	92	3	18	6	48	5	1st	26	44	4
Cummins	28	8	84	2	(4) 19.5	4	53	2	2nd	89	55	29
Lyon	22	4	73	1	(5) 15	4	42	2	3rd	115	179	60
M.R.Marsh	9	1	43	0	(3) 3	1	14	0	4th	131	248	100
Smith	3	1	8	0					5th	368	549	133
									6th	372	560	172
ENGLAND									7th	389	561	196
Anderson	37.3	9	116	4					8th	389	654	210
Broad	35	3	142	0					9th	393	662	211
Woakes	41	8	128	1					10th	403	–	218
Overton	24	1	110	2								
Ali	33	4	120	1								
Root	3	0	13	0								
Malan	6	1	13	0								

Umpires: M.Erasmus (*South Africa*) (47) and C.B.Gaffaney (*New Zealand*) (18).
Referee: Sir R.B.Richardson (*West Indies*) (14). Test No. 2285/344 (A806/E993)

AUSTRALIA v ENGLAND (4th Test)

At Melbourne Cricket Ground, on 26, 27, 28, 29, 30 December 2017.
Toss: Australia. Result: **MATCH DRAWN**.
Debut: England – T.K.Curran.

AUSTRALIA

C.T.Bancroft	lbw b Woakes	26	b Woakes		27
D.A.Warner	c Bairstow b Anderson	103	c Vince b Root		86
U.T.Khawaja	c Bairstow b Broad	17	c Bairstow b Anderson		11
*S.P.D.Smith	b Curran	76	not out		102
S.E.Marsh	lbw b Broad	61	c Bairstow b Broad		4
M.R.Marsh	b Woakes	9	not out		29
†T.D.Paine	b Anderson	24			
P.J.Cummins	c Cook b Broad	4			
J.M.Bird	lbw b Broad	4			
J.R.Hazlewood	not out	1			
N.M.Lyon	lbw b Anderson	0			
Extras	(LB 1, NB 1)	2	(B 4)		4
Total	**(119 overs)**	**327**	**(4 wkts; 124.2 overs)**		**263**

ENGLAND

A.N.Cook	not out	244
M.D.Stoneman	c and b Lyon	15
J.M.Vince	lbw b Hazlewood	17
*J.E.Root	c Lyon b Cummins	61
D.J.Malan	lbw b Hazlewood	14
†J.M.Bairstow	c Paine b Lyon	22
M.M.Ali	c S.E.Marsh b Lyon	20
C.R.Woakes	c Paine b Cummins	26
T.K.Curran	c Paine b Hazlewood	4
S.C.J.Broad	c Khawaja b Cummins	56
J.M.Anderson	c Bancroft b Cummins	0
Extras	(B 4, LB 5, NB 3)	12
Total	**(144.1 overs; 634 mins)**	**491**

ENGLAND	O	M	R	W		O	M	R	W
Anderson	29	11	61	3		30	12	46	1
Broad	28	10	51	4		24	11	44	1
Woakes	22	4	72	2		26	7	62	1
Ali	12	0	57	0	(5)	13.2	2	32	0
Curran	21	5	65	1	(4)	20	6	53	0
Malan	7	1	20	0		8	1	21	0
Root						3	2	1	1

AUSTRALIA	O	M	R	W
Hazlewood	30	5	95	3
Bird	30	5	108	0
Lyon	42	9	109	3
Cummins	29.1	1	117	4
M.R.Marsh	12	1	42	0
Smith	1	0	11	0

FALL OF WICKETS

Wkt	A	E	A
	1st	1st	2nd
1st	122	35	51
2nd	135	80	65
3rd	160	218	172
4th	260	246	178
5th	278	279	–
6th	314	307	–
7th	318	366	–
8th	325	373	–
9th	326	473	–
10th	327	491	–

Umpires: H.D.P.K.Dharmasena (*Sri Lanka*) (50) and S.Ravi (*India*) (24).
Referee: R.S.Madugalle (*Sri Lanka*) (180).   **Test No. 2286/345 (A807/E994)**

AUSTRALIA v ENGLAND (5th Test)

At Sydney Cricket Ground, on 4, 5, 6, 7, 8 January 2018.
Toss: England. Result: **AUSTRALIA** won by an innings and 123 runs.
Debut: England – M.S.Crane.

ENGLAND

A.N.Cook	lbw b Hazlewood	39	b Lyon		10
M.D.Stoneman	c Paine b Cummins	24	lbw b Starc		0
J.M.Vince	c Paine b Cummins	25	c Smith b Cummins		18
*J.E.Root	c M.R.Marsh b Starc	83	retired hurt		58
D.J.Malan	c Smith b Starc	62	lbw b Lyon		5
†J.M.Bairstow	c Paine b Hazlewood	5	lbw b Cummins		38
M.M.Ali	c Paine b Cummins	30	lbw b Lyon		13
T.K.Curran	c Bancroft b Cummins	39	not out		23
S.C.J.Broad	c Smith b Lyon	31	c Paine b Cummins		4
M.S.Crane	run out	4	c Paine b Cummins		2
J.M.Anderson	not out	0	c Paine b Hazlewood		2
Extras	(LB 2, W 2)	4	(LB 2, Pen 5)		7
Total	**(112.3 overs)**	**346**	**(88.1 overs)**		**180**

AUSTRALIA

C.T.Bancroft	b Broad	0
D.A.Warner	c Bairstow b Anderson	56
U.T.Khawaja	st Bairstow b Crane	171
*S.P.D.Smith	c and b Ali	83
S.E.Marsh	run out	156
M.R.Marsh	b Curran	101
†T.D.Paine	not out	38
M.A.Starc	c Vince b Ali	11
P.J.Cummins	not out	24
J.R.Hazlewood		
N.M.Lyon		
Extras	(B 2, LB 4, NB 2, W 1)	9
Total	**(7 wkts dec; 193 overs)**	**649**

AUSTRALIA	O	M	R	W		O	M	R	W
Starc	21	6	80	2		16	4	38	1
Hazlewood	23	4	65	2		17.1	6	36	1
Cummins	24.3	5	80	4	(4)	17	4	39	4
Lyon	37	5	86	1	(3)	35	12	54	3
M.R.Marsh	7	0	33	0	(6)	1	0	1	0
Smith					(5)	2	0	0	0

ENGLAND	O	M	R	W
Anderson	34	14	56	1
Broad	30	2	121	1
Ali	48	10	170	2
Curran	25	3	82	1
Crane	48	3	193	1
Root	8	3	21	0

FALL OF WICKETS			
	E	A	E
Wkt	1st	1st	2nd
1st	28	1	5
2nd	88	86	15
3rd	95	274	43
4th	228	375	68
5th	233	544	121
6th	251	596	144
7th	294	613	148
8th	335	–	156
9th	346	–	180
10th	346	–	–

Umpires: H.D.P.K.Dharmasena (*Sri Lanka*) (51) and J.S.Wilson (*West Indies*) (9).
Referee: R.S.Madugalle (*Sri Lanka*) (181). **Test No. 2287/346 (A808/E995)**
J.E.Root retired hurt overnight at 92-4 and resumed at 121-5. He was taken ill again at 144-5.

NEW ZEALAND v WEST INDIES (1st Test)

At Basin Reserve, Wellington, on 1, 2, 3, 4 December 2017.
Toss: New Zealand. Result: **NEW ZEALAND** won by an innings and 67 runs.
Debuts: New Zealand – T.A.Blundell; West Indies – S.W.Ambris.

WEST INDIES

K.C.Brathwaite	c Nicholls b Wagner	24	lbw b Santner		91
K.O.A.Powell	c Raval b Boult	42	c and b Henry		40
S.O.Hetmyer	c Latham b Wagner	13	c Raval b Henry		66
S.D.Hope	c Blundell b Wagner	0	c Williamson b Boult		37
R.L.Chase	c Raval b Wagner	5	b Henry		18
S.W.Ambris	hit wkt b Wagner	0	c Taylor b de Grandhomme		18
†S.O.Dowrich	run out	18	c Santner b Wagner		3
*J.O.Holder	b Wagner	0	c Boult b Wagner		7
K.A.J.Roach	not out	14	lbw b de Grandhomme		7
M.L.Cummins	b Boult	1	b Boult		14
S.T.Gabriel	c Latham b Wagner	10	not out		4
Extras	(B 2, LB 5)	7	(B 4, LB 4, W 6)		14
Total	**(45.4 overs; 203 mins)**	**134**	**(106 overs; 444 mins)**		**319**

NEW ZEALAND

T.W.M.Latham	c Roach b Holder	37
J.A.Raval	c Dowrich b Roach	42
*K.C.Williamson	c Hope b Roach	1
L.R.P.L.Taylor	lbw b Roach	93
H.M.Nicholls	c Gabriel b Cummins	67
M.J.Santner	b Cummins	17
C.de Grandhomme	c Powell b Chase	105
†T.A.Blundell	not out	107
N.Wagner	b Chase	3
M.J.Henry	c Dowrich b Gabriel	4
T.A.Boult	not out	18
Extras	(B 4, LB 6, NB 15, W 1)	26
Total	**(9 wkts dec; 148.4 overs; 667 mins)**	**520**

NEW ZEALAND	O	M	R	W	O	M	R	W
Boult	16	8	36	2	23	5	87	2
Henry	11	1	39	0	24	6	57	3
De Grandhomme	4	1	13	0	19	3	40	2
Wagner	14.4	2	39	7	22	3	102	2
Santner					17	7	25	1
Williamson					1	1	0	0

WEST INDIES	O	M	R	W
Gabriel	29	4	90	1
Roach	22	6	85	3
Cummins	27	7	92	2
Holder	34	8	102	1
Chase	28	4	95	2
Brathwaite	8.4	0	46	0

FALL OF WICKETS

	WI	NZ	WI
Wkt	1st	1st	2nd
1st	59	65	72
2nd	75	68	166
3rd	79	109	231
4th	80	236	257
5th	80	272	273
6th	97	281	286
7th	97	429	288
8th	104	437	301
9th	105	442	301
10th	134	–	319

Umpires: I.J.Gould (*England*) (63) and R.J.Tucker (*Australia*) (56).
Referee: B.C.Broad (*England*) (89).   Test No. 2288/46 (NZ423/WI529)

NEW ZEALAND v WEST INDIES (2nd Test)

At Seddon Park, Hamilton, on 9, 10 11, 12 December 2017.
Toss: West Indies. Result: **NEW ZEALAND** won by 240 runs.
Debut: West Indies – R.A.Reifer.

NEW ZEALAND

J.A.Raval	c Dowrich b Gabriel	84	c and b Cummins		4
T.W.M.Latham	c Dowrich b Cummins	22	lbw b Reifer		22
*K.C.Williamson	c Dowrich b Cummins	43	b Cummins		54
L.R.P.L.Taylor	c Dowrich b Roach	16	not out		107
H.M.Nicholls	lbw b Reifer	13	c Dowrich b Cummins		5
M.J.Santner	b Gabriel	24	c Ambris b Chase		26
C.de Grandhomme	b Gabriel	58	lbw b Gabriel		22
†T.A.Blundell	b Gabriel	28	c Powell b Gabriel		1
N.Wagner	c Hope b Roach	1	c Hope b Chase		8
T.G.Southee	c and b Roach	31	not out		22
T.A.Boult	not out	37			
Extras	(LB 1, NB 12, W 3)	16	(B 4, LB 2, NB 12, W 2)		20
Total	**(102.2 overs; 469 mins)**	**373**	**(8 wkts dec; 77.4 overs; 351 mins)**		**291**

WEST INDIES

*K.C.Brathwaite	c Southee b de Grandhomme	66	c Williamson b Boult		20
K.O.A.Powell	c Blundell b Southee	0	c Southee b Boult		0
S.O.Hetmyer	c and b Boult	28	c Wagner b Southee		15
S.D.Hope	c Taylor b Southee	15	c de Grandhomme b Wagner		23
R.L.Chase	b de Grandhomme	12	c de Grandhomme b Wagner		64
S.W.Ambris	hit wkt b Boult	2	retired hurt		5
†S.O.Dowrich	c and b Wagner	35	c Nicholls b Wagner		29
R.A.Reifer	not out	23	c Williamson b Southee		29
K.A.J.Roach	c Boult b Wagner	17	b Santner		32
M.L.Cummins	b Boult	15	c Boult b Santner		9
S.T.Gabriel	b Boult	0	not out		0
Extras	(B 1, W 7)	8	(LB 5, W 1)		6
Total	**(66.5 overs; 294 mins)**	**221**	**(63.5 overs; 289 mins)**		**203**

WEST INDIES	O	M	R	W		O	M	R	W
Gabriel	25	4	119	4		15	0	52	2
Roach	23.2	8	58	3		6	1	28	0
Cummins	20	4	57	2		17	1	69	3
Chase	13	1	90	0	(6)	17.4	1	51	2
Reifer	17	8	36	1	(4)	13	1	52	1
Brathwaite	4	0	12	0	(5)	9	0	33	0

NEW ZEALAND	O	M	R	W		O	M	R	W
Southee	19	9	34	2		19	3	71	2
Boult	20.5	5	73	4		16	1	52	2
De Grandhomme	12	1	40	2	(4)	9	5	20	0
Wagner	15	2	73	2	(3)	15	3	42	3
Santner						4.5	0	13	2

FALL OF WICKETS

	NZ	WI	NZ	WI
Wkt	1st	1st	2nd	2nd
1st	65	5	11	4
2nd	154	46	42	27
3rd	159	90	100	43
4th	186	112	161	68
5th	189	117	161	80
6th	265	135	212	158
7th	275	169	235	166
8th	286	204	257	203
9th	312	221	–	203
10th	373	221	–	–

Umpires: B.N.J.Oxenford (*Australia*) (46) and R.J.Tucker (*Australia*) (57).
Referee: B.C.Broad (*England*) (90).   **Test No. 2289/47 (NZ424/WI530)**
S.W.Ambris retired hurt at 80-4.

SOUTH AFRICA v ZIMBABWE (Only Test)

At St George's Park, Port Elizabeth, on 26, 27 December 2017 (day/night).
Toss: South Africa. Result: **SOUTH AFRICA** won by an innings and 120 runs.
Debuts: Zimbabwe – R.P.Burl, B.Muzarabani.

SOUTH AFRICA

D.Elgar	c Moor b Jarvis	31
A.K.Markram	c Taylor b Jarvis	125
H.M.Amla	c Moor b Mpofu	5
*A.B.de Villiers	c and b Mpofu	53
T.Bavuma	c Taylor b Jarvis	44
†Q.de Kock	lbw b Cremer	24
V.D.Philander	lbw b Cremer	10
A.L.Phehlukwayo	not out	4
K.Rabada	run out	1
K.A.Maharaj	c Burl b Mpofu	5
M.Morkel		
Extras	(B 2, LB 2, NB 2, W 1)	7
Total	**(9 wkts dec; 78.3 overs; 335 mins)**	**309**

ZIMBABWE

H.Masakadza	lbw b Morkel	0	c de Villiers b Maharaj	13
C.J.Chibhabha	c Bavuma b Morkel	6	c de Villiers b Rabada	15
C.R.Ervine	lbw b Philander	4	lbw b Phehlukwayo	23
†B.R.M.Taylor	c de Villiers b Morkel	0	c Amla b Maharaj	16
R.P.Burl	b Morkel	16	c de Villiers b Phehlukwayo	0
K.M.Jarvis	c de Villiers b Phehlukwayo	23	(9) b Philander	5
Sikandar Raza	c de Villiers b Morkel	0	(6) c Phehlukwayo b Maharaj	5
P.J.Moor	b Phehlukwayo	9	(7) c de Villiers b Phehlukwayo	1
*A.G.Cremer	c de Villiers b Rabada	2	(8) not out	18
C.B.Mpofu	c Bavuma b Rabada	0	b Maharaj	0
B.Muzarabani	not out	4	b Maharaj	10
Extras	(LB 2, NB 2)	4	(B 8, LB 7)	15
Total	**(30.1 overs; 140 mins)**	**68**	**(42.3 overs; 175 mins)**	**121**

ZIMBABWE	O	M	R	W	O	M	R	W
Jarvis	18	2	57	3				
Muzarabani	13	2	48	0				
Mpofu	13.3	1	58	3				
Chibhabha	11	1	51	0				
Cremer	18	0	66	2				
Sikandar Raza	5	0	25	0				

SOUTH AFRICA	O	M	R	W		O	M	R	W
Morkel	11	5	21	5		4	0	12	0
Philander	10	4	21	1		7	3	10	1
Rabada	6.1	2	12	2	(4)	7	3	12	1
Phehlukwayo	3	0	12	2	(5)	7	2	13	3
Maharaj					(3)	17.3	5	59	5

FALL OF WICKETS			
	SA	Z	Z
Wkt	1st	1st	2nd
1st	72	0	54
2nd	77	11	75
3rd	173	11	75
4th	251	14	80
5th	272	36	80
6th	298	36	87
7th	303	55	91
8th	304	63	98
9th	309	63	103
10th	–	68	121

Umpires: R.A.Kettleborough (*England*) (49) and P.R.Reiffel (*Australia*) (34).
Referee: B.C.Broad (*England*) (91).   Test No. 2290/9 (SA418/Z105)

SOUTH AFRICA v INDIA (1st Test)

At Newlands, Cape Town, on 5, 6, 7 (*no play*), 8 January 2018.
Toss: South Africa. Result: **SOUTH AFRICA** won by 72 runs.
Debut: India – J.J.Bumrah.

SOUTH AFRICA

D.Elgar	c Saha b Kumar	0	(2) c Saha b Pandya		25
A.K.Markram	lbw b Kumar	5	(1) c Kumar b Pandya		34
H.M.Amla	c Saha b Kumar	3	(4) c Sharma b Shami		4
A.B.de Villiers	b Bumrah	65	(5) c Kumar b Bumrah		35
*F.du Plessis	c Saha b Pandya	62	(6) c Saha b Bumrah		0
†Q.de Kock	c Saha b Kumar	43	(7) c Saha b Bumrah		8
V.D.Philander	b Shami	23	(8) lbw b Shami		0
K.A.Maharaj	run out	35	(9) c Saha b Kumar		15
K.Rabada	c Saha b Ashwin	26	(3) c Kohli b Shami		5
D.W.Steyn	not out	16	(11) not out		0
M.Morkel	lbw b Ashwin	2	(10) c Saha b Kumar		2
Extras	(B 2, LB 3, NB 1)	6	(W 2)		2
Total	**(73.1 overs; 327 mins)**	**286**	**(41.2 overs; 203 mins)**		**130**

INDIA

M.Vijay	c Elgar b Philander	1	c de Villiers b Philander	13
S.Dhawan	c and b Steyn	16	c sub (C.H.Morris) b Morkel	16
C.A.Pujara	c du Plessis b Philander	26	c de Kock b Morkel	4
*V.Kohli	c de Kock b Morkel	5	lbw b Philander	28
R.G.Sharma	lbw b Rabada	11	b Philander	10
R.Ashwin	c de Kock b Philander	12	(8) c de Kock b Philander	37
H.H.Pandya	c de Kock b Rabada	93	c de Villiers b Rabada	1
†W.P.Saha	lbw b Steyn	0	(6) lbw b Rabada	8
B.Kumar	c de Kock b Morkel	25	not out	13
Mohammed Shami	not out	4	c du Plessis b Philander	4
J.J.Bumrah	c Elgar b Rabada	2	c du Plessis b Philander	0
Extras	(B 1, LB 13)	14	(LB 1)	1
Total	**(73.4 overs; 344 mins)**	**209**	**(42.4 overs; 201 mins)**	**135**

INDIA	O	M	R	W	O	M	R	W
Kumar	19	4	87	4	11	5	33	2
Mohammed Shami	16	6	47	1	(3) 12	3	28	3
Bumrah	19	1	73	1	(2) 11.2	1	39	3
Pandya	12	1	53	1	6	0	27	2
Ashwin	7.1	1	21	2	1	0	3	0

SOUTH AFRICA	O	M	R	W	O	M	R	W
Philander	14.3	8	33	3	15.4	4	42	6
Steyn	17.3	6	51	2				
Morkel	19	6	57	2	(2) 11	1	39	2
Rabada	16.4	4	34	3	(4) 12	2	41	2
Maharaj	6	0	20	0	(4) 4	1	12	0

FALL OF WICKETS

Wkt	SA 1st	I 1st	SA 2nd	I 2nd
1st	0	16	52	30
2nd	7	18	59	30
3rd	12	27	66	39
4th	126	57	73	71
5th	142	76	82	76
6th	202	81	92	77
7th	221	92	95	82
8th	258	191	122	131
9th	280	199	130	135
10th	286	209	130	135

Umpires: R.A.Kettleborough (*England*) (50) and M.A.Gough (*England*) (5).
Referee: B.C.Broad (*England*) (92). Test No. 2291/34 (SA419/I519)

SOUTH AFRICA v INDIA (2nd Test)

At SuperSport Park, Centurion, on 13, 14, 15, 16, 17 January 2018.
Toss: South Africa. Result: **SOUTH AFRICA** won by 135 runs.
Debut: South Africa – L.T.Ngidi.

SOUTH AFRICA

D.Elgar	c Vijay b Ashwin	31	(2)	c Rahul b Shami	61
A.K.Markram	c Patel b Ashwin	94	(1)	lbw b Bumrah	1
H.M.Amla	run out	82		lbw b Bumrah	1
A.B.de Villiers	b I.Sharma	20		c Patel b Shami	80
*F.du Plessis	b I.Sharma	63		c and b Bumrah	48
†Q.de Kock	c Kohli b Ashwin	0		c Patel b Shami	12
V.D.Philander	run out	0		c Vijay b I.Sharma	26
K.A.Maharaj	c Patel b Shami	18		c Patel b I.Sharma	6
K.Rabada	c Pandya b I.Sharma	11		c Kohli b Shami	4
M.Morkel	c Vijay b Ashwin	6		not out	10
L.T.Ngidi	not out	1		c Vijay b Ashwin	1
Extras	(LB 8, NB 1)	8		(B 2, LB 5, W 1)	8
Total	**(113.5 overs; 488 mins)**	**335**		**(91.3 overs; 413 mins)**	**258**

INDIA

M.Vijay	c de Kock b Maharaj	46		b Rabada	9
K.L.Rahul	c and b Morkel	10		c Maharaj b Ngidi	4
C.A.Pujara	run out	0		run out	19
*V.Kohli	c de Villiers b Morkel	153		lbw b Ngidi	5
R.G.Sharma	lbw b Rabada	10	(6)	c de Villiers b Rabada	47
†P.A.Patel	c de Kock b Ngidi	19	(5)	c Morkel b Rabada	19
H.H.Pandya	run out	15		c de Kock b Ngidi	6
R.Ashwin	c du Plessis b Philander	38		c de Kock b Ngidi	3
Mohammed Shami	c Amla b Morkel	1		c Morkel b Ngidi	28
I.Sharma	c Markram b Morkel	3		not out	4
J.J.Bumrah	not out	0		c Philander b Ngidi	2
Extras	(B 8, LB 1, NB 1, W 2)	12		(B 4, W 1)	5
Total	**(92.1 overs; 422 mins)**	**307**		**(50.2 overs; 245 mins)**	**151**

INDIA	O	M	R	W		O	M	R	W
Bumrah	22	6	60	0	(2)	20	3	70	3
Mohammed Shami	15	2	58	1	(4)	16	3	49	4
I.Sharma	22	4	46	3		17	3	40	2
Pandya	16	4	50	0	(5)	9	1	14	0
Ashwin	38.5	10	113	4	(1)	29.3	6	78	1

SOUTH AFRICA	O	M	R	W		O	M	R	W
Maharaj	20	1	67	1	(5)	6	1	26	0
Morkel	22.1	5	60	4	(4)	8	3	10	0
Philander	16	3	46	1	(1)	9	3	25	0
Rabada	20	1	74	1	(2)	14	3	47	3
Ngidi	14	2	51	1	(3)	12.2	3	39	6

FALL OF WICKETS				
	SA	I	SA	I
Wkt	1st	1st	2nd	2nd
1st	85	28	1	11
2nd	148	28	3	16
3rd	199	107	144	26
4th	246	132	151	49
5th	250	164	163	65
6th	251	209	209	83
7th	282	280	215	87
8th	324	281	245	141
9th	333	306	245	145
10th	335	307	258	151

Umpires: M.A.Gough (*England*) (6) and P.R.Reiffel (*Australia*) (35).
Referee: B.C.Broad (*England*) (93).

Test No. 2292/35 (SA420/I520)

SOUTH AFRICA v INDIA (3rd Test)

At New Wanderers Stadium, Johannesburg, on 24, 25, 26, 27 January 2018.
Toss: India. Result: **INDIA** won by 63 runs.
Debuts: None.

INDIA

M.Vijay	c de Kock b Rabada	8	b Rabada		25
K.L.Rahul	c de Kock b Philander	0	(3) c du Plessis b Philander		16
C.A.Pujara	c de Kock b Phehlukwayo	50	(4) c du Plessis b Morkel		1
*V.Kohli	c de Villiers b Ngidi	54	(5) b Rabada		41
A.M.Rahane	lbw b Morkel	9	(6) c de Kock b Morkel		48
†P.A.Patel	c de Kock b Morkel	2	(2) c Markram b Philander		16
H.H.Pandya	c de Kock b Phehlukwayo	0	c and b Rabada		4
B.Kumar	c Phehlukwayo b Rabada	30	c de Kock b Morkel		33
Mohammed Shami	c Rabada b Philander	8	c de Villiers b Ngidi		27
I.Sharma	c du Plessis b Rabada	0	not out		7
J.J.Bumrah	not out	0	c Rabada b Philander		0
Extras	(B 11, LB 7, NB 2, W 6)	26	(B 5, LB 12, W 12)		29
Total	**(76.4 overs; 353 mins)**	**187**	**(80.1 overs; 384 mins)**		**247**

SOUTH AFRICA

D.Elgar	c Patel b Kumar	4	(2) not out		86
A.K.Markram	c Patel b Kumar	2	(1) c Patel b Shami		4
K.Rabada	c Rahane b Sharma	30	(9) c Pujara b Kumar		0
H.M.Amla	c Pandya b Bumrah	61	(3) c Pandya b Sharma		52
A.B.de Villiers	b Kumar	5	(4) c Rahane b Bumrah		6
*F.du Plessis	b Bumrah	8	(5) b Sharma		2
†Q.de Kock	c Patel b Bumrah	8	(6) lbw b Bumrah		0
V.D.Philander	c Bumrah b Shami	35	(7) b Shami		10
A.L.Phehlukwayo	lbw b Bumrah	9	(8) b Shami		0
M.Morkel	not out	9	b Shami		0
L.T.Ngidi	c Patel b Bumrah	0	c sub (K.D.Karthik) b Shami		4
Extras	(LB 14, W 9)	23	(B 7, W 6)		13
Total	**(65.5 overs; 328 mins)**	**194**	**(73.3 overs; 356 mins)**		**177**

SOUTH AFRICA	O	M	R	W		O	M	R	W
Morkel	17	5	47	2	(3)	21	6	47	3
Philander	19	10	31	2	(1)	21.1	5	61	3
Rabada	18.4	6	39	3	(2)	23	5	69	3
Ngidi	15	7	27	1		12	2	38	1
Phehlukwayo	7	1	25	2		3	0	15	0
INDIA									
Kumar	19	9	44	3		18	4	39	1
Bumrah	18.5	2	54	5	(3)	21	3	57	2
Sharma	14	2	33	1	(4)	16	3	31	2
Mohammed Shami	12	0	46	1	(2)	12.3	2	28	5
Pandya	2	0	3	0		6	1	15	0

FALL OF WICKETS				
	I	SA	I	SA
Wkt	1st	1st	2nd	2nd
1st	7	3	17	5
2nd	13	16	51	124
3rd	97	80	57	131
4th	113	92	100	144
5th	144	107	134	145
6th	144	125	148	157
7th	144	169	203	157
8th	163	175	238	160
9th	166	194	240	161
10th	187	194	247	177

Umpires: I.J.Gould (*England*) (64) and Alim Dar (*Pakistan*) (117).
Referee: A.J.Pycroft (*Zimbabwe*) (57).   **Test No. 2293/36 (SA421/I521)**

BANGLADESH v SRI LANKA (1st Test)

At Zahur Ahmed Chowdhury Stadium, Chittagong, on 31 January, 1, 2, 3, 4, February 2018.
Toss: Bangladesh. Result: **MATCH DRAWN**.
Debut: Bangladesh – Sanjamul Islam.

BANGLADESH

Tamim Iqbal	b Perera	52	c Dickwella b Sandakan		41
Imrul Kayes	lbw b Sandakan	40	c Chandimal b Perera		19
Mominul Haque	c Mendis b Herath	176	c Karunaratne b de Silva		105
Mushfiqur Rahim	c Dickwella b Lakmal	92	c Mendis b Herath		2
†Liton Das	b Lakmal	0	c Perera b Herath		94
*Mahmudullah	not out	83	not out		28
Mosaddek Hossain	c Sandakan b Herath	8	not out		8
Mehedi Hasan	run out	20			
Sanjamul Islam	st Dickwella b Sandakan	24			
Taijul Islam	b Herath	1			
Mustafizur Rahman	c Dickwella b Lakmal	8			
Extras	(NB 4, W 5)	9	(B 3, LB 2, NB 4, W 1)		10
Total	**(129.5 overs)**	**513**	**(5 wkts; 100 overs)**		**307**

SRI LANKA

F.D.M.Karunaratne	c Imrul b Mehedi	0
B.K.G.Mendis	c Mushfiqur b Taijul	196
D.M.de Silva	c Liton b Mustafizur	173
A.R.S.Silva	c Liton b Mehedi	109
*L.D.Chandimal	b Taijul	87
†D.P.D.N.Dickwella	c Liton b Mehedi	62
M.D.K.Perera	lbw b Sanjamul	32
H.M.R.K.B.Herath	lbw b Taijul	24
R.A.S.Lakmal	b Taijul	9
C.B.R.L.S.Kumara	not out	2
P.A.D.L.R.Sandakan		
Extras	(B 11, LB 6, W 2)	19
Total	**(9 wkts dec; 199.3 overs)**	**713**

SRI LANKA	O	M	R	W		O	M	R	W
Lakmal	23.5	4	68	3	(2)	9	1	25	0
Kumara	15	1	79	0	(6)	6	0	16	0
Perera	27	4	112	1	(4)	26	5	74	1
Herath	37	2	150	3	(1)	28	6	80	2
Sandakan	22	1	92	2	(5)	18	2	64	1
De Silva	5	0	12	0	(3)	12	0	41	1
Mendis						1	0	2	0

BANGLADESH	O	M	R	W
Mustafizur Rahman	32	6	113	1
Sanjamul Islam	45	2	153	1
Mehedi Hasan	49	4	174	3
Taijul Islam	67.3	13	219	4
Mosaddek Hossain	3	0	24	0
Mominul Haque	2	0	6	0
Mahmudullah	1	0	7	0

FALL OF WICKETS			
	B	SL	B
Wkt	1st	1st	2nd
1st	72	0	52
2nd	120	308	76
3rd	356	415	81
4th	356	550	261
5th	376	613	279
6th	390	663	–
7th	417	687	–
8th	475	706	–
9th	478	713	–
10th	513	–	–

Umpires: M.Erasmus (*South Africa*) (48) and R.J.Tucker (*Australia*) (58).
Referee: D.C.Boon (*Australia*) (48).   **Test No. 2294/19 (B105/SL268)**

BANGLADESH v SRI LANKA (2nd Test)

At Shere Bangla National Stadium, Mirpur, Dhaka, on 8, 9, 10 February 2018.
Toss: Sri Lanka. Result: **SRI LANKA** won by 215 runs.
Debut: Sri Lanka – M.K.P.A.D.Perera.

SRI LANKA

B.K.G.Mendis	b Razzak	68	(2)	lbw b Razzak	7
F.D.M.Karunaratne	st Liton b Razzak	3	(1)	c Imrul b Mehedi	32
D.M.de Silva	c Sabbir b Taijul	19		b Taijul	28
M.D.Gunathilleke	c Mushfiqur b Razzak	13		lbw b Mustafizur	17
*L.D.Chandimal	b Razzak	0		lbw b Mehedi	30
A.R.S.Silva	c Liton b Taijul	56		not out	70
†D.P.D.N.Dickwella	b Taijul	1		c Mahmudullah b Taijul	10
M.D.K.Perera	c Mominul b Taijul	31		c Liton b Mustafizur	7
M.K.P.A.D.Perera	c Mushfiqur b Mustafizur	20		c Liton b Mustafizur	0
H.M.R.K.B.Herath	c Mushfiqur b Mustafizur	2		b Taijul	21
R.A.S.Lakmal	not out	4		lbw b Taijul	0
Extras	(LB 5)	5		(LB 4)	4
Total	**(65.3 overs)**	**222**		**(73.5 overs)**	**226**

BANGLADESH

Tamim Iqbal	c and b Lakmal	4		lbw b M.D.K.Perera	2
Imrul Kayes	lbw b M.D.K.Perera	19		c Dickwella b Herath	17
Mominul Haque	run out	0		c Dickwella b Herath	33
Mushfiqur Rahim	b Lakmal	1		st Dickwella b Herath	12
†Liton Das	b Lakmal	25		c Mendis b M.K.P.A.D.Perera	12
Mehedi Hasan	not out	38	(8)	c Dickwella b M.K.P.A.D.Perera	7
*Mahmudullah	b M.K.P.A.D.Perera	17	(6)	c Karunaratne b M.K.P.A.D.Perera	6
Sabbir Rahman	c Chandimal b M.K.P.A.D.Perera	1	(7)	c Mendis b M.K.P.A.D.Perera	1
Abdur Razzak	c and b M.K.P.A.D.Perera	1		st Dickwella b M.K.P.A.D.Perera	2
Taijul Islam	run out	1		c Gunathilleke b M.K.P.A.D.Perera	6
Mustafizur Rahman	lbw b M.D.K.Perera	0		not out	5
Extras	(LB 2, NB 1, W 1)	4		(B 6, LB 1)	7
Total	**(45.4 overs)**	**110**		**(29.3 overs)**	**123**

BANGLADESH	O	M	R	W		O	M	R	W
Mehedi Hasan	13	0	54	0	(4)	20	5	37	2
Abdur Razzak	16	2	63	4	(1)	17	2	60	1
Taijul Islam	25.3	2	83	4		19.5	2	76	4
Mustafizur Rahman	11	4	17	2	(2)	17	3	49	3

SRI LANKA	O	M	R	W		O	M	R	W
Lakmal	12	4	25	3		3	0	11	0
M.D.K.Perera	11.4	4	32	2		10	0	32	1
M.K.P.A.D.Perera	10	2	20	3	(4)	5	1	24	5
Herath	12	1	31	0	(3)	11.3	1	49	4

FALL OF WICKETS

Wkt	SL 1st	B 1st	SL 2nd	B 2nd
1st	14	4	19	3
2nd	61	4	53	49
3rd	96	12	80	64
4th	96	45	92	78
5th	109	73	143	100
6th	110	107	170	102
7th	162	107	178	102
8th	205	109	178	104
9th	207	110	226	113
10th	222	110	226	123

Umpires: R.J.Tucker (*Australia*) (59) and J.S.Wilson (*West Indies*) (10).
Referee: D.C.Boon (*Australia*) (49).   **Test No. 2295/20 (B106/SL269)**

INTERNATIONAL UMPIRES AND REFEREES 2018

ELITE PANEL OF UMPIRES 2018

The Elite Panel of ICC Umpires and Referees was introduced in April 2002 to raise standards and guarantee impartial adjudication. Two umpires from this panel stand in Test matches while one officiates with a home umpire from the Supplementary International Panel in limited-overs internationals.

Full Names	Birthdate	Birthplace	Tests	Debut	LOI	Debut
ALIM Sarwar DAR	06.06.68	Jhang, Pakistan	117	2003-04	190	1999-00
DHARMASENA, H.D.P.Kumar	24.04.71	Colombo, Sri Lanka	52	2010-11	84	2008-09
ERASMUS, Marais	27.02.64	George, South Africa	48	2009-10	74	2007-08
GAFFANEY, Christopher Blair	30.11.75	Dunedin, New Zealand	18	2014	57	2010
GOULD, Ian James	19.08.57	Taplow, England	64	2008-09	125	2006
ILLINGWORTH, Richard Keith	23.08.63	Bradford, England	30	2012-13	57	2010
KETTLEBOROUGH, Richard Allan	15.03.73	Sheffield, England	50	2010-11	74	2009
LLONG, Nigel James	11.02.69	Ashford, England	49	2007-08	117	2006
OXENFORD, Bruce Nicholas James	05.03.60	Southport, Australia	46	2010-11	86	2007-08
RAVI, Sundaram	22.04.66	Bangalore, India	25	2013-14	33	2011-12
REIFFEL, Paul Ronald	19.04.66	Box Hill, Australia	35	2012	54	2008-09
TUCKER, Rodney James	28.08.64	Sydney, Australia	59	2009-10	74	2008-09

ELITE PANEL OF REFEREES 2018

Full Names	Birthdate	Birthplace	Tests	Debut	LOI	Debut
BOON, David Clarence	29.12.60	Launceston, Australia	49	2011	105	2011
BROAD, Brian Christopher	29.09.57	Bristol, England	93	2003-04	294	2003-04
CROWE, Jeffrey John	14.09.58	Auckland, New Zealand	86	2004-05	267	2003-04
MADUGALLE, Ranjan Senerath	22.04.59	Kandy, Sri Lanka	181	1993-94	321	1993-94
PYCROFT, Andrew John	06.06.56	Harare, Zimbabwe	57	2009	156	2009
RICHARDSON, Sir Richard Benjamin	12.01.62	Five Islands, Antigua	14	2016	29	2016
SRINATH, Javagal	31.08.69	Mysore, India	37	2006	207	2006-07

INTERNATIONAL UMPIRES PANEL 2018

Nominated by their respective cricket boards, members from this panel officiate in home LOIs and supplement the Elite panel for Test matches. Specialist third umpires have been selected to undertake adjudication involving television replays. The number of Test matches/LOI in which they have stood is shown in brackets.

			Third Umpire
Afghanistan	Ahmed Shah Pakteen (-/8)	Ahmed Shah Durrani (-/3)	Bismallah Jan Shinwari (-/1)
Australia	S.D.Fry (7/43)	P.Wilson (-/8)	S.J.Nogajski (-/4)
			G.A.Abood (-/1)
Bangladesh	Anisur Rahman (-/7)	Sharfuddoula (-/38)	Masudur Rahman (-/1)
England	R.J.Bailey (-/20)	M.A.Gough (6/39)	R.T.Robinson (-/13)
			A.G.Wharf (-/-)
India	C.Shamshuddin (-/34)	A.K.Chaudhary (-/15)	C.K.Nandan (-/5)
			N.N.Menon (-/12)
Ireland	M.Hawthorne (-/26)	R.Black (-/6)	A.J.Neill (-/4)
New Zealand	W.J.Knights (-/10)	C.M.Brown (-/11)	S.B.Haig (-/3)
Pakistan	Shozab Raza (-/19)	Ahsan Raza (-/27)	Ahmed Shahab (-/4)
South Africa	A.T.Holdstock (-/12)	S.George (-/29)	B.P.Jele (-/6)
			Allahudien Paleker (-/-)
Sri Lanka	R.E.J.Martinesz (8/44)	R.S.A.Palliyaguruge (-/60)	R.R.Wimalasiri (-/9)
West Indies	G.O.Brathwaite (-/24)	J.S.Wilson (10/48)	L.S.Reifer (-/2)
			N.Duguid (-/4)
Zimbabwe	R.B.Tiffin (44/152)	T.J.Matibiri (-/22)	L.Rusere (-/5)

Test Match and LOI statistics to 8 March 2018.

TEST MATCH CAREER RECORDS

These records, complete to 28 February 2018, contain all players registered for county cricket in 2018 at the time of going to press, plus those who have played Test cricket since 1 December 2016 (Test No. 2236).

ENGLAND – BATTING AND FIELDING

	M	I	NO	HS	Runs	Avge	100	50	Ct/St
M.M.Ali	49	83	8	155*	2467	32.89	5	12	27
T.R.Ambrose	11	16	1	102	447	29.80	1	3	31
J.M.Anderson	134	186	73	81	1128	9.98	–	1	84
J.M.Bairstow	50	86	6	167*	3130	39.12	4	17	129/8
J.T.Ball	4	8	–	31	67	8.37	–	–	1
G.S.Ballance	23	42	2	156	1498	37.45	4	7	22
G.J.Batty	9	12	2	38	149	14.90	–	–	3
I.R.Bell	118	205	24	235	7727	42.69	22	46	100
R.S.Bopara	13	19	1	143	575	31.94	3	–	6
S.G.Borthwick	1	2	–	4	5	2.50	–	–	2
T.T.Bresnan	23	26	4	91	575	26.13	–	3	8
S.C.J.Broad	114	164	21	169	2956	20.67	1	12	36
J.C.Buttler	18	30	5	85	784	31.36	–	6	54
M.A.Carberry	6	12	–	60	345	28.75	–	1	7
R.Clarke	2	3	–	55	96	32.00	–	1	1
P.D.Collingwood	68	115	10	206	4259	40.56	10	20	96
N.R.D.Compton	16	30	3	117	775	28.70	2	2	7
A.N.Cook	152	275	16	294	12005	46.35	32	55	156
M.S.Crane	1	2	–	4	6	3.00	–	–	–
T.K.Curran	2	3	1	39	66	33.00	–	–	–
L.A.Dawson	3	6	2	66*	84	21.00	–	1	2
B.M.Duckett	4	7	–	56	110	15.71	–	1	1
S.T.Finn	36	47	22	56	279	11.16	–	1	8
J.S.Foster	7	12	3	48	226	25.11	–	–	17/1
A.D.Hales	11	21	–	94	573	27.28	–	5	8
H.Hameed	3	6	1	82	219	43.80	–	2	4
K.K.Jennings	6	12	–	112	294	24.50	1	1	3
C.J.Jordan	8	11	1	35	180	18.00	–	–	14
S.C.Kerrigan	1	1	1	1*	1	–	–	–	–
A.Lyth	7	13	–	107	265	20.38	1	–	8
D.J.Malan	10	17	–	140	572	33.64	1	5	4
E.J.G.Morgan	16	24	1	130	700	30.43	2	3	11
G.Onions	9	10	7	17*	30	10.00	–	–	–
C.Overton	2	4	1	41*	62	20.66	–	–	1
S.R.Patel	6	9	–	42	151	16.77	–	–	3
L.E.Plunkett	13	20	5	55*	238	15.86	–	1	3
W.B.Rankin	1	2	–	13	13	6.50	–	–	–
A.U.Rashid	10	18	2	61	295	18.43	–	2	3
S.D.Robson	7	11	–	127	336	30.54	1	1	5
T.S.Roland-Jones	4	6	2	25	82	20.50	–	–	–
J.E.Root	65	119	12	254	5701	53.28	13	37	76
B.A.Stokes	39	69	1	258	2429	35.72	6	12	38
M.D.Stoneman	8	14	1	56	352	27.07	–	3	–
J.C.Tredwell	2	2	–	37	45	22.50	–	–	2
M.E.Trescothick	76	143	10	219	5825	43.79	14	29	95
I.J.L.Trott	52	93	6	226	3835	44.08	9	19	29
J.M.Vince	12	20	–	83	454	22.70	–	2	6
T.Westley	5	9	1	59	193	24.12	–	1	1
C.R.Woakes	22	37	9	66	789	28.17	–	3	9
M.A.Wood	10	18	5	32*	219	16.84	–	–	3

ENGLAND – BOWLING

	O	M	R	W	Avge	Best	5wI	10wM
M.M.Ali	1472.2	223	5352	133	40.24	6- 53	4	1
J.M.Anderson	4933.2	1239	14333	523	27.40	7- 42	25	3
J.T.Ball	102	23	343	3	114.33	1- 47	–	–
G.S.Ballance	2	1	5	0	–	–	–	–
G.J.Batty	285.4	38	914	15	60.93	3- 55	–	–
I.R.Bell	18	3	76	1	76.00	1- 33	–	–
R.S.Bopara	72.2	10	290	1	290.00	1- 39	–	–
S.G.Borthwick	13	0	82	4	20.50	3- 33	–	–
T.T.Bresnan	779	185	2357	72	32.73	5- 48	1	–
S.C.J.Broad	3922.1	901	11706	399	29.33	8- 15	15	2
R.Clarke	29	11	60	4	15.00	2- 7	–	–
P.D.Collingwood	317.3	51	1018	17	59.88	3- 23	–	–
A.N.Cook	3	0	7	1	7.00	1- 6	–	–
M.S.Crane	48	3	193	1	193.00	1-193	–	–
T.K.Curran	66	14	200	2	100.00	1- 65	–	–
L.A.Dawson	87.4	12	298	7	42.57	4-101	–	–
S.T.Finn	1068.4	190	3800	125	30.40	6- 79	5	–
A.D.Hales	3	1	2	0	–	–	–	–
K.K.Jennings	6	1	22	0	–	–	–	–
C.J.Jordan	255	74	752	21	35.80	4- 18	–	–
S.C.Kerrigan	8	0	53	0	–	–	–	–
A.Lyth	1	1	0	0	–	–	–	–
D.J.Malan	22	3	61	0	–	–	–	–
G.Onions	267.4	50	957	32	29.90	5- 38	1	–
C.Overton	59	4	226	6	37.66	3-105	–	–
S.R.Patel	143	23	421	7	60.14	2- 27	–	–
L.E.Plunkett	443.1	71	1536	41	37.46	5- 64	1	–
W.B.Rankin	20.5	0	81	1	81.00	1- 47	–	–
A.U.Rashid	424	32	1626	38	42.78	5- 64	1	–
T.S.Roland-Jones	89.2	23	334	17	19.64	5- 57	1	–
J.E.Root	271.2	61	817	17	48.05	2- 9	–	–
B.A.Stokes	955.4	175	3224	95	33.93	6- 22	4	–
J.C.Tredwell	131	39	321	11	29.18	4- 47	–	–
M.E.Trescothick	50	6	155	1	155.00	1- 34	–	–
I.J.L.Trott	118	11	400	5	80.00	1- 5	–	–
J.M.Vince	4	1	13	0	–	–	–	–
T.Westley	4	0	12	0	–	–	–	–
C.R.Woakes	658.4	150	2025	60	33.75	6- 70	2	1
M.A.Wood	310.3	72	1057	26	40.65	3- 39	–	–

AUSTRALIA – BATTING AND FIELDING

	M	I	NO	HS	Runs	Avge	100	50	Ct/St
A.C.Agar	4	7	1	98	195	32.50	–	1	–
C.T.Bancroft	5	8	1	82*	179	25.57	–	1	5
G.J.Bailey	5	8	1	53	183	26.14	–	1	10
J.M.Bird	9	9	6	19*	43	14.33	–	–	2
H.W.R.Cartwright	2	2	–	37	55	27.50	–	–	–
P.J.Cummins	10	14	4	44	276	27.60	–	–	4
J.P.Faulkner	1	2	–	23	45	22.50	–	–	–
P.S.P.Handscomb	12	22	5	110	805	47.35	2	4	18
J.R.Hazlewood	36	40	17	39	274	11.91	–	–	15
U.T.Khawaja	29	49	4	174	2061	45.80	6	10	23
N.M.Lyon	74	91	29	40*	720	11.61	–	–	35
C.J.McKay	1	1	–	10	10	10.00	–	–	1
N.J.Maddinson	3	4	–	22	27	6.75	–	–	2
M.R.Marsh	24	39	5	181	994	29.23	2	2	11
S.E.Marsh	28	49	2	182	1921	40.87	6	9	19
G.J.Maxwell	7	14	1	104	339	26.07	1	–	5

TESTS AUSTRALIA – BATTING AND FIELDING (continued)

	M	I	NO	HS	Runs	Avge	100	50	Ct/St
S.N.J.O'Keefe	9	13	4	25	86	9.55	–	–	–
T.D.Paine	9	14	2	92	479	39.91	–	3	41/2
M.T.Renshaw	10	18	1	184	623	36.64	1	3	7
P.M.Siddle	62	86	14	51	1063	14.76	–	2	16
S.P.D.Smith	61	111	16	239	6057	63.75	23	23	89
M.A.Starc	40	60	12	99	1111	23.14	–	9	19
A.C.Voges	20	31	7	269*	1485	61.87	5	4	15
M.S.Wade	22	38	7	106	886	28.58	2	4	63/11
D.A.Warner	71	131	5	253	6146	48.77	21	27	53

AUSTRALIA – BOWLING

	O	M	R	W	Avge	Best	5wI	10wM
A.C.Agar	145.4	31	410	9	45.55	3- 46	–	–
J.M.Bird	322.2	80	1042	34	30.64	5- 59	1	–
H.W.R.Cartwright	9	1	31	0	–	–	–	–
P.J.Cummins	381.1	83	1100	44	25.00	6- 79	1	–
J.P.Faulkner	27.4	4	98	6	16.33	4- 51	–	–
J.R.Hazlewood	1283.4	326	3583	139	25.77	6- 67	6	–
U.T.Khawaja	1	0	1	0	–	–	–	–
N.M.Lyon	2988.1	566	9178	290	31.64	8- 50	12	2
C.J.McKay	28	5	101	1	101.00	1- 56	–	–
N.J.Maddinson	6	0	27	0	–	–	–	–
M.R.Marsh	348.1	63	1219	29	42.03	4- 61	–	–
G.J.Maxwell	77	4	341	8	42.62	4-127	–	–
S.N.J.O'Keefe	371.2	68	1029	35	29.40	6- 35	2	1
P.M.Siddle	2156.5	575	6314	211	29.92	6- 54	8	–
S.P.D.Smith	216.1	20	924	17	54.35	3- 18	–	–
M.A.Starc	1388.2	279	4715	170	27.73	6- 50	8	1
A.C.Voges	12.4	1	44	0	–	–	–	–
M.S.Wade	1	1	0	0	–	–	–	–
D.A.Warner	57	1	269	4	67.25	2- 45	–	–

SOUTH AFRICA – BATTING AND FIELDING

	M	I	NO	HS	Runs	Avge	100	50	Ct/St
K.J.Abbott	11	14	–	17	95	6.78	–	–	4
H.M.Amla	113	193	14	311*	8776	49.08	28	38	99
T.Bavuma	27	42	4	102*	1259	33.13	1	9	13
S.C.Cook	11	19	–	117	632	33.26	3	2	6
T.B.de Bruyn	3	6	–	48	72	12.00	–	–	5
Q.de Kock	29	47	5	129*	1649	39.26	3	11	116/7
M.de Lange	2	2	–	9	9	4.50	–	–	1
A.B.de Villiers	110	183	16	278*	8338	49.92	21	42	211/5
F.du Plessis	48	78	11	137	3022	45.10	7	17	41
J.P.Duminy	46	74	10	166	2103	32.85	6	8	38
D.Elgar	45	74	6	199	2861	42.07	10	10	43
S.R.Harmer	5	6	1	13	58	11.60	–	–	1
Imran Tahir	20	23	9	29*	130	9.28	–	–	8
R.K.Kleinveldt	4	5	2	17*	27	9.00	–	–	2
H.G.Kuhn	4	8	–	34	113	14.12	–	–	1
K.A.Maharaj	16	23	6	41*	306	18.00	–	–	5
A.K.Markram	6	10	–	143	520	52.00	2	2	6
M.Morkel	83	99	22	40	931	12.09	–	–	24
C.H.Morris	4	7	–	69	173	24.71	–	1	5
L.T.Ngidi	2	4	1	4	6	2.00	–	–	–
D.Olivier	5	4	1	4	7	2.33	–	–	–
W.D.Parnell	6	4	–	23	67	16.75	–	–	3
A.L.Phehlukwayo	4	4	2	9	19	9.50	–	–	2
V.D.Philander	50	68	15	74	1290	24.33	–	7	15
K.Rabada	26	34	9	34	336	13.44	–	–	11

	M	I	NO	HS	Runs	Avge	100	50	Ct/St
J.A.Rudolph	48	83	9	222*	2622	35.43	6	11	29
D.W.Steyn	86	107	24	76	1178	14.19	–	2	23
S.van Zyl	12	17	2	101*	395	26.33	1	–	6
D.J.Vilas	6	9	–	26	94	10.44	–	–	13
G.C.Viljoen	1	2	1	20*	26	26.00	–	–	–

SOUTH AFRICA – BOWLING

	O	M	R	W	Avge	Best	5wI	10wM
K.J.Abbott	346.5	95	886	39	22.71	7- 29	3	–
H.M.Amla	9	0	37	0	–	–	–	–
T.Bavuma	15	1	51	1	51.00	1- 29	–	–
S.C.Cook	2	0	16	0	–	–	–	–
T.B.de Bruyn	10	1	48	0	–	–	–	–
M. de Lange	74.4	10	277	9	30.77	7- 81	1	–
A.B.de Villiers	34	6	104	2	52.00	2- 49	–	–
F.du Plessis	13	0	69	0	–	–	–	–
J.P.Duminy	450.3	48	1601	42	38.11	4- 47	–	–
D.Elgar	153.5	10	582	13	44.76	4- 22	–	–
S.R.Harmer	191.2	34	588	20	29.40	4- 61	–	–
Imran Tahir	654.1	86	2294	57	40.24	5- 32	2	–
R.K.Kleinveldt	111.1	21	422	10	42.20	3- 65	–	–
K.A.Maharaj	512.5	106	1527	57	26.78	6- 40	3	–
A.K.Markram	2	0	13	0	–	–	–	–
M.Morkel	2659	580	8256	294	28.08	6- 23	7	–
C.H.Morris	103.5	15	459	12	38.25	3- 38	–	–
L.T.Ngidi	53.2	14	155	9	17.22	6- 39	1	–
D.Olivier	101	19	393	17	23.11	3- 38	–	–
W.D.Parnell	92.4	11	414	15	27.60	4- 51	–	–
A.L.Phehlukwayo	41.4	9	147	11	13.36	3- 13	–	–
V.D.Philander	1521.4	387	4109	188	21.85	6- 42	12	2
K.Rabada	794.4	166	2645	120	22.04	7-112	7	3
J.A.Rudolph	110.4	13	432	4	108.00	1- 1	–	–
D.W.Steyn	2898.3	628	9354	419	22.32	7- 51	26	5
S.van Zyl	67.1	15	148	6	24.66	3- 20	–	–
G.C.Viljoen	19	2	94	1	94.00	1- 79	–	–

WEST INDIES – BATTING AND FIELDING

	M	I	NO	HS	Runs	Avge	100	50	Ct/St
S.W.Ambris	2	4	1	18	25	8.33	–	–	1
D.Bishoo	28	47	12	45	570	16.28	–	–	14
J.Blackwood	27	48	4	112*	1324	30.09	1	10	24
K.C.Brathwaite	44	83	5	212	2920	37.43	6	16	22
S.Chanderpaul	164	280	49	203*	11867	51.37	30	66	66
R.L.Chase	17	31	3	137*	1065	38.03	3	5	7
M.L.Cummins	8	13	3	24*	69	6.90	–	–	1
S.O.Dowrich	18	33	3	103	724	24.13	1	5	40/5
F.H.Edwards	55	88	28	30	394	6.56	–	–	10
S.T.Gabriel	32	46	18	20*	150	5.35	–	–	14
S.O.Hetmyer	5	10	–	66	218	21.80	–	1	2
J.O.Holder	29	50	8	110	1218	29.00	2	6	18
K.A.Hope	5	9	–	43	101	11.22	–	–	3
S.D.Hope	17	32	2	147	996	33.20	2	3	16
A.S.Joseph	6	11	–	8	41	3.72	–	–	2
K.O.A.Powell	31	59	1	134	1620	27.93	3	4	28
R.Rampaul	18	31	8	40*	335	14.56	–	–	3
R.A.Reifer	1	2	1	29	52	52.00	–	–	–
K.A.J.Roach	44	71	12	41	605	10.25	–	–	12
V.A.Singh	3	6	–	32	63	10.50	–	–	2

WEST INDIES – BOWLING

	O	M	R	W	Avge	Best	5wI	10wM
D.Bishoo	1152.2	158	3674	102	36.01	8- 49	4	1
J.Blackwood	54	9	194	2	97.00	2- 14	–	–
K.C.Brathwaite	251.4	22	831	14	59.35	6- 29	1	–
S.Chanderpaul	290	50	883	9	98.11	1- 2	–	–
R.L.Chase	455.3	55	1555	31	50.16	5-121	1	–
M.L.Cummins	206.2	31	713	18	39.61	6- 48	1	–
F.H.Edwards	1600.2	183	6249	165	37.87	7- 87	12	–
S.T.Gabriel	854.1	154	2845	83	34.27	5- 11	2	–
J.O.Holder	788.4	199	2042	53	38.52	5- 30	1	–
A.S.Joseph	187.5	44	583	15	38.86	3- 53	–	–
K.O.A.Powell	1	1	0	0	–	–	–	–
R.Rampaul	573.2	111	1705	49	34.75	4- 48	–	–
R.A.Reifer	30	9	88	2	44.00	1- 36	–	–
K.A.J.Roach	1342.1	277	4326	147	29.42	6- 48	7	1

NEW ZEALAND – BATTING AND FIELDING

	M	I	NO	HS	Runs	Avge	100	50	Ct/St
C.J.Anderson	13	22	1	116	683	32.52	1	4	7
T.A.Blundell	2	3	1	107*	136	68.00	1	–	2
T.A.Boult	52	68	35	52*	529	16.03	–	1	27
D.A.J.Bracewell	27	45	4	47	568	13.85	–	–	10
N.T.Broom	2	3	–	20	32	10.66	–	–	–
C.de Grandhomme	8	12	1	105	391	35.54	1	2	8
G.D.Elliott	5	9	1	25	86	10.75	–	–	2
J.E.C.Franklin	31	46	7	122*	808	20.71	1	2	12
M.J.Henry	9	14	3	66	216	19.63	–	1	5
T.W.M.Latham	34	62	2	177	2295	38.25	6	13	35
J.D.S.Neesham	12	22	1	137*	709	33.76	2	4	12
H.M.Nicholls	16	24	2	118	692	31.45	1	5	10
J.S.Patel	24	38	8	47	381	12.70	–	–	13
J.A.Raval	9	15	1	88	623	44.50	–	6	13
M.J.Santner	17	21	–	73	535	25.47	–	2	7
I.S.Sodhi	14	19	3	63	365	22.81	–	2	8
T.G.Southee	58	88	7	77*	1384	17.08	–	3	36
L.R.P.L.Taylor	83	149	19	290	6246	48.04	17	28	125
N.Wagner	34	44	11	37	402	12.18	–	–	8
B.J.Watling	52	84	13	142*	2702	38.05	6	13	171/6
K.S.Williamson	63	113	10	242*	5214	50.62	17	26	56

NEW ZEALAND – BOWLING

	O	M	R	W	Avge	Best	5wI	10wM
C.J.Anderson	217	34	659	16	41.18	3- 47	–	–
T.A.Boult	1916	426	5712	200	28.56	6- 40	5	1
D.A.J.Bracewell	830.4	147	2796	72	38.83	6- 40	2	–
G.D.Elliott	47	9	140	4	35.00	2- 8	–	–
C.de Grandhomme	202.5	52	522	20	26.10	6- 41	1	–
J.E.C.Franklin	794.3	143	2786	82	33.97	6-119	3	–
M.J.Henry	359.1	65	1163	25	46.52	4- 93	–	–
J.D.S.Neesham	179.2	18	675	14	48.21	3- 42	–	–
J.S.Patel	972.1	202	3078	65	47.35	5-110	1	–
M.J.Santner	450.2	96	1260	34	37.05	3- 60	–	–
I.S.Sodhi	471	72	1774	38	46.68	4- 60	–	–
T.G.Southee	2141.2	477	6543	208	31.45	7- 64	6	1
L.R.P.L.Taylor	16	3	48	2	24.00	2- 4	–	–
N.Wagner	1240.5	248	4014	144	27.87	7- 39	5	–
K.S.Williamson	338.3	47	1129	29	38.93	4- 44	–	–

INDIA – BATTING AND FIELDING

	M	I	NO	HS	Runs	Avge	100	50	Ct/St
R.Ashwin	57	80	10	124	2145	30.64	4	11	21
J.J.Bumrah	3	6	2	2	4	1.00	–	–	–
S.Dhawan	29	49	1	190	2046	42.62	6	5	24
R.A.Jadeja	35	52	12	90	1176	29.40	–	8	28
V.Kohli	66	112	8	243	5554	53.40	21	16	63
Kuldeep Yadav	2	2	–	26	33	16.50	–	–	1
B.Kumar	21	29	4	63*	552	22.08	–	3	8
A.Mishra	22	32	2	84	648	21.60	–	4	8
Mohammed Shami	30	40	13	51*	398	14.74	–	1	6
A.Mukund	7	14	–	81	320	22.85	–	2	6
K.K.Nair	6	7	1	303*	374	62.33	1	–	6
H.H.Pandya	6	9	–	108	297	33.00	1	2	7
P.A.Patel	25	38	8	71	934	31.13	–	6	62/10
C.A.Pujara	57	96	7	206*	4496	50.51	14	17	40
A.M.Rahane	44	75	9	188	2883	43.68	9	12	59
K.L.Rahul	23	37	1	199	1458	40.50	4	10	27
W.P.Saha	32	46	8	117	1164	30.63	3	5	75/10
I.Sharma	81	110	42	31*	572	8.41	–	–	16
R.G.Sharma	25	43	6	177	1479	39.97	3	9	24
M.Vijay	56	96	1	167	3802	40.02	11	15	48
J.Yadav	4	6	1	104	228	45.60	1	1	1
U.T.Yadav	36	40	17	30	226	9.82	–	–	11

INDIA – BOWLING

	O	M	R	W	Avge	Best	5wI	10wM
R.Ashwin	2752.3	558	7951	311	25.56	7-59	26	7
J.J.Bumrah	112.1	16	353	14	25.21	5-54	1	–
S.Dhawan	9	2	18	0	–	–	–	–
R.A.Jadeja	1683.4	446	3917	165	23.73	7-48	9	1
V.Kohli	27.1	2	76	0	–	–	–	–
Kuldeep Yadav	58	9	187	9	20.77	4-40	–	–
B.Kumar	558	141	1644	63	26.09	6-82	4	–
A.Mishra	850.3	123	2715	76	35.72	5-71	1	–
Mohammed Shami	939	164	3180	110	28.90	5-28	3	–
A.Mukund	2	0	14	0	–	–	–	–
K.K.Nair	2	0	11	0	–	–	–	–
H.H.Pandya	83	10	257	7	36.71	2-27	–	–
C.A.Pujara	1	0	2	0	–	–	–	–
I.Sharma	2600	502	8411	234	35.94	7-74	7	1
R.G.Sharma	55.4	3	202	2	101.00	1-26	–	–
M.Vijay	55	5	167	1	167.00	1-12	–	–
J.Yadav	104.3	19	367	11	33.36	3-30	–	–
U.T.Yadav	983	169	3555	99	35.90	5-93	1	–

PAKISTAN – BATTING AND FIELDING

	M	I	NO	HS	Runs	Avge	100	50	Ct/St
Ahmed Shehzad	13	25	1	176	982	40.91	3	4	3
Asad Shafiq	58	97	6	137	3614	39.71	11	18	51
Azhar Ali	62	118	8	302*	5129	46.62	14	27	60
Babar Azam	11	22	2	90*	475	23.75	–	4	9
Haris Sohail	2	4	–	76	176	44.00	–	2	–
Hasan Ali	2	4	2	29	60	30.00	–	–	1
Imran Khan	9	8	2	6	6	1.00	–	–	–
Misbah-ul-Haq	75	132	20	161*	5222	46.62	10	39	50
Mohammad Abbas	5	8	5	4	11	3.66	–	–	1
Mohammad Amir	30	57	8	48	645	13.16	–	–	4
Rahat Ali	20	30	12	35*	136	7.55	–	–	9
Sami Aslam	13	25	1	91	758	31.58	–	7	7
Sarfraz Ahmed	38	67	12	112	2208	40.14	3	14	103/18

PAKISTAN – BATTING AND FIELDING (continued)

	M	I	NO	HS	Runs	Avge	100	50	Ct/St
Shadab Khan	1	2	–	16	17	8.50	–	–	–
Shan Masood	12	24	–	125	565	23.54	1	3	10
Sharjeel Khan	1	2	–	40	44	22.00	–	–	–
Sohail Khan	9	12	2	65	252	25.20	–	1	2
Wahab Riaz	26	40	4	39	299	8.30	–	–	5
Yasir Shah	28	41	6	38*	445	12.71	–	–	18
Younus Khan	118	213	19	313	10099	52.05	34	33	139

PAKISTAN – BOWLING

	O	M	R	W	Avge	Best	5wI	10wM
Ahmed Shehzad	8	0	28	0	–	–	–	–
Asad Shafiq	37.4	1	126	2	63.00	1- 7	–	–
Azhar Ali	138.3	8	589	8	73.62	2- 35	–	–
Haris Sohail	33	5	93	5	18.60	3- 1	–	–
Hasan Ali	71.1	17	164	6	27.33	3- 33	–	–
Imran Khan	248.4	47	844	28	30.14	5- 58	1	–
Mohammad Abbas	201.5	47	491	23	21.34	5- 46	1	–
Mohammad Amir	1069.4	241	3123	95	32.87	6- 44	4	–
Rahat Ali	674.3	124	2171	58	37.43	6-127	2	–
Shadab Khan	40	3	145	1	145.00	1- 90	–	–
Shan Masood	4	1	19	0	–	–	–	–
Sohail Khan	304.4	55	1125	27	41.66	5- 68	2	–
Wahab Riaz	809.2	113	2783	83	33.53	5- 63	2	–
Yasir Shah	1546.1	243	4859	165	29.44	7- 76	13	2
Younus Khan	134	18	491	9	54.55	2- 23	–	–

SRI LANKA – BATTING AND FIELDING

	M	I	NO	HS	Runs	Avge	100	50	Ct/St
P.V.D.Chameera	6	11	1	19	61	6.10	–	–	3
L.D.Chandimal	46	84	6	164	3413	43.75	10	16	73/10
D.M.de Silva	13	25	2	173	1066	46.34	4	2	7
D.P.D.N.Dickwella	17	32	2	83	990	33.00	–	8	42/14
A.N.P.R.Fernando	28	50	17	17*	132	4.00	–	–	5
M.V.T.Fernando	2	4	2	4*	4	2.00	–	–	–
P.L.S.Gamage	4	6	3	1*	3	1.00	–	–	–
D.A.S.Gunaratne	6	10	2	116	455	56.87	1	3	6
M.D.Gunathilleke	2	4	–	17	48	12.00	–	–	2
H.M.R.K.B.Herath	89	137	27	80*	1639	14.90	–	3	22
F.D.M.Karunaratne	49	95	3	196	3186	34.63	7	14	42
C.B.R.L.S.Kumara	9	13	6	10	36	5.14	–	–	3
R.A.S.Lakmal	44	68	19	42	543	11.08	–	–	12
A.D.Mathews	72	128	17	160	4914	44.27	8	28	55
B.K.G.Mendis	24	47	1	196	1712	37.21	4	5	33
M.D.K.Perera	27	48	4	95	915	20.79	–	6	17
M.D.K.J.Perera	10	18	–	110	565	31.38	1	3	16/8
M.K.P.A.D.Perera	1	2	–	20	20	20.00	–	–	1
S.Prasanna	1	1	–	5	5	5.00	–	–	–
P.M.Pushpakumara	2	4	1	16	42	14.00	–	–	–
W.S.R.Samarawickrama	4	8	–	38	125	15.62	–	4	4
P.A.D.L.R.Sandakan	9	13	6	19*	77	11.00	–	–	4
M.D.Shanaka	3	6	1	17	29	5.80	–	–	1
A.R.S.Silva	3	5	2	109	309	103.00	1	3	–
J.K.Silva	37	70	–	139	2058	29.40	3	12	33/1
W.U.Tharanga	31	58	3	165	1754	31.89	3	8	24
H.D.R.L.Thirimanne	29	56	6	155*	1153	23.06	1	5	15

SRI LANKA – BOWLING

	O	M	R	W	Avge	Best	5wI	10wM
P.V.D.Chameera	172.5	10	726	22	33.00	5- 47	1	–
D.M.de Silva	123	9	460	7	65.71	2- 91	–	–
A.N.P.R.Fernando	846.1	130	3003	70	42.90	6-132	1	–
M.V.T.Fernando	28	3	103	3	34.33	2- 87	–	–
P.L.S.Gamage	144.2	30	463	10	46.30	2- 38	–	–
D.A.S.Gunaratne	26	1	114	3	38.00	2- 28	–	–
M.D.Gunathilleke	12	0	57	1	57.00	1- 16	–	–
H.M.R.K.B.Herath	4153.2	780	11694	415	28.17	9-127	33	9
F.D.M.Karunaratne	24	1	97	1	97.00	1-.31	–	–
C.B.R.L.S.Kumara	264	21	1137	23	49.43	6-122	1	–
R.A.S.Lakmal	1374.3	250	4444	102	43.56	5- 63	1	–
A.D.Mathews	638	154	1738	33	52.66	4- 44	–	–
B.K.G.Mendis	12	1	43	1	43.00	1- 10	–	–
M.D.K.Perera	1144	158	3732	106	35.20	6- 70	5	1
M.K.P.A.D.Perera	15	3	44	8	5.50	5- 24	1	–
S.Prasanna	23	3	80	0	–	–	–	–
P.M.Pushpakumara	61.2	4	238	5	47.60	3- 82	–	–
P.A.D.L.R.Sandakan	297	35	1086	28	38.78	5-132	1	–
M.D.Shanaka	73.1	12	261	9	29.00	3- 46	–	–
H.D.R.L.Thirimanne	14	1	51	0	–	–	–	–

A.N.P.R.Fernando is also known as N.Pradeep; M.K.P.A.D.Perera is also known as A.Dananjaya.

ZIMBABWE – BATTING AND FIELDING

	M	I	NO	HS	Runs	Avge	100	50	Ct/St
R.P.Burl	1	2	–	16	16	8.00	–	–	1
R.W.Chakabva	12	24	2	101	618	28.09	1	4	14/3
C.J.Chibhabha	3	6	–	60	124	20.66	–	1	–
T.S.Chisoro	1	1	–	9	9	9.00	–	–	–
A.G.Cremer	19	38	5	102*	540	16.36	1	–	12
C.R.Ervine	15	30	2	160	941	33.60	2	3	15
S.M.Ervine	5	8	–	86	261	32.62	–	3	7
K.M.Jarvis	10	18	8	25*	111	11.10	–	–	3
H.Masakadza	36	72	2	158	2084	29.77	5	7	28
S.F.Mire	2	4	–	47	78	19.50	–	–	–
P.J.Moor	6	12	–	79	374	31.16	–	3	9/1
C.B.Mpofu	15	28	10	33	105	5.83	–	–	4
T.K.Musakanda	1	2	–	6	6	3.00	–	–	–
B.Muzarabani	1	2	1	10	14	14.00	–	–	–
Sikandar Raza	10	20	–	127	762	38.10	1	6	1
B.R.M.Taylor	26	52	3	171	1594	32.53	4	8	25
D.T.Tiripano	6	12	3	49*	219	24.33	–	–	2
M.N.Waller	14	28	1	72*	577	21.37	–	4	10
S.C.Williams	8	16	–	119	421	26.31	1	1	8

ZIMBABWE – BOWLING

	O	M	R	W	Avge	Best	5wI	10wM
C.J.Chibhabha	41	4	162	1	162.00	1- 44	–	–
T.S.Chisoro	41.2	9	113	3	37.66	3-113	–	–
A.G.Cremer	702.2	71	2604	57	45.68	5-125	1	–
S.M.Ervine	95	18	388	9	43.11	4-116	–	–
K.M.Jarvis	317.3	52	1115	36	30.97	5- 54	2	–
T.Kamungozi	26	6	58	1	58.00	1- 51	–	–
H.Masakadza	192	49	482	16	30.12	3- 24	–	–
S.F.Mire	14	2	32	1	32.00	1- 22	–	–
C.B.Mpofu	414.5	86	1392	29	48.00	4- 92	–	–
B.Muzarabani	13	2	48	0	–	–	–	–
Sikandar Raza	225.5	28	763	13	58.69	5- 99	1	–
B.R.M.Taylor	7	0	38	0	–	–	–	–

TESTS **ZIMBABWE – BOWLING (continued)**

	O	M	R	W	Avge	Best	5wI	10wM
D.T.Tiripano	172	33	510	10	51.00	3-91	–	–
M.N.Waller	76	8	218	8	27.25	4-59	–	–
S.C.Williams	189.1	22	605	15	40.33	3-20	–	–

BANGLADESH – BATTING AND FIELDING

	M	I	NO	HS	Runs	Avge	100	50	Ct/St
Abdur Razzak	13	22	6	43	248	15.50	–	–	4
Imrul Kayes	34	66	2	150	1679	26.23	3	4	32
Kamrul Islam	5	10	4	25*	44	7.33	–	–	–
Liton Das	8	13	–	94	385	29.61	–	3	15/2
Mahmudullah	37	70	4	115	2065	31.28	1	15	34/1
Mehedi Hasan	12	23	4	51	346	18.21	–	1	9
Mominul Haque	27	50	4	181	2154	46.82	6	12	19
Mosaddek Hossain	2	4	1	75	104	34.66	–	1	2
Mushfiqur Rahim	60	112	8	200	3636	34.96	5	19	98/13
Mustafizur Rahman	10	15	5	10*	38	3.80	–	–	1
Nasir Hossain	19	32	2	100	1044	34.80	1	6	10
Nazmul Hossain	1	2	–	18	30	15.00	–	–	–
Nurul Hasan	1	2	–	47	47	23.50	–	–	2
Rubel Hossain	25	43	18	45*	237	9.48	–	–	11
Sabbir Rahman	11	22	2	66	481	24.05	–	4	3
Shafiul Islam	11	21	1	53	211	10.55	–	1	2
Shakib Al Hasan	51	96	7	217	3594	40.38	5	22	19
Soumya Sarkar	10	19	–	86	558	29.36	–	4	12
Subashis Roy	4	6	5	12*	14	14.00	–	–	–
Sanjamul Islam	1	1	–	24	24	24.00	–	–	–
Taijul Islam	18	30	4	32	225	8.65	–	–	8
Tamim Iqbal	54	104	1	206	3985	38.68	8	25	13
Taskin Ahmed	5	10	–	33	68	6.80	–	–	1

BANGLADESH – BOWLING

	O	M	R	W	Avge	Best	5wI	10wM
Abdur Razzak	502.3	69	1673	28	59.75	4- 63	–	–
Imrul Kayes	4	0	12	0	–	–	–	–
Kamrul Islam	93	9	398	7	56.85	3- 87	–	–
Mahmudullah	523.3	52	1831	39	46.94	5- 51	1	–
Mehedi Hasan	551	53	1860	48	38.75	6- 77	3	1
Mominul Haque	67.1	2	252	4	63.00	3- 27	–	–
Mosaddek Hossain	10	0	45	0	–	–	–	–
Mustafizur Rahman	258.3	50	819	26	31.50	4- 37	–	–
Nasir Hossain	154	26	442	8	55.25	3- 52	–	–
Nazmul Hossain	0.4	0	13	0	–	–	–	–
Rubel Hossain	661	67	2607	33	79.00	5-166	1	–
Sabbir Rahman	24	1	98	0	–	–	–	–
Shafiul Islam	289	44	942	17	55.41	3- 86	–	–
Shakib Al Hasan	2015.2	371	6086	188	32.37	7- 36	17	2
Soumya Sarkar	42.4	2	159	1	159.00	1- 45	–	–
Subashis Roy	124.5	19	465	9	51.66	3-118	–	–
Sanjamul Islam	45	2	153	1	153.00	1-153	–	–
Taijul Islam	718.2	102	2364	66	35.81	8- 39	3	–
Tamim Iqbal	5	0	20	0	–	–	–	–
Taskin Ahmed	155	16	682	7	97.42	2- 43	–	–

INTERNATIONAL TEST MATCH RESULTS

Complete to 28 February 2018.

	Opponents	Tests	Won by											Tied	Drawn
			E	A	SA	WI	NZ	I	P	SL	Z	B			
England	Australia	346	108	144	–	–	–	–	–	–	–	–	–	–	94
	South Africa	149	61	–	33	–	–	–	–	–	–	–	–	–	55
	West Indies	154	48	–	–	55	–	–	–	–	–	–	–	–	51
	New Zealand	101	48	–	–	–	9	–	–	–	–	–	–	–	44
	India	117	43	–	–	–	–	25	–	–	–	–	–	–	49
	Pakistan	81	24	–	–	–	–	–	20	–	–	–	–	–	37
	Sri Lanka	31	12	–	–	–	–	–	–	8	–	–	–	–	11
	Zimbabwe	6	3	–	–	–	–	–	–	–	0	–	–	–	3
	Bangladesh	10	9	–	–	–	–	–	–	–	–	1	–	–	0
Australia	South Africa	94	–	51	23	–	–	–	–	–	–	–	–	–	20
	West Indies	116	–	58	–	32	–	–	–	–	–	–	–	1	25
	New Zealand	57	–	31	–	–	8	–	–	–	–	–	–	–	18
	India	94	–	41	–	–	–	26	–	–	–	–	–	1	26
	Pakistan	62	–	31	–	–	–	–	14	–	–	–	–	–	17
	Sri Lanka	29	–	17	–	–	–	–	–	4	–	–	–	–	8
	Zimbabwe	3	–	3	–	–	–	–	–	–	0	–	–	–	0
	Bangladesh	6	–	5	–	–	–	–	–	–	–	1	–	–	0
South Africa	West Indies	28	–	–	18	3	–	–	–	–	–	–	–	–	7
	New Zealand	45	–	–	25	–	4	–	–	–	–	–	–	–	16
	India	36	–	–	15	–	–	11	–	–	–	–	–	–	10
	Pakistan	23	–	–	12	–	–	–	4	–	–	–	–	–	7
	Sri Lanka	25	–	–	14	–	–	–	–	5	–	–	–	–	6
	Zimbabwe	9	–	–	8	–	–	–	–	–	0	–	–	–	1
	Bangladesh	12	–	–	10	–	–	–	–	–	–	0	–	–	2
West Indies	New Zealand	47	–	–	–	13	15	–	–	–	–	–	–	–	19
	India	94	–	–	–	30	–	18	–	–	–	–	–	–	46
	Pakistan	52	–	–	–	17	–	–	20	–	–	–	–	–	15
	Sri Lanka	17	–	–	–	3	–	–	–	8	–	–	–	–	6
	Zimbabwe	10	–	–	–	7	–	–	–	–	0	–	–	–	3
	Bangladesh	12	–	–	–	8	–	–	–	–	–	2	–	–	2
New Zealand	India	57	–	–	–	–	10	21	–	–	–	–	–	–	26
	Pakistan	55	–	–	–	–	10	–	24	–	–	–	–	–	21
	Sri Lanka	32	–	–	–	–	14	–	–	8	–	–	–	–	10
	Zimbabwe	17	–	–	–	–	11	–	–	–	0	–	–	–	6
	Bangladesh	13	–	–	–	–	10	–	–	–	–	0	–	–	3
India	Pakistan	59	–	–	–	–	–	9	12	–	–	–	–	–	38
	Sri Lanka	44	–	–	–	–	–	20	–	7	–	–	–	–	17
	Zimbabwe	11	–	–	–	–	–	7	–	–	2	–	–	–	2
	Bangladesh	9	–	–	–	–	–	7	–	–	–	0	–	–	2
Pakistan	Sri Lanka	53	–	–	–	–	–	–	19	16	–	–	–	–	18
	Zimbabwe	17	–	–	–	–	–	–	10	–	3	–	–	–	4
	Bangladesh	10	–	–	–	–	–	–	9	–	–	0	–	–	1
Sri Lanka	Zimbabwe	18	–	–	–	–	–	–	–	13	0	–	–	–	5
	Bangladesh	20	–	–	–	–	–	–	–	16	–	1	–	–	3
Zimbabwe	Bangladesh	14	–	–	–	–	–	–	–	–	6	5	–	–	3
		2295	356	381	158	168	91	144	132	85	11	10		2	757

	Tests	Won	Lost	Drawn	Tied	Toss Won
England	995	356	295	344	–	483
Australia	808†	382†	216	208	2	404†
South Africa	421	158	139	124	–	204
West Indies	530	168	187	174	1	275
New Zealand	424	91	170	163	–	210
India	521	144	160	216	1	264
Pakistan	412	132	122	158	–	195
Sri Lanka	269	85	100	84	–	147
Zimbabwe	105	11	67	27	–	59
Bangladesh	106	10	80	16	–	55

† total includes Australia's victory against the ICC World XI.

INTERNATIONAL TEST CRICKET RECORDS

(To 28 February 2018)

TEAM RECORDS

HIGHEST INNINGS TOTALS

952-6d	Sri Lanka v India	Colombo (RPS)	1997-98
903-7d	England v Australia	The Oval	1938
849	England v West Indies	Kingston	1929-30
790-3d	West Indies v Pakistan	Kingston	1957-58
765-6d	Pakistan v Sri Lanka	Karachi	2008-09
760-7d	Sri Lanka v India	Ahmedabad	2009-10
759-7d	India v England	Chennai	2016-17
758-8d	Australia v West Indies	Kingston	1954-55
756-5d	Sri Lanka v South Africa	Colombo (SSC)	2006
751-5d	West Indies v England	St John's	2003-04
749-9d	West Indies v England	Bridgetown	2008-09
747	West Indies v South Africa	St John's	2004-05
735-6d	Australia v Zimbabwe	Perth	2003-04
730-6d	Sri Lanka v Bangladesh	Dhaka	2013-14
729-6d	Australia v England	Lord's	1930
726-9d	India v Sri Lanka	Mumbai	2009-10
713-3d	Sri Lanka v Zimbabwe	Bulawayo	2003-04
713-9d	Sri Lanka v Bangladesh	Chittagong	2017-18
710-7d	England v India	Birmingham	2011
708	Pakistan v England	The Oval	1987
707	India v Sri Lanka	Colombo (SSC)	2010
705-7d	India v Australia	Sydney	2003-04
701	Australia v England	The Oval	1934
699-5	Pakistan v India	Lahore	1989-90
695	Australia v England	The Oval	1930
692-8d	West Indies v England	The Oval	1995
690	New Zealand v Pakistan	Sharjah	2014-15
687-8d	West Indies v England	The Oval	1976
687-6d	India v Bangladesh	Hyderabad	2016-17
682-6d	South Africa v England	Lord's	2003
681-8d	West Indies v England	Port-of-Spain	1953-54
680-8d	New Zealand v India	Wellington	2013-14
679-7d	Pakistan v India	Lahore	2005-06
676-7	India v Sri Lanka	Kanpur	1986-87
675-5d	India v Pakistan	Multan	2003-04
674	Australia v India	Adelaide	1947-48

674-6	Pakistan v India	Faisalabad	1984-85
674-6d	Australia v England	Cardiff	2009
671-4	New Zealand v Sri Lanka	Wellington	1990-91
668	Australia v West Indies	Bridgetown	1954-55
664	India v England	The Oval	2007
662-9d	Australia v England	Perth	2017-18
660-5d	West Indies v New Zealand	Wellington	1994-95
659-8d	Australia v England	Sydney	1946-47
659-4d	Australia v India	Sydney	2011-12
658-8d	England v Australia	Nottingham	1938
658-9d	South Africa v West Indies	Durban	2003-04
657-8d	Pakistan v West Indies	Bridgetown	1957-58
657-7d	India v Australia	Calcutta	2000-01
656-8d	Australia v England	Manchester	1964
654-5	England v South Africa	Durban	1938-39
653-4d	England v India	Lord's	1990
653-4d	Australia v England	Leeds	1993
652-8d	West Indies v England	Lord's	1973
652	Pakistan v India	Faisalabad	1982-83
652-7d	England v India	Madras	1984-85
652-7d	Australia v South Africa	Johannesburg	2001-02
651	South Africa v Australia	Cape Town	2008-09
650-6d	Australia v West Indies	Bridgetown	1964-65

The highest for Zimbabwe is 563-9d (v WI, Harare, 2001), and for Bangladesh 638 (v SL, Galle, 2012-13).

LOWEST INNINGS TOTALS

† One batsman absent

26	New Zealand v England	Auckland	1954-55
30	South Africa v England	Port Elizabeth	1895-96
30	South Africa v England	Birmingham	1924
35	South Africa v England	Cape Town	1898-99
36	Australia v England	Birmingham	1902
36	South Africa v Australia	Melbourne	1931-32
42	Australia v England	Sydney	1887-88
42	New Zealand v Australia	Wellington	1945-46
42†	India v England	Lord's	1974
43	South Africa v England	Cape Town	1888-89
44	Australia v England	The Oval	1896
45	England v Australia	Sydney	1886-87
45	South Africa v Australia	Melbourne	1931-32
45	New Zealand v South Africa	Cape Town	2012-13
46	England v West Indies	Port-of-Spain	1993-94
47	South Africa v England	Cape Town	1888-89
47	New Zealand v England	Lord's	1958
47	West Indies v England	Kingston	2003-04
47	Australia v South Africa	Cape Town	2011-12
49	Pakistan v South Africa	Johannesburg	2012-13

The lowest for Sri Lanka is 71 (v P, Kandy, 1994-95), for Zimbabwe 51 (v NZ, Napier, 2011-12), and for Bangladesh 62 (v SL, Colombo PPS, 2006-07).

BATTING RECORDS
5000 RUNS IN TESTS

Runs			M	I	NO	HS	Avge	100	50
15921	S.R.Tendulkar	I	200	329	33	248*	53.78	51	68
13378	R.T.Ponting	A	168	287	29	257	51.85	41	62
13289	J.H.Kallis	SA/ICC	166	280	40	224	55.37	45	58
13288	R.S.Dravid	I/ICC	164	286	32	270	52.31	36	63
12400	K.C.Sangakkara	SL	134	233	17	319	57.40	38	52
12005	A.N.Cook	E	152	275	16	294	46.35	32	55
11953	B.C.Lara	WI/ICC	131	232	6	400*	52.88	34	48
11867	S.Chanderpaul	WI	164	280	49	203*	51.37	30	66
11814	D.P.M.D.Jayawardena	SL	149	252	15	374	49.84	34	50
11174	A.R.Border	A	156	265	44	205	50.56	27	63
10927	S.R.Waugh	A	168	260	46	200	51.06	32	50
10122	S.M.Gavaskar	I	125	214	16	236*	51.12	34	45
10099	Younus Khan	P	118	213	19	313	52.05	34	33
9265	G.C.Smith	SA/ICC	117	205	13	277	48.25	27	38
8900	G.A.Gooch	E	118	215	6	333	42.58	20	46
8832	Javed Miandad	P	124	189	21	280*	52.57	23	43
8830	Inzamam-ul-Haq	P/ICC	120	200	22	329	49.60	25	46
8786	H.M.Amla	SA	113	193	14	311*	49.08	28	38
8781	V.V.S.Laxman	I	134	225	34	281	45.97	17	56
8643	M.J.Clarke	A	115	198	22	329*	49.10	28	27
8625	M.L.Hayden	A	103	184	14	380	50.73	30	29
8586	V.Sehwag	I/ICC	104	180	6	319	49.34	23	32
8540	I.V.A.Richards	WI	121	182	12	291	50.23	24	45
8463	A.J.Stewart	E	133	235	21	190	39.54	15	45
8338	A.B.de Villiers	SA	110	183	16	278*	49.92	21	42
8231	D.I.Gower	E	117	204	18	215	44.25	18	39
8181	K.P.Pietersen	E	104	181	8	227	47.28	23	35
8114	G.Boycott	E	108	193	23	246*	47.72	22	42
8032	G.St A.Sobers	WI	93	160	21	365*	57.78	26	30
8029	M.E.Waugh	A	128	209	17	153*	41.81	20	47
7728	M.A.Atherton	E	115	212	7	185*	37.70	16	46
7727	I.R.Bell	E	118	205	24	235	42.69	22	46
7696	J.L.Langer	A	105	182	12	250	45.27	23	30
7624	M.C.Cowdrey	E	114	188	15	182	44.06	22	38
7558	C.G.Greenidge	WI	108	185	16	226	44.72	19	34
7530	Mohammad Yousuf	P	90	156	12	223	52.29	24	33
7525	M.A.Taylor	A	104	186	13	334*	43.49	19	40
7515	C.H.Lloyd	WI	110	175	14	242*	46.67	19	39
7487	D.L.Haynes	WI	116	202	25	184	42.29	18	39
7422	D.C.Boon	A	107	190	20	200	43.65	21	32
7289	G.Kirsten	SA	101	176	15	275	45.27	21	34
7249	W.R.Hammond	E	85	140	16	336*	58.45	22	24
7214	C.H.Gayle	WI	103	182	11	333	42.18	15	37
7212	S.C.Ganguly	I	113	188	17	239	42.17	16	35
7172	S.P.Fleming	NZ	111	189	10	274*	40.06	9	46
7110	G.S.Chappell	A	87	151	19	247*	53.86	24	31
7037	A.J.Strauss	E	100	178	6	177	40.91	21	27
6996	D.G.Bradman	A	52	80	10	334	99.94	29	13
6973	S.T.Jayasuriya	SL	110	188	14	340	40.07	14	31
6971	L.Hutton	E	79	138	15	364	56.67	19	33
6868	D.B.Vengsarkar	I	116	185	22	166	42.13	17	35
6806	K.F.Barrington	E	82	131	15	256	58.67	20	35
6744	G.P.Thorpe	E	100	179	28	200*	44.66	16	39

Runs			M	I	NO	HS	Avge	100	50
6453	B.B.McCullum	NZ	101	176	9	302	38.64	12	31
6361	P.A.de Silva	SL	93	159	11	267	42.97	20	22
6246	L.R.P.L.Taylor	NZ	83	149	19	290	48.04	17	28
6235	M.E.K.Hussey	A	79	137	16	195	51.52	19	29
6227	R.B.Kanhai	WI	79	137	6	256	47.53	15	28
6215	M.Azharuddin	I	99	147	9	199	45.03	22	21
6167	H.H.Gibbs	SA	90	154	7	228	41.95	14	26
6149	R.N.Harvey	A	79	137	10	205	48.41	21	24
6146	D.A.Warner	A	71	131	5	253	48.77	21	27
6080	G.R.Viswanath	I	91	155	10	222	41.93	14	35
6057	S.P.D.Smith	A	61	111	16	239	63.75	23	23
5949	R.B.Richardson	WI	86	146	12	194	44.39	16	27
5842	R.R.Sarwan	WI	87	154	8	291	40.01	15	31
5825	M.E.Trescothick	E	76	143	10	219	43.79	14	29
5807	D.C.S.Compton	E	78	131	15	278	50.06	17	28
5768	Salim Malik	P	103	154	22	237	43.69	15	29
5764	N.Hussain	E	96	171	16	207	37.19	14	33
5762	C.L.Hooper	WI	102	173	15	233	36.46	13	27
5719	M.P.Vaughan	E	82	147	9	197	41.44	18	18
5701	J.E.Root	E	65	119	12	254	53.28	13	37
5570	A.C.Gilchrist	A	96	137	20	204*	47.60	17	26
5554	V.Kohli	I	66	112	8	243	53.40	21	16
5515	M.V.Boucher	SA/ICC	147	206	24	125	30.30	5	35
5502	M.S.Atapattu	SL	90	156	15	249	39.02	16	17
5492	T.M.Dilshan	SL	87	145	11	193	40.98	16	23
5462	T.T.Samaraweera	SL	81	132	20	231	48.76	14	30
5444	M.D.Crowe	NZ	77	131	11	299	45.36	17	18
5410	J.B.Hobbs	E	61	102	7	211	56.94	15	28
5357	K.D.Walters	A	74	125	14	250	48.26	15	33
5345	I.M.Chappell	A	75	136	10	196	42.42	14	26
5334	J.G.Wright	NZ	82	148	7	185	37.82	12	23
5312	M.J.Slater	A	74	131	7	219	42.84	14	21
5248	Kapil Dev	I	131	184	15	163	31.05	8	27
5234	W.M.Lawry	A	67	123	12	210	47.15	13	27
5222	Misbah-ul-Haq	P	75	132	20	161*	46.62	10	39
5214	K.S.Williamson	NZ	63	113	10	242*	50.62	17	26
5200	I.T.Botham	E	102	161	6	208	33.54	14	22
5138	J.H.Edrich	E	77	127	9	310*	43.54	12	24
5129	Azhar Ali	P	62	118	8	302*	46.62	14	27
5105	A.Ranatunga	SL	93	155	12	135*	35.69	4	38
5062	Zaheer Abbas	P	78	124	11	274	44.79	12	20

The most for Zimbabwe is 4794 by A.Flower (112 innings), and for Bangladesh 3985 by Tamim Iqbal (104 innings).

750 RUNS IN A SERIES

Runs			Series	M	I	NO	HS	Avge	100	50
974	D.G.Bradman	A v E	1930	5	7	–	334	139.14	4	–
905	W.R.Hammond	E v A	1928-29	5	9	1	251	113.12	4	–
839	M.A.Taylor	A v E	1989	6	11	1	219	83.90	2	5
834	R.N.Harvey	A v SA	1952-53	5	9	–	205	92.66	4	3
829	I.V.A.Richards	WI v E	1976	4	7	–	291	118.42	3	2
827	C.L.Walcott	WI v A	1954-55	5	10	–	155	82.70	5	2
824	G.St A.Sobers	WI v P	1957-58	5	8	2	365*	137.33	3	3
810	D.G.Bradman	A v E	1936-37	5	9	–	270	90.00	3	1
806	D.G.Bradman	A v SA	1931-32	5	5	1	299*	201.50	4	–

Runs			Series	M	I	NO	HS	Avge	100	50
798	B.C.Lara	WI v E	1993-94	5	8	–	375	99.75	2	2
779	E.de C.Weekes	WI v I	1948-49	5	7	–	194	111.28	4	2
774	S.M.Gavaskar	I v WI	1970-71	4	8	3	220	154.80	4	3
769	S.P.D.Smith	A v I	2014-15	4	8	2	192	128.16	4	2
766	A.N.Cook	E v A	2010-11	5	7	1	235*	127.66	3	2
765	B.C.Lara	WI v E	1995	6	10	1	179	85.00	3	3
761	Mudassar Nazar	P v I	1982-83	6	8	2	231	126.83	4	1
758	D.G.Bradman	A v E	1934	5	8	–	304	94.75	2	1
753	D.C.S.Compton	E v SA	1947	5	8	–	208	94.12	4	2
752	G.A.Gooch	E v I	1990	3	6	–	333	125.33	3	2

HIGHEST INDIVIDUAL INNINGS

400*	B.C.Lara	WI v E	St John's	2003-04
380	M.L.Hayden	A v Z	Perth	2003-04
375	B.C.Lara	WI v E	St John's	1993-94
374	D.P.M.D.Jayawardena	SL v SA	Colombo (SSC)	2006
365*	G.St A.Sobers	WI v P	Kingston	1957-58
364	L.Hutton	E v A	The Oval	1938
340	S.T.Jayasuriya	SL v I	Colombo (RPS)	1997-98
337	Hanif Mohammed	P v WI	Bridgetown	1957-58
336*	W.R.Hammond	E v NZ	Auckland	1932-33
334*	M.A.Taylor	A v P	Peshawar	1998-99
334	D.G.Bradman	A v E	Leeds	1930
333	G.A.Gooch	E v I	Lord's	1990
333	C.H.Gayle	WI v SL	Galle	2010-11
329*	M.J.Clarke	A v I	Sydney	2011-12
329	Inzamam-ul-Haq	P v NZ	Lahore	2001-02
325	A.Sandham	E v WI	Kingston	1929-30
319	V.Sehwag	I v SA	Chennai	2007-08
319	K.C.Sangakkara	SL v B	Chittagong	2013-14
317	C.H.Gayle	WI v SA	St John's	2004-05
313	Younus Khan	P v SL	Karachi	2008-09
311*	H.M.Amla	SA v E	The Oval	2012
311	R.B.Simpson	A v E	Manchester	1964
310*	J.H.Edrich	E v NZ	Leeds	1965
309	V.Sehwag	I v P	Multan	2003-04
307	R.M.Cowper	A v E	Melbourne	1965-66
304	D.G.Bradman	A v E	Leeds	1934
303*	K.K.Nair	I v E	Chennai	2016-17
302*	Azhar Ali	P v WI	Dubai (DSC)	2016-17
302	L.G.Rowe	WI v E	Bridgetown	1973-74
302	B.B.McCullum	NZ v I	Wellington	2013-14
299*	D.G.Bradman	A v SA	Adelaide	1931-32
299	M.D.Crowe	NZ v SL	Wellington	1990-91
294	A.N.Cook	E v I	Birmingham	2011
293	V.Sehwag	I v SL	Mumbai	2009-10
291	I.V.A.Richards	WI v E	The Oval	1976
291	R.R.Sarwan	WI v E	Bridgetown	2008-09
290	L.R.P.L.Taylor	NZ v A	Perth	2015-16
287	R.E.Foster	E v A	Sydney	1903-04
287	K.C.Sangakkara	SL v SA	Colombo (SSC)	2006
285*	P.B.H.May	E v WI	Birmingham	1957
281	V.V.S.Laxman	I v A	Calcutta	2000-01
280*	Javed Miandad	P v I	Hyderabad	1982-83
278*	A.B.de Villiers	SA v P	Abu Dhabi	2010-11

278	D.C.S.Compton	E v P	Nottingham	1954
277	B.C.Lara	WI v A	Sydney	1992-93
277	G.C.Smith	SA v E	Birmingham	2003
275*	D.J.Cullinan	SA v NZ	Auckland	1998-99
275	G.Kirsten	SA v E	Durban	1999-00
275	D.P.M.D.Jayawardena	SL v I	Ahmedabad	2009-10
274*	S.P.Fleming	NZ v SL	Colombo (SSC)	2002-03
274	R.G.Pollock	SA v A	Durban	1969-70
274	Zaheer Abbas	P v E	Birmingham	1971
271	Javed Miandad	P v NZ	Auckland	1988-89
270*	G.A.Headley	WI v E	Kingston	1934-35
270	D.G.Bradman	A v E	Melbourne	1936-37
270	R.S.Dravid	I v P	Rawalpindi	2003-04
270	K.C.Sangakkara	SL v Z	Bulawayo	2004
269*	A.C.Voges	A v WI	Hobart	2015-16
268	G.N.Yallop	A v P	Melbourne	1983-84
267*	B.A.Young	NZ v SL	Dunedin	1996-97
267	P.A.de Silva	SL v NZ	Wellington	1990-91
267	Younus Khan	P v I	Bangalore	2004-05
266	W.H.Ponsford	A v E	The Oval	1934
266	D.L.Houghton	Z v SL	Bulawayo	1994-95
263	A.N.Cook	E v P	Abu Dhabi	2015-16
262*	D.L.Amiss	E v WI	Kingston	1973-74
262	S.P.Fleming	NZ v SA	Cape Town	2005-06
261*	R.R.Sarwan	WI v B	Kingston	2004
261	F.M.M.Worrell	WI v E	Nottingham	1950
260	C.C.Hunte	WI v P	Kingston	1957-58
260	Javed Miandad	P v E	The Oval	1987
260	M.N.Samuels	WI v B	Khulna	2012-13
259*	M.J.Clarke	A v SA	Brisbane	2012-13
259	G.M.Turner	NZ v WI	Georgetown	1971-72
259	G.C.Smith	SA v E	Lord's	2003
258	T.W.Graveney	E v WI	Nottingham	1957
258	S.M.Nurse	WI v NZ	Christchurch	1968-69
258	B.A.Stokes	E v SA	Cape Town	2015-16
257*	Wasim Akram	P v Z	Sheikhupura	1996-97
257	R.T.Ponting	A v I	Melbourne	2003-04
256	R.B.Kanhai	WI v I	Calcutta	1958-59
256	K.F.Barrington	E v A	Manchester	1964
255*	D.J.McGlew	SA v NZ	Wellington	1952-53
254	D.G.Bradman	A v E	Lord's	1930
254	V.Sehwag	I v P	Lahore	2005-06
254	J.E.Root	E v P	Manchester	2016
253*	H.M.Amla	SA v I	Nagpur	2009-10
253	S.T.Jayasuriya	SL v P	Faisalabad	2004-05
253	D.A.Warner	A v NZ	Perth	2015-16
251	W.R.Hammond	E v A	Sydney	1928-29
250	K.D.Walters	A v NZ	Christchurch	1976-77
250	S.F.A.F.Bacchus	WI v I	Kanpur	1978-79
250	J.L.Langer	A v E	Melbourne	2002-03

The highest for Bangladesh is 217 by Shakib Al Hasan (v NZ, Wellington, 2016-17).

20 HUNDREDS

			200	Inn	Opponents									
					E	A	SA	WI	NZ	I	P	SL	Z	B
51	S.R.Tendulkar	I	6	329	7	11	7	3	4	—	2	9	3	5
45	J.H.Kallis	SA	2	280	8	5	—	8	6	7	6	1	3	1
41	R.T.Ponting	A	6	287	8	—	8	7	2	8	5	1	1	1
38	K.C.Sangakkara	SL	11	233	3	1	3	3	4	5	10	—	2	7
36	R.S.Dravid	I	5	286	7	2	2	5	6	—	5	3	3	3
34	Younus Khan	P	6	213	4	4	4	3	2	5	—	8	1	3
34	S.M.Gavaskar	I	4	214	4	8	—	13	2	—	5	2	—	—
34	B.C.Lara	WI	9	232	7	9	4	—	1	2	4	5	1	1
34	D.P.M.D.Jayawardena	SL	7	252	8	2	6	1	3	6	2	—	1	5
32	S.R.Waugh	A	1	260	10	—	2	7	2	2	3	3	1	2
32	A.N.Cook	E	5	275	—	5	2	6	3	6	5	3	—	2
30	M.L.Hayden †	A	2	184	5	—	6	5	1	6	1	3	2	—
30	S.Chanderpaul	WI	2	280	5	5	5	—	2	7	1	—	1	4
29	D.G.Bradman	A	12	80	19	—	4	2	—	4	—	—	—	—
28	H.M.Amla	SA	4	193	6	5	—	1	4	5	2	2	—	3
28	M.J.Clarke	A	4	198	6	—	5	1	4	7	1	3	—	1
27	G.C.Smith	SA	5	205	7	3	—	7	2	—	4	—	1	3
27	A.R.Border	A	2	265	8	—	—	5	4	6	1	3	—	—
26	G.St A.Sobers	WI	2	160	10	4	—	—	1	8	3	—	—	—
25	Inzamam-ul-Haq	P	2	200	5	1	—	4	3	3	—	5	2	2
24	G.S.Chappell	A	4	151	9	—	—	5	3	1	6	—	—	—
24	Mohammad Yousuf	P	4	156	6	1	—	7	1	4	—	2	2	1
24	I.V.A.Richards	WI	3	182	8	5	—	—	1	8	2	—	—	—
23	S.P.D.Smith	A	2	111	8	—	1	2	2	7	2	1	—	—
23	V.Sehwag	I	6	180	2	3	5	2	2	—	4	5	—	—
23	K.P.Pietersen	E	3	181	—	4	3	3	2	6	2	3	—	—
23	J.L.Langer	A	3	182	5	—	2	3	4	3	4	2	—	—
23	Javed Miandad	P	6	189	2	6	—	2	7	5	—	1	—	—
22	W.R.Hammond	E	7	140	—	9	6	1	4	2	—	—	—	—
22	M.Azharuddin	I	1	147	6	2	4	—	2	—	3	5	—	—
22	M.C.Cowdrey	E	2	188	—	5	3	6	2	3	3	—	—	—
22	G.Boycott	E	1	193	—	7	1	5	2	4	3	—	—	—
21	I.R.Bell	E	1	205	—	4	2	2	1	4	4	2	—	2
21	V.Kohli	I	6	112	3	6	2	1	3	—	—	5	—	1
21	D.A.Warner	A	1	131	3	—	4	1	4	4	3	—	—	2
21	R.N.Harvey	A	2	137	6	—	8	3	—	4	—	—	—	—
21	G.Kirsten	SA	3	176	5	2	—	3	2	3	2	1	1	2
21	A.J.Strauss	E	1	178	—	4	3	6	3	3	2	—	—	—
21	A.B.de Villiers	SA	2	183	2	5	—	6	—	3	4	1	—	—
21	D.C.Boon	A	1	190	7	—	—	3	3	6	1	1	—	—
20	K.F.Barrington	E	1	131	—	5	2	3	3	3	4	—	—	—
20	P.A.de Silva	SL	2	159	2	1	—	2	1	5	8	—	—	1
20	M.E.Waugh	A	—	209	6	—	4	4	1	3	1	—	1	—
20	G.A.Gooch	E	2	215	—	4	—	5	4	5	1	1	—	—

† Includes century scored for Australia v ICC in 2005-06.

The most for New Zealand is 17 by K.S.Williamson (113 innings), M.D.Crowe (131) and L.R.P.L.Taylor (149), for Zimbabwe 12 by A.Flower (112), and for Bangladesh 8 by Tamim Iqbal (104).

The most double hundreds by batsmen not included above are 6 by M.S.Atapattu (16 hundreds for Sri Lanka), 4 by L.Hutton (19 for England), 4 by C.G.Greenidge (19 for West Indies), 4 by Zaheer Abbas (12 for Pakistan), and 4 by B.B.McCullum (12 for New Zealand).

HIGHEST PARTNERSHIP FOR EACH WICKET

1st	415	N.D.McKenzie/G.C.Smith	SA v B	Chittagong	2007-08
2nd	576	S.T.Jayasuriya/R.S.Mahanama	SL v I	Colombo (RPS)	1997-98
3rd	624	K.C.Sangakkara/D.P.M.D.Jayawardena	SL v SA	Colombo (SSC)	2006
4th	449	A.C.Voges/S.E.Marsh	A v WI	Hobart	2015-16
5th	405	S.G.Barnes/D.G.Bradman	A v E	Sydney	1946-47
6th	399	B.A.Stokes/J.M.Bairstow	E v SA	Cape Town	2015-16
7th	347	D.St E.Atkinson/C.C.Depeiza	WI v A	Bridgetown	1954-55
8th	332	I.J.L.Trott/S.C.J.Broad	E v P	Lord's	2010
9th	195	M.V.Boucher/P.L.Symcox	SA v P	Johannesburg	1997-98
10th	198	J.E.Root/J.M.Anderson	E v I	Nottingham	2014

BOWLING RECORDS
200 WICKETS IN TESTS

Wkts			M	Balls	Runs	Avge	5 wI	10 wM
800	M.Muralitharan	SL/ICC	133	44039	18180	22.72	67	22
708	S.K.Warne	A	145	40705	17995	25.41	37	10
619	A.Kumble	I	132	40850	18355	29.65	35	8
563	G.D.McGrath	A	124	29248	12186	21.64	29	3
523	J.M.Anderson	E	134	29600	14333	27.40	25	3
519	C.A.Walsh	WI	132	30019	12688	24.44	22	3
434	Kapil Dev	I	131	27740	12867	29.64	23	2
431	R.J.Hadlee	NZ	86	21918	9612	22.30	36	9
421	S.M.Pollock	SA	108	24453	9733	23.11	16	1
419	D.W.Steyn	SA	86	17391	9354	22.32	26	5
417	Harbhajan Singh	I	103	28580	13537	32.46	25	5
415	H.M.R.K.B.Herath	SL	89	24920	11694	28.17	33	9
414	Wasim Akram	P	104	22627	9779	23.62	25	5
405	C.E.L.Ambrose	WI	98	22104	8500	20.98	22	3
399	S.C.J.Broad	E	114	23533	11706	29.33	15	2
390	M.Ntini	SA	101	20834	11242	28.82	18	4
383	I.T.Botham	E	102	21815	10878	28.40	27	4
376	M.D.Marshall	WI	81	17584	7876	20.94	22	4
373	Waqar Younis	P	87	16224	8788	23.56	22	5
362	Imran Khan	P	88	19458	8258	22.81	23	6
362	D.L.Vettori	NZ/ICC	113	28814	12441	34.36	20	3
355	D.K.Lillee	A	70	18467	8493	23.92	23	7
355	W.P.J.U.C.Vaas	SL	111	23438	10501	29.58	12	2
330	A.A.Donald	SA	72	15519	7344	22.25	20	3
325	R.G.D.Willis	E	90	17357	8190	25.20	16	–
313	M.G.Johnson	A	73	16001	8891	28.40	12	3
311	R.Ashwin	I	57	16515	7951	25.56	26	7
311	Z.Khan	I	92	18785	10247	32.94	11	1
310	B.Lee	A	76	16531	9554	30.81	10	–
309	L.R.Gibbs	WI	79	27115	8989	29.09	18	2
307	F.S.Trueman	E	67	15178	6625	21.57	17	3
297	D.L.Underwood	E	86	21862	7674	25.83	17	6
294	M.Morkel	SA	83	15954	8256	28.08	7	–
292	J.H.Kallis	SA/ICC	166	20232	9535	32.65	5	–
291	C.J.McDermott	A	71	16586	8332	28.63	14	2
290	N.M.Lyon	A	74	17929	9178	31.64	12	2
266	B.S.Bedi	I	67	21364	7637	28.71	14	1
261	Danish Kaneria	P	61	17697	9082	34.79	15	2
259	J.Garner	WI	58	13169	5433	20.97	7	–
259	J.N.Gillespie	A	71	14234	6770	26.13	8	–
255	G.P.Swann	E	60	15349	7642	29.96	17	3
252	J.B.Statham	E	70	16056	6261	24.84	9	1
249	M.A.Holding	WI	60	12680	5898	23.68	13	2
248	R.Benaud	A	63	19108	6704	27.03	16	1
248	M.J.Hoggard	E	67	13909	7564	30.50	7	1

Wkts			M	Balls	Runs	Avge	5 wI	10 wM
246	G.D.McKenzie	A	60	17681	7328	29.78	16	3
242	B.S.Chandrasekhar	I	58	15963	7199	29.74	16	2
236	A.V.Bedser	E	51	15918	5876	24.89	15	5
236	J.Srinath	I	67	15104	7196	30.49	10	1
236	Abdul Qadir	P	67	17126	7742	32.80	15	5
235	G.St A.Sobers	WI	93	21599	7999	34.03	6	–
234	A.R.Caddick	E	62	13558	6999	29.91	13	1
234	I.Sharma	I	81	15600	8411	35.94	7	1
233	C.S.Martin	NZ	71	14026	7878	33.81	10	1
229	D.Gough	E	58	11821	6503	28.39	9	–
228	R.R.Lindwall	A	61	13650	5251	23.03	12	–
226	S.J.Harmison	E/ICC	63	13375	7192	31.82	8	1
226	A.Flintoff	E/ICC	79	14951	7410	32.78	3	–
218	C.L.Cairns	NZ	62	11698	6410	29.40	13	1
216	C.V.Grimmett	A	37	14513	5231	24.21	21	7
216	H.H.Streak	Z	65	13559	6079	28.14	7	–
212	M.G.Hughes	A	53	12285	6017	28.38	7	1
211	P.M.Siddle	A	62	12941	6314	29.92	8	–
208	S.C.G.MacGill	A	44	11237	6038	29.02	12	2
208	Saqlain Mushtaq	P	49	14070	6206	29.83	13	3
208	T.G.Southee	NZ	58	12848	6543	31.45	6	1
202	A.M.E.Roberts	WI	47	11136	5174	25.61	11	2
202	J.A.Snow	E	49	12021	5387	26.66	8	1
200	J.R.Thomson	A	51	10535	5601	28.00	8	–
200	T.A.Boult	NZ	52	11496	5712	28.56	5	1

The most for Bangladesh is 188 in 51 Tests by Shakib Al Hasan.

35 OR MORE WICKETS IN A SERIES

Wkts			Series	M	Balls	Runs	Avge	5 wI	10 wM
49	S.F.Barnes	E v SA	1913-14	4	1356	536	10.93	7	3
46	J.C.Laker	E v A	1956	5	1703	442	9.60	4	2
44	C.V.Grimmett	A v SA	1935-36	5	2077	642	14.59	5	3
42	T.M.Alderman	A v E	1981	6	1950	893	21.26	4	–
41	R.M.Hogg	A v E	1978-79	6	1740	527	12.85	5	2
41	T.M.Alderman	A v E	1989	6	1616	712	17.36	6	1
40	Imran Khan	P v I	1982-83	6	1339	558	13.95	4	2
40	S.K.Warne	A v E	2005	5	1517	797	19.92	3	2
39	A.V.Bedser	E v A	1953	5	1591	682	17.48	5	1
39	D.K.Lillee	A v E	1981	6	1870	870	22.30	2	1
38	M.W.Tate	E v A	1924-25	5	2528	881	23.18	5	1
37	W.J.Whitty	A v SA	1910-11	5	1395	632	17.08	2	–
37	H.J.Tayfield	SA v E	1956-57	5	2280	636	17.18	4	1
37	M.G.Johnson	A v E	2013-14	5	1132	517	13.97	3	–
36	A.E.E.Vogler	SA v E	1909-10	5	1349	783	21.75	4	1
36	A.A.Mailey	A v E	1920-21	5	1465	946	26.27	4	2
36	G.D.McGrath	A v E	1997	6	1499	701	19.47	2	–
35	G.A.Lohmann	E v SA	1895-96	3	520	203	5.80	4	2
35	B.S.Chandrasekhar	I v E	1972-73	5	1747	662	18.91	4	–
35	M.D.Marshall	WI v E	1988	5	1219	443	12.65	3	–

The most for New Zealand is 33 by R.J.Hadlee (3 Tests v A, 1985-86), for Sri Lanka 30 by M.Muralitharan (3 Tests v Z, 2001-02), for Zimbabwe 22 by H.H.Streak (3 Tests v P, 1994-95), and for Bangladesh 19 by Mehedi Hasan (2 Tests v E, 2016-17).

79

15 OR MORE WICKETS IN A TEST († On debut)

19- 90	J.C.Laker	E v A	Manchester	1956
17- 159	S.F.Barnes	E v SA	Johannesburg	1913-14
16-136†	N.D.Hirwani	I v WI	Madras	1987-88
16-137†	R.A.L.Massie	A v E	Lord's	1972
16- 220	M.Muralitharan	SL v E	The Oval	1998
15- 28	J.Briggs	E v SA	Cape Town	1888-89
15- 45	G.A.Lohmann	E v SA	Port Elizabeth	1895-96
15- 99	C.Blythe	E v SA	Leeds	1907
15- 104	H.Verity	E v A	Lord's	1934
15- 123	R.J.Hadlee	NZ v A	Brisbane	1985-86
15- 124	W.Rhodes	E v A	Melbourne	1903-04
15- 217	Harbhajan Singh	I v A	Madras	2000-01

The best analysis for South Africa is 13-132 by M.Ntini (v WI, Port-of-Spain, 2004-05), for West Indies 14-149 by M.A.Holding (v E, The Oval, 1976), for Pakistan 14-116 by Imran Khan (v SL, Lahore, 1981-82), for Zimbabwe 11-257 by A.G.Huckle (v NZ, Bulawayo, 1997-98), and for Bangladesh 12-159 by Mehedi Hasan (v E, Dhaka, 2016-17).

NINE OR MORE WICKETS IN AN INNINGS

10- 53	J.C.Laker	E v A	Manchester	1956
10- 74	A.Kumble	I v P	Delhi	1998-99
9- 28	G.A.Lohmann	E v SA	Johannesburg	1895-96
9- 37	J.C.Laker	E v A	Manchester	1956
9- 51	M.Muralitharan	SL v Z	Kandy	2001-02
9- 52	R.J.Hadlee	NZ v A	Brisbane	1985-86
9- 56	Abdul Qadir	P v E	Lahore	1987-88
9- 57	D.E.Malcolm	E v SA	The Oval	1994
9- 65	M.Muralitharan	SL v E	The Oval	1998
9- 69	J.M.Patel	I v A	Kanpur	1959-60
9- 83	Kapil Dev	I v WI	Ahmedabad	1983-84
9- 86	Sarfraz Nawaz	P v A	Melbourne	1978-79
9- 95	J.M.Noreiga	WI v I	Port-of-Spain	1970-71
9-102	S.P.Gupte	I v WI	Kanpur	1958-59
9-103	S.F.Barnes	E v SA	Johannesburg	1913-14
9-113	H.J.Tayfield	SA v E	Johannesburg	1956-57
9-121	A.A.Mailey	A v E	Melbourne	1920-21
9-127	H.M.R.K.B.Herath	SL v P	Colombo (SSC)	2014

The best analysis for Zimbabwe is 8-109 by P.A.Strang (v NZ, Bulawayo, 2000-01), and for Bangladesh 8-39 by Taijul Islam (v Z, Dhaka, 2014-15).

HAT-TRICKS

F.R.Spofforth	Australia v England	Melbourne	1878-79
W.Bates	England v Australia	Melbourne	1882-83
J.Briggs[7]	England v Australia	Sydney	1891-92
G.A.Lohmann	England v South Africa	Port Elizabeth	1895-96
J.T.Hearne	England v Australia	Leeds	1899
H.Trumble	Australia v England	Melbourne	1901-02
H.Trumble	Australia v England	Melbourne	1903-04
T.J.Matthews (2)[2]	Australia v South Africa	Manchester	1912
M.J.C.Allom[1]	England v New Zealand	Christchurch	1929-30
T.W.J.Goddard	England v South Africa	Johannesburg	1938-39
P.J.Loader	England v West Indies	Leeds	1957
L.F.Kline	Australia v South Africa	Cape Town	1957-58
W.W.Hall	West Indies v Pakistan	Lahore	1958-59
G.M.Griffin[7]	South Africa v England	Lord's	1960

L.R.Gibbs	West Indies v Australia	Adelaide	1960-61
P.J.Petherick[1/7]	New Zealand v Pakistan	Lahore	1976-77
C.A.Walsh[3]	West Indies v Australia	Brisbane	1988-89
M.G.Hughes[3/7]	Australia v West Indies	Perth	1988-89
D.W.Fleming[1]	Australia v Pakistan	Rawalpindi	1994-95
S.K.Warne	Australia v England	Melbourne	1994-95
D.G.Cork	England v West Indies	Manchester	1995
D.Gough[7]	England v Australia	Sydney	1998-99
Wasim Akram[4]	Pakistan v Sri Lanka	Lahore	1998-99
Wasim Akram[4]	Pakistan v Sri Lanka	Dhaka	1998-99
D.N.T.Zoysa[5]	Sri Lanka v Zimbabwe	Harare	1999-00
Abdul Razzaq	Pakistan v Sri Lanka	Galle	2000-01
G.D.McGrath	Australia v West Indies	Perth	2000-01
Harbhajan Singh	India v Australia	Calcutta	2000-01
Mohammad Sami[7]	Pakistan v Sri Lanka	Lahore	2001-02
J.J.C.Lawson[7]	West Indies v Australia	Bridgetown	2002-03
Alok Kapali[7]	Bangladesh v Pakistan	Peshawar	2003
A.M.Blignaut	Zimbabwe v Bangladesh	Harare	2003-04
M.J.Hoggard	England v West Indies	Bridgetown	2003-04
J.E.C.Franklin	New Zealand v Bangladesh	Dhaka	2004-05
I.K.Pathan[6/7]	India v Pakistan	Karachi	2005-06
R.J.Sidebottom[7]	England v New Zealand	Hamilton	2007-08
P.M.Siddle	Australia v England	Brisbane	2010-11
S.C.J.Broad	England v India	Nottingham	2011
Sohag Gazi	Bangladesh v New Zealand	Chittagong	2013-14
S.C.J.Broad[7]	England v Sri Lanka	Leeds	2014
H.M.R.K.B.Herath	Sri Lanka v Australia	Galle	2016
M.M.Ali	England v South Africa	The Oval	2017

[1] On debut. [2] Hat-trick in each innings. [3] Involving both innings. [4] In successive Tests. [5] His first 3 balls (second over of the match). [6] The fourth, fifth and sixth balls of the match. [7] On losing side.

WICKET-KEEPING RECORDS
150 DISMISSALS IN TESTS†

Total			Tests	Ct	St
555	M.V.Boucher	South Africa/ICC	147	532	23
416	A.C.Gilchrist	Australia	96	379	37
395	I.A.Healy	Australia	119	366	29
355	R.W.Marsh	Australia	96	343	12
294	M.S.Dhoni	India	90	256	38
270	B.J.Haddin	Australia	66	262	8
270†	P.J.L.Dujon	West Indies	79	265	5
269	A.P.E.Knott	England	95	250	19
256	M.J.Prior	England	79	243	13
241†	A.J.Stewart	England	82	227	14
228	Wasim Bari	Pakistan	81	201	27
219	R.D.Jacobs	West Indies	65	207	12
219	T.G.Evans	England	91	173	46
217	D.Ramdin	West Indies	74	205	12
206	Kamran Akmal	Pakistan	53	184	22
201†	A.C.Parore	New Zealand	67	194	7
198	S.M.H.Kirmani	India	88	160	38
189	D.L.Murray	West Indies	62	181	8
187	A.T.W.Grout	Australia	51	163	24
178†	B.B.McCullum	New Zealand	52	168	11
176	I.D.S.Smith	New Zealand	63	168	8
174	R.W.Taylor	England	57	167	7

Total			Tests	Ct	St
167	B.J.Watling	New Zealand	52	161	6
165	R.C.Russell	England	54	153	12
156	H.A.P.W.Jayawardena	Sri Lanka	58	124	32
152	D.J.Richardson	South Africa	42	150	2
151†	K.C.Sangakkara	Sri Lanka	48	131	20
151†	A.Flower	Zimbabwe	55	142	9

The most for Bangladesh is 106 (93 ct, 13 st) by Mushfiqur Rahim in 60 Tests.

† *Excluding catches taken in the field*

25 OR MORE DISMISSALS IN A SERIES

29	B.J.Haddin	Australia v England	2013
28	R.W.Marsh	Australia v England	1982-83
27 (inc 2st)	R.C.Russell	England v South Africa	1995-96
27 (inc 2st)	I.A.Healy	Australia v England (6 Tests)	1997
26 (inc 3st)	J.H.B.Waite	South Africa v New Zealand	1961-62
26	R.W.Marsh	Australia v West Indies (6 Tests)	1975-76
26 (inc 5st)	I.A.Healy	Australia v England (6 Tests)	1993
26 (inc 1st)	M.V.Boucher	South Africa v England	1998
26 (inc 2st)	A.C.Gilchrist	Australia v England	2001
26 (inc 2st)	A.C.Gilchrist	Australia v England	2006-07
26 (inc 1st)	T.D.Paine	Australia v England	2017-18
25 (inc 2st)	I.A.Healy	Australia v England	1994-95
25 (inc 2st)	A.C.Gilchrist	Australia v England	2002-03
25	A.C.Gilchrist	Australia v India	2007-08

TEN OR MORE DISMISSALS IN A TEST

11	R.C.Russell	England v South Africa	Johannesburg	1995-96
11	A.B.de Villiers	South Africa v Pakistan	Johannesburg	2012-13
10	R.W.Taylor	England v India	Bombay	1979-80
10	A.C.Gilchrist	Australia v New Zealand	Hamilton	1999-00
10	W.P.Saha	India v South Africa	Cape Town	2017-18

SEVEN DISMISSALS IN AN INNINGS

7	Wasim Bari	Pakistan v New Zealand	Auckland	1978-79
7	R.W.Taylor	England v India	Bombay	1979-80
7	I.D.S.Smith	New Zealand v Sri Lanka	Hamilton	1990-91
7	R.D.Jacobs	West Indies v Australia	Melbourne	2000-01

FIVE STUMPINGS IN AN INNINGS

5	K.S.More	India v West Indies	Madras	1987-88

FIELDING RECORDS
100 CATCHES IN TESTS

Total			Tests	Total			Tests
210	R.S.Dravid	India/ICC	164	122	I.V.A.Richards	West Indies	121
205	D.P.M.D.Jayawardena	Sri Lanka	149	121	A.J.Strauss	England	100
200	J.H.Kallis	South Africa/ICC	166	120	I.T.Botham	England	102
196	R.T.Ponting	Australia	168	120	M.C.Cowdrey	England	114
181	M.E.Waugh	Australia	128	115	C.L.Hooper	West Indies	102
171	S.P.Fleming	New Zealand	111	115	S.R.Tendulkar	India	200
169	G.C.Smith	South Africa/ICC	117	112	S.R.Waugh	Australia	168
164	B.C.Lara	West Indies/ICC	131	110	R.B.Simpson	Australia	62
157	M.A.Taylor	Australia	104	110	W.R.Hammond	England	85
156	A.N.Cook	England	152	110†	A.B.de Villiers	South Africa	86
156	A.R.Border	Australia	156	109	G.St A.Sobers	West Indies	93
139	Younus Khan	Pakistan	118	108	S.M.Gavaskar	India	125
135	V.V.S.Laxman	India	134	105	I.M.Chappell	Australia	75
134	M.J.Clarke	Australia	115	105	M.Azharuddin	India	99
128	M.L.Hayden	Australia	103	105	G.P.Thorpe	England	100
125	L.R.P.L.Taylor	New Zealand	83	103	G.A.Gooch	England	118
125	S.K.Warne	Australia	145	100	I.R.Bell	England	118
122	G.S.Chappell	Australia	87				

The most for Zimbabwe is 60 by A.D.R.Campbell (60) and for Bangladesh 34 by Mahmudullah (37).
† *Excluding catches taken when wicket-keeping.*

15 CATCHES IN A SERIES

15	J.M.Gregory	Australia v England	1920-21

SEVEN OR MORE CATCHES IN A TEST

8	A.M.Rahane	India v Sri Lanka	Galle	2015
7	G.S.Chappell	Australia v England	Perth	1974-75
7	Yajurvindra Singh	India v England	Bangalore	1976-77
7	H.P.Tillekeratne	Sri Lanka v New Zealand	Colombo (SSC)	1992-93
7	S.P.Fleming	New Zealand v Zimbabwe	Harare	1997-98
7	M.L.Hayden	Australia v Sri Lanka	Galle	2003-04

FIVE CATCHES IN AN INNINGS

5	V.Y.Richardson	Australia v South Africa	Durban	1935-36
5	Yajurvindra Singh	India v England	Bangalore	1976-77
5	M.Azharuddin	India v Pakistan	Karachi	1989-90
5	K.Srikkanth	India v Australia	Perth	1991-92
5	S.P.Fleming	New Zealand v Zimbabwe	Harare	1997-98
5	G.C.Smith	South Africa v Australia	Perth	2012-13
5	D.J.G.Sammy	West Indies v India	Mumbai	2013-14
5	D.M.Bravo	West Indies v Bangladesh	Kingstown	2014
5	A.M.Rahane	India v Sri Lanka	Galle	2015
5	J.Blackwood	West Indies v Sri Lanka	Colombo (PSS)	2015-16

APPEARANCE RECORDS
100 TEST MATCH APPEARANCES

			Opponents									
			E	A	SA	WI	NZ	I	P	SL	Z	B
200	S.R.Tendulkar	India	32	39	25	21	24	–	18	25	9	7
168†	R.T.Ponting	Australia	35	–	26	24	17	29	15	14	3	4
168	S.R.Waugh	Australia	46	–	16	32	23	18	20	8	3	2

83

		E	A	SA	WI	NZ	I	P	SL	Z	B
166† J.H.Kallis	South Africa/ICC	31	28	–	24	18	18	19	15	6	6
164 S.Chanderpaul	West Indies	35	20	24	–	21	25	14	7	8	10
164† R.S.Dravid	India/ICC	21	32	21	23	15	–	15	20	9	7
156 A.R.Border	Australia	47	–	6	31	23	20	22	7	–	–
152 A.N.Cook	England	–	35	19	20	13	25	18	16	–	6
149 D.P.M.D.Jayawardena	Sri Lanka	23	16	18	11	13	18	29	–	8	13
147† M.V.Boucher	South Africa/ICC	25	20	–	24	17	14	15	17	6	8
145† S.K.Warne	Australia	36	–	24	19	20	14	15	13	1	2
134 J.M.Anderson	England	–	31	24	17	12	22	13	11	2	2
134 V.V.S.Laxman	India	17	29	19	22	10	–	15	13	6	3
134 K.C.Sangakkara	Sri Lanka	22	11	17	12	12	17	23	–	5	15
133† M.Muralitharan	Sri Lanka/ICC	16	12	15	12	14	22	16	–	14	11
133 A.J.Stewart	England	–	33	23	24	16	9	13	9	6	–
132 A.Kumble	India	19	20	21	17	11	–	15	18	7	4
132 C.A.Walsh	West Indies	36	38	10	–	10	15	18	3	2	–
131 Kapil Dev	India	27	20	4	25	10	–	29	14	2	–
131† B.C.Lara	West Indies/ICC	30	30	18	–	11	17	12	8	2	2
128 M.E.Waugh	Australia	29	–	18	28	14	14	15	9	1	–
125 S.M.Gavaskar	India	38	20	–	27	9	–	24	7	–	–
124 Javed Miandad	Pakistan	22	24	–	17	18	28	–	12	3	–
124† G.D.McGrath	Australia	30	–	17	23	14	11	17	8	1	2
121 I.V.A.Richards	West Indies	36	34	–	–	7	28	16	–	–	–
120† Inzamam-ul-Haq	Pakistan/ICC	19	13	13	15	12	10	–	20	11	6
119 I.A.Healy	Australia	33	–	12	28	11	9	14	11	1	–
118 I.R.Bell	England	–	33	11	12	13	20	13	10	–	6
118 G.A.Gooch	England	–	42	3	26	15	19	10	3	–	–
118 Younus Khan	Pakistan	17	11	14	15	11	9	–	29	5	7
117 D.I.Gower	England	–	42	–	19	13	24	17	2	–	–
117† G.C.Smith	South Africa/ICC	21	21	–	14	13	15	16	7	2	8
116 D.L.Haynes	West Indies	36	33	1	–	10	19	16	1	–	–
116 D.B.Vengsarkar	India	26	24	–	25	11	–	22	8	–	–
115 M.A.Atherton	England	–	33	18	27	11	7	11	4	4	–
115† M.J.Clarke	Australia	35	–	14	12	11	22	10	8	–	2
114 S.C.J.Broad	England	–	27	18	15	12	15	14	10	–	3
114 M.C.Cowdrey	England	–	43	14	21	18	8	10	–	–	–
113 H.M.Amla	South Africa	21	17	–	9	14	21	11	10	2	8
113 S.C.Ganguly	India	12	24	17	12	8	–	12	14	9	5
113† D.L.Vettori	New Zealand/ICC	17	18	14	10	–	15	9	11	9	9
111 S.P.Fleming	New Zealand	19	14	15	11	–	13	9	13	11	6
111 W.P.J.U.C.Vaas	Sri Lanka	15	12	11	9	10	14	18	–	15	7
110 A.B.de Villiers	South Africa	20	20	–	13	10	20	12	7	4	4
110 S.T.Jayasuriya	Sri Lanka	14	13	15	10	13	10	17	–	13	5
110 C.H.Lloyd	West Indies	34	29	–	–	8	28	11	–	–	–
108 G.Boycott	England	–	38	7	29	15	13	6	–	–	–
108 C.G.Greenidge	West Indies	29	32	–	–	10	23	14	–	–	–
108 S.M.Pollock	South Africa	23	13	–	16	11	12	12	13	5	3
107 D.C.Boon	Australia	31	–	6	22	17	11	11	9	–	–
105† J.L.Langer	Australia	21	–	11	18	14	14	13	8	3	2
104 K.P.Pietersen	England	–	27	10	14	8	16	14	11	–	4
104† V.Sehwag	India/ICC	17	23	15	10	12	–	9	11	3	4
104 M.A.Taylor	Australia	33	–	11	20	11	9	12	8	–	–
104 Wasim Akram	Pakistan	18	13	4	17	9	12	–	19	10	2
103 C.H.Gayle	West Indies	20	8	16	–	12	14	8	10	8	7
103 Harbhajan Singh	India	14	18	11	11	13	–	9	16	7	4
103† M.L.Hayden	Australia	20	–	19	15	11	18	6	7	2	4
103 Salim Malik	Pakistan	19	15	1	7	18	22	–	15	6	–

		Opponents									
			E	*A*	*SA*	*WI*	*NZ*	*I*	*P*	*SL*	*Z*	*B*
102	I.T.Botham	England	–	36	–	20	15	14	14	3	–	–
102	C.L.Hooper	West Indies	24	25	10	–	2	19	14	6	2	–
101	G.Kirsten	South Africa	22	18	–	13	13	10	11	9	3	2
101	B.B.McCullum	New Zealand	16	16	13	13	–	10	8	12	4	9
101	M.Ntini	South Africa	18	15	–	15	11	10	9	12	3	8
100	A.J.Strauss	England	–	20	16	18	9	12	13	8	–	4
100	G.P.Thorpe	England	–	16	16	27	13	5	8	9	2	4

† Includes appearance in the Australia v ICC 'Test' in 2005-06. The most for Zimbabwe is 67 by G.W.Flower, and for Bangladesh 61 by Mohammad Ashraful.

100 CONSECUTIVE TEST APPEARANCES

153	A.R.Border	Australia	March 1979 to March 1994
150	A.N.Cook	England	May 2006 to January 2018
107	M.E.Waugh	Australia	June 1993 to October 2002
106	S.M.Gavaskar	India	January 1975 to February 1987
101	B.B.McCullum	New Zealand	March 2004 to February 2016

50 TESTS AS CAPTAIN

			Won	*Lost*	*Drawn*	*Tied*
109	G.C.Smith	South Africa	53	29	27	–
93	A.R.Border	Australia	32	22	38	1
80	S.P.Fleming	New Zealand	28	27	25	–
77	R.T.Ponting	Australia	48	16	13	–
74	C.H.Lloyd	West Indies	36	12	26	–
60	M.S.Dhoni	India	27	18	15	–
59	A.N.Cook	England	24	22	13	–
57	S.R.Waugh	Australia	41	9	7	–
56	Misbah-ul-Haq	Pakistan	26	19	11	–
56	A.Ranatunga	Sri Lanka	12	19	25	–
54	M.A.Atherton	England	13	21	20	–
53	W.J.Cronje	South Africa	27	11	15	–
51	M.P.Vaughan	England	26	11	14	–
50	I.V.A.Richards	West Indies	27	8	15	–
50	M.A.Taylor	Australia	26	13	11	–
50	A.J.Strauss	England	24	11	15	–

The most for Zimbabwe is 21 by A.D.R.Campbell and H.H.Streak, and for Bangladesh 34 by Mushfiqur Rahim.

50 TEST UMPIRING APPEARANCES

128	S.A.Bucknor	(West Indies)	28.04.1989 to 22.03.2009
117	Alim Dar	(Pakistan)	21.10.2003 to 27.01.2018
108	R.E.Koertzen	(South Africa)	26.12.1992 to 24.07.2010
95	D.J.Harper	(Australia)	28.11.1998 to 23.06.2011
92	D.R.Shepherd	(England)	01.08.1985 to 07.06.2005
84	B.F.Bowden	(New Zealand)	11.03.2000 to 03.05.2015
78	D.B.Hair	(Australia)	25.01.1992 to 08.06.2008
74	S.J.A.Taufel	(Australia)	26.12.2000 to 20.08.2012
73	S.Venkataraghavan	(India)	29.01.1993 to 20.01.2004
66	H.D.Bird	(England)	05.07.1973 to 24.06.1996
64	I.J.Gould	(England)	19.11.2008 to 27.01.2018
59	R.J.Tucker	(Australia)	15.02.2010 to 10.02.2018
57	S.J.Davis	(Australia)	27.11.1997 to 25.04.2015
51	H.D.P.K.Dharmasena	(Sri Lanka)	04.11.2010 to 08.01.2018
50	R.A.Kettleborough	(England)	15.10.2010 to 08.01.2018

THE FIRST-CLASS COUNTIES
REGISTER, RECORDS AND 2017 AVERAGES

All statistics are to 12 March 2018.

ABBREVIATIONS – General

*	not out/unbroken partnership	IT20	International Twenty20
b	born	l-o	limited-overs
BB	Best innings bowling analysis	LOI	Limited-Overs Internationals
Cap	Awarded 1st XI County Cap	Tests	International Test Matches
f-c	first-class	F-c Tours	Overseas tours involving first-class
HS	Highest Score		appearances

Awards

PCA 2017   Professional Cricketers' Association Player of 2017
Wisden 2016   One of *Wisden Cricketers' Almanack*'s Five Cricketers of 2016
YC 2017   Cricket Writers' Club Young Cricketer of 2017

ECB Competitions

BHC	Benson & Hedges Cup (1972-2002)
CB40	Clydesdale Bank 40 (2010-12)
CC	Specsavers County Championship
CGT	Cheltenham & Gloucester Trophy (2001-06)
FPT	Friends Provident Trophy (2007-09)
NL	National League (1999-2005)
NWT	NatWest Trophy (1981-2000)
P40	NatWest PRO 40 League (2006-09)
RLC	Royal London One-Day Cup (2014-17)
SL	Sunday League (1969-98)
T20	Twenty20 Competition
Y40	Yorkshire Bank 40 (2013)

Education

Ac	Academy
BHS	Boys' High School
C	College
CS	Comprehensive School
GS	Grammar School
HS	High School
I	Institute
S	School
SFC	Sixth Form College
SS	Secondary School
TC	Technical College
U	University
UWIC	University of Wales Institute, Cardiff

Playing Categories

LBG	Bowls right-arm leg-breaks and googlies
LF	Bowls left-arm fast
LFM	Bowls left-arm fast-medium
LHB	Bats left-handed
LM	Bowls left-arm medium pace
LMF	Bowls left-arm medium fast
OB	Bowls right-arm off-breaks
RF	Bowls right-arm fast
RFM	Bowls right-arm fast-medium
RHB	Bats right-handed
RM	Bowls right-arm medium pace
RMF	Bowls right-arm medium-fast
SLA	Bowls left-arm leg-breaks
SLC	Bowls left-arm 'Chinamen'
WK	Wicket-keeper

Teams (see also 230)

AS	Adelaide Strikers
BH	Brisbane Heat
CC&C	Combined Campuses & Colleges
CD	Central Districts

CSK	Chennai Super Kings
DC	Deccan Chargers
DD	Delhi Daredevils
EL	England Lions
EP	Eastern Province
GL	Gujarat Lions
GW	Griqualand West
HB	Habib Bank Limited
HH	Hobart Hurricanes
KKR	Kolkata Knight Riders
KRL	Khan Research Laboratories
KXIP	Kings XI Punjab
KZN	KwaZulu-Natal Inland
ME	Mashonaland Eagles
MI	Mumbai Indians
MR	Melbourne Renegades
MS	Melbourne Stars
MSC	Mohammedan Sporting Club
MT	Matabeleland Tuskers
MWR	Mid West Rhinos
NBP	National Bank of Pakistan
ND	Northern Districts
NSW	New South Wales
NT	Northern Transvaal
NW	North West
(O)FS	(Orange) Free State
PDSC	Prime Doleshwar Sporting Club
PS	Perth Scorchers
PW	Pune Warriors
Q	Queensland
RCB	Royal Challengers Bangalore
RPS	Rising Pune Supergiants
RR	Rajasthan Royals
SA	South Australia
SH	Sunrisers Hyderabad
SJD	Sheikh Jamal Dhanmondi
SLPACC	Sri Lanka Ports Authority CC
SNGPL	Sui Northern Gas Pipelines Limited
SR	Southern Rocks
SS	Sydney Sixers
SSGC	Sui Southern Gas Corporation
ST	Sydney Thunder
Tas	Tasmania
T&T	Trinidad & Tobago
TU	Tamil Union
Vic	Victoria
WA	Western Australia
WAPDA	Water & Power Development Authority
WP	Western Province

DERBYSHIRE

Formation of Present Club: 4 November 1870
Inaugural First-Class Match: 1871
Colours: Chocolate, Amber and Pale Blue
Badge: Rose and Crown
County Champions: (1) 1936
NatWest Trophy Winners: (1) 1981
Benson and Hedges Cup Winners: (1) 1993
Sunday League Winners: (1) 1990
Twenty20 Cup Winners: (0) best – Quarter-Finalist 2005, 2017

18 70
Cricket
DERBYSHIRE

Chief Executive: Simon Storey, Derbyshire County Cricket Club, The 3aaa County Ground, Nottingham Road, Derby, DE21 6DA • Tel: 01332 388101 • Fax: 0844 500 8322 • Email: info@derbyshireccc.com • Web: www. derbyshireccc.com • Twitter: @DerbyshireCCC (39,224 followers)

Cricket Advisor: Kim Barnett. **T20 Head Coach**: John Wright. **Captain**: B.A.Godleman (f-c & l-o), G.C.Wilson (T20). **Vice-Captain**: G.C.Wilson. **Overseas Player**: D.Olivier. **2018 Testimonial**: A.P.Palladino. **Head Groundsman**: Neil Godrich. **Scorer**: John Brown. ‡ New registration. NQ Not qualified for England.

BRODRICK, Calum Ashley James (John Taylor HS, Barton-under-Needwood), b Burton-upon-Trent, Staffs 24 Jan 1998. 5'11''. LHB, RM. Squad No 19. Debut (Derbyshire) 2017. Derbyshire 2nd XI debut 2014. HS 52 v West Indians (Derby) 2017 – only f-c game. T20 HS 14.

CRITCHLEY, Matthew James John (St Michael's HS, Chorley), b Preston, Lancs 13 Aug 1996. 6'2''. RHB, LB. Squad No 20. Debut (Derbyshire) 2015. Derbyshire 2nd XI debut 2014. HS 137* v Northants (Derby) 2015. BB 3-50 v Lancs (Southport) 2015. LO HS 49 v Yorks (Leeds) 2017 (RLC). LO BB 4-48 v Northants (Derby) 2015 (RLC). T20 HS 72*. T20 BB 3-32.

DAVIS, William Samuel (Stafford GS), b 6 Mar 1996. 6'1''. RHB, RFM. Squad No 44. Debut (Derbyshire) 2015. Derbyshire 2nd XI debut 2013. HS 25 v Sussex (Hove) 2016. BB 7-146 v Glamorgan (Colwyn Bay) 2016. LO HS –.

GLEADALL, Alfie Frank (Westfield Sports C), b Chesterfield 28 May 2000. 5'10''. RHB, RMF. Squad No 17. Derbyshire 2nd XI debut 2017. Awaiting f-c debut. LO HS –. LO BB –.

GODLEMAN, Billy Ashley (Islington Green S), b Islington, London 11 Feb 1989. 6'3''. LHB, LB. Squad No 1. Middlesex 2005-09. Essex 2010-12. Derbyshire debut 2013; cap 2015; captain 2016 to date. 1000 runs (1): 1069 (2016). HS 204 v Worcs (Derby) 2016. BB –. LO HS 109* v Northants (Derby) 2015 (RLC). T20 HS 70.

HAMIDULLAH QADRI (Derby Moor S; Chellaston Ac), b Kandahar, Afghanistan 5 Dec 2000. 5'9''. RHB, OB. Squad No 75. Debut (Derbyshire) 2017, taking 5-60 v Glamorgan (Cardiff), the youngest to take 5 wkts on CC debut, and the first born this century to play f-c cricket in England. HS 11* and BB 5-60 (*see above*). LO HS –. LO BB –. T20 BB –.

HOSEIN, Harvey Richard (Denstone C), b Chesterfield 12 Aug 1996. 5'10". RHB, WK. Squad No 16. Debut (Derbyshire) 2014, taking seven catches in an innings and UK record-equalling 11 in match v Surrey (The Oval). Derbyshire 2nd XI debut 2010, aged 13y 287d. HS 108 v Worcs (Worcester) 2016. LO HS 40 v Notts (Mkt Warsop) 2016 (RLC). T20 HS 0*.

HUGHES, Alex Lloyd (Ounsdale HS, Wolverhampton), b Wordsley, Staffs 29 Sep 1991. 5'10". RHB, RM. Squad No 18. Debut (Derbyshire) 2013; cap 2017. HS 142 v Glos (Bristol) 2017. BB 4-46 v Glamorgan (Derby) 2014. LO HS 96* v Leics (Leicester) 2016 (RLC). LO BB 3-31 v Leics (Derby) 2015 (RLC). T20 HS 43*. T20 BB 3-23.

MacDONELL, Charles Michael (Wellingborough S; Collingwood C, Durham U), b Basingstoke, Hants 23 Feb 1995. 5'10". RHB, RM. Squad No 3. Durham MCCU 2015-16. Derbyshire debut 2016. Northamptonshire 2nd XI 2014-15. MCC Univs 2015. Durham 2nd XI 2015. Derbyshire 2nd XI 2015-16. Buckinghamshire 2014-15. HS 91 v Glos (Bristol) 2016. BB 2-57 v West Indians (Derby) 2017. CC BB – . LO HS 19 v Sri Lanka A (Derby) 2016.

MADSEN, Wayne Lee (Kearsney C, Durban; U of South Africa), b Durban, South Africa 2 Jan 1984. Nephew of M.B.Madsen (Natal 1967-68 to 1978-79), T.R.Madsen (Natal 1976-77 to 1989-90) and H.R.Fotheringham (Natal, Transvaal 1971-72 to 1989-90), cousin of G.S.Fotheringham (KwaZulu-Natal 2008-09 to 2009-10). 5'11". RHB, OB. Squad No 77. KwaZulu-Natal 2003-04 to 2007-08. Dolphins 2006-07 to 2007-08. Derbyshire debut 2009, scoring 170 v Glos (Cheltenham) 2009; cap 2011; captain 2012-15; testimonial 2017. Qualified for England by residence in February 2015. 1000 runs (4); most – 1292 (2016). HS 231* v Northants (Northampton) 2012. BB 3-45 KZN v EP (Pt Elizabeth) 2007-08. De BB 2-9 v Sussex (Hove) 2013. LO HS 138 v Hants (Derby) 2014 (RLC). LO BB 3-27 v Durham (Derby) 2013 (Y40). T20 HS 86*. T20 BB 2-20.

‡NQ**OLIVIER, Duanne**, b Groblersdal, South Africa 9 May 1992. RHB, RFM. Squad No 74. Free State 2010-11 to date. Knights 2013-14 to date. Joins Derbyshire for the first half of 2018. Tests (SA): 5 (2016-17 to 2017-18); HS 4 and BB 3-38 v E (Manchester) 2017; BB 3-38 v SL (Johannesburg) 2016-17. F-c Tours (SA): E 2017; A 2016 (SAA); Z 2016 (SAA). HS 72 FS v Namibia (Bloemfontein) 2014-15. BB 6-60 Knights v Titans (Centurion) 2016-17. LO HS 25* and LO BB 4-34 Knights v Lions (Kimberley) 2017-18. T20 HS 11*. T20 BB 4-28.

PALLADINO, Antonio Paul (Cardinal Pole SS; Anglia Polytechnic U), b Tower Hamlets, London 29 Jun 1983. 6'0". RHB, RMF. Squad No 28. Cambridge UCCE 2003-05. Essex 2003-10. Namibia 2009-10. Derbyshire debut 2011; cap 2012; testimonial 2018. HS 106 v Australia A (Derby) 2012. CC HS 68 v Warwks (Birmingham) 2013. 50 wkts (2); most – 56 (2012). BB 7-53 v Kent (Derby) 2012. Hat-trick v Leics (Leicester) 2012. LO HS 31 Namibia v Boland (Windhoek) 2009-10. LO BB 5-49 v Lancs (Derby) 2014 (RLC). T20 HS 14*. T20 BB 4-21.

‡NQ**RAMPAUL, Ravi**, b Preysal, Trinidad 15 Oct 1984. 6'1". LHB, RFM. Squad No 41. Trinidad & Tobago 2001-02 to 2012-13. Surrey 2016-17. IPL: RCB 2013-14. Tests (WI): 18 (2009-10 to 2012-13); HS 40* v A (Adelaide) 2009-10; BB 4-48 v P (Providence) 2011. LOI (WI): 92 (2003-04 to 2015-16); HS 86* v I (Visakhapatnam) 2011-12; BB 5-49 v B (Khulna) 2012-13. IT20 (WI): 23 (2007 to 2015-16); HS 8 v Ire (Providence) 2010; BB 3-16 v A (Colombo, RPS) 2012-13. F-c Tours (WI): E 2007, 2012; A 2009-10; SA 2003-04 (WI A); I 2011-12; B 2011-12, 2012-13. HS 64* WI A v Sri Lanka A (Basseterre) 2006-07. CC HS 13* Sy v Notts (Nottingham) 2016. BB 7-51 T&T v Barbados (Pointe-a-Pierre) 2006-07. CC BB 5-85 Sy v Somerset (Oval) 2016. LO HS 86* (see LOI). LO BB 5-49 (see LOI). T20 HS 23*. T20 BB 5-9.

REECE, Luis Michael (St Michael's HS, Chorley; Leeds Met U), b Taunton, Somerset 4 Aug 1990. 6'1". LHB, LM. Squad No 10. Leeds/Bradford MCCU 2012-13. Lancashire 2013-15, no f-c appearances in 2016. Derbyshire debut 2017. MCC 2014. Unicorns 2011-12. HS 168 v Northants (Derby) 2017, sharing De record 1st wkt partnership of 333 with B.A.Godleman. BB 4-28 LBU v Leics (Leicester) 2013. De BB 3-38 v Kent (Canterbury) 2017. LO HS 59 Unicorns v Derbys (Chesterfield) 2012 (CB40). LO BB 4-35 Unicorns v Glos (Exmouth) 2011 (CB40). T20 HS 97*. T20 BB 3-33.

SLATER, Benjamin Thomas (Netherthorpe S; Leeds Met U), b Chesterfield 26 Aug 1991. 5'10". LHB, OB. Squad No 26. Debut (Leeds/Bradford MCCU) 2012. Southern Rocks 2012-13. Derbyshire debut 2013. HS 119 v Leics (Derby) 2014, also scored 104 in same match. BB –. LO HS 148* v Northants (Northampton) 2016 (RLC). T20 HS 57.

NQSMIT, Daryn (Northwood S; U of SA), b Durban, South Africa 28 Jan 1984. 5'11". RHB, LB, occ WK. Squad No 11. KwaZulu Natal 2004-05 to 2016-17. Dolphins 2005-06 to 2016-17. Derbyshire debut 2017; qualifies as a non-overseas player. 1000 runs (0+1): 1081 (2015-16). HS 156* KZN v NW (Durban) 2015-16. De HS 41 v Glamorgan (Cardiff) 2017. BB 7-27 KZN v SW Districts (Durban) 2013-14. De BB –. LO HS 109 Dolphins v Warriors (East London) 2011-12. LO BB 4-39 KZN v GW (Kimberley) 2013-14. T20 HS 57. T20 BB 3-19.

SONCZAK, Matthew David (Audenshaw S, Manchester), b Hadfield 5 Sep 1998. RHB, SLA. Squad No 69. Debut (Derbyshire) 2017. Derbyshire 2nd XI debut 2017. HS 9 and BB 2-56 v West Indians (Derby) 2017 – only 1st XI game.

TAYLOR, James Philip Arthur (Trentham HS), b Stoke-on-Trent, Staffs 19 Jan 2001. Younger brother of T.A.I.Taylor (*see LEICESTERSHIRE*). 6'2". RHB, RM. Squad No 32. Debut (Derbyshire) 2017. Derbyshire 2nd XI debut 2016. HS 0* and BB 1-14 v West Indians (Derby) 2017 – only 1st XI game.

NQVILJOEN, GC ('Hardus') b Witbank, South Africa 6 Mar 1989. 6'5". RHB, RF. Squad No 7. Easterns 2008-09 to 2011-12. Titans 2009-10 to 2011-12. Lions 2012-13 to date. Kent 2016. Derbyshire debut 2017 (Kolpak signing). **Tests** (SA): 1 (2015-16); HS 20* and BB 1-79 v E (Johannesburg) 2015-16. F-c Tours (SA A): A 2014, 2016; I 2015; Z 2016. HS 72 Lions v Titans (Centurion) 2015-16. CC HS 63 K v Northants (Beckenham) 2016. De HS 19* v Durham (Chester-le-St) 2017. 50 wkts (0+1): 68 (2010-11). BB 8-90 (15-170 match - best match figs for De since 1952) v Sussex (Hove) 2017. LO HS 54* Easterns v Boland (Paarl) 2011-12. LO BB 6-19 Lions v Titans (Centurion) 2012-13. T20 HS 41*. T20 BB 5-16.

NQWILSON, Gary Craig (Methodist C, Belfast; Manchester Met U), b Dundonald, N Ireland 5 Feb 1986. 5'10". RHB, WK. Squad No 14. Ireland 2005 to date. Surrey 2010-16; cap 2014. Derbyshire debut 2017, T20 captain 2018. MCC YC 2005. **LOI** (Ire): 92 (2007 to 2017-18); HS 113 v Netherlands (Dublin) 2010. **IT20** (Ire): 53 (2008 to 2016-17); HS 65* v Scotland (Dubai, DSC) 2016-17. HS 160* Sy v Leics (Oval) 2014. De HS 97 v Kent (Canterbury) 2017 and 97 v Leics (Derby) 2017. BB –. LO HS 113 (*see LOI*). T20 HS 65*.

RELEASED/RETIRED

(Having made a County 1st XI appearance in 2017)

CORK, Gregory Teodor Gerald (Denstone C), b Derby 29 Sep 1994. Son of D.G.Cork (Derbyshire, Lancashire, Hampshire and England 1990-2011). 6'2". RHB, LMF. Derbyshire 2016-17. Derbyshire 2nd XI debut 2011. HS 49 v Worcs (Worcester) 2016. BB –. LO HS 8 v Sri Lanka A (Derby) 2016. LO BB 2-17 v Somerset (Taunton) 2015 (RLC). T20 HS 13*. T20 BB 2-36.

COTTON, Benjamin David (Clayton Hall C; Stoke-on-Trent SFC), b Stoke-on-Trent, Staffs 13 Sep 1993. 6'4". RHB, RMF. Derbyshire 2014-17. Derbyshire 2nd XI debut 2011. HS 43 v Leics (Derby) 2015. BB 4-20 v Leics (Derby) 2014. LO HS 18* v Yorks (Scarborough) 2014 (RLC). LO BB 4-43 v Worcs (Worcester) 2016 (RLC). T20 HS 30*. T20 BB 2-14.

HEMMINGS, Robert Philip (Sir Thomas Boughey S, Stoke-on-Trent; Denstone C), b Newcastle-under-Lyme, Staffs 28 Feb 1996. 6'4". RHB, RM. Derbyshire 2016-17. Derbyshire 2nd XI debut 2015. HS 19 v Leics (Derby) 2017. BB – . LO HS 25* v Sri Lanka A (Derby) 2016. LO BB – .

HENRY, M.J. – *see* KENT.

NQIMRAN TAHIR, Mohammad (Government Pakistan Angels HS and MAO College, Lahore), b Lahore, Pakistan 4 Jun 1979. 5'11". RHB, LB. Lahore City 1996-97 to 1997-98. WAPDA 1998-99. REDCO 1999-00. Lahore Whites 2000-01. SNGPL 2001-02 to 2003-04. Sialkot 2002-03. Middlesex 2003. Lahore Blues 2004-05. PIA 2004-05 to 2006-07. Lahore Ravi 2005-06. Yorkshire (1 match) 2007. Titans 2007-08 to 2009-10. Hampshire 2008-14; cap 2009. Easterns 2008-09 to 2009-10. Warwickshire 2010; cap 2010. Dolphins 2010-11 to date. Lions 2012-13 to 2013-14. Nottinghamshire 2015-16; cap 2015. Derbyshire 2017. Staffordshire 2004-05. Qualified for SA on 1 Apr 2009. IPL: DD 2014-16. RPS 2017. **Tests** (SA): 20 (2011-12 to 2015-16); HS 29* v SL (Centurion) 2011-12; BB 5-32 v P (Dubai) 2013-14. **LOI** (SA): 85 (2010-11 to 2017-18); HS 29 v WI (Bridgetown) 2016; LO BB 7-45 v WI (Basseterre) 2016. **IT20** (SA): 36 (2013 to 2017); HS 9* v Netherlands (Chittagong) 2013-14; BB 5-24 v NZ (Auckland) 2016-17. F-c Tours (SA): E 2012; A 2012-13; NZ 2011-12; I 2015-16; SL 2004-05 (Pak A), 2014; UAE 2013-14 (v P). HS 77* H v Somerset (Southampton) 2009. De HS 18* v Durham (Chester-le-St) 2017. 50 wkts (2+2); most – 74 (2004-05). BB 8-42 (12-133 match) Dolphins v Knights (Kimberley) 2015-16. UK BB 7-66 (12-189 match) H v Lancs (Manchester) 2008. De BB 5-76 v Glos (Bristol) 2017. LO HS 41* Staffs v Lancs (Stone) 2004 (CGT). LO BB 7-45 (*see LOI*). T20 HS 23. T20 BB 5-24.

NQMENDIS, Balapuwaduge Mankulasuriya Amith **Jeevan** (St Thomas C), b Colombo, Sri Lanka 15 Jan 1983. 5'8". LHB, LB. Bloomfield 2000-01. Sinhalese 2002-03 to 2007-08. Tamil Union 2008-09 to date. Kandurata 2008-09 to 2009-10. Derbyshire 2017. IPL: DD 2013. Big Bash: SS 2012-13. **LOI** (SL): 54 (2010 to 2014-15); HS 72 v I (Pallekele) 2012; BB 3-15 v NZ (Hambantota) 2012-13. **IT20** (SL): 19 (2011 to 2017-18); HS 43* and BB 3-24 v Z (Hambantota) 2012-13. F-c Tours (SLA): E 2004; A 2010; WI 2006-07; P 2002-03; B 2005-06. HS 206* Tamil v Colombo (Colombo CC) 2012-13. De HS 27 v Glamorgan (Cardiff) 2017. BB 6-37 (and 109) Tamil v Saracens (Colombo, PSS) 2011. De BB 6-204 v Leics (Derby) 2017. LO HS 99* SL v Worcs (Worcester) 2011. LO BB 5-12 Tamil v Chilaw Marians (Colombo, PSS) 2013-14. T20 HS 67. T20 BB 4-14.

MILNES, Thomas Patrick (Heart of England S, Coventry), b Stourbridge, Worcs 6 Oct 1992. 5'11". RHB, RMF. Warwickshire 2011-15. Derbyshire 2015-17. HS 56 v Glos (Derby) 2016. BB 7-39 Wa v Oxford MCCU (Oxford) 2013. CC BB 6-93 v Essex (Derby) 2016. LO HS 16 Wa v Worcs (Birmingham) 2013 (Y40). LO BB 2-73 Wa v Northants (Birmingham) 2013 (Y40). T20 HS 0. T20 BB – .

SANDHU, Gurjit Singh (Isleworth & Syon S; Heathland S), b W Middlesex Hospital, Isleworth 24 Mar 1992. 6'4". RHB, LMF. Middlesex 2011-14. Durham (1 game) 2016. Derbyshire (1 game) 2017. Hertfordshire 2016. Shropshire 2017. HS 46* and CC BB 3-60 v Durham (Chesterfield) 2017. BB 4-49 M v Cambridge MCCU (Cambridge) 2013. LO HS 3 M v Notts (Lord's) 2015 (RLC). LO BB 3-28 M v Essex (Lord's) 2012 (CB40). T20 HS 2*. T20 BB 2-15.

TAYLOR, T.A.I. – *see LEICESTERSHIRE.*

THAKOR, Shivsinh Jaysinh (Loughborough GS; Uppingham S), b Leicester 22 Oct 1993. 6'1". RHB, RM. Leicestershire 2011-13. No f-c appearances in 2014. Derbyshire 2015-17. Leicestershire 2nd XI debut 2008, aged 14y 218d. England U19 2010-11. HS 134 Le v Loughborough MCCU (Leicester) 2011 – on debut. CC HS 132 v Leics (Derby) 2017. BB 5-63 v Kent (Derby) 2016. LO HS 130 v Northants (Derby) 2017 (RLC). LO BB 4-49 Le v Worcs (Leicester) 2014 (RLC). T20 HS 42. T20 BB 3-17.

WOOD, Thomas Anthony (Heanor Gate Science C), b Derby 11 May 1994. RHB, RM. Derbyshire 2016-17. Derbyshire 2nd XI debut 2014. HS 15 v West Indians (Derby) 2017. CC HS 14 v Leics (Derby) 2016. LO HS 44 v Sri Lanka A (Derby) 2016. T20 HS 24.

COUNTY CAPS AWARDED IN 2017

Derbyshire	A.L.Hughes
Durham	–
Essex	D.W.Lawrence
Glamorgan	C.A.Ingram
Gloucestershire	O.C.Currill, G.S.Drissell, C.J.Liddle
Hampshire	K.J.Abbott, G.J.Bailey
Kent	A.J.Blake
Lancashire	A.L.Davies, L.S.Livingstone
Leicestershire	–
Middlesex	–
Northamptonshire	R.E.Levi, D.Murphy, R.I.Newton
Nottinghamshire	J.L.Pattinson, C.A.Pujara
Somerset	S.M.Davies, D.Elgar, M.J.Leach
Surrey	–
Sussex	J.C.Archer
Warwickshire	–
Worcestershire (colours)	R.Ashwin, P.R.Brown, J.W.Hastings, N.M.Lyon, J.C.Tongue
Yorkshire	–

Durham abolished their capping system after 2005. Gloucestershire award caps on first-class debut. Worcestershire award club colours on Championship debut. Glamorgan's capping system is now based on a player's number of appearances and not on his performances.

DERBYSHIRE 2017

RESULTS SUMMARY

	Place	Won	Lost	Drew	Aband	NR
Specsavers County Champ (2nd Division)	8th	3	3	3	1	
All First-Class Matches		3	7	4	1	
Royal London One-Day Cup (North Group)	7th	2	5			1
NatWest t20 Blast (North Group)	QF	8	6			1

SPECSAVERS COUNTY CHAMPIONSHIP AVERAGES
BATTING AND FIELDING

Cap		M	I	NO	HS	Runs	Avge	100	50	Ct/St
	B.D.Cotton	2	4	3	32	50	50.00	–	–	–
2017	A.L.Hughes	13	22	2	142	800	40.00	2	3	15
2015	B.A.Godleman	12	22	2	156*	799	39.95	3	2	7
	M.J.J.Critchley	5	8	1	102	266	38.00	1	1	2
	B.T.Slater	8	15	2	74*	490	37.69	–	2	3
	L.M.Reece	12	21	1	168	732	36.60	2	5	4
	H.R.Hosein	4	7	2	52	166	33.20	–	1	7
	S.J.Thakor	6	11	1	132	328	32.80	1	–	1
	G.C.Wilson	9	14	1	97	401	30.84	–	3	17
2011	W.L.Madsen	13	22	–	121	667	30.31	1	5	14
	H.W.Podmore	4	6	1	66*	133	26.60	–	1	2
	T.A.I.Taylor	6	10	1	69	183	20.33	–	1	1
	D.Smit	8	13	1	41	237	19.75	–	–	18/3
	T.P.Milnes	3	5	–	53	96	19.20	–	1	2
	W.S.Davis	5	7	2	25	64	12.80	–	–	2
	B.M.A.J.Mendis	7	12	1	27	132	12.00	–	–	3
	Hamidullah Qadri	3	6	4	11*	20	10.00	–	–	2
2012	A.P.Palladino	10	17	2	32	143	9.53	–	–	3
	Imran Tahir	4	6	1	18*	41	8.20	–	–	2
	G.C.Viljoen	5	8	1	19*	36	5.14	–	–	1

Also batted: R.P.Hemmings (1 match) 19; C.McKerr (2) 16*, 0, 17; G.S.Sandhu (1) 46*, 9.

BOWLING

	O	M	R	W	Avge	Best	5wI	10wM
C.McKerr	85.5	19	290	14	20.71	5- 54	2	1
G.C.Viljoen	139.5	27	517	24	21.54	8- 90	3	1
Hamidullah Qadri	101.3	22	288	10	28.80	5- 60	1	–
W.S.Davis	103.5	13	410	14	29.28	4- 60	–	–
B.M.A.J.Mendis	252	24	908	30	30.26	6-204	1	–
Imran Tahir	123.1	16	407	13	31.30	5- 76	2	–
A.P.Palladino	254.4	56	818	24	34.08	4- 36	–	–
T.A.I.Taylor	144	30	548	16	34.25	4- 67	–	–
Also bowled:								
W.L.Madsen	60.3	5	260	7	37.14	2- 12	–	–
S.J.Thakor	64.3	9	302	6	50.33	4- 45	–	–
H.W.Podmore	85.3	12	310	6	51.66	2- 44	–	–
L.M.Reece	127.3	26	473	8	59.12	3- 38	–	–

B.D.Cotton 23-2-123-0; M.J.J.Critchley 10.2-0-66-2; R.P.Hemmings 24-6-94-0; A.L.Hughes 33-8-121-0; T.P.Milnes 64.4-10-306-4; G.S.Sandhu 21.3-2-87-3; B.T.Slater 2-0-6-0; D.Smit 10.5-0-57-0.

The First-Class Averages (pp 230–246) give the records of Derbyshire players in all first-class county matches (Derbyshire's other opponents being the West Indians), with the exception of C.McKerr and H.W.Podmore, whose first-class figures for Derbyshire are as above.

DERBYSHIRE RECORDS

FIRST-CLASS CRICKET

Highest Total	For 801-8d		v	Somerset	Taunton	2007
	V 677-7d		by	Yorkshire	Leeds	2013
Lowest Total	For 16		v	Notts	Nottingham	1879
	V 23		by	Hampshire	Burton upon T	1958
Highest Innings	For 274	G.A.Davidson	v	Lancashire	Manchester	1896
	V 343*	P.A.Perrin	for	Essex	Chesterfield	1904

Highest Partnership for each Wicket

1st	333	L.M.Reece/B.A.Godleman	v	Northants	Derby	2017
2nd	417	K.J.Barnett/T.A.Tweats	v	Yorkshire	Derby	1997
3rd	316*	A.S.Rollins/K.J.Barnett	v	Leics	Leicester	1997
4th	328	P.Vaulkhard/D.Smith	v	Notts	Nottingham	1946
5th	302*†	J.E.Morris/D.G.Cork	v	Glos	Cheltenham	1993
6th	212	G.M.Lee/T.S.Worthington	v	Essex	Chesterfield	1932
7th	258	M.P.Dowman/D.G.Cork	v	Durham	Derby	2000
8th	198	K.M.Krikken/D.G.Cork	v	Lancashire	Manchester	1996
9th	283	A.Warren/J.Chapman	v	Warwicks	Blackwell	1910
10th	132	A.Hill/M.Jean-Jacques	v	Yorkshire	Sheffield	1986

† 346 runs were added for this wicket in two separate partnerships

Best Bowling	For 10- 40	W.Bestwick	v	Glamorgan	Cardiff	1921
(Innings)	V 10- 45	R.L.Johnson	for	Middlesex	Derby	1994
Best Bowling	For 17-103	W.Mycroft	v	Hampshire	Southampton	1876
(Match)	V 16-101	G.Giffen	for	Australians	Derby	1886

Most Runs – Season	2165	D.B.Carr	(av 48.11)	1959
Most Runs – Career	23854	K.J.Barnett	(av 41.12)	1979-98
Most 100s – Season	8	P.N.Kirsten		1982
Most 100s – Career	53	K.J.Barnett		1979-98
Most Wkts – Season	168	T.B.Mitchell	(av 19.55)	1935
Most Wkts – Career	1670	H.L.Jackson	(av 17.11)	1947-63
Most Career W-K Dismissals	1304	R.W.Taylor	(1157 ct; 147 st)	1961-84
Most Career Catches in the Field	563	D.C.Morgan		1950-69

LIMITED-OVERS CRICKET

Highest Total	50ov	366-4		v	Comb Univs	Oxford	1991
	40ov	321-5		v	Essex	Leek	2013
	T20	222-5		v	Yorkshire	Leeds	2010
		222-5		v	Notts	Nottingham	2017
Lowest Total	50ov	73		v	Lancashire	Derby	1993
	40ov	60		v	Kent	Canterbury	2008
	T20	72		v	Leics	Derby	2013
Highest Innings	50ov	173*	M.J.Di Venuto	v	Derbys CB	Derby	2000
	40ov	141*	C.J.Adams	v	Kent	Chesterfield	1992
	T20	111	W.J.Durston	v	Notts	Nottingham	2010
Best Bowling	50ov	8-21	M.A.Holding	v	Sussex	Hove	1988
	40ov	6- 7	M.Hendrick	v	Notts	Nottingham	1972
	T20	5-27	T.Lungley	v	Leics	Leicester	2009

DURHAM

Formation of Present Club: 23 May 1882
Inaugural First-Class Match: 1992
Colours: Navy Blue, Yellow and Maroon
Badge: Coat of Arms of the County of Durham
County Champions: (3) 2008, 2009, 2013
Friends Provident Trophy Winners: (1) 2007
Royal London One-Day Cup Winners: (1) 2014
Twenty20 Cup Winners: (0); best – Finalist 2016

Chief Executive: David Harker, Emirates Riverside, Chester-le-Street, Co Durham DH3 3QR • Tel: 0191 387 1717 • Fax: 0191 387 1616 • Email: marketing@durhamccc.co.uk • Web: www.durhamccc.co.uk • Twitter: @DurhamCricket (52,440 followers)

Head Coach: Jon Lewis. **Bowling Coach**: Alan Walker. **Captains**: P.D.Collingwood (f-c) and T.W.M.Latham (l-o). **Overseas Players**: T.W.M.Latham and A.K.Markram. **2018 Testimonial**: None. **Head Groundsman**: Vic Demain. **Scorer**: William Dobson. ‡ New registration. NQ Not qualified for England.

Durham initially awarded caps immediately after their players joined the staff but revised this policy in 1998, capping players on merit, past 'awards' having been nullified. Durham abolished their capping and 'awards' systems after the 2005 season.

BURNHAM, Jack Tony Arthur (Deerness Valley CS, Durham), b Durham 18 Jan 1997. 6'1". RHB, RM. Squad No 8. Debut (Durham) 2015. Durham 2nd XI debut 2014. Northumberland 2015. Suspended during the 2018 season. HS 135 v Surrey (Oval) 2016. LO HS 26 v Northants (Northampton) 2016 (RLC). T20 HS 53*.

CARSE, Brydon Alexander (Pearson HS, Pt Elizabeth), b Port Elizabeth, South Africa 31 Jul 1995. Son of J.A.Carse (Rhodesia, W Province, E Province, Northants, Border, Griqualand W 1977-78 to 1992-93). 6'2". RHB, RF. Squad No 99. Debut (Durham) 2016. Durham 2nd XI debut 2015. HS 61* v Sussex (Chester-le-St) 2017. BB 3-38 v Lancs (Chester-le-St) 2016. T20 HS 3. T20 BB 1-11.

CLARK, Graham (St Benedict's Catholic HS, Whitehaven), b Whitehaven, Cumbria 16 Mar 1993. Younger brother of J.Clark (*see LANCASHIRE*). 6'1". RHB, LB. Squad No 7. Debut (Durham) 2015. MCC YC 2013. HS 109 v Glamorgan (Chester-le-St) 2017. LO HS 114 v Worcs (Worcester) 2017 (RLC). T20 HS 91*. T20 BB –.

COLLINGWOOD, Paul David (Blackfyne CS; Derwentside C), b Shotley Bridge 26 May 1976. 5'11". RHB, RM. Squad No 5. Debut (Durham) 1996 v Northants (Chester-le-St) taking wicket of D.J.Capel with his first ball before scoring 91 and 16; cap 1998; benefit 2007; captain 2012 (*part*) to date; testimonial 2017. IPL: DD 2009-10. MBE 2005. *Wisden* 2007. **Tests**: 68 (2003-04 to 2010-11); 1000 runs (1): 1121 (2006); HS 206 v A (Adelaide) 2006-07; BB 3-23 v NZ (Wellington) 2007-08. **LOI**: 197 (2001 to 2010-11, 25 as captain); 1000 runs (1): 1064 (2007); HS 120* v A (Melbourne) 2006-07; BB 6-31 v B (Nottingham) 2005 – record analysis for E, and first to score a hundred (112*) and take six wickets in same LOI. **IT20**: 36, inc 1 for a World XI in 2017 (2005 to 2010-11, 30 as captain); HS 79 v WI (Oval) 2007; BB 4-22 v SL (Southampton) 2006. F-c Tours: A 2006-07, 2010-11; SA 2009-10; WI 2003-04, 2008-09; NZ 2007-08; I 2005-06, 2008-09; P 2005-06; SL 2003-04, 2007-08; B 2009-10. 1000 runs (3); most – 1120 (2005). HS 206 (*see Tests*). Du HS 190 v SL (Chester-le-St) 2002 and 190 v Derbys (Derby) 2005, sharing Du record 4th wkt partnership of 250 with D.M.Benkenstein. BB 5-52 v Somerset (Stockton) 2005. LO HS 132 v Northants (Northampton) 2015 (RLC). LO BB 6-31 (*see LOI*). T20 HS 108* v Worcs (Worcester) 2017 – Du record. T20 BB 5-6 v Northants (Chester-le-St) 2011 – Du record.

COUGHLIN, Josh (St Robert of Newminster Catholic CS, Washington), b Sunderland 29 Sep 1997. Younger brother of P.Coughlin (see *NOTTINGHAMSHIRE*); nephew of T.Harland (Durham 1974-78). 6'4". LHB, RM. Squad No 29. Debut (Durham) 2016. Durham 2nd XI debut 2015. England U19 2016. HS 0 and BB 1-10 v Sri Lanka A (Chester-le-St) 2016 – only 1st XI appearance.

HARDING, George Harvey Idris (Brine Leas HS, Nantwich; Myerscough C), b Poole, Dorset 12 Oct 1996. 6'6". RHB, SLA. Squad No 37. Debut (Durham) 2017. Durham 2nd XI debut 2015. Northumberland 2016. HS 0 and BB 4-11 v Glamorgan (Swansea) 2017 – only f-c game. LO HS 18* v Lancs (Chester-le-St) 2017 (RLC). LO BB 2-52 v Worcs (Worcester) 2017 (RLC).

HARTE, Gareth Jason (King Edward VII S), b Johannesburg, South Africa 15 Mar 1993. 5'9". RHB, RM. Squad No 93. Awaiting f-c debut. Somerset 2nd XI 2012. Middlesex 2nd XI 2012. Kent 2nd XI 2014. MCC YCs 2016-17. Sussex 2nd XI 2016. Durham 2nd XI 2017. T20 HS 11.

[NO]**LATHAM, Thomas** William Maxwell, b Christchurch, New Zealand 2 Apr 1992. Son of R.T.Latham (Canterbury and New Zealand 1980-81 to 1994-95). 5'9". LHB, RM, WK. Squad No 48. Canterbury 2010-11 to date. Kent 2016. Durham debut 2017; l-o captain 2018. **Tests** (NZ): 34 (2013-14 to 2017-18); HS 177 v B (Wellington) 2016-17. **LOI** (NZ): 74 (2011-12 to 2017-18); HS 137 v B (Christchurch) 2016-17. **IT20** (NZ): 13 (2012 to 2017-18); HS 39 v I (Delhi) 2017-18. F-c Tours (NZ): E 2013, 2014 (NZ A), 2015; A 2015-16; SA 2016; WI 2014; I 2013-14 (NZ A), 2016-17; SL 2013-14 (NZ A); Z 2016; UAE 2014-15 (v P). HS 261 Cant v CD (Napier) 2013-14. Du HS 124 v Leics (Leicester) 2017. BB 1-7 NZ v Cricket Australia (Sydney) 2015-16. LO HS 137 (see *LOI*). T20 HS 82.

[NO]**McCARTHY, Barry** John (St Michael's C, Dublin; Dublin U), b Dublin, Ireland 13 Sep 1992. 5'11". RHB, RMF. Squad No 60. Debut (Durham) 2015. **LOI** (Ire): 19 (2016 to 2017-18); HS 16* v NZ (Dublin) 2017; BB 5-46 v Afghanistan (Sharjah) 2017-18. **IT20** (Ire): 2 (2016-17); HS 0; BB 4-33 v Afghanistan (Greater Noida) 2016-17. HS 51* v Hants (Chester-le-St) 2016. BB 6-63 v Kent (Canterbury) 2017. LO HS 39 Ire Wolves v Bangladesh A (Cox's Bazar) 2017-18. LO BB 5-46 (see *LOI*). T20 HS 2*. T20 BB 4-33.

[NO]**MAIN, Gavin** Thomas, b Lanark, Scotland 28 Feb 1995. 6'2". RHB, RMF. Squad No 20. Debut (Durham) 2014. Durham 2nd XI debut 2013. **IT20** (Scot): 4 (2015 to 2015-16); HS – ; BB 1-13 v Hong Kong (Nagpur) 2015-16. HS 13 v Northants (Chester-le-St) 2017. BB 3-72 v Notts (Nottingham) 2014. LO BB 2-35 Scot v Nepal (Alloway) 2015. T20 BB 1-13.

‡[NO]**MARKRAM, Aiden** Kyle, b Pretoria, South Africa 4 Oct 1994. RHB, OB Squad No 4. Northerns 2014-15 to 2016-17. Titans 2016-17 to date. Joins Durham for the first part of the 2018 season. **Tests** (SA): 7 (2017-18); HS 143 v A (Durban) 2017-18; BB –. **LOI** (SA): 7 (2017-18); HS 66 v B (East London) 2017-18. F-c Tour (SAA): E 2017. 1000 runs (0+1): 1134 (2017-18). HS 182 Northerns v WP (Cape Town) 2015-16. BB 1-2 Titans v Dolphins (Pietermaritzburg) 2017-18. LO HS 183 Titans v Lions (Johannesburg) 2016-17. LO BB 4-45 SAA v England Lions (Northampton) 2017. T20 HS 82. T20 BB 3-21.

POTTS, Matthew ('**Matty**') James (St Robert of Newminster Catholic S), b Sunderland 29 Oct 1998. 6'0". RHB, RM. Squad No 35. Debut (Durham) 2017. Durham 2nd XI debut 2016. England U19 2017. HS 53* v Derbys (Chester-le-St) 2017. BB 3-48 v Glamorgan (Chester-le-St) 2017.

^{NQ}**POYNTER, Stuart** William (Teddington S), b Hammersmith, London 18 Oct 1990. Younger brother of A.D.Poynter (Middlesex and Ireland 2005-11). 5'9". RHB, WK. Squad No 90. Middlesex 2010. Ireland 2011 to date. Warwickshire 2013. Durham debut 2016. **LOI** (Ire): 16 (2014 to 2017-18); HS 36 v SL (Dublin) 2016. **IT20** (Ire): 14 (2015 to 2016-17); HS 39 v Scotland (Dubai, DSC) 2016-17. F-c Tour (Ire): Z 2015-16. HS 125 Ire v Zimbabwe A (Harare) 2015-16. CC HS 65 v Notts (Chester-le-St) 2017. LO HS 109 Ire v Sri Lanka A (Belfast) 2014. T20 HS 61*.

PRINGLE, Ryan David (Durham SFC), b Sunderland 17 Apr 1992. 6'0". RHB, OB. Squad No 17. Debut (Durham) 2014. Northumberland 2011-12. HS 99 v Hants (Chester-le-St) 2015. BB 7-107 (10-260 match) v Hants (Southampton) 2016. LO HS 125 v Derbys (Derby) 2016 (RLC). LO BB 2-39 v Northants (Northampton) 2016 (RLC). T20 HS 33. T20 BB 3-30.

RICHARDSON, Michael John (Rondebosch HS; Stonyhurst C, Nottingham U), b Pt Elizabeth, South Africa 4 Oct 1986. Son of D.J.Richardson (South Africa, EP and NT 1977-78 to 1997-98), grandson of J.H.Richardson (NE Transvaal and Transvaal B 1952-53 to 1960-61), nephew of R.P.Richardson (WP 1984-85 to 1988-89). 5'10". RHB, WK. Squad No 10. Debut (Durham) 2010. Colombo CC 2014-15. MCC YC 2008-09. 1000 runs (1): 1007 (2015). HS 148 v Yorks (Chester-le-St) 2014. LO HS 100* v Yorks (Leeds) 2017 (RLC). T20 HS 53.

‡^{NQ}**RIMMINGTON, Nathan** John (Wellington C), b Redcliffe, Queensland, Australia 11 Nov 1982. 5'10". RHB, RFM. Squad No 11. Queensland 2005-06 to date. W Australia 2011-12 to 2016-17. Hampshire 2014. Derbyshire (T20 only) 2015. IPL: KXIP 2011. Big Bash: PS 2011-12 to 2012-13. MR 2012-13 to 2016-17. HS 102* WA v NSW (Sydney) 2011-12. CC HS 65* and BB 2-51 H v Essex (Colchester) 2014. BB 5-27 WA v Q (Perth) 2014-15. LO HS 55 WA v Tas (Sydney) 2014-15. LO BB 4-34 WA v SA (Perth) 2016-17 T20 HS 26. T20 BB 5-27.

RUSHWORTH, Christopher (Castle View CS, Sunderland), b Sunderland 11 Jul 1986. Cousin of P.Mustard (see *GLOUCESTERSHIRE*). 6'2". RHB, RMF. Squad No 22. Debut (Durham) 2010. MCC 2013, 2015. Northumberland 2004-05. PCA 2015. HS 57 v Kent (Canterbury) 2017. 50 wkts (2); most – 88 (2015). BB 9-52 (15-95 match – Du record) v Northants (Chester-le-St) 2014. Hat-trick v Hants (Southampton) 2015. LO HS 38* v Derbys (Chester-le-St) 2015 (RLC). LO BB 5-31 v Notts (Chester-le-St) 2010 (CB40). T20 HS 5. T20 BB 3-14.

SMITH, William Rew (Bedford S; Collingwood C, Durham U), b Luton, Beds 28 Sep 1982. 5'9". RHB, OB. Squad No 2. Nottinghamshire 2002-06. Durham UCCE 2003-05; captain 2004-05. British U 2004-05. Durham 2007-13; captain 2009-10 (*part*). Hampshire 2014-17; cap 2015. Bedfordshire 1999-2002. Rejoins Durham in 2018. 1000 runs (1): 1187 (2014). HS 210 v Lancs (Southampton) 2016. Du HS 201* v Surrey (Guildford) 2008. BB 3-34 DU v Leics (Leicester) 2005. CC BB 2-27 H v Kent (Southampton) 2014. Du BB 2-30 v Durham MCCU (Chester-le-St) 2013. LO HS 120* Du v Surrey (Chester-le-St) 2013 (Y40). LO BB 2-19 Du v Derbys (Derby) 2013 (Y40). T20 HS 55. T20 BB 3-15.

STEEL, Cameron Tate (Scotch C, Perth, Australia; Millfield S; Durham U), b San Francisco, USA 13 Sep 1995. 5'10". RHB, LB. Squad No 14. Durham MCCU 2014-16. Durham debut 2017. Middlesex 2nd XI 2013-16. Somerset 2nd XI 2013. Durham 2nd XI debut 2016. HS 224 v Leics (Leicester) 2017. BB 2-24 v Derbys (Chester-le-St) 2017. LO HS 77 v Notts (Nottingham) 2017 (RLC). LO BB –. T20 HS 37. T20 BB 2-60.

STOKES, Benjamin Andrew (Cockermouth S), b Christchurch, Canterbury, New Zealand 4 Jun 1991. 6'1''. LHB, RFM. Squad No 38. Debut (Durham) 2010. IPL: RPS. Big Bash: MR 2014-15. YC 2013. *Wisden* 2015. **ECB Test & LO Central Contract 2017-18. Tests**: 39 (2013-14 to 2017); HS 258 v SA (Cape Town) 2015-16, setting E record fastest double century in 163 balls; BB 6-22 v WI (Lord's) 2017. **LOI**: 67 (2011 to 2017-18); HS 102* v A (Birmingham) 2017; BB 5-61 v A (Southampton) 2013. **IT20**: 21 (2011 to 2016-17); HS 38 v I (Nagpur) 2016-17; BB 3-26 v NZ (Delhi) 2015-16. F-c Tours: A 2013-14; SA 2015-16; WI 2010-11 (EL), 2014-15; I 2016-17; B 2016-17; UAE 2015-16 (v P). HS 258 (*see Tests*). Du HS 185 v Lancs (Chester-le-St) 2011, sharing Du record 4th wkt partnership of 331 with D.M.Benkenstein. BB 7-67 (10-121 match) v Sussex (Chester-le-St) 2014. LO HS 164 v Notts (Chester-le-St) 2014 (RLC) – Du record. LO BB 5-61 (*see LOI*). T20 HS 103*. T20 BB 3-18.

TREVASKIS, Liam (Q Elizabeth GS, Penrith), b Carlisle, Cumberland 18 Apr 1999. 5'8''. LHB, SLA. Squad No 80. Debut (Durham) 2017. Durham 2nd XI debut 2015. HS 9 and BB 1-69 v Worcs (Worcester) 2017 – only f-c game. T20 HS 13*. T20 BB 1-33.

WEIGHELL, William James (Stokesley S), b Middlesbrough, Yorks 28 Jan 1994. 6'4''. LHB, RMF. Squad No 28. Debut (Durham) 2015. Durham 2nd XI debut 2012. Northumberland 2012-15. HS 58 v Sussex (Hove) 2015. BB 5-33 v Warwks (Birmingham) 2016. LO HS 14 v Worcs (Worcester) 2017 (RLC). LO BB 5-57 v Warwks (Birmingham) 2017 (RLC). T20 HS 6*. T20 BB 3-28.

WOOD, Mark Andrew (Ashington HS; Newcastle C), b Ashington 11 Jan 1990. 5'11''. RHB, RF. Squad No 33. Debut (Durham) 2011. Northumberland 2008-10. **ECB L-O Central Contract 2017-18. Tests**: 10 (2015 to 2017); HS 32* v A (Cardiff) 2015; BB 3-39 v P (Dubai, DSC) 2016-17. **LOI**: 26 (2015 to 2017-18); HS 13 v A (Manchester) 2015; BB 4-33 v A (Birmingham) 2017. **IT20**: 4 (2015 to 2017-18); HS 5* v A (Hobart) 2017-18 and 5* v NZ (Wellington) 2017-18; BB 3-26 v NZ (Manchester) 2015. F-c Tours (EL): SA 2014-15; SL 2013-14; UAE 2015-16 (v P). HS 72* v Kent (Chester-le-St) 2017. BB 5-32 EL v Sri Lanka A (Colombo, RPS) 2013-14. Du BB 5-37 v Somerset (Taunton) 2014. LO HS 15* v Lancs (Chester-le-St) 2013 (Y40). LO BB 4-33 (*see LOI*). T20 HS 12. T20 BB 4-25.

RELEASED/RETIRED
(Having made a County 1st XI appearance in 2017)

ARSHAD, Usman (Beckfoot GS, Bingley), b Bradford, Yorks 9 Jan 1993. 5'11''. RHB, RMF. Durham 2013-16. Northumberland 2011. HS 84 v Yorks (Chester-le-St) 2016. BB 4-78 v Northants (Northampton) 2014. LO HS 25 v Surrey (Chester-le-St) 2015 (RLC). LO BB 3-50 v Warwks (Chester-le-St) 2016 (RLC). T20 HS 43. T20 BB 3-18.

NQ**COOK, Stephen** Craig, b Johannesburg, South Africa 29 Nov 1982. Son of S.J.Cook (Transvaal, Somerset & South Africa, 1972-73 to 1994-95). RHB, RM. Gauteng 2000-01 to 2014-15. Lions 2004-05 to date. North West 2015-16. Durham 2017. Tests (SA): 11 (2015-16 to 2016-17); HS 117 v SL (Pt Elizabeth) 2016-17. F-c Tours (SA A)(C=Captain): A 2016C, 2016-17 (SA); NZ 2016-17 (SA); SL 2010; Z 2016C. 1000 runs (0+4); most – 1642 (2009-10). HS 390 Lions v Warriors (East London) 2009-10 – record score in SA. Du HS 89* v Glamorgan (Chester-le-St) 2017. BB 3-42 Lions v Dolphins (Durban) 2008-09. LO HS 127* Lions v Cobras (Johannesburg) 2015-16. LO BB 1-2 Lions v Titans (Johannesburg) 2008-09. T20 HS 66.

COUGHLIN, P. – *see NOTTINGHAMSHIRE*.

HICKEY, Adam James (Biddick S Sports C, Washington), b Darlington 1 Mar 1997. Son of D.J.Hickey (Cumberland 2010). 6'3''. LHB, OB. Durham 2016. Durham 2nd XI debut 2014. HS 36* and BB 2-19 v Somerset (Taunton) 2016. T20 HS 15. T20 BB 1-11.

JENNINGS, K.K. – *see LANCASHIRE*.

ONIONS, G. – *see LANCASHIRE*.

DURHAM 2017

RESULTS SUMMARY

	Place	Won	Lost	Drew	NR
Specsavers County Champ (2nd Division)	8th	3	6	5	
All First-Class Matches		3	6	5	
Royal London One-Day Cup (North Group)	5th	4	3		1
NatWest t20 Blast (North Group)	9th	3	10		1

SPECSAVERS COUNTY CHAMPIONSHIP AVERAGES

BATTING AND FIELDING

Cap		M	I	NO	HS	Runs	Avge	100	50	Ct/St
	T.W.M.Latham	4	7	1	124	382	63.66	2	1	5
1998	P.D.Collingwood	14	24	2	177	1087	49.40	3	5	23
	C.T.Steel	13	24	2	224	899	40.86	2	4	3
	W.J.Weighell	4	7	3	58	162	40.50	–	2	–
	G.Clark	12	21	–	109	769	36.61	1	6	10
	P.Coughlin	8	12	2	73*	364	36.40	–	3	3
	M.A.Wood	5	8	2	72*	195	32.50	–	1	–
	B.J.McCarthy	5	6	2	39	129	32.25	–	–	3
	M.J.Richardson	10	16	1	82	460	30.66	–	4	20
	S.C.Cook	7	14	1	89*	348	26.76	–	2	5
	K.K.Jennings	11	21	2	102*	490	25.78	1	1	13
	R.D.Pringle	13	22	4	71	459	25.50	–	3	9
	J.T.A.Burnham	7	11	2	93*	223	24.77	–	1	1
	S.W.Poynter	9	14	1	65	269	20.69	–	1	30
	M.J.Potts	5	6	2	53*	69	17.25	–	1	–
	C.Rushworth	13	17	3	57	174	12.42	–	1	5
	G.Onions	8	10	–	15	58	5.80	–	–	1

Also batted: B.A.Carse (2 matches) 7, 61*, 23*; G.H.I.Harding (1) 0; G.T.Main (2), 13, 0, 0*; B.A.Stokes (1) 0; L.Trevaskis (1) 5, 9.

BOWLING

	O	M	R	W	Avge	Best	5wI	10wM
K.K.Jennings	64	9	214	12	17.83	3-37	–	–
G.Onions	237	48	725	32	22.65	6-62	1	–
C.Rushworth	436.3	96	1217	47	25.89	5-52	1	–
B.J.McCarthy	164.2	23	653	24	27.20	6-63	1	–
P.Coughlin	208.1	31	804	27	29.77	5-49	2	1
M.A.Wood	123	17	389	13	29.92	5-54	1	–
M.J.Potts	163	37	465	14	33.21	3-48	–	–
W.J.Weighell	94.5	8	438	11	39.81	3-51	–	–
R.D.Pringle	197.5	41	688	15	45.86	4-73	–	–

Also bowled:
C.T.Steel 65.2 3 275 8 34.37 2-24

B.A.Carse 58-4-191-3; P.D.Collingwood 77.2-21-199-4; S.C.Cook 1-0-16-0; G.H.I.Harding 36-2-186-4; G.T.Main 43-3-219-3; B.A.Stokes 20-3-81-0; L.Trevaskis 26-3-126-1.

Durham played no first-class fixtures outside the County Championship in 2017. The First-Class Averages (pp 230–246) give the records of Durham players in all first-class county matches, with the exception of K.K.Jennings, B.A.Stokes and M.A.Wood, whose first-class figures for Durham are as above.

DURHAM RECORDS

FIRST-CLASS CRICKET

Highest Total	For 648-5d		v	Notts	Chester-le-St[2]	2009
	V 810-4d		by	Warwicks	Birmingham	1994
Lowest Total	For 67		v	Middlesex	Lord's	1996
	V 18		by	Durham MCCU	Chester-le-St[2]	2012
Highest Innings	For 273	M.L.Love	v	Hampshire	Chester-le-St[2]	2003
	V 501*	B.C.Lara	for	Warwicks	Birmingham	1994

Highest Partnership for each Wicket

1st	334*	S.Hutton/M.A.Roseberry	v	Oxford U	Oxford	1996
2nd	274	M.D.Stoneman/S.G.Borthwick	v	Middlesex	Chester-le-St[2]	2014
3rd	212	M.J.Di Venuto/D.M.Benkenstein	v	Essex	Chester-le-St[2]	2010
4th	331	B.A.Stokes/D.M.Benkenstein	v	Lancashire	Chester-le-St[2]	2011
5th	247	G.J.Muchall/I.D.Blackwell	v	Worcs	Worcester	2011
6th	249	G.J.Muchall/P.Mustard	v	Kent	Canterbury	2006
7th	315	D.M.Benkenstein/O.D.Gibson	v	Yorkshire	Leeds	2006
8th	147	P.Mustard/L.E.Plunkett	v	Yorkshire	Leeds	2009
9th	150	P.Mustard/P.Coughlin	v	Lancashire	Chester-le-St[2]	2014
10th	103	M.M.Betts/D.M.Cox	v	Sussex	Hove	1996

Best Bowling	For 10- 47	O.D.Gibson	v	Hampshire	Chester-le-St[2]	2007
(Innings)	V 9- 34	J.A.R.Harris	for	Middlesex	Lord's	2015
Best Bowling	For 15- 95	C.Rushworth	v	Northants	Chester-le-St[2]	1995
(Match)	V 13-103	J.A.R.Harris	for	Middlesex	Lord's	2015

Most Runs – Season	1654	M.J.Di Venuto	(av 78.76)	2009
Most Runs – Career	11731	P.D.Collingwood	(av 35.12)	1996-2017
Most 100s – Season	7	K.K.Jennings		2016
Most 100s – Career	25	P.D.Collingwood		1996-2017
Most Wkts – Season	80	O.D.Gibson	(av 20.75)	2007
Most Wkts – Career	527	G.Onions	(av 25.58)	2004-17
Most Career W-K Dismissals	638	P.Mustard	(619 ct; 19 st)	2002-16
Most Career Catches in the Field	235	P.D.Collingwood		1996-2017

LIMITED-OVERS CRICKET

Highest Total	50ov	353-8		v	Notts	Chester-le-St[2]	2014
	40ov	325-9		v	Surrey	The Oval	2011
	T20	225-2		v	Leics	Chester-le-St[2]	2010

Lowest Total	50ov	82		v	Worcs	Chester-le-St[1]	1968
	40ov	72		v	Warwicks	Birmingham	2002
	T20	93		v	Kent	Canterbury	2009

Highest Innings	50ov	164	B.A.Stokes	v	Notts	Chester-le-St[2]	2014
	40ov	150*	B.A.Stokes	v	Warwicks	Birmingham	2011
	T20	108*	P.D.Collingwood	v	Worcs	Worcester	2017

Best Bowling	50ov	7-32	S.P.Davis	v	Lancashire	Chester-le-St[1]	1983
	40ov	6-31	N.Killeen	v	Derbyshire	Derby	2000
	T20	5- 6	P.D.Collingwood	v	Northants	Chester-le-St[2]	2011

[1] Chester-le-Street CC (Ropery Lane) [2] Emirates Durham International Cricket Ground

ESSEX

Formation of Present Club: 14 January 1876
Inaugural First-Class Match: 1894
Colours: Blue, Gold and Red
Badge: Three Seaxes above Scroll bearing 'Essex'
County Champions: (7) 1979, 1983, 1984, 1986, 1991, 1992, 2017
NatWest/Friends Prov Trophy Winners: (3) 1985, 1997, 2008
Benson and Hedges Cup Winners: (2) 1979, 1998
Pro 40/National League (Div 1) Winners: (2) 2005, 2006
Sunday League Winners: (3) 1981, 1984, 1985
Twenty20 Cup Winners: (0); best – Semi-Finalist 2006, 2008, 2010

Chief Executive: Derek Bowden, The Cloudfm County Ground, New Writtle Street, Chelmsford CM2 0PG • Tel: 01245 252420 • Fax: 01245 254030 • Email: administration@essexcricket.org.uk • Web: www.essexcricket.org.uk • Twitter: @EssexCricket (67,639 followers)

Head Coach: Anthony McGrath. **Assistant Head Coach**: Dimitri Mascarenhas. **Captain**: R.N.ten Doeschate. **Vice-Captain**: T.Westley. **Overseas Players**: P.M.Siddle, N.Wagner and A.Zampa (T20 only). **2018 Testimonial**: None. **Head Groundsman**: Stuart Kerrison. **Scorer**: Tony Choat. ‡ New registration. NQ Not qualified for England.

Syed ASHAR Ahmed ZAIDI, b Karachi, Pakistan 13 Jul 1981. LHB, SLA. Squad No 99. UK citizen. Islamabad 1999-00 to 2009-10. PTC 2003-04 to 2005-06. Rawalpindi 2003-04 to 2004-05. KRL 2006-07. Federal Areas 2007-08. Sussex 2013-15. Essex debut 2016. HS 202 Islamabad v Sialkot (Sialkot) 2009-10. CC HS 106 Sx v Warwks (Birmingham) 2015. Ex HS 37 v Glos (Cheltenham) 2016. BB 4-50 Islamabad v Hyderabad (Islamabad) 2009-10. CC BB 4-57 Sx v Yorks (Hove) 2013. Ex BB 3-17 v Somerset (Taunton) 2017. LO HS 141 Rupganj v Old DOHS (Mirpur) 2014-15. LO BB 4-39 Gazi Tank v PDSC (Mirpur) 2013-14. T20 HS 59*. T20 BB 4-11.

BEARD, Aaron Paul (Boswells S, Chelmsford), b Chelmsford 15 Oct 1997. LHB, RFM. Squad No 14. Debut (Essex) 2016. England U19 2016 to 2016-17. HS 58* v Durham MCCU (Chelmsford) 2017. CC HS 4* (twice). BB 4-62 v Sri Lankans (Chelmsford) 2016. CC BB 3-47 v Lancs (Chelmsford) 2017.

BOPARA, Ravinder Singh (Brampton Manor S; Barking Abbey Sports C), b Newham, London 4 May 1985. 5'8". RHB, RM. Squad No 25. Debut (Essex) 2002; cap 2005; benefit 2015; captain (l-o only) 2016. Auckland 2009-10. Dolphins 2010-11. IPL: KXIP 2009 to 2009-10. SH 2015. Big Bash: SS 2013-14. MCC 2006, 2008. YC 2008. **Tests**: 13 (2007-08 to 2012); HS 143 v WI (Lord's) 2009; BB 1-39 v SL (Galle) 2007-08. **LOI**: 120 (2006-07 to 2014-15); HS 101* v Ireland (Dublin) 2013; BB 4-38 v B (Birmingham) 2010. **IT20**: 38 (2008 to 2014); HS 65* v A (Hobart) 2013-14; BB 4-10 v WI (Oval) 2011 – E record. F-c Tours: WI 2008-09, 2010-11 (EL); SL 2007-08, 2011-12. 1000 runs (1): 1256 (2008). HS 229 v Northants (Chelmsford) 2007. BB 5-49 v Derbys (Chelmsford) 2016. LO HS 201* v Leics (Leicester) 2008 (FPT) – Ex record. LO BB 5-63 Dolphins v Warriors (Pietermaritzburg) 2010-11. T20 HS 105*. T20 BB 6-16.

BROWNE, Nicholas Lawrence Joseph (Trinity Catholic HS, Woodford Green), b Leytonstone 24 Mar 1991. 6'3½". LHB, LB. Squad No 10. Debut (Essex) 2013; cap 2015. MCC 2016. 1000 runs (3); most – 1262 (2016). HS 255 v Derbys (Chelmsford) 2016. BB –. LO HS 99 v Glamorgan (Chelmsford) 2016 (RLC). T20 HS 38.

CHOPRA, Varun (Ilford County HS), b Barking, Essex 21 Jun 1987. 6'1". RHB, LB. Squad No 6. Debut (Essex) 2006, scoring 106 v Glos (Chelmsford) on CC debut. Warwickshire 2010-16; cap 2012; captain 2015. Tamil Union 2011-12. F-c Tour (EL): SL 2013-14. 1000 runs (3); most – 1203 (2011). HS 233* TU v Sinhalese (Colombo, PSS) 2011-12. CC HS 228 Wa v Worcs (Worcester) 2011 (in 2nd CC game of season, having scored 210 v Somerset in 1st). Ex HS 155 v Glos (Bristol) 2008. BB –. LO HS 124 v Glamorgan (Cardiff) 2017 (RLC). T20 HS 116.

‡**COLES, Matthew** Thomas (Maplesden Noakes S; Mid-Kent C), b Maidstone, Kent 26 May 1990. 6'3". LHB, RFM. Squad No 1. Kent 2009-17; cap 2012. Hampshire 2013-14. Joins Essex in 2018. HS 103* K v Yorks (Leeds) 2012. 50 wkts (2); most – 67 (2015). BB 6-51 K v Northants (Northampton) 2012. LO HS 100 K v Surrey (Oval) 2015 (RLC). LO BB 6-32 K v Yorks (Leeds) 2012 (CB40). T20 HS 54. T20 BB 4-27.

COOK, Alastair Nathan (Bedford S), b Gloucester 25 Dec 1984. 6'3". LHB, OB. Squad No 26. Debut (Essex) 2003; cap 2005; benefit 2014. MCC 2004-07, 2015. YC 2005. *Wisden* 2011. **ECB Test Central Contract 2017-18. Tests**: 152 (2005-06 to 2017-18, 59 as captain); 1000 runs (5); most – 1364 (2015); HS 294 v I (Birmingham) 2011. Scored 60 and 104* v I (Nagpur) 2005-06 on debut. Second, after M.A.Taylor, to score 1000 runs in the calendar year of his debut. BB 1-6 v I (Nottingham) 2014. **LOI**: 92 (2006 to 2014-15, 69 as captain); HS 137 v P (Abu Dhabi) 2011-12. **IT20**: 4 (2007 to 2009-10); HS 26 v SA (Centurion) 2009-10. F-c Tours (C=Captain): A 2006-07, 2010-11, 2013-14C, 2017-18; SA 2009-10, 2015-16C; WI 2005-06 (Eng A), 2008-09, 2014-15C; NZ 2007-08, 2012-13C; I 2005-06, 2008-09, 2012-13C, 2016-17C; SL 2004-05 (Eng A), 2007-08, 2011-12; B 2009-10C, 2016-17C; UAE 2011-12 (v P), 2015-16C (v P). 1000 runs (7+1); most – 1466 (2005). HS 294 (*see Tests*). CC HS 195 v Northants (Chelmsford) 2005. BB 3-13 v Northants (Chelmsford) 2005. LO HS 137 (*see LOI*). BB –. T20 HS 100*.

COOK, Samuel James (Great Baddow HS & SFC; Loughborough U), b Chelmsford 4 Aug 1997. RHB, RFM. Squad No 16. Loughborough MCCU 2016-17. Essex debut 2017. Essex 2nd XI debut 2014. HS 3 LU v Leics (Leicester) 2017. Scored 0*, 0*, 0, 0* and 0* for Essex. BB 5-18 v Hants (Southampton) 2017.

^{NO}**DIXON, Matt**hew William, b Subiaco, W Australia 12 Jun 1992. RHB, RF. Squad No 30. W Australia 2010-11 to 2015-16. Essex debut 2016. UK passport. HS 22 WA v Q (Perth) 2011-12. Ex HS 14 and BB 5-124 v Kent (Canterbury) 2016. LO HS 12 Cricket Australia XI v WA (Sydney) 2015-16. LO BB 3-40 CA v Tas (Sydney) 2015-16. T20 HS 1. T20 BB 3-32.

FOSTER, James Savin (Forest S, Snaresbrook; Collingwood C, Durham U), b Whipps Cross 15 Apr 1980. 6'0". RHB, WK. Squad No 7. British U 2000-01. Essex debut 2000; cap 2001; captain 2010 (*part*); benefit 2015; benefit 2011. Durham UCCE 2001. MCC 2004, 2008-10. **Tests**: 7 (2001-02 to 2002-03); HS 48 v I (Bangalore) 2001-02. **LOI**: 11 (2001-02); HS 13 v I (Bombay) 2001-02. **IT20**: 5 (2009); HS 14* v P (Oval) 2009. F-c Tours: A 2002-03; WI 2000-01 (Eng A); NZ 2001-02; I 2001-02, 2007-08 (Eng A). 1000 runs (1): 1037 (2004). HS 212 v Leics (Chelmsford) 2004. BB 1-122 v Northants (Northampton) 2008 – in contrived circumstances. LO HS 83* v Durham, inc 5 sixes in 5 balls off S.G.Borthwick (Chester-le-St) 2009 (P40). T20 HS 65*.

^{NO}**HARMER, Simon** Ross, b Pretoria, South Africa 10 Feb 1993. RHB, OB. Squad No 11. Eastern Province 2009-10 to 2011-12. Warriors 2010-11 to date. Essex debut 2017 (Kolpak signing). **Tests** (SA): 5 (2014-15 to 2015-16); HS 13 v I (Nagpur) 2015-16; BB 4-61 v I (Mohali) 2015-16. F-c Tours (SA): A 2014 (SA A); I 2015-16; B 2015; Ire 2012 (SA A). HS 100* EP v Border (East London) 2011-12. Ex HS 64 v Yorks (Chelmsford) 2017. 50 wkts (1+1); most – 74 (2017). BB 9-95 (14-172 match) v Middx (Chelmsford) 2017. LO HS 44* v Surrey (Oval) 2017. LO BB 4-42 Warriors v Lions (Potchefstroom) 2011-12. T20 HS 43. T20 BB 3-28.

KHUSHI, Feroze Isa Nazir (Kelmscott S, Walthamstow; Leyton SFC), b Whipps Cross 23 Jun 1999. RHB. OB. Squad No 23. Essex 2nd XI debut 2015. Awaiting 1st XI debut.

LAWRENCE, Daniel William (Trinity Catholic HS, Woodford Green), b Whipps Cross 12 Jul 1997. 6'2". RHB, LB. Squad No 28. Debut (Essex) 2015; cap 2017. England Lions 2017. Essex 2nd XI debut 2013, aged 15y 321d. England U19 2015. 1000 runs (1): 1070 (2016). HS 161 v Surrey (Oval) 2015. BB 1-5 v Kent (Chelmsford) 2016. LO HS 35 v Kent (Chelmsford) 2016 (RLC). LO BB 3-35 v Middx (Lord's) 2016 (RLC). T20 HS 47. T20 BB 3-21.

NIJJAR, Aron Stuart Singh (Ilford County HS), b Goodmayes 24 Sep 1994. LHB, SLA. Squad No 24. Debut (Essex) 2015. Essex 2nd XI debut 2013. Suffolk 2014. No 1st XI appearances in 2016. HS 53 v Northants (Chelmsford) 2015. BB 2-33 v Lancs (Chelmsford) 2015. LO HS 21 v Yorks (Chelmsford) 2015 (RLC). LO BB 1-39 v Sussex (Hove) 2015 (RLC).

PORTER, James Alexander (Oak Park HS, Newbury Park; Epping Forest C), b Leyton-stone 25 May 1993. 5'11½". RHB, RFM. Squad No 44. Debut (Essex) 2014, taking a wkt with his 5th ball; cap 2015. England Lions 2017. MCC YCs 2011-13. Essex 2nd XI debut 2014. F-c Tour (EL): WI 2017-18. HS 34 v Glamorgan (Cardiff) 2015. 50 wkts (3); most – 85 (2017). BB 7-55 (12-95 match) v Somerset (Chelmsford) 2016. LO HS 5* v Yorks (Chelmsford) 2015 (RLC). LO BB 4-40 v Middx (Chelmsford) 2017 (RLC). T20 HS 1*. T20 BB 4-20.

NQQUINN, Matthew Richard, b Auckland, New Zealand 28 Feb 1993. RHB, RMF. Squad No 94. Auckland 2012-13 to date. Essex debut 2016. UK passport. HS 50 v Auckland v Canterbury (Auckland) 2013-14. Ex HS 15 v Hants (Chelmsford) 2017. BB 7-76 (11-163 match) v Glos (Cheltenham) 2016. LO HS 36 Auckland v CD (Auckland) 2013-14. LO BB 4-71 v Sussex (Hove) 2016 (RLC). T20 HS 8*. T20 BB 4-35.

‡NQSIDDLE, Peter Matthew, b Traralgon, Victoria, Australia 25 Nov 1984. 6'1½". RHB, RFM. Victoria 2005-06 to date. Nottinghamshire 2014; cap 2014. Lancashire 2015. Joins Essex in 2018 for first part of the season. Big Bash: MR 2013-14 to 2014-15. AS 2017-18. **Tests** (A): 62 (2008-09 to 2016-17); HS 51 v I (Delhi) 2012-13; BB 6-54 v E (Brisbane) 2010-11. **LOI** (A): 17 (2008-09 to 2010-11); HS 9* v SL (Sydney) 2010-11; BB 3-55 v E (Centurion) 2009-10. **IT20** (A): 2 (2008-09 to 2010-11); HS 1* and BB 2-24 v NZ (Sydney) 2008-09. F-c Tours (A): E 2009, 2013, 2015; SA 2008-09, 2011-12, 2013-14; WI 2011-12; NZ 2015-16; I 2008-09 (Aus A), 2008-09, 2012-13; SL 2011; Z 2011 (Aus A); UAE 2014-15 (v P). HS 103* Aus A v Scotland (Edinburgh) 2013. CC HS 89 La v Northants (Northampton) 2015. 50 wkts (0+1): 54 (2011-12). BB 8-54 Vic v S Aus (Adelaide) 2014-15. CC BB 4-39 La v Glos (Manchester) 2015. LO HS 62 Vic v Q (N Sydney) 2017-18. LO BB 4-27 Vic v Tas (Hobart) 2008-09. T20 HS 9*. T20 BB 4-29.

TAYLOR, Callum John (Cromer Ac; Eastern C, Norwich), b Norwich, Norfolk 26 Jun 1997. 5'11". RHB, RM. Squad No 67. Debut (Essex) 2015. Essex 2nd XI debut 2013. Norfolk 2013. England U19 2014-15 to 2015. HS 26 v Glamorgan (Cardiff) 2015. BB 2-20 v West Indians (Chelmsford) 2017. T20 HS 14.

NQTen DOESCHATE, Ryan Neil (Fairbairn C; Cape Town U), b Port Elizabeth, South Africa 30 Jun 1980. 5'10½". RHB, RMF. Squad No 27. Debut (Essex) 2003; cap 2006; captain (l-o) 2014-15; captain 2016 to date. EU passport – Dutch ancestry. Netherlands 2005 to 2009-10. Otago 2012-13. IPL: KKR 2011-15. Big Bash: AS 2014-15. **LOI** (Ne): 33 (2006 to 2010-11); HS 119 v E (Nagpur) 2010-11; BB 4-31 v Canada (Nairobi) 2006-07. **IT20** (Ne): 9 (2008 to 2009-10); HS 56 v Kenya (Belfast) 2008; BB 3-23 v Scotland (Belfast) 2008. F-c Tours (Ne): SA 2006-07, 2007-08; K 2005-06, 2009-10; Ireland 2005. 1000 runs (1): 1226 (2016). HS 259* and BB 6-20 (9-112 match) Netherlands v Canada (Pretoria) 2006. Ex HS 168* v Surrey (Guildford) 2017. Ex BB 6-57 v New Zealanders (Chelmsford) 2008. CC BB 5-13 v Hants (Chelmsford) 2010. LO HS 180 v Scotland (Chelmsford) 2013 (Y40) – Ex 40-over record, inc 15 sixes. LO BB 5-50 v Glos (Bristol) 2007 (FPT). T20 HS 121*. T20 BB 4-24.

[NQ]**WAGNER, Neil**, b Pretoria, South Africa 13 Mar 1986. LHB, LMF. Squad No 13. Northerns 2005-06 to 2007-08. Titans 2006-07 to 2007-08. Otago 2008-09 to date. Northamptonshire 2014. Lancashire 2016. Essex debut 2017. **Tests** (NZ): 34 (2012 to 2017-18); HS 37 v WI (Dunedin) 2013-14; BB 7-39 v WI (Wellington) 2017-18. F-c Tours (NZ): E 2013, 2015; SA 2012-13, 2016; WI 2012, 2014; I 2016-17; Z 2007 (SA Acad), 2016; B 2013-14. HS 70 Otago v Wellington (Queenstown) 2009-10. Ex HS 50 v Surrey (Chelmsford) 2017. 50 wkts (0+2); most – 51 (2010-11, 2012-13). BB 7-46 Otago v Wellington (Dunedin) 2011-12. Ex BB 6-48 v Somerset (Taunton) 2017. LO HS 42 Otago v CD (Dunedin) 2014-15. LO BB 5-34 Otago v Wellington (Wellington) 2008-09. T20 HS 14. T20 BB 4-33.

WESTLEY, Thomas (Linton Village C; Hills Road SFC), b Cambridge 13 March 1989. 6'2". RHB, OB. Squad No 21. Debut (Essex) 2007; cap 2013. England Lions 2017. MCC 2007, 2009, 2016. Durham MCCU 2010-11. Cambridgeshire 2005. **Tests**: 5 (2017); HS 59 v SA (Oval) 2017. F-c Tour (EL): SL 2016-17. 1000 runs (1): 1435 (2016). HS 254 v Worcs (Chelmsford) 2016. BB 4-55 DU v Durham (Durham) 2010. CC BB 4-75 v Surrey (Colchester) 2015. LO HS 111* v Yorks (Scarborough) 2014 (RLC). LO BB 4-60 v Northants (Northampton) 2014 (RLC). T20 HS 109*. T20 BB 2-27.

WHEATER, Adam Jack Aubrey (Millfield S), b Whipps Cross 13 Feb 1990. 5'6". RHB, WK. Squad No 31. Debut (Essex) 2008, returned in 2016. Cambridge MCCU 2010. Matabeleland Tuskers 2010-11 to 2012-13. Badureliya Sports Club 2011-12. Northern Districts 2012-13. Hampshire 2013-16; cap 2016. HS 204* H v Warwks (Birmingham) 2016. Ex HS 164 v Northants (Chelmsford) 2011, sharing Ex record 6th wkt partnership of 253 with J.S.Foster. BB 1-86 v Leics (Leicester) 2012 – in contrived circumstances. LO HS 135 v Essex (Chelmsford) 2014 (RLC). T20 HS 78.

‡[NQ]**ZAMPA, Adam**, b Shellharbour, NSW, Australia 31 Mar 1992. RHB, LB. New South Wales 2012-13. S Australia 2013-14 to date. Joins Essex in 2018 (T20 only). IPL: RPS 2016-17. Big Bash: ST 2012-13. AS 2013-14 to 2014-15. MS 2015-16 to date. **LOI** (A): 31 (2015-16 to 2017-18); HS 12 v SA (Centurion) 2016-17; BB 3-16 v WI (Providence) 2016. **IT20** (A): 13 (2015-16 to 2017-18); HS 5* v SA (Durban) 2015-16; BB 3-16 v SL (Colombo, RPS) 2016. HS 74 S Aus v WA (Adelaide) 2014-15. BB 6-62 (10-119 match) S Aus v Q (Adelaide) 2016-17. LO HS 66 S Aus v Q (N Sydney) 2013-14. LO BB 4-18 S Aus v WA (Brisbane) 2014-15. T20 HS 15. T20 BB 6-19.

RELEASED/RETIRED

(Having made a County 1st XI appearance in 2017)

[NQ]**MOHAMMAD AMIR**, b Gujar Khan, Punjab, Pakistan 13 Apr 1992. LHB, LF. Federal Areas 2008-09. National Bank 2008-09 to 2009-10. SSGC 2015-16. Essex 2017. **Tests** (P): 30 (2009 to 2017-18); HS 48 v A (Brisbane) 2016-17; BB 6-44 v WI (Kingston) 2017. **LOI** (P): 40 (2009 to 2017-18); HS 73* v NZ (Abu Dhabi) 2009-10); BB 4-28 v SL (Colombo, RPS) 2009. **IT20** (P): 35 (2009 to 2017-18); HS 21* v A (Birmingham) 2010; BB 4-13 v SL (Lahore) 2017-18. F-c Tours (P): E 2010, 2016; A 2009-10, 2016-17; NZ 2009-10, 2016-17; WI 2017; SL 2009. HS 66 SSGC v Lahore Blues (Lahore) 2015-16. Ex HS 22* v Somerset (Chelmsford) 2017. 50 wkts (0+1); 56 (2008-09). BB 7-61 (10-97 match) NBP v Lahore Shalimar (Lahore) 2008-09. Ex BB 5-18 (10-72 match) v Yorks (Scarborough) 2017. LO HS 73* (*see LOI*). LO BB 5-36 Sindh v Islamabad (Faisalabad) 2016. T20 HS 21*. T20 BB 4-13.

RELEASED/RETIRED continued on p 109

ESSEX 2017

RESULTS SUMMARY

	Place	Won	Lost	Drew	NR
Specsavers County Champ (1st Division)	**1st**	10		4	
All First-Class Matches		10		6	
Royal London One-Day Cup (South Group)	SF	7	2		
NatWest t20 Blast (South Group)	8th	5	7		2

SPECSAVERS COUNTY CHAMPIONSHIP AVERAGES
BATTING AND FIELDING

Cap		M	I	NO	HS	Runs	Avge	100	50	Ct/St
2005	A.N.Cook	7	10	–	193	667	66.70	3	1	13
2017	D.W.Lawrence	13	21	4	141*	761	44.76	3	3	10
2015	N.L.J.Browne	14	22	–	221	952	43.27	1	5	6
2013	T.Westley	11	15	2	111	561	43.15	2	2	5
2006	R.N.ten Doeschate	13	17	1	168*	659	41.18	1	4	8
2005	R.S.Bopara	14	20	2	192	576	32.00	1	2	7
2001	J.S.Foster	10	12	–	121	357	29.75	1	1	48/1
	V.Chopra	9	14	1	100*	372	28.61	1	1	15
	P.I.Walter	5	5	2	32*	76	25.33	–	–	–
	N.Wagner	10	13	3	50	242	24.20	–	1	4
	A.J.A.Wheater	7	10	–	88	223	22.30	–	2	14/2
	S.R.Harmer	14	18	2	64	260	16.25	–	2	11
	A.P.Beard	3	4	3	4*	11	11.00	–	–	–
2015	J.A.Porter	13	15	8	10*	52	7.42	–	–	1
	S.J.Cook	4	4	3	0*	0	0.00	–	–	–

Also batted: Ashar Zaidi (2 matches) 23, 6 (2 ct); Mohammad Amir (3) 22, 22* (1 ct); M.R.Quinn (3) 15, 4, 0 (1 ct).

BOWLING

	O	M	R	W	Avge	Best	5wI	10wM
Mohammad Amir	76.2	19	189	14	13.50	5-18	2	1
S.J.Cook	99.4	24	286	18	15.88	5-18	2	–
J.A.Porter	399	89	1262	75	16.82	7-55	5	1
S.R.Harmer	521.3	121	1382	72	19.19	9-95	4	2
N.Wagner	316.4	54	1095	31	35.32	6-48	1	–
R.S.Bopara	127.1	12	489	12	40.75	2-10	–	–
Also bowled:								
M.R.Quinn	61.5	13	221	6	36.83	3-66	–	–
A.P.Beard	67	10	241	6	40.16	3-47	–	–

Ashar Zaidi 25-5-43-3; D.W.Lawrence 23-6-71-1; R.N.ten Doeschate 13.1-0-60-3; P.I.Walter 75-19-219-3; T.Westley 21.3-5-72-3.

The First-Class Averages (pp 230–246) give the records of Essex players in all first-class county matches (Essex's other opponents being Durham MCCU and the West Indians), with the exception of A.N.Cook, whose first-class figures for Essex are as above, and:
S.J.Cook 5-5-4-0*-0-0.00-0-0-0ct. 128.4-32-360-19-18.94-5/18-2-0.
D.W.Lawrence 15-24-4-141*-828-41.40-3-3-11ct. 27-8-77-2-38.50-1/6-0-0.
J.A.Porter 14-16-8-10*-53-6.62-0-0-2ct. 425-98-1318-79-16.68-7/55-5-1.
T.Westley 12-17-2-111-595-39.66-2-2-8ct. 24.3-5-78-3-26.00-1/6-0-0.

ESSEX RECORDS

FIRST-CLASS CRICKET

Highest Total	For	761-6d		v	Leics	Chelmsford	1990
	V	803-4d		by	Kent	Brentwood	1934
Lowest Total	For	20		v	Lancashire	Chelmsford	2013
	V	14		by	Surrey	Chelmsford	1983
Highest Innings	For	343*	P.A.Perrin	v	Derbyshire	Chesterfield	1904
	V	332	W.H.Ashdown	for	Kent	Brentwood	1934

Highest Partnership for each Wicket

1st	373	N.L.J.Browne/A.N.Cook	v	Middlesex	Chelmsford	2017
2nd	403	G.A.Gooch/P.J.Prichard	v	Leics	Chelmsford	1990
3rd	347*	M.E.Waugh/N.Hussain	v	Lancashire	Ilford	1992
4th	314	Salim Malik/N.Hussain	v	Surrey	The Oval	1991
5th	339	J.C.Mickleburgh/J.S.Foster	v	Durham	Chester-le-St[2]	2010
6th	253	A.J.A.Wheater/J.S.Foster	v	Northants	Chelmsford	2011
7th	261	J.W.H.T.Douglas/J.Freeman	v	Lancashire	Leyton	1914
8th	263	D.R.Wilcox/R.M.Taylor	v	Warwicks	Southend	1946
9th	251	J.W.H.T.Douglas/S.N.Hare	v	Derbyshire	Leyton	1921
10th	218	F.H.Vigar/T.P.B.Smith	v	Derbyshire	Chesterfield	1947

Best Bowling	For	10- 32	H.Pickett	v	Leics	Leyton	1895
(Innings)	V	10- 40	E.G.Dennett	for	Glos	Bristol	1906
Best Bowling	For	17-119	W.Mead	v	Hampshire	Southampton	1895
(Match)	V	17- 56	C.W.L.Parker	for	Glos	Gloucester	1925

Most Runs – Season	2559	G.A.Gooch	(av 67.34)	1984
Most Runs – Career	30701	G.A.Gooch	(av 51.77)	1973-97
Most 100s – Season	9	J.O'Connor		1929, 1934
	9	D.J.Insole		1955
Most 100s – Career	94	G.A.Gooch		1973-97
Most Wkts – Season	172	T.P.B Smith	(av 27.13)	1947
Most Wkts – Career	1610	T.P.B.Smith	(av 26.68)	1929-51
Most Career W-K Dismissals	1231	B.Taylor	(1040 ct; 191 st)	1949-73
Most Career Catches in the Field	519	K.W.R.Fletcher		1962-88

LIMITED-OVERS CRICKET

Highest Total	50ov	391-5		v	Surrey	The Oval	2008
	40ov	368-7		v	Scotland	Chelmsford	2013
	T20	242-3		v	Sussex	Chelmsford	2008
Lowest Total	50ov	57		v	Lancashire	Lord's	1996
	40ov	69		v	Derbyshire	Chesterfield	1974
	T20	74		v	Middlesex	Chelmsford	2013
Highest Innings	50ov	201*	R.S.Bopara	v	Leics	Leicester	2008
	40ov	180	R.N.ten Doeschate	v	Scotland	Chelmsford	2013
	T20	152*	G.R.Napier	v	Sussex	Chelmsford	2008
Best Bowling	50ov	5- 8	J.K.Lever	v	Middlesex	Westcliff	1972
		5- 8	G.A.Gooch	v	Cheshire	Chester	1995
	40ov	8-26	K.D.Boyce	v	Lancashire	Manchester	1971
	T20	6-16	T.G.Southee	v	Glamorgan	Chelmsford	2011

GLAMORGAN

Formation of Present Club: 6 July 1888
Inaugural First-Class Match: 1921
Colours: Blue and Gold
Badge: Gold Daffodil
County Champions: (3) 1948, 1969, 1997
Pro 40/National League (Div 1) Winners: (2) 2002, 2004
Sunday League Winners: (1) 1993
Twenty20 Cup Winners: (0); best – Semi-Finalist 2004, 2017

GLAMORGAN

Chief Executive: Hugh Morris, The SSE SWALEC, Cardiff, CF11 9XR • Tel: 02920 409380 • Fax: 02920 419389 • email: info@glamorgancricket.co.uk • Web: www.glamorgancricket.com • Twitter: @GlamCricket (44,579 followers)

Head Coach: Robert Croft. **2nd XI Coach**: Steve Watkin. **Player Development Manager**: Richard Almond. **Captain**: M.G.Hogan (f-c) and C.A.Ingram (l-o & T20). **Overseas Player**: S.E.Marsh. **2018 Testimonial**: None. **Head Groundsman**: Robin Saxton. **Scorer**: Andrew K.Hignell. ‡ New registration. ᴺᑫ Not qualified for England.

BROWN, Connor Rhys (Y Pant CS; Cardiff U), b Caerphilly 28 Apr 1997. RHB, OB. Squad No 27. Cardiff MCCU 2017. Glamorgan debut 2017. Glamorgan 2nd XI debut 2014. Wales MC 2014-15. HS 35 v Glos (Cardiff) 2017. BB –.

BULL, Kieran Andrew (Q Elizabeth HS, Haverfordwest; Cardiff Met U), b Haverfordwest 5 Apr 1995. 6'2". RHB, OB. Squad No 11. Debut (Glamorgan) 2014. Cardiff MCCU 2015. Wales MC 2012-13. No 1st XI appearances in 2016 and 2017. HS 31 v Glos (Swansea) 2015. BB 4-62 v Kent (Canterbury) 2014. LO HS –. LO BB 1-40 v Middx (Lord's) 2015 (RLC).

CAREY, Lukas John (Pontarddulais CS; Gower SFC), b Carmarthen 17 Jul 1997. 6'0". RHB, RFM. Squad No 17. Debut (Glamorgan) 2016. Glamorgan 2nd XI debut 2014. Wales MC 2016. HS 54 v Worcs (Worcester) 2017. BB 4-85 v Northants (Northampton) 2017. LO HS 9* v Surrey (Cardiff) 2017 (RLC). LO BB 1-21 v Glos (Bristol) 2017 (RLC). T20 BB 1-19.

CARLSON, Kiran Shah (Whitchurch HS), b Cardiff 16 May 1998. 5'8". RHB, OB. Squad No 5. Glamorgan 2nd XI debut 2015. Wales MC 2014. Debut (Glamorgan) 2016. Glamorgan 2nd XI debut 2014. HS 191 v Glos (Cardiff) 2017. BB 5-28 v Northants (Northampton) 2016 – on debut. Youngest ever to score a century & take five wkts in an innings in a f-c career, aged 18y 119d. LO HS 63 v Somerset (Cardiff) 2017 (RLC). LO BB 1-30 v Middx (Radlett) 2017 (RLC). T20 HS 3.

COOKE, Christopher Barry (Bishops S, Cape Town; U of Cape Town), b Johannesburg, South Africa 30 May 1986. 5'11". RHB, WK. Squad No 46. W Province 2009-10. Glamorgan debut 2013; cap 2016. HS 171 v Kent (Canterbury) 2014. LO HS 137* v Somerset (Taunton) 2012 (CB40). T20 HS 65*.

CULLEN, Thomas Nicholas (Aquinas C, Stockport; Cardiff Met U), b Perth, Australia 4 Jan 1992. RHB, WK. Squad No 54. Cardiff MCCU 2015-17. Glamorgan debut 2017. Leicestershire 2nd XI 2015. HS 42 v Sussex (Colwyn Bay) 2017.

NQDe LANGE, Marchant, b Tzaneen, South Africa 13 Oct 1990. RHB, RF. Squad No 90. Easterns 2010-11 to 2015-16. Titans 2010-11 to 2015-16. Knights 2015-17 to date. Free State 2016-17. Glamorgan debut 2017. IPL: KKR 2012. MI 2014-15. Not overseas due to wife's UK passport. **Tests** (SA): 2 (2011-12); HS 9 and BB 7-81 v SL (Durban) 2011-12 – on debut. **LOI** (SA): 4 (2011-12 to 2015-16); HS – ; BB 4-46 v NZ (Auckland) 2011-12. **IT20** (SA): 6 (2011-12 to 2015-16); HS – : BB 2-26 v WI (Durban) 2014-15. F-c Tours (SA): A 2014 (SA A); NZ 2011-12. HS 65 Knights v Lions (Kimberley) 2016-17. Gm HS 39 v Northants (Cardiff) 2017. BB 7-23 Knights v Titans (Centurion) 2016-17. Gm BB 5-95 v Durham (Chester-le-St) 2017. LO HS 53 Knights v Lions (Kimberley) 2017-18. LO BB 5-49 v Hants (Southampton) 2017 (RLC). T20 HS 27*. T20 BB 4-23.

DONALD, Aneurin Henry Thomas (Pontarddulais CS), b Swansea 20 Dec 1996. 6'2". RHB, OB. Squad No 12. Debut (Glamorgan) 2014. Glamorgan 2nd XI debut 2012, aged 15y 189d. Wales MC 2012. HS 234 v Derbys (Colwyn Bay) 2016, in 123 balls, equalling world record for fastest 200, inc 15 sixes, going from 0-127* between lunch and tea, and 127-234 after tea. LO HS 53 v Sussex (Cardiff) 2016 (RLC). T20 HS 76.

HOGAN, Michael Garry, b Newcastle, New South Wales, Australia 31 May 1981. British passport. 6'5". RHB, RFM. Squad No 31. W Australia 2009-10 to 2015-16. Glamorgan debut/cap 2013; captain 2018. Big Bash: HH 2011-12 to 2012-13. HS 57 v Lancs (Colwyn Bay) 2015. 50 wkts (3); most – 67 (2013). BB 7-92 v Glos (Bristol) 2013. LO HS 27 WA v Vic (Melbourne) 2011-12. LO BB 5-44 WA v Vic (Melbourne) 2010-11. T20 HS 13. T20 BB 5-17.

NQINGRAM, Colin Alexander, b Port Elizabeth, South Africa 3 Jul 1985. LHB, LB. Squad No 41. Free State 2004-05 to 2005-06. Eastern Province 2005-06 to 2008-09. Warriors 2006-07 to 2016-17. Somerset 2014. Glamorgan debut 2015 (Kolpak signing); cap 2017; captain (l-o & 2020) 2018. IPL: DD 2011. Big Bash: AS 2017-18. **LOI** (SA): 31 (2010-11 to 2013-14); HS 124 v Z (Bloemfontein) 2010-11 – on debut; BB – . **IT20** (SA): 9 (2010-11 to 2011-12); HS 78 v I (Johannesburg) 2011-12. HS 190 EP v KZN (Port Elizabeth) 2008-09. Gm HS 155* v Notts (Cardiff) 2017. BB 4-16 EP v Boland (Port Elizabeth) 2005-06. Gm BB 3-90 v Essex (Chelmsford) 2015. LO HS 142 v Essex (Cardiff) 2017 (RLC). LO BB 4-39 v Middx (Radlett) 2017 (RLC). T20 HS 114. T20 BB 4-32.

LAWLOR, Jeremy Lloyd (Monmouth S; Cardiff Met U), b Cardiff 4 Nov 1995. Son of P.J.Lawlor (Glamorgan 1981). 6'0". RHB, RM. Squad No 6. Cardiff MCCU 2015-17. Glamorgan debut 2015. Glamorgan 2nd XI debut 2012. Wales MC 2013. No 1st XI appearances in 2016 and 2017. HS 81 CfU v Hants (Southampton) 2016. Gm HS 0. BB 1-26 CfU v Glamorgan (Cardiff) 2017.

LLOYD, David Liam (Darland HS; Shrewsbury S), b St Asaph, Denbighs 15 May 1992. 5'9". RHB, RM. Squad No 73. Debut (Glamorgan) 2012. Wales MC 2010-11. HS 107 v Kent (Canterbury) 2016. BB 3-36 v Northants (Swansea) 2016. LO HS 65 v Kent (Canterbury) 2016 (RLC). BB 5-53 v Kent (Swansea) 2017 (RLC). T20 HS 97*. T20 BB 2-13.

‡NQMARSH, Shaun Edward, b Narrogin, WA, Australia 9 Jul 1983. Son of G.R.Marsh (WA and Australia 1977-78 to 1993-94) and elder brother of M.R.Marsh (WA and Australia 2009-10 to date). 6'0". LHB, SLA. Squad No 43. Western Australia 2000-01 to date. Yorkshire 2017. IPL: KXIP 2007-08 to 2017. Big Bash: PS 2011-12 to date. **Tests** (A): 29 (2011 to 2017-18); HS 182 v WI (Hobart) 2015-16. **LOI** (A): 53 (2008 to 2016-17); HS 151 v Scotland (Edinburgh) 2013. **IT20** (A): 15 (2008 to 2015-16); HS 47* v SL (Melbourne) 2012-13. F-c Tours (A): E 2015; SA 2011-12, 2013 (Aus A), 2013-14, 2017-18; WI 2015; I 2016-17; SL 2011, 2016. HS 182 (*see Tests*). CC HS 125* Y v Surrey (Oval) 2017. BB 2-20 WA v NSW (Sydney) 2003-04. LO HS 186 WA v Cricket Australia (Sydney) 2015-16. LO BB 1-14 WA v Vic (Perth) 2002-03. T20 HS 115. T20 BB –.

MESCHEDE, Craig Anthony Joseph (King's C, Taunton), b Johannesburg, South Africa 21 Nov 1991. 6'1''. RHB, RMF. Squad No 44. Somerset 2011-14. Glamorgan debut 2015. HS 107 v Northants (Cardiff) 2015. BB 5-84 v Essex (Chelmsford) 2016. LO HS 45 v Hants (Swansea) 2016 (RLC). LO BB 4-5 Sm v Leics (Taunton) 2013 (Y40). T20 HS 53. T20 BB 3-9.

MORGAN, Alan Owen (Ysgol Gyfun yr Strade, Llanelli; Cardiff U), b Swansea 14 Apr 1994. 5'11''. RHB, SLA. Squad No 29. Cardiff MCCU 2014. Glamorgan debut 2016. MCC Univs 2013. Glamorgan 2nd XI debut 2014. Wales MC 2012-16. HS 103* v Worcs (Worcester) 2016. BB 2-37 v Northants (Northampton) 2016. LO HS 29 and LO BB 2-49 v Pakistan A (Newport) 2016.

MURPHY, Jack Roger (Greenhill S, Tenby; Cardiff Met U), b Haverfordwest 15 Jul 1995. 6'7''. LHB, LFM. Squad No 7. Cardiff MCCU 2015. Glamorgan debut 2017. Glamorgan 2nd XI debut 2011. Wales MC 2011-13. HS 27 v Sussex (Colwyn Bay) 2017. BB 2-90 CfU v Glamorgan (Cardiff) 2015. LO HS 6 v Pakistan A (Newport) 2016. LO BB –.

SALTER, Andrew Graham (Milford Haven SFC; Cardiff Met U), b Haverfordwest 1 Jun 1993. 5'9''. RHB, OB. Squad No 21. Cardiff MCCU 2012-14. Glamorgan debut 2013. Glamorgan 2nd XI debut 2010. Wales MC 2010-11. HS 88 v Glos (Cardiff) 2017. BB 3-5 v Northants (Cardiff) 2015. LO HS 51 v Pakistan A (Newport) 2016. LO BB 2-41 v Notts (Nottingham) 2012 (CB40) and 2-41 v Notts (Lord's) 2013 (Y40). T20 HS 37*. T20 BB 2-19.

SELMAN, Nicholas James (Matthew Flinders Anglican C, Buderim), b Brisbane, Australia 18 Oct 1995. 6'4''. RHB, RM. Squad No 9. Debut (Glamorgan) 2016. Kent 2nd XI debut 2014. Gloucestershire 2nd XI 2015. HS 142* v Glos (Cardiff) 2017. BB –. LO HS 6 v Pakistan A (Newport) 2016. T20 HS 66.

[NO]**SMITH, Ruaidhri** Alexander James (Llandaff Cathedral S; Shrewsbury S; Bristol U), b Glasgow, Scotland 5 Aug 1994. 6'1''. RHB, RM. Squad No 20. Debut (Glamorgan) 2013. Scotland 2017. Wales MC 2010-16. Glamorgan 2nd XI debut 2011. **LOI** (Scot): 2 (2016); HS 10 and BB 1-34 v Afghanistan (Edinburgh) 2016. HS 57* v Glos (Bristol) 2014. BB 3-23 v Derbys (Chesterfield) 2015. LO HS 10 (*see LOI*). LO BB 4-76 v Pakistan A (Newport) 2016. T20 HS 16*. T20 BB 1-11.

[NQ]**van der GUGTEN, Timm**, b Hornsby, Sydney, Australia 25 Feb 1991. 6'1½''. RHB, RFM. Squad No 64. New South Wales 2011-12. Netherlands 2012 to date. Glamorgan debut 2016. Big Bash: NH 2014-15. **LOI** (Ne): 4 (2011-12 to 2013); HS 2 (twice); BB 5-24 v Canada (King City, NW) 2013. **IT20** (Ne): 25 (2011-12 to 2016-17); HS 12* v Nepal (Rotterdam) 2015; BB 3-18 v B (The Hague) 2012. HS 57 Neth v Papua New Guinea (Amstelveen) 2015. Gm HS 36 v Derbys (Derby) 2016. 50 wkts (1): 56 (2016). BB 7-68 (10-121 match) Neth v Namibia (Windhoek) 2013. Gm BB 5-52 v Leics (Leicester) 2016. LO HS 36 Neth v Nepal (Amstelveen) 2016; LO BB 5-24 (*see LOI*). T20 HS 16. T20 BB 5-21.

WAGG, Graham Grant (Ashlawn S, Rugby), b Rugby, Warwks 28 Apr 1983. 6'0''. RHB, LM. Squad No 8. Warwickshire 2002-04. Derbyshire 2006-10; cap 2007. Glamorgan debut 2011; cap 2013. F-c Tour (Eng A): I 2003-04. HS 200 v Surrey (Guildford) 2015. 50 wkts (2); most – 59 (2008). BB 6-29 v Surrey (Oval) 2014. LO HS 62* v Essex (Cardiff) 2015 (RLC). LO BB 4-35 De v Durham (Derby) 2008 (FPT). T20 HS 62. T20 BB 5-14 v Worcs (Worcester) 2013 – Gm record.

(Having made a County 1st XI appearance in 2017)

BRAGG, William David (Rougemont S, Newport; UWIC), b Newport, Monmouthshire 24 Oct 1986. 5'9". LHB, RM. Glamorgan 2007-17; cap 2015. Wales MC 2004-09. 1000 runs (3); most – 1126 (2016). HS 161* v Essex (Cardiff) 2016. BB 2-10 v Worcs (Cardiff) 2013. LO HS 94 v Kent (Swansea) 2017 (RLC). LO BB 1-11 v Glos (Cardiff) 2013 (Y40). T20 HS 15.

NQ**MILLER, David** Andrew (Maritzburg C), b Pietermaritzburg, South Africa 10 Jun 1989. 5'11". LHB, OB. Dolphins 2007-08 to 2015-16. KwaZulu-Natal 2008-09 to 2013-14. Knights 2016-17 to date. Yorkshire 2012 (l-o and T20 only). Glamorgan 2017 (T20 only). IPL: KXIP 2012 to date. **LOI** (SA): 105 (2010 to 2017-18); HS 138* v Z (Hamilton) 2014-15. **IT20** (SA): 60 (2010 to 2017-18); HS 101* v B (Potchefstroom) 2017-18. HS 177 Knights v Lions (Kimberley) 2016-17. LO HS 138* (*see LOI*). T20 HS 120*.

NQ**RUDOLPH, Jacobus** Andries ('**Jacques**') (Afrikaanse Hoer Seunskool), b Springs, Transvaal, South Africa 4 May 1981. Elder brother of G.J.Rudolph (Limpopo and Namibia 2006-07 to 2012-13). 5'11". LHB, LBG. Northerns 1997-98 to 2003-04. Titans 2004-05 to 2014-15. Eagles 2005-06 to 2007-08. Yorkshire 2007-11 (Kolpak registration); scored 122 v Surrey (Oval) on debut; cap 2007. Surrey 2012. Glamorgan 2014-17; cap 2014; captain 2015-17. **Tests** (SA): 48 (2003 to 2012-13); HS 222* v B (Chittagong) 2003 – on debut; BB 1-1 v E (Leeds) 2003. **LOI** (SA): 45 (2003 to 2005-06); HS 81 v B (Dhaka) 2003. **IT20** (SA): 1 (2005-06); HS 6* v A (Brisbane) 2005-06. F-c Tours (SA): E 2003, 2012; A 2001-02, 2005-06, 2012-13; WI 2004-05; NZ 2003-04, 2011-12; I 2004-05; SL 2004, 2005-06, 2006; B 2003. 1000 runs (4+1); most – 1375 (2010). HS 228* Y v Durham (Leeds) 2010. Gm HS 142 v Cardiff MCCU (Cardiff) 2017. BB 5-80 Eagles v Cape Cobras (Cape Town) 2007-08. CC BB 1-5 v Glos (Bristol) 2016. LO HS 169* v Sussex (Hove) 2014 (RLC) – Gm record. LO BB 4-41 SA A v New Zealand A (Colombo) 2005-06. T20 HS 101*. T20 BB 3-16.

ESSEX RELEASED/RETIRED (continued from p 103)

NQ**TAMIM IQBAL** Khan, b Chittagong, Bangladesh 20 Mar 1989. Younger brother of Nafees Iqbal (Chittagong and Bangladesh 2000-01 to date). LHB, OB. Chittagong 2004-05 to 2015-16. Essex 2017 (T20 only). *Wisden* 2010. **Tests** (B): 54 (2007-08 to 2017-18); HS 206 v P (Khulna) 2015; BB –. **LOI** (B): 179 (2006-07 to 2017-18); HS 154 v Z (Bulawayo) 2009 – B record; BB –. **IT20** (B): 63 (2007 to 2017-18); HS 103* v Oman (Dharamsala) 2015-16 – B record. F-c Tours (B): E 2008 (B A), 2010; SA 2008-09, 2017-18; WI 2009, 2014; NZ 2007-08, 2009-10, 2016-17; I 2016-17; SL 2012-13, 2016-17; Z 2011, 2013. HS 206 (*see Tests*). BB –. LO HS 157 Mohammedan SC v Kala Bagan Krira Chakra (Savar) 2017. LO BB –. T20 HS 130. T20 BB –.

WALTER, Paul Ian (Billericay S), b Basildon 28 May 1994. LHB, LMF. Essex 2016-17. Essex 2nd XI debut 2015. HS 68* v West Indians (Chelmsford) 2017. CC HS 47 and BB 3-44 v Derbys (Derby) 2016. LO HS 11* v Somerset (Taunton) 2017 (RLC). LO BB 4-37 v Middx (Chelmsford) 2017 (RLC). T20 HS 20*. T20 BB 3-24.

K.S.Velani left the staff without making a County 1st XI appearance in 2017.

GLAMORGAN 2017

RESULTS SUMMARY

	Place	Won	Lost	Drew	NR
Specsavers County Champ (2nd Division)	7th	3	7	4	
All First-Class Matches		3	7	5	
Royal London One-Day Cup (South Group)	4th	4	4		
NatWest t20 Blast (South Group)	SF	8	4		4

SPECSAVERS COUNTY CHAMPIONSHIP AVERAGES

BATTING AND FIELDING

Cap		M	I	NO	HS	Runs	Avge	100	50	Ct/St
2016	C.B.Cooke	12	21	5	113*	695	43.43	1	4	39
	A.G.Salter	12	19	4	88	619	41.26	–	5	5
2017	C.A.Ingram	12	20	2	155*	672	37.33	2	1	5
	N.J.Selman	14	26	2	142*	872	36.33	4	3	15
	C.A.J.Meschede	6	8	–	87	290	36.25	–	1	2
	K.S.Carlson	8	13	–	191	443	34.07	1	1	4
2014	J.A.Rudolph	11	20	1	111	492	25.89	1	1	3
	A.H.T.Donald	11	20	1	66*	487	25.63	–	4	12
	R.A.J.Smith	3	4	–	38	89	22.25	–	–	–
	T.N.Cullen	2	4	–	42	84	21.00	–	–	8/1
	C.R.Brown	2	4	–	35	83	20.75	–	–	–
2013	G.G.Wagg	3	6	1	33*	93	18.60	–	–	2
	L.J.Carey	10	14	2	54	219	18.25	–	1	3
	D.L.Lloyd	8	15	1	88	247	17.64	–	1	4
	J.R.Murphy	4	6	–	27	97	16.16	–	–	1
	M.de Lange	11	17	1	39	254	15.87	–	–	5
2013	M.G.Hogan	12	17	10	29*	100	14.28	–	–	4
2015	W.D.Bragg	3	6	1	30	65	13.00	–	–	2
	T.van der Gugten	5	7	–	21	64	9.14	–	–	–
	H.W.Podmore	2	4	1	10	21	7.00	–	–	1
	A.O.Morgan	3	6	–	17	28	4.66	–	–	1

BOWLING

	O	M	R	W	Avge	Best	5wI	10wM
M.G.Hogan	370.4	84	1044	50	20.88	6- 43	3	1
T.van der Gugten	158.2	43	505	22	22.95	5-101	1	–
L.J.Carey	271.3	49	1051	35	30.02	4- 85	–	–
C.A.J.Meschede	126	18	450	13	34.61	4- 61	–	–
M.de Lange	345.5	41	1315	34	38.67	5- 95	1	–
A.G.Salter	155.4	12	646	14	46.14	3- 60	–	–
Also bowled:								
G.G.Wagg	60	10	206	7	29.42	2- 14	–	–
R.A.J.Smith	69.4	6	302	9	33.55	3- 64	–	–

C.R.Brown 4-0-14-0; C.A.Ingram 37.1-0-155-2; D.L.Lloyd 69.7-320-4; H.W.Podmore 28.1-3-124-3.

The First-Class Averages (pp 230–246) give the records of Glamorgan players in all first-class county matches (Glamorgan's other opponents being Cardiff MCCU), with the exception of C.R.Brown, T.N.Cullen and H.W.Podmore, whose first-class figures for Glamorgan are as above.

GLAMORGAN RECORDS

FIRST-CLASS CRICKET

Highest Total	For 718-3d		v	Sussex	Colwyn Bay	2000
	V 712		by	Northants	Northampton	1998
Lowest Total	For 22		v	Lancashire	Liverpool	1924
	V 33		by	Leics	Ebbw Vale	1965
Highest Innings	For 309*	S.P.James	v	Sussex	Colwyn Bay	2000
	V 322*	M.B.Loye	for	Northants	Northampton	1998

Highest Partnership for each Wicket

1st	374	M.T.G.Elliott/S.P.James	v	Sussex	Colwyn Bay	2000
2nd	252	M.P.Maynard/D.L.Hemp	v	Northants	Cardiff	2002
3rd	313	D.E.Davies/W.E.Jones	v	Essex	Brentwood	1948
4th	425*	A.Dale/I.V.A.Richards	v	Middlesex	Cardiff	1993
5th	264	M.Robinson/S.W.Montgomery	v	Hampshire	Bournemouth	1949
6th	240	J.Allenby/M.A.Wallace	v	Surrey	The Oval	2009
7th	211	P.A.Cottey/O.D.Gibson	v	Leics	Swansea	1996
8th	202	D.Davies/J.J.Hills	v	Sussex	Eastbourne	1928
9th	203*	J.J.Hills/J.C.Clay	v	Worcs	Swansea	1929
10th	143	T.Davies/S.A.B.Daniels	v	Glos	Swansea	1982

Best Bowling	For	10- 51	J.Mercer	v	Worcs	Worcester	1936
(Innings)	V	10- 18	G.Geary	for	Leics	Pontypridd	1929
Best Bowling	For	17-212	J.C.Clay	v	Worcs	Swansea	1937
(Match)	V	16- 96	G.Geary	for	Leics	Pontypridd	1929

Most Runs – Season		2276	H.Morris	(av 55.51)	1990
Most Runs – Career		34056	A.Jones	(av 33.03)	1957-83
Most 100s – Season		10	H.Morris		1990
Most 100s – Career		54	M.P.Maynard		1985-2005
Most Wkts – Season		176	J.C.Clay	(av 17.34)	1937
Most Wkts – Career		2174	D.J.Shepherd	(av 20.95)	1950-72
Most Career W-K Dismissals		933	E.W.Jones	(840 ct; 93 st)	1961-83
Most Career Catches in the Field		656	P.M.Walker		1956-72

LIMITED-OVERS CRICKET

Highest Total	50ov	429		v	Surrey	The Oval	2002
	40ov	328-4		v	Lancashire	Colwyn Bay	2011
	T20	240-3		v	Surrey	The Oval	2015
Lowest Total	50ov	68		v	Lancashire	Manchester	1973
	40ov	42		v	Derbyshire	Swansea	1979
	T20	90		v	Yorkshire	Cardiff	2016
Highest Innings	50ov	169*	J.A.Rudolph	v	Sussex	Hove	2014
	40ov	155*	J.H.Kallis	v	Surrey	Pontypridd	1999
	T20	116*	I.J.Thomas	v	Somerset	Taunton	2004
Best Bowling	50ov	6-20	S.D.Thomas	v	Comb Univs	Cardiff	1995
	40ov	7-16	S.D.Thomas	v	Surrey	Swansea	1998
	T20	5-14	G.G.Wagg	v	Worcs	Worcester	2013

GLOUCESTERSHIRE

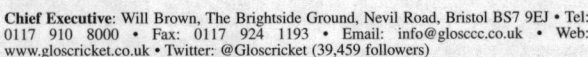

Formation of Present Club: 1871
Inaugural First-Class Match: 1870
Colours: Blue, Gold, Brown, Silver, Green and Red
Badge: Coat of Arms of the City and County of Bristol
County Champions (since 1890): (0); best – 2nd 1930, 1931,
1947, 1959, 1969, 1986
Gillette/NatWest/C&G Trophy Winners: (5) 1973, 1999,
2000, 2003, 2004
Benson and Hedges Cup Winners: (3) 1977, 1999, 2000
Pro 40/National League (Div 1) Winners: (1) 2000
Royal London One-Day Cup Winners: (1) 2015
Twenty20 Cup Winners: (0); best – Finalist 2007

Chief Executive: Will Brown, The Brightside Ground, Nevil Road, Bristol BS7 9EJ • Tel:
0117 910 8000 • Fax: 0117 924 1193 • Email: info@glosccc.co.uk • Web:
www.gloscricket.co.uk • Twitter: @Gloscricket (39,459 followers)

Head Coach: Richard Dawson. **Asst Head Coach**: Ian Harvey. **Captains**: C.D.J.Dent (f-c
& l-o) and M.Klinger (T20). **Overseas Players**: M.Klinger, A.J.Tye (T20 only) and
D.J.Worrall. **2018 Testimonial**: None. **Head Groundsman**: Sean Williams. **Scorer**: Adrian
Bull. ‡ New registration. NQ Not qualified for England.

*Gloucestershire revised their capping policy in 2004 and now award players with their
County Caps when they make their first-class debut.*

BRACEY, James Robert (Filton CS), b Bristol 3 May 1997. Younger brother of S.N.Bracey
(Cardiff MCCU 2014-15). 6'1". LHB, WK. Debut (Gloucestershire) 2016; cap 2016.
Loughborough MCCU 2017. Gloucestershire 2nd XI debut 2015. HS 156 v Glamorgan
(Cardiff) 2017.

COCKBAIN, Ian Andrew (Maghull HS), b Bootle, Liverpool 17 Feb 1987. Son of
I.Cockbain (Lancs and Minor Cos 1979-94). 6'0". RHB, RM. Squad No 28. Debut
(Gloucestershire) 2011; cap 2011. MCC YC 2008-10. HS 151* v Surrey (Bristol) 2014. BB
1-23 v Durham MCCU (Bristol) 2016. LO HS 108* v Middx (Lord's) 2017 (RLC). T20 HS
91*.

CURRILL, Oliver Charles (Chipping Camden Academy), b Banbury, Oxon 27 Feb 1997.
6'4". RHB, RMF. Debut (Gloucestershire) 2017; cap 2017. Gloucestershire 2nd XI debut
2015. BB –.

DENT, Christopher David James (Backwell CS; Alton C), b Bristol 20 Jan 1991. 5'9".
LHB, WK, occ SLA. Squad No 15. Debut (Gloucestershire) 2010; cap 2010; captain 2018.
1000 runs (3); most – 1336 (2016). HS 268 v Glamorgan (Bristol) 2016. BB 2-21 v Sussex
(Hove) 2016. LO HS 151* v Glamorgan (Cardiff) 2013 (Y40). LO BB 4-43 v Leics (Bristol)
2012 (CB40). T20 HS 63*. T20 BB 1-4.

DRISSELL, George Samuel (Bedminster Down SS; Filton C), b Bristol 20 Jan 1999. RHB,
OB. Debut (Gloucestershire) 2017. Gloucestershire 2nd XI debut 2016. HS 0 and BB– v
Northants (Northampton) 2017 – only 1st XI appearance.

HAMMOND, Miles Arthur Halhead (St Edward's S, Oxford), b Cheltenham 11 Jan 1996. 5'11". LHB, OB. Squad No 88. Debut (Gloucestershire) 2013; cap 2013. England U19 2012-13. Gloucestershire 2nd XI debut 2010, aged 14y 120d. No 1st XI appearances 2016-17. HS 30 v Glamorgan (Swansea) 2015. BB 1-96 v Glamorgan (Bristol) 2013. LO HS 0. LO BB 2-18 v Northants (Northampton) 2015 (RLC). T20 HS and BB –.

HANKINS, George Thomas (Millfield S), b Bath, Somerset 4 Jan 1997. 6'1½". RHB, OB. Squad No 21. Debut (Gloucestershire) 2016; cap 2016. Gloucestershire 2nd XI debut 2014. England U19 2016. HS 116 v Northants (Northampton) 2016. BB –. LO HS 67 v Sussex (Eastbourne) 2017 (RLC). T20 HS 14.

‡HIGGINS, Ryan Francis (Bradfield C), b Harare, Zimbabwe 6 Jan 1995. 5'10". RHB, OB. Squad No 29. Middlesex 2018. Joins Gloucestershire in 2018. Middlesex 2nd XI debut 2012. HS 45 M v Warwks (Birmingham) 2017. BB 4-75 M v Warwks (Lord's) 2017. LO HS 48* M v Sussex (Lord's) 2017 (RLC). LO BB 3-32 M v Glamorgan (Radlett) 2017 (RLC). T20 HS 68*. T20 BB 5-13.

HOWELL, Benny Alexander Cameron (The Oratory S), b Bordeaux, France 5 Oct 1988. Son of J.B.Howell (Warwickshire 2nd XI 1978). 5'11". RHB, RM. Squad No 13. Hampshire 2011. Gloucestershire debut/cap 2012. Berkshire 2007. HS 163 v Glamorgan (Cardiff) 2017. BB 5-57 v Leics (Leicester) 2013. LO HS 122 v Surrey (Croydon) 2011 (CB40). LO BB 3-37 v Yorks (Leeds) 2015 (RLC). T20 HS 57. T20 BB 4-26.

NQKLINGER, Michael (Scopus Memorial C, Kew), b Kew, Melbourne, Australia 4 Jul 1980. 5'10½". RHB. Squad No 2. Victoria 1999-00 to 2007-08. S Australia 2008-09 to 2013-14. Worcestershire 2012; cap 2012. Gloucestershire debut/cap 2013; captain 2013-15; l-o captain 2016 to date. W Australia 2014-15 to 2016-17. Big Bash: AS 2011-12 to 2013-14. PS 2014-15 to date. IT20 (A): 3 (2016-17); HS 62 v SL (Adelaide) 2016-17. 1000 runs (1+2); most – 1203 (2008-09). HS 255 S Aus v WA (Adelaide) 2008-09. Gs HS 163 v Hants (Bristol) 2013. LO HS 166* v Hants (Bristol) 2016 (RLC). T20 HS 126* v Essex (Bristol) 2015 – Gs record.

LIDDLE, Christopher John (Nunthorpe CS; Teesside Tertiary C), b Middlesbrough, Yorks 1 Feb 1984. 6'5". RHB, LFM. Squad No 23. Leicestershire 2005-06. Sussex 2007-15. Gloucestershire debut/cap 2017. HS 53 Sx v Worcs (Hove) 2007. Gs HS 21 v Durham (Bristol) 2017. BB 3-42 Le v Somerset (Leicester) 2006. Gs BB 2-30 v Durham MCCU (Bristol) 2017. LO HS 18 Sx v Warwks (Rugby) 2015 (RLC). LO BB 5-18 Sx v Netherlands (Amstelveen) 2011 (CB40). T20 HS 16. T20 BB 5-17.

MILES, Craig Neil (Bradon Forest S, Swindon; Filton C, Bristol), b Swindon, Wilts 20 July 1994. Brother of A.J.Miles (Cardiff MCCU 2012). 6'4". RHB, RMF. Squad No 34. Debut (Gloucestershire) 2011; cap 2011. Gloucestershire 2nd XI debut 2009, aged 14y 318d. HS 62* v Worcs (Cheltenham) 2014. 50 wkts (2); most – 57 (2016). BB 6-63 v Northants (Northampton) 2015. Hat-trick v Essex (Cheltenham) 2016. LO HS 16 v Somerset (Taunton) 2016 (RLC). LO BB 4-29 v Yorks (Scarborough) 2015 (RLC). T20 HS 8. T20 BB 3-25.

MUSTARD, Philip (Usworth CS), b Sunderland, Co Durham 8 Oct 1982. Cousin of C.Rushworth (see DURHAM). 5'11". LHB, WK. Squad No 19. Durham 2002-16; captain 2010 (part) to 2012 (part). Mountaineers 2011-12. Auckland 2012-13. Lancashire 2015 (on loan). Gloucestershire debut/cap 2016. LOI: 10 (2007-08); HS 83 v NZ (Napier) 2007-08. IT20: 2 (2007-08); HS 40 v NZ (Christchurch) 2007-08. HS 130 Du v Kent (Canterbury) 2006. Gs HS 107* v Derbys (Derby) 2016. BB 1-9 Du v Sussex (Hove) 2013. LO HS 143 Du v Surrey (Chester-le-St) 2012 (CB40). T20 HS 97*.

NQNOEMA-BARNETT, Kieran, b Dunedin, New Zealand 4 Jun 1987. 6'1". LHB, RM. Squad No 11. Central Districts 2008-09 to 2016-17. Gloucestershire debut/cap 2015. HS 107 CD v Auckland (Auckland) 2011-12. Gs HS 84 v Worcs (Bristol) 2016. BB 4-20 CD v Otago (Dunedin) 2010-11. Gs BB 4-31 v Worcs (Cheltenham) 2017. LO HS 74 CD v ND (New Plymouth) 2016-17. LO BB 3-42 CD v Auckland (Auckland) 2013-14. T20 HS 57*. T20 BB 2-13.

NORWELL, Liam Connor (Redruth SS), b Bournemouth, Dorset 27 Dec 1991. 6'3". RHB, RMF. Squad No 24. Debut (Gloucestershire) 2011, taking 6-46 v Derbys (Bristol); cap 2011. HS 102 v Derbys (Bristol) 2016. 50 wkts (2); most – 68 (2015). BB 8-43 (10-95 match) v Leics (Leicester) 2017. LO HS 16 v Somerset (Bristol) 2017 (RLC). LO BB 6-52 v Leics (Leicester) 2012 (CB40). T20 HS 2*. T20 BB 3-27.

PAYNE, David Alan (Lytchett Minster S), b Poole, Dorset, 15 Feb 1991. 6'2". RHB, LMF. Squad No 14. Debut (Gloucestershire) 2011; cap 2011. Dorset 2009. HS 67* v Glamorgan (Cardiff) 2016. BB 6-26 v Leics (Bristol) 2011. LO HS 23 v Kent (Canterbury) 2016 (RLC). LO BB 7-29 v Essex (Chelmsford) 2010 (CB40), inc 4 wkts in 4 balls and 6 wkts in 9 balls – Gs record. T20 HS 10. T20 BB 5-24 v Middx (Richmond) 2015 – Gs record.

NQRODERICK, Gareth Hugh (Maritzburg C), b Durban, South Africa 29 Aug 1991. 6'0". RHB, WK. Squad No 27. UK passport. KZN 2010-11 to 2011-12. Gloucestershire debut/cap 2013; captain 2016-17. HS 171 v Leics (Bristol) 2014. LO HS 104 v Leics (Leicester) 2015 (RLC). T20 HS 32.

SMITH, Thomas Michael John (Seaford Head Community C; Sussex Downs C), b Eastbourne, Sussex 29 Aug 1987. 5'9". RHB, SLA. Squad No 6. Sussex 2007-09. Surrey 2009 (l-o only). Middlesex 2010-13. Gloucestershire debut/cap 2013. HS 80 v Surrey (Bristol) 2014. BB 4-35 v Kent (Canterbury) 2014. LO HS 65 Sy v Leics (Leicester) 2009 (P40). LO BB 4-26 v Sussex (Cheltenham) 2016 (RLC). T20 HS 36*. T20 BB 5-24.

TAVARÉ, William Andrew (Bristol GS; Loughborough U), b Bristol 1 Jan 1990. Nephew of C.J.Tavaré (Kent, Somerset & England 1974-93). 6'0". RHB, RM. Squad No 4. Loughborough MCCU 2010-12. Gloucestershire debut/cap 2014. 1000 runs (1): 1014 (2014). HS 139 v Hants (Bristol) 2014 – on CC debut. BB –. LO HS 77 v Hants (Bristol) 2014 (RLC) – on l-o debut.

TAYLOR, Jack Martin Robert (Chipping Norton S), b Banbury, Oxfordshire 12 Nov 1991. Elder brother of M.D.Taylor (*see below*). 5'11". RHB, OB. Squad No 10. Debut (Gloucestershire) 2010; cap 2010. Oxfordshire 2009-11. HS 156 v Northants (Cheltenham) 2015. BB 4-16 v Glamorgan (Bristol) 2016. LO HS 68 v Somerset (Bristol) 2017 (RLC). LO BB 4-38 v Hants (Bristol) 2014 (RLC). T20 HS 80. T20 BB 4-16.

TAYLOR, Matthew David (Chipping Norton S), b Banbury, Oxfordshire 8 Jul 1994. Younger brother of J.M.R.Taylor (*see above*). 6'0". RHB, LM. Squad No 36. Debut (Gloucestershire) 2013; cap 2013. Gloucestershire 2nd XI debut 2011. Oxfordshire 2011-12. HS 36 v Kent (Canterbury) 2017. BB 5-75 v Hants (Bristol) 2014. LO HS 16 v Kent (Canterbury) 2016 (RLC). LO BB 3-48 v Somerset (Bristol) 2017 (RLC). T20 HS 9*. T20 BB 3-16.

NQTYE, Andrew James (Padbury Senior HS, WA), b Perth, Australia 12 Dec 1986. 6'4". RHB, RMF. Squad No 68. W Australia 2014-15 to date. Gloucestershire debut 2016 (T20 only). IPL: GL 2017. Big Bash: ST 2013-14. PS 2014-15 to date. **LOI** (A): 4 (2017-18); HS 8 and BB 5-46 v E (Perth) 2017-18. **IT20** (A): 12 (2015-16 to 2017-18); HS 4 v I (Melbourne) 2015-16; BB 4-23 v NZ (Sydney) 2017-18. HS 10 WA v Tas (Hobart) 2014-15. BB 3-47 WA v Q (Brisbane) 2014-15. LO HS 28* WA v NSW (Sydney) 2013-14. LO BB 5-46 WA v Tas (Sydney) 2013-14. T20 HS 42. T20 BB 5-17.

[NQ]**van BUUREN, Graeme** Lourens, b Pretoria, South Africa 22 Aug 1990. 5'6". RHB, SLA. Squad No 12. Northerns 2009-10 to 2015-16. Titans 2012-13 to 2014-15. Gloucestershire (Centurion) 2014-15. Gs HS 172* v Worcs (Worcester) 2016. BB 4-12 Northerns v SW Districts (Oudtshoorn) 2012-13. Gs BB 4-18 v Durham MCCU (Bristol) 2017. CC BB 3-15 v Glamorgan (Bristol) 2016. LO HS 119* Northerns v EP (Pt Elizabeth, Grey HS) 2013-14. LO BB 5-35 Northerns v SW Districts (Pretoria) 2011-12. T20 HS 64. T20 BB 5-8.

[NQ]**WORRALL, Daniel** James (Kardina International C; U of Melbourne), b Melbourne, Australia 10 Jul 1991. RHB, RFM. S Australia 2012-13 to date. Joins Gloucestershire for first part off the season. Big Bash: MS 2013-14 to date. LOI (A): 3 (2016-17); HS 6* v SA (Centurion) 2016-17; BB 1-43 v SA (Benoni) 2016-17. HS 26 S Aus v Tas (Adelaide) 2016-17. BB 6-96 S Aus v Vic (Adelaide) 2015-16. LO HS 16 SS Aus v Tas (N Sydney) 2017-18. LO BB 5-62 S Aus v Vic (Hobart) 2017-18.

RELEASED/RETIRED

(Having made a County 1st XI appearance in 2017)

BANCROFT, C.T. – see SOMERSET.

GILMOUR, Brandon Stuart (Park House S), b Bulawayo, Zimbabwe 11 Apr 1996. 5'10". LHB, RM. Gloucestershire 2nd XI debut 2014. Awaiting 1st XI debut.

[NQ]**PERERA**, Narangoda Liyanaarachchilage **Thisara** Chirantha (St Joseph's C, Maradana), b Colombo, Sri Lanka 3 Apr 1989. 6'1". LHB, RMF. Colts CC 2008-09 to 2013-14. Wayamba 2008-09. Gloucestershire 2017 (T20 only). IPL: CSK 2009-10. MI 2012. SH 2013. KXIP 2015. RPS 2016. Big Bash: BH 2012-13. MR 2016-17. **Tests** (SL): 6 (2011 to 2012); HS 75 and BB 4-63 v P (Pallekele) 2012. **LOI** (SL): 133 (2009-10 to 2017-18); HS 80* v B (Dhaka) 2013-14; BB 6-44 v P (Pallekele) 2012. **IT20** (SL): 71 (2010 to 2017-18); HS 49 v E (Oval) 2014; BB 3-24 v P (Abu Dhabi) 2017-18. F-c Tours (SL): E 2011; SA 2011-12. HS 113* and BB 5-69 CCC v Moors (Colombo, CCC) 2009-10. LO HS 80* (see LOI). LO BB 6-44 (see LOI). T20 HS 84. T20 BB 5-26.

B.S.Gilmour and P.J.Grieshaber left the staff without making a County 1st XI appearance in 2017.

GLOUCESTERSHIRE 2017

RESULTS SUMMARY

	Place	Won	Lost	Drew	Tied	NR
Specsavers County Champ (2nd Division)	6th	3	4	7		
All First-Class Matches		3	4	8		
Royal London One-Day Cup (South Group)	7th	3	4			1
NatWest t20 Blast (South Group)	9th	4	6		1	3

SPECSAVERS COUNTY CHAMPIONSHIP AVERAGES
BATTING AND FIELDING

Cap†		M	I	NO	HS	Runs	Avge	100	50	Ct/St
2016	J.R.Bracey	4	6	1	156	370	74.00	1	2	6
2010	C.D.J.Dent	13	24	3	135*	894	42.57	2	7	12
2016	C.T.Bancroft	11	21	4	206*	685	40.29	1	4	14
2010	J.M.R.Taylor	14	20	3	143	645	39.11	2	2	10
2013	G.H.Roderick	8	12	1	96	400	36.36	–	4	23/1
2011	D.A.Payne	10	11	5	54*	203	33.83	–	1	1
2016	P.Mustard	14	20	–	72	573	28.65	–	3	21
2014	W.A.Tavaré	10	17	1	101	422	26.37	1	2	6
2016	G.T.Hankins	11	17	1	79*	387	24.18	–	3	20
2015	K.Noema-Barnett	11	14	1	59	291	22.38	–	1	6
2016	G.L.van Buuren	7	12	1	88*	233	21.18	–	2	3
2013	M.D.Taylor	5	7	3	36	55	13.75	–	–	–
2017	C.J.Liddle	5	7	3	21	54	13.50	–	–	1
2011	L.C.Norwell	11	13	5	24	99	12.37	–	–	4
2011	C.N.Miles	10	13	1	47	137	11.41	–	–	2
2016	J.Shaw	4	5	–	13	23	4.60	–	–	–

Also batted: I.A.Cockbain (1 match – cap 2011) 27; G.S.Drissell (1 – cap 2017) 0; B.A.C.Howell (2 – cap 2012) 163, 36, 5; T.M.J.Smith (2 – cap 2013) 8, 9, 14*.

BOWLING

	O	M	R	W	Avge	Best	5wI	10wM
L.C.Norwell	321	66	1026	59	17.38	8- 43	5	2
K.Noema-Barnett	254.4	59	737	23	32.04	4- 31	–	–
D.A.Payne	259.1	49	816	25	32.64	3- 37	–	–
C.N.Miles	245	35	974	27	36.07	5- 99	1	–
J.Shaw	101.5	15	443	11	40.27	5-118	1	–
J.M.R.Taylor	146.2	15	619	13	47.61	3- 50	–	–
M.D.Taylor	127	19	492	10	49.20	3- 80	–	–

Also bowled:

T.N.J.Smith	70.4	7	263	9	29.22	3- 73	–	–
C.J.Liddle	119.1	23	438	8	54.75	2- 46	–	–
G.L.van Buuren	114.3	23	342	5	68.40	2- 28	–	–

C.T.Bancroft 7-0-67-1; C.D.J.Dent 16.4-0-130-1; G.S.Drissell 12-0-58-0; G.T.Hankins 2.1-0-13-0; B.A.C.Howell 21-2-82-1; P.Mustard 20-2-141-0; W.A.Tavaré 8-1-52-0.

The First-Class Averages (pp 230–246) give the records of Gloucestershire players in all first-class county matches (Gloucestershire's other opponents being Durham MCCU), with the exception of J.R.Bracey and J.Shaw, whose first-class figures for Gloucestershire are as above.

† Gloucestershire revised their capping policy in 2004 and now award players with their County Caps when they make their first-class debut.

GLOUCESTERSHIRE RECORDS

FIRST-CLASS CRICKET

Highest Total	For	695-9d		v	Middlesex	Gloucester	2004
	V	774-7d		by	Australians	Bristol	1948
Lowest Total	For	17		v	Australians	Cheltenham	1896
	V	12		by	Northants	Gloucester	1907
Highest Innings	For	341	C.M.Spearman	v	Middlesex	Gloucester	2004
	V	319	C.J.L.Rogers	for	Northants	Northampton	2006

Highest Partnership for each Wicket

1st	395	D.M.Young/R.B.Nicholls	v	Oxford U	Oxford	1962
2nd	256	C.T.M.Pugh/T.W.Graveney	v	Derbyshire	Chesterfield	1960
3rd	392	G.H.Roderick/A.P.R.Gidman	v	Leics	Bristol	2014
4th	321	W.R.Hammond/W.L.Neale	v	Leics	Gloucester	1937
5th	261	W.G.Grace/W.O.Moberley	v	Yorkshire	Cheltenham	1876
6th	320	G.L.Jessop/J.H.Board	v	Sussex	Hove	1903
7th	248	W.G.Grace/E.L.Thomas	v	Sussex	Hove	1896
8th	239	W.R.Hammond/A.E.Wilson	v	Lancashire	Bristol	1938
9th	193	W.G.Grace/S.A.P.Kitcat	v	Sussex	Bristol	1896
10th	137	C.N.Miles/L.C.Norwell	v	Worcs	Cheltenham	2014

Best Bowling	For	10-40	E.G.Dennett	v	Essex	Bristol	1906
(Innings)	V	10-66	A.A.Mailey	for	Australians	Cheltenham	1921
		10-66	K.Smales	for	Notts	Stroud	1956
Best Bowling	For	17-56	C.W.L.Parker	v	Essex	Gloucester	1925
(Match)	V	15-87	A.J.Conway	for	Worcs	Moreton-in-M	1914

Most Runs – Season	2860	W.R.Hammond	(av 69.75)	1933
Most Runs – Career	33664	W.R.Hammond	(av 57.05)	1920-51
Most 100s – Season	13	W.R.Hammond		1938
Most 100s – Career	113	W.R.Hammond		1920-51
Most Wkts – Season	222	T.W.J.Goddard	(av 16.80)	1937
	222	T.W.J.Goddard	(av 16.37)	1947
Most Wkts – Career	3170	C.W.L.Parker	(av 19.43)	1903-35
Most Career W-K Dismissals	1054	R.C.Russell	(950 ct; 104 st)	1981-2004
Most Career Catches in the Field	719	C.A.Milton		1948-74

LIMITED-OVERS CRICKET

Highest Total	50ov	401-7		v	Bucks	Wing	2003
	40ov	344-6		v	Northants	Cheltenham	2001
	T20	254-3		v	Middlesex	Uxbridge	2011
Lowest Total	50ov	82		v	Notts	Bristol	1987
	40ov	49		v	Middlesex	Bristol	1978
	T20	68		v	Hampshire	Bristol	2010
Highest Innings	50ov	177	A.J.Wright	v	Scotland	Bristol	1997
	40ov	153	C.M.Spearman	v	Warwicks	Gloucester	2003
	T20	126*	M.Klinger	v	Essex	Bristol	2015
Best Bowling	50ov	6-13	M.J.Proctor	v	Hampshire	Southampton	1977
	40ov	7-29	D.A.Payne	v	Essex	Chelmsford	2010
	T20	5-24	D.A.Payne	v	Middlesex	Richmond	2015

HAMPSHIRE

HAMPSHIRE
CRICKET

Formation of Present Club: 12 August 1863
Inaugural First-Class Match: 1864
Colours: Blue, Gold and White
Badge: Tudor Rose and Crown
County Champions: (2) 1961, 1973
NatWest/C&G/FP Trophy Winners: (3) 1991, 2005, 2009
Benson and Hedges Cup Winners: (2) 1988, 1992
Sunday League Winners: (3) 1975, 1978, 1986
Clydesdale Bank Winners: (1) 2012
Twenty20 Cup Winners: (2) 2010, 2012

Chairman: David Mann, The Ageas Bowl, Botley Road, West End, Southampton SO30 3XH • Tel: 023 8047 2002 • Fax: 023 8047 2122 • Email: enquiries@ageasbowl.com • Web: www.ageasbowl.com • Twitter: @hantscricket (53,195 followers)

CEO: David Mann. **Cricket Operations Manager**: Tim Tremlett. **Director of Cricket**: Giles White. **1st XI Coach**: Craig White. **Batting Coach**: Tony Middleton. **Captain**: J.M.Vince. **Overseas Player**: H.M.Amla. **2018 Testimonial**: None. **Head Groundsman**: Karl McDermott. **Scorer**: Kevin Baker. ‡ New registration. [NQ] Not qualified for England.

[NQ]**ABBOTT, Kyle John**, b Empangeni, South Africa 18 Jun 1987. RHB, RFM. Squad No 87. KwaZulu-Natal 2008-09 to 2009-10. Dolphins 2008-09 to 2014-15. Hampshire debut 2014; cap 2017 (Kolpak signing). Worcestershire 2016. IPL: KXIP 2016. **Tests** (SA): 11 (2012-13 to 2016-17; HS 17 v A (Adelaide) 2016-17; BB 7-29 v P (Centurion) 2012-13. **LOI** (SA): 28 (2012-13 to 2016-17); HS 23 v Z (Bulawayo) 2014; BB 4-21 v Ireland (Canberra) 2014-15. **IT20** (SA): 21 (2012-13 to 2015-16); HS 9* v NZ (Centurion) 2015; BB 3-20 v B (Dhaka) 2015. F-c Tours (SA): A 2016-17; I 2015-16. HS 97* v Lancs (Manchester) 2017. 50 wkts (1+1): 65 (2012-13). BB 8-45 (12-96 match) Dolphins v Cobras (Cape Town) 2012-13. H BB 7-41 v Yorks (Leeds) 2017. LO HS 56 v Surrey (Oval) 2017 (RLC). LO BB 4-21 (*see LOI*). T20 HS 16*. T20 BB 5-14.

ADAMS, James Henry Kenneth (Sherborne S; University C, London; Loughborough U), b Winchester 23 Sep 1980. 6'2". LHB, LM. Squad No 4. British U 2002-04. Hampshire debut 2002; cap 2006; captain 2012-15; benefit 2015. Loughborough UCCE 2003-04 – scoring 107 v Somerset (Taunton) on debut. MCC 2013. Dorset 1998. F-c Tour (EL): WI 2010-11. 1000 runs (5); most – 1351 (2009). HS 262* v Notts (Nottingham) 2006. BB 2-16 v Durham (Chester-le-St) 2004. LO HS 131 v Warwks (Birmingham) 2010 (CB40). LO BB 1-34 v Essex (Chelmsford) 2007 (FPT). T20 HS 101*. T20 BB –.

ALSOP, Thomas Philip (Lavington S), b High Wycombe, Bucks 26 Nov 1995. Younger brother of O.J.Alsop (Wiltshire 2010-12). 5'11". LHB, WK, occ SLA. Squad No 9. Debut (Hampshire) 2014. England Lions 2016-17. MCC 2017. Hampshire 2nd XI debut 2013. England U19 2014 to 2015. No 1st XI appearances in 2015. HS 117 v Surrey (The Oval) 2016. LO HS 116 v Surrey (Southampton) 2016 (RLC). T20 HS 85.

‡**NQAMLA, Hashim** Mahomed, b Durban, South Africa 31 Mar 1983. Younger brother of A.M.Amla (Natal B, KZN, Dolphins 1997-98 to 2012-13). RHB, RM/OB. Squad No 1. KZN 1999-00 to 2003-04. Dolphins 2004-05 to 2011-12. Essex 2009. Nottinghamshire 2010; cap 2010. Surrey 2013-14. Derbyshire 2015. Cape Cobras 2015-16 to date. Joins Hampshire for the first part of 2018. IPL: KXIP 2016 to date. *Wisden* 2012. **Tests** (SA): 114 (2004-05 to 2017-18, 14 as captain); 1000 runs (3); most – 1249 (2010); HS 311* v E (Oval) 2012; BB –. **LOI** (SA): 164 (2007-08 to 2017-18, 9 as captain); 1000 runs (2); most – 1062 (2015); HS 159 v Ireland (Canberra) 2014-15. **IT20** (SA): 43 (2008-09 to 2017-18, 2 as captain); HS 97* v A (Cape Town) 2015-16. F-c Tours (SA) (C=Captain): E 2008, 2012, 2017; A 2008-09, 2012-13, 2016-17; WI 2010; NZ 2011-12, 2016-17; I 2004-05, 2007-08 (SA A), 2007-08, 2009-10, 2015-16C; P 2007-08; SL 2005-06 (SA A), 2006, 2014C; Z 2004 (SA A), 2007 (SA A), 2014C; B 2007-08, 2015C; UAE 2010-11, 2013-14 (v P). 1000 runs (0+2); most – 1126 (2005-06). HS 311* *(see Tests)*. CC HS 181 Ex v Glamorgan (Chelmsford) 2009 – on debut. BB 1-10 SA A v India A (Kimberley) 2001-02. LO HS 159 *(see LOI)*. T20 HS 104*.

BERG, Gareth Kyle (South African College S), b Cape Town, South Africa 18 Jan 1981. 6'0". RHB, RMF. Squad No 13. England qualified through residency. Middlesex 2008-14; cap 2010. Hampshire debut 2015; cap 2016. Italy (T20 only) 2011-12 to date. HS 130* M v Leics (Leicester) 2011, sharing M record 9th wkt partnership of 172 with T.J.Murtagh. H HS 99* v Yorks (Southampton) 2017. BB 6-56 v Yorks (Southampton) 2016. LO HS 75 M v Glamorgan (Lord's) 2013 (Y40). LO BB 4-24 M v Worcs (Worcester) 2011 (CB40). T20 HS 90. T20 BB 4-20.

CRANE, Mason Sydney (Lancing C), b Shoreham-by-Sea, Sussex 18 Feb 1997. 5'7". RHB, LB. Squad No 32. Debut (Hampshire) 2015. NSW 2016-17. England Lions 2017 to 2017-18. MCC 2017. Hampshire 2nd XI debut 2013. **Test**: 1 (2017-18); HS 4 and BB 1-193 v A (Sydney) 2017-18. F-c Tours: A 2017-18; WI 2017-18 (EL). HS 29 v Somerset (Taunton) 2017. BB 5-35 v Warwks (Southampton) 2015. LO HS 16* v Kent (Canterbury) 2015 (RLC). LO BB 4-30 v Middx (Southampton) 2015 (RLC). T20 HS 3*. T20 BB 3-15.

DAWSON, Liam Andrew (John Bentley S, Calne), b Swindon, Wilts 1 Mar 1990. 5'8". RHB, SLA. Squad No 8. Debut (Hampshire) 2007; cap 2013. Mountaineers 2011-12. Essex 2015 (on loan). Wiltshire 2006-07. **Tests**: 3 (2016-17 to 2017); HS 66* v I (Chennai) 2016-17; BB 2-34 v SA (Lord's) 2017. **LOI**: 1 (2016); HS 10 and BB 2-70 v P (Cardiff) 2016. **IT20**: 6 (2016 to 2017-18); HS 10 v NZ (Hamilton) 2017-18; BB 3-27 v SL (Southampton) 2016. F-c Tour: I 2016-17. HS 169 v Somerset (Southampton) 2011. BB 7-51 Mountaineers v ME (Mutare) 2011-12 (also scored 110* in same match). H BB 5-29 v Leics (Southampton) 2012. LO HS 113* SJD v Kalabagan (Savar) 2014-15. LO BB 6-47 v Sussex (Southampton) 2015 (RLC). T20 HS 76*. T20 BB 5-17.

DICKINSON, Calvin Miles (St Edward's S, Oxford; Oxford Brookes U), b Durban, South Africa 3 Nov 1996. RHB, WK. UK passport. Oxford MCCU 2016. Worcestershire 2nd XI 2015. Essex 2nd XI 2016. HS 99 v South Africa A (Southampton) 2017. LO HS 21 v T&T (Lucas Street) 2017-18. T20 HS 51.

NQEDWARDS, Fidel Henderson (St James's SS), b Gays, St Peter, Barbados 6 Feb 1982. 5'11". RHB, RFM. Squad No 82. Half-brother of P.T.Collins (Barbados, Surrey, Middlesex & West Indies 1996-97 to 2011-12). Barbados 2001-02 to 2013-14. Hampshire debut 2015 (Kolpak signing). IPL: DC 2009 to 2009-10. Big Bash: ST 2011-12. **Tests** (WI): 55 (2003 to 2012-13); HS 30 v I (Roseau) 2011; BB 7-87 v NZ (Napier) 2008-09. **LOI** (WI): 50 (2003-04 to 2009); HS 13 v NZ (Wellington) 2008-09; BB 6-22 v Z (Harare) 2003-04 – on debut. **IT20** (WI): 20 (2007-08 to 2012-13); HS 7* v E (Oval) 2011; BB 3-23 v A (Bridgetown) 2011-12. F-c Tours (WI): E 2004, 2007, 2009, 2012; A 2005-06; SA 2003-04, 2007-08; NZ 2005-06, 2008-09; I 2011-12, 2013-14 (WI A); P 2006-07; Z 2003-04; B 2011-12, 2012-13. HS 40 Bar v Jamaica (Bridgetown) 2007-08. H HS 20 v Surrey (Southampton) 2017. BB 7-87 *(see Tests)*. H BB 6-88 (10-145 match) v Notts (Nottingham) 2015. LO HS 21* Bar v Jamaica (Providence) 2007-08. LO BB 6-22 *(see LOI)*. T20 HS 11*. T20 BB 5-22.

ERVINE, Sean Michael (Lomagundi C, Chinhoyi), b Harare, Zimbabwe 6 Dec 1982. Elder brother of C.R.Ervine (Midlands, SR, MT, Bulawayo Metropolitan Tuskers and Zimbabwe 2003-04 to date); son of R.M.Ervine (Rhodesia 1977-78); grandson of M.A.Den (Rhodesia 1935-36); nephew of N.B.Ervine (Rhodesia 1977-78) and G.M.Den (Rhodesia and Eastern Province 1963-64 to 1969-70). 6'2". LHB, RMF. Squad No 7. CFX Academy 2000-01 to 2001. Midlands 2001-02 to 2003-04. Hampshire debut/cap 2005; qualified for England in 2013 season; benefit 2016. W Australia 2006-07 to 2007-08. Southern Rocks 2009-10. Matabeleland Tuskers 2011-12 to 2012-13. **Tests** (Z): 5 (2003 to 2003-04); HS 86 v B (Harare) 2003-04; BB 4-146 v A (Perth) 2003-04. **LOI** (Z): 42 (2001-02 to 2003-04); HS 100 v I (Adelaide) 2003-04; BB 3-29 v P (Sharjah) 2001-02. F-c Tours (Z): E 2003; A 2003-04. 1000 runs (1): 1090 (2016). HS 237* v Somerset (Southampton) 2010. BB 6-82 Midlands v Mashonaland (Kwekwe) 2002-03. H BB 5-60 v Glamorgan (Cardiff) 2005. LO HS 167* v Ireland (Southampton) 2009 (FPT). LO BB 5-50 v Glamorgan (Cardiff) 2005 (CGT). T20 HS 82. T20 BB 4-12.

HART, Asher Hale-Bopp Joseph Arthur (Ullswater Community C), b Carlisle 30 Mar 1997. 6'0". RHB, RM. Squad No 28. Debut (Hampshire) 2017. Durham 2nd XI 2016. Northumberland 2016. HS 36 v South Africa A (Southampton) 2017. BB 3-17 v Cardiff MCCU (Southampton) 2017. Awaiting CC debut. LO HS 21 v Windward Is (Bridgetown) 2017-18. LO BB 2-34 v CC&C (Bridgetown) 2017-18.

NQ**HOLLAND, Ian** Gabriel (Ringwood Secondary C, Melbourne), b Stevens Point, Wisconsin, USA 3 Oct 1990. 6'0". RHB, RMF. Squad No 22. Victoria 2015-16. Hampshire debut 2017. HS 58* v Surrey (Oval) 2017. BB 4-16 v Somerset (Southampton) 2017. LO HS 11* v Glamorgan (Southampton) 2017 (RLC). LO BB 2-57 v Kent (Canterbury) 2017 (RLC). T20 BB 1-33.

McMANUS, Lewis David (Clayesmore S, Bournemouth), b Poole, Dorset 9 Oct 1994. 5'10". RHB, WK. Squad No 18. Debut (Hampshire) 2015. Hampshire 2nd XI debut 2011. Dorset 2011-13. HS 132* v Surrey (Southampton) 2016. LO HS 47 v Barbados (Bridgetown) 2017-18. T20 HS 59.

‡**NORTHEAST, Sam** Alexander (Harrow S), b Ashford, Kent 16 Oct 1989. 5'11". RHB, LB. Squad No 17. Kent 2007-17; cap 2012; captain 2016-17. MCC 2013. 1000 runs (3); most – 1402 (2016). HS 191 K v Derbys (Canterbury) 2016. BB 1-60 K v Glos (Cheltenham) 2013. LO HS 132 K v Somerset (Taunton) 2014 (RLC). T20 HS 114 K v Somerset (Taunton) 2015 – K record.

ORGAN, Felix Spencer (Canford S), b Sydney, Australia 2 Jun 1999. 5'9". RHB, OB. Debut (Hampshire) 2017. Hampshire 2nd XI debut 2015. HS 16 v Middx (Uxbridge) 2017. LO HS 0. LO BB 1-6 v CC&C (Lucas Street) 2017.

NQ**ROSSOUW, Rilee** Roscoe, b Bloemfontein, South Africa, 9 Oct 1989. LHB, OB. Squad No 30. Free State 2007-08 to 2012-13. Eagles 2008-09 to 2009-10. Knights 2010-11 to 2016-17. Hampshire debut 2017 (Kolpak signing). IPL: RCB 2014-15. **LOI** (SA): 36 (2014 to 2016-17); HS 132 v WI (Centurion) 2014-15; BB 1-17 v Z (Harare) 2014. **IT20** (SA): 15 (2014-15 to 2015-16); HS 78 v A (Adelaide) 2014-15. F-c Tours (SA A): A 2014; SL 2010; B 2010. 1000 runs (0+1): 1261 (2009-10). HS 319 Eagles v Titans (Centurion) 2009-10, sharing in 3rd highest 2nd wkt partnership in all f-c cricket of 480 with D.Elgar. H HS 99 v Middx (Southampton) 2017. BB 1-1 Knights v Cobras (Cape Town) 2013-14. LO HS 156 v Somerset (Taunton) 2017 (RLC). LO BB 1-17 (see LOI). T20 HS 78. T20 BB 1-8.

NQSOLE, Christopher Barclay (Merchiston Castle S), b Edinburgh, Scotland 24 Feb 1994. Older brother of T.B.Sole (see *NORTHAMPTONSHIRE*); son of D.M.B.Sole (Scotland Grand Slam-winning rugby union captain); nephew of C.R.Trembath (Gloucestershire 1982-84). Debut (Scotland) 2016. Hampshire 2nd XI debut 2017. **LOI** (Scot): 8 (2016 to 2017-18); HS 4 v PNG (Port Moresby) 2017-18; BB 4-28 v Hong Kong (Edinburgh) 2016. **IT20** (Scot): 1 (2016-17); BB –. HS 21 Scot v PNG (Port Moresby) 2017-18. BB 3-79 Scot v Ire (Dubai, DSC) 2017-18. LO HS 10* Scot v Namibia (Edinburgh) 2017. LO BB 4-24 Scot v Kenya (Dubai, DSC) 2017-18. T20 BB –.

STEVENSON, Ryan Anthony (King Edward VI Community C), b Torquay, Devon 2 Apr 1992. 6'2". RHB, RMF. Squad No 47. Debut (Hampshire) 2015. Devon 2015. HS 30 v Durham (Chester-le-St) 2015. BB 1-15 v Notts (Nottingham) 2015. LO HS 0. LO BB 1-28 v Essex (Southampton) 2016 (RLC). T20 HS 3. T20 BB 2-40.

TAYLOR, Bradley Jacob (Eggar's S, Alton), b Winchester 14 Mar 1997. 5'11". RHB, OB. Squad No 93. Debut (Hampshire) 2013. Hampshire 2nd XI debut 2011. England U19 2014 to 2014-15. HS 36 v Cardiff MCCU (Southampton) 2013. CC HS 20 and BB 4-64 v Lancs (Southport) 2013. LO HS 69 v C&C (Bridgetown) 2017-18. LO BB 4-26 v CC&C (Lucas Street) 2017-18. T20 HS 9*. T20 BB 2-20.

TOPLEY, Reece James William (Royal Hospital S, Ipswich), b Ipswich, Suffolk 21 February 1994. Son of T.D.Topley (Surrey, Essex, GW 1985-94) and nephew of P.A.Topley (Kent 1972-75). 6'7". RHB, LMF. Squad No 6. Essex 2011-15; cap 2013. Hampshire debut 2018 – missed all bar one game due to injuries. Signed white-ball-only contract for 2018. Essex 2nd XI debut 2010, aged 16y 156d. England U19 2012-13. **LOI**: 10 (2015 to 2015-16); HS 6 v A (Manchester) 2015; BB 4-50 v SA (Pt Elizabeth) 2015-16. **IT20**: 6 (2015 to 2015-16); HS 1* v SA (Johannesburg) 2015-16; BB 3-24 v P (Dubai, DSC) 2015-16. F-c Tour (EL): SL 2013-14. HS 16 and H BB 1-56 v Yorks (Southampton) 2017. BB 6-29 (11-85 match) Ex v Worcs (Chelmsford) 2013. LO HS 19 Ex v Somerset (Taunton) 2011 (CB40). LO BB 4-26 Ex v Derbys (Colchester) 2013 (Y40). T20 HS 5*. T20 BB 4-26.

VINCE, James Michael (Warminster S), b Cuckfield, Sussex 14 Mar 1991. 6'2". RHB, RM. Squad No 14. Debut (Hampshire) 2009; cap 2013; captain 2016 to date. Wiltshire 2007-08. Big Bash: ST 2016-17 to date. **Tests**: 12 (2016 to 2017-18); HS 83 v A (Brisbane) 2017-18; BB –. **LOI**: 5 (2015 to 2016-17); HS 51 v SL (Cardiff) 2016. **IT20**: 7 (2015-16 to 2017-18); HS 46 v P (Sharjah) 2015-16. F-c Tours: A 2017-18; SA 2014-15 (EL); SL 2013-14 (EL). 1000 runs (2); most – 1525 (2014). HS 240 v Essex (Southampton) 2014. BB 5-41 v Loughborough MCCU (Southampton) 2013. CC BB 2-2 v Lancs (Southport) 2013. LO 178 v Glamorgan (Southampton) 2017 (RLC) – H record. LO BB 1-18 EL v Australia A (Sydney) 2012-13. T20 HS 107*. T20 BB 1-5.

WEATHERLEY, Joe James (King Edward VI S, Southampton), b Winchester 19 Jan 1997. 6'1". RHB, OB. Squad No 5. Debut (Hampshire) 2016. Kent 2017 (on loan). Hampshire 2nd XI debut 2014. England U19 2014-15. HS 83 v Cardiff MCCU (Southampton) 2016. CC HS 36 K v Glos (Canterbury) 2017. BB 1-46 v Surrey (Southampton) 2017. LO HS 56* v CC&C (Lucas Street) 2017-18. LO BB 4-25 v T&T (Cave Hill) 2017-18. T20 HS 43. T20 BB –.

NQWHEAL, Bradley Thomas James (Clifton C), b Durban, South Africa 28 Aug 1996. 5'9". RHB, RMF. Squad No 58. Debut (Hampshire) 2015. **LOI** (Scot): 7 (2015-16 to 2017-18); HS 2* v Hong Kong (Mong Kok) 2015-16; BB 3-36 v Afghanistan (Bulawayo) 2017-18. **IT20** (Scot): 5 (2015-16 to 2016-17); HS 2* and BB 3-20 v Hong Kong (Mong Kok) 2015-16. HS 18 v Yorks (Leeds) 2017. BB 6-51 v Notts (Nottingham) 2016. LO HS 18* v CC&C (Bridgetown) 2017-18. LO BB 4-38 v Kent (Southampton) 2016 (RLC). T20 HS 16. T20 BB 3-20.

WOOD, Christopher Philip (Alton C), b Basingstoke 27 June 1990. 6'2". RHB, LM. Squad No 25. Debut (Hampshire) 2010. Missed most of 2016 due to knee ligament injury. HS 105* v Leics (Leicester) 2012. BB 5-39 v Kent (Canterbury) 2014. LO HS 41 v Essex (Southampton) 2013 (Y40). LO BB 5-22 v Glamorgan (Cardiff) 2012 (CB40). T20 HS 27. T20 BB 4-16.

RELEASED/RETIRED

(Having made a County 1st XI appearance in 2017)

[NQ]**BAILEY, George** John, b Launceston, Tasmania, Australia 7 Sep 1982. 5'10". RHB, RM. Tasmania 2004-05 to date. Hampshire 2013-17; cap 2017. Middlesex 2016. Sussex 2015 (l-o and T20 only). IPL: CSK 2009 to 2009-10. KXIP 2014-15. RPS 2016. Big Bash: MS 2011-12. HH 2012-13 to date. **Tests** (A): 5 (2013-14); HS 53 v E (Adelaide) 2013-14. **LOI** (A): 90 (2011-12 to 2016-17); HS 156 v I (Nagpur) 2013-14. **IT20** (A): 30 (2011-12 to 2017); HS 63 v WI (Colombo, RPS) 2012-13. F-c Tours (Aus A): E 2012; I 2008-09. HS 200* Tas v NSW (Wollongong) 2016-17. H HS 161 v Surrey (Oval) 2017. BB –. LO HS 156 (see LOI). LO BB 1-19 Tas v Vic (Melbourne) 2004-05. T20 HS 89*.

CARBERRY, M.A. – see LEICESTERSHIRE.

SALISBURY, Matthew Edward Thomas (Shenfield HS; Anglia Ruskin U), b Chelmsford, Essex 18 Apr 1993. 6'0½". RHB, RMF. Cambridge MCCU 2012-13. Essex 2014-15. Hampshire 2017 (non-contract player). Suffolk 2016. HS 24 Ex v Leics (Chelmsford) 2015. H HS 17* v Warwks (Southampton) 2017. BB 4-50 Ex v Worcs (Worcester) 2014. H BB 3-65 v South Africa A (Southampton) 2017. LO HS 5* Ex v Leics (Chelmsford) 2014 (RLC). LO BB 4-55 Ex v Lancs (Chelmsford) 2014 (RLC). T20 HS 1*. T20 BB 2-19.

[NQ]**SHAHID KHAN AFRIDI**, Sahibzaha Mohammad (Ibrahim Alibhai S; Islamia Science C, Karachi) b Kohat, Pakistan, 1 Mar 1980. Brother of Tariq Afridi (Karachi 1999-00) and Ashfaq Afridi (Karachi Blues 2008-09). RHB, LBG. Debut Combined XI v Eng A 1995-96. Karachi 1995-96 to 2003-04. HB 1997-98 to 2015-16. Leicestershire 2001; cap 2001. Derbyshire 2003. GW 2003-04. Sind 2007-08 to 2008-09. MCC 2001. Hampshire 2016-17 (l-o & T20 only). IPL: DC 2007-08. Big Bash: MR 2011-12. **Tests** (P): 27 (1998-99 to 2010, 1 as captain); HS 156 v I (Faisalabad) 2005-06; BB 5-52 v A (Karachi) 1998-99 – on debut. **LOI** (P): 398 (1996-97 to 2014-15, 38 as captain); HS 124 v B (Dambulla) 2010; BB 7-12 v WI (Providence) 2013, 2nd best analysis in all LOIs. Scored a 37-ball hundred which included then joint record 11 sixes v SL (Nairobi) 1996-97 in his first LOI innings. **IT20** (P): 98 (2006-07 to 2015-16, 39 as captain); HS 54* v SL (Lord's) 2009; BB 4-11 v Netherlands (Lord's) 2009. F-c Tours (P): E 2006, 2010; A 1996-97, 2004-05; WI 1999-00, 2005; I 1998-99, 2004-05; SL 2005-06; Z 2002-03; B 1998-99. HS 164 Le v Northants (Northampton) 2001. BB 6-101 HB v KRL (Rawalpindi) 1997-98. UK BB 5-84 Le v Essex (Chelmsford) 2001. LO HS 124 (see LOI). LO BB 7-12 (see LOI). T20 HS 101. T20 BB 5-7.

SMITH, W.R. – see DURHAM.

HAMPSHIRE 2017

RESULTS SUMMARY

	Place	Won	Lost	Drew	NR
Specsavers County Champ (1st Division)	5th	3	3	8	
All First-Class Matches		3	4	9	
Royal London One-Day Cup (South Group)	6th	3	4		1
NatWest t20 Blast (South Group)	SF	8	7		1

SPECSAVERS COUNTY CHAMPIONSHIP AVERAGES

BATTING AND FIELDING

Cap		M	I	NO	HS	Runs	Avge	100	50	Ct/St
2017	G.J.Bailey	10	16	–	161	610	38.12	2	3	5
	I.G.Holland	8	11	4	58*	233	33.28	–	2	1
2013	J.M.Vince	12	19	–	147	626	32.94	2	1	13
2006	J.H.K.Adams	12	17	–	166	558	32.82	2	1	14
2016	G.K.Berg	14	20	–	99*	568	31.55	–	2	2
2017	K.J.Abbott	14	18	4	97*	418	29.85	–	2	1
2005	S.M.Ervine	14	21	1	203	572	28.60	1	2	13
2006	M.A.Carberry	7	11	–	98	272	24.72	–	2	2
	L.D.McManus	10	14	2	41*	285	23.75	–	–	28/3
2013	L.A.Dawson	10	16	–	75	334	20.87	–	2	5
	R.R.Rossouw	8	13	–	99	253	19.46	–	1	7
	T.P.Alsop	5	7	–	40	118	16.85	–	–	9
	M.S.Crane	7	8	3	29	66	13.20	–	–	3
	J.J.Weatherley	3	4	–	35	45	11.25	–	–	–
	B.T.J.Wheal	4	4	1	18	31	10.33	–	–	–
	F.H.Edwards	9	10	4	20	43	7.16	–	–	–

Also batted: C.M.Dickinson (1 match) 1; F.S.Organ (1) 16; M.E.T.Salisbury (2) 17*, 14, 0; B.J.Taylor (1) 18, 17*; R.J.W.Topley (2) 16, 0*, 7*.

BOWLING

	O	M	R	W	Avge	Best	5wI	10wM
K.J.Abbott	415.3	131	1092	60	18.20	7-41	4	–
I.G.Holland	133	38	351	19	18.47	4-16	–	–
F.H.Edwards	208.1	31	772	30	25.73	5-49	2	–
L.A.Dawson	333.2	87	809	31	26.09	4-22	–	–
G.K.Berg	391.5	103	987	37	26.67	4-28	–	–
B.T.J.Wheal	84.5	11	352	11	32.00	4-98	–	–
M.S.Crane	193.1	32	715	16	44.68	5-40	1	–

Also bowled:

S.M.Ervine 126.4 29 331 6 55.16 2- 1 – –

J.H.K.Adams 1-1-0-0; G.J.Bailey 2-0-9-0; M.A.Carberry 2-1-1-0; M.E.T.Salisbury 46.2-7-177-4; B.J.Taylor 40-1-180-2; R.J.W.Topley 44.2-6-178-2; J.M.Vince 8.5-0-38-1; J.J.Weatherley 15-3-55-1.

The First-Class Averages (pp 230–246) give the records of Hampshire players in all first-class county matches (Hampshire's other opponents being Cardiff MCCU and South Africa A), with the exception of J.J.Weatherley, whose first-class figures for Hampshire are as above, and:

M.A.Carberry 8-12-0-100-372-31.00-1-2-2ct. 5-2-5-0.
M.S.Crane 8-10-3-29-66-9.42-0-0-3ct. 223.1-34-830-16-51.87-5/40-1-0.
L.A.Dawson 11-18-0-75-386-21.44-0-2-5ct. 350.2-94-835-32-26.09-4/22-0-0.

HAMPSHIRE RECORDS

FIRST-CLASS CRICKET

Highest Total	For 714-5d		v	Notts	Southampton	2005
	V 742		by	Surrey	The Oval	1909
Lowest Total	For 15		v	Warwicks	Birmingham	1922
	V 23		by	Yorkshire	Middlesbrough	1965
Highest Innings	For 316	R.H.Moore	v	Warwicks	Bournemouth	1937
	V 303*	G.A.Hick	for	Worcs	Southampton	1997

Highest Partnership for each Wicket

1st	347	V.P.Terry/C.L.Smith	v	Warwicks	Birmingham	1987
2nd	373	J.H.K.Adams/M.A.Carberry	v	Somerset	Taunton	2011
3rd	523	M.A.Carberry/N.D.McKenzie	v	Yorkshire	Southampton	2011
4th	367	J.H.K.Adams/S.M.Ervine	v	Warwicks	Southampton	2017
5th	235	G.Hill/D.F.Walker	v	Sussex	Portsmouth	1937
6th	411	R.M.Poore/E.G.Wynyard	v	Somerset	Taunton	1899
7th	325	G.Brown/C.H.Abercrombie	v	Essex	Leyton	1913
8th	257	N.Pothas/A.J.Bichel	v	Glos	Cheltenham	2005
9th	230	D.A.Livingstone/A.T.Castell	v	Surrey	Southampton	1962
10th	192	H.A.W.Bowell/W.H.Livsey	v	Worcs	Bournemouth	1921

Best Bowling	For 9- 25	R.M.H.Cottam	v	Lancashire	Manchester	1965
(Innings)	V 10- 46	W.Hickton	for	Lancashire	Manchester	1870
Best Bowling	For 16- 88	J.A.Newman	v	Somerset	Weston-s-Mare	1927
(Match)	V 17-103	W.Mycroft	for	Derbyshire	Southampton	1876

Most Runs – Season	2854	C.P.Mead	(av 79.27)	1928
Most Runs – Career	48892	C.P.Mead	(av 48.84)	1905-36
Most 100s – Season	12	C.P.Mead		1928
Most 100s – Career	138	C.P.Mead		1905-36
Most Wkts – Season	190	A.S.Kennedy	(av 15.61)	1922
Most Wkts – Career	2669	D.Shackleton	(av 18.23)	1948-69
Most Career W-K Dismissals	700	R.J.Parks	(630 ct; 70 st)	1980-92
Most Career Catches in the Field	629	C.P.Mead		1905-36

LIMITED-OVERS CRICKET

Highest Total	50ov	371-4	v	Glamorgan	Southampton	1975
	40ov	353-8	v	Middlesex	Lord's	2005
	T20	249-8	v	Derbyshire	Derby	2017
Lowest Total	50ov	50	v	Yorkshire	Leeds	1991
	40ov	43	v	Essex	Basingstoke	1972
	T20	85	v	Sussex	Southampton	2008
Highest Innings	50ov	178	J.M.Vince	v	Glamorgan	Southampton	2017
	40ov	172	C.G.Greenidge	v	Surrey	Southampton	1987
	T20	124*	M.J.Lumb	v	Essex	Southampton	2009
Best Bowling	50ov	7-30	P.J.Sainsbury	v	Norfolk	Southampton	1965
	40ov	6-20	T.E.Jesty	v	Glamorgan	Cardiff	1975
	T20	5-14	A.D.Mascarenhas	v	Sussex	Hove	2004

KENT

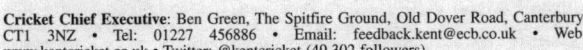

Formation of Present Club: 1 March 1859
Substantial Reorganisation: 6 December 1870
Inaugural First-Class Match: 1864
Colours: Maroon and White
Badge: White Horse on a Red Ground
County Champions: (6) 1906, 1909, 1910, 1913, 1970, 1978
Joint Champions: (1) 1977
Gillette Cup Winners: (2) 1967, 1974
Benson and Hedges Cup Winners: (3) 1973, 1976, 1978
Pro 40/National League (Div 1) Winners: (1) 2001
Sunday League Winners: (4) 1972, 1973, 1976, 1995
Twenty20 Cup Winners: (1) 2007

Cricket Chief Executive: Ben Green, The Spitfire Ground, Old Dover Road, Canterbury, CT1 3NZ • Tel: 01227 456886 • Email: feedback.kent@ecb.co.uk • Web: www.kentcricket.co.uk • Twitter: @kentcricket (49,302 followers)

Director of Cricket: Paul Downton. **Head Coach**: Matt Walker. **Assistant Coach**: Allan Donald. **Captain**: S.W.Billings. **Overseas Players**: M.J.Henry and M.P.Stoinis (T20 only). **2018 Testimonial**: None. **Head Groundsman**: Simon Williamson. **Scorer**: Lorne Hart. ‡ New registration. NQ Not qualified for England.

BELL-DRUMMOND, Daniel James (Millfield S), b Lewisham, London 4 Aug 1993. 5'10". RHB, RMF. Squad No 23. Debut (Kent) 2011; cap 2015. MCC 2014. Kent 2nd XI debut 2009, aged 16y 21d. England U19 2010 to 2010-11. 1000 runs (1): 1058 (2014). HS 206* v Loughborough MCCU (Canterbury) 2016. CC 153 v Hants (Southampton) 2014. BB –. LO HS 171* EL v Sri Lanka A (Canterbury) 2016. LO BB –. T20 HS 112*.

BILLINGS, Samuel William (Haileybury S; Loughborough U), b Pembury 15 Jun 1991. 5'11". RHB, WK. Squad No 7. Loughborough MCCU 2011, scoring 131 v Northants (Loughborough) on f-c debut. Kent debut 2011; cap 2015; captain 2018. England Lions 2017. MCC 2015. IPL: DD 2016-17. Big Bash: SS 2016-17 to date. **LOI**: 13 (2015 to 2017); HS 62 v B (Chittagong) 2016-17. **IT20**: 17 (2015 to 2017-18); HS 53 v P (Dubai, DSC) 2015-16. HS 171 v Glos (Bristol) 2016. LO HS 175 EL v Pakistan A (Canterbury) 2016. T20 HS 78*.

BLAKE, Alexander James (Hayes SS; Leeds Met U), b Farnborough 25 Jan 1989. 6'1". LHB, RMF. Squad No 10. Debut (Kent) 2008; cap 2017. Leeds/Bradford UCCE 2009-11 (not f-c). HS 105* v Yorks (Leeds) 2010. BB 2-9 v Pakistanis (Canterbury) 2010. CC BB 1-60 v Hants (Southampton) 2010. LO HS 116 v Somerset (Taunton) 2017 (RLC). LO BB 2-13 v Yorks (Leeds) 2011 (CB40). T20 HS 71*.

CLAYDON, Mitchell Eric (Westfield Sports HS, Sydney), b Fairfield, NSW, Australia 25 Nov 1982. 6'4". LHB, RMF. Squad No 8. Yorkshire 2005-06. Durham 2007-13. Canterbury 2010-11. Kent debut 2013; cap 2015. HS 77 v Leics (Leicester) 2014. 50 wkts (2); most – 59 (2014). BB 6-104 Du v Somerset (Taunton) 2011. K BB 5-42 v Worcs (Canterbury) 2016. LO HS 19 Du v Glos (Bristol) 2009 (FPT) and 19 v Middx (Canterbury) 2017 (RLC). LO BB 5-31 v Guyana (North Sound) 2017-18. T20 HS 19. T20 BB 5-26.

CRAWLEY, Zak (Tonbridge S), b Bromley 3 Feb 1998. 6'6". RHB, RM. Squad No 16. Debut (Kent) 2017. Kent 2nd XI debut 2013, aged 15y 199d. HS 62 v West Indians (Canterbury) 2017. CC HS 37 v Glamorgan (Canterbury) 2017. LO HS 99* v Leeward Is (North Sound) 2017-18.

DENLY, Joseph Liam (Chaucer TC), b Canterbury 16 Mar 1986. 6'0''. RHB, LB. Squad No 6. Kent debut 2004; cap 2008. Middlesex 2012-14; cap 2012. MCC 2013. **LOI**: 9 (2009 to 2009-10); HS 67 v Ireland (Belfast) 2009 – on debut. **IT20**: 5 (2009 to 2009-10); HS 14 and BB 1-9 v SA (Centurion) 2009-10. F-c Tours (Eng A): NZ 2008-09; I 2007-08. 1000 runs (4); most – 1266 (2017). HS 227 v Worcs (Worcester) 2017. BB 3-43 v Surrey (Oval) 2011. LO HS 115 v Warwks (Birmingham) 2009 (FPT). LO BB 4-35 v Jamaica (North Sound) 2017-18. T20 HS 127 v Essex (Chelmsford) 2017 – K record. T20 BB 1-9.

NQDICKSON, Sean Robert, b Johannesburg, South Africa 2 Sep 1991. 5'10''. RHB, RM. Squad No 58. Northerns 2013-14 to 2014-15. Kent debut 2015. UK passport holder. HS 318 v Northants (Beckenham) 2017, 2nd highest score in K history, sharing K record 2nd wkt partnership of 382 with J.L.Denly. BB 1-15 Northerns v GW (Centurion) 2014-15. K BB –. LO HS 99 v Middx (Lord's) 2016 (RLC). T20 HS 53. T20 BB 1-9.

GIDMAN, William Robert Simon (Wycliffe C; Berkshire C of Agriculture), b High Wycombe, Bucks 14 Feb 1985. Younger brother of A.P.R.Gidman (Gloucestershire, Worcestershire 2002-15). 6'2''. LHB, RM. Squad No 42. Durham 2007. No f-c appearances in 2008-10. Gloucestershire 2011-14; cap 2011, becoming first player for Gs to score 1000 runs and take 50 wkts in debut season. Nottinghamshire 2015. Kent debut 2016. MCC YC 2004-06. 1000 runs (1): 1006 (2011). HS 143 and BB 6-15 (10-43 match) Gs v Leics (Bristol) 2013 – only the fifth Gs player to score a century and take ten wkts in a match. K HS 99* v Sussex (Hove) 2016. 50 wkts (2); most – 55 (2013). K BB 3-0 v Leeds/Bradford MCCU (Canterbury) 2017. LO HS 94 v Windward Is (Coolidge) 2016-17. LO BB 4-20 v Guyana (Coolidge) 2017-18. T20 HS 40*. T20 BB 2-23.

HAGGETT, Calum John (Millfield S), b Taunton, Somerset 30 Oct 1990. 6'3''. LHB, RMF. Squad No 25. Debut (Kent) 2013. HS 80 v Surrey (Oval) 2015. BB 4-15 v Derbys (Derby) 2016. LO HS 45 v Leeward Is (Coolidge) 2016-17. LO BB 4-59 v Windward Is (Coolidge) 2016-17. T20 HS 11. T20 BB 2-12.

‡**NQHENRY, Matthew** James, b Christchurch, New Zealand 14 Dec 1991. RHB, RFM. Canterbury 2010-11 to date. Worcestershire 2016. Derbyshire 2017 (T20 only). Joins Kent for first part of 2018 season. IPL: KXIP 2017. **Tests** (NZ): 9 (2015 to 2017-18); HS 66 v A (Christchurch) 2015-16; BB 4-93 v E (Lord's) 2015 and 4-93 v SA (Hamilton) 2016-17. **LOI** (NZ): 35 (2013-14 to 2017-18); HS 48* v P (Wellington) 2015-16; BB 5-30 v P (Abu Dhabi) 2014-15. **IT20** (NZ): 6 (2014-15 to 2016-17); HS 10 v P (Auckland) 2015-16; BB 3-44 v SL (Mt Maunganui) 2015-16. F-c Tours (NZ): E 2014 (NZ A), 2015; A 2015-16; I 2016-17, 2017-18 (NZA); SL 2013-14 (NZ A). HS 75* Canterbury v CD (Rangiora) 2015-16. CC HS 49* Wo v Leics (Leicester) 2016. BB 5-18 NZ A v Surrey (Oval) 2014. CC BB 5-36 Wo v Northants (Northampton) 2016. LO HS 48* (see **LOI**). LO BB 6-45 Canterbury v Auckland (Auckland) 2012-13. T20 HS 42. T20 BB 4-43.

HUNN, Matthew David (St Joseph's C, Ipswich), b Colchester, Essex 22 Mar 1994. 6'4''. RHB, RMF. Squad No 14. Debut (Kent) 2013. Essex 2nd XI 2012. Suffolk 2011-13. HS 32* v Glos (Canterbury) 2016. BB 5-99 v Australians (Canterbury) 2015. CC BB 4-47 v Essex (Tunbridge W) 2015. LO HS 5* v Lancs (Canterbury) 2015 (RLC). LO BB 2-31 v Sussex (Canterbury) 2015 (RLC). T20 HS –. T20 BB 3-30.

IMRAN QAYYUM (Villiers HS, Southall; Greenford SFC; City U), b Ealing, Middx 23 May 1993. 6'0''. RHB, SLA. Squad No 11. Debut (Kent) 2016. Kent 2nd XI debut 2013. Northamptonshire 2nd XI 2013. HS 39 v Leics (Canterbury) 2017. BB 3-158 v Northants (Northampton) 2016. LO HS 18 v Leeward Is (Coolidge) 2016-17. LO BB 4-33 v USA (North Sound) 2017-18. T20 HS 6. T20 BB 2-19.

‡**NOKUHN, Heino** Gunther, b Piet Relief, Mpumalanga, South Africa 1 Apr 1984. RHB, WK. Northerns 2004-05 to 2015-16. Titans 2005-06 to date. Joins Kent in 2018 (Kolpak signing). **Tests** (SA): 4 (2017); HS 34 v E (Nottingham) 2017. **IT20** (SA): 7 (2009-10 to 2016-17); HS 29 v SL (Johannesburg) 2016-17. F-c Tours (SAA): E 2017 (SA); A 2014; SL 2010; Z 2016; B 2010; Ire 2012. 1000 runs (0+1): 1159 (2015-16). HS 244* Titans v Lions (Benoni) 2014-15. Scored 200* SAA v Hants (Southampton) 2017 on UK debut. LO HS 141* SAA v Bangladesh A (Benoni) 2011. T20 HS 83*.

RILEY, Adam Edward Nicholas (Beths GS, Bexley; Loughborough U), b Sidcup 23 Mar 1992. 6'2''. RHB, OB. Squad No 33. Debut (Kent) 2011. Loughborough MCCU 2012-14. MCC 2015. F-c Tour (EL): SA 2014-15. HS 34 v Derbys (Canterbury) 2015. 50 wkts (1): 57 (2014). BB 7-150 v Hants (Southampton) 2013. LO HS 21* v Leeward Is (Coolidge) 2016-17. LO BB 4-40 v Leeward Is (Coolidge) 2017-18. T20 HS 5*. T20 BB 4-22.

ROBINSON, Oliver Graham (Hurtsmere S, Greenwich), b Sidcup 1 Dec 1998. 5'8''. RHB, WK, occ RM. Squad No 21. Kent 2nd XI debut 2015. England U19 2017. Awaiting f-c debut. LO HS –.

ROUSE, Adam Paul (Perrins Community Sports C; Peter Symonds C, Winchester), b Harare, Zimbabwe 30 Jun 1992. 5'10''. RHB, WK. Squad No 12. Hampshire 2013. Gloucestershire 2014; cap 2014. Kent debut 2016. HS 95* v Derbys (Canterbury) 2017. LO HS 75* v Jamaica (North Sound) 2017-18. T20 HS 35*.

STEVENS, Darren Ian (Hinckley C), b Leicester 30 Apr 1976. 5'11''. RHB, RM. Squad No 3. Leicestershire 1997-2004; cap 2002. Kent debut/cap 2005; benefit 2016. MCC 2002. F-c Tour (ECB Acad): SL 2002-03. 1000 runs (3); most – 1304 (2013). HS 208 v Glamorgan (Canterbury) 2005 and 208 v Middx (Uxbridge) 2009. 50 wkts (3); most – 63 (2017). BB 8-75 v Leics (Canterbury) 2017. LO HS 147 v Glamorgan (Swansea) 2017 (RLC) – K record. LO BB 5-32 v Scotland (Edinburgh) 2005 (NL). T20 HS 90. T20 BB 4-14.

NOSTEWART, Grant (All Saints C, Maitland; U of Newcastle), b Kalgoorlie, W Australia 19 Feb 1994. 6'2''. RHB, RMF. Squad No 9. UK qualified due to Italian mother. Debut (Kent) 2017. HS 15* and BB 2-52 v Glamorgan (Canterbury) 2017 – only f-c game. LO HS 44 v USA (North Sound) 2017-18. LO BB 3-17 v Guyana (Coolidge) 2017-18.

NOSTOINIS, Marcus Peter (Hale S, Wembley Downs, Perth; U of WA), b Perth, W Australia 16 Aug 1989. RHB, RMF. W Australia 2008-09 to date. Victoria 2012-13 to 2016-17. Joins Kent in 2018 (T20 only). IPL: KXIP 2016-17. Big Bash: PS 2012-13. MS 2013-14 to date. Kent 2nd XI 2012. **LOI** (A): 13 (2015 to 2017-18); HS 146* and BB 3-49 v NZ (Auckland) 2016-17. **IT20** (A): 7 (2015 to 2017-18); HS 10* v E (Cardiff) 2015; BB 1-16 v E (Hobart) 2017-18. F-c Tour (Aus A): I 2015. HS 170 Vic v Tas (Melbourne) 2013-14. BB 4-82 WA v Vic (Perth) 2017-18. LO HS 146* (*see LOI*). LO BB 4-43 Vic v S Aus (Sydney, BO) 2015-16. T20 HS 99. T20 BB 4-15.

THOMAS, Ivan Alfred Astley (John Roan S, Blackheath; Leeds U), b Greenwich, London 25 Sep 1991. 6'4''. RHB, RMF. Squad No 5. Leeds/Bradford MCCU 2012-14. Kent debut 2012. HS 13 v Australians (Canterbury) 2015. CC HS 7* v Glos (Bristol) 2015. BB 4-48 v Leics (Canterbury) 2015. LO HS 6 v Guyana (North Sound) 2017-18. LO BB 4-30 v Jamaica (North Sound) 2017-18. T20 HS 3*. T20 BB 2-42.

TREDWELL, James Cullum (Southlands Community CS, New Romney), b Ashford 27 Feb 1982. 6'0''. LHB, OB. Squad No 15. Debut (Kent) 2001; cap 2007; captain 2013; testimonial 2017. Sussex (on loan) 2014. MCC 2004, 2008, 2016. Tests: 2 (2009-10 to 2014-15); HS 37 v B (Dhaka) 2009-10; BB 4-47 v WI (North Sound) 2014-15. LOI: 45 (2009-10 to 2014-15); HS 30 v I (Nottingham) 2014; BB 4-41 v Scotland (Aberdeen) 2014. IT20: 17 (2012-13 to 2014); HS 22 and BB 1-16 v WI (Bridgetown) 2013-14. F-c Tours: WI 2014-15; NZ 2012-13 (part); I 2003-04 (Eng A, captain); B 2009-10. HS 124 v Essex (Chelmsford) 2016, sharing K record 8th wkt partnership of 222 with S.A.Northeast. 50 wkts (1): 69 (2009). BB 8-66 (11-120 match) v Glamorgan (Canterbury) 2009. LO HS 88 v Surrey (Oval) 2007 (FPT). LO BB 6-27 v Middx (Southgate) 2009 (FPT). T20 HS 34*. T20 BB 4-21.

RELEASED/RETIRED

(Having made a County 1st XI appearance in 2017)

BALL, Adam James (Beths GS, Bexley) b Greenwich, London 1 March 1993. 6'2''. RHB, LFM. Debut (Kent) 2011. HS 69 v Lancs (Canterbury) 2013. BB 3-36 v Leics (Leicester) 2011. LO HS 40* v Windward Is (Coolidge) 2016-17. LO BB 3-36 v Sussex (Horsham) 2013 (Y40). T20 HS 18. T20 BB 2-18.

COLES, M.T. – *see ESSEX.*

HARTLEY, Charles Frederick (Millfield S), b Redditch, Worcs 4 Jan 1994. 6'2''. RHB, RMF. Debut (Kent) 2014. Kent 2nd XI debut 2013. HS 5 and BB 4-80 v West Indians (Canterbury) 2017. CC HS 2 and CC BB 2-40 v Leics (Leicester) 2014. LO HS 15 and LO BB 2-23 v Glos (Canterbury) 2016 (RLC).

NQ**MILNE, Adam** Fraser, b Palmerston North, New Zealand 13 Apr 1992. RHB, RMF. Central Districts 2009-10 to date. Kent 2017. IPL: RCB 2016-17. LOI (NZ): 40 (2012-13 to 2017-18); HS 36 v A (Wellington) 2015-16; BB 3-49 v P (Auckland) 2015-16. IT20 (NZ): 19 (2010-11 to 2017-18); HS 10* v SA (Centurion) 2015; BB 4-37 v P (Auckland) 2015-16. F-c Tour (NZ A): SL 2013-14. HS 97 and BB 5-47 CD v Otago (Napier) 2012-13. K HS 51 v Notts (Nottingham) 2017. K BB 4-68 v Durham (Chester-le-St) 2017. LO HS 45 NZ A v Sri Lanka A (Lincoln) 2015-16. LO BB 5-61 NZ A v Sri Lanka A (Pallekele) 2013-14. T20 HS 18*. T20 BB5-11 v Somerset (Taunton) 2017 – K record.

NQ**NEESHAM, James** Douglas Sheahan, b Auckland, New Zealand 17 Sep 1990. LHB, RM. Auckland 2009-10 to 2010-11. Otago 2011-12 to date. Derbyshire 2016 (l-o and T20 only). Kent 2017 (T20 only). IPL: DD 2014. Tests (NZ): 12 (2013-14 to 2016-17); HS 137* v I (Wellington) 2013-14; BB 3-42 v SL (Wellington) 2014-15. LOI (NZ): 41 (2012-13 to 2017); HS 74 v A (Canberra) 2016-17; BB 4-42 v B (Dhaka) 2013-14. IT20 (NZ): 15 (2012-13 to 2016-17); HS 28 v SA (Centurion) 2015; BB 3-16 v WI (Auckland) 2013-14. F-c Tours (NZ): A 2015-16; WI 2014; I 2013-14 (NZ A), 2016-17; UAE (v P) 2014-15. HS 147 Otago v CD (Nelson) 2013-14. LO HS 5-65 Otago v ND (Whangarei) 2013-14. LO HS 74 (*see LOI*). LO BB 5-44 Otago v Wellington (Wellington) 2011-12. T20 HS 59*. T20 BB 4-35.

NORTHEAST, S.A. – *see HAMPSHIRE.*

NO PARNELL, Wayne Dillon (Grey HS), b Port Elizabeth, South Africa 30 Jul 1989. 6'1".
LHB, LFM. E Province 2006-07 to 2010-11. Warriors 2008-09 to 2014-15. Kent 2009-17.
Sussex 2011. Cape Cobras 2015-16 to date. Glamorgan 2015 (T20 only). IPL: PW 2011-13.
DD 2014. **Tests** (SA): 6 (2009-10 to 2017-18); HS 23 and BB 4-51 v SL (Johannesburg)
2016-17. **LOI** (SA): 65 (2008-09 to 2017); HS 56 v P (Sharjah) 2013-14; BB 5-48 v E
(Cape Town) 2009-10. **IT20** (SA): 40 (2008-09 to 2017); HS 29* v A (Johannesburg)
2011-12; BB 4-13 v WI (Oval) 2009. F-c Tours (SA A): A 2016; I 2009-10 (SA), 2015; Ire
2012. HS 111* CC v Warriors (Paarl) 2015-16. CC HS 90 v Glamorgan (Canterbury) 2009.
BB 7-51 CC v Dolphins (Cape Town) 2015-16. CC BB 4-78 v Essex (Chelmsford) 2009.
LO HS 129 Warriors v Lions (Potchefstroom) 2013-14. LO BB 6-51 Warriors v Knights
(Kimberley) 2013-14. T20 HS 99. T20 BB 4-13.

NO YASIR SHAH, b Swabi, NW Frontier Province, Pakistan 2 May 1986. RHB, LB. Rest of
NWFP 2001-02. SNGPL 2004-15 to date. Pakistan Customs 2007-08. NWFP 2007-08 to
2008-09. Khyber Pakhtunkhwa 2010-11 to 2011-12. Abbottabad 2012-13. Kent 2017. Big
Bash: BH 2017-18. **Tests** (P): 28 (2014-15 to 2017-18); HS 38* v WI (Roseau) 2017; BB
7-76 v SL (Galle) 2015. **LOI** (P): 17 (2011 to 2016); HS 32* v Z (Harare) 2015-16; BB
6-26 v Z (Harare) 2015-16 (separate matches). **IT20** (P): 2 (2011-12); HS 11* v Z (Harare)
2011-12; BB –. F-c Tours (P): E 2016; A 2016-17; WI 2010-11 (P A), 2016-17; NZ
2016-17; SL 2010 (P A), 2015; B 2014-15. HS 71 SNGPL v HB (Lahore) 2008-09. K HS 48
v Durham (Canterbury) 2017. BB 7-76 (*see Tests*). K BB 5-132 v Worcs (Worcester) 2017.
LO HS 66* Abbottabad v Islamabad (Islamabad) 2012-13. BB 6-26 (*see LOI*). T20 HS 28.
T20 BB 4-7.

H.R.Bernard and F.K.Cowdrey left the staff without making a County 1st XI appearance in
2017.

KENT 2017

RESULTS SUMMARY

	Place	Won	Lost	Tied	Drew	Aband
Specsavers County Champ (2nd Division)	5th	4	2		7	1
All First-Class Matches		5	2		8	1
Royal London One-Day Cup (South Group)	9th	1	7			
NatWest t20 Blast (South Group)	6th	6	7	1		

SPECSAVERS COUNTY CHAMPIONSHIP AVERAGES

BATTING AND FIELDING

Cap		M	I	NO	HS	Runs	Avge	100	50	Ct/St
2008	J.L.Denly	13	23	2	227	1165	55.47	4	5	8
2012	S.A.Northeast	13	23	3	173*	1017	50.85	3	4	5
2015	S.W.Billings	6	8	2	70*	262	43.66	–	1	12
	Yasir Shah	3	4	1	48	131	43.66	–	–	1
2005	D.I.Stevens	12	20	3	100	707	41.58	1	5	2
	S.R.Dickson	12	21	–	318	804	38.28	1	4	9
	J.A.R.Harris	4	6	2	34	146	36.50	–	–	1
	A.P.Rouse	10	16	2	95*	491	35.07	–	3	26/1
2007	J.C.Tredwell	6	9	2	55	184	26.28	–	1	5
2015	D.J.Bell-Drummond	13	23	1	90	561	25.50	–	3	10
	J.J.Weatherley	5	8	–	36	190	23.75	–	–	1
2012	M.T.Coles	11	16	2	56*	304	21.71	–	1	12
	A.F.Milne	5	8	2	51	121	20.16	–	–	1
	W.R.S.Gidman	8	14	–	51	236	16.85	–	1	14
2016	M.E.Claydon	9	13	5	21*	111	13.87	–	–	1
	Z.Crawley	4	6	–	37	75	12.50	–	–	3
	Imran Qayyum	3	5	1	39	40	10.00	–	–	2
	C.J.Haggett	3	5	–	21	35	7.00	–	–	–

Also played: M.D.Hunn (2 matches) did not bat; W.D.Parnell (2) 51*, 41, 8; G.Stewart (1) 15*, 0.

BOWLING

	O	M	R	W	Avge	Best	5wI	10wM
D.I.Stevens	395.4	102	1121	62	18.08	8- 75	7	–
J.A.R.Harris	114.2	25	400	19	21.05	4- 56	–	–
Yasir Shah	155.5	22	533	14	38.07	5-132	1	–
M.E.Claydon	241.5	45	884	23	38.43	5- 54	1	–
M.T.Coles	335	60	1313	32	41.03	6- 84	1	–
A.F.Milne	184	51	572	13	44.00	4- 68	–	–
Also bowled:								
W.D.Parnell	57.1	16	162	7	23.14	3- 48	–	–
M.D.Hunn	46.5	7	202	7	28.85	3- 90	–	–
J.L.Denly	66.3	11	228	7	32.57	2- 49	–	–
Imran Qayyum	50.5	5	198	6	33.00	2- 25	–	–
C.J.Haggett	96	30	256	7	36.57	3- 40	–	–
W.R.S.Gidman	56	7	230	5	46.00	2- 48	–	–

D.J.Bell-Drummond 1-0-10-0; G.Stewart 20-5-89-2; J.C.Tredwell 66-11-228-3.

The First-Class Averages (pp 230–246) give the records of Kent players in all first-class county matches (Kent's other opponents being Leeds/Bradford MCCU and the West Indians), with the exception of J.A.R.Harris and J.J.Weatherley, whose first-class figures for Kent are as above, and:
S.W.Billings 7-9-2-70*-287-41.00-0-1-12ct.

KENT RECORDS

FIRST-CLASS CRICKET

Highest Total	For 803-4d		v	Essex	Brentwood	1934
	V 676		by	Australians	Canterbury	1921
Lowest Total	For 18		v	Sussex	Gravesend	1867
	V 16		by	Warwicks	Tonbridge	1913
Highest Innings	For 332	W.H.Ashdown	v	Essex	Brentwood	1934
	V 344	W.G.Grace	for	MCC	Canterbury	1876

Highest Partnership for each Wicket

1st	300	N.R.Taylor/M.R.Benson	v	Derbyshire	Canterbury	1991
2nd	382	S.R.Dickson/J.L.Denly	v	Northants	Beckenham	2017
3rd	323	R.W.T.Key/M.van Jaarsveld	v	Surrey	Tunbridge Wells	2005
4th	368	P.A.de Silva/G.R.Cowdrey	v	Derbyshire	Maidstone	1995
5th	277	F.E.Woolley/L.E.G.Ames	v	N Zealanders	Canterbury	1931
6th	315	P.A.de Silva/M.A.Ealham	v	Notts	Nottingham	1995
7th	248	A.P.Day/E.Humphreys	v	Somerset	Taunton	1908
8th	222	S.A.Northeast/J.C.Tredwell	v	Essex	Chelmsford	2016
9th	171	M.A.Ealham/P.A.Strang	v	Notts	Nottingham	1997
10th	235	F.E.Woolley/A.Fielder	v	Worcs	Stourbridge	1909

Best Bowling	For	10- 30	C.Blythe	v	Northants	Northampton	1907
(Innings)	V	10- 48	C.H.G.Bland	for	Sussex	Tonbridge	1899
Best Bowling	For	17- 48	C.Blythe	v	Northants	Northampton	1907
(Match)	V	17-106	T.W.J.Goddard	for	Glos	Bristol	1939

Most Runs – Season	2894	F.E.Woolley	(av 59.06)	1928
Most Runs – Career	47868	F.E.Woolley	(av 41.77)	1906-38
Most 100s – Season	10	F.E.Woolley		1928, 1934
Most 100s – Career	122	F.E.Woolley		1906-38
Most Wkts – Season	262	A.P.Freeman	(av 14.74)	1933
Most Wkts – Career	3340	A.P.Freeman	(av 17.64)	1914-36
Most Career W-K Dismissals	1253	F.H.Huish	(901 ct; 352 st)	1895-1914
Most Career Catches in the Field	773	F.E.Woolley		1906-38

LIMITED-OVERS CRICKET

Highest Total	50ov	384-6		v	Berkshire	Finchampstead	1994
	40ov	337-7		v	Sussex	Canterbury	2013
	T20	231-7		v	Surrey	The Oval	2015
Lowest Total	50ov	60		v	Somerset	Taunton	1979
	40ov	83		v	Middlesex	Lord's	1984
	T20	72		v	Hampshire	Southampton	2011
Highest Innings	50ov	147	D.I.Stevens	v	Glamorgan	Swansea	2017
	40ov	146	A.Symonds	v	Lancashire	Tunbridge Wells	2004
	T20	127	J.L.Denly	v	Essex	Chelmsford	2017
Best Bowling	50ov	8-31	D.L.Underwood	v	Scotland	Edinburgh	1987
	40ov	6- 9	R.A.Woolmer	v	Derbyshire	Chesterfield	1979
	T20	5-11	A.F.Milne	v	Somerset	Taunton	2017

LANCASHIRE

Formation of Present Club: 12 January 1864
Inaugural First-Class Match: 1865
Colours: Red, Green and Blue
Badge: Red Rose
County Champions (since 1890): (8) 1897, 1904, 1926, 1927, 1928, 1930, 1934, 2011
Joint Champions: (1) 1950
Gillette/NatWest Trophy Winners: (7) 1970, 1971, 1972, 1975, 1990, 1996, 1998
Benson and Hedges Cup Winners: (4) 1984, 1990, 1995, 1996
Pro 40/National League (Div 1) Winners: (1) 1999.
Sunday League Winners: (4) 1969, 1970, 1989, 1998
Twenty20 Cup Winners: (1) 2015

Chief Executive: Daniel Gidney, Emirates Old Trafford, Talbot Road, Manchester M16 0PX • Tel: 0161 868 6700 • Email: enquiries@lccc.co.uk • Web: www.lccc.co.uk • Twitter: @LancsCCC (77,656 followers)

Director of Cricket: Paul Allott. **Head Coach**: Glen Chapple. **Assistant Coach**: Mark Chilton. **Captain**: L.S.Livingstone. **Overseas Players**: J.P.Faulkner (T20 only) and J.M.Mennie. **2018 Testimonial**: S.J.Croft. **Head Groundsman**: Matthew Merchant. **Scorer**: Chris Rimmer. ‡ New registration. [NQ] Not qualified for England.

ANDERSON, James Michael (St Theodore RC HS and SFC, Burnley), b Burnley 30 Jul 1982. 6'2". LHB, RFM. Squad No 9. Debut (Lancashire) 2002; cap 2003; benefit 2012. YC 2003. *Wisden* 2008. **ECB Test Central Contract 2017-18. Tests**: 134 (2003 to 2017-18); HS 81 v I (Nottingham) 2014, sharing a world Test record 10th wkt partnership of 198 with J.E.Root; 50 wkts (3); most – 57 (2010); BB 7-42 v WI (Lord's) 2017. **LOI**: 194 (2002-03 to 2014-15); HS 28 v NZ (Southampton) 2013; BB 5-23 v SA (Port Elizabeth) 2009-10. Hat-trick v P (Oval) 2003 – 1st for E in 373 LOI. **IT20**: 19 (2006-07 to 2009-10); HS 1* v A (Sydney) 2006-07; BB 3-23 v Netherlands (Lord's) 2009. F-c Tours: A 2006-07, 2010-11, 2013-14, 2017-18; SA 2004-05, 2009-10, 2015-16; WI 2003-04, 2005-06 (Eng A) (*part*), 2008-09, 2014-15; NZ 2007-08, 2012-13; I 2005-06 (*part*), 2008-09, 2012-13, 2016-17; SL 2003-04, 2007-08, 2011-12; UAE 2011-12 (v P), 2015-16 (v P). HS 81 (*see Tests*). La HS 42 v Surrey (Manchester) 2015. 50 wkts (4); most – 60 (2005, 2017). BB 7-42 (*see Tests*). La BB 7-77 v Essex (Chelmsford) 2015. Hat-trick v Essex (Manchester) 2003. LO HS 28 (*see LOI*). LO BB 5-23 (*see LOI*). T20 HS 16. T20 BB 3-23.

BAILEY, Thomas Ernest (Our Lady's Catholic HS, Preston), b Preston 21 Apr 1991. 6'4". RHB, RMF. Squad No 8. Debut (Lancashire) 2012. HS 58 v Middx (Southport) 2017. BB 5-12 v Leics (Leicester) 2015. LO HS 11 v Northants (Liverpool) 2017 (RLC). LO BB 3-31 v Middx (Blackpool) 2015 (RLC). T20 HS 10. T20 BB 2-24.

BOHANNON, Joshua James (Harper Green HS), b Bolton 9 Apr 1997. 5'8". RHB, RMF. Squad No 20. Lancashire 2nd XI debut 2014. Awaiting 1st XI debut.

BROWN, Karl Robert (Hesketh Fletcher HS, Atherton), b Bolton 17 May 1988. 5'10". RHB, RMF. Squad No 14. Debut (Lancashire) 2006; cap 2015. Moors Sports Club 2011-12. HS 132 v Glamorgan (Manchester) 2015. BB 2-30 v Notts (Nottingham) 2009. LO HS 129 v Yorks (Manchester) 2014 (RLC). T20 HS 69.

BUTTLER, Joseph Charles (King's C, Taunton), b Taunton, Somerset 8 Sep 1990. 6'0". RHB, WK. Squad No 6. Somerset 2009-13; cap 2013. Lancashire debut 2014. IPL: MI 2016-17. Big Bash: MR 2013-14, ST 2017-18. **ECB L-O Central Contract 2017-18. Tests**: 18 (2014 to 2016-17); HS 85 v I (Southampton) 2014. **LOI**: 109 (2011-12 to 2017-18); HS 129 v NZ (Birmingham) 2015. **IT20**: 61 (2011 to 2017-18); HS 73* v SL (Southampton) 2016. T20 HS 144 Sm v Hants (Southampton) 2010. La HS 100* v Durham (Chester-le-St) 2014. BB –. LO HS 129 (see LOI). T20 HS 81.

NQ**CHANDERPAUL, Shivnarine** (Cove and John SS, Unity Village), b Unity Village, Demerara, Guyana 16 Aug 1974. 5'8". LHB, LB. Squad No 11. Guyana 1991-92 to date. Durham 2007-09. Lancashire debut/cap 2010; returned in 2017 (Kolpak signing). Warwickshire 2011. Derbyshire 2013-14; cap 2014. IPL: RCB 2007-08. *Wisden* 2007. **Tests** (WI): 164 (1993-94 to 2015, 14 as captain); 1000 runs (1): 1065 (2002); HS 203* v SA (Georgetown) 2004-05; BB 1-2 v A (Adelaide) 1996-97. **LOI** (WI): 268 (1994-95 to 2010-11, 16 as captain); HS 150 v SA (E London) 1998-99; BB 3-18 v I (Sharjah) 1997-98. **IT20** (WI): 22 (2005-06 to 2010); HS 41 v E (Oval) 2007. F-c Tours (WI) (C=Captain): E 1995, 2000, 2004, 2007, 2009, 2012; A 1996-97, 1995-96, 1996-97, 2000-01, 2005-06C, 2009-10; SA 1998-99, 2003-04, 2007-08, 2014-15; NZ 1994-95, 1999-00, 2005-06C, 2008-09, 2013-14; I 1994-95, 2002-03, 2011-12, 2013-14; P 1997-98, 2001-02 (Sharjah), 2006-07; SL 2005C, 2010-11; Z 2001, 2003-04; B 1999-00, 2002-03, 2011-12, 2012-13; K 2001. 1000 runs (1+1); most – 1107 (2004-05). HS 303* Guyana v Jamaica (Kingston) 1995-96. CC HS 201* Du v Worcs (Worcester) 2009. La HS 182 v Surrey (Oval) 2017. BB 4-48 Guyana v Leeward Is (Basseterre) 1992-93. LO HS 150 (see LOI). LO BB 4-22 Guyana v Trinidad (Hampton Court) 1995-96. T20 HS 87*.

CLARK, Jordan (Sedbergh S), b Whitehaven, Cumbria 14 Oct 1990. Elder brother of G.Clark (see DURHAM). 6'4". RHB, RMF, occ WK. Squad No 16. Debut (Lancashire) 2015. HS 140 v Surrey (Oval) 2017. BB 4-81 v Warwks (Birmingham) 2017. LO HS 79* and LO BB 4-34 v Worcs (Manchester) 2017 (RLC). T20 HS 44. T20 BB 4-22.

CROFT, Steven John (Highfield HS, Blackpool; Myerscough C), b Blackpool 11 Oct 1984. 5'10". RHB, OB. Squad No 15. Debut (Lancashire) 2005; cap 2010; captain 2017; testimonial 2018. Auckland 2008-09. HS 156 v Northants (Manchester) 2014. BB 6-41 v Worcs (Manchester) 2012. LO HS 127 v Warwks (Birmingham) 2017 (RLC). LO BB 4-24 v Scotland (Manchester) 2008 (FPT). T20 HS 94*. T20 BB 3-6.

DAVIES, Alexander Luke (Queen Elizabeth GS, Blackburn), b Darwen 23 Aug 1994. 5'7". RHB, WK. Squad No 17. Debut (Lancashire) 2012; cap 2017. Lancashire 2nd XI debut 2011. F-c Tour (EL): WI 2017-18. 1000 runs (1): 1046 (2017). HS 140* v Essex (Chelmsford) 2017. LO HS 73* v Warwks (Manchester) 2015 (RLC). T20 HS 47.

NQ**FAULKNER, James** Peter, b Launceston, Tasmania, Australia 29 Apr 1990. Son of P.I.Faulkner (Tasmania 1982-83 to 1989-90). 6'1". RHB, LMF. Tasmania 2008-09 to date. Lancashire 2015, returning in 2018 for 2018 only. IPL: PW 2011. KXIP 2012. RR 2013-15. GL 2016-17 Big Bash: MS 2011-12 to date. **Tests** (A): 1 (2013); HS 23 and BB 4-51 (Oval) 2013. **LOI** (A): 69 (2012-13 to 2017-18); HS 116 v I (Bangalore) 2013-14; BB 4-32 v P (Brisbane) 2016-17. **IT20** (A): 24 (2011-12 to 2016-17); HS 41* v SA (Adelaide) 2014-15; BB 5-27 v P (Mohali) 2015-16. F-c Tour (A): E 2013. HS 121 v Surrey (Oval) 2015. BB 5-5 Tas v S Aus (Hobart) 2010-11. La BB 5-39 v Essex (Manchester) 2015. LO HS 116 (see LOI). LO BB 4-20 Tas v Vic (Melbourne) 2010-11. T20 HS 73. T20 BB 5-16.

GUEST, Brooke David (Kent Street Senior HS, Perth, WA; Murdoch U, Perth), b Whitworth Park, Manchester 14 May 1997. 5'11". RHB, WK. Squad No 29. Lancashire 2nd XI debut 2016. Awaiting 1st XI debut. Summer contract.

HAMEED, Haseeb (Bolton S), b Bolton 17 Jan 1997. 6'2". RHB, LB. Squad No 23. Debut (Lancashire) 2015; cap 2016. England Lions 2017. Lancashire 2nd XI debut 2013. England U19 2014-15 to 2015. **Tests**: 3 (2016-17); HS 82 v I (Rajkot) 2016-17 – on debut. F-c Tours: WI 2017-18 (EL); I 2016-17; SL 2016-17 (EL). 1000 runs (1): 1198 (2016). HS 122 v Notts (Nottingham) 2016. BB –. LO HS 88 v Leics (Manchester) 2017 (RLC).

HURT, Liam Jack (Balshaw's CE HS, Leyland), b Preston 15 Mar 1994. 6'4". RHB, RMF. Squad No 22. Lancashire 2nd XI debut 2013. Played 2nd XI cricket for six other counties. Awaiting f-c debut. LO HS 15 and LO BB 2-59 Le v Durham (Leicester) 2015 (RLC) – only 1st XI appearance.

‡JENNINGS, Keaton Kent (King Edward VII S, Johannesburg), b Johannesburg, South Africa 19 Jun 1992. Son of R.V.Jennings (Transvaal 1973-74 to 1992-93), brother of D.Jennings (Gauteng and Easterns 1999 to 2003-04), nephew of K.E.Jennings (Northern Transvaal 1981-82 to 1982-83). 6'4". LHB, RMF. Squad No 1. Gauteng 2011-12. Durham 2012-17; captain 2017 (l-o only). England Lions 2017. Joins Lancashire in 2018. **Tests**: 6 (2016-17 to 2017); HS 112 v I (Mumbai), on debut; BB –. F-c Tours (C=Captain): WI 2017-18 (EL)C; I 2016-17 (EL). 1000 runs (1): 1602 (2016), inc seven hundreds (Du record). HS 221* Du v Yorks (Chester-le-St) 2016. BB 3-37 Du v Sussex (Chester-le-St) 2017. LO HS 139 Du v Warwks (Birmingham) 2017 (RLC). LO BB 1-9 Du v Surrey (Chester-le-St) 2014 (RLC). T20 HS 88. T20 BB 4-37.

JONES, Robert Peter (Bridgewater HS), b Warrington, Cheshire 3 Nov 1995. 5'10". RHB, LB. Squad No 12. Debut (Lancashire) 2016. Lancashire 2nd XI debut 2013. Cheshire 2014. England U19 2014. HS 106* v Middx (Manchester) 2016.

KERRIGAN, Simon Christopher (Corpus Christi RC HS, Preston), b Preston 10 May 1989. 5'9". RHB, SLA. Squad No 10. Debut (Lancashire) 2010; cap 2013. Northampton-shire 2017 (on loan). MCC 2013. **Tests**: 1 (2013); HS 1* and BB – v A (Oval) 2013. F-c Tour (EL): SL 2013-14. HS 62* v Hants (Southport) 2013. 50 wkts (2); most – 58 (2013). BB 9-51 (12-192 match) v Hants (Liverpool) 2011. LO HS 10 v Middx (Lord's) 2012 (CB40). LO BB 3-21 EL v Sri Lanka A (Northampton) 2011. T20 HS 4*. T20 BB 3-17.

LAMB, Daniel John (St Michael's HS, Chorley; Cardinal Newman C, Preston), b Preston 7 Sep 1995. RHB, RM. Squad No 26. Lancashire 2nd XI debut 2013. Awaiting f-c debut. LO HS 4* and LO BB 2-51 v Durham (Chester-le-St) 2017 (RLC). T20 HS 22. T20 BB 3-30.

LESTER, Toby James (Rossall S; Loughborough U), b Blackpool 5 Apr 1993. 6'4". LHB, LFM. Squad No 5. Loughborough MCCU 2012-14. Lancashire debut 2015. No 1st XI appearances in 2017. MCC Univs 2012-14. HS 2* LU v Sussex (Hove) 2014. La HS 1 v Middx (Manchester) 2016. BB 3-50 v Essex (Manchester) 2015.

LILLEY, Arron Mark (Mossley Hollins HS; Ashton SFC), b Tameside 1 Apr 1991. 6'1". RHB, OB. Squad No 19. Debut (Lancashire) 2013. HS 63 and BB 5-23 v Derbys (Southport) 2015. LO HS 10 v Hants (Manchester) 2013 (Y40). LO BB 4-30 v Derbys (Manchester) 2013 (Y40). T20 HS 38. T20 BB 3-31.

LIVINGSTONE, Liam Stephen (Chetwynde S, Barrow-in-Furness), b Barrow-in-Furness, Cumberland 4 Aug 1993. 6'1". RHB, LB. Squad No 7. Debut (Lancashire) 2016; cap 2017; captain 2018. England Lions 2017. Lancashire 2nd XI debut 2012. **IT20**: 2 (2017); HS 16 v SA (Taunton) 2017. F-c Tours (EL): WI 2017-18; SL 2016-17. HS 224 v Warwks (Manchester) 2017. BB 6-52 v Surrey (Manchester) 2017. LO HS 129 EL v South Africa A (Northampton) 2017. LO BB 3-51 v Yorks (Manchester) 2016 (RLC). T20 HS 61. T20 BB 2-11.

MAHMOOD, Saqib (Matthew Moss HS, Rochdale), b Birmingham, Warwks 25 Feb 1997. 6'3". RHB, RFM. Squad No 25. Debut (Lancashire) 2016. England U19 2014. F-c Tour (EL): WI 2017-18. HS 9 EL v West Indies A (North Sound) 2017-18. La HS 4* v Yorks (Leeds) 2017. BB 4-50 v Surrey (Manchester) 2017. LO HS 27* North v South (Dubai, DCS) 2016-17. LO BB 3-55 v Northants (Northampton) 2016 (RLC). T20 BB 3-12.

‡NQ**MENNIE, Joe** Matthew, b Coffs Harbour, NSW, Australia 24 Dec 1988. 6'3". RHB, RMF. South Australia 2011-12 to date. Joins Lancashire in 2018. Big Bash: PS 2012-13 to 2013-14. HH 2014-15 to 2015-16. SS 2015-16. MR 2017-18. **Tests** (A): 1 (2016-17); HS 10 and BB 1-85 v SA (Hobart) 2016-17. **LOI** (A): 2 (2016-17); HS 1 v SA (Johannesburg) 2016-17; BB 3-49 v SA (Cape Town) 2016-17. HS 79* S Aus v Q (Brisbane) 2012-13. 50 wkts (0+1): 51 (2015-16). BB 7-96 S Aus v WA (Perth) 2011-12. LO HS 43* S Aus v Cricket Australia (Brisbane, AB) 2017-18. LO BB 5-36 S Aus v Q (Brisbane, AB) 2017-18. T20 HS 4. T20 BB 3-20.

‡**ONIONS, Graham** (St Thomas More RC S, Blaydon), b Gateshead, Tyne & Wear 9 Sep 1982. 6'1". RHB, RFM. Squad No 99. Durham 2004-17; benefit 2015. Dolphins 2013-14. Joins Lancashire in 2018. MCC 2007-08, 2015-16. *Wisden* 2009. **Tests**: 9 (2009 to 2012); HS 17* v A (Lord's) 2009; BB 5-38 v WI (Lord's) 2009 – on debut. **LOI**: 4 (2009 to 2009-10); HS 1 v A (Centurion) 2009-10; BB 2-58 v SL (Johannesburg) 2009-10. F-c Tours: SA 2009-10; NZ 2012-13; I 2007-08 (EL), 2012-13; SL 2013-14; B 2006-07 (Eng A); UAE 2011-12 (*part*). HS 65 Du v Notts (Chester-le-St) 2016. 50 wkts (7); most – 73 (2013). BB 9-67 Du v Notts (Nottingham) 2012. LO HS 19 Du v Derbys (Derby) 2008 (FPT). LO BB 4-45 Du v Lancs (Chester-le-St) 2013 (Y40). T20 HS 31. T20 BB 3-15.

PARKINSON, Matthew William (Bolton S), b Bolton 24 Oct 1996. Twin brother of C.F.Parkinson (*see LEICESTERSHIRE*). 6'0". RHB, LB. Squad No 28. Debut (Lancashire) 2016. Lancashire 2nd XI debut 2013. Staffordshire 2014. England U19 2015. HS 13 v Middx (Lord's) 2017. BB 5-49 v Warwks (Manchester) 2016 – on debut. LO HS 15* and LO BB 2-33 EL v West Indies A (Coolidge) 2017-18. T20 HS 7*. T20 BB 4-23.

PARRY, Stephen David (Audenshaw HS), b Manchester 12 Jan 1986. 6'0". RHB, SLA. Squad No 4. Debut (Lancashire) 2007, taking 5-23 v Durham U (Durham); cap 2015. Cumberland 2005-06. Big Bash: BH 2014-15. **LOI**: 2 (2013-14); HS – ; BB 3-32 v WI (North Sound) 2013-14. **IT20**: 5 (2013-14 to 2015-16); HS 1 v Netherlands (Chittagong) 2013-14; BB 2-33 v P (Dubai, DSC) 2015-16. HS 44 v Somerset (Manchester) 2017. CC BB 5-45 v Middx (Southport) 2017. BB 5-23 (*see above*). LO HS 31 v Essex (Chelmsford) 2009 (FPT). LO BB 5-17 v Surrey (Manchester) 2016 (Y40). T20 HS 15*. T20 BB 5-13 v Worcs (Manchester) 2016 – La record.

NQ**VILAS, Dane** James, b Johannesburg, South Africa 10 Jun 1985. 6'2". RHB, WK. Squad No 33. Gauteng 2006-07 to 2009-10. Lions 2008-09 to 2009-10. W Province 2010-11. Cape Cobras 2011-12 to 2016-17. Lancashire debut 2017 (Kolpak signing). Dolphins 2017-18 **Tests** (SA): 6 (2015 to 2015-16); HS 26 v E (Johannesburg) 2015-16. **IT20** (SA): 1 (2011-12); HS – . F-c Tours (SA): A 2016 (SA A), I 2015 (SA A), 2015-16; Z 2016 (SA A), B 2015. HS 244 v Hants (Manchester) 2017. LO HS 120 Gauteng v Namibia (Windhoek) 2009-10 and 120 WP v Namibia (Windhoek) 2010-11. T20 HS 71*

RELEASED/RETIRED

(Having made a County 1st XI appearance in 2017)

NQJARVIS, Kyle Malcolm (St John's C, Harare), b Harare, Zimbabwe 16 Feb 1989. Son of M.P.Jarvis (Zimbabwe 1979-80 to 1994-95). 6'4". RHB, RFM. Mashonaland Eagles 2009-10 to 2012-13. C Districts 2011-12 to 2012-13. Lancashire 2013-17; cap 2015. MWR 2014-15. Midlands Rhinos 2017-18. **Tests** (Z): 10 (2011 to 2017-18); HS 25* v P (Bulawayo) 2011; BB 5-54 v WI (Bridgetown) 2012-13. **LOI** (Z): 31 (2009-10 to 2017-18); HS 20 v Afghanistan (Sharjah) 2017-18; BB 3-36 v Kenya (Harare) 2009-10. **IT20** (Z): 11 (2011 to 2017-18); HS 9* v SA (Hambantota) 2012-13; BB 3-15 v P (Harare) 2011. F-c Tours (Z): SA 2017-18; WI 2012-13. HS 57 v Yorks (Manchester) 2016. 50 wkts (2); most – 62 (2015). BB 7-35 ME v MT (Bulawayo) 2012-13. La BB 6-61 v Hants (Southampton) 2017. LO HS 33* MWR v Mountaineers (Kwekwe) 2014-15. LO BB 4-31 v Derbys (Derby) 2016 (RLC). T20 HS 10. T20 BB 3-15.

NQJUNAID KHAN, Mohammad, b Matra, NW Frontier, Pakistan 24 Dec 1989. RHB, LMF. Abbottabad 2006-07 to 2011-12. NW Frontier Province 2008-09. KRL 2008-09. Lancashire 2011-14; T20 only in 2017. WAPDA 2012-13 to 2016-17. Habib Bank 2017-18. **Tests** (P): 22 (2011 to 2015); HS 17 v Z (Harare) 2013; BB 5-38 v SL (Abu Dhabi) 2011-12. **LOI** (P): 66 (2011 to 2017-18); HS 25 v SA (Benoni) 2012-13; BB 4-12 v Ireland (Belfast) 2011. **IT20** (P): 9 (2011 to 2013-14); HS 3* v WI (Gros Islet) 2011; BB 3-24 v Afghanistan (Sharjah) 2013-14. F-c Tours (P): SA 2012-13; WI 2010-11; SL 2010 (P A), 2012, 2014, 2015; Z 2011, 2013; B 2015; UAE 2011-12 (v E), 2013-14 (v SA), 2013-14 (v SL). HS 71 Abbottabad v Rawalpindi (Abbottabad) 2007-08. La HS 16 v Durham (Liverpool) 2011. BB 7-46 (13-77 match) Abbottabad v Peshawar (Peshawar) 2007-08. La BB 3-84 v Middx (Manchester) 2014. LO HS 32 P A v South Africa A (Colombo, PSS) 2010. LO BB 5-45 Fighters v Warriors (Karachi) 2014-15. T20 HS 36. T20 BB 4-12.

NQMcLAREN, Ryan (Grey C, Bloemfontein; Free State U), b Kimberley, South Africa 9 Feb 1983. 6'4". Son of P.McLaren (GW 1977-78 to 1994-95), nephew of Keith McLaren (GW 1971-72 to 1984-85), cousin of A.P.McLaren (GW 1998-99 to 2011-12, Eagles 2007-08 to 2008-09, Knights 2010-11, SW Districts 2012-13 to 2013-14, Warriors 2012-13). LHB, RFM. FS 2003-04 to 2004-05. Eagles 2004-05 to 2009-10. Kent 2007-09; cap 2007. Knights 2010-11 to date. Dolphins 2014-15. Hampshire 2015-16. Lancashire 2017. IPL: MI 2009-10. KXIP 2011. KKR 2013. **Tests** (SA): 2 (2009-10 to 2013-14); HS 33* v E (Johannesburg) 2009-10; BB 2-72 v A (Centurion) 2013-14. **LOI** (SA): 54 (2009-10 to 2014-15); HS 71* v I (Cardiff) 2013; BB 4-19 v P (Birmingham) 2013. **IT20** (SA): 12 (2009-10 to 2014-15); HS 6* and BB 5-19 (SA record analysis) v WI (North Sound) 2009-10. F-c Tour (SA A): Ire 2012. HS 140 Eagles v Warriors (Bloemfontein) 2005-06. CC HS 107 v Hants (Manchester) 2017. 50 wkts (1+1); most – 54 (2006-07). BB 8-38 Eagles v Cobras (Stellenbosch) 2006-07. CC BB 6-75 K v Notts (Nottingham) 2008. La BB 4-37 v Somerset (Manchester) 2017. LO HS 88 Knights v Cobras (Bloemfontein) 2013-14. LO BB 5-38 Knights v Warriors (Kimberley) 2012-13. T20 HS 77. T20 BB 5-19.

PROCTER, L.A. – *see NORTHAMPTONSHIRE.*

LANCASHIRE 2017

RESULTS SUMMARY

	Place	Won	Lost	Tied	Drew	NR
Specsavers County Champ (1st Division)	2nd	5	3		6	
All First-Class Matches		6	3		6	
Royal London One-Day Cup (North Group)	4th	4	4			
NatWest t20 Blast (North Group)	7th	5	6	1		2

SPECSAVERS COUNTY CHAMPIONSHIP AVERAGES

BATTING AND FIELDING

Cap		M	I	NO	HS	Runs	Avge	100	50	Ct/St
2010	S.Chanderpaul	13	19	3	182	831	51.93	3	1	3
2017	L.S.Livingstone	11	19	2	224	803	47.23	2	3	12
2017	A.L.Davies	14	24	1	140*	916	39.82	3	3	42/6
	R.McLaren	14	19	1	107	602	33.44	1	2	6
	D.J.Vilas	14	22	2	244	662	33.10	1	2	13
2010	S.J.Croft	9	15	1	115	409	29.21	1	–	6
2016	H.Hameed	12	21	3	88	513	28.50	–	3	6
	J.Clark	11	14	1	140	364	28.00	1	–	–
2003	J.M.Anderson	5	6	5	13*	23	23.00	–	–	3
	T.E.Bailey	8	11	1	58	216	21.60	–	1	1
	S.D.Parry	13	16	–	44	293	18.31	–	–	5
	R.P.Jones	3	5	–	35	87	17.40	–	–	3
	J.C.Buttler	4	6	–	49	103	17.16	–	–	3
	L.A.Procter	4	6	–	24	71	11.83	–	–	1
2015	K.M.Jarvis	9	11	2	30	106	11.77	–	–	3
	M.W.Parkinson	5	6	3	13	20	6.66	–	–	1
	S.Mahmood	3	4	3	4*	5	5.00	–	–	1

Also batted: S.C.Kerrigan (2 matches – cap 2013) 20*, 59 (1 ct).

BOWLING

	O	M	R	W	Avge	Best	5wI	10wM
S.Mahmood	69.3	10	256	12	21.33	4-50	–	–
M.W.Parkinson	76.4	7	308	14	22.00	4-68	–	–
K.M.Jarvis	255.3	62	779	33	23.60	6-61	2	–
J.M.Anderson	162.3	46	373	15	24.86	4-20	–	–
R.McLaren	379.1	87	1130	45	25.11	4-37	–	–
T.E.Bailey	217.2	48	629	25	25.16	5-44	2	1
S.D.Parry	322.3	68	777	25	31.08	5-45	1	–
J.Clark	179.5	23	643	19	33.84	4-81	–	–

Also bowled:

L.A.Procter	46	6	160	6	26.66	3-43	–	–
L.S.Livingstone	109	16	345	7	49.28	6-52	1	–
S.C.Kerrigan	83	14	287	5	57.40	2-35	–	–

S.J.Croft 24.5-2-58-0; H.Hameed 4-1-9-0.

The First-Class Averages (pp 230–246) give the records of their players in all first-class county matches (Lancashire's other opponents being Cambridge MCCU), with the exception of S.C.Kerrigan and L.A.Procter, whose first-class figures for Lancashire are as above, and:
J.M.Anderson 6-7-5-13*-33-16.50-0-0-3ct. 178.3-53-388-21-18.47-5/10-1-0.
H.Hameed 13-22-4-88-520-28.88-0-3-6ct. 4-1-9-0.
L.S.Livingstone 12-21-2-224-805-42.36-2-3-12ct. 115-19-353-9-39.22-6/52-1-0.

LANCASHIRE RECORDS

FIRST-CLASS CRICKET

Highest Total	For 863		v	Surrey	The Oval	1990
	V 707-9d		by	Surrey	The Oval	1990
Lowest Total	For 25		v	Derbyshire	Manchester	1871
	V 20		by	Essex	Chelmsford	2013
Highest Innings	For 424	A.C.MacLaren	v	Somerset	Taunton	1895
	V 315*	T.W.Hayward	for	Surrey	The Oval	1898

Highest Partnership for each Wicket

1st	368	A.C.MacLaren/R.H.Spooner	v	Glos	Liverpool	1903
2nd	371	F.B.Watson/G.E.Tyldesley	v	Surrey	Manchester	1928
3rd	501	A.N.Petersen/A.G.Prince	v	Glamorgan	Colwyn Bay	2015
4th	358	S.P.Titchard/G.D.Lloyd	v	Essex	Chelmsford	1996
5th	360	S.G.Law/C.L.Hooper	v	Warwicks	Birmingham	2003
6th	278	J.Iddon/H.R.W.Butterworth	v	Sussex	Manchester	1932
7th	248	G.D.Lloyd/I.D.Austin	v	Yorkshire	Leeds	1997
8th	158	J.Lyon/R.M.Ratcliffe	v	Warwicks	Manchester	1979
9th	142	L.O.S.Poidevin/A.Kermode	v	Sussex	Eastbourne	1907
10th	173	J.Briggs/R.Pilling	v	Surrey	Liverpool	1885

Best Bowling	For	10-46	W.Hickton	v	Hampshire	Manchester	1870
(Innings)	V	10-40	G.O.B.Allen	for	Middlesex	Lord's	1929
Best Bowling	For	17-91	H.Dean	v	Yorkshire	Liverpool	1913
(Match)	V	16-65	G.Giffen	for	Australians	Manchester	1886

Most Runs – Season	2633	J.T.Tyldesley	(av 56.02)		1901
Most Runs – Career	34222	G.E.Tyldesley	(av 45.20)		1909-36
Most 100s – Season	11	C.Hallows			1928
Most 100s – Career	90	G.E.Tyldesley			1909-36
Most Wkts – Season	198	E.A.McDonald	(av 18.55)		1925
Most Wkts – Career	1816	J.B.Statham	(av 15.12)		1950-68
Most Career W-K Dismissals	925	G.Duckworth	(635 ct; 290 st)		1923-38
Most Career Catches in the Field	556	K.J.Grieves			1949-64

LIMITED-OVERS CRICKET

Highest Total	50ov	381-3		v	Herts	Radlett	1999
	40ov	324-4		v	Worcs	Worcester	2012
	T20	231-4		v	Yorkshire	Manchester	2015
Lowest Total	50ov	59		v	Worcs	Worcester	1963
	40ov	68		v	Yorkshire	Leeds	2000
		68		v	Surrey	The Oval	2002
	T20	91		v	Derbyshire	Manchester	2003
Highest Innings	50ov	162*	A.R.Crook	v	Bucks	Wormsley	2005
	40ov	143	A.Flintoff	v	Essex	Chelmsford	1999
	T20	103*	A.N.Petersen	v	Leics	Leicester	2016
Best Bowling	50ov	6-10	C.E.H.Croft	v	Scotland	Manchester	1982
	40ov	6-25	G.Chapple	v	Yorkshire	Leeds	1998
	T20	5-13	S.D.Parry	v	Worcs	Manchester	2016

LEICESTERSHIRE

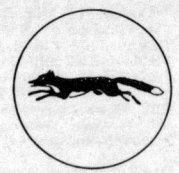

Formation of Present Club: 25 March 1879
Inaugural First-Class Match: 1894
Colours: Dark Green and Scarlet
Badge: Gold Running Fox on Green Ground
County Champions: (3) 1975, 1996, 1998
Benson and Hedges Cup Winners: (3) 1972, 1975, 1985
Sunday League Champions: (2) 1974, 1977
Twenty20 Cup Winners: (3) 2004, 2006, 2011

Chief Executive: Wasim Khan, Fischer County Ground, Grace Road, Leicester LE2 8EB •
Tel: 0116 283 2128 • Fax: 0116 244 0363 • Email: enquiries@leicestershireccc.co.uk • Web:
www.leicestershireccc.co.uk • Twitter: @leicsccc (35,754 followers)

Head Coach: Paul Nixon. **Assistant Coach**: John Sadler. **Captain**: M.A.Carberry.
Overseas Players: C.N.Ackermann, Mohammad Abbas, Mohammad Nabi (T20 only) and
Sohail Khan. **2018 Testimonial**: None. **Head Groundsman**: Andy Ward. **Scorer**: Paul
Rogers. ‡ New registration. NQ Not qualified for England.

NQ**ACKERMANN, Colin** Niel (Grey HS, Port Elizabeth; U of SA), b George, South Africa
4 Apr 1991. RHB, OB. Squad No 48. Eastern Province 2010-11 to 2015-16. Warriors
2013-14 to date. Leicestershire debut 2017 (two-year contract). 1000 runs (0+1): 1200
(2013-14). HS 187* Warriors v Knights (Kimberley) 2017-18. Le HS 118 v Derbys (Derby)
2017. BB 3-45 v Northants (Northampton) 2017. LO HS 92 Warriors v Cobras (Port
Elizabeth) 2015-16. LO BB 4-48 Warriors v Dolphins (Durban) 2017-18. T20 HS 79*. T20
BB 3-21.

ALI, Aadil Masud (Lancaster S, Leicester; Q Elizabeth C), b Leicester 29 Dec 1994. 5'11".
RHB, OB. Squad No 14. Debut (Leicestershire) 2015. Leicestershire 2nd XI debut 2013. HS
80 v Glos (Leicester) 2015. BB 1-10 v Worcs (Worcester) 2017. LO HS 88 v Worcs
(Leicester) 2017 (RLC). LO BB 1-31 v Notts (Mkt Warsop) 2017 (RLC). T20 HS 35*. T20
BB 2-22.

CARBERRY, Michael Alexander (St John Rigby Catholic C), b Croydon, Surrey 29 Sep
1980. 6'0". LHB, RM. Squad No 15. Surrey 2001-02. Kent 2003-05. Hampshire 2006-17;
cap 2006. Leicestershire debut 2017; captain 2018. MCC 2008, 2015. Big Bash: PS
2014-15. **Tests**: 6 (2009-10 to 2013-14); HS 60 v A (Adelaide) 2013-14. **LOI**: 6 (2013 to
2014); HS 63 v A (Cardiff) 2013. **IT20**: 1 (2014); HS 7 v SL (Oval) 2014. F-c Tours: A
2013-14; B 2006-07 (Eng A), 2009-10. 1000 runs (4); most – 1275 (2015). HS 300* H v
Yorks (Southampton) 2011, sharing in UK 3rd highest and UK record 3rd-wkt partnership
of 523 with N.D.McKenzie. Le HS 18 v Kent (Canterbury) 2017. BB 2-85 H v Durham
(Chester-le-St) 2006. LO HS 150* H v Lancs (Southampton) 2013 (Y40). LO BB 3-37 H v
Derbys (Derby) 2013 (Y40). T20 HS 100*. T20 BB 1-16.

CHAPPELL, Zachariah John ('**Zak**') (Stamford S), b Grantham, Lincs 21 Aug 1996. 6'4".
RHB, RFM. Squad No 32. Debut (Leicestershire) 2015. HS 96 v Derbys (Derby) 2015. BB
4-108 v Derbys (Derby) 2017. LO HS 59* v Durham (Gosforth) 2017 (RLC). LO BB 2-44
v Notts (Mkt Warsop) 2017 (RLC). T20 BB –.

NQCOSGROVE, Mark James, b Elizabeth, Adelaide, S Australia 14 Jun 1984. 5'9". LHB, RM. Squad No 55. S Australia 2002-03 to 2015-16. Glamorgan 2006-10; cap 2006. Tasmania 2010-11 to 2013-14. Leicestershire debut/cap 2015; captain 2015-17. Big Bash: HH 2011-12. ST 2012-13 to 2014-15. SS 2013-14. **LOI** (A): 3 (2005-06 to 2006-07); HS 74 v B (Fatullah) 2005-06 – on debut; BB 1-1 v WI (Kuala Lumpur) 2006-07. 1000 runs (4); most – 1279 (2016). HS 233 Gm v Derbys (Derby) 2006. Le HS 188 v Derbys (Derby) 2017. BB 3-3 S Aus v Tas (Adelaide) 2006-07. CC BB Gm 3-30 v Derbys (Derby) 2009. Le BB 2-14 v Worcs (Worcester) 2016. LO HS 121 S Aus v WA (Perth) 2005-06. LO BB 2-21 S Aus v Q (Brisbane) 2005-06. T20 HS 89. T20 BB 2-11.

DEARDEN, Harry Edward (Tottington HS), b Bury, Lancs 7 May 1997. LHB, OB. Squad No 5. Debut (Leicestershire) 2016. Lancashire 2nd XI 2014-15. Cheshire 2016. HS 87 v Glamorgan (Leicester) 2017. BB 1-0 v Kent (Leicester) 2017.

NQDELPORT, Cameron Scott (Kloof Senior S, Durban; Westville BHS), b Durban, South Africa 12 May 1989. 5'10". LHB, RM. Squad No 24. KwaZulu-Natal 2008-09 to 2016-17. Dolphins 2008-09 to 2011-12. Leicestershire debut 2017, but played l-o and T20 in 2016. Big Bash: ST 2014-15. HS 163 KZN v Northerns (Centurion) 2010-11. Le HS 20 v Glamorgan (Leicester) 2017. BB 2-10 KZN v Northern Cape (Chatsworth) 2016-17. LO HS 169* Dolphins v Knights (Bloemfontein) 2014-15. LO BB 4-42 Dolphins v Titans (Durban) 2011-12. T20 HS 109*. T20 BB 4-17.

DEXTER, Neil John (Northwood HS, Durban; Varsity C; U of South Africa), b Johannesburg, South Africa 21 Aug 1984. 6'0". RHB, RMF. Squad No 17. Kent 2005-08. Essex 2008. Middlesex 2009-15; cap 2010; captain 2010 (*part*) to 2013. Leicestershire debut 2016. Qualified for England in 2010. HS 163* M v Northants (Northampton) 2014. Le HS 136 v Glos (Leicester) 2016. BB 6-63 M v Lancs (Lord's) 2014. Le BB 5-52 v Sussex (Leicester) 2016. LO HS 135* K v Glamorgan (Cardiff) 2006 (CGT). Le BB 4-22 v Lancs (Leicester) 2016 (RLC). T20 HS 73. T20 BB 4-21.

ECKERSLEY, Edmund John Holden ('Ned') (St Benedict's GS, Ealing), b Oxford 9 Aug 1989. 6'0". RHB, WK, occ OB. Squad No 3. Debut (Leicestershire) 2011; cap 2013. Mountaineers 2011-12. MCC 2013. 1000 runs (1): 1302 (2013). HS 158 v Derbys (Derby) 2017. BB 2-29 v Lancs (Manchester) 2013. LO HS 108 v Yorks (Leicester) 2013 (Y40). T20 HS 43.

EVANS, Samuel Thomas (Lancaster S, Leicester; Wyggeston & QE I C; Leicester U), b Leicester 20 Dec 1997. RHB. Squad No 21. Loughborough MCCU 2017. Leicestershire debut 2017. Leicestershire 2nd XI debut 2015. HS 114 LU v Northants (Northampton) 2017. Le HS 29 v Northants (Leicester) 2017.

GRIFFITHS, Gavin Timothy (St Mary's C, Crosby), b Ormskirk, Lancs 19 Nov 1993. 6'2". RHB, RMF. Squad No 93. Debut (Leicestershire) 2017. Lancashire 2014-15 (l-o only). Hampshire 2016 (T20 only). England U19 2012-13. HS 14* v Kent (Leicester) 2017. BB 4-101 v Glos (Bristol) 2017. LO HS 5* La v Kent (Canterbury) 2015 (RLC). LO BB 3-35 v Warwks (Leicester) 2017 (RLC). T20 HS 11. T20 BB 3-33.

HILL, Lewis John (Hastings HS, Hinckley; Open Cleveland C), b Leicester 5 Oct 1990. 5'7½". RHB, WK, occ RM. Squad No 23. Debut (Leicestershire) 2015. Unicorns 2012-13. HS 126 v Surrey (Oval) 2015. LO HS 86 v Durham (Leicester) 2015 (RLC). T20 HS 31*.

HORTON, Paul James (St Margaret's HS, Liverpool), b Sydney, Australia 20 Sep 1982. 5'10". RHB, RM. Squad No 2. UK resident since 1997. Lancashire 2003-15; cap 2007. Matabeleland Tuskers 2010-11 to 2011-12. Leicestershire debut 2016. 1000 runs (3); most – 1116 (2007). HS 209 MT v SR (Masvingo) 2010-11. CC HS 173 La v Somerset (Taunton) 2009. Le HS 117* v Worcs (Worcester) 2016. BB 2-6 v Sussex (Leicester) 2016. LO HS 111* La v Derbys (Manchester) 2009 (FPT). LO BB 1-7 v Lancs (Leicester) 2016 (RLC). T20 HS 71*.

‡**JAVID, Ateeq** (Aston Manor S), b Birmingham 15 Oct 1991. 5'8". RHB, OB. Squad No 99. Warwickshire 2009-17. Joins Leicestershire in 2018. HS 133 Wa v Somerset (Birmingham) 2013. BB 1-1 Wa v Lancs (Manchester) 2014. LO HS 43 Wa v Kent (Canterbury) 2013 (Y40). LO BB 4-42 Wa v Yorks (Leeds) 2016 (RLC). T20 HS 51*. T20 BB 4-17.

JONES, Richard Alan (Grange HS and King Edward VI C, Stourbridge; Loughborough U), b Wordsley, Stourbridge, Worcs 6 Nov 1986. 6'2". RHB, RMF. Squad No 25. Worcestershire 2007-13; cap 2007. Matabeleland Tuskers 2011-12. Warwickshire 2014-15. Leicestershire debut 2014 (on loan). HS 62 MT v SR (Bulawayo) 2011-12. UK HS 53* Wo v Durham (Worcester) 2009. Le HS 33 v Worcs (Worcester) 2016. BB 7-115 Wo v Sussex (Hove) 2010. Le BB 2-41 v Glos (Cheltenham) 2016. LO HS 26 Wa v Notts (Nottingham) 2016 (RLC). LO BB 1-25 MT v ME (Bulawayo) 2011-12. T20 HS 9. T20 BB 5-34.

NQ**KLEIN, Dieter** (Hoerskool, Lichtenburg), b Lichtenburg, South Africa 31 Oct 1988. 5'10". RHB, LMF. Squad No 77. North West 2007-08 to 2015-16. Lions 2012-13 to 2013-14. Leicestershire debut 2016. HS 66 NW v Border (E London) 2014-15. Le HS 26 v Worcs (Worcester) 2017. BB 8-72 NW v Northerns (Potchefstroom) 2014-15. Le BB 6-80 v Northants (Northampton) 2017. LO HS 26 v Durham (Gosforth) 2017 (RLC). LO BB 5-35 NW v Northerns (Pretoria) 2012-13. T20 HS 16. T20 BB 3-27.

‡NQ**MOHAMMAD ABBAS**, b Sialkot, Pakistan 10 Mar 1990. RHB, RMF. Squad No 26. Sialkot 2008-09 to 2012-13. KRL 2015-16 to 2016-17. SNGPL 2017-18. Joins Leicestershire in 2018. Tests (P): 5 (2017 to 2017-18); HS 4 and BB 5-46 v WI (Roseau) 2017. F-c Tour (P): WI 2017. HS 40 and BB 8-46 (14-93 match) KRL v Karachi Whites (Karachi) 2016-17. 50 wkts (0+2); most 71 (2016-17). LO HS 15* KRL v HB (Karachi) 2016-17. LO BB 4-31 KRL v SNGPL (Karachi) 2016-17. T20 HS 7*. T20 BB 2-18.

‡NQ**MOHAMMAD NABI** Eisakhil, b Peshawar, Pakistan 7 Mar 1985. RHB, OB. Squad No 7. MCC2007-11. Pakistan Customs 2007-08 to 2009-10. Afghanistan 2009 to date. Joins Leicestershire for T20 only. IPL: SH 2017. Big Bash: MR 2017-18. **LOI** (Afghan): 94 (2009 to 2017-18); HS 116 v Z (Bulawayo) 2015-16; BB 4-30 v Ireland (Greater Noida) 2016-17. **IT20** (Afghan): 60 (2009-10 to 2017-18); HS 89 v Ireland (Greater Noida) 2016-17. BB 4-10 v Ireland (Dubai, DSC) 2016-17. HS 117 Afg v UAE (Sharjah) 22011-12. BB 6-33 Afg v Namibia (Windhoek) 2013. LO HS 146 MSC v PDSC (Bogra) 2013-14. LO BB 5-12 Afg v Namibia (Windhoek) 2013. T20 HS 89. T20 BB 4-10.

PARKINSON, Callum Francis (Bolton S), b Bolton, Lancs 24 Oct 1996. Twin brother of M.W.Parkinson (see LANCASHIRE). RHB, SLA. Squad No 10. Derbyshire 2016. Leicestershire debut 2017. Staffordshire 2015-16. HS 75 v Kent (Canterbury) 2017. BB 8-148 (10-185 match) v Worcs (Worcester) 2017. LO HS 3 and LO BB 1-44 v Yorks (Leeds) 2017 (RLC). T20 HS 8*. T20 BB 3-20.

PETTINI, Mark Lewis (Comberton Village C; Hills Road SFC, Cambridge; Cardiff U), b Brighton, Sussex 7 Aug 1983. 5'10". RHB, RM. Squad No 6. Essex 2001-15; cap 2006; captain 2007 (part) to 2010 (part). Mountaineers 2011-12 to 2014-15. Mashonaland Eagles 2015-16. Leicestershire debut 2016; captain (l-o only) 2016. MCC 2005. 1000 runs (1): 1218 (2006). HS 209 Mountaineers v MT (Bulawayo) 2013-14. CC HS 208* Ex v Derbys (Chelmsford) 2006. Le HS 142* v Sussex (Hove) 2016. BB 1-72 Ex v Leics (Leicester) 2012 – in contrived circumstances. LO HS 159 v Warwks (Leicester) 2017 (RLC). T20 HS 95*.

RAINE, Benjamin Alexander (St Aidan's RC SS, Sunderland) b Sunderland, Co Durham 14 Sep 1991. 6'0''. LHB, RMF. Squad No 44. Durham 2011. Leicestershire debut 2013. HS 72 v Lancs (Manchester) 2013. 50 wkts (1): 61 (2015). BB 6-66 v Notts (Leicester) 2017. LO HS 43 v Yorks (Leicester) 2014 (RLC). LO BB 3-62 v Derbys (Derby) 2016 (RLC). T20 HS 48. T20 BB 3-7.

SAYER, Robert John (Ramsey Abbey C; Leeds Beckett U), b Huntingdon, Cambridgeshire 25 Jan 1995. 6'3''. RHB, OB. Squad No 12. Debut (Leicestershire) 2015. Leicestershire 2nd XI debut 2013. Cambridgeshire 2013. HS 34 v Glos (Leicester) 2015. BB 2-41 v Sri Lankans (Leicester) 2016. CC BB 2-59 v Derbys (Leicester) 2015. LO HS 26 v Notts (Leicester) 2016 (RLC). LO BB 2-65 v Worcs (Leicester) 2017 (RLC). T20 HS 9. T20 BB 2-16.

‡[NQ]**SOHAIL KHAN**, b Malakand, Pakistan 6 Mar 1984. Brother of Murad Khan (SNGC 2008-09). RHB, RFM. Squad No 19. SSGC 2007-08 to 2015-16. Sind 2007-08 to 2010-11. Karachi Whites 2010-11 to 2012-13. Karachi Blues 2011-12. Port Qasim Authority 2013-14 to 2014-15. United Bank 2017-18. Joins Leicestershire as overseas player for part of 2018. **Tests** (P): 9 (2009 to 2016-17); HS 65 v A (Melbourne) 22016-17; BB 5-68 v E (The Oval) 2016. **LOI** (P): 13 (2007-08 to 2016-17); HS 7 and BB 5-55 v I (Adelaide) 2014-15. **IT20** (P): 5 (2008-09 to 2016-17); HS 1* v World XI (Lahore) 2017; BB 2-13 v Z (Harare) 2011. F-c Tours (P): E 2016; A 2016-17; NZ 2016-17; Z 2011. HS 65 (*see Tests*). 50 wkts (0+4): most – 91 (2007-08). BB 9-109 (16-189 match) SNGC v WAPDA (Karachi) 2007-08. LO HS 39 Karachi Zebras v Lahore Eagles (Karachi) 2011-12. LO BB 6-44 Karachi Zebras v Lahore Lions (Karachi) 2010-11. T20 HS 45*. T20 BB 5-23.

SWINDELLS, Harry John, (Brockington C; Lutterworth C), b Leicester 21 Feb 1999. 5'7''. RHB, WK. Squad No 28. Leicestershire 2nd XI debut 2015. England U19 2017. Awaiting 1st XI debut.

‡**TAYLOR, Thomas** Alex Ian (Trentham HS, Stoke-on-Trent), b Stoke-on-Trent, Staffs 21 Dec 1994. Elder brother of J.P.A.Taylor (*see DERBYSHIRE*). 6'2''. RHB, RMF. Squad No 16. Derbyshire 2014-17. Derbyshire 2nd XI debut 2011. HS 80 De v Kent (Derby) 2016. BB 6-61 De v Lancs (Derby) 2015. LO HS –. LO BB 3-48 De v Worcs (Worcester) 2014 (RLC).

WELLS, Thomas Joshua (Gartree HS; Beauchamp C, Leicester), b Grantham, Lincs 15 Mar 1993. Father, John Wells, played rugby for Leicester. 6'2''. RHB, RMF. Squad No 83. Debut (Leicestershire) 2013. Leicestershire 2nd XI debut 2010. HS 87* v Sri Lankans (Leicester) 2016. CC HS 82 v Hants (Leicester) 2013. BB 4-46 v Loughborough MCCU (Leicester) 2017. CC BB 3-68 v Lancs (Leicester) 2015. LO HS 67 and LO BB 3-44 v Warwks (Leicester) 2017 (RLC). T20 HS 64*. T20 BB 1-5.

RELEASED/RETIRED

(Having made a County 1st XI appearance in 2017)

BURKE, James Edward (Plymouth C), b Plymouth, Devon 25 Jan 1991. 6'2''. RHB, RMF. Somerset 2012. Surrey 2015-16. Devon 2008-13. Leicestershire 2017 (1 game). HS 79 Sy v Derbys (Oval) 2015. BB 4-19 Sy v Leics (Leicester) 2015. LO HS 26* Sy v Northants (Oval) 2015 (RLC). LO BB 5-28 Sy v Derbys (Guildford) 2015 (RLC). T20 HS 8. T20 BB 3-23.

FAZAKERLEY, William Nicholas (Lancing C), b Guernsey 19 Jun 1998. 6'3''. RHB, RFM. Leicestershire 2017. Leicestershire 2nd XI debut 2016. HS 0 and BB 1-32 v Sussex (Arundel) 2017 – only 1st XI game.

^{NQ}**McKAY, Clinton** James, b Melbourne, Australia 22 Feb 1983. 6'4".. RHB, RFM. Victoria 2006-07 to 2015-16. Leicestershire 2015-17; cap 2015; captain 2017 (l-o only). IPL: MI 2012. Big Bash: MS 2011-12 to 2014-15. ST 2015-16 to 2016-17. **Tests** (A): 1 (2009-10); HS 10 and BB 1-56 v WI (Perth) 2009-10. **LOI** (A): 59 (2009-10 to 2013-14); HS 30 v SL (Oval) 2013; BB 5-28 v SL (Adelaide) 2011-12. **IT20** (A): 6 (2010-11 to 2013-14); HS 7 and BB 2-24 v WI (Bridgetown) 2011-12. HS 66 v Kent (Leicester) 2017. 50 wkts (2); most – 58 (2015). BB 6-40 Vic v Tas (Melbourne) 2011-12. Le BB 6-54 v Kent (Canterbury) 2015. LO HS 57 Vic v Tas (Brisbane) 2014-15. LO BB 5-28 (*see LOI*). T20 HS 21*. T20 BB 5-11 v Worcs (Worcester) 2017 – Le record.

^{NQ}**RONCHI, Luke**, b Dannevirke, Manawatu, New Zealand 23 Apr 1981. 5'11". RHB, WK. W Australia 2002-03 to 2011-12. Wellington 2011-12 to date. Somerset 2015. Warwickshire 2016 (T20 only). Leicestershire 2017 (T20 only). IPL: MI 2007-08 to 2009. Big Bash: PS 2011-12 to 2012-13. **Tests** (NZ): 4 (2015 to 2016-17); HS 88 v E (Leeds) 2015. **LOI** (A/NZ): 85 (4 for A 2008; 81 for NZ 2013 to 2017); HS 170* v SL (Dunedin) 2014-15. **IT20** (A/NZ): 32 (3 for A 2008 to 2008-09; 29 for NZ 2013-14 to 2016-17); HS 51* v WI (Wellington) 2013-14. F-c Tours: E 2015 (NZ); I 2008-09 (Aus A), 2013 (NZ A), 2016-17 (NZ); P 2007-08 (Aus A); SL 2013-14 (NZ A). HS 148 WA v NSW (Sydney) 2009-10. CC HS 51 Sm v Warwks (Taunton) 2015. LO HS 170* (*see LOI*). T20 HS 102.

SHRECK, Charles Edward (Truro S), b Truro, Cornwall 6 Jan 1978. 6'7". RHB, RFM. Nottinghamshire 2003-11; cap 2006. Wellington 2005-06 to 2007-08. Kent 2012-13. Leicestershire 2014-17. MCC 2008. Cornwall 1997-2002. HS 56 v Surrey (Oval) 2014. 50 wkts (4); most – 61 (2006, 2008). BB 8-31 (12-129 match) Nt v Middx (Nottingham) 2006. Le BB 5-71 v Essex (Chelmsford) 2015. Hat-trick Nt v Middx (Lord's) 2006. LO HS 9* Wellington v CD (Palmerston N) 2005-06. LO BB 5-19 Cornwall v Worcs (Truro) 2002 (CGT). T20 HS 10. T20 BB 4-22.

SYKES, James Stuart (St Ives S, Huntingdon), b Hinchingbrooke, Cambs 26 Apr 1992. 6'2". LHB, SLA. Leicestershire 2013-16. Cambridgeshire 2010. HS 34 v Lancs (Manchester) 2013. BB 4-176 v Essex (Chelmsford) 2013 – on debut. LO HS 15 v Glos (Bristol) 2013 (Y40). LO BB 4-57 v Lancs (Manchester) 2017 (RLC). T20 HS 2*. T20 BB 2-24.

A.J.Robson left the staff without making a 1st XI appearance in 2017.

143

LEICESTERSHIRE 2017

RESULTS SUMMARY

	Place	Won	Lost	Drew	NR
Specsavers County Champ (2nd Division)	10th	9	5		
All First-Class Matches		9	6		
Royal London One-Day Cup (North Group)	6th	3	4		1
NatWest t20 Blast (North Group)	QF	8	6		1

SPECSAVERS COUNTY CHAMPIONSHIP AVERAGES
BATTING AND FIELDING

Cap		M	I	NO	HS	Runs	Avge	100	50	Ct/St
	C.F.Parkinson	5	6	4	75	103	51.50	–	1	3
2015	M.J.Cosgrove	12	23	–	188	1112	48.34	2	6	1
	L.J.Hill	11	19	3	85*	527	32.93	–	2	22/2
	C.N.Ackermann	12	22	3	118	618	32.52	2	1	2
	Z.J.Chappell	6	10	2	66	258	32.25	–	1	–
2013	E.J.H.Eckersley	14	26	2	158	716	29.83	1	3	16
	M.L.Pettini	7	12	1	110*	303	27.54	1	2	1
	P.J.Horton	10	19	–	71	504	26.52	–	2	8
2015	C.J.McKay	11	18	4	66	347	24.78	–	1	2
	B.A.Raine	9	17	4	57	301	23.15	–	2	1
	N.J.Dexter	8	15	2	114	300	23.07	1	–	2
	R.A.Jones	2	4	2	23*	45	22.50	–	–	1
	A.M.Ali	3	5	–	40	110	22.00	–	–	2
	H.E.Dearden	10	19	–	87	401	21.10	–	2	11
	A.Harinath	2	4	–	26	68	17.00	–	–	–
	M.W.Pillans	4	7	–	56	107	15.28	–	1	1
	D.Klein	9	14	3	26	138	12.54	–	–	5
	R.J.Sayer	3	5	–	31	39	7.80	–	–	2
	M.A.Carberry	4	8	–	18	59	7.37	–	–	1
	G.T.Griffiths	5	7	2	14*	28	5.60	–	–	–

Also played: C.S.Delport (1 match) 20, 1; S.T.Evans (1) 8, 29 (1 ct); W.N.Fazakerley 0, 0; A.Shahzad did not bat (1 ct); C.E.Shreck (1) 26; T.J.Wells (2) 46, 16, 24 (1 ct).

BOWLING

	O	M	R	W	Avge	Best	5wI	10wM
B.A.Raine	256.1	54	777	33	23.54	6- 66	2	–
N.J.Dexter	121	23	456	14	32.57	5- 71	2	–
C.F.Parkinson	147.2	14	556	17	32.70	8-148	1	1
D.Klein	206	21	958	28	34.21	6- 80	2	–
M.W.Pillans	101.1	9	416	12	34.66	3- 63	–	–
C.J.McKay	315.3	97	809	22	36.77	4- 35	–	–
Also bowled:								
R.A.Jones	58	5	228	5	45.60	2- 50	–	–
Z.J.Chappell	114.5	13	514	9	57.11	4-108	–	–
C.N.Ackermann	104	9	394	6	65.66	3- 45	–	–
G.T.Griffiths	124	20	403	5	80.60	4-101	–	–

A.M.Ali 6-0-46-1; M.J.Cosgrove 39-1-163-2; H.E.Dearden 18.4-0-95-2; C.S.Delport 7-1-30-0; E.J.H.Eckersley 1-0-2-0; W.N.Fazakerley 12-2-83-1; A.Harinath 1-0-5-0; P.J.Horton 0.4-0-6-0; R.J.Sayer 102-9-379-2; A.Shahzad 25-1-104-0; C.E.Shreck 42-7-141-1; T.J.Wells 15-1-120-2.

The First-Class Averages (pp 230–246) give the records of Leicestershire players in all first-class county matches (Leicestershire's other opponents being Loughborough MCCU), with the exception of M.A.Carberry, S.T.Evans and A.Shahzad, whose first-class figures for Leicestershire are as above.

LEICESTERSHIRE RECORDS

FIRST-CLASS CRICKET

Highest Total	For 701-4d		v	Worcs	Worcester	1906
	V 761-6d		by	Essex	Chelmsford	1990
Lowest Total	For 25		v	Kent	Leicester	1912
	V 24		by	Glamorgan	Leicester	1971
	24		by	Oxford U	Oxford	1985
Highest Innings	For 309*	H.D.Ackerman	v	Glamorgan	Cardiff	2006
	V 355*	K.P.Pietersen	for	Surrey	The Oval	2015

Highest Partnership for each Wicket

1st	390	B.Dudleston/J.F.Steele	v	Derbyshire	Leicester	1979
2nd	289*	J.C.Balderstone/D.I.Gower	v	Essex	Leicester	1981
3rd	436*	D.L.Maddy/B.J.Hodge	v	L'boro UCCE	Leicester	2003
4th	360*	J.W.A.Taylor/A.B.McDonald	v	Middlesex	Leicester	2010
5th	330	J.W.A.Taylor/S.J.Thakor	v	L'boro MCCU	Leicester	2011
6th	284	P.V.Simmons/P.A.Nixon	v	Durham	Chester-le-St[2]	1996
7th	219*	J.D.R.Benson/P.Whitticase	v	Hampshire	Bournemouth	1991
8th	195	J.W.A.Taylor/J.K.H.Naik	v	Derbyshire	Leicester	2009
9th	160	R.T.Crawford/ W.W.Odell	v	Worcs	Leicester	1902
10th	228	R.Illingworth/K.Higgs	v	Northants	Leicester	1977

Best Bowling	For 10- 18	G.Geary		v	Glamorgan	Pontypridd	1929
(Innings)	V 10- 32	H.Pickett		for	Essex	Leyton	1895
Best Bowling	For 16- 96	G.Geary		v	Glamorgan	Pontypridd	1929
(Match)	V 16-102	C.Blythe		for	Kent	Leicester	1909

Most Runs – Season		2446	L.G.Berry	(av 52.04)	1937
Most Runs – Career		30143	L.G.Berry	(av 30.32)	1924-51
Most 100s – Season		7	L.G.Berry		1937
		7	W.Watson		1959
		7	B.F.Davison		1982
Most 100s – Career		45	L.G.Berry		1924-51
Most Wkts – Season		170	J.E.Walsh	(av 18.96)	1948
Most Wkts – Career		2131	W.E.Astill	(av 23.18)	1906-39
Most Career W-K Dismissals		905	R.W.Tolchard	(794 ct; 111 st)	1965-83
Most Career Catches in the Field		426	M.R.Hallam		1950-70

LIMITED-OVERS CRICKET

Highest Total	50ov	406-5		v	Berkshire	Leicester	1996
	40ov	344-4		v	Durham	Chester-le-St[2]	1996
	T20	221-3		v	Yorkshire	Leeds	2004
Lowest Total	50ov	56		v	Northants	Leicester	1964
		56		v	Minor Cos	Wellington	1982
	40ov	36		v	Sussex	Leicester	1973
	T20	90		v	Notts	Nottingham	2014
Highest Innings	50ov	201	V.J.Wells	v	Berkshire	Leicester	1996
	40ov	154*	B.J.Hodge	v	Sussex	Horsham	2004
	T20	111	D.L.Maddy	v	Yorkshire	Leeds	2004
Best Bowling	50ov	6-16	C.M.Willoughby	v	Somerset	Leicester	2005
	40ov	6-17	K.Higgs	v	Glamorgan	Leicester	1973
	T20	5-11	C.J.McKay	v	Worcs	Worcester	2017

MIDDLESEX

Formation of Present Club: 2 February 1864
Inaugural First-Class Match: 1864
Colours: Blue
Badge: Three Seaxes
County Champions (since 1890): (11) 1903, 1920, 1921, 1947, 1976, 1980, 1982, 1985, 1990, 1993, 2016
Joint Champions: (2) 1949, 1977
Gillette/NatWest Trophy Winners: (4) 1977, 1980, 1984, 1988
Benson and Hedges Cup Winners: (2) 1983, 1986
Sunday League Winners: (1) 1992
Twenty20 Cup Winners: (1) 2008

Chief Executive: Richard Goatley, Lord's Cricket Ground, London NW8 8QN • Tel: 020 7289 1300 • Fax: 020 7289 5831 • Email: enquiries@middlesexccc.com • Web: www.middlesexccc.com • Twitter: @Middlesex_CCC (47,299 followers)

Managing Director of Cricket: Angus Fraser. **Head Coach**: Richard Scott. **Assistant Coach**: Richard Johnson. **T20 Coach**: Daniel Vettori. **Captain**: D.J.Malan. **Overseas Player**: tba. **2018 Beneficiary**: N.R.D.Compton. **Head Groundsman**: Mick Hunt. **Scorer**: Don Shelley. ‡ New registration. NQ Not qualified for England.

ANDERSSON, Martin Kristoffer (Reading Blue Coat S), b Reading, Berks 6 Sep 1996. 6'1". RHB, RM. Squad No 24. Debut (Leeds/Bradford MCCU) 2017. Middlesex 2nd XI debut 2013. Berkshire 2015-16. Awaiting 1st XI debut. HS 12 LBU v Yorks (Leeds) 2017.

BAMBER, Ethan Read (Mill Hill S), b Westminster 17 Dec 1998. RHB, RM. Middlesex 2nd XI debut 2015. Berkshire 2017. Awaiting 1st XI debut.

BARBER, Thomas Edward (Bournemouth GS), b Poole, Dorset 31 May 1994. 6'3". RHB, LFM. Squad No 25. Hampshire 2nd XI 2013-15. Somerset 2nd XI 2016. Dorset 2016. Awaiting f-c debut. LO HS 0. LO BB 2-22 H v Yorks (Southampton) 2014 (RLC). T20 HS 0. T20 BB 1-32.

COMPTON, Nicholas Richard Denis (Harrow S; Durham U), b Durban, South Africa 26 Jun 1983. Son of R.Compton (Natal 1978-79 to 1980-81), grandson of D.C.S.Compton (Middlesex, England, Holkar, Europeans, Commonwealth and Cavaliers 1936-64), great-nephew of L.H.Compton (Middlesex 1938-56). 6'1". RHB, OB. Squad No 3. Middlesex debut 2004; cap 2006; testimonial 2018. Somerset 2010-14; cap 2011. Mashonaland Eagles 2010-11. Worcestershire (1 game) 2013. SLPACC 2017-18. MCC 2007, 2015. PCA 2012. *Wisden* 2012. **Tests**: 16 (2012-13 to 2016); HS 117 v NZ (Dunedin) 2012-13. F-c Tours: SA 2015-16; NZ 2012-13; I 2012-13; B 2006-07 (Eng A). 1000 runs (6); most – 1494 (2012). Scored 685 runs in April 2012 – a record for April. HS 254* Sm v Durham (Chester-le-St) 2011. M HS 190 v Durham (Lord's) 2006. BB 1-1 Sm v Hants (Southampton) 2010. M BB 1-94 v Sussex (Southgate) 2007. LO HS 131 v Kent (Canterbury) 2009 (FPT). LO BB 1-0 v Scotland v 2009 (FPT). T20 HS 78.

NQ**ESKINAZI, Stephen** Sean (Christ Church GS, Claremont; U of WA), b Johannesburg, South Africa 28 Mar 1994. 6'2". RHB, WK. Squad No 28. Debut (Middlesex) 2015. Middlesex 2nd XI debut 2013. UK passport. HS 179 v Warwks (Birmingham) 2017. T20 HS 57*.

FINN, Steven Thomas (Parmiter's S, Garston), b Watford, Herts 4 Apr 1989. 6'7½". RHB, RFM. Squad No 9. Debut (Middlesex) 2005; cap 2009. Otago 2011-12. YC 2010. **Tests**: 36 (2009-10 to 2016-17); HS 56 v NZ (Dunedin) 2012-13; BB 6-79 v A (Birmingham) 2015. **LOI**: 69 (2010-11 to 2017); HS 35 v A (Brisbane) 2010-11; BB 5-33 v I (Brisbane) 2014-15. **IT20**: 21 (2011 to 2015); HS 8* v I (Colombo, RPS) 2012-13; BB 3-16 v NZ (Pallekele) 2012-13. F-c Tours: A 2010-11, 2013-14; SA 2015-16; NZ 2012-13; I 2012-13; SL 2011-12; B 2009-10, 2016-17; UAE 2011-12 (v P). HS 56 (see Tests). M HS 41* v Oxford MCCU (Oxford) 2015. CC HS 37* v Warwks (Birmingham) 2014. 50 wkts (2); most – 64 (2010). BB 9-37 (14-106 match) v Worcs (Worcester) 2010. LO HS 42* v Glamorgan (Cardiff) 2014 (RLC). LO BB (see LOI) and 5-33 v Derbys (Lord's) 2011 (CB40). T20 HS 8*. T20 BB 4-24.

NQFRANKLIN, James Edward Charles (Wellington C; Victoria U), Wellington, New Zealand 7 Nov 1980. 6'4½". LHB, LM. Squad No 74. Irish passport. Wellington 1998-99 to 2014-15. Gloucestershire 2004-10; cap 2004. Glamorgan 2006; cap 2006. Nottinghamshire 2014; cap 2014. Middlesex debut/cap 2015; captain (f-c & l-o) 2017 (l-o only in 2016). IPL: MI 2011-12. Big Bash: AS 2011-12. **Tests** (NZ): 31 (2000-01 to 2012-13); HS 122* v SA (Cape Town) 2006-07; BB 6-119 v A (Auckland) 2004-05. Hat-trick v B (Dhaka) 2004-05. **LOI** (NZ): 110 (2000-01 to 2013); HS 98* v I (Bangalore) 2010-11; BB 5-42 v E (Chester-le-St) 2004. **IT20** (NZ): 38 (2005-06 to 2013); HS 60 v Z (Hamilton) 2011-12; BB 4-15 v E (Hamilton) 2012-13. F-c Tours (NZ): A 2004-05; SA 2004-05 (NZ A), 2005-06, 2012-13; I 2012; SL 2012-13; Z 2005, 2010-11 (NZ A); B 2004-05. HS 219 Wellington v Auckland (Auckland) 2008-09. HS 135 v Worcs (Uxbridge) 2015. M BB 7-14 Gs v Derbys (Bristol) 2010. M BB 4-40 v Surrey (Lord's) 2017. Hat-tricks (see above) Gs v Derbys (Cheltenham) 2009, also scoring 109 in same match. LO HS 133* Gs v Derbys (Bristol) 2010 (CB40). LO BB 5-42 (see LOI). T20 HS 90. T20 BB 5-21.

FULLER, James Kerr (Otago U, NZ), b Cape Town, South Africa 24 Jan 1990. UK passport. 6'3". RHB, RFM. Squad No 26. Otago 2009-10 to 2012-13. Gloucestershire 2011-15; cap 2011. Middlesex debut 2016. HS 93 v Somerset (Taunton) 2016. BB 6-24 (10-79 match) Otago v Wellington (Dunedin) 2012-13. CC BB 6-47 Gs v Surrey (Oval) 2014. M BB 5-70 v Hants (Northwood) 2016. Hat-trick v Worcs (Cheltenham) 2013. LO HS 45 Gs v Surrey (Bristol) 2015 (RLC). LO BB 6-35 v Netherlands (Amstelveen) 2012 (CB40). T20 HS 36. T20 BB 4-24.

GUBBINS, Nicholas Richard Trail (Radley C; Leeds U), b Richmond, Surrey 31 Dec 1993. 6'0½". LHB, LB. Squad No 18. Leeds/Bradford MCCU 2013-15. Middlesex debut 2014; cap 2016. England Lions 2017. Middlesex 2nd XI debut 2012. F-c Tours (EL): WI 2017-18; SL 2016-17; UAE 2016-17 (v Afghan). 1000 runs (1): 1409 (2016). HS 201* v Lancs (Lord's) 2016. LO HS 141 v Sussex (Hove) 2015 (RLC). T20 HS 46.

HARRIS, James Alexander Russell (Pontardulais CS; Gorseinon C), b Morriston, Swansea, Glamorgan 16 May 1990. 6'0". RHB, RMF. Squad No 7. Glamorgan 2007-14, making debut aged 16y 351d – youngest Gm player to take an f-c wicket; cap 2010. Middlesex debut 2013; cap 2015. Kent 2017 (on loan). MCC 2016. Wales MC 2005-08. F-c Tours (EL): WI 2010-11; SL 2013-14. HS 87* Gm v Notts (Swansea) 2007. HS 78 v Somerset (Taunton) 2015. 50 wkts (2); most – 73 (2015). BB 9-34 (13-103 match) v Durham (Lord's) 2015 – record innings and match analysis v Durham. Took 12-118 in match for Gm v Glos (Bristol) 2007 – youngest (17y 3d) to take 10 wickets in any CC match. LO HS 32 v Hants (Southampton) 2015 (RLC). LO BB 4-38 v Glamorgan (Lord's) 2015 (RLC). T20 HS 18. T20 BB 4-23.

HELM, Thomas George (Misbourne S, Gt Missenden), b Stoke Mandeville Hospital, Bucks 7 May 1994. 6'4". RHB, RMF. Squad No 7. Debut (Middlesex) 2013. Glamorgan 2014 (on loan). England Lions 2017. Middlesex 2nd XI debut 2011. Buckinghamshire 2011. F-c Tour (EL): SL 2016-17. HS 28 v Somerset (Lord's) 2017. BB 5-59 v Warwks (Birmingham) 2017. LO HS 25 v Glamorgan (Radlett) 2017 (RLC). LO BB 5-33 EL v Sri Lanka A (Colombo, CCC) 2016-17. T20 HS 4-. T20 BB 5-11 v Essex (Lord's) 2017 – M record.

· **HOLDEN, Max** David Edward (Sawston Village C; Hills Road SFC, Cambridge), b Cambridge 18 Dec 1997. 5'11". LHB, OB. Squad No 4. Middlesex 2nd XI debut 2013. England U19 2014-15 to 2016-17. Northamptonshire 2017 (on loan). Middlesex debut 2017. HS 153 and BB 2-59 Nh v Kent (Beckenham) 2017. M HS 35 v Hants (Uxbridge) 2017. LO HS Nh v South Africans (Northampton) 2017.

LACE, Thomas Cresswell (Millfield S), b Hammersmith 27 May 1998. 5'8". RHB, WK. Squad No 27. Middlesex 2nd XI debut 2015. Awaiting 1st XI debut. Summer contract.

MALAN, Dawid Johannes (Paarl HS), b Roehampton, Surrey 3 Sep 1987. Son of D.J.Malan (WP B and Transvaal B 1978-79 to 1981-82), elder brother of C.C.Malan (Loughborough MCCU 2009-10). 6'0". LHB, LB. Squad No 29. Boland 2005-06. MCC YC 2006-07. Middlesex debut 2008, scoring 132* v Northants (Uxbridge); cap 2010; T20 captain 2016 to date; captain 2018. MCC 2010-11, 2013. **Tests**: 10 (2017 to 2017-18); HS 140 v A (Perth) 2017-18; BB –. **IT20**: 5 (2017 to 2017-18); HS 78 v SA (Cardiff) 2017; BB 1-27 v NZ (Hamilton) 2017-18. F-c Tour: A 2017-18. 1000 runs (2); most – 1137 runs (2014). HS 182* v Notts (Nottingham) 2015. BB 5-61 v Lancs (Liverpool) 2012. LO HS 185* EL v Sri Lanka A (Northampton) 2016. LO BB 4-25 PDSC v Partex (Savar) 2014-15. T20 HS 115*. T20 BB 2-10.

MORGAN, Eoin Joseph Gerard (Catholic University S), b Dublin, Ireland 10 Sep 1986. 6'0". LHB, RM. Squad No 16. UK passport. Ireland 2004 to 2007-08. Middlesex debut 2006; cap 2008; l-o captain 2014-15. IPL: RCB 2009-10. KKR 2011-13. SH 2015-16. KXIP 2017. Big Bash: ST 2013-14 to 2016-17. *Wisden* 2010. **ECB L-O Central Contract 2017-18. Tests**: 16 (2010 to 2011-12); HS 130 v P (Nottingham) 2010. **LOI** (E/Ire): 200 (23 for Ire 2006 to 2008-09; 177 for E 2009 to 2017-18, 78 as captain); HS 124* v Ireland (Dublin) 2013. **IT20**: 72 (2009 to 2017-18, 29 as captain); HS 85* v SA (Johannesburg) 2009-10. F-c Tours (Ire): A 2010-11 (E); NZ 2008-09 (Eng A); Namibia 2005-06; UAE 2006-07, 2007-08, 2011-12 (v P). 1000 runs (1): 1085 (2008). HS 209* Ire v UAE (Abu Dhabi) 2006-07. M HS 191 v Notts (Nottingham) 2014. BB 2-24 v Notts (Lord's) 2007. LO HS 161 v Kent (Canterbury) 2009 (FPT). LO BB –. T20 HS 85*.

NQ**MURTAGH, Timothy** James (John Fisher S; St Mary's C), b Lambeth, London 2 Aug 1981. Elder brother of C.P.Murtagh (Loughborough UCCE and Surrey 2005-09), nephew of A.J.Murtagh (Hampshire and EP 1973-77). 6'0". LHB, RFM. Squad No 34. British U 2000-03. Surrey 2001-06. Middlesex debut 2007; cap 2008; benefit 2015. Ireland 2012-13 to date. MCC 2010. **LOI** (Ire): 38 (2012 to 2017-18); HS 23* v Scotland (Belfast) 2013; BB 4-32 v Z (Harare) 2015-16. **IT20** (Ire): 14 (2012 to 2015-16); HS 12* v UAE (Abu Dhabi) 2015-16; BB 3-23 v PNG (Townsville) 2015-16. HS 74* Sy v Middx (Oval) 2004 and 74* Sy v Warwks (Croydon) 2005. M HS 55 v Leics (Leicester) 2011, sharing M record 9th wkt partnership of 172 with G.K.Berg. 50 wkts (6); most – 85 (2011). BB 7-82 v Derbys (Derby) 2009. LO HS 35* v Surrey (Lord's) 2008 (FPT). LO BB 4-14 Sy v Derbys (Derby) 2005 (NL). T20 HS 40*. T20 BB 6-24 Sy v Middx (Lord's) 2005 – Sy record and 5th best UK figs.

PATEL, Ravi Hasmukh (Merchant Taylors' S, Northwood; Loughborough U), b Harrow 4 Aug 1991. 5'8". RHB, SLA. Squad No 36. Debut (Middlesex) 2010. Loughborough MCCU 2011. Essex 2015 (on loan). HS 26* v Warwks (Uxbridge) 2013. BB 7-81 (12-173 match) v Somerset (Taunton) 2017. LO HS 18* v Essex (Chelmsford) 2017 (RLC). LO BB 3-71 EL v Sri Lanka A (Taunton) 2014. T20 HS 11*. T20 BB 4-18.

PODMORE, Harry William (Twyford HS), b Hammersmith, London 23 Jul 1994. 6'3". RHB, RM. Squad No 23. Glamorgan 2016-17 (on loan). Middlesex debut 2016. Derbyshire 2017 (on loan). Middlesex 2nd XI debut 2011. MCC YC 2013. HS 66* De v Sussex (Hove) 2017. M HS 21 v Warwks (Birmingham) 2016. BB 4-54 v Somerset (Taunton) 2016. LO HS 1* v Notts (Lord's) 2014 (RLC). LO BB 2-46 v Somerset (Lord's) 2014 (RLC). T20 HS 9. T20 BB 3-13.

RAYNER, Oliver Philip (St Bede's S, Upper Dicker), b Fallingbostel, W Germany, 1 Nov 1985. 6'5". RHB, OB. Squad No 2. Sussex 2006-11, scoring 101 v Sri Lankans (Hove) – first hundred on debut for Sussex since 1920. Middlesex debut 2011; cap 2015. MCC 2014. F-c Tours (EL): SL 2013-14, 2016-17; UAE 2016-17 (v Afghan). HS 143* v Notts (Nottingham) 2012. 50 wkts (1): 51 (2016). BB 8-46 (15-118 match) v Surrey (Oval) 2013. LO HS 61 Sx v Lancs (Hove) 2006 (P40). LO BB 4-35 v Notts (Lord's) 2015 (RLC). T20 HS 41*. T20 BB 5-18.

ROBSON, Sam David (Marcellin C, Randwick), b Paddington, Sydney, Australia 1 Jul 1989. Elder brother of A.J.Robson (see SUSSEX). 6'0". RHB, LB. Squad No 12. Qualified for England in April 2013. Debut (Middlesex) 2009; cap 2013. England Lions 2017. **Tests**: 7 (2014); HS 127 v SL (Leeds) 2014. F-c Tours (EL): SA 2014-15; SL 2013-14. 1000 runs (2); most – 1180 (2013). HS 231* v Warwks (Lord's) 2013. BB 1-4 EL v Sri Lanka A (Dambulla) 2013-14. M BB –. LO HS 88 v Notts (Lord's) 2015 (RLC). T20 HS 28*.

ROLAND-JONES, Tobias Skelton ('**Toby**') (Hampton S; Leeds U), b Ashford 29 Jan 1988. 6'4". RHB, RFM. Squad No 21. Debut (Middlesex) 2010; cap 2012. MCC 2011. Wisden 2018. Leeds/Bradford UCCE 2009 (not f-c). **ECB Incremental Central Contract 2017-18**. **Tests**: 4 (2017); HS 25 and BB 5-57 v SA (Oval) 2017. **LOI**: 1 (2017); HS 37* and BB 1-34 v SA (Lord's) 2017. F-c Tours (EL): WI 2017-18; SL 2016-17; UAE 2016-17 (v Afghan). HS 103* v Yorks (Lord's) 2015. 50 wkts (2); most – 64 (2012). BB 6-50 (12-105 match) v Northants (Northampton) 2014. Hat-tricks (2): v Derbys (Lord's) 2013, and v Yorks (Lord's) 2016 – at end of match to secure the Championship. LO HS 65 v Glos (Lord's) 2017 (RLC). LO BB 4-10 v Hants (Southampton) 2017 (RLC). T20 HS 30. T20 BB 4-25.

SCOTT, George Frederick Buchan (Beechwood Park S; St Albans S; Leeds U), b Hemel Hempstead, Herts 6 Nov 1995. Younger brother of J.E.B.Scott (Hertfordshire 2013 to date). 6'2". RHB, RM. Squad No 17. Leeds/Bradford MCCU 2015-16. Middlesex 2nd XI debut 2013. Hertfordshire 2011-14. Awaiting Middlesex f-c debut. HS 16* LBU v Sussex (Hove) 2016. BB 2-67 LBU v Sussex (Hove) 2015. LO HS 4 v Notts (Lord's) 2015 (RLC). LO BB –. T20 HS 38*. T20 BB 1-22.

SIMPSON, John Andrew (St Gabriel's RC HS), b Bury, Lancs 13 Jul 1988. 5'10". LHB, WK. Squad No 20. Debut (Middlesex) 2009; cap 2011. Cumberland 2007. MCC YCs 2008. HS 143 v Surrey (Lord's) 2011. LO HS 82* v Sussex (Lord's) 2017 (RLC). T20 HS 84*.

[NQ]**SOWTER, Nathan** Adam (Hill Sport HS, NSW), b Penrith, NSW, Australia 12 Oct 1992. 5'10". RHB, LB. Squad No 72. Debut (Middlesex) 2017. HS 37 and BB 1-23 v Warwks (Lord's) 2017. LO HS 0. LO BB –. T20 HS 12. T20 BB 4-23.

[NQ]**STIRLING, Paul** Robert (Belfast HS), b Belfast, N Ireland 3 Sep 1990. Father Brian Stirling was an international rugby referee. 5'10". RHB, OB. Squad No 39. Ireland 2007-08 to date. Middlesex debut 2013; cap 2016. **LOI** (Ire): 93 (2008 to 2017-18); HS 177 v Canada (Toronto) 2010; BB 6-55 v Afghanistan (Greater Noida) 2016-17 – Ire record figures. **IT20** (Ire): 44 (2009 to 2016-17); HS 79 v Afghanistan (Dubai, DSC) 2011-12; BB 3-21 v B (Belfast) 2012. F-c Tours (Ire): WI 2009-10; Kenya 2011-12; Z 2015-16; UAE 2013-14. HS 146 Ire v UAE (Dublin) 2015. M HS 111 v Yorks (Leeds) 2017. BB 2-27 Ire v Namibia (Windhoek) 2015-16. M BB 2-31 v Oxford MCCU (Oxford) 2015. CC BB 2-43 v Surrey (Lord's) 2013. LO HS 177 (see LOI). LO BB 6-55 (see LOI). T20 HS 90. T20 BB 4-10.

WHITE, Robert George (Harrow S; Loughborough U), b 15 Sep 1995. 5'9". RHB, WK, occ RM. Squad No 14. Loughborough MCCU 2015-17. Middlesex 2nd XI debut 2013. Awaiting 1st XI debut. HS 69 LU v Northants (Northampton) 2017.

RELEASED/RETIRED

(Having made a County 1st XI appearance in 2017)

HIGGINS, R.F. – *see GLOUCESTERSHIRE.*

^{NQ}**McCULLUM, Brendon** Barrie, b Dunedin, New Zealand 27 Sep 1981. Son of S.J.McCullum (Otago 1976-77 to 1990-91), younger brother of N.L.McCullum (Otago and Glamorgan 1999-00 to date). RHB, RM, WK. Otago 1999-00 to 2014-15. Canterbury 2003-04 to 2006-07. Glamorgan 2006; cap 2006. Middlesex 2016-17 (T20 only). IPL: KKR 2007-08 to 2013. CSK 2014-15. GL 2016-17. Big Bash: BH 2011-12 to date. **Tests** (NZ): 101 (2003-04 to 2015-16, 31 as captain); 1000 runs (1): 1164 (2014); HS 302 v I (Wellington) 2013-14 – NZ record; BB 1-1 v P (Dubai) 2014-15. Scored fastest Test century (54 balls) in final Test, v A (Christchurch) 2015-16. **LOI** (NZ): 260 (2001-02 to 2015-16, 62 as captain); HS 166 v Ireland (Aberdeen) 2008. **IT20** (NZ): 71 (2004-05 to 2015, 28 as captain); HS 123 v B (Pallekele) 2012-13. F-c Tours (NZ)(C=Captain): E 2004, 2008, 2013C, 2015C; A 2004-05, 2008-09, 2011-12, 2015-16C; SA 2005-06, 2007-08, 2012-13C; WI 2012, 2014C; I 2010-11, 2012; SL 2009, 2012-13; Z 2005, 2011-12; B 2004-05, 2008-09, 2013-14C; UAE (v P) 2014-15C. HS 302 (*see Tests*). CC HS 160 Gm v Leics (Cardiff) 2006 – on Gm debut. BB 1-1 (*see Tests*). LO HS 170 Otago v Auckland (Auckland) 2007-08. T20 HS 158* Wa v Derbys (Birmingham) 2015 – Wa record & joint 4th highest score in all T20 cricket, and 158* KKR v RCB (Bangalore) 2007-08.

^{NQ}**SOUTHEE, Tim**othy Grant, b Whangarei, New Zealand 11 Dec 1988. RHB, RMF. Northern Districts 2006-07 to date. Middlesex 2017 (T20 only). IPL: CSK 2011. RR 2014-15. MI 2016-17. **Tests** (NZ): 58 (2007-08 to 2017-18); HS 77* v E (Napier) 2007-08 – on debut; BB 7-64 v I (Bangalore) 2012. **LOI** (NZ): 133 (2008 to 2017-18); HS 55 v I (Dharamsala) 2016-17; BB 7-33 v E (Wellington) 2014-15 – NZ record. **IT20** (NZ): 51 (2007-08 to 2017-18); HS 23 v WI (Lauderhill) 2012; BB 5-18 v P (Auckland) 2010-11 – NZ record. F-c Tours (NZ): E 2008, 2013, 2015; A 2008-09, 2011-12, 2015-16; SA 2016; WI 2012, 2014; I 2010-11, 2012; SL 2012-13; Z 2016; UAE (v P) 2014-15. HS 156 ND v Wellington (Wellington) 2012-13. BB 8-27 ND v Wellington (Hamilton) 2009-10. LO HS 66* ND v Auckland (Hamilton) 2012-13. LO BB 7-33 (*see LOI*). T20 HS 74. T20 BB 6-16.

^{NQ}**VOGES, Adam** Charles (Edith Cowan U, Perth), b Perth, Australia 4 Oct 1979. 6'0''. RHB, SLA. W Australia 2002-03 to date. Nottinghamshire 2008-12; cap 2008. Middlesex 2013-17; captain 2015-16; cap 2016. IPL: RR 2009-10. Big Bash: MS: 2011-12. PS 2012-13 to date. **Tests** (A): 20 (2015 to 2016-17); 1000 runs (1): 1028 (2015) – becoming only the 3rd batsman to score 1000 runs in the year of his debut; HS 269* v WI (Hobart) 2015-16; scored a record 614 Test runs between dismissals (269*, 106* and 239 v WI); BB –. **LOI** (A): 31 (2006-07 to 2013-14); HS 112* v WI (Melbourne) 2012-13. BB 1-3 v E (Birmingham) 2013. **IT20** (A): 7 (2007-08 to 2012-13); HS 51 v WI (Brisbane) 2012-13; BB 2-5 v I (Melbourne) 2007-08. F-c Tours (A): E 2015; WI 2015; NZ 2015-16; I 2008-09 (Aus A); P 2007-08 (Aus A); SL 2016. 1000 runs (0+1): 1132 (2014-15). HS 269* (*see Tests*). UK HS 165 Nt v Oxford MCCU (Oxford) 2011. M HS 160* v Hants (Northwood) 2016. BB 4-92 WA v S Aus (Adelaide) 2006-07. UK BB 3-21 Nt v Durham (Nottingham) 2008. M BB 2-20 v Durham (Lord's) 2015. LO HS 112* (*see LOI*). LO BB 3-20 WA v Q (Sydney) 2015-16. T20 HS 82*. T20 BB 2-4.

A.Godsal left the staff without making a County 1st XI appearance in 2017.

MIDDLESEX 2017

RESULTS SUMMARY

	Place	Won	Lost	Tied	Drew	NR
Specsavers County Champ (1st Division)	7th	3	4		7	
All First-Class Matches		3	4		7	
Royal London One-Day Cup (South Group) 8th		2	4			2
NatWest t20 Blast (South Group)	7th	5	7	1		1

SPECSAVERS COUNTY CHAMPIONSHIP AVERAGES
BATTING AND FIELDING

Cap		M	I	NO	HS	Runs	Avge	100	50	Ct/St
2013	S.D.Robson	11	20	–	159	785	39.25	2	4	10
2016	A.C.Voges	9	14	3	92	402	36.54	–	3	12
2010	D.J.Malan	8	16	2	115	493	35.21	1	2	4
2016	P.R.Stirling	8	13	–	111	454	34.92	1	3	4
	S.S.Eskinazi	14	25	2	179	793	34.47	2	4	11
2011	J.A.Simpson	14	22	2	90	570	28.50	–	3	53/1
2006	N.R.D.Compton	11	19	2	120	446	26.23	1	–	5
2016	N.R.T.Gubbins	7	13	–	101	314	24.15	1	2	–
2015	J.E.C.Franklin	10	14	1	112	296	22.76	1	1	4
2015	O.P.Rayner	11	15	2	52*	274	21.07	–	1	15
2012	T.S.Roland-Jones	9	14	2	53	252	21.00	–	1	2
	R.F.Higgins	4	7	–	45	129	18.42	–	–	–
2015	J.A.R.Harris	6	10	1	19	110	12.22	–	–	1
2008	T.J.Murtagh	12	17	6	27	134	12.18	–	–	2
2009	S.T.Finn	11	14	6	31*	95	11.87	–	–	6
	T.G.Helm	5	7	1	28	65	10.83	–	–	2
	R.H.Patel	2	4	2	7*	12	6.00	–	–	1

Also batted (1 match each): M.D.E.Holden 35; N.A.Sowter 0, 37.

BOWLING

	O	M	R	W	Avge	Best	5wI	10wM
R.H.Patel	70	7	221	12	18.41	7- 81	2	1
J.E.C.Franklin	102	21	280	12	23.33	4- 40	–	–
R.F.Higgins	98	24	281	12	23.41	4- 75	–	–
T.J.Murtagh	372	93	995	36	27.63	6- 63	1	–
S.T.Finn	287.2	45	1045	34	30.73	8- 79	1	–
T.S.Roland-Jones	277.2	63	880	28	31.42	4- 66	–	–
T.G.Helm	167.5	30	602	19	31.68	5- 59	1	–
J.A.R.Harris	154.5	32	490	15	32.66	4-119	–	–
O.P.Rayner	265.3	62	778	20	38.90	4- 35	–	–
Also bowled:								
D.J.Malan	38	4	125	7	17.85	2- 1	–	–

N.R.D.Compton 1-0-2-0; N.R.T.Gubbins 1-0-4-0; J.A.Simpson 2-0-21-0; N.A.Sowter 10.1-1-25-1; P.R.Stirling 57-8-165-4; A.C.Voges 17-0-80-1.

Middlesex played no first-class fixtures outside the County Championship in 2017. The First-Class Averages (pp 230–246) give the records of their players in all first-class county matches, with the exception of N.R.T.Gubbins, J.A.R.Harris, T.G.Helm, M.D.E.Holden, D.J.Malan, H.W.Podmore, S.D.Robson and T.S.Roland-Jones, whose first-class figures for Middlesex are as above.

MIDDLESEX RECORDS

FIRST-CLASS CRICKET

Highest Total	For 642-3d		v	Hampshire	Southampton	1923
	V 850-7d		by	Somerset	Taunton	2007
Lowest Total	For 20		v	MCC	Lord's	1864
	V 31		by	Glos	Bristol	1924
Highest Innings	For 331*	J.D.B.Robertson	v	Worcs	Worcester	1949
	V 341	C.M.Spearman	for	Glos	Gloucester	2004

Highest Partnership for each Wicket

1st	372	M.W.Gatting/J.L.Langer	v	Essex	Southgate	1998
2nd	380	F.A.Tarrant/J.W.Hearne	v	Lancashire	Lord's	1914
3rd	424*	W.J.Edrich/D.C.S.Compton	v	Somerset	Lord's	1948
4th	325	J.W.Hearne/E.H.Hendren	v	Hampshire	Lord's	1919
5th	338	R.S.Lucas/T.C.O'Brien	v	Sussex	Hove	1895
6th	270	J.D.Carr/P.N.Weekes	v	Glos	Lord's	1994
7th	271*	E.H.Hendren/F.T.Mann	v	Notts	Nottingham	1925
8th	182*	M.H.C.Doll/H.R.Murrell	v	Notts	Lord's	1913
9th	172	G.K.Berg/T.J.Murtagh	v	Leics	Leicester	2011
10th	230	R.W.Nicholls/W.Roche	v	Kent	Lord's	1899

Best Bowling	For 10- 40	G.O.B.Allen	v	Lancashire	Lord's	1929
(Innings)	V 9- 38	R.C.R.Glasgow†	for	Somerset	Lord's	1924
Best Bowling	For 16-114	G.Burton	v	Yorkshire	Sheffield	1888
(Match)	16-114	J.T.Hearne	v	Lancashire	Manchester	1898
	V 16-100	J.E.B.B.P.Q.C.Dwyer	for	Sussex	Hove	1906

Most Runs – Season	2669	E.H.Hendren	(av 83.41)		1923
Most Runs – Career	40302	E.H.Hendren	(av 48.81)		1907-37
Most 100s – Season	13	D.C.S.Compton			1947
Most 100s – Career	119	E.H.Hendren			1907-37
Most Wkts – Season	158	F.J.Titmus	(av 14.63)		1955
Most Wkts – Career	2361	F.J.Titmus	(av 21.27)		1949-82
Most Career W-K Dismissals	1223	J.T.Murray	(1024 ct; 199 st)		1952-75
Most Career Catches in the Field	561	E.H.Hendren			1907-37

LIMITED-OVERS CRICKET

Highest Total	50ov	367-6	v	Sussex	Hove	2015
	40ov	350-6	v	Lancashire	Lord's	2012
	T20	221-2	v	Sussex	Hove	2015
Lowest Total	50ov	41	v	Essex	Westcliff	1972
	40ov	23	v	Yorkshire	Leeds	1974
	T20	92	v	Surrey	Lords	2013
Highest Innings	50ov	163	A.J.Strauss	v	Surrey	The Oval	2008
	40ov	147*	M.R.Ramprakash	v	Worcs	Lord's	1990
	T20	129	D.T.Christian	v	Kent	Canterbury	2014
Best Bowling	50ov	7-12	W.W.Daniel	v	Minor Cos E	Ipswich	1978
	40ov	6- 6	R.W.Hooker	v	Surrey	Lord's	1969
	T20	5-11	T.G.Helm	v	Essex	Lord's	2017

† R.C.Robertson-Glasgow

NORTHAMPTONSHIRE

Formation of Present Club: 31 July 1878
Inaugural First-Class Match: 1905
Colours: Maroon
Badge: Tudor Rose
County Champions: (0); best – 2nd 1912, 1957, 1965, 1976
Gillette/NatWest/C&G/FP Trophy Winners: (2) 1976, 1992
Benson and Hedges Cup Winners: (1) 1980
Twenty20 Cup Winners: (2) 2013, 2016

est. 1878
NORTHAMPTONSHIRE
COUNTY CRICKET CLUB

Chief Executive: Ray Payne, County Ground, Abington Avenue, Northampton, NN1 4PR •
Tel: 01604 514455 • Fax: 01604 609288 • Email: post@nccc.co.uk • Web: www.nccc.co.uk
• Twitter: @NorthantsCCC (44,260 followers)

Head Coach: David Ripley. **Assistant/Bowling Coach**: Phil Rowe. **Batting Coach**: David
Sales. **Captain**: A.G.Wakely. **Overseas Players**: D.A.J.Bracewell, R.K.Kleinveldt and
S.Prasanna (T20 only). **2018 Beneficiary**: None. **Head Groundsman**: Craig Harvey.
Scorer: Tony Kingston. ‡ New registration. NQ Not qualified for England

‡NQBRACEWELL, Douglas Andrew John, b Tauranga, New Zealand 28 Sep 1990. Son of
B.P.Bracewell (Central Districts, Otago, Northern Districts & New Zealand 1977-78 to
1989-90); nephew of J.G.Bracewell (Otago, Auckland and New Zealand 1978-79 to
1989-90), D.W.Bracewell (Canterbury and Central Districts 1974-75 to 1979-80) and
M.A.Bracewell (Otago 1977-78); cousin of M.G.Bracewell (Otago and Wellington 2010-11
to date). RHB, RM. Central Districts 2008-09 to date. Joins Northamptonshire for the first
part of the season. IPL: DD 2012. **Tests**: 27 (2011-12 to 2016); HS 47 v SL (Dunedin)
2015-16; BB 6-40 v A (Hobart) 2011-12. LOI (NZ): 16 (2011-12 to 2017-18); HS 30 v SL
(Nelson) 2015-16; BB 4-55 v WI (Whangarei) 2017-18. **IT20** (NZ): 17 (2011-12 to
2017-18); HS 21* v SA (Durban) 2012-13; BB 3-25 v Z (Harare) 2011-12. F-c Tours (NZ):
E 2013, 2015; A 2011-12, 2015-16; SA 2012-13, 2016; WI 2012; I 2012, 2013-14 (NZA);
SL 2012-13, 2013-14 (NZA); Z 2011-12; B 2013-14. HS 105 CD v Otago (Queenstown)
2014-15. BB 7-35 CD v Canterbury (Rangiora) 2012-13. LO HS CD v ND (Whangarei)
2015-16. LO BB 4-43 CD v Canterbury (Rangiora) 2010-11. T20 HS 37. T20 BB 3-21.

BUCK, Nathan Liam (Newbridge HS; Ashby S), b Leicester 26 Apr 1991. 6'2" RHB,
RMF. Squad No 11. Leicestershire 2009-14; cap 2011. Lancashire 2015-16. Northampton-
shire 2017. F-c Tour (EL): WI 2010-11. HS 43 v Derbys (Derby) 2017. BB 6-34 v Durham
(Chester-le-St) 2017. LO HS 21 Le v Glamorgan (Leicester) 2009 (P40). LO BB 4-39 EL v
Sri Lanka A (Dambulla) 2011-12. T20 HS 8*. T20 BB 4-26.

COBB, Joshua James (Oakham S), b Leicester 17 Aug 1990. Son of R.A.Cobb (Leics and
N Transvaal 1980-89). 5'11½". RHB, OB. Squad No 4. Leicestershire 2007-14; l-o captain
2014. Northamptonshire debut 2015. HS 148* Le v Middx (Lord's) 2008. Nh HS 96 v
Durham (Chester-le-St) 2017. BB 2-11 Le v Glos (Leicester) 2008. Nh BB 2-44 v
Loughborough MCCU (Northampton) 2017. LO HS 137 Le v Lancs (Manchester) 2012
(CB40). LO BB 3-34 Le v Glos (Leicester) 2013 (Y40). T20 HS 84. T20 BB 4-22.

CROOK, Steven Paul (Rostrevor C; Magill U), b Modbury, S Australia 28 May 1983.
Younger brother of A.R.Crook (S Australia, Aus Academy, Lancashire, Northamptonshire
1998-99 to 2008). 5'11". RHB, RFM. Squad No 25. UK passport. Lancashire 2003-05.
Northamptonshire debut 2005; cap 2013. Middlesex 2011-14. Aus Academy 2001-02. HS
145 v Worcs (Worcester) 2016. BB 5-48 M v Lancs (Lord's) 2012. Nh BB 5-71 v Essex

(Northampton) 2009. LO HS 100 SJD v PDSC (Savar) 2013-14. LO BB 5-36 v Warwks (Northampton) 2013 (Y40). T20 HS 63. T20 BB 3-19.

DUCKETT, Ben Matthew (Stowe S), b Farnborough, Kent 17 Oct 1994. 5'7''. LHB, WK, occ OB. Squad No 17. Debut (Northamptonshire) 2013; cap 2016. MCC 2017. Northamptonshire 2nd XI debut 2011. England U19 2012-13. PCA 2016. YC 2016. *Wisden* 2016. **Tests**: 4 (2016-17); HS 56 v B (Dhaka) 2016-17. **LOI**: 3 (2016-17); HS 63 v B (Chittagong) 2016-17. F-c Tours: I 2016-17; B 2016-17. 1000 runs (2); most – 1338 (2016). HS 282* v Sussex (Northampton) 2016. BB 1-21 v Kent (Beckenham) 2017. LO HS 220* EL v Sri Lanka A (Canterbury) 2016. T20 HS 92*.

GLEESON, Richard James, b Blackpool, Lancs 2 Dec 1987. RHB, RMF. Squad No 33. Debut (Northamptonshire) 2015. Cumberland 2010-15. F-c Tour (EL): WI 2017-18. HS 31 v Glos (Bristol) 2016. BB 5-46 v Glos (Northampton) 2017. LO HS 13 EL v West Indies A (Coolidge) 2017-18. LO BB 5-47 v Worcs (Worcester) 2016 (RLC). T20 HS 7*. T20 BB 3-12.

‡**HUTTON, Brett** Alan (Worksop C), b Doncaster, Yorks 6 Feb 1993. 6'2''. RHB, RM. Squad No 16. Nottinghamshire 2011-17. Joins Northamptonshire in 2018. HS 74 Nt v Durham (Nottingham) 2016. BB 5-29 (10-106 match) Nt v Durham (Nottingham) 2015. LO HS 33* Nt v Lancs (Liverpool) 2015 (RLC). LO BB 3-72 Nt v Kent (Nottingham) 2015 (RLC). T20 HS 4*. T20 BB 1-24.

KEOGH, Robert Ian (Queensbury S; Dunstable C), b Luton, Beds 21 Oct 1991. 5'11''. RHB, OB. Squad No 14. Debut (Northamptonshire) 2012. Bedfordshire 2009-10. HS 221 v Hants (Southampton) 2013. BB 9-52 (13-125 match) v Glamorgan (Northampton) 2016. LO HS 134 v Durham (Northampton) 2016 (RLC). LO BB 1-49 v Somerset (Northampton) 2015 (RLC). T20 HS 41*. T20 BB 2-27.

NQ**KLEINVELDT, Rory** Keith, b Cape Town, South Africa 15 Mar 1983. Cousin of M.C.Kleinveldt (W Province 2010-11 to date). Nephew of J.Kleinveldt (W Province and Transvaal 1979-80 to 1982-83). 6'2''. RHB, RMF. Squad No 6. W Province 2002-03 to 2005-06. Cape Cobras 2005-06 to date. Hampshire 2008 (1 game). Northamptonshire debut 2015; cap 2016. **Tests** (SA): 4 (2012-13); HS 17* v A (Brisbane) 2012-13; BB 3-65 v A (Adelaide) 2012-13. **LOI** (SA): 10 (2012-13 to 2013); HS 43 v E (Oval) 2013; BB 4-22 v P (Bloemfontein) 2012-13. **IT20** (SA): 6 (2008-09 to 2012-13); HS 22 v P (Centurion) 2012-13; BB 3-18 v NZ (Durban) 2012-13. F-c Tours (SA A): A 2012-13 (SA); I 2007-08; SL 2010. HS 115* WP v KZN (Chatsworth) 2005-06. Nh HS 97 v Derbys (Northampton) 2016. 50 wkts (2); most – 57 (2015). BB 9-65 (13-98 match) v Notts (Northampton) 2017. LO HS 128 v Notts (Nottingham) 2016 (RLC). LO BB 4-22 (*see LOI*). T20 HS 46. T20 BB 3-14.

NQ**LEVI, Richard** Ernst, b Johannesburg, South Africa 14 Jan 1988. 5'11''. RHB, RM. Squad No 88. W Province 2006-07 to date. Cape Cobras 2008-09 to date. Northamptonshire debut 2014 (Kolpak signing); cap 2017. **IT20** (SA): 13 (2011-12 to 2012-13); HS 117* v NZ (Hamilton) 2011-12. HS 168 v Essex (Northampton) 2015. LO HS 166 Cobras v Titans (Paarl) 2012-13. T20 HS 117*.

NEWTON, Robert Irving (Framlingham C), b Taunton, Somerset 18 Jan 1990. 5'8''. RHB, OB. Squad No 10. Debut (Northamptonshire) 2010; cap 2017. 1000 runs (1): 1060 (2017). HS 202* v Leics (Northampton) 2016. BB 1-82 v Derbys (Derby) 2017. LO HS 107 v Worcs (Northampton) 2017 (RLC). T20 HS 38.

NQPRASANNA, Seekkuge (Rewatha C), b Balapitiya, Sri Lanka 27 Jun 1985. 5'9". RHB, LB. Squad No 41. Sri Lanka Army 2006-07 to date. Kandurata 2008-09 to 2009-10. Northamptonshire debut 2016, returning in 2018 for T20 only. **Tests** (SL): 1 (2011); HS 5 and BB – v A (Pallekele) 2011. **LOI** (SL): 38 (2011 to 2017-18); HS 95 v Ireland (Dublin) 2016; BB 3-32 v A (Colombo, RPS) 2011. **IT20** (SL): 20 (2013-14 to 2017-18); HS 37* v SA (Cape Town) 2016-17; BB 2-45 v P (Dubai, DSC) 2013-14. F-c Tour (SL A): E 2011. HS 81 SL Army v Colts (Panagoda) 2012-13. HS 31 v Worcs (Northampton) 2016. 50 wkts (0+4); most – 71 (2008-09). BB 8-59 (12-95 match) SL Army v Bloomfield (Panagoda) 2008-09. NH BB 5-97 v Glos (Bristol) 2016. LO HS 95 (*see LOI*). LO BB 6-23 SL A v England Lions (Worcester) 2011. T20 HS 53. T20 BB 4-19.

PROCTER, Luke Anthony (Counthill S, Oldham), b Oldham 24 June 1988. 5'11". LHB, RM. Squad No 2. Lancashire 2010-17. Northamptonshire debut 2017. Cumberland 2007. HS 137 v Hants (Manchester) 2016. Nh HS 94 v Leics (Leicester) 2017. BB 7-71 v Surrey (Liverpool) 2012. Nh BB 1-67 v Sussex (Northampton) 2017. LO HS 97 v West Indies A (Manchester) 2010. LO BB 3-29 v Unicorns (Colwyn Bay) 2010 (CB40). T20 HS 25*. T20 BB 3-22.

ROSSINGTON, Adam Matthew (Mill Hill S), b Edgware, Middx 5 May 1993. 5'11". RHB, WK, occ RM. Squad No 7. Middlesex 2010-14. Northamptonshire debut 2014. Middlesex 2nd XI debut 2010. England U19 2010-11, scoring 113 v SL on debut. HS 138* v Sussex (Arundel) 2016. Won 2013 Walter Lawrence Trophy with 55-ball century v Cambridge MCCU (Cambridge). LO HS 97 v Notts (Nottingham) 2016 (RLC). T20 HS 85.

SANDERSON, Ben William (Ecclesfield CS; Sheffield C), b Sheffield, Yorks 3 Jan 1989. 6'0". RHB, RMF. Squad No 26. Yorkshire 2008-10. Northamptonshire debut 2015. Shropshire 2013-15. HS 42 v Kent (Canterbury) 2015. 50 wkts (1): 55 (2016). BB 8-73 v Glos (Northampton) 2016. LO HS 19* and LO BB 3-36 v Durham (Chester-le-St) 2017 (RLC). T20 HS 12*. T20 BB 4-21.

SOLE, Thomas Barclay (Merchiston Castle S; Cardiff Met U), b Edinburgh, Scotland 12 Jun 1996. Younger brother of C.B.Sole (*see HAMPSHIRE*); son of D.M.B.Sole (Scotland Grand Slam-winning rugby union captain); nephew of C.R.Trembath (Gloucestershire 1982-84). RHB, OB. Squad No 90. Northamptonshire 2nd XI debut 2015. Awaiting f-c debut. **LOI** (Scot): 3 (2017-18); HS 20 v Ireland (Dubai, ICCA) 2017-18; BB 4-15 v Hong Kong (Bulawayo) 2017-18. LO HS 54 v S Africans (Northampton) 2017. LO BB 4-15 (*see LOI*).

NQVASCONCELOS, Ricardo Surrador (St Stithians), b Johannesburg, South Africa 27 Oct 1997. LHB, WK. Boland 2016-17 to date. South Africa U19 2016. Joins Northamptonshire in May 2018. Holds Portuguese passport. HS 140 Boland v Namibia (Windhoek) 2017-18. LO HS 56 Boland v Namibia (Windhoek) 2017-18. T20 HS 45*.

WADE, Gareth (Prudhoe Community HS; Sunderland U), b Hexham, Northumberland 11 Jan 1991. RHB, RMF. Squad No 9. Debut (Northamptonshire) 2017. Northumberland 2014 to date. BB 1-100 v Loughborough MCCU (Northampton) 2017.

WAKELY, Alexander George (Bedford S), b Hammersmith, London 3 Nov 1988. 6'2". RHB, RM. Squad No 8. Debut (Northamptonshire) 2007; cap 2012; captain 2015 to date. Bedfordshire 2004-05. HS 123 v Leics (Northampton) 2015. BB 2-62 v Somerset (Taunton) 2007. LO HS 109* v Lancs (Liverpool) 2017 (RLC). LO BB 2-14 v Lancs (Northampton) 2007 (P40). T20 HS 64. T20 BB –.

WHITE, Graeme Geoffrey (Stowe S), b Milton Keynes, Bucks 18 Apr 1987. 5'11". RHB, SLA. Squad No 87. Debut (Northamptonshire) 2006. Nottinghamshire 2010-13. HS 65 v Glamorgan (Colwyn Bay) 2007. BB 6-44 v Glamorgan (Northampton) 2016. LO HS 40 v Notts (Nottingham) 2016 (RLC) and 40 v Yorks (Northampton) 2017 (RLC). LO BB 6-37 v Lancs (Northampton) 2016 (RLC). T20 HS 34. T20 BB 5-22 Nt v Lancs (Nottingham) 2013 – Nt record.

ZAIB, Saif Ali (RGS High Wycombe), b High Wycombe, Bucks 22 May 1998. LHB, SLA. Squad No 5. Debut (Northamptonshire) 2015. Northamptonshire 2nd XI debut 2013, aged 15y 90d. HS 65* v Glamorgan (Swansea) 2016. BB 6-115 v Loughborough MCCU (Northampton) 2016 CC BB 5-148 v Leics (Northampton) 2016. LO HS 17 and LO BB 2-22 v South Africans (Northampton) 2017.

RELEASED/RETIRED

(Having made a County 1st XI appearance in 2017, even if not formally contracted. Some may return in 2018.)

AZHARULLAH, Mohammad, b Burewala, Punjab, Pakistan 25 Dec 1983. 5'7". RHB, RFM. Multan 2004-05 to 2006-07. WAPDA 2004-05 to 2012-13. Quetta 2005-06. Baluchistan 2007-08 to 2008-09. Northamptonshire 2013-17; cap 2015. UK qualified through residency and British wife. HS 58* v Kent (Canterbury) 2015. BB 7-74 Quetta v Lahore Ravi (Quetta) 2005-06. Nh BB 7-76 (10-158 match) v Sussex (Northampton) 2014. LO HS 9 (twice). LO BB 5-38 v Hants (Southampton) 2014 (RLC). T20 HS 6*. T20 BB 4-14.

CARTER, Andrew (Lincoln C), b Lincoln 27 Aug 1988. 6'4". RHB, RM. Nottinghamshire 2009-15. Essex 2010 (on loan). Glamorgan 2015 (on loan). Derbyshire 2016. Hampshire 2016 (on loan). Northamptonshire 2017. Lincolnshire 2007-10. HS 39 De v Glamorgan (Derby) 2016. Nh HS 8 and Nh BB 3-51 v Worcs (Worcester) 2017. BB 5-40 Ex v Kent (Canterbury) 2010. LO HS 12 Nt v Sussex (Hove) 2009 (P40). LO BB 4-45 Nt v Durham (Nottingham) 2012 (CB40). T20 HS 5*. T20 BB 4-20.

HUGHES, Chesney Francis (Albena Lake Hodge CS, Anguilla), b Anguilla 20 January 1991. 6'2". LHB, SLA. UK passport. Derbyshire 2010-16. Leeward Is 2015-16 to date. Northamptonshire 2017. HS 270* De v Yorks (Leeds) 2013. Nh HS 21 v Durham (Chester-le-St) 2017. BB 3-87 v Glos (Bristol) 2016. LO HS 81 Leeward Is v Windward Is (Kingston) 2010-11. LO BB 5-29 v Unicorns (Wormsley) 2012 (CB40). T20 HS 65. T20 BB 4-23.

[NO]**MURPHY, David** (Richard Hale S, Hertford; Loughborough U), b Welwyn Garden City, Herts 24 June 1989. 5'11". RHB, WK. Loughborough MCCU 2009-11. Northamptonshire 2009-17; cap 2017. **LOI** (Scot): 8 (2012-13 to 2013); HS 20* v Ireland (Belfast) 2013. **IT20** (Scot): 4 (2012-13 to 2013-14); HS 20 v Kenya (Dubai) 2013-14. HS 135* v Surrey (Oval) 2015. BB 1-40 v Leics (Northampton) 2016. LO HS 31* v Netherlands (Northampton) 2010 (CB40). T20 HS 20.

RICHARDSON, Miles Andrew (Sackville S), b Maidstone, Kent 26 Aug 1991. RHB, RMF. Debut (Northamptonshire) 2017, without batting or taking a wicket. LO HS 1* v Derbys (Derby) 2017 (RLC). LO BB –.

RELEASED/RETIRED continued on p 170

NORTHAMPTONSHIRE 2017

RESULTS SUMMARY

	Place	Won	Lost	Tied	Drew	NR
Specsavers County Champ (2nd Division)	3rd	9	3		2	
All First-Class Matches		9	3		3	
Royal London One-Day Cup (North Group) 8th		1	4	1		2
NatWest t20 Blast (North Group)	6th	6	5			3

SPECSAVERS COUNTY CHAMPIONSHIP AVERAGES

BATTING AND FIELDING

Cap		M	I	NO	HS	Runs	Avge	100	50	Ct/St
	L.A.Procter	2	4	–	94	235	58.75	–	3	2
2017	R.E.Levi	10	19	3	115	734	45.87	2	3	12
2016	B.M.Duckett	11	19	–	193	799	42.05	3	3	16
	M.D.E.Holden	9	16	–	153	629	39.31	2	2	4
2017	R.I.Newton	13	24	–	108	894	37.25	1	10	1
2012	A.G.Wakely	13	24	3	112	658	31.33	1	2	14
	A.M.Rossington	8	13	1	112	358	29.83	1	2	19/2
	J.J.Cobb	10	18	4	96	410	29.28	–	1	3
	S.C.Kerrigan	4	5	1	62	98	24.50	–	1	2
	G.G.White	3	4	–	47	88	22.00	–	–	–
2016	R.K.Kleinveldt	12	19	1	86	394	21.88	–	1	8
	R.I.Keogh	12	22	3	105*	408	21.47	1	1	5
	N.L.Buck	8	13	3	43	201	20.10	–	–	4
2013	S.P.Crook	5	8	1	30	128	18.28	–	–	2
2015	M.Azharullah	7	10	5	23	73	14.60	–	–	1
	R.J.Gleeson	7	9	4	25	63	12.60	–	–	1
	C.F.Hughes	3	6	–	21	60	10.00	–	–	3
2017	D.Murphy	5	7	–	30	67	9.57	–	–	12/3
	B.W.Sanderson	10	16	5	16*	72	6.54	–	–	3

Also batted (1 match each): A.Carter 3, 8; A.Sheikh 7.

BOWLING

	O	M	R	W	Avge	Best	5wI	10wM
R.J.Gleeson	222.2	44	745	40	18.62	5-46	3	–
N.L.Buck	222.4	37	770	36	21.38	6-34	3	–
B.W.Sanderson	334.1	93	860	40	21.50	5-39	2	–
M.Azharullah	192	36	677	31	21.83	5-63	2	–
R.K.Kleinveldt	350.1	68	1153	50	23.06	9-65	2	1
S.C.Kerrigan	120.4	24	389	12	32.41	4-62	–	–

Also bowled:

A.Carter	22	5	90	5	18.00	3-51	–	–
R.I.Keogh	112.1	17	461	9	51.22	3-44	–	–

J.J.Cobb 32-0-113-1; S.P.Crook 74.4-6-333-4; B.M.Duckett 9-0-41-1; M.D.E.Holden 33-2-159-3; C.H.Hughes 2-0-16-0; R.I.Newton 9-0-82-1; L.A.Procter 31-3-138-1; A.M.Rossington 12-1-48-0; A.Sheikh 8-1-36-1; A.G.Wakely 9.2-0-75-0; G.G.White 72-9-305-3.

The First-Class Averages (pp 230–246) give the records of Northamptonshire players in all first-class county matches (Northamptonshire's other opponents being Loughborough MCCU), with the exception of S.C.Kerrigan and L.A.Procter, whose first-class figures for Northamptonshire are as above, and:
M.D.E.Holden 10-18-1-153-723-42.52-2-3-5ct. 43-3-203-4-50.75-2/59-0-0.

NORTHAMPTONSHIRE RECORDS

FIRST-CLASS CRICKET

Highest Total	For	781-7d		v	Notts	Northampton	1995
	V	701-7d		by	Kent	Beckenham	2017
Lowest Total	For	12		v	Glos	Gloucester	1907
	V	33		by	Lancashire	Northampton	1977
Highest Innings	For	331*	M.E.K.Hussey	v	Somerset	Taunton	2003
	V	333	K.S.Duleepsinhji	for	Sussex	Hove	1930

Highest Partnership for each Wicket

1st	375	R.A.White/M.J.Powell	v	Glos	Northampton	2002
2nd	344	G.Cook/R.J.Boyd-Moss	v	Lancashire	Northampton	1986
3rd	393	A.Fordham/A.J.Lamb	v	Yorkshire	Leeds	1990
4th	370	R.T.Virgin/P.Willey	v	Somerset	Northampton	1976
5th	401	M.B.Loye/D.Ripley	v	Glamorgan	Northampton	1998
6th	376	R.Subba Row/A.Lightfoot	v	Surrey	The Oval	1958
7th	293	D.J.G.Sales/D.Ripley	v	Essex	Northampton	1999
8th	179	A.J.Hall/J.D.Middlebrook	v	Surrey	The Oval	2011
9th	156	R.Subba Row/S.Starkie	v	Lancashire	Northampton	1955
10th	148	B.W.Bellamy/J.V.Murdin	v	Glamorgan	Northampton	1925

Best Bowling	For	10-127	V.W.C.Jupp	v	Kent	Tunbridge W	1932
(Innings)	V	10- 30	C.Blythe	for	Kent	Northampton	1907
Best Bowling	For	15- 31	G.E.Tribe	v	Yorkshire	Northampton	1958
(Match)	V	17- 48	C.Blythe	for	Kent	Northampton	1907

Most Runs – Season	2198	D.Brookes	(av 51.11)	1952
Most Runs – Career	28980	D.Brookes	(av 36.13)	1934-59
Most 100s – Season	8	R.A.Haywood		1921
Most 100s – Career	67	D.Brookes		1934-59
Most Wkts – Season	175	G.E.Tribe	(av 18.70)	1955
Most Wkts – Career	1102	E.W.Clark	(av 21.26)	1922-47
Most Career W-K Dismissals	810	K.V.Andrew	(653 ct; 157 st)	1953-66
Most Career Catches in the Field	469	D.S.Steele		1963-84

LIMITED-OVERS CRICKET

Highest Total	50ov	425		v	Notts	Nottingham	2016
	40ov	324-6		v	Warwicks	Birmingham	2013
	T20	224-5		v	Glos	Milton Keynes	2005
Lowest Total	50ov	62		v	Leics	Leicester	1974
	40ov	41		v	Middlesex	Northampton	1972
	T20	47		v	Durham	Chester-le-St^2	2011
Highest Innings	50ov	161	D.J.G.Sales	v	Yorkshire	Northampton	2006
	40ov	172*	W.Larkins	v	Warwicks	Luton	1983
	T20	111*	L.Klusener	v	Worcs	Kidderminster	2007
Best Bowling	50ov	7-10	C.Pietersen	v	Denmark	Brondby	2005
	40ov	7-39	A.Hodgson	v	Somerset	Northampton	1976
	T20	6-21	A.J.Hall	v	Worcs	Northampton	2008

NOTTINGHAMSHIRE

NOTTINGHAMSHIRE
COUNTY CRICKET CLUB

Formation of Present Club: March/April 1841
Substantial Reorganisation: 11 December 1866
Inaugural First-Class Match: 1864
Colours: Green and Gold
Badge: Badge of City of Nottingham
County Champions (since 1890): (6) 1907, 1929, 1981, 1987, 2005, 2010
NatWest Trophy Winners: (1) 1987
Benson and Hedges Cup Winners: (1) 1989
Sunday League Winners: (1) 1991
Yorkshire Bank 40 Winners: (1) 2013
Royal London Cup Winners: (1) 2017
Twenty20 Cup Winners: (1) 2017

Chief Executive: Lisa Pursehouse, Trent Bridge, West Bridgford, Nottingham NG2 6AG • Tel: 0115 982 3000 • Fax: 0115 982 3037 • Email: administration@nottsccc.co.uk • Web: www.trentbridge.co.uk • Twitter: @TrentBridge (60,647 followers)

Director of Cricket: Mick Newell. **Head Coach**: Peter Moores. **Assistant Head Coach**: Paul Franks. **Bowling Coach**: Andy Pick. **Captains**: S.J.Mullaney (f-c & l-o) and D.T.Christian (T20). **Overseas Players**: D.T.Christian, I.S.Sodhi (T20 only) and L.R.P.L.Taylor. **2018 Testimonial**: None. **Head Groundsman**: Steve Birks. **Scorer**: Roger Marshall. ‡ New registration. NQ Not qualified for England.

BALL, Jacob Timothy ('**Jake**') (Meden CS), b Mansfield 14 Mar 1991. Nephew of B.N.French (Notts and England 1976-95). 6'0". RHB, RM. Squad No 28. Debut (Nottinghamshire) 2011; cap 2016. MCC 2016. **ECB L-O Central Contract 2017-18. Tests**: 3 (2016 to 2017-18); HS 31 and BB 1-47 v I (Mumbai) 2016-17. **LOI**: 17 (2016-17 to 2017-18); HS 28 v B (Dhaka) 2016-17; BB 5-51 v B (Dhaka) 2016-17 – different games. F-c Tours: A 2017-18; I 2016-17. HS 49* v Warwks (Nottingham) 2015. 50 wkts (1): 54 (2016). BB 6-49 v Sussex (Nottingham) 2015. Hat-trick v Middx (Nottingham) 2016. LO HS 28 (see LOI). BB 5-51 (see LOI). T20 HS 8*. T20 BB 3-36.

BLATHERWICK, Jack Morgan (Holgate Ac, Hucknall; Central C, Nottingham), b Nottingham 4 June 1998. RHB, RMF. Squad No 80. Nottinghamshire 2nd XI debut 2016. England U19 2017. Awaiting 1st XI debut.

BROAD, Stuart Christopher John (Oakham S), b Nottingham 24 Jun 1986. 6'6". LHB, RFM. Squad No 8. Son of B.C.Broad (Glos, Notts, OFS and England 1979-94). Debut (Leicestershire) 2005; cap 2007. Nottinghamshire debut/cap 2008. Big Bash: HH 2016-17. YC 2006. *Wisden* 2009. **ECB Test Central Contract 2017-18. Tests**: 114 (2007-08 to 2017-18); HS 169 v P (Lord's) 2010, sharing in record Test and UK f-c 8th-wkt partnership of 332 with I.J.L.Trott; 50 wkts (2); most – 62 (2013); BB 8-15 v A (Nottingham) 2015. Hat-tricks (2): v I (Nottingham) 2011, and v SL (Leeds) 2014. **LOI**: 121 (2006 to 2015-16, 3 as captain); HS 45* v I (Manchester) 2007; BB 5-23 v SA (Nottingham) 2008. **IT20**: 56 (2006 to 2013-14, 27 as captain); HS 18* v SA (Chester-le-St) 2012 and 18* v A (Melbourne) 2013-14; BB 4-24 v NZ (Auckland) 2012-13. F-c Tours: A 2010-11, 2013-14, 2017-18; SA 2009-10, 2015-16; WI 2005-06 (Eng A), 2008-09, 2014-15; NZ 2007-08, 2012-13; I 2008-09, 2012-13, 2016-17; SL 2007-08, 2011-12; B 2006-07 (Eng A), 2009-10, 2016-17; UAE 2011-12 (v P), 2015-16 (v P). HS 169 (see Tests). CC HS 91* Le v Derbys (Leicester) 2007. Nt HS 60 v Worcs (Nottingham) 2009. BB 8-15 (see Tests). CC BB 8-52 (11-131 match) Nt v Warwks (Birmingham) 2010. LO HS 45* (see LOI). LO BB 5-23 (see LOI). T20 HS 18*. T20 BB 4-24.

CARTER, Matthew (Branston S), b Lincoln 26 May 1996. Younger brother of A.Carter (*see NORTHAMPTONSHIRE*). RHB, OB. Squad No 20. Debut (Nottinghamshire) 2015, taking 7-56 v Somerset (Taunton) – the best debut figures for Nt since 1914. Nottinghamshire 2nd XI debut 2013. Lincolnshire 2013-17. HS 33 v Sussex (Hove) 2017. BB 7-56 (10-195 match) (*see above*).

NQCHRISTIAN, Daniel Trevor, b Camperdown, NSW, Australia 4 May 1983. RHB, RFM. Squad No 54. S Australia 2007-08 to 2012-13. Hampshire 2010. Gloucestershire 2013; cap 2013. Victoria 2013-14 to date. Nottinghamshire debut/cap 2016, having joined in 2015 for l-o and T20 only; captain 2016 to date (T20 only). IPL: DC 2011-12. RCB 2013. RPS 2017. Big Bash: BH 2011-12 to 2014-15. HH 2015-16 to date. **LOI** (A): 19 (2011-12 to 2013-14); HS 39 v I (Adelaide) 2011-12; BB 5-31 v SL (Melbourne) 2011-12. **IT20** (A): 16 (2009-10 to 2017-18); HS 9 v I (Ranchi) 2017-18; BB 3-27 v WI (Gros Islet) 2011-12. HS 131* S Aus v NSW (Adelaide) 2011-12. CC HS 36 and CC BB 2-115 H v Somerset (Taunton) 2010. Nt HS 31 v Hants (Southampton) 2016. BB 5-24 S Aus v WA (Perth) (2009-10). Nt BB 1-22 v Warwks (Birmingham) 2016. LO HS 117 Vic v NSW (Sydney) 2013-14. LO BB 6-48 S Aus v Vic (Geelong) 2010-11. T20 HS 129 M v Kent (Canterbury) 2014 – M record. T20 BB 5-14.

‡**COUGHLIN, Paul** (St Robert of Newminster Catholic CS, Washington), b Sunderland, Co Durham 23 Oct 1992. Elder brother of J.Coughlin (*see DURHAM*); nephew of T.Harland (Durham 1974-78). 6'3". RHB, RM. Squad No 29. Durham 2012-17. Joins Nottinghamshire in 2018. Northumberland 2011. F-c Tour (EL): WI 2017-18. HS 85 Du v Lancs (Chester-le-St) 2014, sharing Du record 9th wkt partnership of 150 with P.Mustard. BB 5-49 (10-133 match) Du v Northants (Chester-le-St) 2017. LO HS 22 Du v Notts (Nottingham) 2017 (RLC) and 22 Du v Lancs (Chester-le-St) 2017 (RLC). LO BB 3-36 Du v Worcs (Worcester) 2017 (RLC). T20 HS 53. T20 BB 5-42.

FLETCHER, Luke Jack (Henry Mellish S, Nottingham), b Nottingham 18 Sep 1988. 6'6". RHB, RMF. Squad No 19. Debut (Nottinghamshire) 2008; cap 2014. Surrey 2015 (on loan). Derbyshire 2016 (on loan). HS 92 v Hants (Southampton) 2009 and 92 v Durham (Chester-le-St) 2017. BB 5-52 v Warwks (Nottingham) 2013. LO HS 40* v Durham (Chester-le-St) 2009 (P40). LO BB 4-44 v Warwks (Nottingham) 2014 (RLC). T20 HS 11*. T20 BB 4-30.

FOOTITT, Mark Harold Alan (Carlton le Willows S; West Notts C), b Nottingham 25 Nov 1985. 6'2". RHB, LFM. Squad No 7. Nottinghamshire debut 2005, returned in 2017. Derbyshire 2010-15; cap 2014. Surrey 2016-17. MCC 2006. F-c Tour: SA 2015-16. HS 34 De v Leics (Leicester) 2015. Nt HS 19* v Hants (Southampton) 2005. 50 wkts (2); most – 84 (2014). BB 7-62 Sy v Lancs (Oval) 2016. Nt BB 5-45 v West Indies A (Nottingham) 2006. LO HS 11* De v Notts (Nottingham) 2014 (RLC). LO BB 5-28 De v Scotland (Edinburgh) 2013 (Y40). T20 HS 2*. T20 BB 3-22.

GURNEY, Harry Frederick (Garendon HS; Loughborough GS; Leeds U), b Nottingham 25 Oct 1986. 6'2". RHB, LFM. Squad No 11. Leicestershire 2007-11. Nottinghamshire debut 2012; cap 2014. MCC 2014. Bradford/Leeds UCCE 2006-07 (not f-c). **LOI**: 10 (2014 to 2014-15); HS 6* v SL (Colombo, RPS) 2014-15; BB 4-55 v SL (Lord's) 2014. **IT20**: 2 (2014); BB 2-26 v SL (Oval) 2014. HS 42* v Sussex (Hove) 2014. BB 6-61 v Durham (Chester-le-St) 2016. Hat-trick v Sussex (Hove) 2013. LO HS 13* v Durham (Chester-le-St) 2012 (CB40). LO BB 5-24 Le v Hants (Leicester) 2010 (CB40). T20 HS 5*. T20 BB 4-17.

HALES, Alexander Daniel (Chesham HS), b Hillingdon, Middx 3 Jan 1989. 6'5''. RHB, OB, occ WK. Squad No 10. Debut (Nottinghamshire) 2008; cap 2011. Agreed white-ball-only contract for 2018. Worcestershire 2014 (1 game, on loan). Buckinghamshire 2006-07. MCC YCs 2006-07. Big Bash: MR 2012-13. AS 2013-14. HH 2014-15. **ECB L-O Central Contract 2017-18. Tests**: 11 (2015-16 to 2016); HS 94 v SL (Lord's) 2016; BB –. **LOI**: 59 (2014 to 2017-18); HS 171 v P (Nottingham) 2016. **IT20**: 52 (2011 to 2017-18); HS 116* v SL (Chittagong) 2013-14 – E record. 1000 runs (3); most – 1127 (2011). HS 236 v Yorks (Nottingham) 2015. BB 2-63 v Yorks (Nottingham) 2009. LO HS 187* v Surrey (Lord's) 2017 (RLC) – Nt record. T20 HS 116*.

KITT, Benjamin Michael, b Plymouth, Devon 18 Jan 1995. RHB, RMF. Squad No 17. Nottinghamshire 2nd XI debut 2012. Cornwall 2011-12. Awaiting 1st XI debut.

LIBBY, Jacob ('Jake') Daniel (Plymouth C; UWIC), b Plymouth, Devon 3 Jan 1993. 5'9''. RHB, OB. Squad No 2. Cardiff MCCU 2014. Nottinghamshire debut 2014, scoring 108 v Sussex (Nottingham). Northamptonshire 2016 (on loan). Cornwall 2011-14. HS 144 v Durham (Chester-le-St) 2016. BB 1-13 Nh v Leics (Leicester) 2016.

MILNES, Matthew Edward (West Bridgford CS; Durham U), b Nottingham 29 Jul 1994. RHB, RMF. Squad No 16. Durham MCCU 2014. Durham 2nd XI 2014-15. MCC Univs 2015. Nottinghamshire 2nd XI debut 2016. Awaiting 1st XI debut. HS 9 and BB 2-37 DU v Durham (Chester-le-St) 2014.

MOORES, Thomas James (Loughborough GS), b Brighton, Sussex 4 Sep 1996. Son of P.Moores (Worcestershire, Sussex & OFS 1983-98); nephew of S.Moores (Cheshire 1995). LHB, WK. Squad No 23. Lancashire 2016 (on loan). Nottinghamshire debut 2016. Nottinghamshire 2nd XI debut 2014. HS 41 v Yorks (Scarborough) 2016. LO HS 10 La v Leics (Leicester) 2016 (RLC). T20 HS 57.

MULLANEY, Steven John (St Mary's RC S, Astley), b Warrington, Cheshire 19 Nov 1986. 5'9''. RHB, RM. Squad No 5. Lancashire 2006-08. Nottinghamshire debut 2010, scoring 100* v Hants (Southampton); cap 2013; captain 2018. 1000 runs (1): 1148 (2016). HS 168 v Kent (Nottingham) 2017. BB 5-32 v Glos (Nottingham) 2017. LO HS 111 v Essex (Chelmsford) 2017 (RLC). LO BB 4-29 v Kent (Nottingham) 2013 (Y40). T20 HS 53. T20 BB 4-19.

‡**NASH, Christopher** David (Collyer's SFC; Loughborough U), b Cuckfield, Sussex 19 May 1983. 5'11''. RHB, OB. Squad No 3. Sussex 2002-17; cap 2008; testimonial 2017. Loughborough UCCE 2003-04. British U 2004. Joins Nottinghamshire in 2018. 1000 runs (4); most – 1321 (2009). HS 184 Sx v Leics (Leicester) 2010. BB 4-12 Sx v Glamorgan (Cardiff) 2010. LO HS 124* Sx v Kent (Canterbury) 2011 (CB40). LO BB 4-40 Sx v Yorks (Hove) 2009 (FPT). T20 HS 112*. T20 BB 4-7.

PATEL, Samit Rohit (Worksop C), b Leicester 30 Nov 1984. Elder brother of A.Patel (Derbyshire and Notts 2007-11). 5'8''. RHB, SLA. Squad No 21. Debut (Nottinghamshire) 2002; cap 2008; testimonial 2017. MCC 2014, 2016. **Tests**: 6 (2011-12 to 2015-16); HS 42 v P (Sharjah) 2015-16; BB 2-27 v SL (Galle) 2011-12. **LOI**: 36 (2008 to 2012-13); HS 70* v I (Mohali) 2011-12; BB 5-41 v SA (Oval) 2008. **IT20**: 18 (2011 to 2012-13); HS 67 v SL (Pallekele) 2012-13; BB 2-6 v Afghanistan (Colombo, RPS) 2012-13. F-c Tours: NZ 2008-09 (Eng A); I 2012-13; UAE 2015-16 (v P). 1000 runs (2); most – 1125 (2014). HS 257* v Glos (Bristol) 2011. BB 7-68 (11-111 match) v Hants (Southampton) 2011. LO HS 129* v Warwks (Nottingham) 2013 (Y40). LO BB 6-13 v Ireland (Dublin) 2009 (FPT). T20 HS 90*. T20 BB 4-20.

ROOT, William (**'Billy'**) Thomas (Worksop C; Leeds Beckett U), b Sheffield, Yorks 5 Aug 1992. Younger brother of J.E.Root (*see YORKSHIRE*). LHB, OB. Squad No 66. Leeds/Bradford MCCU 2015-16. Nottinghamshire debut 2015. Suffolk 2014. HS 133 LBU v Sussex (Hove) 2016. Nt HS 132 and BB 3-29 v Sussex (Hove) 20117. LO HS 107* v Warwks (Birmingham) 2017 (RLC). LO BB –. T20 HS 37. T20 BB –.

^{NQ}**SODHI,** Inderbir Singh (**'Ish'**), b Ludhiana, Punjab, India 31 Oct 1992. RHB, LBG. Squad No 61. Northern Districts 2012-13 to date. Nottinghamshire debut 2017 (T20 only). Big Bash: AS 2016-17. **Tests** (NZ): 14 (2013-14 to 2016-17); HS 63 v P (Abu Dhabi) 2014-15; BB 4-60 v Z (Bulawayo) 2016. **LOI** (NZ): 22 (2015 to 2017-18); HS 5 v SA (Durban) 2015 and 5 v E (Christchurch) 2017-18; BB 4-58 v E (Dunedin) 2017-18. **IT20** (NZ): 26 (2014 to 2017-18); HS 15 v P (Auckland) 2017-18; BB 3-18 v I (Nagpur) 2015-16. F-c Tours (NZ): WI 2014; I 2013-14, 2016-17. 2013-14 (NZ A); SL 2013-14 (NZ A); Z 2016; B 2013-14; UAE 2014-15 (v P). HS 82* ND v Otago (Dunedin) 2014-15. BB 7-59 (11-189 match) ND v Otago (Dunedin) 2017-18. LO HS 444* ND v CD (Whangarei) 2017-18. LO BB 4-10 NZ A v Sri Lanka A (Bristol) 2014. T20 HS 51. T20 BB 6-11 – 6th best analysis in all T20.

‡^{NQ}**TAYLOR,** Luteru **Ross** Poutoa Lote, b Lower Hutt, Wellington, New Zealand 8 Mar 1984. 6'0". RHB, OB. Squad No 16. Central Districts 2002-03 to date. Sussex 2016. Joins Nottinghamshire in 2018 for first part of the season. IPL: RCB 2007-08 to 2009-10. RR 2011. DD 2012-14. PW 2013. **Tests** (NZ): 83 (2007-08 to 2017-18, 14 as captain); HS 290 v A (Perth) 2015-16; BB 2-4 v I (Ahmedabad) 2010-11. **LOI** (NZ): 204 (2005-06 to 2017-18, 20 as captain); 1000 runs (1): 1046 (2015); HS 181* v E (Dunedin) 2017-18; BB – . **IT20** (NZ): 81 (2006-07 to 2017-18, 13 as captain); HS 63 v WI (Auckland) 2008-09. F-c Tours (NZ) (C=Captain): E 2008, 2013, 2015; A 2008-09, 2011-12C, 2015-16; SA 2004 (NZ A), 2007-08, 2016; WI 2012C; I 2010-11, 2012C, 2014, 2016-17; SL 2009, 2012-13C; Z 2011-12C, 2016; B 2008-09, 2013-14; UAE 2014-15 (v P). HS 290 (*see Tests*). CC HS 142* Sx v Kent (Tunbridge W) 2016. BB 2-4 (*see Tests*). LO HS 181* (*see LOI*). LO BB 1-13 CD v Canterbury (Christchurch) 2005-06. T20 HS 111*. T20 BB 3-28.

WESSELS, Mattheus Hendrik (**'Riki'**) (Woodridge C, Pt Elizabeth; Northampton U), b Marogudoore, Queensland, Australia 12 Nov 1985. Left Australia when 2 months old. Qualified for England after gaining a UK passport in July 2016. Son of K.C.Wessels (OFS, Sussex, WP, NT, Q, EP, GW, Australia and South Africa 1973-74 to 1999-00). 5'11". RHB, WK. Squad No 9. MCC 2004. Northamptonshire 2005-09. Nondescripts 2007-08. MWR 2009-10 to 2011-12. Nottinghamshire debut 2011; cap 2014. Big Bash: SS 2014-15. 1000 runs (2); most – 1213 (2014). HS 202* v Sussex (Nottingham) 2017. BB 1-10 MWR v MT (Bulawayo) 2009-10. LO HS 146 v Northants (Nottingham) 2016 (RLC). LO BB 1-0 MWR v MT (Bulawayo) 2009-10. T20 HS 110 v Debys (Nottingham) 2017 – Nt record.

WOOD, Luke (Portland CS, Worksop), b Sheffield, Yorks 2 Aug 1995. 5'9". LHB, LM. Squad No 14. Debut (Nottinghamshire) 2014. Nottinghamshire 2nd XI debut 2012. England U19 2014. HS 100 v Sussex (Nottingham) 2015. BB 5-40 v Cambridge MCCU (Cambridge) 2016. CC BB 4-31 v Northants (Northampton) 2017. LO HS 52 and LO BB 2-44 v Leics (Leicester) 2016 (RLC). T20 HS 1*. T20 BB 2-15.

RELEASED/RETIRED

(Having made a County 1st XI appearance in 2017)

HUTTON, B.A. – *see NORTHAMPTONSHIRE.*

LUMB, Michael John (St Stithians C, Johannesburg), b Johannesburg, South Africa 12 Feb 1980. Son of R.G.Lumb (Yorkshire 1970-84), nephew of A.J.S.Smith (SAU and Natal 1972-73 to 1983-84). 6'0". LHB, RM. Yorkshire 2000-06; ECB qualified and CC debut 2001; cap 2003. Hampshire 2007-11; cap 2008. Nottinghamshire 2012-17; cap 2012. IPL: RR 2009-10. DC 2011. Big Bash: SS 2011-12 to 2016-17. **LOI**: 3 (2013-14); HS 106 v WI (North Sound) 2013-14, becoming only the 2nd England player after D.L.Amiss to score a century on LOI debut. **IT20**: 27 (2009-10 to 2013-14); HS 63 v WI (Bridgetown) 2013-14. F-c Tour (Eng A): I 2003-04. 1000 runs (3); most – 1120 (2013). HS 221* v Derbys (Nottingham) 2013. BB 2-10 Y v Kent (Canterbury) 2001. LO HS 184 v Northants (Nottingham) 2016. LO BB –. T20 HS 124* H v Essex (Southampton) 2009. T20 BB 3-32.

NQPATTINSON, James Lee, b Melbourne, Australia 3 May 1990. Younger brother of D.J.Pattinson (Victoria, Nottinghamshire and England 2006-07 to 2011-12). LHB, RFM. Victoria 2008-09 to date. Nottinghamshire 2017; cap 2017. Big Bash: MR 2013-14 to 2016-17. **Tests** (A): 17 (2011-12 to 2015-16); HS 42 v SA (Adelaide) 2012-13; BB 5-27 v NZ (Brisbane) 2011-12 and 5-27 v WI (Hobart) 2015-16. **LOI** (A): 15 (2011 to 2015); HS 13 v E (Manchester) 2012; BB 4-51 v SL (Melbourne) 2011-12. **IT20** (A): 4 (2011-12); HS 5* and BB 2-17 v SA (Johannesburg) 2011-12. F-c Tours (A): E 2013; SA 2013-14; WI 2011-12; NZ 2015-16; I 2012-13. HS 89* and Nt BB 5-29 v Leics (Leicester) 2017. BB 6-32 Vic v Q (Brisbane) 2012-13. LO HS 44 Vic v Q (Sydney) 2015-16. LO BB 6-48 Vic v NSW (Sydney) 2009-10. T20 HS 13. T20 BB 4-24.

PUJARA, C.A. – *see YORKSHIRE.*

READ, Christopher Mark Wells (Torquay GS; Bath U), b Paignton, Devon 10 Aug 1978. 5'8". RHB, WK. Gloucestershire (l-o only) 1997. Debut 1997-98 for England A in Kenya. Nottinghamshire 1998-2017; cap 1999; captain 2008-17; benefit 2009. MCC 2002. Devon 1995-97. *Wisden* 2010. **Tests**: 15 (1999 to 2006-07); HS 55 v P (Leeds) 2006. Made six dismissals twice in successive innings 2006-07 to establish an Ashes record. **LOI**: 36 (1999-00 to 2006-07); HS 30* v SA (Manchester) 2003. **IT20**: 1 (2006); HS 13 v P (Bristol) 2006. F-c Tours: A 2006-07; SA 1998-99 (Eng A), 1999-00; WI 2000-01 (Eng A), 2003-04, 2005-06 (Eng A); SL 1997-98 (Eng A), 2002-03 (ECB Acad), 2003-04; Z 1998-99 (Eng A); B 2003-04; K 1997-98 (Eng A). 1000 runs (3); most – 1203 (2009). HS 240 v Essex (Chelmsford) 2007. BB –. LO HS 135 v Durham (Nottingham) 2006 (CGT). T20 HS 58*.

SMITH, Gregory Philip (Oundle S; St Hild & St Bede C, Durham U), b Leicester 16 Nov 1988. 6'0". RHB, LBG. Leicestershire 2008-14, returned in 2015 on loan. Durham MCCU 2009-11. Badureliya 2013-14. Colombo CC 2014-15. Nottinghamshire 2015-17. HS 158* Le v Glos (Leicester) 2010. Nt HS 73 v Cambridge MCCU (Cambridge) 2017. BB 1-64 Le v Glos (Leicester) 2008. LO HS 135* Le v Somerset (Leicester) 2013 (Y40). T20 HS 102.

NQTAYLOR, Brendan Ross Murray (St John's C), b Harare, Zimbabwe 6 Feb 1986. RHB, WK, OB. Mashonaland 2001-02 to 2004-05. Northerns (Zim) 2007-08 to 2008-09. MRW 2009-10 to 2013-14. Nottinghamshire 2015-17; cap 2015. Midlands Rhinos 2017-18. **Tests** (Z): 26 (2004 to 2017-18, 13 as captain); HS 171 v B (Harare) 2013; BB – . **LOI** (Z): 179 (2004 to 2017-18, 34 as captain); HS 145* v SA (Bloemfontein) 2010-11; BB 3-54 v B (Dhaka) 2004-05. **IT20** (Z): 28 (2006-07 to 2017-18, 17 as captain); HS 75* v NZ (Hamilton) 2011-12; BB 1-16 v SA (Kimberley) 2010-11. F-c Tours (Z) (C=Captain): SA 2004-05, 2007-08, 2017-18; WI 2010, 2012-13C; NZ 2011-12C; I 2005-06; P 2004-05, 2007-08; B 2003-04 (ZA), 2004-05, 2014-15C. 1000 runs (1+1); most – 1070 (2015). HS 217 MWR v SR (Masvingo) 2009-10. Nt HS 152 v Somerset (Taunton) 2015. BB 2-36 Mashonaland v Manicaland (Mutare) 2003-04. LO HS 154 v Somerset (Taunton) 2017 (RLC). LO BB 5-28 Zim A v India A (Harare) 2004. T20 HS 101*. T20 BB 3-38.

NOTTINGHAMSHIRE 2017

RESULTS SUMMARY

	Place	Won	Lost	Drew	NR
Specsavers County Champ (2nd Division)	2nd	7	2	5	
All First-Class Matches		8	2	5	
Royal London One-Day Cup (North Group)	Winners	7	3		1
NatWest t20 Blast (North Group)	Winners	11	4		2

SPECSAVERS COUNTY CHAMPIONSHIP AVERAGES
BATTING AND FIELDING

Cap		M	I	NO	HS	Runs	Avge	100	50	Ct/St
2008	S.R.Patel	14	19	2	257*	906	53.29	2	2	6
2017	J.L.Pattinson	5	5	1	89*	197	49.25	–	2	–
2014	M.H.Wessels	14	18	1	202*	823	48.41	3	2	21
2011	A.D.Hales	7	9	–	218	424	47.11	1	1	–
2008	S.C.J.Broad	5	5	1	57	171	42.75	–	3	4
2013	S.J.Mullaney	11	15	–	168	620	41.33	1	4	15
1999	C.M.W.Read	14	18	2	124	622	38.87	1	3	53
2016	J.T.Ball	7	9	4	43	174	34.80	–	–	1
	L.Wood	6	9	3	44	199	33.16	–	–	2
2012	M.J.Lumb	8	9	–	117	292	32.44	1	–	2
	G.P.Smith	3	5	2	60*	91	30.33	–	1	5
2017	C.A.Pujara	8	12	–	112	333	27.75	1	1	7
2015	B.R.M.Taylor	4	5	–	61	123	24.60	–	1	6
	J.D.Libby	14	20	1	109	464	24.42	1	–	4
2014	L.J.Fletcher	9	10	2	92	139	17.37	–	1	2
	B.A.Hutton	9	13	–	61	210	16.15	–	1	6
2014	H.F.Gurney	11	12	5	42*	60	8.57	–	–	1

Also played: M.Carter (1 match) 33 (1 ct); M.H.A.Footitt (1) did not bat; T.J.Moores (1) 1, 0; W.T.Root (2) 11, 7, 132.

BOWLING

	O	M	R	W	Avge	Best	5wI	10wM
J.L.Pattinson	139.3	34	386	32	12.06	5-29	2	–
S.J.Mullaney	177	58	486	25	19.44	5-32	1	–
S.C.J.Broad	122.1	23	334	16	20.87	3-40	–	–
L.J.Fletcher	252.3	48	808	36	22.44	4-35	–	–
J.T.Ball	183.2	39	675	27	25.00	3-36	–	–
B.A.Hutton	289.2	64	995	37	26.89	5-52	2	1
L.Wood	130.2	15	512	18	28.44	4-31	–	–
S.R.Patel	223	55	682	19	35.89	3-17	–	–
H.F.Gurney	288	48	985	27	36.48	3-55	–	–

Also bowled: M.Carter 25-3-161-4; M.H.A.Footitt 27.2-4-95-4; J.D.Libby 10-0-41-0; M.J.Lumb 2-0-5-0; C.A.Pujara 5-0-17-0; W.T.Root 7.2-1-29-3; M.H.Wessels 5-0-15-0.

The First-Class Averages (pp 230–246) give the records of Nottinghamshire players in all first-class county matches (Nottinghamshire's other opponents being Cambridge MCCU), with the exception of M.H.A.Footitt, whose first-class figures for Nottinghamshire are as above, and:
S.C.J.Broad 6-6-1-57-189-37.80-0-3-5ct. 140.1-29-360-18-20.00-3/40-0-0.

NOTTINGHAMSHIRE RECORDS

FIRST-CLASS CRICKET

Highest Total	For	791		v	Essex	Chelmsford	2007
	V	781-7d		by	Northants	Northampton	1995
Lowest Total	For	13		v	Yorkshire	Nottingham	1901
	V	16		by	Derbyshire	Nottingham	1879
		16		by	Surrey	The Oval	1880
Highest Innings	For	312*	W.W.Keeton	v	Middlesex	The Oval	1939
	V	345	C.G.Macartney	for	Australians	Nottingham	1921

Highest Partnership for each Wicket

1st	406*	D.J.Bicknell/G.E.Welton	v	Warwicks	Birmingham	2000
2nd	398	A.Shrewsbury/W.Gunn	v	Sussex	Nottingham	1890
3rd	367	W.Gunn/J.R.Gunn	v	Leics	Nottingham	1903
4th	361	A.O.Jones/J.R.Gunn	v	Essex	Leyton	1905
5th	359	D.J.Hussey/C.M.W.Read	v	Essex	Nottingham	2007
6th	372*	K.P.Pietersen/J.E.Morris	v	Derbyshire	Derby	2001
7th	301	C.C.Lewis/B.N.French	v	Durham	Chester-le-St[2]	1993
8th	220	G.F.H.Heane/R.Winrow	v	Somerset	Nottingham	1935
9th	170	J.C.Adams/K.P.Evans	v	Somerset	Taunton	1994
10th	152	E.B.Alletson/W.Riley	v	Sussex	Hove	1911
	152	U.Afzaal/A.J.Harris	v	Worcs	Nottingham	2000

Best Bowling	For	10-66	K.Smales	v	Glos	Stroud	1956
(Innings)	V	10-10	H.Verity	for	Yorkshire	Leeds	1932
Best Bowling	For	17-89	F.C.L.Matthews	v	Northants	Nottingham	1923
(Match)	V	17-89	W.G.Grace	for	Glos	Cheltenham	1877

Most Runs – Season	2620	W.W.Whysall	(av 53.46)	1929
Most Runs – Career	31592	G.Gunn	(av 35.69)	1902-32
Most 100s – Season	9	W.W.Whysall		1928
	9	M.J.Harris		1971
	9	B.C.Broad		1990
Most 100s – Career	65	J.Hardstaff jr		1930-55
Most Wkts – Season	181	B.Dooland	(av 14.96)	1954
Most Wkts – Career	1653	T.G.Wass	(av 20.34)	1896-1920
Most Career W-K Dismissals	983	C.M.W.Read	(939 ct; 44 st)	1998-2017
Most Career Catches in the Field	466	A.O.Jones		1892-1914

LIMITED-OVERS CRICKET

Highest Total	50ov	445-8		v	Northants	Nottingham	2016
	40ov	296-7		v	Somerset	Taunton	2002
	T20	227-3		v	Derbyshire	Nottingham	2017
Lowest Total	50ov	74		v	Leics	Leicester	1987
	40ov	57		v	Glos	Nottingham	2009
	T20	91		v	Lancashire	Manchester	2006
Highest Innings	50ov	187*	A.D.Hales	v	Surrey	Lord's	2017
	40ov	150*	A.D.Hales	v	Worcs	Nottingham	2009
	T20	110	M.H.Wessels	v	Derbyshire	Nottingham	2017
Best Bowling	50ov	6-10	K.P.Evans	v	Northumb	Jesmond	1994
	40ov	6-12	R.J.Hadlee	v	Lancashire	Nottingham	1980
	T20	5-22	G.G.White	v	Lancashire	Nottingham	2013

SOMERSET

Formation of Present Club: 18 August 1875
Inaugural First-Class Match: 1882
Colours: Black, White and Maroon
Badge: Somerset Dragon
County Champions: (0); best – 2nd (Div 1) 2001, 2010, 2012, 2016
Gillette/NatWest/C&G Trophy Winners: (3) 1979, 1983, 2001
Benson and Hedges Cup Winners: (2) 1981, 1982
Sunday League Winners: (1) 1979
Twenty20 Cup Winners: (1) 2005

Chief Executive: Lee Cooper, Cooper Associates County Ground, Taunton TA1 1JT • Tel: 0845 337 1875 • Fax: 01823 332395 • Email: enquiries@somersetcountycc.co.uk • Web: www.somersetcountycc.co.uk • Twitter: @SomersetCCC (77,646 followers)

Director of Cricket: Andy Hurry. **Head Coach**: Jason Kerr. **Academy Director**: Steve Snell. **Captains**: T.B.Abell (f-c and l-o) and L.Gregory (T20). **Overseas Players**: C.J.Anderson (T20 only) and C.T.Bancroft. **2018 Testimonial**: M.E.Trescothick. **Groundsman**: Simon Lee. **Scorers**: Gerald Stickley and Polly Rhodes. ‡ New registration. NQ Not qualified for England.

ABELL, Thomas Benjamin (Taunton S; Exeter U), b Taunton 5 Mar 1994. 5'10''. RHB, RM. Squad No 28. Debut (Somerset) 2014; captain 2017. Somerset 2nd XI debut 2010. HS 135 v Lancs (Manchester) 2016. BB 1-11 v Yorks (Taunton) 2015. LO HS 106 v Sussex (Taunton) 2016 (RLC). T20 HS 7.

NQANDERSON, Corey James, b Christchurch, New Zealand 13 Dec 1990. LHB, LMF. Canterbury 2006-07 to 2009-10. Northern Districts 2011-12 to date. Somerset debut 2017 (T20 only). IPL: MI 2014-15. DD 2017. **Tests** (NZ): 13 (2013-14 to 2015-16); HS 116 v B (Dhaka) 2013-14; BB 3-47 v WI (Hamilton) 2013-14. **LOI** (NZ): 49 (2013 to 2017); HS 131* v WI (Queenstown) 2013-14; BB 5-63 v I (Auckland) 2013-14. **IT20** (NZ): 29 (2012-13 to 2016-17); HS 94* v B (Mt Maunganui) 2014-15; BB 2-17 v P (Wellington) 2015-16. F-c Tours (NZ): E 2015; I 2013-14 (NZA); SL 2013-14 (NZA); B 2013-14; UAE 2014-15 (v P). HS 167 ND v Otago (Hamilton) 2012-13. BB 5-22 ND v Canterbury (Hamilton) 2009-10. LO HS 131* (*see LOI*). LO BB 5-26 ND v Canterbury (Hamilton) 2009-10. T20 HS 95*. T20 BB 2-17.

‡NQBANCROFT, Cameron Timothy (Aquinas C, Perth), b Attadale, Perth, Australia 19 Nov 1992. 6'0''. RHB, RM, WK. Squad No 4. W Australia 2013-14 to date. Gloucestershire 2016-17; cap 2016. Big Bash: PS 2014-15 to date. **Tests** (A): 7 (2017-18); HS 82* v E (Brisbane) 2017-18. **IT20** (A): 1 (2015-16); HS 0* v I (Sydney) 2015-16. F-c Tours (A): SA 2017-18; I 2015 (Aus A). HS 228* WA v SA (Perth) 2017-18. Gs HS 206* v Kent (Bristol) 2017. LO HS 176 WA v S Aus (Sydney Hurtsville) 2015-16. T20 HS 75*.

BANTON, Thomas (Bromsgrove S), b Chiltern, Bucks 11 Nov 1998. Son of C.Banton (Nottinghamshire 1995). 6'2''. RHB, WK. Squad No 18. Awaiting f-c debut. Warwickshire 2nd XI 2015. Somerset 2nd XI debut 2016. T20 HS 4.

BARTLETT, George Anthony (Millfield S), b Frimley, Surrey 14 Mar 1998. 6'0''. RHB, OB. Squad No 14. Debut (Somerset) 2017. Somerset 2nd XI debut 2015. England U19 2016 to 2017. HS 28 v Surrey (Oval) 2017.

BESS, Dominic Mark (Blundell's S), b Exeter, Devon 22 Jul 1997. Cousin of Z.G.G.Bess (Devon 2015 to date) and J.J.Bess (Devon 2007 to date). RHB, OB. Squad No 22. Debut (Somerset) 2016. Somerset 2nd XI debut 2013. Devon 2015-16. F-c Tour (EL): WI 2017-18. HS 55 v Surrey (Taunton) 2017. BB 7-117 (10-162 match) v Hants (Taunton) 2017. LO HS 19 EL v West Indies A (Coolidge) 2017-18. LO BB 1-40 EL v West Indies A (Coolidge) 2017-18 – different games. T20 HS 1. T20 BB 1-31.

BYROM, Edward James (St John's C, Harare), b Harare, Zimbabwe 17 Jun 1997. 5'11". LHB, OB. Squad No 97. Irish passport. Debut (Somerset) 2017. Rising Stars 2017-18. Somerset 2nd XI debut 2015. HS 152 RS v MT (Kwekwe) 2017-18. Sm HS 56 v Middx (Taunton) 2017.

NQDAVEY, Joshua Henry (Culford S), b Aberdeen, Scotland 3 Aug 1990. 5'11". RHB, RMF. Squad No 38. Middlesex 2010-12. Scotland 2011-12 to date. Somerset debut 2015. Suffolk 2014. **LOI** (Scot): 29 (2010 to 2017); HS 64 v Afghanistan (Sharjah) 2012-13; BB 6-28 v Afghanistan (Abu Dhabi) 2014-15. **IT20** (Scot): 14 (2012 to 2016-17); HS 24 v Z (Nagpur) 2015-16; BB 4-34 v Netherlands (Abu Dhabi) 2016-17. HS 72 M v Oxford MCCU (Oxford) 2010 – on debut. CC HS 61 M v Glos (Bristol) 2010. Sm HS 47 v Middx (Lord's) 2017. BB 4-53 Scot v Afghanistan (Abu Dhabi) 2012-13. Sm BB 2-33 v Lancs (Manchester) 2017. LO HS 91 Scot v Warwks (Birmingham) 2011 (CB40). LO BB 6-28 (*see LOI*). T20 HS 24. T20 BB 4-34.

DAVIES, Steven Michael (King Charles I S, Kidderminster), b Bromsgrove, Worcs 17 Jun 1986. 5'10". LHB, WK. Squad No 11. Worcestershire 2005-09. Surrey 2010-16; cap 2011. Somerset debut/cap 2017. MCC 2006-07, 2011. **LOI**: 8 (2009-10 to 2010-11); HS 87 v P (Chester-le-St) 2010. **IT20**: 5 (2008-09 to 2010-11); HS 33 v P (Cardiff) 2010. F-c Tours: A 2010-11; B 2006-07 (Eng A); UAE 2011-12 (v P). 1000 runs (6); most – 1147 (2016). HS 200* Sy v Glamorgan (Cardiff) 2015. Sm HS 142 v Surrey (Taunton) 2017. LO HS 127* Sy v Hants (Oval) 2013 (Y40). T20 HS 99*.

GREEN, Benjamin George Frederick (Exeter S), b Exeter, Devon 28 Sep 1997. 6'2". RHB, RFM. Squad No 54. Somerset 2nd XI debut 2014. Devon 2014-15. England U19 2014-15 to 2017. Awaiting f-c debut. T20 HS 12*.

GREGORY, Lewis (Hele's S, Plympton), b Plymouth, Devon 24 May 1992. 6'0". RHB, RMF. Squad No 24. Debut (Somerset) 2011; cap 2015; T20 captain 2018. MCC 2017. Devon 2008. HS 137 v Middx (Lord's) 2017. BB 6-47 (11-122 match) v Northants (Northampton) 2014. LO HS 105* v Durham (Taunton) 2014 (RLC). LO BB 4-23 v Essex (Chelmsford) 2016 (RLC). T20 HS 37*. T20 BB 4-15.

GROENEWALD, Timothy Duncan (Maritzburg C; South Africa U), b Pietermaritzburg, South Africa 10 Jan 1984. 6'0". RHB, RFM. Squad No 5. Debut Cambridge UCCE 2006. Warwickshire 2006-08. Derbyshire 2009-14; cap 2011. Somerset debut 2014; cap 2016. HS 78 Wa v Bangladesh A (Birmingham) 2008. CC HS 76 Wa v Durham (Chester-le-St) 2008. Sm HS 47 v New Zealanders (Taunton) 2015. BB 6-50 De v Surrey (Croydon) 2009. Sm BB 5-58 v Warwks (Birmingham) 2017. Hat-trick De v Essex (Chelmsford) 2014. LO HS 57 v Warwks (Birmingham) 2014 (RLC). LO BB 4-22 De v Worcs (Worcester) 2011 (CB40). T20 HS 41. T20 BB 4-21.

HILDRETH, James Charles (Millfield S), b Milton Keynes, Bucks 9 Sep 1984. 5'10", RHB, RMF. Squad No 25. Debut (Somerset) 2003; cap 2007; testimonial 2017. MCC 2017. F-c Tour (EL): WI 2010-11. 1000 runs (6); most – 1620 (2015). HS 303* v Warwks (Taunton) 2009. BB 2-39 v Hants (Taunton) 2004. LO HS 151 v Scotland (Taunton) 2009 (FPT). LO BB 2-26 v Worcs (Worcester) 2008 (FPT). T20 HS 107*. T20 BB 3-24.

LEACH, Matthew Jack (Bishop Fox's Community S, Taunton; Richard Huish C; UWIC), b Taunton 22 Jun 1991. 6'0". LHB, SLA. Squad No 17. Cardiff MCCU 2012. Somerset debut 2012; cap 2012. England Lions 2017. MCC 2017. Dorset 2011. F-c Tours (EL): WI 2017-18; SL 2016-17; UAE 2016-17 (v Afghan). HS 52 v Lancs (Manchester) 2017. 50 wkts (2); most – 68 (2016). BB 7-106 (11-180 match) v Warwks (Taunton) 2015. LO HS 18 v Surrey (Oval) 2014 (RLC). LO BB 3-7 EL v UAE (Dubai, DSC) 2016-17.

^{NO}**MYBURGH, Johannes** Gerhardus (Pretoria BHS; U of SA), b Pretoria, South Africa 22 Oct 1980. Elder brother of S.J.Myburgh (Northerns, KZN and Netherlands 2005-06 to date), brother-in-law of F.de Wet (Northerns, NW, Lions, Hampshire, Dolphins and South Africa 2001-02 to 2011-12). 5'7". RHB, OB. Squad No 9. Northerns 1997-98 to 2006-07. Titans 2004-05. Canterbury 2007-08 to 2009-10. Hampshire 2011. Durham 2012. Somerset debut 2014. EU qualified through wife's visa. HS 203 Northerns B v Easterns (Pretoria) 1997-98. Sm HS 150 v Durham MCCU (Taunton Vale) 2015. CC HS 118 v Durham (Taunton) 2014. BB 4-56 Canterbury v ND (Hamilton) 2008-09. Sm BB 3-57 v Yorks (Taunton) 2015. LO HS 112 Canterbury v Auckland (Christchurch) 2009-10. LO BB 2-22 Canterbury v CD (Christchurch) 2009-10. T20 HS 88. T20 BB 3-16.

OVERTON, Craig (West Buckland S), b Barnstaple, Devon 10 Apr 1994. Twin brother of Jamie Overton (*see below*). 6'5". RHB, RMF. Squad No 12. Debut (Somerset) 2012; cap 2016. MCC 2017. Somerset 2nd XI debut 2011. Devon 2010-11. **Tests**: 2 (2017-18); HS 41* and BB 3-105 v A (Adelaide) 2017-18. F-c Tour: A 2017-18. HS 138 v Hants (Taunton) 2016. BB 6-74 v Warwks (Birmingham) 2015. LO HS 60* EL v Sri Lanka A (Dambulla) 2016-17. LO BB 3-21 v Sussex (Hove) 2017. T20 HS 35*. T20 BB 3-17.

OVERTON, Jamie (West Buckland S), b Barnstaple, Devon 10 Apr 1994. Twin brother of Craig Overton (*see above*). 6'5". RHB, RFM. Squad No 8. Debut (Somerset) 2012. England Lions 2017. Somerset 2nd XI debut 2011. Devon 2010-11. HS 56 v Warwks (Birmingham) 2014. BB 6-95 v Middx (Taunton) 2013. LO HS 40* v Glos (Taunton) 2016 (RLC). LO BB 4-42 v Durham (Chester-le-St) 2012 (CB40). T20 HS 31. T20 BB 4-22.

ROUSE, Timothy David (Kingswood S, Bath; Cardiff U), b Sheffield, Yorks 9 Apr 1996. Younger brother of H.P.Rouse (Leeds/Bradford MCCU 2013-15). 5'11. RHB, OB. Squad No 44. Cardiff MCCU 2015-17. Somerset debut 2016. Somerset 2nd XI debut 2012. HS 69 v Yorks (Scarborough) 2017. BB 2-31 CfU v Glamorgan (Cardiff) 2017.

SALE, Oliver Richard Trethowan (Sherborne S), b Newcastle-under-Lyme, Staffs 30 Sep 1995. 6'1". RHB, RFM. Squad No 82. Somerset 2nd XI debut 2014. Awaiting f-c debut. T20 HS 1.

TREGO, Peter David (Wyvern CS, W-s-M), b Weston-super-Mare 12 Jun 1981. 6'0". RHB, RMF. Squad No 7. Debut (Somerset) 2000; cap 2007; benefit 2015. Kent 2003. Middlesex 2005. C Districts 2013-14. MCC 2013. Herefordshire 2005. 1000 runs (1): 1070 (2016). HS 154* v Lancs (Manchester) 2016, sharing Sm record 8th wkt partnership of 236 with R.C.Davies. 50 wkts (1): 50 (2012). BB 7-84 (11-153 match) v Yorks (Leeds) 2014. LO HS 147 v Glamorgan (Taunton) 2010 (CB40). LO BB 5-40 EL v West Indies A (Worcester) 2010. T20 HS 94*. T20 BB 4-27.

TRENOUTH, Finlay Robert (Clifton C; Millfield S), b London 22 Sep 1998. 6'1". RHB, occ WK. Somerset 2nd XI debut 2016. Awaiting 1st XI debut. Summer contract.

TRESCOTHICK, Marcus Edward (Sir Bernard Lovell S), b Keynsham 25 Dec 1975. 6'2". LHB, RM, occ WK. Squad No 2. Debut (Somerset) 1993; cap 1999; joint captain 2002; benefit 2008; captain 2010-15; testimonial 2018. PCA 2000, 2009, 2011. *Wisden* 2004. MBE 2005. **Tests**: 76 (2000 to 2006, 2 as captain); HS 219 v SA (Oval) 2003; BB 1-34 v P (Karachi) 2000-01. **LOI**: 123 (2000 to 2006, 10 as captain); HS 137 v P (Lord's) 2001; BB 2-7 v Z (Manchester) 2000. **IT20**: 3 (2005 to 2006); HS 72 v SL (Southampton) 2006. F-c Tours: A 2002-03; SA 2004-05; WI 2003-04; NZ 1999-00 (Eng A), 2001-02; I 2001-02, 2005-06 (*part*); P 2000-01, 2005-06; SL 2000-01, 2003-04; B 1999-00 (Eng A), 2003-04. 1000 runs (8); most – 1817 (2009). HS 284 v Northants (Northampton) 2007. BB 4-36 (inc hat-trick) v Young A (Taunton) 1995. CC BB 4-82 v Yorks (Leeds) 1998. Hat-trick 1995 (*see above*). LO HS 184 v Glos (Taunton) 2008 (P40) – Sm l-o record. LO BB 4-50 v Northants (Northampton) 2000 (NL). T20 HS 108*.

NQ**VAN DER MERWE, Roelof** Erasmus (Pretoria HS), b Johannesburg, South Africa 31 Dec 1984. RHB, SLA. Squad No 52. Northerns 2006-07 to 2013-14. Titans 2007-08 to 2014-15. Netherlands 2015 to date. Somerset debut 2016. IPL: RCB 2009 to 2009-10. DD 2011-13. Big Bash: BH 2011-12. **LOI** (SA): 13 (2008-09 to 2010); HS 12 v I (Gwalior) 2009-10; BB 3-27 v Z (Centurion) 2009-10. **IT20** (SA/Neth): 24 (13 for SA 2008-09 to 2010; 11 for Neth 2015 to 2016-17); HS 48 v A (Centurion) 2008-09; BB 2-3 v Ireland (Dharamsala) 2015-16. HS 205* Titans v Warriors (Benoni) 2014-15. Sm HS 102* v Hants (Taunton) 2016. BB 4-22 v Middx (Taunton) 2017. LO HS 165* v Surrey (Taunton) 2017 (RLC). LO BB 5-26 Titans v Knights (Centurion) 2012-13. T20 HS 89*. T20 BB 3-13.

NQ**VAN MEEKEREN, Paul** Adriaan, b Amsterdam, Netherlands 15 Jan 1993. RHB, RMF. Squad No 47. Netherlands 2013 to date. Somerset debut 2016. **LOI** (Neth): 2 (2013 to 2013-14); HS 15* and BB 1-54 v SA (Amstelveen) 2013. **IT20** (Neth): 18 (2013 to 2016-17); HS 18 v Hong Kong (Dubai, DSC) 2016-17; BB 4-11 v Ireland (Dharamsala) 2015-16. HS 34 Neth v PNG (Amstelveen) 2017. Sm HS 1* and BB 4-60 v Essex (Chelmsford) 2017. LO HS 15* (*see LOI*). LO BB 3-22 Neth v UAE (Amstelveen) 2017. T20 HS 18. T20 BB 4-11.

WALLER, Maximilian Thomas Charles (Millfield S; Bournemouth U), b Salisbury, Wiltshire 3 March 1988. 6'0". RHB, LB. Squad No 10. Debut (Somerset) 2009. Dorset 2007-08. No f-c appearances since 2012. HS 28 v Hants (Southampton) 2009. BB 3-33 v Cardiff MCCU (Taunton Vale) 2012. CC BB 2-27 v Sussex (Hove) 2009. LO HS 25* v Glamorgan (Taunton) 2013 (Y40). LO BB 3-37 v Glos (Bristol) 2017 (RLC). T20 HS 17. T20 BB 4-16.

RELEASED/RETIRED

(Having made a County 1st XI appearance in 2017)

ALLENBY, James (Christ Church GS, Perth), b Perth, W Australia 12 Sep 1982. 6'0". RHB, RM. Leicestershire 2006-09. Glamorgan 2009-14; cap 2010; captain (T20) 2014. Somerset 2015-17; captain (l-o) 2016-17. 1000 runs (1): 1202 (2015). HS 138* Le v Bangladesh A (Leicester) 2008 and 138* Gm v Leics (Leicester) 2013. Sm HS 64 v Notts (Nottingham) 2015. 50 wkts (1): 54 (2014). BB 6-54 (10-128 match) Gm v Hants (Cardiff) 2014. Sm BB 4-67 v Middx (Taunton) 2016. LO HS 144* v Glamorgan (Cardiff) 2017 (RLC). LO BB 5-43 Le v Derbys (Leicester) 2007 (FPT). T20 HS 110. T20 BB 5-21 Le v Lancs (Manchester) 2008, inc 4 wkts in 4 balls.

DAVIES, Ryan Christopher (Sandwich TS), b Thanet, Kent 5 Nov 1996. 5'9". RHB, WK. Kent 2015. Somerset 2016. Kent 2nd XI debut 2013. England U19 2014-15 to 2015. HS 86 v Lancs (Manchester) 2016, sharing Sm record 8th wkt partnership of 236 with P.D.Trego. LO HS 46 v Warwks (Birmingham) 2016 (RLC). T20 HS 6.

^{NQ}**ELGAR, Dean**, b Welkom, OFS, South Africa 11 Jun 1987. LHB, SLA. Free State 2005-06 to 2010-11. Eagles 2006-07 to 2009-10. Knights 2010-11 to 2013-14. Somerset 2013-17; cap 2017. Titans 2014-15 to date. Surrey 2015. **Tests** (SA): 47 (2012-13 to 2017-18); 1000 runs (1): 1128 (2017); HS 199 v B (Potchefstroom) 2017-18; BB 4-22 v I (Mohali) 2015-16. **LOI** (SA): 6 (2012 to 2015-16); HS 42 v E (Oval) 2012; BB 1-11 v E (Southampton) 2012. F-c Tours (SA): E 2017; A 2012-13, 2016 (SA A), 2016-17; NZ 2016-17; I 2015-16; SL 2010 (SA A), 2014; Z 2014; B 2010 (SA A), 2015; UAE (v P) 2013-14; Ire 2012 (SA A). 1000 runs (0+2); most – 1193 (2009-10). HS 268 SA A v Australia A (Pretoria) 2013. CC HS 158 v Middx (Lord's) 2017. BB 4-22 (*see Tests*). CC BB 1-4 v Essex (Taunton) 2017. LO HS 131* v Sussex (Hove) 2017 (RLC). LO BB 3-43 Titans v Dolphins (Durban) 2014-15. T20 HS 72. T20 BB 4-23.

HOSE, A.J. – *see WARWICKSHIRE.*

NORTHAMPTONSHIRE RELEASED/RETIRED (continued from p 156)

^{NQ}**LEASK, Michael** Alexander, b Aberdeen, Scotland 29 Oct 1990. RHB, OB. Northamptonshire (l-o only) 2014. Somerset 2016-17 (T20 only). **LOI** (Scot): 26 (2013-14 to 2017-18); HS 59* v Z (Edinburgh) 2017; BB 4-37 v Z (Bulawayo) 2017-18. **IT20** (Scot): 14 (2013 to 2016-17); HS 58 v Netherlands (Abu Dhabi) 2013-14; BB 3-20 v UAE (Edinburgh) 2015. LO HS 59* (*see LOI*). LO BB 4-37 (*see LOI*). T20 HS 58. T20 BB 3-20.

^{NQ}**SHAMSI, Tabraiz**, b Johannesburg, South Africa 18 Feb 1990. RHB, SLC. Gauteng 2009-10. Lions 2009-10. Dolphins 2010-11 to 2013-14. KwaZulu-Natal 2010-11. KZN Inland 2011-12 to 2013-14. Easterns 2014-15 to 2015-16. Titans 2015-16 to date. Warriors 2017-18. Northamptonshire 2017 (T20 only). IPL: RCB 2016. **Tests** (SA): 1 (2016-17); HS 18* and BB 1-49 v A (Adelaide) 2016-17. **LOI** (SA): 7 (2016 to 2017-18); HS 0*; BB 3-36 v A (Port Elizabeth) 2016-17. **IT20** (SA): 5 (2017 to 2017-18); HS 0*; BB 1-31 v I (Cape Town) 2017-18. F-c Tour (SA): A 2016-17. HS 30* KZN Inland v Easterns (Benoni) 2012-13. 50 wkts (0+2); most – 57 (2015-16). BB 8-85 (13-120 match) KZN Inland v KZN (Chatsworth) 2013-14. LO HS 15* Titans v Dolphins (Pietermaritzburg) 2017-18. LO BB 5-40 Titans v Lions (Benoni) 2017-18. T20 HS 15*. T20 BB 4-10.

SHEIKH, Atif (Bluecoat S), b Nottingham 18 Feb 1991. 6'0". RHB, LFM. Derbyshire 2010. Leicestershire 2014-16. Northamptonshire 2017. HS 12 Le v Essex (Leicester) 2014. Nh HS 7 and Nh BB 1-36 v Glos (Northampton) 2017. BB 4-97 Le v Glos (Bristol) 2014, inc hat-trick. LO HS 22 and LO BB 3-49 v Australians (Leicester) 2015. T20 HS 14. T20 BB 2-11.

SOMERSET 2017

RESULTS SUMMARY

	Place	Won	Lost	Drew	NR
Specsavers County Champ (1st Division)	6th	4	6	4	
All First-Class Matches		4	6	4	
Royal London One-Day Cup (South Group)	QF	5	3		1
NatWest t20 Blast (South Group)	QF	6	7		2

SPECSAVERS COUNTY CHAMPIONSHIP AVERAGES

BATTING AND FIELDING

Cap		M	I	NO	HS	Runs	Avge	100	50	Ct/St
2017	D.Elgar	6	12	1	158	517	47.00	2	2	3
2017	S.M.Davies	14	24	2	142	775	35.22	2	3	39/7
	A.J.Hose	3	6	–	68	194	32.33	–	2	1
2007	J.C.Hildreth	14	26	1	109	756	30.24	2	2	12
1999	M.E.Trescothick	14	27	2	119*	714	28.56	2	1	21
	E.J.Byrom	8	15	–	56	401	26.73	–	1	2
	T.B.Abell	13	25	3	96	572	26.00	–	4	12
2015	L.Gregory	7	12	–	137	299	24.91	1	–	1
2016	T.D.Groenewald	10	14	8	41*	146	24.33	–	–	1
2007	P.D.Trego	8	12	–	68	257	21.41	–	2	1
	D.M.Bess	9	14	4	55	198	19.80	–	1	5
	T.D.Rouse	3	5	–	69	83	16.60	–	1	1
2016	C.Overton	13	21	3	44*	287	15.94	–	–	9
2017	M.J.Leach	14	21	5	52	237	14.81	–	1	4
	J.H.Davey	3	5	1	47	58	14.50	–	–	2
	G.A.Bartlett	4	8	1	28	100	14.28	–	–	3
	J.Overton	5	8	1	37	92	13.14	–	–	1
	R.E.van der Merwe	3	5	–	24	33	6.60	–	–	2

Also batted: J.Allenby (2 matches) 19, 9 (5 ct); P.A.van Meekeren (1) 0, 1* (1 ct).

BOWLING

	O	M	R	W	Avge	Best	5wI	10wM
R.E.van der Merwe	68.4	17	189	11	17.18	4- 22	–	–
C.Overton	373.5	106	1030	46	22.39	5- 47	2	–
L.Gregory	176.3	49	484	21	23.04	5- 74	1	–
D.M.Bess	265.5	60	843	36	23.41	7-117	3	1
T.D.Groenewald	243.4	71	646	26	24.84	5- 58	1	–
M.J.Leach	520.1	150	1315	51	25.78	6- 78	4	–
J.Overton	103	22	312	12	26.00	3- 30	–	–
Also bowled:								
P.D.Trego	79.5	13	265	7	37.85	5- 67	1	–

T.B.Abell 27-6-96-2; J.Allenby 14-6-25-0; J.H.Davey 75-17-186-3; D.Elgar 1-0-4-1; T.D.Rouse 1-0-1-0; P.A.van Meekeren 34.9-9-132-4.

Somerset played no first-class fixtures outside the County Championship in 2017. The First-Class Averages (pp 230–246) give the records of Somerset players in all first-class county matches, with the exceptions of D.Elgar, M.J.Leach, J.Overton and T.D.Rouse, whose first-class figures for Somerset are as above.

SOMERSET RECORDS

FIRST-CLASS CRICKET

Highest Total	For 850-7d		v	Middlesex	Taunton	2007
	V 811		by	Surrey	The Oval	1899
Lowest Total	For 25		v	Glos	Bristol	1947
	V 22		by	Glos	Bristol	1920
Highest Innings	For 342	J.L.Langer	v	Surrey	Guildford	2006
	V 424	A.C.MacLaren	for	Lancashire	Taunton	1895

Highest Partnership for each Wicket

1st	346	L.C.H.Palairet/ H.T.Hewett	v	Yorkshire	Taunton	1892
2nd	450	N.R.D.Compton/J.C.Hildreth	v	Cardiff MCCU	Taunton Vale	2012
3rd	319	P.M.Roebuck/M.D.Crowe	v	Leics	Taunton	1984
4th	310	P.W.Denning/I.T.Botham	v	Glos	Taunton	1980
5th	320	J.D.Francis/I.D.Blackwell	v	Durham UCCE	Taunton	2005
6th	265	W.E.Alley/K.E.Palmer	v	Northants	Northampton	1961
7th	279	R.J.Harden/G.D.Rose	v	Sussex	Taunton	1997
8th	236	P.D.Trego/R.C.Davies	v	Lancashire	Manchester	2016
9th	183	C.H.M.Greetham/H.W.Stephenson	v	Leics	Weston-s-Mare	1963
	183	C.J.Tavaré/N.A.Mallender	v	Sussex	Hove	1990
10th	163	I.D.Blackwell/N.A.M.McLean	v	Derbyshire	Taunton	2003

Best Bowling	For 10- 49	E.J.Tyler	v	Surrey	Taunton	1895
(Innings)	V 10- 35	A.Drake	for	Yorkshire	Weston-s-Mare	1914
Best Bowling	For 16- 83	J.C.White	v	Worcs	Bath	1919
(Match)	V 17-137	W.Brearley	for	Lancashire	Manchester	1905

Most Runs – Season	2761	W.E.Alley	(av 58.74)	1961
Most Runs – Career	21142	H.Gimblett	(av 36.96)	1935-54
Most 100s – Season	11	S.J.Cook		1991
Most 100s – Career	51	M.E.Trescothick		1993-2017
Most Wkts – Season	169	A.W.Wellard	(av 19.24)	1938
Most Wkts – Career	2165	J.C.White	(av 18.03)	1909-37
Most Career W-K Dismissals	1007	H.W.Stephenson	(698 ct; 309 st)	1948-64
Most Career Catches in the Field	417	M.E.Trescothick		1993-2017

LIMITED-OVERS CRICKET

Highest Total	50ov	413-4		v	Devon	Torquay	1990
	40ov	377-9		v	Sussex	Hove	2003
	T20	250-3		v	Glos	Taunton	2006
Lowest Total	50ov	58		v	Middlesex	Southgate	2000
	40ov	58		v	Essex	Chelmsford	1977
	T20	82		v	Kent	Taunton	2010
Highest Innings	50ov	177	S.J.Cook	v	Sussex	Hove	1990
	40ov	184	M.E.Trescothick	v	Glos	Taunton	2008
	T20	151*	C.H.Gayle	v	Kent	Taunton	2015
Best Bowling	50ov	8-66	S.R.G.Francis	v	Derbyshire	Derby	2004
	40ov	6-16	Abdur Rehman	v	Notts	Taunton	2012
	T20	6- 5	A.V.Suppiah	v	Glamorgan	Cardiff	2011

SURREY

Formation of Present Club: 22 August 1845
Inaugural First-Class Match: 1864
Colours: Chocolate
Badge: Prince of Wales' Feathers
County Champions (since 1890): (18) 1890, 1891, 1892, 1894, 1895, 1899, 1914, 1952, 1953, 1954, 1955, 1956, 1957, 1958, 1971, 1999, 2000, 2002
Joint Champions: (1) 1950
NatWest Trophy Winners: (1) 1982
Benson and Hedges Cup Winners: (3) 1974, 1997, 2001
Pro 40/National League (Div 1) Winners: (1) 2003
Sunday League Winners: (1) 1996
Clydesdale Bank 40 Winners: (1) 2011
Twenty20 Cup Winners: (1) 2003

Chief Executive: Richard Gould, The Kia Oval, London, SE11 5SS • Tel: 0203 946 1000 • Fax: 020 7820 5601 • Email: enquiries@surreycricket.com • Web: www.kiaoval.com • Twitter: @surreycricket (76,492 followers)

Director of Cricket: Alec Stewart. **Head Coach**: Michael Di Venuto. **Captains**: R.J.Burns (f-c and l-o) and J.W.Dernbach (T20). **Overseas Players**: A.J.Finch (T20 only) and M.R.Marsh. **2018 Testimonial**: None. **Head Groundsman**: Lee Fortiss. **Scorer**: Philip Makepeace. ‡ New registration. NQ Not qualified for England.

ATKINSON, Angus ('**Gus**') Alexander Patrick (Bradfield C), b Chelsea, Middx 19 Jan 1998. 6'2". RHB, RM. Squad No 37. Surrey 2nd XI debut 2016. Awaiting 1st XI debut.

BATTY, Gareth Jon (Bingley GS), b Bradford, Yorks 13 Oct 1977. Younger brother of J.D.Batty (Yorkshire and Somerset 1989-96). 5'11". RHB, OB. Squad No 3. Yorkshire 1997. Surrey debut 1999; cap 2011; captain 2015-17; testimonial 2017. Worcestershire 2002-09. MCC 2012. **Tests**: 9 (2003-04 to 2016-17); HS 38 v SL (Kandy) 2003-04; BB 3-55 v SL (Galle) 2003-04. Took wicket with his third ball in Test cricket. **LOI**: 10 (2002-03 to 2008-09); HS 17 v WI (Bridgetown) 2008-09; BB 2-40 v WI (Gros Islet, St Lucia) 2003-04. **IT20**: 1 (2008-09); HS 4 v WI (Port of Spain) 2008-09. F-c Tours: WI 2003-04, 2005-06; NZ 2008-09 (Eng A); I 2016-17; SL 2002-03 (ECB Acad), 2003-04; B 2003-04, 2016-17. HS 133 Wo v Surrey (Oval) 2004. Sy HS 110* v Hants (Southampton) 2016, sharing Sy record 8th wkt partnership of 222* with B.T.Foakes. 50 wkts (2); most – 60 (2003). BB 8-68 v Essex (Chelmsford) 2014. Hat-trick v Derbys (Oval) 2015. LO HS 83* v Yorks (Oval) 2001 (NL). LO BB 5-35 Wo v Hants (Southampton) 2009 (FPT). T20 HS 87. T20 BB 4-13.

BORTHWICK, Scott George (Farringdon Community Sports C, Sunderland), b Sunderland, Co Durham 19 Apr 1990. 5'9". LHB, LBG. Squad No 6. Durham 2009-16. Wellington 2015-16 to 2016-17. Surrey debut 2017. **Tests**: 1 (2013-14); HS 4 and BB 3-33 v A (Sydney) 2013-14. **LOI**: 2 (2011 to 2011-12); HS 15 v Ireland (Dublin) 2011; BB –. **IT20**: 1 (2011); HS 14 and BB 1-15 v WI (Oval) 2011. F-c Tours: A 2013-14; SL 2013-14 (EL). 1000 runs (5); most – 1390 (2015). HS 216 Du v Middx (Chester-le-St) 2014, sharing Du record 2nd wkt partnership of 274 with M.D.Stoneman. Sy HS 108* v Lancs (Oval) 2017. BB 6-70 Du v Surrey (Oval) 2013. Sy BB 1-5 v Oxford MCCU (Oxford) 2017. LO HS 87 and LO BB 5-38 Du v Leics (Leicester) 2015 (RLC). T20 HS 62. T20 BB 4-18.

BURNS, Rory Joseph (City of London Freemen's S), b Epsom 26 Aug 1990. 5'10". LHB, WK, occ RM. Squad No 17. Debut (Surrey) 2011; cap 2014; captain 2018. MCC 2016. MCC Univs 2010. 1000 runs (4); most – 1248 (2016). HS 219* v Hants (Oval) 2017. BB 1-18 v Middx (Lord's) 2013. LO HS 95 v Glos (Bristol) 2015 (RLC). T20 HS 46*.

CLARKE, Rikki (Broadwater SS; Godalming C), b Orsett, Essex 29 Sep 1981. 6'4''. RHB, RMF. Squad No 81. Debut (Surrey) 2002, scoring 107* v Cambridge U (Cambridge); cap 2005. Derbyshire cap/captain 2008. Warwickshire 2008-17; cap 2011. MCC 2006, 2016. YC 2002. **Tests**: 2 (2003-04); HS 55 and BB 2-7 v B (Chittagong) 2003-04. **LOI**: 20 (2003 to 2006); HS 39 v P (Lord's) 2006; BB 2-28 v B (Dhaka) 2003-04. F-c Tours: WI 2003-04, 2005-06; SL 2002-03 (ECB Acad), 2004-05; B 2003-04. 1000 runs (1): 1027 (2006). HS 214 v Somerset (Guildford) 2006. BB 7-55 v Somerset (Oval) 2017. Took seven catches in an innings Wa v Lancs (Liverpool) 2011 to equal world record. LO HS 98* v Derbys (Derby) 2002 (NL). LO BB 5-26 Wa v Worcs (Birmingham) 2016 (RLC). T20 HS 79*. T20 BB 4-16

CURRAN, Samuel Matthew (Wellington C), b Northampton 3 Jun 1998. Son of K.M.Curran (Glos, Natal, Northants, Boland and Zimbabwe 1980-81 to 1999), grandson of K.P.Curran (Rhodesia 1947-48 to 1954-55), younger brother of T.K.Curran (*see below*). 5'9''. LHB, LMF. Squad No 58. Debut (Surrey) 2015, taking 5-101 v Kent (Oval). Surrey 2nd XI debut 2013. England Lions 2017. F-c Tours (EL): SL 2016-17; UAE 2016-17 (v Afghan). HS 96 v Lancs (Oval) 2016. BB 7-58 v Durham (Chester-le-St) 2016. LO HS 57 v Glos (Oval) 2016 (RLC). LO BB 4-32 v Northants (Oval) 2015 (RLC). T20 HS 50. T20 BB 4-13.

CURRAN, Thomas Kevin (Hilton C, Durban), b Cape Town, South Africa 12 Mar 1995. Son of K.M.Curran (Glos, Natal, Northants, Boland and Zimbabwe 1980-81 to 1999), grandson of K.P.Curran (Rhodesia 1947-48 to 1954-55), elder brother of S.M.Curran (*see above*). 6'0''. RHB, RFM. Squad No 59. Debut (Surrey) 2014; cap 2016. Surrey 2nd XI debut 2012. **Tests**: 2 (2017-18); HS 39 v A (Sydney) 2017-18; BB 1-65 v A (Melbourne) 2017-18. **LOI**: 8 (2017 to 2017-18); HS 35 v A (Adelaide) 2017-18; BB 5-35 v A (Perth) 2017-18. **IT20**: 6 (2017 to 2017-18); HS 6 v A (Hobart) 2017-18; BB 3-33 v SA (Taunton) 2017. F-c Tours: A 2017-18; SL 2016-17 (EL); UAE 2016-17 (v Afghan). HS 60 v Leics (Leicester) 2015. 50 wkts (1): 76 (2015). BB 7-20 v Glos (Oval) 2015. LO HS 44 v Yorks (Oval) 2015 (RLC). Lo BB 5-16 EL v UAE (Dubai, DSC) 2016-17. T20 HS 51*. T20 BB 4-35.

DERNBACH, Jade Winston (St John the Baptist S), b Johannesburg, South Africa 3 Mar 1986. 6'1½''. RHB, RFM. Squad No 16. Italian passport. UK resident since 1998. Debut (Surrey) 2003; cap 2011; captain 2018 (T20 only). **LOI**: 24 (2011 to 2013); HS 5 v SL (Leeds) 2011; BB 4-45 v P (Dubai) 2011-12. **IT20**: 34 (2011 to 2013-14); HS 12 v I (Colombo, RPS) 2012-13; BB 4-22 v I (Manchester) 2011. F-c Tour (EL): WI 2010-11. HS 56* v Northants (Northampton) 2010. 50 wkts (1): 51 (2010). BB 6-47 v Leics (Leicester) 2009. LO HS 31 v Somerset (Taunton) 2010 (CB40). LO BB 6-35 v Glos (Lord's) 2015 (RLC). T20 HS 24*. T20 BB 4-22.

DUNN, Matthew Peter (Bearwood C, Wokingham), b Egham 5 May 1992. 6'1''. LHB, RFM. Squad No 4. Debut (Surrey) 2010. No 1st XI appearances in 2017. MCC 2015. HS 31* v Kent (Guildford) 2014. BB 5-48 v Glos (Oval) 2014. LO HS –. LO BB 2-32 England Dev XI v Sri Lanka A (Manchester) 2011. T20 HS 2. BB 3-8.

NOFINCH, Aaron James, b Colac, Victoria, Australia 17 Nov 1986. 5'9''. RHB, SLA. Squad No 15. Victoria 2007-08 to date. Yorkshire 2014-15. Surrey debut 2016. IPL: RR: 2009-10. DD 2011-12. PW 2013. SH 2014. MI 2015. GL 2016-17. Big Bash: MR 2011-12 to date. **LOI** (A): 88 (2012-13 to 2017-18); HS 148 v Scotland (Edinburgh) 2013; BB 1-2 v I (Pune) 2013-14. **IT20** (A): 36 (2010-11 to 2017-18); HS 156 v E (Southampton) 2013 – world record IT20 score. F-c Tours (Aus A): SA/Z 2013; Z 2011. HS 288* Cricket A v New Zealanders (Sydney) 2015-16. CC HS 110 Y v Warwks (Birmingham) 2014, and 110 v Warwks (Guildford) 2016. BB 1-0 Vic v WA (Perth) 2013-14. CC BB 1-20 Y v Sussex (Arundel) 2014. LO HS 154 Vic v Q (Brisbane) 2012-13. LO BB 2-44 Aus A v EL (Hobart) 2012-13. T20 HS 156. T20 BB 1-9.

FOAKES, Benjamin Thomas (Tendring TC), b Colchester, Essex 15 Feb 1993. 6'1". RHB, WK. Squad No 7. Essex 2011-14. Surrey debut 2015; cap 2016. England Lions 2017. MCC 2016. Essex 2nd XI debut 2008, aged 15y 172d. England U19 2010-11. F-c Tours (EL): WI 2017-18; SL 2013-14, 2016-17; UAE 2016-17 (v Afghan). HS 141* v Hants (Southampton) 2016, sharing SR record 8th wkt partnership of 222* with G.J.Batty. LO HS 92 v Somerset (Taunton) 2016 (RLC). T20 HS 49.

HARINATH, Arun (Tiffin Boys GS; Loughborough U), b Sutton 26 Mar 1987. 5'11". LHB, OB. Squad No 10. Loughborough UCCE 2007-09. Surrey debut 2009; cap 2016. Leicestershire 2017 (on loan). MCC 2008. Buckinghamshire 2007-08. HS 154 v Derbys (Derby) 2013. BB 2-1 v Glamorgan (Colwyn Bay) 2014. LO HS 52 v Derbys (Oval) 2013 (Y40). LO BB –.

JACKS, William George (St George's C, Weybridge), b Chertsey 21 Nov 1998. 6'1". RHB, RM. Squad No 9. Surrey 2nd XI debut 2016. England U19 2016-17 to 2017. Awaiting 1st XI debut.

McKERR, Conor (St John's C, Johannesburg), b 19 Jan 1998. 6'6". RHB, RFM. Squad No 83. UK passport. Derbyshire 2017 (on loan), taking wkt of J.D.Libby with 4th ball in f-cricket. Surrey debut 2017. Surrey 2nd XI debut 2016. UK passport. HS 17 and BB 5-54 (10-141 match) De v Northants (Northampton) 2017. Sy HS 1 and Sy BB 1-102 v Hants (Oval) 2017.

‡**NQMARSH, Mitchell** Ross, b Attadale, Perth, W Australia 20 Oct 1991. Son of G.R.Marsh (W Australia and Australia 1977-78 to 1993-94) and younger brother of S.E.Marsh (W Australia, Yorkshire and Australia 2000-01 to date). 6'3". RHB, RMF. Squad No 8. W Australia 2009-10 to date. IPL: DC 2009-10. PW 2011-13. RPS 2016. Big Bash: PS 2011-12 to date. Joins Surrey in 2018. **Tests** (A): 26 (2014-15 to 2017-18); HS 181 v E (Perth) 2017-18; BB 4-61 v WI (Melbourne) 2015-16. **LOI** (A): 53 (2011-12 to 2017-18); HS 102* v I (Sydney) 2015-16; BB 5-33 v E (Melbourne) 2014-15. **IT20** (A): 9 (2011-12 to 2015-16); HS 36 v SA (Johannesburg) 2011-12; BB 1-17 v SA (Durban) 2015-16. F-c Tours (A): E 2015; SA 2013 (Aus A); WI 2015; NZ 2015-16; I 2016-17; SL 2016; Z 2011 (Aus A); UAE 2014-15 (v P). HS 211 Aus A v India A (Brisbane, AB) 2014. BB 6-84 WA v Q (Perth) 2011-12. LO HS 124 WA v S Aus (Sydney, DO) 2017-18. LO BB 5-33 (see LOI). T20 HS 77*. T20 BB 4-6.

MEAKER, Stuart Christopher (Cranleigh S), b Durban, South Africa 21 Jan 1989. Moved to UK in 2001. 6'1". RHB, RFM. Squad No 18. Debut (Surrey) 2008; cap 2012. Auckland 2017-18. **LOI**: 2 (2011-12); HS 1 and BB 1-45 v I (Mumbai) 2011-12. **IT20**: 2 (2012-13); BB 1-28 v I (Pune) 2012-13. F-c Tour: I 2012-13. HS 94 v Bangladeshis (Oval) 2010. CC HS 72 v Essex (Colchester) 2009. 50 wkts (1): 51 (2012). BB 8-52 (11-167 match) v Somerset (Oval) 2012. LO HS 21* v Glamorgan (Oval) 2012 (CB40). LO BB 4-37 v Kent (Oval) 2017 (RLC). T20 HS 17. T20 BB 4-30.

PATEL, Ryan (Whitgift S), b Sutton 26 Oct 1997. 5'10". LHB, RMF. Squad No 26. Debut (Surrey) 2017. Surrey 2nd XI debut 2016. England U19 2017. HS 81 v Hants (Southampton) 2017. BB 1-11 v Somerset (Oval) 2017.

NQPILLANS, Mathew William (Pretoria BHS; U of Pretoria), b Durban, South Africa 4 Jul 1991. 6'6". RHB, RF. Squad No 47. Northerns 2012-13. KwaZula Natal Inland 2013-14 to date. Dolphins 2013-14 to 2015-16. Surrey debut 2016. Leicestershire 2017 (on loan). HS 56 Le v Northants (Northampton) 2017. Sy HS 34* v Somerset (Taunton) 2016. BB 6-67 (10-129 match) Dolphins v Knights (Durban) 2014-15. CC BB 3-63 Le v Sussex (Arundel) 2017. Sy BB –. LO HS 20* KZN v NW (Pietermaritzburg) 2013-14. LO BB 3-14 KZN v Namibia (Pietermaritzburg) 2015-16. T20 HS 34*. T20 BB 3-15.

175

POPE, Oliver John Douglas (Cranleigh S), b Chelsea, Middx 2 Jan 1998. 5'9". RHB, WK. Squad No 32. Debut (Surrey) 2017. Surrey 2nd XI debut 2015. England U19 2016 to 2016-17. HS 100* v Hants (Southampton) 2017. LO HS 55 v Sussex (Hove) 2017 (RLC). T20 HS 46.

ROY, Jason Jonathan (Whitgift S), b Durban, South Africa 21 Jul 1990. 6'0". RHB, RM. Squad No 20. Debut (Surrey) 2010; cap 2014. IPL: GL 2017. Big Bash: ST 2014-15. SS 2016-17 to date. **ECB L-O Central Contract 2017-18. LOI**: 57 (2015 to 2017-18); HS 180 v A (Melbourne) 2017-18 – E record. **IT20**: 27 (2014 to 2017-18); HS 78 v NZ (Delhi) 2015-16. 1000 runs (1): 1078 (2014). HS 143 v Lancs (Oval) 2015. BB 3-9 v Glos (Bristol) 2014. LO HS 180 (*see LOI*). LO BB –. T20 HS 122* v Somerset (Oval) 2015 – Sy record. T20 BB 1-23.

STONEMAN, Mark Daniel (Whickham CS), b Newcastle upon Tyne, Northumb 26 Jun 1987. 5'10". LHB, OB. Squad No 23. Durham 2007-16; captain (l-o only) 2015-16. Surrey debut 2017. England Lions 2017. **Tests**: 8 (2017 to 2017-18); HS 56 v A (Perth) 2017-18. F-c Tour: A 2017-18. 1000 runs (5); most – 1481 (2017). HS 197 v Essex (Guildford) 2017. BB –. LO HS 144* v Notts (Lord's) 2017 (RLC). T20 HS 89*.

VAN DEN BERGH, Frederick Oliver Edward (Whitgift S, Croydon; Hatfield C, Durham U), b Farnborough, Kent 14 Jun 1992. 6'0". RHB, SLA. Squad No 5. Debut (Surrey) 2011. Durham MCCU 2013-14. No 1st XI appearances in 2015 or 2016. HS 34 and BB 4-84 DU v Notts (Nottingham) 2013. Sy HS 16* v Leeds/Bradford MCCU (Oval) 2012. CC HS 5 and CC BB 3-84 v Yorks (Oval) 2017. Sy BB 3-79 v Cambridge MCCU (Cambridge) 2011. LO HS 29* v Sussex (Oval) 2014 (RLC). LO BB –.

VIRDI, Guramar Singh ('**Amar**') (Guru Nanak Sikh Ac, Hayes), b Chiswick, Middx 19 Jul 1998. 5'10". RHB, OB. Squad No 19. Debut (Surrey) 2017. Surrey 2nd XI debut 2016. England U19 2016 to 2017. HS 8* and BB 3-82 v Essex (Chelmsford) 2017.

RELEASED/RETIRED

(Having made a County 1st XI appearance in 2017)

ANSARI, Zafar Shahaan (Hampton S; Trinity Hall, Cambridge), b Ascot, Berks 10 Dec 1991. Younger brother of A.S.Ansari (Cambridge U 2008-13). 5'11". LHB, SLA. Cambridge MCCU 2011-13. Surrey 2011-17; cap 2014. MCC 2015. **Tests**: 3 (2016-17); HS 32 v I (Rajkot) 2016-17; BB 2-76 v B (Dhaka) 2016-17. **LOI**: 1 (2015) did not bat or bowl. 1000 runs (1): 1029 (2014). HS 112 v Glamorgan (Colwyn Bay) 2014. BB 6-30 v Glos (Oval) 2015. LO HS 66* v Yorks (Oval) 2013 (RLC). LO BB 4-42 v Scotland (Oval) 2013 (Y40). T20 HS 67*. T20 BB 3-17.

FOOTITT, M.H.A. – *see NOTTINGHAMSHIRE*.

[NQ]**HENRIQUES, Moises** Constantino, b Funchal, Madeira, Portugal 1 Feb 1987. 6'1½". RHB, RFM. New South Wales 2006-07 to date. Glamorgan 2012. Surrey 2015-17 (T20 only). IPL: KKR 2009. DD 2009-10. RCB 2013. SH 2014-17. Big Bash: SS 2011-12 to date. **Tests** (A): 4 (2012-13 to 2016); HS 81* and BB 1-48 v I (Chennai) 2012-13. **LOI** (A): 11 (2009-10 to 2017); HS 18 v NZ (Birmingham) 2017; BB 3-32 v SL (Hobart) 2012-13. **IT20** (A): 11 (2009-10 to 2017-18); HS 62* v I (Guwahati) 2017-18; BB 2-35 v E (Hobart) 2013-14. F-c Tours (A): SA/Z 2013 (Aus A); I 2012-13; SL 2016; Scot/Ire 2013 (Aus A). HS 265 NSW v Q (Sydney) 2016-17. BB 5-17 NSW v Q (Brisbane) 2006-07. LO HS 164* NSW v Cricket Aus (Sydney) 2016-17. LO BB 4-17 NSW v Tas (Sydney) 2013-14. T20 HS 77. T20 BB 3-11.

PIETERSEN, Kevin Peter (Maritzburg C; Natal U), b Pietermaritzburg, South Africa 27 Jun 1980. British passport (English mother) – qualified for England Oct 2004. 6'4". RHB, OB. Natal/KZN 1997-98 to 1999-00. Nottinghamshire 2001-04; cap 2002. Hampshire 2005-08; cap 2005. Surrey 2010-15; T20 only in 2017. Dolphins 2010-11. MCC 2004. IPL: RCB 2009-10. DD 2012-14. RPS 2016. Big Bash: MS 2014-15 to date. MBE 2005. *Wisden* 2005. **Tests:** 104 (2005 to 2013-14, 3 as captain); 1000 runs (4); most – 1343 (2006); HS 227 v A (Adelaide) 2010-11; BB 3-52 v SA (Leeds) 2012. **LOI:** 134 (2004-05 to 2013, 12 as captain; +2 for ICC World XI; HS 130 v P (Dubai) 2011-12; BB 2-22 v SA (Leeds) 2008. **IT20:** 37 (2005 to 2013); HS 79 v Z (Cape Town) 2007-08; BB 1-27 v SA (Centurion) 2009-10. F-c Tours: A 2006-07, 2010-11, 2013-14; SA 2009-10; WI 2008-09; NZ 2007-08, 2012-13; I 2003-04 (Eng A), 2005-06, 2008-09 (Captain), 2012-13; P 2005-06; SL 2007-08, 2011-12; B 2009-10; UAE 2011-12 (v P). 1000 runs (3); most – 1546 (2003). HS 355* v Leics (Oval) 2015 – record score v Le. BB 4-31 Nt v Durham U (Nottingham) 2003. CC BB 3-72 Nt v Hants (Nottingham) 2004. Sy BB 2-24 v Notts (Oval) 2012. LO HS 147 Nt v Somerset (Taunton) 2002 (NL). LO BB 3-14 Nt v Middx (Lord's) 2004 (NL). T20 HS 115*. T20 BB 3-33.

RAMPAUL, R. – *see DERBYSHIRE*.

[NQ]**SANGAKKARA, Kumar** Chokshanada (Trinity C, Kandy; Colombo U), b Matale, Sri Lanka, 27 Oct 1977. 5'11". LHB, WK, occ OB. Nondescripts 1997-98 to 2007-08. Central Province 2003-04 to 2004-05. Warwickshire 2007; cap 2007. Durham 2014. Surrey 2015-17; cap 2015. IPL: KXIP 2007-10. DC 2011-12. SH 2013. Big Bash: HH 2015-16 to 2016-17. *Wisden* 2011. **Tests** (SL): 134 (2000 to 2015, 15 as captain); 1000 runs (5); most – 1438 (2014); HS 319 v B (Chittagong) 2013-14 (also scored 105 to become only the 2nd man, after G.A.Gooch, to score a treble century and a century in the same match). Scored 287 v SA (Colombo, SSC) 2006, sharing in world record f-c partnership for any wkt of 624 with D.P.M.D.Jayawardena; BB –. **LOI** (SL): 397 (2000 to 2014-15, 45 as captain; +4 for Asia XI, +3 for ICC World XI; 1000 runs (6); most – 1333 (2006); HS 169 v SA (Colombo, RPS) 2013. **IT20** (SL): 56 (2006 to 2013-14, 22 as captain); HS 78 v I (Nagpur) 2009-10. F-c Tours (SL) (C=Captain): E 2002, 2006, 2011, 2014; A 2004, 2007-08, 2012-13; SA 1999-00 (SL A), 2000-01, 2002-03, 2011-12; WI 2003, 2007-08; NZ 2004-05, 2006-07, 2014-15; I 2005-06, 2009-10C; P 2001-02, 2004-05, 2008-09; Z 2004, 2008-09; B 2005-06, 2008-09, 2013-14; UAE 2011-12 (v P), 2013-14 (v P). 1000 runs (2+1): 1491 (2017), ave of 106.50 was 2nd highest on record. HS 319 (*see Tests*). Sy HS 200 v Essex (Chelmsford) 2017 – his 5th consecutive century. BB 1-13 SL v Zim A (Harare) 2004. LO HS 169 (*see LOI*). T20 HS 94.

SIBLEY, D.P. – *see WARWICKSHIRE*.

SURREY 2017

RESULTS SUMMARY

	Place	Won	Lost	Drew	NR
Specsavers County Champ (1st Division)	3rd	2	2	10	
All First-Class Matches		2	2	11	
Royal London One-Day Cup (South Group)	Finalist	6	4		1
NatWest t20 Blast (South Group)	QF	7	6		2

SPECSAVERS COUNTY CHAMPIONSHIP AVERAGES

BATTING AND FIELDING

Cap		M	I	NO	HS	Runs	Avge	100	50	Ct/St
2015	K.C.Sangakkara	10	16	2	200	1491	106.50	8	2	6
	M.D.Stoneman	12	19	–	197	1156	60.84	4	4	4
2014	R.J.Burns	14	22	1	219*	1041	49.57	1	8	7
2014	J.J.Roy	5	7	1	87	257	42.83	–	2	–
2016	B.T.Foakes	14	20	4	110	680	42.50	1	4	29/2
	O.J.D.Pope	5	8	2	100*	226	37.66	1	1	2
	D.P.Sibley	7	12	2	69	330	33.00	–	4	3
	R.Patel	4	6	–	81	170	28.33	–	1	2
2016	T.K.Curran	9	11	2	53	247	27.44	–	1	3
	S.M.Curran	13	17	1	90	423	26.43	–	4	4
	S.G.Borthwick	12	19	1	108*	446	24.77	1	1	21
2005	R.Clarke	6	7	–	50	157	22.42	–	1	7
2011	G.J.Batty	12	14	4	33	175	17.50	–	–	–
2012	S.C.Meaker	9	13	3	49	174	17.40	–	–	3
	G.S.Virdi	3	4	1	8*	18	6.00	–	–	–
2011	J.W.Dernbach	5	5	1	8*	17	4.25	–	–	–
	R.Rampaul	2	4	2	3	4	2.00	–	–	–
	M.H.A.Footitt	7	8	1	4	7	1.00	–	–	2

Also batted: Z.S.Ansari (1 match – cap 2014) 3; A.J.Finch (1) 39; C.McKerr (2) 1; F.O.E.van den Bergh (1) 5.

BOWLING

	O	M	R	W	Avge	Best	5wI	10wM
R.Clarke	166.2	52	436	22	19.81	7-55	1	–
M.H.A.Footitt	178.3	25	686	23	29.82	6-14	2	–
G.J.Batty	308.1	64	857	25	34.28	3-70	–	–
T.K.Curran	256.3	50	832	24	34.66	4-69	–	–
S.C.Meaker	215.3	33	869	21	41.38	4-92	–	–
J.W.Dernbach	140.3	32	433	10	43.30	3-51	–	–
S.M.Curran	339.5	60	1179	25	47.16	3-74	–	–

Also bowled: A.Virdi 88 13 271 6 45.16 3-82 – –

Z.S.Ansari 27-5-88-0; S.G.Borthwick 77.1-1-347-4; C.McKerr 25-1-102-1; R.Patel 42-8-128-2; R.Rampaul 62-15-193-3; D.P.Sibley 6.4-0-50-1; F.O.E.van den Bergh 57-13-145-4.

The First-Class Averages (pp 230–246) give the records of Surrey players in all first-class county matches (Surrey's other opponents being Oxford MCCU), with the exception of R.Clarke, B.T.Foakes and C.McKerr, whose first-class figures for Surrey are as above, and: S.M.Curran 14-19-1-90-446-24.77-0-4-5ct. 359.5-66-1227-27-45.44-3/74-0-0. M.H.A.Footitt 8-8-1-4-7-1.00-0-0-2ct. 193.3-29-719-27-26.62-6/14-2-0. D.P.Sibley 8-14-4-104*-494-49.40-1-5-3ct. 6.4-0-50-1-50.00-1/50-0-0. M.D.Stoneman 13-21-0-197-1217-57.95-4-4-6ct.

SURREY RECORDS

FIRST-CLASS CRICKET

Highest Total	For 811		v	Somerset	The Oval	1899
	V 863		by	Lancashire	The Oval	1990
Lowest Total	For 14		v	Essex	Chelmsford	1983
	V 16		by	MCC	Lord's	1872
Highest Innings	For 357*	R.Abel	v	Somerset	The Oval	1899
	V 366	N.H.Fairbrother	for	Lancashire	The Oval	1990

Highest Partnership for each Wicket

1st	428	J.B.Hobbs/A.Sandham	v	Oxford U	The Oval	1926
2nd	371	J.B.Hobbs/E.G.Hayes	v	Hampshire	The Oval	1909
3rd	413	D.J.Bicknell/D.M.Ward	v	Kent	Canterbury	1990
4th	448	R.Abel/T.W.Hayward	v	Yorkshire	The Oval	1899
5th	318	M.R.Ramprakash/Azhar Mahmood	v	Middlesex	The Oval	2005
6th	298	A.Sandham/H.S.Harrison	v	Sussex	The Oval	1913
7th	262	C.J.Richards/K.T.Medlycott	v	Kent	The Oval	1987
8th	222*	B.T.Foakes/G.J.Batty	v	Hampshire	Southampton	2016
9th	168	E.R.T.Holmes/E.W.J.Brooks	v	Hampshire	The Oval	1936
10th	173	A.Ducat/A.Sandham	v	Essex	Leyton	1921

Best Bowling	For	10-43	T.Rushby	v	Somerset	Taunton	1921
(Innings)	V	10-28	W.P.Howell	for	Australians	The Oval	1899
Best Bowling	For	16-83	G.A.R.Lock	v	Kent	Blackheath	1956
(Match)	V	15-57	W.P.Howell	for	Australians	The Oval	1899

Most Runs – Season	3246	T.W.Hayward	(av 72.13)	1906
Most Runs – Career	43554	J.B.Hobbs	(av 49.72)	1905-34
Most 100s – Season	13	T.W.Hayward		1906
	13	J.B.Hobbs		1925
Most 100s – Career	144	J.B.Hobbs		1905-34
Most Wkts – Season	252	T.Richardson	(av 13.94)	1895
Most Wkts – Career	1775	T.Richardson	(av 17.87)	1892-1904
Most Career W-K Dismissals	1221	H.Strudwick	(1035 ct; 186 st)	1902-27
Most Career Catches in the Field	605	M.J.Stewart		1954-72

LIMITED-OVERS CRICKET

Highest Total	50ov	496-4	v	Glos	The Oval	2007
	40ov	386-3	v	Glamorgan	The Oval	2010
	T20	224-5	v	Glos	Bristol	2006
Lowest Total	50ov	74	v	Kent	The Oval	1967
	40ov	64	v	Worcs	Worcester	1978
	T20	88	v	Kent	The Oval	2012
Highest Innings	50ov	268	A.D.Brown	v	Glamorgan	The Oval	2002
	40ov	203	A.D.Brown	v	Hampshire	Guildford	1997
	T20	122*	J.J.Roy	v	Somerset	The Oval	2015
Best Bowling	50ov	7-33	R.D.Jackman	v	Yorkshire	Harrogate	1970
	40ov	7-30	M.P.Bicknell	v	Glamorgan	The Oval	1999
	T20	6-24	T.J.Murtagh	v	Middlesex	Lord's	2005

SUSSEX

Formation of Present Club: 1 March 1839
Substantial Reorganisation: August 1857
Inaugural First-Class Match: 1864
Colours: Dark Blue, Light Blue and Gold
Badge: County Arms of Six Martlets
County Champions: (3) 2003, 2006, 2007
Gillette/NatWest/C&G Trophy Winners: (5) 1963, 1964, 1978, 1986, 2006
Pro 40/National League (Div 1) Winners: (2) 2008, 2009
Sunday League Winners: (1) 1982
Twenty20 Cup Winners: (1) 2009

Chief Executive: Rob Andrew, The 1st Central County Ground, Eaton Road, Hove BN3 3AN • Tel: 0844 264 0202 • Fax: 01273 771549 • Email: info@sussexcricket.co.uk • Web: www.sussexcricket.co.uk • Twitter: @SussexCCC (59,161 followers)

Director of Cricket: Keith Greenfield. **Head Coach**: Jason Gillespie. **Batting Coach**: Michael Yardy. **Captain**: B.C.Brown. **Overseas Players**: Rashid Khan and I.Sharma. **2018 Beneficiary**: E.C.Joyce. **Head Groundsman**: Andy Mackay. **Scorer**: M.J. (Mike) Charman. ‡ New registration. NQ Not qualified for England.

NQARCHER, Jofra Chioke (Christchurch Foundation), b Bridgetown, Barbados 1 Apr 1995. 6'3". RHB, RFM. Squad No 22. Debut (Sussex) 2016; cap 2017. Big Bash: HH 2017-18. HS 81* v Northants (Northampton) 2017. 50 wkts (1): 61 (2017). BB 7-67 v Kent (Hove) 2017. LO HS 45 v Essex (Chelmsford) 2017 (RLC). LO BB 5-42 v Somerset (Taunton) 2016 (RLC). T20 HS 36. T20 BB 4-18.

BARTON, Adam Paul (Anglia Ruskin U), b Epsom, Surrey 17 Apr 1995. RHB, LMF. Cambridge MCCU 2014-17. Sussex debut 2017. HS 13* v Notts (Nottingham) 20117. BB 5-31 CU v Lancs (Cambridge) 2017. Sx BB –.

BEER, William Andrew Thomas (Reigate GS; Collyer's C, Horsham), b Crawley 8 Oct 1988. 5'10". RHB, LB. Squad No 18. Debut (Sussex) 2008. HS 39 v Middx (Lord's) 2013. BB 6-29 (11-91 match) v South Africa A (Arundel) 2017. CC BB 3-31 v Worcs (Worcester) 2010. LO HS 45* v Durham (Hove) 2014 (RLC). LO BB 3-27 v Warwks (Hove) 2012 (CB40). T20 HS 37. T20 BB 3-14.

BRIGGS, Danny Richard (Isle of Wight C), b Newport, IoW, 30 Apr 1991. 6'2". RHB, SLA. Squad No 21. Hampshire 2009-15; cap 2012. Sussex debut 2016. **LOI**: 1 (2011-12); BB 2-39 v P (Dubai) 2011-12. **IT20**: 7 (2012 to 2013-14); HS 0*; BB 2-25 v A (Chester-le-St) 2013. F-c Tour (EL): WI 2010-11. HS 120* v South Africa A (Arundel) 2017. CC HS 54 H v Glos (Bristol) 2013. Sx HS 49 v Essex (Colchester) 2016. BB 6-45 EL v Windward Is (Roseau) 2010-11. CC BB 6-65 H v Notts (Southampton) 2011. Sx BB 5-93 v Glos (Bristol) 2016. LO HS 25 and LO BB 4-32 H v Glamorgan (Cardiff) 2012 (CB40). T20 HS 13. T20 BB 5-19.

BROWN, Ben Christopher (Ardingly C), b Crawley 23 Nov 1988. 5'8". RHB, WK. Squad No 26. Debut (Sussex) 2007; cap 2014. captain 2017 to date. 1000 runs (1): 1031 (2015). HS 163 v Durham (Hove) 2014. BB 1-48 v Essex (Colchester) 2016. LO HS 62 v Hants (Hove) 2016 (RLC). T20 HS 68.

BURGESS, Michael Gregory Kerran (Cranleigh S; Loughborough U), b Epsom, Surrey 8 Jul 1994. RHB, RM, occ WK. Squad No 5. Loughborough MCCU 2014-15. Leicestershire 2016. Sussex debut 2017. Surrey 2nd XI 2011-13. HS 146 v Notts (Hove) 2017. LO HS 49 v Glos (Leicester) 2015 (RLC).

EVANS, Laurie John (Whitgift S; The John Fisher S; St Mary's C, Durham U), b Lambeth, London 12 Oct 1987. 6'0". RHB, RM. Squad No 32. Durham UCCE 2007. MCC 2007. Surrey 2009-10. Warwickshire 2010-16. Northamptonshire 2016 (on loan). Sussex debut 2017. HS 213* and BB 1-29 Wa v Sussex (Birmingham) 2015, sharing Wa 6th wkt record partnership of 327 with T.R.Ambrose. Sx HS 19 v Durham (Chester-le-St) 2017. LO HS 134* v Kent (Canterbury) 2017 (RLC). LO BB –. T20 HS 69*. T20 BB 1-5.

FINCH, Harry Zachariah (St Richard's Catholic C, Bexhill; Eastbourne C), b Hastings 10 Feb 1995. 5'8". RHB, RM. Squad No 6. Debut (Sussex) 2013. Sussex 2nd XI debut 2011, aged 16y 69d. England U19 2012-13. HS 135* and BB 1-9 v Leeds/Bradford MCCU (Hove) 2016. CC HS 82 v Worcs (Worcester) 2017. CC BB 1-30 v Northants (Arundel) 2016. LO HS 92* v Glamorgan (Hove) 2014 (RLC). LO BB –. T20 HS 35*.

GARTON, George Henry Simmons (Hurstpierpoint C), b Brighton 15 Apr 1997. 5'10½". LHB, LF. Squad No 15. Debut (Sussex) 2016). England Lions 2017. Sussex 2nd XI debut 2014. HS 18* v Glamorgan (Cardiff) 2016. BB 3-20 v Durham (Chester-le-St) 2017. LO HS 7* v Somerset (Hove) 2017 (RLC). LO BB 4-43 EL v Sri Lanka A (Canterbury) 2016. T20 HS 2*. T20 BB 4-16.

HAINES, Thomas Jacob (Tanbridge House S, Horsham; Hurstpierpoint C), b Crawley 28 Oct 1998. 5'10". LHB, RM. Squad No 20. Debut (Sussex) 2016. Sussex 2nd XI debut 2014. No 1st XI appearances in 2017. HS 11 v Kent (Hove) 2016. BB –.

JENNER, Jonty William (Hurstpierpoint C), b Jersey 2 Dec 1997. RHB, OB. Debut (Sussex) 2017. Sussex 2nd XI debut 2015. HS 68 v South Africa A (Arundel) 2017 – only 1st XI appearance.

JORDAN, Christopher James (Comber Mere S, Barbados; Dulwich C), b Christ Church, Barbados 4 Oct 1988. 6'0". RHB, RFM. Squad No 8. Surrey 2007-12. Barbados 2011-12 to 2012-13. Sussex debut 2013; cap 2014. IPL: RCB 2016. SH 2017. Big Bash: AS 2016-17. **Tests**: 8 (2014 to 2014-15); HS 35 v SL (Lord's) 2014; BB 4-18 v I (Oval) 2014. **LOI**: 31 (2013 to 2016); HS 38* v SL (Oval) 2014; BB 5-29 v SL (Manchester) 2014. **IT20**: 30 (2013-14 to 2017-18); HS 27* v WI (Bridgetown) 2013-14; BB 4-28 v SL (Delhi) 2015-16. F-c Tour: WI 2014-15. HS 147 v Notts (Hove) 2017. 50 wkts (1): 61 (2013). BB 7-43 Barbados v CC&C (Bridgetown) 2012-13. Sx BB 6-48 v Yorks (Leeds) 2013. LO HS 55 v Surrey (Guildford) 2016 (RLC). LO BB 5-28 v Middx (Hove) 2016 (RLC). T20 HS 45*. T20 BB 4-11.

MILLS, Tymal Solomon (Mildenhall TC), b Dewsbury, Yorks 12 Aug 1992. 6'1". RHB, LF. Squad No 7. Essex 2011-14. Sussex debut 2015; has played T20 only since 2016. IPL: RCB 2017. Big Bash: BH 2016-17. HH 2017-18. **IT20**: 4 (2016 to 2017); HS 0; BB 1-27 v I (Kanpur) 2016-17. F-c Tour (EL): SL 2013-14. HS 31* EL v Sri Lanka A (Colombo, RPS) 2013-14. CC HS 30 Ex v Kent (Canterbury) 2014. Sx HS 8 v Worcs (Hove) 2015. BB 4-25 Ex v Glamorgan (Cardiff) 2012. Sx BB 2-28 v Hants (Southampton) 2015. LO HS 3* v Notts (Hove) 2015 (RLC). LO BB 3-23 Ex v Durham (Chelmsford) 2013 (Y40). T20 HS 8*. T20 BB 4-22.

‡**NQRASHID KHAN** Arman, b Nangarhar, Afghanistan 20 Sep 1998. RHB, LBG. Squad No 1. Afghanistan 2016-17 to date. Joins Sussex in 2018 for T20 only. IPL: SH 2017. Big Bash: AS 2017-18. **LOI** (Afg): 40 (2015-16 to 2017-18); HS 60* v Ireland (Belfast) 2016; BB 7-18 v WI (Gros Islet) 2017 – 4th best analysis in all LOI. **IT20** (Afg): 29 (2015-16 to 2017-18); HS 33 v WI (Basseterre) 2017; BB 5-3 v Ireland (Greater Noida) 2016-17 – joint 4th best analysis in all IT20. HS 52 and BB 8-74 (12-122 match) Afg v England Lions (Abu Dhabi) 2016-17, LO HS 60* (*see LOI*). LO BB 7-18 (*see LOI*). T20 HS 33. T20 BB 5-3.

RAWLINS, Delray Millard Wendell (Bede's S, Upper Dicker), b Bermuda 14 Sep 1997. 6'1". LHB, SLA. Squad No 9. Debut (Sussex) 2017. Sussex 2nd XI debut 2015. England U19 2016-17. HS 96 v South Africa A (Arundel) 2017. CC HS 55 v Notts (Hove) 2017. BB 1-46 v Kent (Hove) 2017. LO HS 41 v South Africans (Hove) 2017. LO BB –.

ROBINSON, Oliver Edward (King's S, Canterbury), b Margate, Kent 1 Dec 1993. 6'1". RHB, RM/OB. Squad No 25. Debut (Sussex) 2015. Kent 2nd XI 2011-12. Leicestershire 2nd XI 2013. Yorkshire 2nd XI 2013-14. HS 110 v Durham (Chester-le-St) 2015, on debut, sharing Sx record 10th wkt partnership of 164 with M.E.Hobden. BB 6-33 v Warwks (Hove) 2015. LO HS 30 v Kent (Canterbury) 2015 (RLC). LO BB 2-61 v Middx (Hove) 2015 (RLC). T20 HS 10. T20 BB 3-16.

SAKANDE, Abidine (Ardingly C; St John's C, Oxford), b Chester 22 Sep 1994. 6'1". RHB, RFM. Squad No 11. Oxford U 2014-15. Oxford MCCU 2015-16. Sussex debut 2016. Sussex 2nd XI debut 2011. HS 33 OU v Cambridge U (Cambridge) 2015. Sx HS 17 and BB 5-43 v South Africa A (Arundel) 2017. CC HS 7* and CC BB 2-53 v Glos (Hove) 2017. LO HS 7* and LO BB 2-62 v South Africans (Hove) 2017.

SALT, Philip Dean (Reed's S, Cobham), b Bodelwyddan, Denbighs 28 Aug 1996. 5'10". RHB, OB. Squad No 28. Debut (Sussex) 2013. Sussex 2nd XI debut 2014. HS 72 v Durham (Chester-le-St) 2017. LO HS 81 v Middx (Hove) 2016 (RLC). T20 HS 33.

‡^{NO}**SHARMA, Ishant**, b Delhi, India 2 Sep 1988. RHB, RFM. Squad No 97. Delhi 2006-07 to date. Joins Sussex for first two months of 2018 season. IPL: KKR 2007-08 to 2009-10. DC 2011. SH 2013-15. RPS 2016. KXIP 2017. **Tests** (I): 81 (2007 to 2017-18); HS 31* v SL (Galle) 2010; BB 7-74 v E (Lord's) 2014. **LOI** (I): 80 (2007 to 2015-16); HS 13 v SL (Colombo, RPS) 2009; BB 4-34 v SL (Cuttack) 2014-15. **IT20** (I): 14 (2007-08 to 2013-14); HS 5* v SL (Nagpur) 2009-10; BB 2-34 v B (Nottingham) 2009. F-c Tours (I): E 2007, 2011, 2014; A 2007-08, 2011-12, 2014-15; SA 2010-11, 2013-14, 2017-18; WI 2011, 2016; NZ 2008-09, 2013-14; SL 2008, 2010, 2015. HS 31* (*see Tests*). BB 7-24 (*see Tests*). LO HS 31 Delhi v Punjab (Mohali) 2010-11. LO BB 5-21 Delhi v Vidarbha (Delhi) 2015-16. T20 HS 9. T20 BB 5-12.

^{NO}**VAN ZYL, Stiaan**, b Cape Town, South Africa 19 Sep 1987. 5'11½". LHB, RM. Squad No 74. Boland 2006-07 to 2010-11. Cape Cobras 2007-08 to date. W Province 2014-15 to 2016-17. Sussex debut 2017 (Kolpak signing). **Tests** (SA): 12 (2014-15 to 2016); HS 101* v WI (Centurion) 2014-15 – on debut; BB 3-20 v E (Durban) 2015-16. F-c Tours (SA): A 2016 (SA A), I 2015 (SA A), 2015-16; SL 2010 (SA A); B 2010 (SA A), 2015; Ire 2012 (SA A). 1000 runs (1): 1023 (2017). HS 228 Cobras v Lions (Paarl) 2017-18. Sx 166* v Leics (Arundel) 2017. BB 5-32 Boland v Northerns (Paarl) 2010-11. Sx 2-25 v Derbys (Hove) 2017. LO HS 114* Cobras v Eagles (Kimberley) 2009-10. LO BB 4-24 Boland v Gauteng (Stellenbosch) 2010-11. T20 HS 86*. T20 BB 2-14.

WELLS, Luke William Peter (St Bede's S, Upper Dicker), b Eastbourne 29 Dec 1990. Son of A.P.Wells (Border, Kent, Sussex and England 1981-2000); elder brother of D.A.C.Wells (Oxford MCCU 2017); nephew of C.M.Wells (Border, Derbyshire, Sussex and WP 1979-96). 6'4". LHB, LB. Squad No 31. Debut (Sussex) 2010; cap 2016. Colombo CC 2011-12. 1000 runs (2); most – 1292 (2017). HS 258 v Durham (Hove) 2017. BB 3-35 v Durham (Arundel) 2015. LO HS 23 v Notts (Horsham) 2014 (RLC). BB 3-19 v Netherlands (Amstelveen) 2011 (CB40). T20 HS 11.

^{NO}**WHITTINGHAM, Stuart** Gordon (Christ's Hospital, Horsham; Loughborough U), b Derby 10 Feb 1994. 6'0". RHB, RFM. Squad No 29. Loughborough MCCU 2015. Sussex debut 2016. Sussex 2nd XI debut 2014. MCC Universities 2013. **LOI** (Scot): 4 (2017-18); HS 3* and BB 3-58 v Ireland (Dubai, ICCA) 2017-18. HS 22 v Notts (Hove) 2017. BB 5-70 Scot v Ireland (Dubai, DSC) 2017-18. BB 5-80 v Derbys (Hove) 2017. LO HS 3* (*see LOI*). LO BB 3-35 Scot v Nepal (Bulawayo) 2017-18.

^{NQ}**WIESE, David** (Witbank HS), b Roodepoort, South Africa 18 May 1985. 6'3". RHB, RMF. Squad No 96. Easterns 2005-06 to 2011-12. Titans 2009-10 to 2016-17. Sussex debut/cap 2016 (Kolpak signing). IPL: RCB 2015-16. **LOI** (SA): 6 (2015 to 2015-16); HS 41* and BB 3-50 v E (Cape Town) 2015-16. **IT20** (SA): 20 (2013 to 2015-16); HS 28 v WI (Nagpur) 2015-16; BB 5-23 v WI (Durban) 2014-15. F-c Tour (SA): A 2014. HS 208 Easterns v GW (Benoni) 2008-09. Sx HS 70* and Sx BB 4-18 v Worcs (Hove) 2016. BB 6-58 Titans v Knights (Centurion) 2014-15. LO HS 106 Easterns v FS (Bloemfontein) 2007-08. LO BB 5-25 Easterns v Boland (Benoni) 2010-11. T20 HS 71*. T20 BB 5-19.

WRIGHT, Luke James (Belvoir HS; Ratcliffe C; Loughborough U), b Grantham, Lincs 7 Mar 1985. Younger brother of A.S.Wright (Leicestershire 2001-02). 5'11". RHB, RMF. Squad No 10. Leicestershire 2003 (one f-c match). Sussex debut 2004; cap 2007; T20 captain & benefit 2015; captain 2016-17. IPL: PW 2012-13. Big Bash: MS 2011-12 to date. **LOI**: 50 (2007 to 2013-14); HS 52 v NZ (Birmingham) 2008; BB 2-34 v NZ (Bristol) 2008 and 2-34 v A (Southampton) 2010. **IT20**: 51 (2007-08 to 2013-14); HS 99* v Afghanistan (Colombo, RPS) 2012-13; BB 2-24 v NZ (Hamilton) 2012-13. F-c Tour (EL): NZ 2008-09. 1000 runs (1): 1220 (2015). HS 226* v Worcs (Worcester) 2015, sharing Sx record 6th wkt partnership of 335 with B.C.Brown. BB 5-65 v Derbys (Derby) 2010. LO HS 143* EL v Bangladesh A (Bristol) 2013. LO BB 4-12 v Middx (Hove) 2004 (NL). T20 HS 153* v Essex (Chelmsford) 2014 – Sx record. T20 BB 3-17.

RELEASED/RETIRED

(Having made a County 1st XI appearance in 2017)

HUTSON, Jacob William (Kemnal TC, Bromley; NW Kent C; U of Brighton), b Sidcup, Kent 22 Jun 1994. RHB, WK. Sussex 2017. Sussex 2nd XI debut 2016. Kent 2nd XI 2016. HS 25 v South Africa A (Arundel) 2017 – only 1st XI appearance.

MAGOFFIN, S.J. – *see WORCESTERSHIRE*.

NASH, C.D. – *see NOTTINGHAMSHIRE*.

^{NQ}**PHILANDER, Vernon** Darryl, b Bellville, Cape Province, South Africa 24 Jun 1985. RHB, RMF. Western Province 2003-04 to 2015-16. WP Boland 2004-05. Cape Cobras 2005-06 to date. Middlesex 2008. Somerset 2012. Kent 2013. Nottinghamshire 2015; cap 2015. Sussex 2017. Devon 2004. **Tests** (SA): 52 (2011-12 to 2017-18); HS 74 v P (Centurion) 2012-13; BB 6-42 v I (Cape Town) 2017-18. **LOI** (SA): 30 (2007 to 2015); HS 30* v NZ (Potchefstroom) 2015; BB 4-12 v Ireland (Belfast) 2007 – on debut. **IT20** (SA): 7 (2007-08); HS 6 v E (Cape Town) 2007-08; BB 2-23 v E (Cape Town) 2007-08. F-c Tours (SA): E 2012, 2017; A 2012-13, 2016-17; NZ 2011-12, 2016-17; I 2015-16; SL 2010 (SA A), 2014; Z 2014, 2016; B 2010 (SA A), 2015; UAE (v P) 2013-14. HS 168 WP v GW (Kimberley) 2004-05. Sx HS 73* v Kent (Tunbridge Wells) 2017 and 73* v Leics (Leicester) 2017. 50 wkts (0+2); most – 59 (2009-10). BB 7-61 Cobras v Knights (Cape Town) 2011-12. CC BB 5-43 Sm v Middx (Taunton) 2012. Sx 4-39 v Durham (Hove) 2017. LO HS 79* SA A v Bangladesh A (East London) 2010-11. LO BB 4-12 (*see LOI*). T20 HS 56*. T20 BB 5-17.

ROBSON, Angus James (Marcellin C, Randwick; Australian C of PE), b Darlinghurst, Sydney, Australia 19 Feb 1992. Younger brother of S.D.Robson (*see MIDDLESEX*). 5'9". RHB, LB. Leicestershire 2013-16. Sussex 2017. 1000 runs (2); most – 1086 (2014). HS 120 v Essex (Chelmsford) 2015. Sx HS 72 v Northants (Northampton) 2017. BB –. LO HS 90 v Yorks (Leeds) 2015 (RLC).

RELEASED/RETIRED continued on p 190

SUSSEX 2017

RESULTS SUMMARY

	Place	Won	Lost	Tied	Drew	NR
Specsavers County Champ (2nd Division)	4th	7	5		2	
All First-Class Matches		8	5		2	
Royal London One-Day Cup (South Group)	5th	3	3			2
NatWest t20 Blast (South Group)	5th	5	5	1		3

SPECSAVERS COUNTY CHAMPIONSHIP AVERAGES
BATTING AND FIELDING

Cap		M	I	NO	HS	Runs	Avge	100	50	Ct/St
2016	L.W.P.Wells	12	22	2	258	1292	64.60	4	4	4
	V.D.Philander	5	7	3	73*	211	52.75	–	2	1
	S.van Zyl	13	22	1	166*	1023	48.71	2	4	6
	M.G.K.Burgess	6	10	1	146	434	48.22	1	2	18
2017	J.C.Archer	13	20	6	81*	638	45.57	–	5	9
2014	B.C.Brown	8	14	1	90	483	37.15	–	5	23
2007	L.J.Wright	12	21	1	118	742	37.10	1	4	6
2014	C.J.Jordan	11	17	3	147	438	31.28	1	2	13
2008	C.D.Nash	12	21	–	118	578	27.52	1	3	12
2016	D.Wiese	10	15	–	66	404	26.93	–	2	3
	P.D.Salt	2	4	–	72	100	25.00	–	1	1
	A.J.Robson	4	8	1	72	169	24.14	–	1	3
	H.Z.Finch	11	20	2	82	405	22.50	–	3	14
	D.R.Briggs	8	12	5	27	116	16.57	–	–	5
	O.E.Robinson	4	8	1	41*	116	16.57	–	–	2
	D.M.W.Rawlins	4	8	–	55	121	15.12	–	1	–
	G.H.S.Garton	2	4	–	18	43	10.75	–	–	2
	S.G.Whittingham	5	8	2	22	43	7.16	–	–	1
	L.J.Evans	4	8	–	19	48	6.00	–	–	4

Also batted: A.P.Barton (1 match) 13*, 5; W.A.T.Beer (1) 25; S.J.Magoffin (2 – cap 2013) 5, 0*; A.Sakande (3) 7*, 6, 1*; A.Shahzad (1) 1, 5.

BOWLING

	O	M	R	W	Avge	Best	5wI	10wM
O.E.Robinson	149.3	30	412	19	21.68	5-69	1	–
J.C.Archer	475.1	91	1543	61	25.29	7-67	4	1
V.D.Philander	121.3	29	429	16	26.81	4-39	–	–
C.J.Jordan	353.5	57	1182	36	32.83	5-46	1	–
S.G.Whittingham	105.5	12	494	15	32.93	5-80	1	–
S.van Zyl	116.1	24	368	10	36.80	2-25	–	–
D.Wiese	248.3	44	834	22	37.90	4-63	–	–
D.R.Briggs	218.1	36	677	14	48.35	3-40	–	–
Also bowled:								
S.J.Magoffin	27	10	69	5	13.80	5-51	1	–
G.H.S.Garton	56	0	262	9	29.11	3-20	–	–
A.Sakande	51.4	8	212	7	30.28	2-53	–	–
A.Shahzad	48	6	187	6	31.16	3-91	–	–

A.P.Barton 11-0-81-0; W.A.T.Beer 27.3-1-88-4; H.Z.Finch 1-0-2-0; C.D.Nash 24-6-66-0; D.M.W.Rawlins 39.1-1-154-1.

The First-Class Averages (pp 230–246) give the records of Sussex players in all first-class county matches (Sussex's other opponents being South Africa A), with the exception of V.D.Philander and A.Shahzad, whose first-class figures for Sussex are as above, and:
A.P.Barton 2-3-1-13*-20-10.00-0-0-0ct. 24-3-115-0.
G.H.S.Garton 3-5-0-18-43-8.60-0-0-2ct. 67-4-329-10-32.90-3/20-0-0.

SUSSEX RECORDS

FIRST-CLASS CRICKET

Highest Total	For 742-5d		v	Somerset	Taunton	2009
	V 726		by	Notts	Nottingham	1895
Lowest Total	For 19		v	Surrey	Godalming	1830
	19		v	Notts	Hove	1873
	V 18		by	Kent	Gravesend	1867
Highest Innings	For 344*	M.W.Goodwin	v	Somerset	Taunton	2009
	V 322	E.Paynter	for	Lancashire	Hove	1937

Highest Partnership for each Wicket

1st	490	E.H.Bowley/J.G.Langridge	v	Middlesex	Hove	1933
2nd	385	E.H.Bowley/M.W.Tate	v	Northants	Hove	1921
3rd	385*	M.H.Yardy/M.W.Goodwin	v	Warwicks	Hove	2006
4th	363	M.W.Goodwin/C.D.Hopkinson	v	Somerset	Taunton	2009
5th	297	J.H.Parks/H.W.Parks	v	Hampshire	Portsmouth	1937
6th	335	L.J.Wright/B.C.Brown	v	Durham	Hove	2014
7th	344	K.S.Ranjitsinhji/W.Newham	v	Essex	Leyton	1902
8th	291	R.S.C.Martin-Jenkins/M.J.G.Davis	v	Somerset	Taunton	2002
9th	178	H.W.Parks/A.F.Wensley	v	Derbyshire	Horsham	1930
10th	164	O.E.Robinson/M.E.Hobden	v	Durham	Chester-le-St[2]	2015

Best Bowling	For 10- 48	C.H.G.Bland	v	Kent	Tonbridge	1899
(Innings)	V 9- 11	A.P.Freeman	for	Kent	Hove	1922
Best Bowling	For 17-106	G.R.Cox	v	Warwicks	Horsham	1926
(Match)	V 17- 67	A.P.Freeman	for	Kent	Hove	1922

Most Runs – Season	2850	J.G.Langridge	(av 64.77)	1949
Most Runs – Career	34150	J.G.Langridge	(av 37.69)	1928-55
Most 100s – Season	12	J.G.Langridge		1949
Most 100s – Career	76	J.G.Langridge		1928-55
Most Wkts – Season	198	M.W.Tate	(av 13.47)	1925
Most Wkts – Career	2211	M.W.Tate	(av 17.41)	1912-37
Most Career W-K Dismissals	1176	H.R.Butt	(911 ct; 265 st)	1890-1912
Most Career Catches in the Field	779	J.G.Langridge		1928-55

LIMITED-OVERS CRICKET

Highest Total	50ov	384-9		v	Ireland	Belfast	1996
	40ov	399-4		v	Worcs	Horsham	2011
	T20	242-5		v	Glos	Bristol	2016
Lowest Total	50ov	49		v	Derbyshire	Chesterfield	1969
	40ov	59		v	Glamorgan	Hove	1996
	T20	67		v	Hampshire	Hove	2004
Highest Innings	50ov	158*	M.W.Goodwin	v	Essex	Chelmsford	2006
	40ov	163	C.J.Adams	v	Middlesex	Arundel	1999
	T20	153*	L.J.Wright	v	Essex	Chelmsford	2014
Best Bowling	50ov	6- 9	A.I.C.Dodemaide	v	Ireland	Downpatrick	1990
	40ov	7-41	A.N.Jones	v	Notts	Nottingham	1986
	T20	5-11	Mushtaq Ahmed	v	Essex	Hove	2005

WARWICKSHIRE

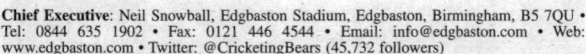

Formation of Present Club: 8 April 1882
Substantial Reorganisation: 19 January 1884
Inaugural First-Class Match: 1894
Colours: Dark Blue, Gold and Silver
Badge: Bear and Ragged Staff
County Champions: (7) 1911, 1951, 1972, 1994, 1995, 2004, 2012
Gillette/NatWest Trophy Winners: (5) 1966, 1968, 1989, 1993, 1995
Benson and Hedges Cup Winners: (2) 1994, 2002
Sunday League Winners: (3) 1980, 1994, 1997
Clydesdale Bank 40 Winners: (1) 2010
Royal London Cup Winners: (1) 2015
Twenty20 Cup Winners: (1) 2014

Chief Executive: Neil Snowball, Edgbaston Stadium, Edgbaston, Birmingham, B5 7QU • Tel: 0844 635 1902 • Fax: 0121 446 4544 • Email: info@edgbaston.com • Web: www.edgbaston.com • Twitter: @CricketingBears (45,732 followers)

Sport Director: Ashley Giles. **1st Team Coach**: Jim Troughton. **Batting Coach**: Tony Frost. **Bowling Coach**: Graeme Welch. **Captains**: J.S.Patel (f-c & l-o), G.D.Elliott (T20). **Vice-Captain**: D.P.Sibley. **Overseas Players**: C.de Grandhomme (T20 only), G.D.Elliott (T20 only) and J.S.Patel. **2018 Testimonial**: None. **Head Groundsman**: Gary Barwell. **Scorer**: Mel Smith. ‡ New registration. ᴺᑫ Not qualified for England.

AMBROSE, Timothy Raymond (Merewether HS, NSW; TAFE C), b Newcastle, NSW, Australia 1 Dec 1982. ECB qualified – British/EU passport. 5'7''. RHB, WK. Squad No 11. Sussex 2001-05; cap 2003. Warwickshire debut 2006; cap 2007; benefit 2016. **Tests**: 11 (2007-08 to 2008-09); HS 102 v NZ (Wellington) 2007-08. **LOI**: 5 (2008); HS 6 v NZ (Oval) 2008. **IT20**: 1 (2008); HS –. F-c Tours: WI 2008-09; NZ 2007-08. HS 251* v Worcs (Worcester) 2007. LO HS 135 v Durham (Birmingham) 2007 (FPT). T20 HS 77.

BANKS, Liam (Newcastle-under-Lyme S & SFC), b Newcastle-under-Lyme, Staffs 3 Jun 1999. 5'10''. RHB, RM. Squad No 8. Debut (Warwickshire) 2017. Warwickshire 2nd XI debut 2015. England U19 2017. HS 29 v Yorks (Leeds) 2017.

BARKER, Keith Hubert Douglas (Moorhead HS; Fulwood C, Preston), b Manchester 21 Oct 1986. Son of K.H.Barker (British Guiana 1960-61 to 1963-64). Played football for Blackburn Rovers and Rochdale. 6'3''. LHB, LMF. Squad No 13. Debut (Warwickshire) 2009; cap 2013. HS 125 v Surrey (Guildford) 2013. 50 wkts (3); most – 62 (2016). BB 6-40 v Somerset (Taunton) 2012. LO HS 56 v Scotland (Birmingham) 2011 (CB40). LO BB 4-33 v Scotland (Birmingham) 2010 (CB40). T20 HS 46. T20 BB 4-19.

BELL, Ian Ronald (Princethorpe C), b Walsgrave-on-Sowe 11 Apr 1982. 5'9''. RHB, RM. Squad No 4. Debut (Warwickshire) 1999; cap 2001; benefit 2011; captain 2016-17. MCC 2004, 2016. YC 2004. MBE 2005. *Wisden* 2007. **Tests**: 118 (2004 to 2015-16); 1000 runs (1): 1005 (2013); HS 235 v I (Oval) 2011; BB 1-33 v P (Faisalabad) 2005-06. **LOI**: 161 (2004-05 to 2014-15); 1000 runs (1): 1080 (2007); HS 141 v A (Hobart) 2014-15; BB 3-9 v Z (Bulawayo) 2004-05 – taking a wicket with his third ball in LOI. **IT20**: 8 (2006 to 2014); HS 60* v NZ (Manchester) 2008. F-c Tours: A 2006-07, 2010-11, 2013-14; SA 2009-10; WI 2000-01 (Eng A – *part*), 2008-09, 2014-15; NZ 2007-08, 2012-13; I 2005-06, 2008-09, 2012-13; P 2005-06; SL 2002-03 (ECB Acad), 2004-05, 2007-08, 2011-12; B 2009-10; UAE 2011-12 (v P), 2015-16 (v P). 1000 runs (2); most – 1714 (2004). HS 262* v Sussex (Horsham) 2004. BB 4-4 v Middx (Lord's) 2004. LO HS 158 EL v India A (Worcester) 2010. LO BB 5-41 v Essex (Chelmsford) 2003 (NL). T20 HS 90. T20 BB 1-12.

BROOKES, Henry James Hamilton (Tudor Grange Acad, Solihull), b Solihull 21 Aug 1999. RHB, RMF. Squad No 10. Debut (Warwickshire) 2017. Warwickshire 2nd XI debut 2016. England U19 2016-17 to 2017. HS 11 and BB- v Essex (Birmingham) 2017 – only 1st XI appearance.

^{NQ}**DE GRANDHOMME, Colin**, b Harare, Zimbabwe 22 Jul 1986. Son of L.L.de Grandhomme (Rhodesia B and Zimbabwe 1979-80 to 1987-88). RHB, RMF. Squad No 77. Zimbabwe A 2005-06. Auckland 2006-07 to date. Warwickshire debut 2017 (T20 only). IPL: KKR 2017. **Tests** (NZ): 8 (2016-17 to 2017-18); HS 105 v WI (Wellington) 2017-18; BB 6-41 v P (Christchurch) 2016-17 – on debut. **LOI** (NZ): 19 (2011-12 to 2017-18); HS 74* v P (Hamilton) 2017-18; BB 2-40 v SA (Wellington) 2016-17. **IT20** (NZ): 19 (2011-12 to 2017-18); HS 41* v B (Napier) 2016-17; BB 2-22 v SA (Auckland) 2016-17. F-c Tours: E 2014 (NZ A); SA 2005-06 (Z U23). HS 144* Auckland v Otago (Auckland) 2016-17. BB 6-24 Auckland v Wellington (Auckland) 2013-14. LO HS 151 NZ A v Northants (Northampton) 2014. LO BB 4-37 Auckland v Wellington (Wellington) 2015-16. T20 HS 72*. T20 BB 3-4.

^{NQ}**ELLIOTT, Grant** David (St Stithians) b Johannesburg, South Africa 21 Mar 1979. 6'1''. RHB, RMF. Squad No 88. Transvaal B 1996-97. Griqualand West 1999-00 to 2000-01. Gauteng 2001-02 to 2002-03. Wellington 2005-06 to 2013-14. Surrey 2009 (1 match). Leicestershire 2015 (T20 only). Warwickshire debut 2017 (T20 only); T20 captain 2018. Qualified for NZ in 2007. **Tests** (NZ): 5 (2007-08 to 2009-10); HS 25 v P (Dunedin) 2009-10. BB 2-8 v P (Wellington) 2009-10. **LOI** (NZ): 83 (2008 to 2015-16); HS 115 v A (Sydney) 2008-09; BB 4-31 v E (Johannesburg) 2009-10. **IT20** (NZ): 16 (2008-09 to 2015-16, +1 for World XI); HS 27 v A (Dharmasala) 2015-16; BB 4-22 v SL (Auckland) 2015-16. F-c Tours (NZ): E 2008; A 2008-09; B 2008-09. HS 196* Wellington v Auckland (Wellington) 2007-08. CC HS 22 Sy v Middx (Oval) 2009. BB 5-33 Wellington v ND (Whangarei) 2013-14. LO HS 115 (*see LOI*). LO BB 5-34 Wellington v Otago (Wellington) 2007-08. T20 HS 70. T20 BB 4-15.

HAIN, Samuel Robert (Southport S, Gold Coast), b Hong Kong 16 July 1995. 5'10''. RHB, OB. Squad No 16. Debut (Warwickshire) 2014. Warwickshire 2nd XI debut 2011. UK passport (British parents). HS 208 v Northants (Birmingham) 2014. LO HS 144 v West Indies A (Coolidge) 2017-18. T20 HS 92*.

HANNON-DALBY, Oliver James (Brooksbank S, Leeds Met U), b Halifax, Yorkshire 20 Jun 1989. 6'7''. LHB, RMF. Squad No 20. Yorkshire 2008-12. Warwickshire debut 2013. HS 40 v Somerset (Taunton) 2014. BB 5-68 Y v Warwks (Birmingham) and 5-68 Y v Somerset (Leeds) 2010 – in consecutive matches. Wa BB 4-29 v Hants (Birmingham) 2017. LO HS 21* Y v Warwks (Scarborough) 2012 (CB40). LO BB 5-27 v Glamorgan (Birmingham) 2015 (RLC). T20 HS 9*. T20 BB 4-29.

HOSE, Adam John (Carisbrooke S), b Newport, IoW 25 Oct 1992. 6'2''. RHB, RMF. Squad No 21. Somerset 2016-17. MCC YC 2011-14. HS 68 Sm v Yorks (Taunton) 2016. LO HS 101* Sm v Glos (Bristol) 2017 (RLC). T20 HS 76.

LAMB, Matthew James (North Bromsgrove HS; Bromsgrove S), b Wolverhampton, Staffs 19 July 1996. 6'1''. RHB, RM. Squad No 7. Debut (Warwickshire) 2016. Warwickshire 2nd XI debut 2015. HS 71 v Middx (Lord's) 2017. BB 1-19 v Somerset (Birmingham) 2017. LO HS 12 v Lancs (Birmingham) 2017 (RLC).

MELLOR, Alexander James (Westwood C, Leek; Staffordshire U), b Stoke-on-Trent, Staffs 22 Jul 1991. 5'10''. LHB, WK. Squad No 15. Derbyshire 2016. Warwickshire debut 2016. Staffordshire 2014-15. HS 59 v Oxford MCCU (Oxford) 2017. CC HS 44 De v Essex (Derby) 2016. LO HS –. T20 HS 18*.

PANAYI, George David (Shrewsbury S), b Enfield, Middx 23 Sep 1997. 6'3". RHB, RFM. Squad No 33. Debut (Warwickshire) 2017. Warwickshire 2nd XI debut 2015. England U19 2017. HS 16 and BB 3-41 v Lancs (Birmingham) 2017.

[NQ]**PATEL, Jeetan** Shashi, b Wellington, New Zealand 7 May 1980. 5'10". RHB, OB. Squad No 5. Wellington 1999-00 to date. Warwickshire debut 2009; cap 2012; captain 2018. *Wisden* 2014. **Tests** (NZ): 24 (2006-07 to 2016-17); HS 47 v I (Kolkata) 2016-17; BB 5-110 v WI (Napier) 2008-09. **LOI** (NZ): 43 (2005 to 2017); HS 34 v SL (Kingston) 2006-07; BB 3-11 v SA (Mumbai, BS) 2006-07. **IT20** (NZ): 11 (2005-06 to 2008-09); HS 5 v E (Auckland) 2007-08; BB 3-20 v SA (Johannesburg) 2005-06. F-c career (NZ): E 2008; SA 2005-06, 2012-13; I 2010-11, 2012, 2016-17; SL 2009, 2012-13; Z 2010-11, 2011-12; B 2008-09. HS 120 v Yorks (Birmingham) 2009. 50 wkts (5); most – 69 (2016). BB 7-38 v Somerset (Taunton) 2015. LO HS 50 v Kent (Birmingham) 2013 (Y40). LO BB 5-43 v Somerset (Birmingham) 2016 (RLC). T20 HS 34*. T20 BB 4-11.

POLLOCK, Edward John (RGS Worcester; Shrewsbury S; Collingwood C, Durham U), b High Wycombe, Bucks 10 Jul 1995. Son of A.J.Pollock (Cambridge U 1982-84); younger brother of A.W.Pollock (Cambridge MCCU & U 2013-15). LHB, OB. Squad No 28. Durham MCCU 2015-17. Awaiting Warwickshire f-c debut. Durham 2nd XI 2015. Warwickshire 2nd XI debut 2015. Herefordshire 2014-16. HS 52 DU v Glos (Bristol) 2017. T20 HS 66.

POYSDEN, Joshua Edward (Cardinal Newman S, Hove; Anglia RU), b Shoreham-by-Sea, Sussex 8 Aug 1991. 5'9". LHB, LB. Squad No 14. Cambridge MCCU 2011-13. Warwickshire debut 2015. Unicorns (l-o) 2013. HS 47 CU v Surrey (Cambridge) 2011. Wa HS 7* v Surrey (Guildford) 2016. BB 5-53 v Middx (Birmingham) 2016. LO HS 10* Unicorns v Glos (Wormsley) 2013 (Y40). LO BB 3-33 Unicorns v Middx (Lord's) 2013 (Y40). T20 BB 9*. T20 BB 4-51.

[NQ]**RANKIN, William Boyd** (Strabane GS; Harper Adams UC), b Londonderry, Co Derry, N Ireland 5 Jul 1984. Brother of R.J.Rankin (Ireland U19 2003-04). 6'8". LHB, RFM. Squad No 30. Ireland 2006-07 to date. Derbyshire 2007. Warwickshire debut 2008; cap 2013. Became available for England in 2012, before rejoining Ireland in 2015-16. **Tests**: 1 (2013-14); HS 13 and BB 1-47 v A (Sydney) 2013-14. **LOI** (E/Ire): 54 (47 for Ire 2006-07 to 2017-18, 7 for E 2013 to 2013-14); HS 18* Ire v SL (Dublin) 2016; BB 4-46 Ire v UAE (Harare) 2017-18. **IT20** (E/Ire): 26 (24 for Ire 2009 to 2016-17, 2 for E 2013); HS 16* Ire v UAE (Abu Dhabi) 2015-16; BB 3-16 Ire v UAE (Dubai, DSC) 2016-17. F-c Tour: A 2013-14. HS 56* v Worcs (Birmingham) 2015. 50 wkts (1): 55 (2011). BB 6-55 v Yorks (Leeds) 2015. LO HS 18* v Northants (Northampton) 2013 (Y40) and *see LOI*. LO BB 4-15 (*see LOI*). T20 HS 16*. T20 BB 4-9.

‡**RHODES, William** Michael Henry (Cottingham HS, Cottingham SFC, Hull), b Nottingham 2 Mar 1995. 6'2". LHB, RMF. Squad No 35. Yorkshire 2014-15 to 2016. Essex 2016 (on loan). Yorkshire 2nd XI debut 2012. England U19 2014. HS 95 v MCC (Abu Dhabi) 2015-16. CC HS 79 Y v Warwks (Birmingham) 2015. BB 3-42 Y v Middx (Leeds) 2015. LO HS 46 Y v Leics (Leeds) 2015 (RLC). LO BB 2-22 Y v Essex (Chelmsford) 2015 (RLC). T20 HS 45. T20 BB 3-27.

SIBLEY, Dominic Peter (Whitgift S, Croydon), b Epsom, Surrey 5 Sep 1995. 6'0". RHB, OB. Squad No 45. Surrey 2013-17. Warwickshire debut 2017. Surrey 2nd XI debut 2011, aged 15y 302d. England U19 2012-13 to 2014. HS 242 Sy v Yorks (Oval) 2013. Wa HS 92* v Hants (Birmingham) 2017. BB 2-103 Sy v Hants (Southampton) 2016. Wa BB –. LO HS 37 Sy v Durham (Chester-le-St) 2013 (Y40) and 37 Sy v Somerset (Taunton) 2017. LO BB 1-20 Sy v Essex (Chelmsford) 2016 (RLC). T20 HS 74*. T20 BB 2-33.

SIDEBOTTOM, Ryan Nathan, b Shepparton, Victoria, Australia 14 Aug 1989. UK passport. RHB, RMF. Squad No 22. Victoria 2012-13. Warwickshire debut 2017. HS 13 v Hants (Birmingham) 2017. BB 4-29 v Middx (Lord's) 2017.

STONE, Oliver Peter (Thorpe St Andrew HS), b Norwich, Norfolk 9 Oct 1993. 6'1". RHB, RMF. Squad No 6. Northamptonshire 2012-16. Warwickshire debut 2017. Northamptonshire 2nd XI debut 2010. Norfolk 2011. Captained England U19 2012-13. HS 60 Nh v Kent (Northampton) 2016. Wa HS 32 and Wa BB 1-70 v Lancs (Manchester) 2017. BB 5-44 Nh v Kent (Northampton) 2015. LO HS 24* Nh v Derbys (Derby) 2015 (RLC). LO BB 3-34 Nh v Glos (Northampton) 2015 (RLC). T20 HS 8*. T20 BB 3-29.

SUKHJIT SINGH ('**Sunny**') (George Dixon International S, Birmingham; South & City C), b India 30 Mar 1996. 5'10". LHB, SLA. Squad No 58. Debut (Warwickshire) 2017. Warwickshire 2nd XI debut 2014. HS 6* and BB 6-144 v Hants (Southampton) 2017.

THOMASON, Aaron Dean (Barr Beacon S, Walsall), b Birmingham 26 Jun 1997. 5'10". RHB, RMF. Squad No 26. Warwickshire 2nd XI debut 2014. England U19 2015. Awaiting f-c debut. LO HS 28 and LO BB 4-64 v Durham (Birmingham) 2017 (RLC). T20 HS 42. T20 BB 3-33.

THOMSON, Alexander Thomas (Kings S, Macclesfield; Denstone C; Cardiff Met U), b Macclesfield, Cheshire 30 Oct 1993. RHB, OB. Squad No 29. Cardiff MCCU 2014-16. Warwickshire debut 2017. Leicestershire 2nd XI 2013-15. MCC Univs 2014-17. Staffordshire 2013-16. HS 26 v Hants (Birmingham) 2017. BB 6-138 CfU v Hants (Southampton) 2016. Wa BB – .

TROTT, Ian Jonathan Leonard (Rondebosch BHC; Stellenbosch U), b Cape Town, South Africa 22 Apr 1981. Stepbrother of K.C.Jackson (WP and Boland 1988-89 to 2001-02). 6'0". RHB, RM. Squad No 9. Boland 2000-01. W Province 2001-02. EU/British passport. Warwickshire debut 2003, scoring 134 v Sussex (Birmingham); cap 2005; benefit 2014. Otago 2005-06. *Wisden* 2010. **Tests**: 52 (2009 to 2014-15); 1000 runs (2); most – 1325 (2010); HS 226 v B (Lord's) 2010; scored 119 v A (Oval) 2009 on debut. BB 1-5 v SL (Lord's) 2011. **LOI**: 68 (2009 to 2013); 1000 runs (1): 1315 (2011); HS 137 v A (Sydney) 2010-11; BB 2-31 v A (Adelaide) 2010-11. **IT20**: 7 (2007 to 2009-10); HS 51 v SA (Centurion) 2009-10. F-c Tours: A 2010-11, 2013-14 (*part*); SA 2009-10, 2014-15 (EL); WI 2014-15; NZ 2008-09 (EL), 2012-13; I 2007-08 (EL), 2012-13; SL 2011-12; B 2009-10; UAE 2011-12 (v P). 1000 runs (8); most – 1400 (2009). HS 226 (*see Tests*). Wa HS 219* v Middx (Lord's) 2016. BB 7-39 v Kent (Canterbury) 2003. LO HS 137 (*see LOI*). LO BB 4-55 v Hants (Lord's) 2005 (CGT). T20 HS 86*. T20 BB 2-19.

UMEED, Andrew Robert Isaac (High School of Glasgow), b Glasgow 19 Apr 1996. 6'1". RHB, LB. Squad No 23. Scotland 2015. Warwickshire debut 2016, scoring 101 v Durham (Birmingham). Warwickshire 2nd XI debut 2014. HS 113 v Lancs (Birmingham) 2017.

WOAKES, Christopher Roger (Barr Beacon Language S, Walsall), b Birmingham 2 March 1989. 6'2". RHB, RFM. Squad No 19. Debut (Warwickshire) 2006; cap 2009. MCC 2009. Herefordshire 2006-07. *Wisden* 2016. **ECB Test & LO Central Contract 2017-18. Tests**: 22 (2013 to 2017-18); HS 66 v SL (Lord's) 2016; BB 6-70 v P (Lord's) 2016. **LOI**: 76 (2010-11 to 2017-18); HS 95* v SL (Nottingham) 2016; BB 6-45 v A (Brisbane) 2010-11. **IT20**: 8 (2010-11 to 2015-16); HS 37 v P (Sharjah) 2015-16; BB 2-40 v P (Dubai, DSC) 2015-16. F-c Tours: A 2017-18; SA 2015-16; WI 2010-11 (EL); I 2016-17; SL 2013-14 (EL); B 2016-17; UAE 2015-16 (v P). HS 152* v Derbys (Derby) 2013. 50 wkts (3); most – 59 (2016). BB 9-36 v Durham (Birmingham) 2016. LO HS 95* (*see LOI*). LO BB 6-45 (*see LOI*). T20 HS 55*. T20 BB 4-21.

WRIGHT, Christopher Julian Clement (Eggars S, Alton; Anglia Ruskin U), b Chipping Norton, Oxon 14 Jul 1985. 6'3". RHB, RFM. Squad No 31. Cambridge UCCE 2004-05. Middlesex 2004-07. Tamil Union 2005-06. Essex 2008-11. Warwickshire debut 2011; cap 2013. HS 77 Ex v Cambridge MCCU (Cambridge) 2011. CC HS 71* Ex v Middx (Chelmsford) 2008. Wa HS 65 v Notts (Birmingham) 2014 and 65 v Sussex (Birmingham) 2015. 50 wkts (1): 67 (2012). BB 6-22 Ex v Leics (Leicester) 2008. Wa BB 6-31 v Durham (Birmingham) 2013. LO HS 42 Ex v Glos (Cheltenham) 2011 (CB40). LO BB 4-20 Ex v Unicorns (Chelmsford) 2011 (CB40). T20 HS 6*. T20 BB 4-24.

RELEASED/RETIRED

(Having made a County 1st XI appearance in 2017)

ADAIR, Mark Richard (Sullivan Upper S, Hollywood), b Belfast, N Ireland 27 Mar 1996. 6'2". RHB, RFM. Debut (Warwickshire) 2015. Warwickshire 2nd XI debut 2013. HS 32 v Notts (Birmingham) 2016. BB 1-61 v Somerset (Taunton) 2015. LO HS 0* v Derbys (Derby) 2017 (RLC). LO BB –. T20 HS 7. T20 BB 2-18.

CLARKE, R. – see SURREY.

JAVID, A. – see LEICESTERSHIRE.

NQPORTERFIELD, William Thomas Stuart (Strabane GS; Leeds Met U), b Londonderry, N.Ireland 6 Sep 1984. 5'11". LHB, OB. Ireland 2006-07 to 2008-09. Gloucestershire 2008-10; cap 2008. Warwickshire 2011-17; cap 2014. MCC 2007. **LOI** (Ire): 116 (2006 to 2017-18, 93 as captain); HS 139 v UAE (Dubai, ICCA) 2017-18. **IT20** (Ire): 56 (2008 to 2016-17, 56 as captain); HS 72 v UAE (Abu Dhabi) 2015-16. HS 186 Ire v Namibia (Windhoek) 2015-16. CC HS 175 Gs v Worcs (Cheltenham) 2010. Wa HS 118 v Somerset (Birmingham) 2014. BB 1-29 Ire v Jamaica (Spanish Town) 2009-10. UK BB 1-57 Gs v Loughborough UCCE (Bristol) 2008. LO HS 139 (see LOI). T20 HS 127*.

WESTWOOD, Ian James (Wheelers Lane S; Solihull SFC), b Birmingham 13 Jul 1982. 5'7½". LHB, OB. Warwickshire 2003-17; cap 2008; captain 2009-10; benefit 2015. HS 196 v Yorks (Leeds) 2015. BB 2-39 v Hants (Southampton) 2009. LO HS 65 v Northants (Northampton) 2008 (FPT). BB 1-28 Wa CB v Cambs (March) 2001 (CGT). T20 HS 49*. T20 BB 3-29.

SUSSEX RELEASED/RETIRED (continued from p 183)

SHAHZAD, Ajmal (Woodhouse Grove S; Bradford U), b Huddersfield, Yorkshire 27 Jul 1985. 6'0". RHB, RFM. Yorkshire 2006-12 (first British-born Asian to play for Yorkshire); cap 2010. Lancashire 2012 (on loan). Nottinghamshire 2013-14. Sussex 2015-17. Leicestershire 2017. **Tests**: 1 (2010); HS 5 and BB 3-45 v B (Manchester) 2010. **LOI**: 11 (2009-10 to 2010-11); HS 9 v A (Brisbane) 2010-11; BB 3-41 v B (Bristol) 2010. **IT20**: 3 (2009-10 to 2010-11); HS 0*; BB 2-38 v P (Dubai) 2009-10. F-c Tours: A 2010-11; B 2009-10. HS 88 Y v Sussex (Hove) 2009. Sx HS 45* and BB 5-46 v Worcs (Hove) 2015. LO HS 59* Y v Kent (Leeds) 2011 (CB40). LO BB 5-51 Y v Sri Lanka A (Leeds) 2007. T20 HS 20. T20 BB 3-26.

SMITH, Liam James (Malvern C), b Pontefract, Yorks 25 Sep 1996. RHB, RMF. Sussex 2017. Worcestershire 2nd XI 2013-15. Herefordshire 2016. HS 0.

NQTAYLOR, Jerome Everton, b St Elizabeth, Jamaica 22 Jun 1984. 5'11". RHB, RF. Squad No 75. Jamaica 2002-03 to 2016-17. Leicestershire 2007. Sussex 2017 (l-o only). IPL: PW 2011. **Tests** (WI): 46 (2003 to 2015-16); HS 106 v NZ (Dunedin) 2008-09; BB 6-47 v A (Kingston) 2015. **LOI** (WI): 90 (2003 to 2017); HS 43* v SA (Durban) 2007-08); BB 5-48 v Z (Bulawayo) 2007-08. **IT20** (WI): 30 (2005-06 to 2017-18); HS 21 v P (Dubai, DSC) 2016-17; BB 3-6 v SA (Pt Elizabeth) 2007-08. F-c Tours (WI): E 2007, 2009; A 2009-10, 2015-16; SA 2007-08, 2014-15; NZ 2005-06, 2008-09; P 2006-07; SL 2015-16; Z 2003-04. HS 106 (see Tests). CC HS 40 Le v Derbys (Leicester) 2007. BB 8-59 Jamaica v T&T (Port of Spain) 2002-03. CC BB 6-35 Le v Middx (Southgate) 2007. LO HS 43* (see LOI). LO BB 5-40 Jamaica v Guyana (Bridgetown) 2016-17. T20 HS 21. T20 BB 5-10.

TAYLOR, L.R.P.L. – see NOTTINGHAMSHIRE.

E.C.Joyce and M.W.Machan left the staff during the season without making a County 1st XI appearance in 2017.

WARWICKSHIRE 2017

RESULTS SUMMARY

	Place	Won	Lost	Drew	NR
Specsavers County Champ (1st Division)	8th	1	9	4	
All First-Class Matches		1	9	5	
Royal London One-Day Cup (North Group)	9th	2	6		
NatWest t20 Blast (North Group)	Finalists	10	6		1

SPECSAVERS COUNTY CHAMPIONSHIP AVERAGES
BATTING AND FIELDING

Cap		M	I	NO	HS	Runs	Avge	100	50	Ct/St
2005	I.J.L.Trott	14	26	–	175	967	37.19	3	5	10
2008	I.J.Westwood	4	7	–	153	253	36.14	1	1	1
2013	K.H.D.Barker	12	22	4	70*	536	29.77	–	6	2
	D.P.Sibley	6	12	1	92*	310	28.18	–	3	4
2012	J.S.Patel	13	24	2	100	608	27.63	1	2	9
2001	I.R.Bell	13	24	1	99	596	25.91	–	5	9
2009	C.R.Woakes	2	4	–	53	100	25.00	–	1	–
	M.J.Lamb	7	14	–	71	329	23.50	–	2	3
	A.R.I.Umeed	8	14	–	113	325	23.21	1	–	9
2007	T.R.Ambrose	13	24	1	104	513	22.30	1	2	25/3
2011	R.Clarke	8	14	–	83	265	18.92	–	2	6
2013	C.J.C.Wright	8	16	3	41	241	18.53	–	–	2
	A.T.Thomson	2	4	–	26	70	17.50	–	–	1
	S.R.Hain	8	14	–	58	216	15.42	–	1	4
	W.T.S.Porterfield	5	9	–	45	137	15.22	–	–	3
	L.Banks	2	4	–	29	57	14.25	–	–	1
2013	W.B.Rankin	5	9	4	21*	61	12.20	–	–	1
	A.J.Mellor	3	6	–	18	59	9.83	–	–	3
	O.J.Hannon-Dalby	4	7	2	12	44	8.80	–	–	–
	R.N.Sidebottom	6	12	5	13	26	3.71	–	–	1
	Sukhjit Singh	4	7	2	16*	18	3.60	–	–	–

Also batted: H.J.H.Brookes (1 match) 4, 11; A.Javid (1) 14, 8; G.D.Panayi (2) 16, 1, 0; O.P.Stone (1) 32, 7*; G.T.Thornton (2) 0*, 10, 9.

BOWLING

	O	M	R	W	Avge	Best	5wI	10wM
R.N.Sidebottom	129.5	28	510	23	22.17	4- 29	–	–
O.J.Hannon-Dalby	89.1	22	269	11	24.45	4- 29	–	–
J.S.Patel	482	149	1222	41	29.80	6- 50	1	–
Sukhjit Singh	122.4	13	400	13	30.76	6-144	2	–
W.B.Rankin	114.2	13	423	12	35.25	3- 48	–	–
K.H.D.Barker	301	59	950	26	36.53	3- 21	–	–
R.Clarke	199	41	615	15	41.00	3- 29	–	–
C.J.C.Wright	199.3	37	694	16	43.37	5-113	1	–

Also bowled:
C.R.Woakes	44	7	159	7	22.71	3- 38	–	–

H.J.H.Brookes 11-1-43-0; A.Javid 4-0-15-0; M.J.Lamb 20-4-66-3; G.D.Panayi 38.3-7-141-4; D.P.Sibley 2-0-17-0; O.P.Stone 17-3-70-1; G.T.Thornton 14-0-73-2; G.T.Thornton 36.2-4-138-4; I.J.L.Trott 36.4-111-1; A.R.I.Umeed 14-0-73-2.

The First-Class Averages (pp 230–246) give the records of Warwickshire players in all first-class county matches (Warwickshire's other opponents being Oxford MCCU), with the exception of D.P.Sibley and C.R.Woakes, whose first-class figures for Warwickshire are as above, and:
R.Clarke 9-15-1-83-281-20.07-0-2-7ct. 211.4-44-659-16-41.18-3/29-0-0.

WARWICKSHIRE RECORDS

FIRST-CLASS CRICKET

Highest Total	For	810-4d			v	Durham	Birmingham	1994
	V	887			by	Yorkshire	Birmingham	1896
Lowest Total	For	16			v	Kent	Tonbridge	1913
	V	15			by	Hampshire	Birmingham	1922
Highest Innings	For 501*		B.C.Lara		v	Durham	Birmingham	1994
	V	322	I.V.A.Richards		for	Somerset	Taunton	1985

Highest Partnership for each Wicket

1st	377*	N.F.Horner/K.Ibadulla	v	Surrey	The Oval	1960
2nd	465*	J.A.Jameson/R.B.Kanhai	v	Glos	Birmingham	1974
3rd	327	S.P.Kinneir/W.G.Quaife	v	Lancashire	Birmingham	1901
4th	470	A.I.Kallicharran/G.W.Humpage	v	Lancashire	Southport	1982
5th	335	J.O.Troughton/T.R.Ambrose	v	Hampshire	Birmingham	2009
6th	327	L.J.Evans/T.R.Ambrose	v	Sussex	Birmingham	2015
7th	289*	I.R.Bell/T.Frost	v	Sussex	Horsham	2004
8th	228	A.J.W.Croom/R.E.S.Wyatt	v	Worcs	Dudley	1925
9th	233	I.J.L.Trott/J.S.Patel	v	Yorkshire	Birmingham	2009
10th	214	N.V.Knight/A.Richardson	v	Hampshire	Birmingham	2002

Best Bowling	For	10-41	J.D.Bannister	v	Comb Servs	Birmingham	1959
(Innings)	V	10-36	H.Verity	for	Yorkshire	Leeds	1931
Best Bowling	For	15-76	S.Hargreave	v	Surrey	The Oval	1903
(Match)	V	17-92	A.P.Freeman	for	Kent	Folkestone	1932

Most Runs – Season	2417	M.J.K.Smith	(av 60.42)	1959
Most Runs – Career	35146	D.L.Amiss	(av 41.64)	1960-87
Most 100s – Season	9	A.I.Kallicharran		1984
	9	B.C.Lara		1994
Most 100s – Career	78	D.L.Amiss		1960-87
Most Wkts – Season	180	W.E.Hollies	(av 15.13)	1946
Most Wkts – Career	2201	W.E.Hollies	(av 20.45)	1932-57
Most Career W-K Dismissals	800	E.J.Smith	(662 ct; 138 st)	1904-30
Most Career Catches in the Field	422	M.J.K.Smith		1956-75

LIMITED-OVERS CRICKET

Highest Total	50ov	392-5		v	Oxfordshire	Birmingham	1984
	40ov	321-7		v	Leics	Birmingham	2010
	T20	242-2		v	Derbyshire	Birmingham	2015
Lowest Total	50ov	94		v	Glos	Bristol	2000
	40ov	59		v	Yorkshire	Leeds	2001
	T20	73		v	Somerset	Taunton	2013
Highest Innings	50ov	206	A.I.Kallicharran	v	Oxfordshire	Birmingham	1984
	40ov	137	I.R.Bell	v	Yorkshire	Birmingham	2005
	T20	158*	B.B.McCullum	v	Derbyshire	Birmingham	2015
Best Bowling	50ov	7-32	R.G.D.Willis	v	Yorkshire	Birmingham	1981
	40ov	6-15	A.A.Donald	v	Yorkshire	Birmingham	1995
	T20	5-19	N.M.Carter	v	Worcs	Birmingham	2005

WORCESTERSHIRE

Formation of Present Club: 11 March 1865
Inaugural First-Class Match: 1899
Colours: Dark Green and Black
Badge: Shield Argent a Fess between three Pears Sable
County Championships: (5) 1964, 1965, 1974, 1988, 1989
NatWest Trophy Winners: (1) 1994
Benson and Hedges Cup Winners: (1) 1991
Pro 40/National League (Div 1) Winners: (1) 2007
Sunday League Winners: (3) 1971, 1987, 1988
Twenty20 Cup Winners: (0); best – Quarter-Finalist 2004, 2007, 2012, 2014, 2015

Interim Chief Executive: Matt Rawnsley, County Ground, New Road, Worcester, WR2 4QQ • Tel: 01905 748474 • Fax: 01905 748005 • Email: info@wccc.co.uk • Web: www.wccc.co.uk • Twitter: @WorcsCCC (50,931 followers)

Head Coach: Kevin Sharp. **Head Bowling Coach**: Alan Richardson. **Second XI Coach**: Alex Gidman. **Captain**: J.Leach. **Overseas Player**: T.M.Head. **2018 Testimonial**: None. **Head Groundsman**: Tim Packwood. **Scorer**: Sue Drinkwater (home) and Philip Mellish (away). ‡ New registration. ^NQ Not qualified for England.

Worcestershire revised their capping policy in 2002 and now award players with their County Colours when they make their Championship debut.

ALI, Moeen Munir (Moseley S), b Birmingham, Warwks 18 Jun 1987. Brother of A.K.Ali (Worcs, Glos and Leics 2000-12), cousin of Kabir Ali (Worcs, Rajasthan, Hants and Lancs 1999-2014). 6'0". LHB, OB. Squad No 8. Warwickshire 2005-06. Worcestershire debut 2007. Moors SC 2011-12. MT 2012-13. MCC 2012. PCA 2013. *Wisden* 2014. **ECB Test & L-O Central Contract 2017-18. Tests**: 49 (2014 to 2017-18); 1000 runs (1): 1078 (2016); HS 155* v SL (Chester-le-St) 2016; BB 6-53 v SA (Lord's) 2017. Hat-trick v SA (Oval) 2017. **LOI**: 73 (2013-14 to 2017-18); HS 128 v Scotland (Christchurch) 2014-15; BB 3-32 v A (Manchester) 2015. **IT20**: 22 (2013-14 to 2016-17); HS 72* v A (Cardiff) 2015; BB 2-21 v I (Kanpur) 2016-17. F-c Tours: A 2017-18; SA 2015-16; WI 2014-15; I 2016-17; SL 2013-14 (EL); B 2016-17; UAE 2015-16 (v P). 1000 runs (2); most – 1420 (2013). HS 250 v Glamorgan (Worcester) 2013. BB 6-29 (12-96 match) v Lancs (Manchester) 2012. LO HS 158 v Sussex (Horsham) 2011 (CB40). LO BB 3-28 v Notts (Nottingham) 2013 (Y40). T20 HS 90. T20 BB 5-34.

BARNARD, Edward George (Shrewsbury S), b Shrewsbury, Shrops 20 Nov 1995. Younger brother of M.R.Barnard (Oxford MCCU 2010). 6'1". RHB, RMF. Squad No 30. Debut (Worcestershire) 2015. Shropshire 2012. England U19 2012-13 to 2014. HS 75 v Durham (Worcester) 2017. BB 4-23 v Glos (Worcester) 2017. LO HS 51 v Somerset (Taunton) 2015 (RLC). LO BB 3-37 v Derbys (Derby) 2017 (RLC). T20 HS 34*. T20 BB 2-18.

BROWN, Patrick Rhys (Bourne GS, Lincs), b Peterborough, Cambs 23 Aug 1998. 6'2". RHB, RM. Squad No 36. Debut (Worcestershire) 2017. Worcestershire 2nd XI debut 2016. Lincolnshire 2016. HS 5* v Sussex (Worcester) 2017. BB 2-15 v Leics (Worcester) 2017. T20 HS 0. T20 BB 1-22.

CLARKE, Joe Michael (Llanfyllin HS), b Shrewsbury, Shrops 26 May 1996. 5'11". RHB, WK. Squad No 33. Debut (Worcestershire) 2015. England Lions 2017. MCC 2017. Worcestershire 2nd XI debut 2013. Shropshire 2012-13. England U19 2014. F-c Tours (EL): WI 2017-18; UAE 2016-17 (v Afghan). 1000 runs (1): 1325 (2016). HS 194 v Derbys (Worcester) 2016. BB –. LO HS 131* v Glos (Worcester) 2015 (RLC). T20 HS 124*.

COX, Oliver Ben (Bromsgrove S), b Wordsley, Stourbridge 2 Feb 1992. 5'10". RHB, WK. Squad No 10. Debut (Worcestershire) 2009. MCC 2017. HS 124 v Glos (Cheltenham) 2017. LO HS 82 v Northants (Northampton) 2017 (RLC). T20 HS 59*.

D'OLIVEIRA, Brett Louis (Worcester SFC), b Worcester 28 Feb 1992. Son of D.B.D'Oliveira (Worcs 1982-95), grandson of B.L.D'Oliveira (Worcs, EP and England 1964-80). 5'9". RHB, LB. Squad No 15. Debut (Worcestershire) 2012. HS 202* v Glamorgan (Cardiff) 2016. BB 5-48 v Durham (Chester-le-St) 2015. LO HS 73* v Durham (Worcester) 2017 (RLC). LO BB 3-35 v Warwks (Worcester) 2013 (Y40). T20 HS 62*. T20 BB 3-20.

FELL, Thomas Charles (Oakham S; Oxford Brookes U), b Hillingdon, Middx 17 Oct 1993. 6'1". RHB, WK, occ OB. Squad No 29. Oxford MCCU 2013. Worcestershire debut 2013. Worcestershire 2nd XI debut 2010. 1000 runs (1): 1127 (2015). HS 171 v Middx (Worcester) 2015. LO HS 116* v Lancs (Worcester) 2016 (RLC).

FINCH, Adam William (Kingswinford S; Oldswinford Hospital SFC), b Wordsley, Stourbridge 28 May 2000. RHB, RMF. Squad No 61. Worcestershire 2nd XI debut 2017. Awaiting 1st XI debut.

HAYNES, Jack Alexander (Malvern C), b Worcester 30 Jan 2001. Son of G.R.Haynes (Worcestershire 1991-99). RHB, OB. Squad No 17. Worcestershire 2nd XI debut 2016. Awaiting 1st XI debut.

‡NOHEAD, Travis Michael, b Adelaide, Australia 29 Dec 1993. 5'9". LHB, OB. Squad No 62. S Australia 2011-12 to date. Yorkshire 2016. Joins Worcestershire in 2018. IPL: RCB 2016-17. Big Bash: AS 2012-13 to date. MCC YC 2013. **LOI** (A): 34 (2016 to 2017/18); HS 128 v P (Adelaide) 2016-17; BB 2-22 v SL (Pallekele) 2016. **IT20** (A): 10 (2015-16 to 2017/18); HS 48* v I (Guwahati) 2017-18; BB 1-16 v SL (Adelaide) 2016-17. F-c Tour (Aus A): I 2015. HS 192 S Aus v Tas (Adelaide) 2015-16. CC HS 54 Y v Warwks (Leeds) 2016. BB 3-42 S Aus v NSW (Adelaide) 2015-16. LO HS 202 S Aus v WA (Sydney) 2015-16. LO BB 2-9 S Aus v NSW (Brisbane) 2014-15. T20 HS 101*. T20 BB 3-16.

HEPBURN, Alex (Aquinas C, Perth), b Subiaco, W Australia 21 Dec 1995. 5'10". RHB, RM. Squad No 26. Worcestershire 2nd XI debut 2013. Awaiting f-c debut. LO HS 32 v Derbys (Derby) 2015 (RLC). LO BB 4-34 v Leics (Worcester) 2015 (RLC). T20 HS 10. T20 BB 5-24 v Notts (Worcester) 2017 – Wo record.

LEACH, Joseph (Shrewsbury S; Leeds U), b Stafford 30 Oct 1990. Elder brother of S.G.Leach (Oxford MCCU 2014-16). 6'1". RHB, RMF. Squad No 23. Leeds/Bradford MCCU 2012. Worcestershire debut 2012; captain 2017 to date. Staffordshire 2008-09. HS 114 v Glos (Cheltenham) 2013. 50 wkts (3); most – 69 (2017). BB 6-73 v Warwks (Birmingham) 2015. LO HS 63 v Yorks (Leeds) 2016 (RLC). LO BB 4-30 v Northants (Worcester) 2015 (RLC). T20 HS 20. T20 BB 5-33.

NOMAGOFFIN, Stephen James (Indooroopilly HS; Curtin U, Perth), b Corinda, Queensland, Australia 17 Dec 1979. 6'4". LHB, RFM. Squad No 64. W Australia 2004-05 to 2010-11. Surrey 2007 (1 game). Worcestershire 2008, returns in 2018. Queensland 2011-12. Sussex 2012-17; cap 2013. HS 79 WA v Tas (Perth) 2008-09. CC HS 51 Sx v Northants (Northampton) 2014. Wo HS 33 v Derbys (Chesterfield) 2008. 50 wkts (5); most – 73 (2015). BB 8-20 (12-31 match) Sx v Somerset (Horsham) 2013. Wo BB 4-49 v Northants (Northampton) 2017. LO HS 24* Wo v Hants (Southampton) 2008 (FPT). LO BB 4-58 Sy v Kent (Oval) 2007 (FPT). T20 HS 11*. T20 BB 2-15.

MILTON, Alexander Geoffrey (Malvern C; Cardiff U), b Redhill, Surrey 19 May 1996. 5'7". RHB, LB, occ WK. Squad No 12. Cardiff MCCU 2016. Awaiting 1st XI debut. Worcestershire 2nd XI debut 2012. Glamorgan 2nd XI 2015. Herefordshire 2016. HS 12 CfU v Hants (Southampton) 2016.

MITCHELL, Daryl Keith Henry (Prince Henry's HS; University C, Worcester), b Badsey, near Evesham 25 Nov 1983. 5'10". RHB, RM. Squad No 27. Debut (Worcestershire) 2005; captain 2011-16; benefit 2016. Mountaineers 2011-12. MCC 2015. 1000 runs (5); most – 1334 (2014). HS 298 v Somerset (Taunton) 2009. BB 4-49 v Yorks (Leeds) 2009. LO HS 107 v Sussex (Hove) 2013 (Y40). LO BB 4-19 v Northants (Milton Keynes) 2014 (RLC). T20 HS 68*. T20 BB 5-28.

MORRIS, Charles Andrew John (King's C, Taunton; Oxford Brookes U), b Hereford 6 Jul 1992. 6'0". RHB, RMF. Squad No 31. Oxford MCCU 2012-14. Worcestershire debut 2013. No 1st XI appearances in 2017. MCC Univs 2012. Devon 2011-12. HS 33* OU v Warwks (Oxford) 2013. Wo HS 25* v Australians (Worcester) 2013. CC HS 24 v Glos (Worcester) 2014 and 24 v Sussex (Hove) 2015. 50 wkts (2); most – 56 (2014). BB 5-54 v Derbys (Derby) 2014. LO HS 16* v Northants (Milton Keynes) 2014 (RLC). LO BB 3-46 v Derbys (Derby) 2015 (RLC). T20 HS 3. T20 BB 2-30.

PENNINGTON, Dillon Young (Wrekin C), b Shrewsbury, Shrops 26 Feb 1999. RHB, RMF. Squad No 22. Worcestershire 2nd XI debut 2017. Shropshire 2017. Awaiting 1st XI debut.

RHODES, George Harry (Chase HS & SFC, Malvern), b Birmingham 26 Oct 1993. Son of S.J.Rhodes (Yorkshire, Worcestershire & England 1981-2004) and grandson of W.E.Rhodes (Nottinghamshire 1961-64). 6'0". RHB, OB. Squad No 34. Debut (Worcestershire) 2016. Worcestershire 2nd XI debut 2012. HS 59 v Essex (Chelmsford) 2016. BB 2-83 v Kent (Canterbury) 2016. LO HS 5* v Lancs (Worcester) 2016 (RLC). LO BB 2-34 v Yorks (Leeds) 2016 (RLC). T20 HS 17*. T20 BB 4-13.

SCRIMSHAW, George Louis Sheridan (John Taylor HS, Burton), b Burton-on-Trent, Staffs 10 Feb 1998. 6'6". RHB, RMF. Squad No 9. Worcestershire 2nd XI debut 2016. Awaiting f-c debut. T20 HS 1*. T20 BB 1-20.

SHANTRY, Jack David (Priory SS; Shrewsbury SFC; Liverpool U), b Shrewsbury, Shrops 29 Jan 1988. Son of B.K.Shantry (Gloucestershire 1978-79), brother of A.J.Shantry (Northants, Warwicks, Glamorgan 2003-11). 6'4". LHB, LM. Squad No 11. Debut (Worcestershire) 2009. Shropshire 2007-09. HS 106 v Glos (Worcester) 2016. 50 wkts (2); most – 67 (2015). BB 7-60 v Oxford MCCU (Oxford) 2013. CC BB 7-69 v Essex (Worcester) 2013. LO HS 31 v Somerset (Taunton) 2015 (RLC). LO BB 4-29 v Northants (Worcester) 2015 (RLC). T20 HS 12*. T20 BB 4-33.

TONGUE, Joshua Charles (King's S, Worcester; Worcester SFC), b Redditch 15 Nov 1997. 6'5". RHB, RM. Squad No 24. Debut (Worcestershire) 2016. Worcestershire 2nd XI debut 2015. HS 41 and BB 6-97 v Glamorgan (Worcester) 2017. LO HS 11* v Surrey (Worcester) 2017 (RLC). LO BB 2-46 v Lancs (Manchester) 2017 (RLC). T20 HS 2*. T20 BB 2-32.

TWOHIG, Benjamin Jake (Malvern C), b Dewsbury, Yorks 13 Apr 1998. 5'9". RHB, SLA. Squad No 42. Worcestershire 2nd XI debut 2014. Awaiting 1st XI debut.

WESTBURY, Oliver Edward (Ellowes Hall Sports C, Dudley; Shrewsbury S), b Dudley, Warwicks 2 Jul 1997. 5'10". RHB, OB. Squad No 19. Worcestershire 2nd XI debut 2015. England U19 2016. Awaiting 1st XI debut.

WHITELEY, Ross Andrew (Repton S), b Sheffield, Yorks 13 Sep 1988. 6'2". LHB, LM. Squad No 44. Derbyshire 2008-13. Worcestershire debut 2013. HS 130* De v Kent (Derby) 2011. Wo HS 101 v Yorks (Scarborough) 2015. BB 2-6 De v Hants (Derby) 2012. Wo BB 1-23 v Hants (Worcester) 2013. LO HS 77 v Yorks (Worcester) 2015 (RLC). LO BB 1-17 De v Unicorns (Wormsley) 2012 (CB40). T20 HS 91*. T20 BB 1-10.

RELEASED/RETIRED

(Having made a County 1st XI appearance in 2017)

NQ**ASHWIN, Ravi**chandran, b Madras, India 17 Sep 1986. RHB, OB. Tamil Nadu 2006-07 to date. Worcestershire 2017. IPL: CSK 2009-15. RPS 2016. **Tests** (I): 57 (2011-12 to 2017-18); HS 124 v WI (Kolkata) 2013-14; 50 wkts (3); most 72 (2016); BB 7-59 (13-140 match) v NZ (Indore) 2016-17. **LOI** (I): 111 (2010 to 2017); HS 65 v NZ (Auckland) 2013-14; BB 4-25 v UAE (Perth) 2014-15. **IT20** (I): 46 (2010 to 2017); HS 31* v SL (Pune) 2015-16; BB 4-8 v SL (Visakhapatnam) 2015-16. F-c Tours (I): E 2014; A 2011-12, 2014-15; SA 2013-14, 2017-18; WI 2016; SL 2007-08 (TN), 2015, 2017; B 2015. HS 124 (*see Tests*). Wo HS 82 v Durham (Worcester) 2017. 50 wkts (0+1): 82 (2016-17). BB 7-59 (*see Tests*). Wo BB 5-68 v Glos (Worcester) 2017. LO HS 79 South Zone v Central Zone (Vadodara) 2009-10. LO BB 4-25 (*see LOI*). T20 HS 46. T20 BB 4-8.

NQ**HASTINGS, John** Wayne (St Dominic's Catholic C, Sydney; Australian C of PE), b Penrith, NSW, Australia 4 Nov 1985. 6'6". RHB, RFM. Victoria 2007-08 to date. Durham 2014-15. Worcestershire 2017. IPL: CSK 2014. KKR 2016. Big Bash: MS 2012-13 to date. **Tests** (A): 1 (2012-13); HS 32 and BB 1-51 v SA (Perth) 2012-13. **LOI** (A): 29 (2010-11 to 2017); HS 51 v SA (Centurion) 2016-17. BB 6-45 v SL (Dambulla) 2016. **IT20** (A): 9 (2010-11 to 2016); HS 15 v SL (Perth) 2010-11; BB 3-14 v SL (Pallekele) 2011. HS 93 Vic v Tas (Hobart) 2008-09. CC HS 91 Du v Sussex (Arundel) 2015. Wo HS 51 v Glamorgan (Cardiff) 2017. BB 7-60 Du v Worcs (Worcester) 2015. BB 3-44 v Durham (Chester-le-St) 2017. LO HS 69* Vic v S Australia (Adelaide) 2012-13. LO BB 6-45 (*see LOI*). T20 HS 80*. T20 BB 4-26.

KOHLER-CADMORE, T. – *see YORKSHIRE.*

NQ**LYON, Nathan** Michael, b Young, NSW, Australia 20 Nov 1987. RHB, OB. S Australia 2010-11 to 2012-13. New South Wales 2013-14 to date. Big Bash: AS 2011-12 to 2012-13. SS 2013-14 to date. Worcestershire 2017. **Tests** (A): 76 (2011 to 2017-18); HS 40* v WI (Bridgetown) 2011-12; 50 wkts (1): 63 (2017); BB 8-50 v I (Bangalore) 2016-17. **LOI** (A): 13 (2011-12 to 2016); HS 30 v SA (Providence) 2016; BB 4-44 v Z (Harare) 2014. **IT20** (A): 1 (2015-16); BB –. F-c Tours (A): E 2012 (Aus A), 2013, 2015; SA 2011-12, 2013-14, 2017-18; WI 2011-12, 2015; NZ 2015-16; I 2012-13, 2016-17; SL 2011, 2016; B 2017; UAE (v P) 2014-15. HS 75 NSW v Vic (Alice Springs) 2015-16. Wo HS 6* v Glamorgan (Worcester) 2017. BB 8-50 (*see Tests*). Wo BB 3-94 v Northants (Northampton) 2017. LO HS 37* S Aus v WA (Adelaide) 2011-12. LO BB 4-10 NSW v Q (Sydney) 2016-17. T20 HS 11. T20 BB 5-23.

NQ**SANTNER, Mitchell** Josef, b Hamilton, New Zealand 5 Feb 1992. LHB, SLA. N Districts 2011-12 to date. Worcestershire 2016; 2017 (T20 only). **Tests** (NZ): 17 (2015-16 to 2017-18); HS 73 v B (Wellington) 2016-17; BB 3-60 v I (Kolkata) 2016-17. **LOI** (NZ): 53 (2015 to 2017-18); HS 67 v E (Christchurch) 2017-18; BB 5-50 v Ire (Dublin) 2017. **IT20** (NZ): 27 (2015 to 2017-18); HS 37 v P (Auckland) 2017-18; BB 4-11 v I (Nagpur) 2015-16. F-c Tours (NZ): E 2015; A 2015-16; SA 2016; I 2016-17; Z 2016. HS 118 ND v Canterbury (Gisborne) 2013-14. Wo HS 23* v Glamorgan (Cardiff) 2016. BB 3-51 ND v Auckland (Whangarei) 2014-15. LO HS 86 ND v CD (New Plymouth) 2014-15. LO BB 5-50 (*see LOI*). T20 HS 45*. T20 BB 4-11.

A.N.Kervezee left the staff without making a County 1st XI appearance in 2017.

WORCESTERSHIRE 2017

RESULTS SUMMARY

	Place	Won	Lost	Tied	Drew	NR
Specsavers County Champ (2nd Division)	1st	9	3		2	
All First-Class Matches		9	3		2	
Royal London One-Day Cup (North Group)	SF	6	2	1		
NatWest t20 Blast (North Group)	8th	3	10			1

SPECSAVERS COUNTY CHAMPIONSHIP AVERAGES

BATTING AND FIELDING

Cap†		M	I	NO	HS	Runs	Avge	100	50	Ct/St
2005	D.K.H.Mitchell	14	26	3	161	1266	55.04	7	3	21
2014	T.Kohler-Cadmore	4	5	–	102	242	48.40	1	1	4
2015	J.M.Clarke	14	26	5	142	920	43.80	2	3	9
2017	R.Ashwin	4	6	1	82	214	42.80	–	1	2
2008	M.M.Ali	3	5	–	63	208	41.60	–	3	2
2015	E.G.Barnard	14	20	4	75	580	36.25	–	5	8
2012	B.L.D'Oliveira	14	25	–	150	891	35.64	3	3	10
2009	O.B.Cox	14	21	1	124	675	33.75	1	3	42/1
2016	G.H.Rhodes	8	15	2	52	379	29.15	–	2	5
2009	J.D.Shantry	6	8	4	30*	94	23.50	–	–	3
2013	R.A.Whiteley	5	9	1	53	170	21.25	–	1	6
2012	J.Leach	14	19	2	57*	347	20.41	–	2	7
2017	J.W.Hastings	6	8	1	51	139	19.85	–	1	5
2013	T.C.Fell	13	23	1	47	323	14.68	–	–	7
2017	J.C.Tongue	14	18	3	41	138	9.20	–	–	2
2017	N.M.Lyon	4	5	3	6*	15	7.50	–	–	2
2017	P.R.Brown	4	5	3	5*	12	6.00	–	–	1

BOWLING

	O	M	R	W	Avge	Best	5wI	10wM
J.Leach	397.5	73	1338	69	19.39	5-32	4	1
E.G.Barnard	321.3	48	1187	47	25.25	4-23	–	–
J.C.Tongue	333.4	46	1212	47	25.78	6-97	2	–
J.D.Shantry	100.3	19	310	11	28.18	3-54	–	–
R.Ashwin	184.2	29	583	20	29.15	5-68	2	–
J.W.Hastings	161.1	41	550	16	34.37	3-44	–	–

Also bowled:

	O	M	R	W	Avge	Best		
P.R.Brown	42.4	4	199	6	33.16	2-15		
N.M.Lyon	131.4	21	403	6	67.16	3-94		

M.M.Ali 41-4-166-3; B.L.D'Oliveira 60-0-271-0; D.K.H.Mitchell 7.4-0-37-1; G.H.Rhodes 38-7-202-3; R.A.Whiteley 2-0-20-0.

Worcestershire played no first-class fixtures outside the County Championship in 2017. The First-Class Averages (pp 230–246) give the records of Worcestershire players in all first-class county matches, with the exception of M.M.Ali, J.M.Clarke and T.Kohler-Cadmore, whose first-class figures for Worcestershire are as above.

† Worcestershire revised their capping policy in 2002 and now award players with their County Colours when they make their Championship debut.

WORCESTERSHIRE RECORDS

FIRST-CLASS CRICKET

Highest Total	For 701-6d		v	Surrey	Worcester	2007
	V 701-4d		by	Leics	Worcester	1906
Lowest Total	For 24		v	Yorkshire	Huddersfield	1903
	V 30		by	Hampshire	Worcester	1903
Highest Innings	For 405*	G.A.Hick	v	Somerset	Taunton	1988
	V 331*	J.D.B.Robertson	for	Middlesex	Worcester	1949

Highest Partnership for each Wicket

1st	309	H.K.Foster/F.L.Bowley	v	Derbyshire	Derby	1901
2nd	316	S.C.Moore/V.S.Solanki	v	Glos	Cheltenham	2008
3rd	438*	G.A.Hick/T.M.Moody	v	Hampshire	Southampton	1997
4th	330	B.F.Smith/G.A.Hick	v	Somerset	Taunton	2006
5th	393	E.G.Arnold/W.B.Burns	v	Warwicks	Birmingham	1909
6th	265	G.A.Hick/S.J.Rhodes	v	Somerset	Taunton	1988
7th	256	D.A.Leatherdale/S.J.Rhodes	v	Notts	Nottingham	2002
8th	184	S.J.Rhodes/S.R.Lampitt	v	Derbyshire	Kidderminster	1991
9th	181	J.A.Cuffe/R.D.Burrows	v	Glos	Worcester	1907
10th	119	W.B.Burns/G.A.Wilson	v	Somerset	Worcester	1906

Best Bowling	For 9- 23	C.F.Root	v	Lancashire	Worcester	1931
(Innings)	V 10- 51	J.Mercer	for	Glamorgan	Worcester	1936
Best Bowling	For 15- 87	A.J.Conway	v	Glos	Moreton-in-M	1914
(Match)	V 17-212	J.C.Clay	for	Glamorgan	Swansea	1937

Most Runs – Season	2654	H.H.I.H.Gibbons	(av 52.03)	1934
Most Runs – Career	34490	D.Kenyon	(av 34.18)	1946-67
Most 100s – Season	10	G.M.Turner		1970
	10	G.A.Hick		1988
Most 100s – Career	106	G.A.Hick		1984-2008
Most Wkts – Season	207	C.F.Root	(av 17.52)	1925
Most Wkts – Career	2143	R.T.D.Perks	(av 23.73)	1930-55
Most Career W-K Dismissals	1095	S.J.Rhodes	(991 ct; 104 st)	1985-2004
Most Career Catches in the Field	528	G.A.Hick		1984-2008

LIMITED-OVERS CRICKET

Highest Total	50ov	404-3		v	Devon	Worcester	1987
	40ov	376-6		v	Surrey	Oval	2010
	T20	227-6		v	Northants	Kidderminster	2007
Lowest Total	50ov	58		v	Ireland	Worcester	2009
	40ov	86		v	Yorkshire	Leeds	1969
	T20	53		v	Lancashire	Manchester	2016
Highest Innings	50ov	180*	T.M.Moody	v	Surrey	The Oval	1994
	40ov	160	T.M.Moody	v	Kent	Worcester	1991
	T20	127	T.Kohler-Cadmore	v	Durham	Worcester	2004
Best Bowling	50ov	7-19	N.V.Radford	v	Beds	Bedford	1991
	40ov	6-16	Shoaib Akhtar	v	Glos	Worcester	2005
	T20	5-24	A.Hepburn	v	Notts	Worcester	2017

YORKSHIRE

Formation of Present Club: 8 January 1863
Substantial Reorganisation: 10 December 1891
Inaugural First-Class Match: 1864
Colours: Dark Blue, Light Blue and Gold
Badge: White Rose
County Championships (since 1890): (32) 1893, 1896, 1898, 1900, 1901, 1902, 1905, 1908, 1912, 1919, 1922, 1923, 1924, 1925, 1931, 1932, 1933, 1935, 1937, 1938, 1939, 1946, 1959, 1960, 1962, 1963, 1966, 1967, 1968, 2001, 2014, 2015
Joint Champions: (1) 1949
Gillette/C&G Trophy Winners: (3) 1965, 1969, 2002
Benson and Hedges Cup Winners: (1) 1987
Sunday League Winners: (1) 1983
Twenty20 Cup Winners: (0); best – Finalist 2012

Chief Executive: Mark Arthur, Emerald Headingley, Kirkstall Lane, Headingley, Leeds, LS6 3DP • Tel: 0843 504 3099 • Email: cricket@yorkshireccc.com • Web: www.yorkshireccc.com • Twitter: @Yorkshireccc (106,934 followers)

Director of Cricket: Martyn Moxon. **1st XI Coach**: Andrew Gale. **Bowling Coach**: Richard Pyrah. **Captain**: G.S.Ballance. **Vice-Captain**: T.T.Bresnan. **Overseas Players**: C.A.Pujara, B.Stanlake (T20 only) and K.S.Williamson. **2018 Testimonial**: A.U.Rashid. **Head Groundsman**: Andy Fogarty. **Scorer**: John Potter. ‡ New registration. [NQ] Not qualified for England.

AZEEM Muhammad **RAFIQ** (Holgate S Sports C; Barnsley C), b Karachi, Pakistan 27 Feb 1991. 5'11". RHB, OB. Squad No 30. Yorkshire debut 2009; cap 2016. Derbyshire (on loan) 2011. HS 100 v Worcs (Worcester) 2009. BB 5-50 v Essex (Chelmsford) 2012. LO HS 52* v Leics (Leeds) 2017 (RLC). LO BB 5-30 v Bangladesh A (Leeds) 2013. T20 HS 21*. T20 BB 5-19.

BAIRSTOW, Jonathan Marc (St Peter's S, York; Leeds Met U), b Bradford 26 Sep 1989. Son of D.L.Bairstow (Yorkshire, GW and England 1970-90); brother of A.D.Bairstow (Derbyshire 1995). 6'0". RHB, WK, occ RM. Squad No 21. Debut (Yorkshire) 2009; cap 2011. Inaugural winner of Young Wisden Schools Cricketer of the Year 2008. YC 2011. **ECB Test & L-O Central Contract 2017-18. Tests**: 50 (2012 to 2017-18); 1000 runs (1): 1470 (2016); HS 167* v SL (Lord's) 2016. Took a world record 70 dismissals in 2016, as well as scoring a record number of runs in a calendar year for a keeper. **LOI**: 42 (2011 to 2017-18); HS 141* v WI (Southampton) 2017. **IT20**: 23 (2011 to 2017); HS 60* v P (Dubai) 2011-12 and 60* v SA (Southampton) 2017. F-c Tours: A 2013-14, 2017-18; SA 2014-15 (EL), 2015-16; WI 2010-11 (EL); I 2012-13, 2016-17; SL 2013-14 (EL); B 2016-17; UAE 2015-16 (v P). 1000 runs (3); most – 1286 (2016). HS 246 v Hants (Leeds) 2016. LO HS 174 v Durham (Leeds) 2017 (RLC). T20 HS 102*.

BALLANCE, Gary Simon (Peterhouse S, Marondera, Zimbabwe; Harrow S; Leeds Met U), b Harare, Zimbabwe 22 Nov 1989. Nephew of G.S.Ballance (Rhodesia B 1978-79) and D.L.Houghton (Rhodesia/Zimbabwe 1978-79 to 1997-98). 6'0". LHB, LB. Squad No 19. Debut (Yorkshire) 2008; cap 2012; captain 2017 to date. MWR 2010-11 to 2011-12. England Lions 2017. *Wisden* 2014. **Tests**: 23 (2013-14 to 2017); HS 156 v I (Southampton) 2014; BB –. **LOI**: 16 (2013 to 2014-15); HS 79 v A (Melbourne) 2013-14. F-c Tours: A 2013-14; WI 2014-15; B 2016-17. 1000 runs (2+1); most – 1363 (2013). HS 210 MWR v SR (Masvingo) 2011-12. Y HS 203* v Hants (Southampton) 2017. BB –. LO HS 152* v Northants (Northampton) 2013 (RLC). T20 HS 68.

BRESNAN, Timothy Thomas (Castleford HS and TC; Pontefract New C), b Pontefract 28 Feb 1985. 6'0". RHB, RFM. Squad No 16. Debut (Yorkshire) 2003; cap 2006; benefit 2014. MCC 2006, 2009. Big Bash: HH 2014-15. PS 2016-17 to date. *Wisden* 2011. **Tests**: 23 (2009 to 2013-14); HS 91 v B (Dhaka) 2009-10; BB 5-48 v I (Nottingham) 2011. **LOI**: 85 (2006 to 2015); HS 80 v SA (Centurion) 2009-10; BB 5-48 v I (Bangalore) 2010-11. **IT20**: 34 (2006 to 2013-14); HS 47* v WI (Bridgetown) 2013-14; BB 3-10 v P (Cardiff) 2010. F-c Tours: A 2010-11, 2013-14; I 2012-13; SL 2011-12; B 2006-07 (Eng A), 2009-10. HS 169* v Durham (Chester-le-St) 2015, sharing Y record 7th wkt partnership of 366* with J.M.Bairstow. BB 5-36 v Notts (Scarborough) 2016. LO HS 95* v Notts (Scarborough) 2016 (RLC). BB 5-48 (*see LOI*). T20 HS 51. T20 BB 6-19 v Lancs (Leeds) 2017 – Y record.

BROOK, Harry Cherrington (Sedbergh S), b Keighley 22 Feb 1999. 5'11". RHB, RM. Squad No 88. Debut (Yorkshire) 2016. Yorkshire 2nd XI debut 2015. England U19 2016-17 to 2017. HS 38 v Middx (Lord's) 2017. BB 1-54 v Somerset (Scarborough) 2017. LO HS –.

BROOKS, Jack Alexander (Wheatley Park S), b Oxford 4 Jun 1984. 6'2". RHB, RFM. Squad No 70. Northamptonshire 2009-12; cap 2012. Yorkshire debut 2013; cap 2013. Oxfordshire 2004-09. F-c Tour (EL): SA 2014-15. HS 109* v Lancs (Manchester) 2017. 50 wkts (3); most – 71 (2014). BB 6-65 v Middx (Lord's) 2016. LO HS 10 Nh v Middx (Uxbridge) 2009 (P40). LO BB 3-30 v Hants (Southampton) 2014 (RLC). T20 HS 33*. T20 BB 5-21.

CARVER, Karl (Thirsk S & SFC), b Northallerton 26 Mar 1996. 5'10". LHB, SLA. Squad No 29. Debut (Yorkshire) 2014. Yorkshire 2nd XI debut 2013. HS 20 v Somerset (Taunton) 2017. BB 4-106 v MCC (Abu Dhabi) 2015-16. CC BB 2-10 v Essex (Chelmsford) 2017. LO HS 35* v Somerset (Scarborough) 2015 (RLC). LO BB 3-5 v Lancs (Manchester) 2016 (RLC). T20 HS 2. T20 BB 3-40.

COAD, Benjamin Oliver (Thirsk S & SFC), b Harrogate 10 Jan 1994. 6'2". RHB, RM. Squad No 10. Debut (Yorkshire) 2016. Yorkshire 2nd XI debut 2012. HS 28 v Essex (Scarborough) 2017. 50 wkts (1): 53 (2017). BB 6-25 v Lancs (Leeds) 2017. LO HS 2* v Sri Lanka A (Leeds) 2014. LO BB 1-34 v Glos (Bristol) 2013 (Y40). T20 HS 2*. T20 BB 2-24.

FISHER, Matthew David (Easingwold SS), b York 9 Nov 1997. 6'1". RHB, RFM. Squad No 7. Debut (Yorkshire) 2015. Yorkshire 2nd XI debut 2013, aged 15y 201d. England U19 2014. Missed almost all of 2016 season through injury. HS 37 and BB 5-54 v Warwks (Leeds) 2017. LO HS 36* v Worcs (Worcester) 2017 (RLC). LO BB 3-32 v Leics (Leeds) 2015 (RLC). T20 HS 6*. T20 BB 5-22.

HODD, Andrew John (Bexhill C; Loughborough U), b Chichester, Sussex 12 Jan 1984. 5'9". RHB, WK. Squad No 4. Sussex 2003-11. Surrey 2005 (1 match). Yorkshire debut 2012 (on loan); cap 2016. HS 123 Sx v Yorks (Hove) 2007. Y HS 96* v Notts (Scarborough) 2016. LO HS 91 Sx v Lancs (Hove) 2010 (CB40). T20 HS 70.

KOHLER-CADMORE, Tom (Malvern C), b Chatham, Kent 19 Aug 1994. 6'2". RHB, OB. Squad No 32. Worcestershire 2014-17. Yorkshire debut 2017. Worcestershire 2nd XI debut 2010, aged 15y 342d. HS 169 Wo v Glos (Worcester) 2016. Y HS 78 v Surrey (Oval) 2017. LO HS 119 Wo v Northants (Worcester) 2016 (RLC). T20 HS 127 Wo v Durham (Worcester) 2016 – Wo record, winning Walter Lawrence Trophy for fastest 100 (43 balls).

LEANING, Jack Andrew (Archbishop Holgate's S, York; York C), b Bristol, Glos 18 Oct 1993. 5'10". RHB, RMF. Squad No 34. Debut (Yorkshire) 2013; cap 2016. Yorkshire 2nd XI debut 2011. YC 2015. HS 123 v Somerset (Taunton) 2014. BB 1-82 v Notts (Nottingham) 2015. LO HS 131* v Leics (Leicester) 2016 (RLC). LO BB 5-22 v Unicorns (Leeds) 2013 (Y40). T20 HS 64. T20 BB –.

LEES, Alexander Zak (Holy Trinity SS, Halifax), b Halifax 14 Apr 1993. 6'3''. LHB, LB. Squad No 14. Debut (Yorkshire) 2010; cap 2014; captain (l-o) 2016. MCC 2017. YC 2014. 1000 runs (2); most – 1199 (2016). HS 275* v Derbys (Chesterfield) 2013. BB 2-51 v Middx (Lord's) 2016. LO HS 102 v Northants (Northampton) 2014 (RLC). T20 HS 67*.

LYTH, Adam (Caedmon S, Whitby; Whitby Community C), b Whitby 25 Sep 1987. 5'8''. LHB, RM. Squad No 9. Debut (Yorkshire) 2007; cap 2010. MCC 2017. PCA 2014. *Wisden* 2014. **Tests**: 7 (2015); HS 107 v NZ (Leeds) 2015. F-c Tours (EL): SA 2014-15; WI 2010-11. 1000 runs (3); most – 1619 (2014). HS 251 v Lancs (Manchester) 2014, sharing in Y record 6th wicket partnership of 296 with A.U.Rashid. BB 2-9 v Middx (Scarborough) 2016. LO HS 136 v Lancs (Manchester) 2016 (RLC). LO BB 1-6 v Middx (Leeds) 2013 (Y40). T20 HS 161 v Northants (Leeds) 2017 – Y & UK record; 3rd highest score in all T20 cricket. T20 BB 2-5.

PATTERSON, Steven Andrew (Malet Lambert CS; St Mary's SFC, Hull; Leeds U), b Hull 3 Oct 1983. 6'4''. RHB, RMF. Squad No 17. Debut (Yorkshire) 2005; cap 2012; testimonial 2017. Bradford/Leeds UCCE 2003 (not f-c). HS 63* v Warwks (Birmingham) 2016. 50 wkts (2); most – 53 (2012). BB 6-56 v Durham (Chester-le-St) 2016. LO HS 25* v Worcs (Leeds) 2006 (P40). LO BB 6-32 v Derbys (Leeds) 2010. T20 HS 3*. T20 BB 4-30.

PLUNKETT, Liam Edward (Nunthorpe SS; Teesside Tertiary C), b Middlesbrough, Yorks 6 Apr 1985. 6'3''. RHB, RFM. Squad No 28. Durham 2003-12. Dolphins 2007-08. Yorkshire debut 2013; cap 2013. England Lions 2017. **ECB L-O Central Contract 2017-18. Tests**: 13 (2005-06 to 2014); HS 55* v I (Lord's) 2014; BB 5-64 v SL (Leeds) 2014. **LOI**: 65 (2005-06 to 2017-18); HS 56 v P (Lahore) 2005-06; BB 5-52 v WI (Bristol) 2017. **IT20**: 15 (2006 to 2017-18); HS 18 v WI (Chester-le-St) 2017; BB 3-21 v P (Dubai, DSC) 2015-16. F-c Tours (EL): SA 2014-15; WI 2010-11; NZ 2008-09; I 2005-06 (E), 2007-08; P 2005-06 (E); SL 2013-14. HS 126 v Hants (Leeds) 2016. 50 wkts (2); most – 60 (2009). BB 6-33 v Leeds/Bradford MCCU (Leeds) 2013 on Y debut. CC BB 6-63 (11-119 match) Du v Worcs (Chester-le-St) 2009. LO HS 72 Du v Somerset (Chester-le-St) 2008 (P40). LO BB 5-52 (*see LOI*). T20 HS 41. T20 BB 5-31.

NQPUJARA, Cheteshwar Arvindbhai, b Rajkot, India 25 Jan 1988. RHB, LB. Squad No 27. Son of A.S.Pujara (Saurashtra 1976-77 to 1979-80), nephew of B.S.Pujara (Saurashtra 1983-84 to 1996-97). Saurashtra 2005-06 to date. Derbyshire 2014. Yorkshire debut 2015. Nottinghamshire 2017; cap 2017. IPL: KKR 2009-10. RCB 2011-13. KXIP 2014. **Tests** (I): 57 (2010-11 to 2017-18); 1000 runs (1): 1140 (2017); HS 206* v E (Ahmedabad) 2012-13. **LOI**: 5 (2013 to 2014); HS 27 v B (Dhaka) 2014. F-c Tours (I): E 2010 (I A), 2014; A 2006 (I A), 2014-15; SA 2010-11, 2013 (I A), 2013-14, 2017-18; WI 2012 (I A), 2016; NZ 2013-14; SL 2015, 2017; Z/Ken 2007-08 (I A). 1000 runs (0+3); most – 2064 (2016-17). HS 352 Saur v Karnataka (Rajkot) 2012-13. Y HS 133* v Hants (Leeds) 2015. BB 2-4 Saur v Rajasthan (Jaipur) 2007-08. LO HS 158* Ind B v India A (Rajkot) 2012-13. T20 HS 81.

RASHID, Adil Usman (Belle Vue S, Bradford), b Bradford 17 Feb 1988. 5'8''. RHB, LBG. Squad No 3. Debut (Yorkshire) 2006; cap 2008; testimonial 2018; signed white-ball-only contract in 2018. MCC 2007-09. Big Bash: AS 2015-16. YC 2007. Match double (114, 48, 8-157 and 2-45) for England U19 v India U19 (Taunton) 2006. **ECB L-O Central Contract 2017-18. Tests**: 10 (2015-16 to 2016-17); HS 61 v P (Dubai, DSC) 2015-16; BB 5-64 v P (Abu Dhabi) 2015-16 – on debut. **LOI**: 64 (2009 to 2017-18); HS 69 v NZ (Birmingham) 2015; BB 5-27 v Ireland (Bristol) 2017. **IT20**: 20 (2009 to 2017-18); HS 9* v SA (Nottingham) 2009; BB 3-25 v WI (Chester-le-St) 2017. F-c Tours: WI 2010-11 (EL); I 2007-08 (EL), 2016-17; B 2006-07 (Eng A), 2016-17; UAE 2015-16 (v P). HS 180 v Somerset (Leeds) 2013. 50 wkts (2); most – 65 (2008). BB 7-107 v Hants (Southampton) 2008. LO HS 71 v Glos (Leeds) 2014 (RLC). LO BB 5-27 (*see LOI*). T20 HS 36*. T20 BB 4-19.

ROOT, Joseph Edward (King Ecgbert S, Sheffield; Worksop C), b Sheffield 30 Dec 1990. Elder brother of W.T.Root (*see NOTTINGHAMSHIRE*). 6'0". RHB, OB. Squad No 5. Debut (Yorkshire) 2010; cap 2012. YC 2012. **ECB Test & L-O Central Contract 2017-18. Tests**: 65 (2012-13 to 2017-18, 12 as captain); 1000 runs (2); most – 1477 (2016); HS 254 v P (Manchester) 2016. **LOI**: 107 (2012-13 to 2017-18); HS 133* v B (Oval) 2013; BB 3-52 v Ireland (Lord's) 2017. **IT20**: 25 (2012-13 to 2017); HS 90* v A (Southampton) 2013; BB 2-9 v WI (Kolkata) 2015-16. F-c Tours(C=Captain): A 2013-14, 2017-18C; SA 2015-16; WI 2014-15; NZ 2012-13; I 2012-13, 2016-17; B 2016-17; UAE 2015-16 (v P). 1000 runs (3); most – 1228 (2013). HS 254 (*see Tests*). CC HS 236 v Derbys (Leeds) 2013. BB 3-33 v Warwks (Leeds) 2011. LO HS 133* (*see LOI*). LO BB 3-52 (*see LOI*). T20 HS 92*. T20 BB 2-9.

SHAW, Joshua (Crofton HS, Wakefield; Skills Exchange C), b Wakefield, Yorks 3 Jan 1996. Son of C.Shaw (Yorkshire 1984-88). 6'1". RHB, RMF. Squad No 25. Gloucestershire 2016-17 (on loan); cap 2016. Yorkshire debut 2016. Yorkshire 2nd XI debut 2012. England U19 2012-13 to 2014. HS 29 Gs v Leics (Cheltenham) 2016. Y HS 24 v Durham (Chester-le-St) 2016. BB 5-79 Gs v Sussex (Bristol) 2016. Y BB 3-58 v Pakistan A (Leeds) 2016. T20 HS 1. T20 BB –.

‡[NO]**STANLAKE, Billy**, b Hervey Bay, Queensland, Australia 4 Nov 1994. RHB, RFM. Queensland 2015-16. Joins Yorkshire in 2018 (T20 only). IPL: RCB 2017. Big Bash: AS 2015-16 to date. **LOI** (A): 2 (2016-17); HS 1* v P (Brisbane) 2016-17; BB 1-55 v P (Perth) 2016-17. **IT20** (A): 6 (2016-17 to 2017-18); HS – ; BB 3-15 v NZ (Sydney) 2017-18. HS 1* and BB 3-50 Q v S Aus (Brisbane) 2015-16. LO HS 1* (*see LOI*). LO BB 4-37 Q v WA (Sydney, DO) 2015-16. T20 HS 4*. T20 BB 3-15.

TATTERSALL, Jonathan Andrew (King James S, Knaresborough), b Harrogate 15 Dec 1994. 5'8". RHB, LB. Squad No 12. Yorkshire 2nd XI debut 2012. Awaiting f-c debut. No 1st XI appearances 2014-16. England U19s 2012-13 to 2014. LO HS 0.

THOMPSON, Jordan Aaron (Benton Park S), b Leeds 9 Oct 1996. 5'11". LHB, RM. Squad No 44. Yorkshire 2nd XI debut 2014. Awaiting 1st XI debut.

WAINMAN, James Charles (Leeds GS), b Harrogate 25 Jan 1993. 6'4". RHB, LMF. Squad No 15. Awaiting f-c debut. No 1st XI appearances in 2017. LO HS 33 and LO BB 3-51 v Sri Lanka A (Leeds) 2014. T20 HS 12*. T20 BB 1-27.

WAITE, Matthew James (Brigshaw HS), b Leeds 24 Dec 1995. 6'0". RHB, RFM. Squad No 6. Debut (Yorkshire) 2017. Yorkshire 2nd XI debut 2014. HS 18 and BB 2-41 v Somerset (Taunton) 2017. LO HS 71 v Warwks (Birmingham) 2017 (RLC). LO BB 4-65 v Worcs (Worcester) 2017 (RLC). T20 HS 19*. T20 BB 1-6.

WARNER, Jared David (Kettleborough Park HS; Silcoates SFC), b Wakefield 14 Nov 1996. 6'1". RHB, RFM. Squad No 45. Yorkshire 2nd XI debut 2015. England U19 2014-15 to 2015. Awaiting 1st XI debut.

WILLEY, David Jonathan (Northampton S), b Northampton 28 Feb 1990. Son of P.Willey (Northants, Leics and England 1966-91). 6'1". LHB, LMF. Squad No 72. Northamptonshire 2009-15; cap 2013. Yorkshire debut/cap 2016. Bedfordshire 2008. Big Bash: PS 2015-16 to date. **ECB L-O Central Contract 2017-18. LOI**: 34 (2015 to 2017-18); HS 26 v SA (Lord's) 2017; BB 4-34 v SL (Cardiff) 2016. **IT20**: 20 (2015 to 2017-18); HS 21 v NZ (Wellington) 2017-18; HS 21 and BB 3-20 v WI (Kolkata) 2015-16. HS 104* Nh v Glos (Northampton) 2015. Y HS 22 v Middx (Lord's) 2016. BB 5-29 (10-75 match) Nh v Glos (Northampton) 2011. Y BB 3-55 v Surrey (Leeds) 2016. LO HS 167 Nh v Warwks (Birmingham) 2013 (Y40). LO BB 5-62 EL v New Zealand A (Bristol) 2014. T20 HS 118. T20 BB 4-9.

NOWILLIAMSON, Kane Stuart (Tauranga Boys' C), b Tauranga, New Zealand 8 Aug 1990. Cousin of D.Cleaver (C Districts 2010-11 to date). 5'8". RHB, OB. Squad No 8. N Districts 2007-08 to date. Gloucestershire 2011-12; cap 2011. Yorkshire debut 2013. IPL: SH 2015-17. **Tests** (NZ): 63 (2010-11 to 2017-18, 15 as captain); 1000 runs (1): 1172 (2015); HS 242* v SL (Wellington) 2014-15; scored 131 v I (Ahmedabad) 2010-11 on debut; BB 4-44 v E (Auckland) 2012-13. **LOI** (NZ): 127 (2010 to 2017-18, 53 as captain); 1000 runs (1): 1376 (2015); HS 145* v SA (Kimberley) 2012-13; BB 4-22 v SA (Paarl) 2012-13. **IT20** (NZ): 51 (2011-12 to 2017-18, 33 as captain); HS 73* v B (Napier) 2016-17; BB 2-16 v B (Mt Maunganui) 2016-17. F-c Tours (NZ)(C=Captain): E 2013, 2015; A 2011-12, 2015-16; SA 2012-13, 2016C; WI 2012, 2014; I 2010-11, 2012, 2016-17C; SL 2012-13; Z 2011-12, 2016C; B 2013-14; UAE 2014-15 (v P). HS 284* ND v Wellington (Lincoln) 2011-12. Y HS 189 v Sussex (Scarborough) 2014. BB 5-75 ND v Canterbury (Christchurch) 2008-09. CC BB 3-58 Gs v Northants (Northampton) 2012. Y BB 2-44 v Sussex (Hove) 2013. LO HS 145* (see LOI). LO BB 5-51 ND v Auckland (Auckland) 2009-10. T20 HS 101*. T20 BB 3-33.

RELEASED/RETIRED

(Having made a County 1st XI appearance in 2017)

NOBRATHWAITE, Kraigg Clairmonte (Combermere S), b Belfield, St Michael, Barbados 1 Dec 1992. RHB, OB. Barbados 2008-08 to date. Sagicor High Performance Centre 2014. Yorkshire 2017. **Tests** (WI): 44 (2011 to 2017-18); HS 212 v B (Kingstown) 2014; BB 6-29 v SL (Colombo, PSS) 2015-16. **LOI** (WI): 10 (2016-17); HS 78 v Z (Bulawayo) 2016-17; BB 1-56 v SL (Bulawayo) 2016-17. F-c Tours (WI): E 2010 (WI A), 2017; A 2015-16; SA 2014-15; NZ 2013-14, 2017-18; I 2011-12, 2013-14 (WI A); SL 2014-15 (WI A), 2015-16; Z 2017-18; B 2011-12; UAE (v P) 2016-17. HS 212 (see Tests). BB 6-29 (see Tests). LO HS 108 Barb v ICC Americas (Lucas Street) 2016-17. LO BB 2-54 WI A v Sri Lanka A (Dambulla) 2014-15.

CALLIS, Elliot (Worksop C), b Doncaster 8 Nov 1994. 6'2". RHB, LB. Yorkshire 2016-17. Yorkshire 2nd XI debut 2013. Bedfordshire 2015. HS 84 v Pakistan A (Leeds) 2016. LO HS 10 v Sri Lanka A (Leeds) 2014.

GIBSON, Ryan (Fylinghall S), b Middlesbrough 22 Jan 1996. 6'4". RHB, RM. Squad No 24. Yorkshire 2016. Yorkshire 2nd XI debut 2012. HS 0 and BB 1-42 v Pakistan A (Leeds) 2016. LO HS 9 v Sri Lanka A (Leeds) 2014. LO BB 1-17 v Bangladesh A (Leeds) 2013. T20 HS 18. T20 BB –.

NOHANDSCOMB, Peter Stephen Patrick (Mt Waverley SC; Deakin U, Melbourne), b Melbourne, Australia 26 Apr 1991. RHB, WK. British passport (English parents). Victoria 2011-12 to date. Gloucestershire 2015; cap 2015. Yorkshire 2017. IPL: RPS 2016. Big Bash: MS 2012-13 to date. **Tests** (A): 12 (2016-17 to 2017-18); HS 110 v P (Sydney) 2016-17. **LOI** (A): 8 (2016-17 to 2017-18); HS 82 v P (Perth) 2016-17. F-c Tours (A): I 2015 (Aus A), 2016-17; B 2017. HS 215 Vic v NSW (Sydney) 2016-17. Y HS 101* v Lancs (Manchester) 2017. LO HS 140 v Derbys (Leeds) 2017 (RLC). T20 HS 103*.

MARSH, S.E. – see GLAMORGAN.

READ, Jonathan (Lady Lumley's S & SFC), b Scarborough 2 Feb 1998. 5'7". RHB, WK. Yorkshire 2016. Yorkshire 2nd XI debut 2015. HS 14 v Pakistan A (Leeds) 2016. LO HS –.

RHODES, W.M.H. – see WARWICKSHIRE.

^{NQ}**SARFRAZ AHMED**, b Karachi, Pakistan 22 May 1987. RHB, WK, occ OB. Karachi Harbour 2005-06 to 2006-07. PIA 2006-07 to 2013-14. Sind 2006-07 to 2011-12. Karachi Whites 2012-13. Yorkshire 2017 (T20 only). **Tests** (P): 38 (2009-10 to 2017-18, 2 as captain); HS 112 v NZ (Dubai, DSC) 2014-15. **LOI** (P): 85 (2007-08 to 2017-18, 19 as captain); HS 105 v E (Lord's) 2016. **IT20** (P): 38 (2009-10 to 2017-18, 17 as captain); HS 76* v NZ (Dubai, DSC) 2014-15. F-c Tours (P), exc Tests in UAE: E 2016; A 2009 (P A), 2009-10, 2016-17; SA 2012-13; WI 2010-11 (P A), 2017; NZ 2016-17; SL 2009 (P A), 2014, 2015; B 2015. HS 213* Sind v Punjab (Lahore) 2010-11. LO HS 105 (*see LOI*). T20 HS 76*.

SIDEBOTTOM, Ryan Jay (King James's GS, Almondbury), b Huddersfield 15 Jan 1978. Son of A.Sidebottom (Yorkshire, OFS and England 1973-91). 6'3". LHB, LFM. Yorkshire 1997-2017; cap 2000; testimonial 2017. Nottinghamshire 2004-10; cap 2004; benefit 2010. *Wisden* 2007. **Tests**: 22 (2001 to 2009-10); HS 31 v SL (Kandy) 2007-08; BB 7-47 v NZ (Napier) 2007-08. Hat-trick v NZ (Hamilton) 2007-08. **LOI**: 25 (2001-02 to 2009-10); HS 24 v A (Southampton) 2009; BB 3-19 v SL (Dambulla) 2007-08. **IT20**: 18 (2007 to 2010); HS 5* and BB 3-16 v NZ (Auckland) 2007-08. F-c Tours: SA 2009-10; WI 2000-01 (Eng A), 2008-09; NZ 2007-08; SL 2007-08. HS 61 v Worcs (Worcester) 2011. 50 wkts (4); most – 62 (2011). BB 7-37 (11-98 match) v Somerset (Leeds) 2011. LO HS 32 Nt v Middx (Nottingham) 2005 (NL). LO BB 6-40 v Glamorgan (Cardiff) 1998 (SL). T20 HS 17*. T20 BB 4-25.

YORKSHIRE 2017

RESULTS SUMMARY

	Place	Won	Lost	Tied	Drew	NR
Specsavers County Champ (1st Division)	4th	4	5		5	
All First-Class Matches		5	5		5	
Royal London One-Day Cup (North Group)	QF	6	3			
NatWest t20 Blast (North Group)	5th	6	5	1		2

SPECSAVERS COUNTY CHAMPIONSHIP AVERAGES

BATTING AND FIELDING

Cap		M	I	NO	HS	Runs	Avge	100	50	Ct/St
2012	G.S.Ballance	12	18	4	203*	951	67.92	3	4	3
	P.S.P.Handscomb	9	14	1	101*	441	33.92	1	2	7
2016	J.A.Leaning	10	15	–	118	454	30.26	1	2	5
2010	A.Lyth	13	23	1	100	555	25.22	1	2	19
	T.Kohler-Cadmore	3	6	–	78	151	25.16	–	1	1
2014	A.Z.Lees	14	25	3	102	531	24.13	1	2	7
2016	A.J.Hodd	12	19	1	59	428	23.77	–	4	39
2008	A.U.Rashid	7	10	1	65	211	23.44	–	1	–
	M.D.Fisher	2	4	–	37	86	21.50	–	–	–
2013	J.A.Brooks	8	11	2	109*	178	19.77	1	–	2
2000	R.J.Sidebottom	8	11	8	12*	57	19.00	–	–	2
2006	T.T.Bresnan	11	15	–	61	284	18.93	–	1	8
2012	S.A.Patterson	9	13	4	44*	165	18.33	–	–	5
	H.C.Brook	4	6	–	38	82	13.66	–	–	1
	K.Carver	2	4	–	20	48	12.00	–	–	2
	B.O.Coad	12	16	5	28	128	11.63	–	–	1
	K.C.Brathwaite	2	4	–	18	40	10.00	–	–	1
2016	Azeem Rafiq	5	7	–	17	54	7.71	–	–	–

Also batted: J.M.Bairstow (2 matches – cap 2011) 7, 1 (7 ct); S.E.Marsh (2) 22, 78, 125* (1 ct); L.E.Plunkett (2 – cap 2013) 19, 39, 34; J.E.Root (2 – cap 2012) 8, 2, 12*; J.Shaw (1) 3, 0; M.J.Waite (1) 4, 18; D.J.Willey (2 – cap 2016) 19, 8.

BOWLING

	O	M	R	W	Avge	Best	5wI	10wM
R.J.Sidebottom	186.4	43	518	25	20.72	5- 56	1	–
B.O.Coad	356.4	93	1043	50	20.86	6- 25	4	1
S.A.Patterson	280.2	72	754	23	32.78	4- 46	–	–
T.T.Bresnan	240	49	887	27	32.85	4- 53	–	–
J.A.Brooks	205	24	865	23	37.60	5-113	1	–
A.U.Rashid	108	10	500	10	50.00	3- 94	–	–
Also bowled:								
L.E.Plunkett	43	11	136	6	22.66	4- 73	–	–
M.D.Fisher	60.3	11	195	8	24.37	5- 54	1	–
Azeem Rafiq	107	13	393	5	78.60	3-128	–	–

H.C.Brook 19-4-65-1; K.Carver 35.2-4-118-4; J.A.Leaning 6-0-26-0; A.Lyth 39.3-2-127-2; J.E.Root 13.4-0-53-1; J.Shaw 16-3-59-0; M.J.Waite 16-0-70-3; D.J.Willey 60-15-148-4.

The First-Class Averages (pp 230–246) give the records of Yorkshire players in all first-class county matches (Yorkshire's other opponents being Leeds-Bradford MCCU), with the exception of J.M.Bairstow, K.C.Brathwaite, T.Kohler-Cadmore, L.E.Plunkett and J.E.Root, whose first-class figures for Yorkshire are as above, and:
G.S.Ballance 13-19-4-203*-1023-68.20-3-5-3ct.
J.Shaw 2-2-0-3-1.50-0-0-0ct. 41.1-7-151-3-50.33-2/35-0-0.

YORKSHIRE RECORDS

FIRST-CLASS CRICKET

Highest Total	For 887		v	Warwicks	Birmingham	1896
	V 681-7d		by	Leics	Bradford	1996
Lowest Total	For 23		v	Hampshire	Middlesbrough	1965
	V 13		by	Notts	Nottingham	1901
Highest Innings	For 341	G.H.Hirst	v	Leics	Leicester	1905
	V 318*	W.G.Grace	for	Glos	Cheltenham	1876

Highest Partnership for each Wicket

1st	555	P.Holmes/H.Sutcliffe	v	Essex	Leyton	1932
2nd	346	W.Barber/M.Leyland	v	Middlesex	Sheffield	1932
3rd	346	J.J.Sayers/A.McGrath	v	Warwicks	Birmingham	2009
4th	372	J.E.Root/J.M.Bairstow	v	Surrey	Leeds	2016
5th	340	E.Wainwright/G.H.Hirst	v	Surrey	The Oval	1899
6th	296	A.Lyth/A.U.Rashid	v	Lancashire	Manchester	2014
7th	366*	J.M.Bairstow/T.T.Bresnan	v	Durham	Chester-le-St[2]	2015
8th	292	R.Peel/Lord Hawke	v	Warwicks	Birmingham	1896
9th	246	T.T.Bresnan/J.N.Gillespie	v	Surrey	The Oval	2007
10th	149	G.Boycott/G.B.Stevenson	v	Warwicks	Birmingham	1982

Best Bowling	For 10-10	H.Verity	v	Notts	Leeds	1932
(Innings)	V 10-37	C.V.Grimmett	for	Australians	Sheffield	1930
Best Bowling	For 17-91	H.Verity	v	Essex	Leyton	1933
(Match)	V 17-91	H.Dean	for	Lancashire	Liverpool	1913

Most Runs – Season	2883	H.Sutcliffe	(av 80.08)	1932
Most Runs – Career	38558	H.Sutcliffe	(av 50.20)	1919-45
Most 100s – Season	12	H.Sutcliffe		1932
Most 100s – Career	112	H.Sutcliffe		1919-45
Most Wkts – Season	240	W.Rhodes	(av 12.72)	1900
Most Wkts – Career	3597	W.Rhodes	(av 16.02)	1898-1930
Most Career W-K Dismissals	1186	D.Hunter	(863 ct; 323 st)	1888-1909
Most Career Catches in the Field	665	J.Tunnicliffe		1891-1907

LIMITED-OVERS CRICKET

Highest Total	50ov	411-6		v	Devon	Exmouth	2004
	40ov	352-6		v	Notts	Scarborough	2001
	T20	260-4		v	Northants	Leeds	2017
Lowest Total	50ov	76		v	Surrey	Harrogate	1970
	40ov	54		v	Essex	Leeds	2003
	T20	90-9		v	Durham	Chester-le-St[2]	2009
Highest Innings	50ov	175	T.M.Head	v	Leics	Leicester	2016
	40ov	191	D.S.Lehmann	v	Notts	Scarborough	2001
	T20	161	A.Lyth	v	Northants	Leeds	2017
Best Bowling	50ov	7-27	D.Gough	v	Ireland	Leeds	1997
	40ov	7-15	R.A.Hutton	v	Worcs	Leeds	1969
	T20	6-19	T.T.Bresnan	v	Lancashire	Leeds	2017

FIRST-CLASS UMPIRES 2018

† New appointment. See page 86 for key to abbreviations.

BAILEY, Robert John (Biddulph HS), b Biddulph, Staffs 28 Oct 1963. 6'3". RHB, OB. Northamptonshire 1982-99; cap 1985; benefit 1993; captain 1996-97. Derbyshire 2000-01; cap 2000. Staffordshire 1980. YC 1984. **Tests:** 4 (1988 to 1989-90); HS 43 v WI (Oval) 1988. **LOI:** 4 (1984-85 to 1989-90); HS 43* v SL (Oval) 1988. F-c Tours: SA 1991-92 (Nh); WI 1989-90; Z 1994-95 (Nh). 1000 runs (13); most – 1987 (1990). HS 224* Nh v Glamorgan (Swansea) 1986. BB 5-54 Nh v Notts (Northampton) 1993. F-c career: 374 matches; 21844 runs @ 40.52, 47 hundreds; 121 wickets @ 42.51; 272 ct. Appointed 2006. Umpired 20 LOI (2011 to 2017). **ICC International Panel 2011 to date.**

BAINTON, Neil Laurence, b Romford, Essex 2 October 1970. No f-c appearances. Appointed 2006.

BALDWIN, Paul Kerr, b Epsom, Surrey 18 Jul 1973. No f-c appearances. Umpired 18 LOI (2006 to 2009). Reserve List 2010-14. Appointed 2015.

†BLACKWELL, Ian David (Brookfield Community S), b Chesterfield, Derbys 10 Jun 1978. 6'2". LHB, SLA. Derbyshire 1997-99. Somerset 2000-08; cap 2001; captain 2006 (*part*). Durham 2009-12. Warwickshire 2012 (on loan). MCC 2012. **Tests:** 1 (2005-06); HS 4 and BB-v I (Nagpur) 2005-06. **LOI:** 34 (2002-03 to 2005-06); HS 82 v I (Colombo) 2002-03; BB 3-26 v A (Adelaide) 2002-03. F-c Tour: I 2005-06. 1000 runs (2); most – 1256 (2005). HS 247* Sm v Derbys (Taunton) 2003 – off 156 balls and including 204 off 98 balls in reduced post-lunch session. BB 7-52 Du v Australia A (Chester-le-St) 2012. CC BB 7-85 Du v Lancs (Manchester) 2009. F-c career: 210 matches; 11595 runs @ 39.57, 27 hundreds; 398 wickets @ 35.91; 66 ct. Reserve List 2015-17. Appointed 2018.

BURNS, Michael (Walney CS), b Barrow-in-Furness, Lancs 6 Feb 1969. 6'0". RHB, RM, WK. Warwickshire 1992-96. Somerset 1997-2005; cap 1999; captain 2003-04. 1000 runs (2); most – 1133 (2003). HS 221 Sm v Yorks (Bath) 2001. BB 6-54 Sm v Leics (Taunton) 2001. F-c career: 154 matches; 7648 runs @ 32.68, 8 hundreds; 68 wickets @ 42.42; 142 ct, 7 st. Appointed 2016.

COOK, Nicholas Grant Billson (Lutterworth GS), b Leicester 17 Jun 1956. 6'0". RHB, SLA. Leicestershire 1978-85; cap 1982. Northamptonshire 1986-94; cap 1987; benefit 1995. **Tests:** 15 (1983 to 1989); HS 31 v A (Oval) 1989; BB 6-65 (11-83 match) v P (Karachi) 1983-84. **LOI:** 3 (1983-84 to 1989-90); HS – ; BB 2-18 v P (Peshawar) 1987-88. F-c Tours: NZ 1979-80 (DHR), 1983-84; P 1983-84, 1987-88; SL 1985-86 (Eng B); Z 1980-81 (Le), 1984-85 (EC). HS 75 Le v Somerset (Taunton) 1980. 50 wkts (8); most – 90 (1982). BB 7-34 (10-97 match) Nh v Essex (Chelmsford) 1992. F-c career: 356 matches; 3137 runs @ 11.66; 879 wickets @ 29.01; 197 ct. Appointed 2009.

†DEBENHAM, Benjamin John, b Chelmsford, Essex 11 Oct 1967. LHB. No f-c appearances. Reserve List 2012-17. Appointed 2018.

EVANS, Jeffery Howard, b Llanelli, Carms 7 Aug 1954. No f-c appearances. Appointed 2001. Umpired in Indian Cricket League 2007-08.

GOUGH, Michael Andrew (English Martyrs RCS; Hartlepool SFC), b Hartlepool, Co Durham 18 Dec 1979. Son of M.P.Gough (Durham 1974-77). 6'5". RHB, OB. Durham 1998-2003. F-c Tours (Eng A): NZ 1999-00; B 1999-00. HS 123 Du v CU (Cambridge) 1998. CC HS 103 Du v Essex (Colchester) 2002. BB 5-56 Du v Middx (Chester-le-St) 2001. F-c career: 67 matches; 2952 runs @ 25.44, 2 hundreds; 30 wickets @ 45.00; 57 ct. Reserve List 2006-08. Appointed 2009. Umpired 6 Tests (2016 to 2017-18) and 40 LOI (2013 to 2017-18). **ICC International Panel 2012 to date.**

GOULD, Ian James (Westgate SS, Slough), b Taplow, Bucks 19 Aug 1957. 5'8". LHB, WK. Middlesex 1975 to 1980-81, 1996; cap 1977. Auckland 1979-80. Sussex 1981-90; cap 1981; captain 1987; benefit 1990. MCC YC. **LOI:** 18 (1982-83 to 1983); HS 42 v A (Sydney) 1982-83. F-c Tours: A 1982-83; P 1980-81 (Int); Z 1980-81 (M). HS 128 M v Worcs (Worcester) 1978. BB 3-10 Sx v Surrey (Oval) 1989. Middlesex coach 1991-2000. Reappeared in one match (v OU) 1996. F-c career: 298 matches; 8756 runs @ 26.05, 4 hundreds; 7 wickets @ 52.14; 603 dismissals (536 ct, 67 st). Appointed 2002. Umpired 64 Tests (2008-09 to 2017-18) and 125 LOI (2006 to 2017-18), including 2010-11 and 2014-15 World Cups. **ICC Elite Panel 2009 to date.**

HARTLEY, Peter John (Greenhead GS; Bradford C), b Keighley, Yorks 18 Apr 1960. 6'0". RHB, RMF. Warwickshire 1982. Yorkshire 1985-97; cap 1987; benefit 1996. Hampshire 1998-2000; cap 1998. F-c Tours: (Y): SA 1991-92; WI 1986-87; Z 1995-96. HS 127* Y v Lancs (Manchester) 1988. 50 wkts (7); most – 81 (1995). BB 9-41 (inc hat-trick, 4 wkts in 5 balls and 5 in 9; 11-68 match) Y v Derbys (Chesterfield) 1995. Hat-trick 1995. F-c career: 232 matches; 4321 runs @ 19.91, 2 hundreds; 683 wickets @ 30.21; 68 ct. Appointed 2003. Umpired 6 LOI (2007 to 2009). **ICC International Panel 2006-09.**

ILLINGWORTH, Richard Keith (Salts GS), b Bradford, Yorks 23 Aug 1963. 5'11". RHB, SLA. Worcestershire 1982-2000; cap 1986; benefit 1997. Natal 1988-89. Derbyshire 2001. Wiltshire 2005. **Tests:** 9 (1991 to 1995-96); HS 28 v SA (Pt Elizabeth) 1995-96; BB 4-96 v WI (Nottingham) 1995. Took wicket of P.V.Simmons with his first ball in Tests – v WI (Nottingham) 1991. **LOI:** 25 (1991 to 1995-96); HS 14 v P (Melbourne) 1991-92; BB 3-33 v Z (Albury) 1991-92. F-c Tours: SA 1995-96; NZ 1991-92; P 1990-91 (Eng A); SL 1990-91 (Eng A); Z 1989-90 (Eng A), 1990-91 (Wo), 1993-94 (Wo), 1996-97 (Wo). HS 120* Wo v Warwks (Worcester) 1987 – as night-watchman. Scored 106 for England A v Z (Harare) 1989-90 – also as night-watchman. 50 wkts (5); most – 75 (1990). BB 7-50 Wo v OU (Oxford) 1985. F-c career: 376 matches; 7027 runs @ 22.45, 4 hundreds; 831 wickets @ 31.54; 161 ct. Appointed 2006. Umpired 30 Tests (2012-13 to 2017) and 57 LOI (2010 to 2017-18), including 2014-15 World Cup. **ICC Elite Panel 2013 to date.**

KETTLEBOROUGH, Richard Allan (Worksop C), b Sheffield, Yorks 15 Mar 1973. 6'0". LHB, RM. Yorkshire 1994-97. Middlesex 1998-99. F-c Tour: (Y): Z 1995-96. HS 108 Y v Essex (Leeds) 1996. BB 2-26 Y v Notts (Scarborough) 1996. F-c career: 33 matches; 1258 runs @ 25.16, 1 hundred; 3 wickets @ 81.00; 20 ct. Appointed 2006. Umpired 50 Tests (2010-11 to 2017-18) and 74 LOI (2009 to 2017-18), including 2010-11 and 2014-15 World Cups. **ICC Elite Panel 2011 to date.**

LLONG, Nigel James (Ashford North S), b Ashford, Kent 11 Feb 1969. 6'0". LHB, OB. Kent 1990-98; cap 1993. F-c Tour (K): Z 1992-93. HS 130 K v Hants (Canterbury) 1996. BB 5-21 K v Middx (Canterbury) 1996. F-c career: 68 matches; 3024 runs @ 31.17, 6 hundreds; 35 wickets @ 35.97; 59 ct. Appointed 2002. Umpired 49 Tests (2007-08 to 2017-18) and 117 LOI (2006 to 2017-18), including 2010-11 and 2014-15 World Cups. **ICC Elite Panel 2012 to date.**

LLOYD, Graham David (Hollins County HS), b Accrington, Lancs 1 Jul 1969. Son of D.Lloyd (Lancs and England 1965-83). 5'9". RHB, RM. Lancashire 1988-2002; cap 1992; benefit 2001. **LOI:** 6 (1996 to 1998-99); HS 22 v A (Oval) 1997. F-c Tours: A 1992-93 (Eng A); WI 1995-96 (La). 1000 runs (5); most – 1389 (1992). HS 241 La v Essex (Chelmsford) 1996. BB 1-4. F-c career: 203 matches; 11279 runs @ 38.23, 24 hundreds; 2 wickets @ 220.00; 140 ct. Reserve List 2009-13. Appointed 2014.

LLOYDS, Jeremy William (Blundell's S), b Penang, Malaya 17 Nov 1954. 6'0". LHB, OB. Somerset 1979-84; cap 1982. Gloucestershire 1985-91; cap 1985. OFS 1983-84 to 1987-88. F-c Tour (Gl): SL 1986-87. 1000 runs (3); most – 1295 (1986). HS 132* Sm v Northants (Northampton) 1982. BB 7-88 Sm v Essex (Chelmsford) 1982. F-c career: 267 matches; 10679 runs @ 31.04, 10 hundreds; 333 wickets @ 38.86; 229 ct. Appointed 1998. Umpired 5 Tests (2003-04 to 2004-05) and 18 LOI (2000 to 2005-06). **ICC International Panel 2003-06.**

MALLENDER, Neil Alan (Beverley GS), b Kirk Sandall, Yorks 13 Aug 1961. 6'0". RHB, RFM. Northamptonshire 1980-86 and 1995-96; cap 1984. Somerset 1987-94; cap 1987; benefit 1994. Otago 1983-84 to 1992-93; captain 1990-91 to 1992-93. **Tests:** 2 (1992); HS 4 v P (Oval) 1992; BB 5-50 v P (Leeds) 1992 – on debut. F-c Tour (Nh): Z 1994-95. HS 100* Otago v CD (Palmerston N) 1991-92. UK HS 87* Sm v Sussex (Hove) 1990. 50 wkts (6); most – 56 (1983). BB 7-27 Otago v Auckland (Auckland) 1984-85. UK BB 7-41 Nh v Derbys (Northampton) 1982. F-c career: 345 matches; 4709 runs @ 17.18, 1 hundred; 937 wickets @ 26.31; 111 ct. Appointed 1999. Umpired 3 Tests (2003-04) and 22 LOI (2001 to 2003-04), including 2002-03 World Cup. **ICC Elite Panel 2004**.

MILLNS, David James (Garibaldi CS; N Notts C; Nottingham Trent U), b Clipstone, Notts 27 Feb 1965. 6'3". LHB, RF. Nottinghamshire 1988-89, 2000-01; cap 2000. Leicestershire 1990-99; cap 1991; benefit 1999. Tasmania 1994-95. Boland 1996-97. F-c Tours: A 1992-93 (Eng A); SA 1996-97 (Le). HS 121 Le v Northants (Northampton) 1997. 50 wkts (4); most – 76 (1994). BB 9-37 (12-91 match) Le v Derbys (Derby) 1991. F-c career: 171 matches; 3082 runs @ 22.01, 3 hundreds; 553 wickets @ 27.35; 76 ct. Reserve List 2007-08. Appointed 2009.

O'SHAUGHNESSY, Steven Joseph (Harper Green SS, Franworth), b Bury, Lancs 9 Sep 1961. 5'10½". RHB, RM. Lancashire 1980-87; cap 1985. Worcestershire 1988-89. Scored 100 in 35 min to equal world record for La v Leics (Manchester) 1983. 1000 runs (1): 1167 (1984). HS 159* La v Somerset (Bath) 1984. BB 4-66 La v Notts (Nottingham) 1982. F-c career: 112 matches; 3720 runs @ 24.31, 5 hundreds; 114 wickets @ 36.03; 57 ct. Reserve List 2009-10. Appointed 2011.

†POLLARD, Paul Raymond (Gedling CS), b Carlton, Nottingham 24 Sep 1968. 5'11". LHB, RM. Nottinghamshire 1987-98; cap 1992. Worcestershire 1999-2001. F-c Tour (Nt): SA 1996-97. 1000 runs (3); most – 1463 (1993). HS 180 Nt v Derbys (Nottingham) 1993. BB 2-79 Nt v Glos (Bristol) 1993. F-c career: 192 matches; 9685 runs @ 31.44, 15 hundreds; 4 wkts @ 68.00; 158 ct. Reserve List 2012-17. Appointed 2018.

ROBINSON, Robert Timothy (Dunstable GS; High Pavement SFC; Sheffield U), b Sutton in Ashfield, Notts 21 Nov 1958. 6'0". RHB, RM. Nottinghamshire 1978-99; cap 1983; captain 1988-95; benefit 1992. *Wisden* 1985. **Tests:** 29 (1984-85 to 1989); HS 175 v A (Leeds) 1985. LOI: 26 (1984-85 to 1988); HS 83 v P (Sharjah) 1986-87. F-c Tours: A 1987-88; SA 1989-90 (Eng XI), 1996-97 (Nt); NZ 1987-88; WI 1985-86; I/SL 1984-85; P 1987-88. 1000 runs (14) inc 2000 (1): 2032 (1984). HS 220* Nt v Yorks (Nottingham) 1990. BB 1-22. F-c career: 425 matches; 27571 runs @ 42.15, 63 hundreds; 4 wickets @ 72.25; 257 ct. Appointed 2007. Umpired 13 LOI (2013 to 2017). **ICC International Panel (Third Umpire) 2012 to date.**

SAGGERS, Martin John (Springwood HS, King's Lynn; Huddersfield U), b King's Lynn, Norfolk 23 May 1972. 6'2". RHB, RMF. Durham 1996-98. Kent 1999-2009; cap 2001; benefit 2009. MCC 2004. Essex 2007 (on loan). Norfolk 1995-96. **Tests:** 3 (2003-04 to 2004); HS 1 and BB 2-29 v B (Chittagong) 2003-04 – on debut. F-c Tour: B 2003-04. HS 64 K v Worcs (Canterbury) 2004. 50 wkts (4); most – 83 (2002). BB 7-79 K v Durham (Chester-le-St) 2000. F-c career: 119 matches; 1165 runs @ 11.20; 415 wickets @ 25.33; 27 ct. Reserve List 2010-11. Appointed 2012.

TAYLOR, Billy Victor (Bitterne Park S, Southampton), b Southampton 11 Jan 1977. Younger brother of J.L.Taylor (Wiltshire 1998-2002). 6'3". LHB, RMF. Sussex 1999-2003. Hampshire 2004-09; cap 2006; testimonial 2010. Wiltshire 1996-98. HS 40 v Essex (Southampton) 2004. BB 6-32 v Middlesex (Southampton) 2006 (inc hat-trick). F-c career: 54 matches; 431 runs @10.26; 136 wickets @ 33.34; 6 ct. Reserve list 2011-16. Appointed 2017.

†**WARREN, Russell** John (Kingsthorpe Upper S), b Northampton 10 Sep 1971. 6'1". RHB, OB, WK. Northamptonshire 1992-2002; cap 1995. Nottinghamshire 2003-06; cap 2004. 1000 runs (1): 1030 (2001). HS 201* Nh v Glamorgan (Northampton) 2001. F-c career: 146 matches; 7776 runs @ 36.67, 15 hundreds; 128 ct, 5 st. Reserve List 2015-17. Appointed 2018.

WHARF, Alexander George (Buttershaw Upper S; Thomas Danby C), b Bradford, Yorks 4 Jun 1975. 6'5". RHB, RMF. Yorkshire 1994-97. Nottinghamshire 1998-99. Glamorgan 2000-08, scoring 100* v OU (Oxford) on debut; cap 2000; benefit 2009. **LOI**: 13 (2004 to 2004-05); HS 9 v India (Lord's) 2004; BB 4-24 v Z (Harare) 2004-05. F-c Tour (Eng A): WI 2005-06. HS 128* Gm v Glos (Bristol) 2007. 50 wkts (1): 52 (2003). BB 6-59 Gm v Glos (Bristol) 2005. F-c career: 121 matches; 3570 runs @ 23.03, 6 hundreds; 293 wickets @ 37.34; 63 ct. Reserve List 2011-13. Appointed 2014. **ICC International Panel 2018.**

RESERVE FIRST-CLASS LIST: Tom Lungley, James D.Middlebrook, Mark Newell, Ian N.Ramage, Christopher M.Watts, Robert A.White.

Test Match and LOI statistics to 13 March 2018.

TOURING TEAMS REGISTER 2017

SOUTH AFRICA

Full Names	Birthdate	Birthplace	Team	Type	F-C Debut
AMLA, Hashim Mahomed	31.03.83	Durban	Cape Cobras	RHB/RM	1999-00
BAVUMA, Temba	17.05.90	Cape Town	Lions	RHB/RM	2008-09
DE BRUYN, Theunis Booysen	08.10.92	Pretoria	Knights	RHB/RMF	2013-14
DE KOCK, Quinton	17.12.92	Johannesburg	Titans	LHB/WK	2009-10
DU PLESSIS, Francois 'Faf'	13.07.84	Pretoria	Titans	RHB/LB	2003-04
DUMINY, Jean-Paul	14.04.84	Cape Town	Cape Cobras	LHB/OB	2001-02
ELGAR, Dean	11.06.87	Welkom	Titans	LHB/SLA	2005-06
KUHN, Heino Gunther	01.04.84	Piet Relief	Titan	RHB/WK	2004-05
MAHARAJ, Keshav Athmanand	07.02.90	Durban	Dolphins	RHB/SLA	2006-07
MORKEL, Morne	06.10.84	Vereeniging	Titans	LHB/RF	2003-04
MORRIS, Christopher Henry	30.04.87	Pretoria	Titans	RHB/RFM	2009-10
OLIVIER, Duanne	09.05.92	Groblersdal	Knights	RHB/RF	2010-11
PHILANDER, Vernon Darryl	24.06.85	Bellville	Cape Cobras	RHB/RMF	2003-04
RABADA, Kagiso	25.05.95	Johannesburg	Lions	LHB/RF	2013-14

SOUTH AFRICA A

Full Names	Birthdate	Birthplace	Team	Type	F-C Debut
BAVUMA, Temba	17.05.90	Cape Town	Lions	RHB/RM	2008-09
DALA, Carl Junior	29.12.89	Lusaka, Zambia	Titan	RHB/RFM	2011-12
DE BRUYN, Theunis Booysen	08.10.92	Pretoria	Knights	RHB/RMF	2013-14
HENDRICKS, Beuran Eric	08.06.90	Cape Town	Lions	LHB/LFM	2009-10
KLAASEN, Heinrich	30.07.91	Pretoria	Titans	RHB/WK	2012-13
KUHN, Heino Gunther	01.04.84	Piet Relief	Titan	RHB/WK	2004-05
MARKRAM, Aiden Kyle	04.10.94	Pretoria	Titans	RHB/OB	2014-15
MULDER, Peter Wiaan Adriaan	19.02.98	Johannesburg	Lions	RHB/RM	2016-17
OLIVIER, Duanne	09.05.92	Groblersdal	Knights	RHB/RF	2010-11
PATERSON, Dane	04.04.89	Cape Town	Cape Cobras	RHB/RFM	2009-10
PIEDT, Dane Lee-Roy	06.03.90	Cape Town	Cape Cobras	RHB/OB	2009-10
SECOND, Rudi Stewart	17.07.89	Queenstown	Knights	RHB/OB	2011-12
SMITH, Jason Franswyn	11.10.94	Johannesburg	Cape Cobras	RHB/RMF	2012-13
ZONDO, Khayelihle	07.03.90	Durban	Dolphins	RHB/OB	2007-08

WEST INDIES

Full Names	Birthdate	Birthplace	Team	Type	F-C Debut
BISHOO, Devendra	06.11.85	New Amsterdam	Guyana	LHB/LB	2007-08
BLACKWOOD, Jermaine	20.11.91	St Elizabeth	Jamaica	RHB/OB	2011-12
BRATHWAITE, Kraigg Clairmonte	01.12.92	St Michael	Barbados	RHB/OB	2008-09
CHASE, Roston Lamar	22.03.92	Christ Church	Barbados	RHB/OB	2010-11
CUMMINS, Miguel Lamar	05.09.90	St Michael	Barbados	LHB/RF	2011-12
DOWRICH, Shane Omari	30.10.91	St James	Barbados	RHB/WK	2009-10
GABRIEL, Shannon Terry	28.04.88	Trinidad	Trinidad	RHB/RFM	2009-10
HETMYER, Shimron Odilon	26.12.96	Georgetown	Guyana	LHB/WK	2013-14
HOLDER, Jason Omar	05.11.91	St George	Barbados	RHB/RMF	2008-09
HOPE, Kyle Antonio	20.11.88	St Michael	Trinidad	RHB/OB	2009-10
HOPE, Shai Diego	10.11.93	Barbados	Barbados	RHB/WK	2012-13
JOSEPH, Alzarri Shaheim	20.11.96	Antigua	Leeward Is	RHB/RFM	2014-15
POWELL, Kieran Omar Akeem	06.03.90	Charlestown	Leeward Is	LHB/RM	2007-08
REIFER, Raymon Anton	11.05.91	St Lucy	Guyana	LHB/LM	2010-11
ROACH, Kemar Andre Jamal	30.06.88	St Lucy	Barbados	RHB/RF	2007-08

UNIVERSITIES REGISTER 2017

CAMBRIDGE († = Blue)

Full Names	Birthdate	Birthplace	College	Bat/Bowl	F-C Debut
ARIF, Adil Tahir	06.11.94	Sharjah, UAE	Anglia RU	RHB/RM	2014
BARTON, Adam Paul	17.04.95	Epsom	Anglia RU	RHB/LMF	2014
CHAPMAN, Luke James	21.08.98	Stevenage	Anglia RU	RHB/OB	2017
†CHOHAN, Darshan	04.11.95	Singapore	St Catharine's	LHB/SLA	2015
†COLVERD, Thomas Gerald Lancaster	13.11.95	Tokyo, Japan	Robinson	RHB/OB	2016
†CRICHARD, Ruari James	09.01.95	Hammersmith	St John's	RHB/RMF	2015
†DALGLEISH, Angus Duncan	01.02.96	Bexley	Trinity Hall	RHB/LM	2016
†DEWHURST, Alasdair Charles H.	05.11.96	Hammersmith	Robinson	RHB/RM	2017
GREENIDGE, Akil Diara	24.12.96	Barbados	Anglia RU	RHB/OB	2017
GUEST, Callum Jake	.05.95	Hastings	Anglia RU	RHB/OB	2017
†MOSES, Timothy Haydn	01.12.94	Lewes	Hughes Hall	LHB/RMF	2017
PALMER, Harrison John	13.10.96	Enfield	Anglia RU	RHB/WK	2016
†POULSON, James Edward	20.02.95	Bury St Edmunds	Homerton	RHB/RM	2014
RIPPINGTON, Samuel Edward	08.01.94	Waltham Forest	Anglia RU	LHB/LM	2017
†SALE, Rory Alexander	.07.96	Hexham	Fitzwilliam	RHB/SLA	2017
†SENARATNE, Nipuna Vikum S.	19.10.93	Leeds	Jesus	RHB/RM	2013
TETLEY, Joseph William	14.04.95	Sheffield	Anglia RU	LHB/WK	2017
†TICE, Patrick James Aikman	30.06.94	Basingstoke	Fitzwilliam	RHB/WK	2015
†WINDER, Nicholas James	.06.97	Hounslow	Robinson	LHB/SLA	2017
ZAIDI, Misemali Syed	24.06.98	Paris, France	Anglia RU	RHB/LB	2017

CARDIFF

Full Names	Birthdate	Birthplace	College	Bat/Bowl	F-C Debut
BRAND, Neil	12.04.96	Johannesburg, SA	Cardiff Met	LHB/SLA	2015
BREWSTER, Andrew David Francis	01.02.97	York	Cardiff Met	RHB/RFM	2017
BROWN, Connor Rhys	28.04.97	Caerphilly	Cardiff Met	RHB/OB	2017
CULLEN, Thomas Nicholas	04.01.92	Perth, Australia	Cardiff Met	RHB/WK	2015
LAWLOR, Jeremy Lloyd	04.11.95	Cardiff	Cardiff Met	RHB/RM	2015
LEVEROCK, Kamau Sadiki	19.10.94	Bermuda	Cardiff Met	LHB/RFM	2014
NIJJAR, Aron Stuart Singh	24.09.94	Goodmayes	Cardiff Met	LHB/SLA	2015
NORRIS, Matthew Jonathan	18.12.92	Cape Town, SA	Cardiff Met	LHB/SLA	2015
O'SULLIVAN, David	11.06.97	Sydney, Aus	Cardiff Met	RHB/RM	2017
PIKE, Oliver Lee	02.04.98	Bridgend	Cardiff	RHB/RFM	2017
ROUSE, Timothy David	09.04.96	Sheffield	Cardiff	RHB/OB	2015
SCRIVEN, Jack Ashley Luke	04.06.95	Oxford	U of S Wales	RHB/OB	2014

DURHAM

Full Names	Birthdate	Birthplace		Bat/Bowl	F-C Debut
ABHIRAJ Rajdeep SINGH	27.05.95	Mumbai, India		LHB/SLA	2017
CLARK, Jack	26.09.94	Ashington		LHB/LM	2016
COOKE, Joseph Michael	30.05.97	Hemel Hempstead		LHB/RFM	2017
FRAINE, William Alan Richard	13.06.96	Huddersfield		RHB/RM	2017
GRAVES, Benedict William M.	.11.96	Hammersmith		SLA	2017
JAHANFAR, Matthew Francis	.08.97	Chelmsford		LHB/WK	2017
McCOLLUM, James Arthur	01.08.95	Craigavon		RHB/RM	2017
McGRATH, Alex Halliday	12.05.97	Bishop Auckland		RHB/LM	2017
MARSHALL, Jason David	20.06.96	Westminster		RHB	2017
OWEN, Xavier George	.08.97	High Wycombe		RHB/RM	2017
POLLOCK, Edward John	10.07.95	High Wycombe		LHB/OB	2015
SIMON, Frederic Peter Andre	14.10.95	Cheltenham		RHB/RMF	2017
STEWART-TAYLOR, Sebastian Ken	02.07.95			RHB/WK	2017
WILLIAMS, Darrel Ryan	21.09.95	Banbury		RHB/LB	2015

LEEDS/BRADFORD

Full Names	Birthdate	Birthplace		Bat/Bowl	F-C Debut
ANDERSSON, Martin Kristoffer	06.09.96	Reading		RHB/RM	2017
ASHRAF, Moin Aqeeb	05.01.92	Bradford		RHB/RMF	2010
BOCKING, Oliver Stuart	25.04.96	Colchester		RHB/RFM	2017
BULLEN, Steven Frank Gregory	12.07.92	Watford		RHB/WK	2015
COOK, William	11.10.95	Wolverhampton		RHB/RFM	2017
FESZCZUR-HATCHETT, Sebastian Alex	21.10.95	Hendon		LMF	2017
GRAHAM, Oliver Jonathan George	03.01.95	Haywards Heath		RHB/OB	2017
HOUGHTON, Daniel	05.07.98	Ormskirk		RHB/RM	2017
McDERMOTT, Peter Frederick	27.01.96	Newham		RHB/RM	2017
POTTICARY, Jack Terence	16.11.96	Harold Wood		RHB/WK	2017
SHOARE, Benjamin John	21.09.95	Crawley		RHB/OB	2017
WALLACE, Craig Donald	27.06.90	Dundee		RHB/WK	2013

LOUGHBOROUGH

Full Names	Birthdate	Birthplace		Bat/Bowl	F-C Debut
AKRAM, Basil Mohammad Ramzan	23.02.93	Waltham Forest		RHB/RMF	2014
BRACEY, James Robert	03.05.97	Bristol		LHB/WK	2016
COOK, Samuel James	04.08.97	Chelmsford		RHB/RFM	2016
EVANS, Samuel Thomes	20.12.97	Leicester		RHB/	2017
GAMBLE, Robert Neil	25.01.95	Nottingham		RHB/RMF	2015
HASAN AZAD, Mohammad	07.01.94	Quetta, Pakistan		LHB/OB	2015
KUMAR, Nitish Roenik	21.05.94	Scarborough, Can		RHB/OB	2009
LADD-GIBBON, Ben Ian William	20.05.94	Dorchester		RHB/RM	2017
THURSTON, Charles Oliver	17.08.96	Cambridge		RHB/RM	2017
TILLCOCK, Adam David	13.10.93	Nottingham		RHB/SLA	2017
WHITE, Robert George	15.09.95	Ealing		RHB/RFM	2015

OXFORD († = Blue)

Full Names	Birthdate	Birthplace	College	Bat/Bowl	F-C Debut
†BROCK, Thomas Michael J.	.11.94	Yeovil		RHB/RM	2017
BROUGHTON, Bruno Miles	10.10.94	Lambeth	Brookes U	RHB/SLA	2016
ELLIS, Edward John	09.05.95	Ascot	Brookes U	RHB/WK	2015
†ESCOTT, Daniel Alexander	26.09.96	Torbay	Lincoln	RHB/LB	2016
†GNODDE, James Spencer Drury	09.11.95	Westminster	Pembroke	LHB/SLA	2017
GRUNDY, Jack Oliver	25.06.94	Warwick	Brookes U	RHB/LMF	2015
†HARRISON, Jack	04.10.95	Leeds		RHB/WK	2017
HEATHFIELD, Thomas David	10.05.97	Northampton	Brookes U	RHB/RMF	2017
†HUGHES, Matthew Stephen Turner	17.04.96	Manchester	Hertford	RHB/RM	2015
HUSSAIN, Reece	08.12.95	Harold Wood	Brookes U	LHB/OB	2017
LAKE, Malcolm Blair	03.08.94	Harare, Zimbabwe	Brookes U	LHB/RM	2015
McIVER, Jack Nathan	26.04.92	Hammersmith	Brookes U	RHB/OB	2015
†MARSDEN, Jonathan	07.04.93	Tunbridge Wells	St Hilda's	RHB/RFM	2013
MARTIN, Alexander Thomas A.	07.11.92	Huntingdon	Brookes U	RHB/WK	2014
†NAYLOR, Andrew			Merton	RHB/RM	2017
†PETTMAN, Toby Henry Somerville	11.05.98	Kingston-upon-T	Jesus	RHB/RFM	2017
†RACKOW, Alexander Joseph W.	.01.97	Wandsworth	St Hilda's	RHB/OB	2017
SCOTT, David Neil Cullinan	27.07.98		Brookes U	RHB/RM	2017
†SWANSON, Ben				LHB/SLA	2017
†TAYLOR, Nicholas Philip	20.03.96	Huntingdon	St Catherine's	RHB/WK	2017
WELLS, Daniel Alan C.	.06.95	Eastbourne	Brookes U	LHB	2017
WILKINSON, Alex Ross	04.09.96	Birmingham	Brookes U	LHB/LFM	2017

THE 2017 FIRST-CLASS SEASON STATISTICAL HIGHLIGHTS

FIRST TO INDIVIDUAL TARGETS

1000 RUNS	K.C.Sangakkara	Surrey	27 June
2000 RUNS	–	Most – 1491 K.C.Sangakkara (Surrey)	
50 WICKETS	S.R.Harmer	Essex	7 August
100 WICKETS	–	Most – 85 J.A.Porter (Essex)	

TEAM HIGHLIGHTS
HIGHEST INNINGS TOTALS

701-7d	Kent v Northamptonshire	Beckenham
668	Sussex v Durham	Hove
648-7d	Hampshire v Surrey	The Oval
619	Leicestershire v Derbyshire	Derby

HIGHEST FOURTH INNINGS TOTAL

401-6	Worcestershire (set 399) v Kent	Worcester

LOWEST INNINGS TOTALS († One man short)

56	Cambridge MCCU v Lancashire (2nd innings)	Cambridge
61	Gloucestershire v Kent	Canterbury
62	Cambridge MCCU v Lancashire (1st innings)	Cambridge
74	Yorkshire v Essex	Chelmsford
76	Essex v Hampshire	Southampton
76	Hampshire v Essex	Southampton
79	Cambridge MCCU v Nottinghamshire	Cambridge
81	Leicestershire v Nottinghamshire	Leicester
91	Warwickshire v Surrey	The Oval
94	Warwickshire v Essex	Chelmsford
98	Cardiff MCCU v Hampshire	Southampton
98	Derbyshire v Worcestershire	Derby

HIGHEST MATCH AGGREGATES

1497-33	England (258 & 490-8d) v West Indies (427 & 322-5)	Leeds
1471-36	Kent (260 & 474) v Worcestershire (336 & 401-6)	Worcester

BATSMEN'S MATCH (Qualification: 1200 runs, average 60 per wicket)

72.65 (1453-20)	Kent (701-7d & 184-3d) v Northamptonshire (568)	Beckenham
64.85 (1297-20)	Hampshire (648-7d) v Surrey (483 & 166-3d)	The Oval
61.34 (1411-23)	Leicestershire (619 & 217-3d) v Derbyshire (533 & 42-0)	Derby

LARGE MARGINS OF VICTORY

376 runs	Essex (227 & 334-7d) beat Yorkshire (111 & 74)	Chelmsford
344 runs	Notts (309 & 207-2d) beat Cambridge MCCU (123 & 79)	Cambridge
340 runs	South Africa (335 & 343-9d) beat England (205 & 133)	Nottingham
340 runs	Lancs (338-6d & 120-7d) beat Cambridge MCCU (62 & 56)	Cambridge
Inns & 280 runs	Nottinghamshire (548-9d) v Leicestershire (134 & 134)	Nottingham
Inns & 224 runs	Yorkshire (543-5d) beat Leeds/Bradford MCCU (137 & 182)	Leeds
Inns & 209 runs	England (514-8d) beat West Indies (168 & 137) (1st Test)	Birmingham

NARROW MARGINS OF VICTORY

2 runs	Northants (261 & 289-7d) beat Leics (157 & 391)	Northampton
3 runs	Yorkshire (202 & 283) beat Somerset (224 & 258)	Taunton
1 wkt	Middlesex (334 & 123-9) beat Warwickshire (334 & 233)	Birmingham
1 wkt	Sussex (268 & 211-9) beat Glamorgan (294 & 182)	Colwyn Bay

VICTORY AFTER FOLLOWING ON

Essex (76 & 362) beat Hampshire (254 & 76) by 108 runs   Southampton

ALL ELEVEN SCORING DOUBLE FIGURES

Kent (298, lowest score 10) v Gloucestershire   Canterbury

SIX FIFTIES IN AN INNINGS

England (490-8d) v West Indies (*2nd Test*)   Leeds

MOST EXTRAS IN AN INNINGS

	B	LB	W	NB			
60	8	2	5	45	Kent (370-6d) v Leeds/Bradford MCCU	Canterbury

Under ECB regulations, Test matches excluded, two penalty extras were scored for each no-ball.

BATTING HIGHLIGHTS
TRIPLE HUNDRED

S.R.Dickson   318   Kent v Northamptonshire   Beckenham

DOUBLE HUNDRED

G.S.Ballance	203*	Yorkshire v Hampshire	Southampton
C.T.Bancroft	206*	Gloucestershire v Kent	Bristol
N.L.J.Browne	221	Essex v Middlesex	Chelmsford
R.J.Burns	219*	Surrey v Hampshire	The Oval
A.N.Cook	243	England v West Indies (*1st Test*)	Birmingham
J.L.Denly	227	Kent v Worcestershire	Worcester
S.M.Ervine	203	Hampshire v Warwickshire	Southampton
A.D.Hales	218	Nottinghamshire v Derbyshire	Derby
H.G.Kuhn	200*	South Africa A v Hampshire	Southampton
L.S.Livingstone	224	Lancashire v Middlesex	Manchester
S.R.Patel (2)	257*	Nottinghamshire v Gloucestershire	Bristol
	247	Nottinghamshire v Leicestershire	Nottingham
K.S.Sangakkara	200	Surrey v Essex	Chelmsford
C.T.Steel	224	Durham v Leicestershire	Leicester
D.J.Vilas	244	Lancashire v Hampshire	Manchester
L.W.P.Wells	258	Sussex v Durham	Hove
M.H.Wessels	202*	Nottinghamshire v Sussex	Nottingham

HUNDREDS IN FIVE CONSECUTIVE INNINGS

K.C.Sangakkara	136		Surrey v Lancashire	The Oval
	105		Surrey v Warwickshire	Birmingham
	114	120	Surrey v Middlesex	Lord's
	200		Surrey v Essex	Chelmsford

He made 84 in the second innings v Essex, narrowly failing to equal the first-class record of six consecutive hundreds.

HUNDREDS IN THREE CONSECUTIVE INNINGS

K.C.Sangakkara	180*	Surrey v Yorkshire	Leeds
	164	Surrey v Yorkshire	The Oval
	157	Surrey v Somerset	The Oval

DOUBLE HUNDRED AND A HUNDRED IN A MATCH

G.S.Ballance   108   203*   Yorkshire v Hampshire   Southampton

HUNDRED IN EACH INNINGS OF A MATCH

J.M.Clarke	142	110*	Worcestershire v Kent	Worcester
S.D.Hope	147	118*	West Indies v England (*2nd Test*)	Leeds
K.C.Sangakkara	114	120	Surrey v Middlesex	Lord's

FASTEST HUNDRED AGAINST GENUINE BOWLING

A.M.Rossington (117) 66 balls Northamptonshire v Loughborough MCCU   Northampton

FASTEST DOUBLE HUNDRED AGAINST GENUINE BOWLING

M.H.Wessels   (202*) 170 balls Nottinghamshire v Sussex   Nottingham

MOST RUNS IN AN OVER

34   L.W.P.Wells (off R.D.Pringle)   Sussex v Durham   Hove
6, 6, 6, 4, 4, 6 NB, 0

200 RUNS IN A DAY

S.R.Dickson (0-210*)	Kent v Northamptonshire	Beckenham
A.D.Hales (0-218)	Nottinghamshire v Derbyshire	Derby
L.W.P.Wells (16*-258)	Sussex v Durham	Hove

He moved from 200 to 250 in 18 balls.

| M.H.Wessels (0-202*) | Nottinghamshire v Sussex | Nottingham |

150 OR MORE RUNS FROM BOUNDARIES IN AN INNINGS

Runs	6s	4s			
178	7	34	L.W.P.Wells	Sussex v Durham	Hove
158	1	38	A.D.Hales	Nottinghamshire v Derbyshire	Derby

HUNDRED ON FIRST-CLASS DEBUT IN BRITAIN

H.Klaasen	103	South Africa A v Hampshire	Southampton
H.G.Kuhn	200*	South Africa A v Hampshire	Southampton
A.K.Markram	102*	South Africa A v Hampshire	Southampton

CARRYING BAT THROUGH COMPLETED INNINGS

C.T.Bancroft	206*	Gloucestershire (385) v Kent	Bristol
D.J.Bell-Drummond	84*	Kent (180) v Nottinghamshire	Nottingham
R.J.Burns	219*	Surrey (483) v Hampshire	The Oval
D.Elgar	113*	Somerset (278) v Lancashire	Manchester
K.K.Jennings	102*	Durham (250) v Nottinghamshire	Chester-le-Street
D.P.Sibley	92*	Warwickshire (188) v Hampshire	Birmingham

60% OF A COMPLETED INNINGS TOTAL

| 62.38% | L.S.Livingstone | (68/109) | Lancashire v Somerset | Manchester |
| 60.17% | A.Lyth | (68/113) | Yorkshire v Essex | Scarborough |

LONG INNINGS (Qualification 600 mins and/or 400 balls)

Mins	Balls				
603	423	R.J.Burns	(219*)	Surrey v Hampshire	The Oval
588	407	A.N.Cook	(243)	England v West Indies (*1st Test*)	Birmingham
520	408	S.R.Dickson	(318)	Kent v Northamptonshire	Beckenham
593	427	C.A.Ingram	(155*)	Glamorgan v Nottinghamshire	Cardiff
496	452	S.R.Patel	(257*)	Nottinghamshire v Gloucestershire	Bristol
501	408	C.T.Steel	(224)	Durham v Leicestershire	Leicester

FIRST-WICKET PARTNERSHIP OF 100 IN EACH INNINGS

241/146	S.D.Robson/N.R.T.Gubbins	Middlesex v Essex	Lord's
103/109	R.J.Burns/M.D.Stoneman	Surrey v Hampshire	The Oval

OTHER NOTABLE PARTNERSHIPS († *Team record*)

Qualifications: 1st-4th wkts: 250 runs; 5th-6th: 225; 7th: 200; 8th: 175; 9th: 150; 10th: 100.

First Wicket

373†	N.L.J.Browne/A.N.Cook	Essex v Middlesex	Chelmsford
333†	L.M.Reece/B.A.Godleman	Derbyshire v Northamptonshire	Derby

Second Wicket

382†	S.R.Dickson/J.L.Denly	Kent v Northamptonshire	Beckenham

Third Wicket

376	L.W.P.Wells/S.van Zyl	Sussex v Durham	Hove
256	S.G.Borthwick/K.C.Sangakkara	Surrey v Lancashire	The Oval

Fourth Wicket

367†	J.H.K.Adams/S.M.Ervine	Hampshire v Warwickshire	Southampton
258	K.C.Sangakkara/B.T.Foakes	Surrey v Yorkshire	The Oval

Fifth Wicket

239	M.D.E.Holden/A.M.Rossington	Northamptonshire v Kent	Beckenham

Sixth Wicket

249	D.Elgar/L.Gregory	Somerset v Middlesex	Lord's
242	W.T.Root/C.M.W.Read	Nottinghamshire v Sussex	Hove
231	D.J.Vilas/R.McLaren	Lancashire v Hampshire	Manchester
229	R.S.Bopara/J.S.Foster	Essex v Warwickshire	Chelmsford
226*	C.A.Ingram/C.B.Cooke	Glamorgan v Nottinghamshire	Cardiff

Seventh Wicket

243	S.Chanderpaul/J.Clark	Lancashire v Surrey	The Oval

Tenth Wicket

122	L.J.Hill/C.F.Parkinson	Leicestershire v Kent	Canterbury
111	C.T.Bancroft/M.D.Taylor	Gloucestershire v Kent	Bristol
102	B.A.Godleman/G.S.Sandhu	Derbyshire v Durham	Chesterfield

BOWLING HIGHLIGHTS
EIGHT OR MORE WICKETS IN AN INNINGS

S.T.Finn	8- 79	Middlesex v Lancashire	Lord's
S.R.Harmer (2)	9- 95	Essex v Middlesex	Chelmsford
	8- 36	Essex v Warwickshire	Chelmsford
R.K.Kleinveldt	9- 65	Northamptonshire v Nottinghamshire	Northampton
L.C.Norwell	8- 43	Gloucestershire v Leicestershire	Leicester
C.F.Parkinson	8-148	Leicestershire v Worcestershire	Worcester
D.I.Stevens	8- 75	Kent v Leicestershire	Canterbury
G.C.Viljoen	8- 90	Derbyshire v Sussex	Hove

TEN OR MORE WICKETS IN A MATCH

M.M.Ali	10-112	England v South Africa (*1st Test*)	Lord's
J.C.Archer	11-137	Sussex v Leicestershire	Leicester
T.E.Bailey	10- 98	Lancashire v Middlesex	Lord's
W.A.T.Beer	11- 91	Sussex v South Africa A	Arundel
D.M.Bess	10-162	Somerset v Hampshire	Taunton
B.O.Coad	10-102	Yorkshire v Warwickshire	Birmingham
P.Coughlin	10-133	Durham v Northamptonshire	Chester-le-Street
R.J.Crichard	11-142	Cambridge U v Oxford U	Cambridge
S.R.Harmer (2)	14-128	Essex v Warwickshire	Chelmsford
	14-172	Essex v Middlesex	Chelmsford

M.G.Hogan	10- 87	Glamorgan v Kent	Canterbury
B.A.Hutton	10-126	Nottinghamshire v Derbyshire	Derby
R.K.Kleinveldt	13- 98	Northamptonshire v Nottinghamshire	Northampton
J.Leach	10-122	Worcestershire v Northamptonshire	Worcester
C.McKerr	10-141	Derbyshire v Northamptonshire	Northampton
Mohammad Amir	10- 72	Essex v Yorkshire	Scarborough
L.C.Norwell (2)	10- 99	Gloucestershire v Leicestershire	Bristol
	10- 95	Gloucestershire v Leicestershire	Leicester
C.F.Parkinson	10-185	Leicestershire v Worcestershire	Worcester
R.H.Patel	12-173	Middlesex v Somerset	Taunton
J.A.Porter	12- 95	Essex v Somerset	Chelmsford
G.C.Viljoen	15-170	Derbyshire v Sussex	Hove

FIVE WICKETS IN AN INNINGS ON FIRST-CLASS DEBUT

| L.Chapman | 6- 78 | Cambridge MCCU v Nottinghamshire | Cambridge |
| Hamidullah Qadri | 5- 60 | Derbyshire v Glamorgan | Cardiff |

HAT-TRICK

| M.M.Ali | | England v South Africa (*3rd Test*) | The Oval |

200 RUNS CONCEDED IN AN INNINGS

| B.M.A.J.Mendis 52.3-3-204-6 | Derbyshire v Leicestershire | Derby |

MOST OVERS BOWLED IN AN INNINGS

| Yasir Shah | 57-10-165-4 | Kent v Northamptonshire | Beckenham |

ALL-ROUND HIGHLIGHTS
MATCH DOUBLE (HUNDRED AND FIVE WICKETS IN AN INNINGS)

| J.S.Patel (100 & 6-50) | Warwickshire v Yorkshire | Leeds |

WICKET-KEEPING HIGHLIGHTS
SIX WICKET-KEEPING DISMISSALS IN AN INNINGS

| A.L.Davies | 6ct | Lancashire v Middlesex | Southport |
| S.O.Dowrich | 5ct, 1st | West Indians v Derbyshire | Derby |

NINE OR MORE WICKET-KEEPING DISMISSALS IN A MATCH

| A.L.Davies | 9ct, 1st | Lancashire v Middlesex | Southport |
| J.A.Simpson | 9ct | Middlesex v Warwickshire | Lord's |

NO BYES CONCEDED IN AN INNINGS OF 600 OR MORE

| D.Smit | | Derbyshire (619) v Leicestershire | Derby |

FIELDING HIGHLIGHTS
FOUR OR MORE CATCHES IN THE FIELD IN AN INNINGS

H.Z.Finch	5ct	Sussex v Worcestershire	Worcester
S.G.Borthwick	4ct	Surrey v Warwickshire	The Oval
P.D.Collingwood	4ct	Durham v Gloucestershire	Bristol
T.B.de Bruyn	4ct	South Africa v England (*4th Test*)	Manchester
W.R.S.Gidman	4ct	Kent v Worcestershire	Worcester
O.P.Rayner	4ct	Middlesex v Surrey	Lord's

SIX CATCHES IN THE FIELD IN A MATCH

| H.Z.Finch | 6ct | Sussex v Worcestershire | Worcester |

COUNTY CHAMPIONSHIP 2017
SPECSAVERS FINAL TABLES

DIVISION 1

	P	W	L	D	Bat	Bowl	Deduct Points	Total Points
1 **ESSEX** (-)	14	10	–	4	40	28	–	248
2 Lancashire (7)	14	5	3	6	37	29	–	176
3 Surrey (5)	14	2	2	10	34	47	–	163
4 Yorkshire (3)	14	4	5	5	35	24	–	148
5 Hampshire (8)	14	3	3	8	36	24	–	148
6 Somerset (2)	14	4	6	4	39	24	–	147
7 Middlesex (1)	14	3	4	7	37	28	2	146
8 Warwickshire (6)	14	1	9	4	31	19	–	86

DIVISION 2

	P	W	L	D	A	Bat	Bowl	Deduct Points	Total Points
1 Worcestershire (3)	14	9	3	2	–	39	45	–	238
2 Nottinghamshire (-)	14	7	2	5	–	41	44	–	222
3 Northamptonshire (5)	14	9	3	2	–	39	29	5	217
4 Sussex (4)	14	7	5	2	–	39	35	–	196
5 Kent (4)	14	4	2	7	1	36	35	–	175
6 Gloucestershire (6)	14	3	4	7	–	35	29	–	147
7 Glamorgan (8)	14	3	7	4	–	40	25	–	133
8 Derbyshire (9)	14	3	7	3	1	30	29	–	127
9 Durham (7)	14	3	6	5	–	37	36	48	98
10 Leicestershire (7)	14	–	9	5	–	34	32	16	75

Middlesex deducted 2 points for slow over rate.
Northamptonshire deducted 5 points for slow over rate.
Leicestershire deducted 16 points for a breach in player conduct.
Durham deducted 48 points for accepting a financial aid package during 2016.

SCORING OF CHAMPIONSHIP POINTS 2017

(a) For a win, 16 points, plus any points scored in the first innings.

(b) In a tie, each side to score eight points, plus any points scored in the first innings.

(c) In a drawn match, each side to score five points, plus any points scored in the first innings (see also paragraph (e) below).

(d) If the scores are equal in a drawn match, the side batting in the fourth innings to score eight points plus any points scored in the first innings, and the opposing side to score three points plus any points scored in the first innings.

(e) **First Innings Points** (awarded only for performances **in the first 110 overs** of each first innings and retained whatever the result of the match).

    (i) A maximum of five batting points to be available as under:
        200 to 249 runs – 1 point; 250 to 299 runs – 2 points; 300 to 349 runs – 3 points; 350 to 399 runs – 4 points; 400 runs or over – 5 points.

    (ii) A maximum of three bowling points to be available as under:
        3 to 5 wickets taken – 1 point; 6 to 8 wickets taken – 2 points; 9 to 10 wickets taken – 3 points.

(f) If a match is abandoned without a ball being bowled, each side to score five points.

(g) The side which has the highest aggregate of points gained at the end of the season shall be the Champion County of their respective Division. Should any sides in the Championship table be equal on points, the following tie-breakers will be applied in the order stated: most wins, fewest losses, team achieving most points in contests between teams level on points, most wickets taken, most runs scored. At the end of the season, the top two teams from the Second Division will be promoted and the bottom two teams from the First Division will be relegated.

COUNTY CHAMPIONS

The English County Championship was not officially constituted until December 1889. Prior to that date there was no generally accepted method of awarding the title; although the 'least matches lost' method existed, it was not consistently applied. Rules governing playing qualifications were agreed in 1873 and the first unofficial points system 15 years later.

Research has produced a list of champions dating back to 1826, but at least seven different versions exist for the period from 1864 to 1889 (see *The Wisden Book of Cricket Records*). Only from 1890 can any authorised list of county champions commence.

That first official Championship was contested between eight counties: Gloucestershire, Kent, Lancashire, Middlesex, Nottinghamshire, Surrey, Sussex and Yorkshire. The remaining counties were admitted in the following seasons: 1891 – Somerset, 1895 – Derbyshire, Essex, Hampshire, Leicestershire and Warwickshire, 1899 – Worcestershire, 1905 – Northamptonshire, 1921 – Glamorgan, and 1992 – Durham.

The Championship pennant was introduced by the 1951 champions, Warwickshire, and the Lord's Taverners' Trophy was first presented in 1973. The first sponsors, Schweppes (1977-83), were succeeded by Britannic Assurance (1984-98), PPP Healthcare (1999-2000), CricInfo (2001), Frizzell (2002-05), Liverpool Victoria (2006-15) and Specsavers (from 2016). Based on their previous season's positions, the 18 counties were separated into two divisions in 2000. From 2000 to 2005 the bottom three Division 1 teams were relegated and the top three Division 2 sides promoted. This was reduced to two teams from the end of the 2006 season.

1890	Surrey	1935	Yorkshire	1979	Essex
1891	Surrey	1936	Derbyshire	1980	Middlesex
1892	Surrey	1937	Yorkshire	1981	Nottinghamshire
1893	Yorkshire	1938	Yorkshire	1982	Middlesex
1894	Surrey	1939	Yorkshire	1983	Essex
1895	Surrey	1946	Yorkshire	1984	Essex
1896	Yorkshire	1947	Middlesex	1985	Middlesex
1897	Lancashire	1948	Glamorgan	1986	Essex
1898	Yorkshire	1949 {	Middlesex	1987	Nottinghamshire
1899	Surrey	{	Yorkshire	1988	Worcestershire
1900	Yorkshire	1950 {	Lancashire	1989	Worcestershire
1901	Yorkshire	{	Surrey	1990	Middlesex
1902	Yorkshire	1951	Warwickshire	1991	Essex
1903	Middlesex	1952	Surrey	1992	Essex
1904	Lancashire	1953	Surrey	1993	Middlesex
1905	Yorkshire	1954	Surrey	1994	Warwickshire
1906	Kent	1955	Surrey	1995	Warwickshire
1907	Nottinghamshire	1956	Surrey	1996	Leicestershire
1908	Yorkshire	1957	Surrey	1997	Glamorgan
1909	Kent	1958	Surrey	1998	Leicestershire
1910	Kent	1959	Yorkshire	1999	Surrey
1911	Warwickshire	1960	Yorkshire	2000	Surrey
1912	Yorkshire	1961	Hampshire	2001	Yorkshire
1913	Kent	1962	Yorkshire	2002	Surrey
1914	Surrey	1963	Yorkshire	2003	Sussex
1919	Yorkshire	1964	Worcestershire	2004	Warwickshire
1920	Middlesex	1965	Worcestershire	2005	Nottinghamshire
1921	Middlesex	1966	Yorkshire	2006	Sussex
1922	Yorkshire	1967	Yorkshire	2007	Sussex
1923	Yorkshire	1968	Yorkshire	2008	Durham
1924	Yorkshire	1969	Glamorgan	2009	Durham
1925	Yorkshire	1970	Kent	2010	Nottinghamshire
1926	Lancashire	1971	Surrey	2011	Lancashire
1927	Lancashire	1972	Warwickshire	2012	Warwickshire
1928	Lancashire	1973	Hampshire	2013	Durham
1929	Nottinghamshire	1974	Worcestershire	2014	Yorkshire
1930	Lancashire	1975	Leicestershire	2015	Yorkshire
1931	Yorkshire	1976	Middlesex	2016	Middlesex
1932	Yorkshire	1977 {	Kent	2017	Essex
1933	Yorkshire	{	Middlesex		
1934	Lancashire	1978	Kent		

COUNTY CHAMPIONSHIP RESULTS 2017

DIVISION 1

	ESSEX	HANTS	LANCS	MIDDX	SOM'T	SURREY	WARWKS	YORKS
ESSEX		C'ford	C'ford	C'ford*	C'ford	C'ford	C'ford	C'ford
	–	E I/97	Drawn	E I/34	E 179	Drawn	E I/164	E 376
HANTS	So'ton		So'ton	So'ton	So'ton*	So'ton	So'ton	So'ton
	E 108	–	Drawn	Drawn	Drawn	Drawn	H I/94	Drawn
LANCS	Man	Man		S'port	Man	Man	Man	Man
	Drawn	La I/30	–	La 8w	La 164	La 7w	La 8w	Drawn
MIDDX	Lord's	Uxbrg	Lord's		Lord's	Lord's	Lord's	Lord's
	Drawn	Drawn	M 36	–	Drawn	Drawn	Wa 190	M I/64
SOM'T	Taunton	Taunton	Taunton	Taunton		Taunton	Taunton	Taunton
	E 8w	H 90	Sm 7w	Sm 231	–	Drawn	Drawn	Y 3
SURREY	G'ford	Oval	Oval	Oval	Oval		Oval	Oval
	E 8w	Drawn	Drawn	Drawn	Sy 6w	–	Sy I/1	Drawn
WARWKS	B'ham	B'ham	B'ham*	B'ham	B'ham	B'ham		B'ham
	E I/56	Drawn	Drawn	M 1w	Sm 169	Drawn	–	Y I/88
YORKS	Scar	Leeds	Leeds	Leeds	Scar	Leeds*	Leeds	
	E 8w	H 4w	Y 10w	Drawn	Sm 179	Drawn	Y 2w	–

DIVISION 2

	DERBYS	DURHAM	GLAM	GLOS	KENT	LEICS	N'HANTS	NOTTS	SUSSEX	WORCS
DERBYS		C'field	Derby		C'field	Derby	Derby	Derby		Derby
	–	Du 6w	Drawn	–	Aband	Drawn	Nh 3w	Nt I/61	–	Wo I/42
DURHAM	C-le-St		C-le-St	–	C-le-St	–	C-le-St	C-le-St	C-le-St	C-le-St*
	Du 9w	–	Du 9w	–	Drawn	–	Nh 2w	Nt 9w	Sx 132	Drawn
GLAM	Cardiff*	Swansea		Cardiff			Cardiff	Cardiff	Col B	Cardiff
	De 39	Gm 3w	–	Drawn	–	–	Nh 7w	Drawn	Sx 1w	Wo 8w
GLOS	Bristol	Bristol	Chelt'm		Bristol	Bristol		Bristol		Chelt'm
	De 157	Drawn	Gs 10w	–	Drawn	Gs I/6	–	Drawn	–	Drawn
KENT	Cant	Cant	Cant	Cant		Cant	Beck'm		Tun W	·
	K 169	Drawn	Gm 5w	K 334	–	Drawn	Drawn	–	K 147	·
LEICS		Leics	Leics	Leics	Leics		Leics	Leics	Leics	
	–	Drawn	Drawn	Gs 10w	Drawn	–	Nh 6w	Nt 10w	Sx 5w	–
N'HANTS	No'ton		No'ton	No'ton		No'ton*		No'ton	No'ton	No'ton
	Nh 128	–	Nh I/22	Drawn	–	Nh 2	–	Nh 124	Nh 6w	Wo 8w
NOTTS	N'ham			N'ham	N'ham*	N'ham	N'ham		N'ham	N'ham
	Drawn	– ·	–	Nt I/50	Drawn	Nt I/280	Nt 163	–	Nt I/88	Wo 8w
SUSSEX	Hove	Hove		Hove*	Hove	Arundel		Hove		Hove
	De 45	Sx I/177	–	Drawn	K 226	Sx 231	–	Drawn	–	Sx I/7
WORCS		Worcs	Worcs	Worcs	Worcs	Worcs	Worcs		Worcs	
	–	Wo 137	Gm 9w	Wo 189	Wo 4w	Wo 6w	Wo 20	–	Sx 9w	–

* = Floodlit match

COUNTY CHAMPIONSHIP FIXTURES 2018

DIVISION 1

	ESSEX	HANTS	LANCS	NOTTS	SOM'T	SURREY	WORCS	YORKS
ESSEX	-	C'ford	C'ford	C'ford	C'ford*	C'ford	C'ford	C'ford
HANTS	So'ton	-	So'ton	So'ton	So'ton	So'ton	So'ton	So'ton*
LANCS	Man	Man	-	Man	Man	Man	S'port	Man
NOTTS	N'ham	N'ham	N'ham	-	N'ham	N'ham	N'ham*	N'ham
SOM'T	Taunton	Taunton	Taunton	Taunton	-	Taunton	Taunton	Taunton
SURREY	Oval	Oval	Oval*	Oval	G'ford	-	Oval	Oval
WORCS	Worcs	Worcs	Worcs	Worcs	Worcs	Worcs	-	Worcs
YORKS	Leeds	Leeds	Leeds	Leeds	Leeds	Scar	Scar	-

DIVISION 2

	DERBYS	DURHAM	GLAM	GLOS	KENT	LEICS	MIDDX	N'HANTS	SUSSEX	WARWKS
DERBYS	-	Derby	Derby	Derby	Derby	Derby*	Derby	C'field		
DURHAM	C-le-St	-			C-le-St	C-le-St	C-le-St	C-le-St	C-le-St	C-le-St*
GLAM	Swan	Cardiff	-		Cardiff	Cardiff		Cardiff		Col B
GLOS		Chelt	Bristol	-	Bristol	Bristol	Bristol	Bristol	Chelt	
KENT			Cant	Cant	-	Cant	Cant*	Cant	Cant	Tun W
LEICS	Leics	Leics	Leics		Leics	-	Leics		Leics	Leics
MIDDX	Lord's		Lord's	Lord's	Lord's		-	Lord's	Lord's	Lord's
N'HANTS	No'ton	No'ton		No'ton*		No'ton	No'ton	-	No'ton	No'ton
SUSSEX	Hove	Arundel	Hove*	Hove		Hove	Hove		-	Hove
WARWKS	Birm	Birm	Birm	Birm	Birm			Birm	Birm	-

* = Floodlit match

ROYAL LONDON ONE-DAY CUP 2017

This latest format of limited-overs competition was launched in 2014, and is now the only List-A tournament played in the UK. The top team from each group went through to the semi-finals, with a home draw; the second team from each group (drawn at home) played off against the third team from the other division to qualify for the semi-finals. The winner is decided in the final at Lord's.

NORTH GROUP	P	W	L	T	NR	Pts	Net RR
1 Worcestershire (4)	8	6	1	1	–	13	+0.02
2 Yorkshire (3)	8	6	2	–	–	12	+0.86
3 Nottinghamshire (6)	8	4	3	–	1	9	–0.05
4 Lancashire (9)	8	4	4	–	–	8	+0.19
5 Durham (4)	8	4	3	–	1	7	+0.24
6 Leicestershire (8)	8	3	4	–	1	7	–0.001
7 Derbyshire (7)	8	2	5	–	1	5	–0.33
8 Northamptonshire (1)	8	1	4	1	2	5	–0.72
9 Warwickshire (2)	8	2	6	–	–	4	–0.52

SOUTH GROUP	P	W	L	T	NR	Pts	Net RR
1 Essex (3)	8	7	1	–	–	14	+0.88
2 Somerset (1)	8	5	2	–	1	11	+0.54
3 Surrey (4)	8	4	3	–	1	9	+0.10
4 Glamorgan (7)	8	4	4	–	–	8	–0.66
5 Sussex (9)	8	3	3	–	2	8	+0.53
6 Hampshire (5)	8	3	4	–	1	7	–0.10
7 Gloucestershire (8)	8	3	4	–	1	7	–0.43
8 Middlesex (6)	8	2	4	–	2	6	–0.24
9 Kent (2)	8	1	7	–	–	2	–0.40

Win = 2 points. Tie (T)/No Result (NR) = 1 point.
Durham deducted 2 points as part of a package of ECB financial assistance.

Positions of counties finishing equal on points are decided by most wins or, if equal, the team with the higher net run rate (ie deducting from the average runs per over scored by that team in matches where a result was achieved, the average runs per over scored against that team); if still equal, the team that achieved the most points in the matches played between them. In the event the teams still cannot be separated, the winner will be decided by drawing lots.

Statistical Highlights in 2017

Highest total	429-9	Nottinghamshire v Somerset	Taunton
Biggest victory (runs)	170	Somerset beat Glamorgan	Cardiff
Biggest victory (wkts)	10	Warwickshire beat Northants	Northampton
Most runs	636 (ave 79.50)	A.N.Cook (Essex)	
Highest innings	187*	A.D.Hales	Nottinghamshire v Surrey	Lord's
Most sixes inns	14	D.I.Stevens	Kent v Glamorgan	Swansea
Highest partnership	221	J.M.Vince/L.A.Dawson	Hampshire v Glamorgan	Southampton
Most wickets	20 (ave 24.90)	S.M.Curran (Surrey)	
Best bowling	5-36	L.C.Norwell	Gloucestershire v Middlesex	Lord's
	5-36	C.J.Liddle	Gloucestershire v Kent	Bristol
Most economical	10-1-29-1	C.Rushworth	Durham v Leicestershire	Gosforth
	10-1-29-1	J.C.Tredwell	Kent v Middlesex	Canterbury
Most expensive	10-0-97-1	J.W.Hastings	Worcestershire v Kent	Worcester
Most w/k dismissals	19	B.T.Foakes (Surrey)	
Most w/k dismissals (inns)	5	C.B.Cooke	Glamorgan v Kent	Swansea
Most catches	9	R.J.Burns (Surrey), A.Lyth (Yorkshire)	
Most catches (inns)	4	S.R.Hain	Warwickshire v Leics	Leicester
	4	R.E.van der Merwe	Somerset v Gloucestershire	Bristol

2017 ROYAL LONDON ONE-DAY CUP FINAL
NOTTINGHAMSHIRE v SURREY

At Lord's, London, on 1 July.
Result: **NOTTINGHAMSHIRE** won by four wickets.
Toss: Surrey. Award: A.D.Hales.

SURREY		Runs	Balls	4/6	Fall
J.J.Roy	c Mullaney b Patel	23	25	3	1- 83
M.D.Stoneman	not out	144	149	12	
K.C.Sangakkara	c Read b Mullaney	30	36	3	2-141
S.G.Borthwick	c Mullaney b Patel	14	20	1	3-172
† B.T.Foakes	b Mullaney	1	2	–	4-175
O.J.Pope	c Mullaney b Patel	4	3	1	5-180
S.M.Curran	b Pattinson	24	31	2	6-228
T.K.Curran	run out	16	18	1	7-255
* G.J.Batty	b Fletcher	11	11	1	8-282
J.W.Dernbach	c Wessels b Gurney	5	6	–	9-296
R.Rampaul	not out	0	–	–	
Extras	(B 1, LB 12, NB 2, W 10)	25			
Total	(9 wkts; 50 overs; 210 mins)	**297**			

NOTTINGHAMSHIRE		Runs	Balls	4/6	Fall
M.J.Lumb	lbw b S.M.Curran	4	9	–	1- 25
A.D.Hales	not out	187	167	20/4	
M.H.Wessels	lbw b Rampaul	6	9	1	2- 60
S.R.Patel	c S.M.Curran b Rampaul	7	11	–	3-104
B.R.M.Taylor	c Foakes b Dernbach	11	10	1	4-128
S.J.Mullaney	lbw b S.M.Curran	5	17	–	5-150
*†C.M.W.Read	c Stoneman b S.M.Curran	58	57	7	6-287
J.L.Pattinson	not out	9	9	1	
S.C.J.Broad					
L.J.Fletcher					
H.F.Gurney					
Extras	(LB 3, NB 4, W 4)	11			
Total	(6 wkts; 47.5 overs; 200 mins)	**298**			

NOTTINGHAMSHIRE	O	M	R	W	SURREY	O	M	R	W
Fletcher	5	0	37	1	Dernbach	10	0	53	1
Gurney	7	0	47	1	S.M.Curran	9.5	0	68	3
Pattinson	10	0	48	1	T.K.Curran	6	0	52	0
Patel	10	0	51	3	Rampaul	10	0	52	2
Broad	9	0	51	0	Borthwick	3	0	29	0
Mullaney	9	0	50	2	Batty	9	0	41	0

Umpires: R.T.Robinson and A.G.Wharf

SEMI-FINALS

At County Ground, Chelmsford, on 16 June. Toss: Essex. **NOTTINGHAMSHIRE** won by five wickets. Essex 370-5 (50; A.N.Cook 133, R.N.ten Doeschate 102*). Nottinghamshire 373-5 (49.3; S.R.Patel 122*, S.J.Mullaney 111, B.R.M.Taylor 62, J.A.Porter 3-56). Award: S.J.Mullaney.

At New Road, Worcester, on 17 June. Toss: Surrey. **SURREY** won by 153 runs. Surrey 363-7 (50; J.J.Roy 92, B.T.Foakes 86, K.C.Sangakkara 73). Worcestershire 210 (33.2; R.A.Whiteley 55, B.L.D'Oliveira 53, G.J.Batty 5-40). Award: G.J.Batty.

PRINCIPAL LIST A RECORDS 1963-2017

These records cover all the major limited-overs tournaments played by the counties since the inauguration of the Gillette Cup in 1963.

Highest Totals		496-4	Surrey v Glos	The Oval	2007
		445-8	Notts v Northants	Nottingham	2016
Highest Total Batting Second		429	Glamorgan v Surrey	The Oval	2002
Lowest Totals		23	Middlesex v Yorks	Leeds	1974
		36	Leics v Sussex	Leicester	1973
Largest Victory (Runs)		346	Somerset beat Devon	Torquay	1990
		304	Sussex beat Ireland	Belfast	1996
Highest Scores		268	A.D.Brown	Surrey v Glamorgan	The Oval	2002
		206	A.I.Kallicharran	Warwicks v Oxfords	Birmingham	1984
		203	A.D.Brown	Surrey v Hampshire	Guildford	1997
		201*	R.S.Bopara	Essex v Leics	Leicester	2008
		201	V.J.Wells	Leics v Berkshire	Leicester	1996
Fastest Hundred		36 balls	G.D.Rose	Somerset v Devon	Torquay	1990
		43 balls	R.R.Watson	Scotland v Somerset	Edinburgh	2003
		44 balls	M.A.Ealham	Kent v Derbyshire	Maidstone	1995
		44 balls	T.C.Smith	Lancashire v Worcs	Worcester	2012
		44 balls	D.I.Stevens	Kent v Sussex	Canterbury	2013
Most Sixes (Inns)		15	R.N.ten Doeschate	Essex v Scotland	Chelmsford	2013

Highest Partnership for each Wicket

1st	342	M.J.Lumb/M.H.Wessels	Notts v Northants	Nottingham	2016
2nd	302	M.E.Trescothick/C.Kieswetter	Somerset v Glos	Taunton	2008
3rd	309*	T.S.Curtis/T.M.Moody	Worcs v Surrey	The Oval	1994
4th	234*	D.Lloyd/C.H.Lloyd	Lancashire v Glos	Manchester	1978
5th	221*	R.R.Sarwan/M.A.Hardinges	Glos v Lancashire	Manchester	2005
6th	226	N.J.Llong/M.V.Fleming	Kent v Cheshire	Bowdon	1999
7th	170	D.R.Brown/A.F.Giles	Warwicks v Essex	Birmingham	2003
8th	174	R.W.T.Key/J.C.Tredwell	Kent v Surrey	The Oval	2007
9th	155	C.M.W.Read/A.J.Harris	Notts v Durham	Nottingham	1984
10th	82	G.Chapple/P.J.Martin	Lancashire v Worcs	Manchester	1996

Best Bowling		8-21	M.A.Holding	Derbyshire v Sussex	Hove	1988
		8-26	K.D.Boyce	Essex v Lancashire	Manchester	1971
		8-31	D.L.Underwood	Kent v Scotland	Edinburgh	1987
		8-66	S.R.G.Francis	Somerset v Derbys	Derby	2004
Four Wkts in Four Balls			A.Ward	Derbyshire v Sussex	Derby	1970
			S.M.Pollock	Warwickshire v Leics	Birmingham	1996
			V.C.Drakes	Notts v Derbyshire	Nottingham	1999
			D.A.Payne	Gloucestershire v Essex	Chelmsford	2010
			G.R.Napier	Essex v Surrey	Chelmsford	2013

Most Economical Analyses

8-8-0-0	B.A.Langford	Somerset v Essex	Yeovil	1969
8-7-1-1	D.R.Doshi	Notts v Northants	Northampton	1977
12-9-3-1	J.Simmons	Lancashire v Suffolk	Bury St Eds	1985
8-6-2-3	F.J.Titmus	Middlesex v Northants	Northampton	1972

Most Expensive Analyses

9-0-108-3	S.D.Thomas	Glamorgan v Surrey	The Oval	2002
10-0-107-0	J.W.Dernbach	Surrey v Essex	The Oval	2008
11-0-103-0	G.Welch	Warwicks v Lancs	Birmingham	1995
10-0-101-1	M.J.J.Critchley	Derbyshire v Worcs	Worcester	2016

Century and Five Wickets in an Innings

154*, 5-26	M.J.Procter	Glos v Somerset	Taunton	1972
206, 6-32	A.I.Kallicharran	Warwicks v Oxfords	Birmingham	1984
103, 5-41	C.L.Hooper	Kent v Essex	Maidstone	1993
125, 5-41	I.R.Bell	Warwicks v Essex	Chelmsford	2003

Most Wicket-Keeping Dismissals in an Innings

8 (8 ct)	D.J.S.Taylor	Somerset v British Us	Taunton	1982
8 (8 ct)	D.J.Pipe	Worcs v Herts	Hertford	2001

Most Catches in an Innings by a Fielder

5	J.M.Rice	Hampshire v Warwicks	Southampton	1978
5	D.J.G.Sales	Northants v Essex	Northampton	2007

NATWEST t20 BLAST 2017

In 2017, the Twenty20 competition was sponsored by NatWest. Between 2003 and 2009, three regional leagues competed to qualify for the knockout stages, but this was reduced to two leagues in 2010, before returning to the three-division format in 2012. In 2014, the competition reverted to two regional leagues. (2016's positions in brackets.)

NORTH GROUP

	P	W	L	T	NR	Pts	Net RR
Nottinghamshire (1)	14	8	4	–	2	18	+0.48
Derbyshire (7)	14	8	5	–	1	17	+0.45
Warwickshire (6)	14	8	5	–	1	17	+0.23
Leicestershire (9)	14	8	5	–	1	17	+0.13
Yorkshire (3)	14	6	5	1	2	15	+1.12
Northamptonshire (2)	14	6	5	–	3	15	–0.63
Lancashire (5)	14	5	6	1	2	13	+0.17
Worcestershire (8)	14	3	10	–	1	7	–0.71
Durham (4)	14	3	10	–	1	3	–1.20

SOUTH GROUP

	P	W	L	T	NR	Pts	Net RR
Glamorgan (2)	14	7	3	–	4	18	+0.04
Surrey (5)	14	7	5	–	2	16	–0.13
Hampshire (8)	14	7	6	–	1	15	–0.02
Somerset (9)	14	6	6	–	2	14	+0.49
Sussex (6)	14	5	5	1	3	14	+0.42
Kent (7)	14	6	7	1	–	13	–0.15
Middlesex (3)	14	5	7	1	1	12	+0.22
Essex (4)	14	5	7	–	2	12	–0.20
Gloucestershire (1)	14	4	6	1	3	12	–0.64

Durham deducted 4 points for accepting a financial aid package during 2016.

QUARTER-FINALS: HAMPSHIRE beat Derbyshire by 101 runs at Hove.
GLAMORGAN beat Leicestershire by nine wickets at Cardiff.
NOTTINGHAMSHIRE beat Somerset by five wickets at Nottingham.
WARWICKSHIRE beat Surrey by six wickets at The Oval.

SEMI-FINALS: WARWICKSHIRE beat Glamorgan by 11 runs at Birmingham.
NOTTINGHAMSHIRE beat Warwickshire by 22 runs at Birmingham.

LEADING AGGREGATES AND RECORDS 2017

BATTING (550 runs)

	M	I	NO	HS	Runs	Avge	100	50	R/100b	Sixes
J.L.Denly (Kent)	14	14	1	127	567	43.61	2	1	150.7	25
M.H.Wessels (Notts)	16	16	3	110	559	43.00	1	1	151.4	28

BOWLING (20 wkts)

	O	M	R	W	Avge	BB	4w	R/Over
C.J.McKay (Leics)	43.0	1	328	23	14.26	5-11	1	7.62
J.T.Ball (Notts)	48.4	1	428	22	19.45	3-27	–	8.79
H.F.Gurney (Notts)	56.1	–	500	21	23.80	4-17	1	8.90
M.G.Hogan (Glam)	46.5	2	390	20	19.50	5-17	2	8.32
J.S.Patel (Warwks)	64.0	1	437	20	21.85	4-22	1	6.82

Highest total	260-4		Yorkshire v Northamptonshire	Leeds
Highest innings	161	A.Lyth	Yorkshire v Northamptonshire	Leeds
Most sixes	30	C.A.Ingram (Glamorgan)		
Highest partnership	207	J.L.Denly/D.J.Bell-Drummond	Kent v Essex	Chelmsford
Best bowling	6-19	T.T.Bresnan	Yorkshire v Lancashire	Leeds
Most economical	4-0-8-1	B.A.C.Howell	Gloucestershire v Essex	Bristol
Most expensive	4-0-77-0	B.W.Sanderson	Northamptonshire v Yorkshire	Leeds
Most w/k dismissals	13	B.C.Brown (Sussex), T.J.Moores (Nottinghamshire)		
Most catches	13	S.R.Hain (Warwickshire)		
Most catches (inns)	4	E.J.G.Morgan	Middlesex v Essex	Lord's

2017 NATWEST t20 BLAST FINAL
NOTTINGHAMSHIRE v WARWICKSHIRE

At Edgbaston, Birmingham, on 2 September (floodlit).
Result: **NOTTINGHAMSHIRE** won by 22 runs.
Toss: Warwickshire. Award: S.R.Patel.

NOTTINGHAMSHIRE		Runs	Balls	4/6	Fall
M.H.Wessels	c Ambrose b Woakes	19	12	4	3- 30
A.D.Hales	b Woakes	7	6	–/1	1- 21
† T.J.Moores	c Sibley b Woakes	0	3	–	2- 21
B.R.M.Taylor	c Sibley b de Grandhomme	65	49	9/1	4-162
S.R.Patel	not out	64	42	4/4	
* D.T.Christian	not out	24	8	2/2	
S.J.Mullaney					
W.T.Root					
I.S.Sodhi					
J.T.Ball					
H.F.Gurney					
Extras	(B 1, LB 7, W 3)	11			
Total	(4 wkts; 20 overs)	**190**			

WARWICKSHIRE		Runs	Balls	4/6	Fall
E.J.Pollock	run out	14	11	1	2- 16
D.P.Sibley	b Gurney	2	5	–	1- 12
S.R.Hain	c Christian b Gurney	72	44	5/3	6-157
A.J.Hose	b Ball	7	8	1	3- 36
* G.D.Elliott	lbw b Christian	9	11	–	4- 63
C.de Grandhomme	b Gurney	27	19	–/2	5-118
A.D.Thomason	c Moores b Gurney	26	13	–/2	7-160
C.R.Woakes	not out	4	4	–	
J.S.Patel	b Ball	4	3	–	8-166
† T.R.Ambrose	not out	1	2	–	
O.P.Stone					
Extras	(LB 1, W 1)	2			
Total	(8 wkts; 20 overs)	**168**			

WARWICKSHIRE	O	M	R	W	NOTTINGHAMSHIRE	O	M	R	W
Patel	4	0	24	0	Patel	4	0	42	0
Stone	4	0	50	0	Gurney	4	0	17	4
Woakes	4	0	29	3	Ball	4	0	26	2
Thomason	2	0	26	0	Christian	4	0	43	1
Elliott	2	0	20	0	Mullaney	3	0	28	0
Sibley	3	0	29	0	Sodhi	1	0	11	0
De Grandhomme	1	0	4	1					

Umpires: M.A.Gough and A.G.Wharf

TWENTY20 CUP WINNERS

2003	Surrey	2008	Middlesex	2013	Northamptonshire
2004	Leicestershire	2009	Sussex	2014	Warwickshire
2005	Somerset	2010	Hampshire	2015	Lancashire
2006	Leicestershire	2011	Leicestershire	2016	Northamptonshire
2007	Kent	2012	Hampshire	2017	Nottinghamshire

PRINCIPAL TWENTY20 CUP RECORDS 2003-17

Highest Total	260-4		Yorkshire v Northants	Leeds	2017
Highest Total Batting 2nd	226-3		Sussex v Essex	Chelmsford	2014
Lowest Total	47		Northants v Durham	Chester-le-St	2011
Largest Victory (Runs)	143		Somerset v Essex	Chelmsford	2011
Largest Victory (Balls)	75		Hampshire v Glos	Bristol	2010
Highest Scores	161	A.Lyth	Yorkshire v Northants	Leeds	2017
	158*	B.B.McCullum	Warwickshire v Derbys	Birmingham	2015
	153*	L.J.Wright	Sussex v Essex	Chelmsford	2014
	152*	G.R.Napier	Essex v Sussex	Chelmsford	2008
	151*	C.H.Gayle	Somerset v Kent	Taunton	2015
Fastest Hundred	34 balls	A.Symonds	Kent v Middlesex	Maidstone	2004
Most Sixes (Innings)	16	G.R.Napier	Essex v Sussex	Chelmsford	2008
Most Runs in Career	3518	J.L.Denly	Kent, Middlesex		2004-17

Highest Partnership for each Wicket

1st	207	J.L.Denly/D.J.Bell-Drummond	Kent v Sussex	Chelmsford	2017
2nd	186	J.L.Langer/C.L.White	Somerset v Glos	Taunton	2006
3rd	153	M.H.Wessels/B.R.M.Taylor	Nottinghamshire v Derbys	Nottingham	2017
4th	159*	L.J.Wright/M.W.Machan	Sussex v Essex	Chelmsford	2014
5th	117*	M.N.W.Spriegel/G.C.Wilson	Surrey v Middlesex	Lord's	2012
6th	126*	C.S.MacLeod/J.W.Hastings	Durham v Northants	Chester-le-St	2014
7th	80	D.T.Christian/T.S.Roland-Jones	Middlesex v Kent	Canterbury	2014
8th	86*	J.A.Simpson/T.G.Southee	Middlesex v Hampshire	Southampton	2017
9th	69	C.J.Anderson/J.H.Davey	Somerset v Surrey	The Oval	2017
10th	59	H.H.Streak/J.E.Anyon	Warwickshire v Worcs	Birmingham	2005

Best Bowling

	6- 5	A.V.Suppiah	Somerset v Glamorgan	Cardiff	2011
	6-16	T.G.Southee	Essex v Glamorgan	Chelmsford	2011
	6-19	T.T.Bresnan	Yorkshire v Lancashire	Leeds	2017
	6-21	A.J.Hall	Northants v Worcs	Northampton	2008
	6-24	T.J.Murtagh	Surrey v Middlesex	Lord's	2005
Most Wkts in Career	156	Yasir Arafat	Hants, Kent, Lancs, Somerset, Surrey, Sussex		2006-16

Most Economical Innings Analyses (Qualification: 4 overs)

4-2-5-2	A.C.Thomas	Somerset v Hampshire	Southampton	2010
4-0-5-3	D.R.Briggs	Hampshire v Kent	Canterbury	2010
4-1-6-2	J.Louw	Northants v Warwicks	Birmingham	2004
4-0-6-1	M.W.Alleyne	Glos v Worcs	Worcester	2005

Most Maiden Overs in an Innings

4-2-9-1	M.Morkel	Kent v Surrey	Beckenham	2007
4-2-5-2	A.C.Thomas	Somerset v Hampshire	Southampton	2010

Most Expensive Innings Analyses

4-0-77-0	B.W.Sanderson	Northants v Yorkshire	Leeds	2017
4-0-67-1	R.J.Kirtley	Sussex v Essex	Chelmsford	2008
4-0-65-2	M.J.Hoggard	Yorkshire v Lancs	Leeds	2005
4-0-65-1	P.I.Walter	Essex v Kent	Chelmsford	2017

Most Wicket-Keeping Dismissals in Career

114	J.S.Foster	Essex		2003-17

Most Wicket-Keeping Dismissals in an Innings

5 (5 ct)	M.J.Prior	Sussex v Middlesex	Richmond	2006
5 (4 ct, 1 st)	G.L.Brophy	Yorkshire v Durham	Chester-le-St	2008
5 (3 ct, 2 st)	B.J.M.Scott	Worcs v Yorkshire	Worcester	2011
5 (4 ct, 1 st)	G.C.Wilson	Surrey v Hampshire	The Oval	2014
5 (5 ct)	N.J.O'Brien	Leics v Northants	Leicester	2014
5 (3 ct, 2 st)	J.A.Simpson	Middlesex v Surrey	Lord's	2014
5 (4 ct, 1 st)	C.B.Cooke	Glamorgan v Surrey	Cardiff	2016

Most Catches in Career

78	S.J.Croft	Lancashire		2006-16

Most Catches in an Innings by a Fielder

5	M.W.Machan	Sussex v Glamorgan	Hove	2016

YOUNG CRICKETER OF THE YEAR

This annual award, made by The Cricket Writers' Club, is currently restricted to players qualified for England, Andrew Symonds meeting that requirement at the time of his award, and under the age of 23 on 1st May. In 1986 their ballot resulted in a dead heat. Up to 21 March 2018 their selections have gained a tally of 2,640 international Test match caps (shown in brackets).

1950	R.Tattersall (16)	1973	M.Hendrick (30)	1995	A.Symonds (26 – Australia)
1951	P.B.H.May (66)	1974	P.H.Edmonds (51)	1996	C.E.W.Silverwood (6)
1952	F.S.Trueman (67)	1975	A.Kennedy	1997	B.C.Hollioake (2)
1953	M.C.Cowdrey (114)	1976	G.Miller (34)	1998	A.Flintoff (79)
1954	P.J.Loader (13)	1977	I.T.Botham (102)	1999	A.J.Tudor (10)
1955	K.F.Barrington (82)	1978	D.I.Gower (117)	2000	P.J.Franks
1956	B.Taylor	1979	P.W.G.Parker (1)	2001	O.A.Shah (6)
1957	M.J.Stewart (8)	1980	G.R.Dilley (41)	2002	R.Clarke (2)
1958	A.C.D.Ingleby-Mackenzie	1981	M.W.Gatting (79)	2003	J.M.Anderson (134)
1959	G.Pullar (28)	1982	N.G.Cowans (19)	2004	I.R.Bell (118)
1960	D.A.Allen (39)	1983	N.A.Foster (29)	2005	A.N.Cook (152)
1961	P.H.Parfitt (37)	1984	R.J.Bailey (4)	2006	S.C.J.Broad (114)
1962	P.J.Sharpe (12)	1985	D.V.Lawrence (5)	2007	A.U.Rashid (10)
1963	G.Boycott (108)	1986 {	A.A.Metcalfe	2008	R.S.Bopara (13)
1964	J.M.Brearley (39)		J.J.Whitaker (1)	2009	J.W.A.Taylor (7)
1965	A.P.E.Knott (95)	1987	R.J.Blakey (2)	2010	S.T.Finn (36)
1966	D.L.Underwood (86)	1988	M.P.Maynard (4)	2011	J.M.Bairstow (50)
1967	A.W.Greig (58)	1989	N.Hussain (96)	2012	J.E.Root (65)
1968	R.M.H.Cottam (4)	1990	M.A.Atherton (115)	2013	B.A.Stokes (39)
1969	A.Ward (5)	1991	M.R.Ramprakash (52)	2014	A.Z.Lees
1970	C.M.Old (46)	1992	I.D.K.Salisbury (15)	2015	J.A.Leaning
1971	J.Whitehouse	1993	M.N.Lathwell (2)	2016	B.M.Duckett (4)
1972	D.R.Owen-Thomas	1994	J.P.Crawley (37)	2017	D.W.Lawrence

THE PROFESSIONAL CRICKETERS' ASSOCIATION

PLAYER OF THE YEAR

Founded in 1967, the Professional Cricketers' Association introduced this award, decided by their membership, in 1970. The award, now known as the Reg Hayter Cup, is presented at the PCA's Annual Awards Dinner in London.

1970 {	M.J.Procter	1986	C.A.Walsh	2003	Mushtaq Ahmed
	J.D.Bond	1987	R.J.Hadlee	2004	A.Flintoff
1971	L.R.Gibbs	1988	G.A.Hick	2005	A.Flintoff
1972	A.M.E.Roberts	1989	S.J.Cook	2006	M.R.Ramprakash
1973	P.G.Lee	1990	G.A.Gooch	2007	O.D.Gibson
1974	B.Stead	1991	Waqar Younis	2008	M.van Jaarsveld
1975	Zaheer Abbas	1992	C.A.Walsh	2009	M.E.Trescothick
1976	P.G.Lee	1993	S.L.Watkin	2010	N.M.Carter
1977	M.J.Procter	1994	B.C.Lara	2011	M.E.Trescothick
1978	J.K.Lever	1995	D.G.Cork	2012	N.R.D.Compton
1979	J.K.Lever	1996	P.V.Simmons	2013	M.M.Ali
1980	R.D.Jackman	1997	S.P.James	2014	A.Lyth
1981	R.J.Hadlee	1998	M.B.Loye	2015	C.Rushworth
1982	M.D.Marshall	1999	S.G.Law	2016	B.M.Duckett
1983	K.S.McEwan	2000	M.E.Trescothick	2017	S.R.Patel
1984	R.J.Hadlee	2001	D.P.Fulton		
1985	N.V.Radford	2002	M.P.Vaughan		

2017 FIRST-CLASS AVERAGES

These averages involve the 517 players who appeared in the 151 first-class matches played by 29 teams in England and Wales during the 2017 season.

'Cap' denotes the season in which the player was awarded a 1st XI cap by the county he represented in 2017. If he played for more than one county in 2017, the county(ies) who awarded him his cap is (are) underlined. Durham abolished both their capping and 'awards' system after the 2005 season. Glamorgan's capping system is based on a player's number of appearances. Gloucestershire now cap players on first-class debut. Worcestershire now award county colours when players make their Championship debut.

Team abbreviations: CU – Cambridge University/Cambridge MCCU; CfU – Cardiff MCCU; De – Derbyshire; Du – Durham; DU – Durham MCCU; E – England; EL – England Lions; Ex – Essex; Gm – Glamorgan; Gs – Gloucestershire; H – Hampshire; K – Kent; La – Lancashire; LBU – Leeds/Bradford MCCU; Le – Leicestershire; LU – Loughborough MCCU; M – Middlesex; Nh – Northamptonshire; Nt – Nottinghamshire; OU – Oxford University/Oxford MCCU; Sm – Somerset; SA – South Africa(ns); SAA – South Africa A; Sy – Surrey; Sx – Sussex; Wa – Warwickshire; WI – West Indies/Indians; Wo – Worcestershire; Y – Yorkshire.

† Left-handed batsman. Cap: a dash (–) denotes a non-county player. A blank denotes uncapped by his current county.

BATTING AND FIELDING

	Cap	M	I	NO	HS	Runs	Avge	100	50	Ct/St
K.J.Abbott (H)	2017	14	18	4	97*	418	29.85	–	2	1
T.B.Abell (Sm)		13	25	2	96	572	26.00	–	4	12
† Abhiraj Singh (DU)	–	2	2	–	44	44	22.00	–	–	2
C.N.Ackermann (Le)		12	22	3	118	618	32.52	2	1	2
† J.H.K.Adams (H)	2006	13	19	–	166	580	30.52	2	1	15
B.M.R.Akram (LU)	–	2	2	–	44	51	25.50	–	–	2
A.M.Ali (Le)		3	5	–	40	110	22.00	–	–	2
† M.M.Ali (E/Wo)	2007	10	17	1	87	569	35.56	–	6	6
J.Allenby (Sm)		2	2	–	19	28	14.00	–	–	5
† T.P.Alsop (H)		7	11	–	62	235	21.36	–	2	9
T.R.Ambrose (Wa)	2007	14	26	2	104	542	22.58	1	2	28/3
H.M.Amla (SA)		5	9	–	91	420	46.66	–	4	3
† J.M.Anderson (E/La)	2003	13	16	11	13*	60	12.00	–	–	8
M.K.Anderson (LBU)	–	2	4	–	12	16	4.00	–	–	4
† Z.S.Ansari (Sy)	2014	2	3	–	37	52	17.33	–	–	–
J.C.Archer (Sx)	2017	13	20	6	81*	638	45.57	–	5	9
A.T.Arif (CU)		1	2	–	9	9	4.50	–	–	–
† Ashar Zaidi (Ex)		2	2	–	23	29	14.50	–	–	2
M.A.Ashraf (LBU)	–	1	2	1	24	24	24.00	–	–	–
R.Ashwin (WI)	2017	4	6	1	82	214	42.80	–	1	2
Azeem Rafiq (Y)	2016	6	7	–	17	54	7.71	–	–	–
M.Azharullah (Nh)	2015	7	10	5	23	73	14.60	–	–	1
G.J.Bailey (H)	2017	11	18	–	161	651	36.16	2	3	5
T.E.Bailey (La)		9	12	2	58	226	22.60	–	1	1
J.M.Bairstow (E/Y)	2011	9	14	–	99	397	28.35	–	3	33/2
A.J.Ball (K)		2	3	–	50	55	18.33	–	1	3
J.T.Ball (Nt)	2016	7	9	4	43	174	34.80	–	–	1
† G.S.Ballance (E/EL/Y)	2012	16	24	4	203*	1164	58.20	3	6	5
C.T.Bancroft (Gs)	2016	11	21	4	206*	685	40.29	1	4	14
L.Banks (Wa)		2	4	–	29	57	14.25	–	–	1
† K.H.D.Barker (Wa)	2013	13	23	5	70*	552	30.66	–	6	2
E.G.Barnard (Wo)	2015	14	20	4	75	580	36.25	–	5	8
G.A.Bartlett (Sm)		4	8	1	28	100	14.28	–	–	3
A.P.Barton (CU/Sx)		4	7	1	13*	22	4.40	–	–	2

	Cap	M	I	NO	HS	Runs	Avge	100	50	Ct/St
G.J.Batty (Sy)	2011	13	15	4	33	176	16.00	–	–	–
T.Bavuma (SA/SAA)	–	7	13	1	85*	448	37.33	–	4	3
† A.P.Beard (Ex)		5	6	4	58*	79	39.50	–	1	–
W.A.T.Beer (Sx)		2	2	–	27	52	26.00	–	–	–
I.R.Bell (Wa)	2001	14	25	1	99	629	26.20	–	5	9
D.J.Bell-Drummond (K)	2015	14	24	1	90	561	24.39	–	3	10
G.K.Berg (H)	2016	14	20	2	99*	568	31.55	–	2	2
D.M.Bess (Sm)		9	14	4	55	198	19.80	–	1	5
S.W.Billings (EL/K)	2015	8	10	2	70*	289	36.12	–	1	13
† D.Bishoo (WI)	–	4	5	1	23	41	10.25	–	–	–
J.Blackwood (WI)	–	6	11	3	79*	350	43.75	–	3	4
† A.J.Blake (K)		1	2	1	46*	65	65.00	–	–	1
O.S.Bocking (LBU)	–	2	4	1	1*	1	0.33	–	–	–
R.S.Bopara (Ex)	2005	15	22	2	192	690	34.50	1	3	7
S.G.Borthwick (Sy)		13	21	1	108*	500	25.00	1	1	21
† J.R.Bracey (Gs/LU)	2016	6	8	1	156	449	64.14	1	3	6
† W.D.Bragg (Gm)	2015	3	6	1	30	65	13.00	–	–	2
† N.Brand (CfU)	–	2	3	1	44*	44	22.00	–	–	1
K.C.Brathwaite (WI/Y)		8	16	–	134	408	25.50	1	2	4
T.T.Bresnan (Y)	2006	12	16	–	61	330	20.62	–	1	9
A.D.F.Brewster (CfU)	–	2	1	1	1*	1	1.00	–	–	–
D.R.Briggs (Sx)		9	13	6	120*	236	33.71	1	–	5
† S.C.J.Broad (E/Nt)	2008	13	16	3	57*	318	24.46	–	4	7
T.M.J.Brock (OU)	–	1	2	–	2	2	1.00	–	–	–
† C.A.J.Brodrick (De)		1	1	–	52	52	52.00	–	1	1
H.C.Brook (Y)		4	6	–	38	82	13.66	–	–	1
H.J.H.Brookes (Wa)		1	2	–	11	15	7.50	–	–	–
J.A.Brooks (Y)	2013	8	11	2	109*	178	19.77	1	–	2
B.M.Broughton (OU)	–	2	4	2	46	86	43.00	–	–	3
B.C.Brown (Sx)	2014	8	14	1	90	483	37.15	–	5	23
C.R.Brown (CfU/Gm)		4	7	–	35	154	22.00	–	–	–
P.R.Brown (Wo)	2017	4	5	3	5*	12	6.00	–	–	1
† N.L.J.Browne (Ex)	2015	16	25	–	221	1147	45.88	2	6	7
N.L.Buck (Nh)		9	13	3	43	201	20.10	–	–	6
S.F.G.Bullen (LBU)	–	2	4	–	29	61	15.25	–	–	–
M.G.K.Burgess (Sx)		6	10	1	146	434	48.22	1	2	18
J.E.Burke (Le)		1	1	–	0	0	0.00	–	–	–
J.T.A.Burnham (Du)		7	11	2	93*	223	24.77	–	1	1
† R.J.Burns (Sy)	2014	15	24	1	219*	1106	48.08	1	8	9
J.C.Buttler (La)		4	6	–	49	103	17.16	–	–	3
† E.J.Byrom (Sm)		8	15	–	56	401	26.73	–	1	2
E.Callis (Y)		1	1	–	17	17	17.00	–	–	–
† M.A.Carberry (H/Le)	2006	12	20	–	100	431	21.55	1	2	3
L.J.Carey (Gm)		11	14	2	54	219	18.25	–	1	3
K.S.Carlson (Gm)		9	14	–	191	469	33.50	1	1	4
B.A.Carse (Du)		2	3	2	61*	91	91.00	–	1	–
A.Carter (Nh)		1	2	–	8	11	5.50	–	–	–
M.Carter (Nt)		1	1	–	33	33	33.00	–	–	–
† K.Carver (Y)		2	4	–	20	48	12.00	–	–	2
† S.Chanderpaul (La)		13	19	3	182	831	51.93	3	1	3
L.J.Chapman (CU)	–	2	4	–	13	18	4.50	–	–	1
Z.J.Chappell (Le)		7	11	2	66	267	29.66	–	1	–
R.L.Chase (WI)	–	5	10	3	110*	381	54.42	1	3	1
† D.Chohan (CU)	–	1	2	–	26	30	15.00	–	–	–
V.Chopra (Ex)		11	17	1	100*	418	26.12	1	1	18
G.Clark (Du)		12	21	–	109	769	36.61	1	6	10

	Cap	M	I	NO	HS	Runs	Avge	100	50	Ct/St
J.Clark (La)		12	16	1	140	434	28.93	1	1	–
† J.Clark (DU)	–	2	3	–	18	18	6.00	–	–	–
J.M.Clarke (EL/Wo)	2015	15	26	5	142	920	43.80	2	3	10
R.Clarke (Sy/Wa)	2005/2011	15	22	1	83	438	20.85	–	3	14
† M.E.Claydon (K)	2016	10	13	5	21*	111	13.87	–	–	1
B.O.Coad (Y)		13	16	5	28	128	11.63	–	–	1
J.J.Cobb (Nh)		11	19	5	96	473	33.78	–	2	4
I.A.Cockbain (Gs)	2011	1	1	–	27	27	27.00	–	–	1
M.T.Coles (K)	2012	11	16	2	56*	304	21.71	–	1	12
P.D.Collingwood (Du)	1998	14	24	2	177	1087	49.40	3	5	23
T.G.L.Colverd (CU)	–	3	6	–	64	103	17.16	–	1	–
N.R.D.Compton (M)	2006	11	19	2	120	446	26.23	1	–	5
† A.N.Cook (E/Ex)	2005	14	23	–	243	1239	53.78	4	3	25
S.C.Cook (Du)		7	14	1	89*	348	26.76	–	2	5
S.J.Cook (Ex/LU)		7	7	4	3	4	1.33	–	–	–
W.Cook (LBU)		2	4	–	42	45	11.25	–	–	–
C.B.Cooke (Gm)	2016	13	22	5	113*	705	41.47	1	4	40
† J.M.Cooke (DU)	–	2	2	–	21	28	14.00	–	–	6
G.T.G.Cork (De)		1	1	–	0	0	0.00	–	–	1
† M.J.Cosgrove (Le)	2015	13	25	1	188	1161	48.37	2	6	1
B.D.Cotton (De)		2	4	3	32	50	50.00	–	–	–
P.Coughlin (Du)		8	12	2	73*	364	36.40	–	3	3
O.B.Cox (Wo)	2009	14	21	1	124	675	33.75	1	3	42/1
M.S.Crane (EL/H)		9	10	3	29	66	9.42	–	–	3
Z.Crawley (K)		5	7	–	62	137	19.57	–	1	4
R.J.Crichard (CU)	–	1	1	–	17	17	17.00	–	–	1
M.J.J.Critchley (De)		5	8	1	102	266	38.00	1	1	2
S.J.Croft (La)	2010	10	17	1	115	487	30.43	1	1	7
S.P.Crook (Nh)	2013	6	9	1	30	131	16.37	–	–	2
T.N.Cullen (CfU/Gm)		4	6	–	42	112	18.66	–	–	12/1
† M.L.Cummins (WI)	–	3	3	2	8*	8	8.00	–	–	–
† S.M.Curran (EL/Sy)		15	21	2	90	471	24.78	–	4	5
T.K.Curran (Sy)	2016	9	11	2	53	247	27.44	–	1	3
O.C.Currill (Gs)	2017	1	–	–	–	–	–	–	–	–
C.J.Dala (SAA)	–	3	4	1	14	25	8.33	–	–	–
A.D.Dalgleish (CU)	–	1	2	–	25	44	22.00	–	–	1
J.H.Davey (Sm)		3	5	1	47	58	14.50	–	–	2
A.L.Davies (La)	2017	15	26	2	140*	1046	43.58	3	5	46/7
† S.M.Davies (Sm)	2017	14	24	2	142	775	35.22	2	3	39/7
W.S.Davis (De)		5	7	2	25	64	12.80	–	–	2
L.A.Dawson (E/H)	2013	13	22	1	75	404	19.23	–	2	7
T.B.de Bruyn (SA/SAA)	–	5	9	1	72*	151	18.87	–	1	8
† Q.de Kock (SA)	–	5	9	–	68	236	26.22	–	3	18/2
M.de Lange (Gm)		11	17	1	39	254	15.87	–	–	5
† H.E.Dearden (Le)		11	21	–	87	445	21.19	–	2	12
† C.S.Delport (Le)		1	2	–	20	21	10.50	–	–	–
J.L.Denly (K)	2008	14	24	1	227	1266	57.54	5	5	8
† C.D.J.Dent (Gs)	2010	14	25	3	135*	978	44.45	2	8	13
J.W.Dernbach (Sy)	2011	6	5	1	8*	17	4.25	–	–	–
A.C.H.Dewhurst (CU)	–	1	2	–	91	94	47.00	–	1	1
N.J.Dexter (Le)		8	15	2	114	300	23.07	1	–	2
C.M.Dickinson (H)		2	3	–	99	113	37.66	–	1	4
S.R.Dickson (K)		14	24	–	318	982	40.91	2	4	9
M.W.Dixon (Ex)		2	2	–	8	12	6.00	–	–	–
B.L.D'Oliveira (Wo)	2012	14	25	–	150	891	35.64	3	3	10
A.H.T.Donald (Gm)		12	21	1	66*	550	27.50	–	5	12

	Cap	M	I	NO	HS	Runs	Avge	100	50	Ct/St
S.O.Dowrich (WI)	–	6	9	2	44*	120	17.14	–	–	15/2
G.S.Drissell (Gs)	2017	1	1	–	0	0	0.00	–	–	–
F.du Plessis (SA)	–	3	6	–	63	171	28.50	–	2	7
† B.M.Duckett (Nh)	2016	11	19	–	193	799	42.05	3	3	16
† J.P.Duminy (SA)	–	2	3	–	25	42	14.00	–	–	–
E.J.H.Eckersley (Le)	2013	15	28	3	158	787	31.48	1	3	17
F.H.Edwards (H)		10	11	4	20	43	6.14	–	–	–
† D.Elgar (Sm/SA)	2017	11	21	1	158	813	40.65	3	4	4
E.J.Ellis (OU)	–	2	3	1	18	27	13.50	–	–	5
† S.M.Ervine (H)	2005	15	23	1	203	653	29.68	1	3	14
D.A.Escott (OU)	–	1	2	–	22	36	18.00	–	–	3
S.S.Eskinazi (M)		14	25	2	179	793	34.47	2	4	11
L.J.Evans (Sx)		4	8	–	19	48	6.00	–	–	4
S.T.Evans (Le/LU)		3	4	–	114	163	40.75	1	–	1
W.N.Fazackerley (Le)		1	2	–	0	0	0.00	–	–	–
T.C.Fell (Wo)	2013	13	23	1	47	323	14.68	–	–	7
S.A.Feszczur-Hatchett (LBU)	–	2	4	1	24*	35	11.66	–	–	–
A.J.Finch (Sy)		1	1	–	39	39	39.00	–	–	–
H.Z.Finch (Sx)		12	21	–	82	453	23.84	–	3	16
S.T.Finn (M)	2009	11	14	6	31*	95	11.87	–	–	6
M.D.Fisher (Y)		–	2	–	37	86	21.50	–	–	–
L.J.Fletcher (Nt)	2014	10	11	3	92	140	17.50	–	1	2
B.T.Foakes (EL/Sy)	2016	15	22	5	127*	841	49.47	2	4	32/2
M.H.A.Footitt (Nt/Sy)		9	8	1	4	7	1.00	–	–	2
J.S.Foster (Ex)	2001	10	12	–	121	357	29.75	1	1	48/1
W.A.R.Fraine (DU)	–	2	3	–	23	48	16.00	–	–	–
† J.E.C.Franklin (M)	2015	10	14	1	112	296	22.76	1	1	4
S.T.Gabriel (WI)	–	3	3	1	10	10	5.00	–	–	–
R.N.Gamble (LU)	–	2	2	–	32	32	16.00	–	–	1
† G.H.S.Garton (EL/Sx)		4	5	–	18	43	8.60	–	–	2
† W.R.S.Gidman (K)		10	17	–	51	319	18.76	–	1	14
R.J.Gleeson (Nh)		7	9	4	25	63	12.60	–	–	1
† J.S.D.Gnodde (OU)	–	1	2	–	54	58	29.00	–	1	–
† B.A.Godleman (De)	2015	12	22	2	156*	799	39.95	3	2	7
O.J.G.Graham (LBU)	–	2	4	–	41	56	14.00	–	–	1
† B.W.M.Graves (DU)	–	1	1	–	0	0	0.00	–	–	–
A.D.Greenidge (CU)	–	2	4	–	22	35	8.75	–	–	1
L.Gregory (Sm)	2015	7	12	–	137	299	24.91	1	–	1
G.T.Griffiths (Le)		6	8	3	14*	37	7.40	–	–	1
T.D.Groenewald (Sm)	2016	10	14	8	41*	146	24.33	–	–	1
J.O.Grundy (M)	–	2	2	–	24	32	16.00	–	–	1
† N.R.T.Gubbins (EL/M)	2016	8	15	–	101	381	25.40	1	3	–
C.J.Guest (CU)	–	2	4	–	9	21	5.25	–	–	2
H.F.Gurney (Nt)	2014	12	13	5	42*	62	7.75	–	–	1
† C.J.Haggett (K)		5	8	3	29*	73	14.60	–	–	1
S.R.Hain (Wa)		9	16	1	81	312	20.80	–	2	4
A.D.Hales (Nt)	2011	8	11	–	218	463	42.09	1	1	1
H.Hameed (EL/La)	2016	14	24	4	88	522	26.10	–	3	8
Hamidullah Qadri (De)		3	6	4	11*	20	10.00	–	–	2
P.S.P.Handscomb (Y)		9	14	1	101*	441	33.92	1	2	7
G.T.Hankins (Gs)	2016	12	18	1	79*	446	26.23	–	4	20
† O.J.Hannon-Dalby (Wa)		5	8	3	12	47	9.40	–	–	1
G.H.I.Harding (Du)		1	1	–	0	0	0.00	–	–	–
† A.Harinath (Le)		2	4	–	26	68	17.00	–	–	1
S.R.Harmer (Ex)		15	20	3	64	281	16.52	–	2	12
J.A.R.Harris (K/M)	2015	10	16	3	34	256	19.69	–	–	2

233

	Cap	M	I	NO	HS	Runs	Avge	100	50	Ct/St
J.Harrison (OU)	–	1	2	–	38	52	26.00	–	–	5/1
A.J.H.A.Hart (H)	–	2	4	1	36	44	14.66	–	–	1
C.F.Hartley (K)	–	1	1	–	5	5	5.00	–	–	–
† Hasan Azad (LU)	–	2	2	–	80	85	42.50	–	1	1
J.W.Hastings (Wo)	2017	6	8	1	51	139	19.85	–	1	5
T.D.Heathfield (OU)	–	2	2	2	12*	12	–	–	–	–
T.G.Helm (EL/M)	–	7	8	1	28	85	12.14	–	–	3
R.P.Hemmings (De)	–	1	1	–	19	19	19.00	–	–	–
† B.E.Hendricks (SAA)	–	2	3	1	20	35	17.50	–	–	–
† S.O.Hetmyer (WI)	–	1	2	–	43*	43	43.00	–	–	3
R.F.Higgins (M)	–	4	7	–	45	129	18.42	–	–	–
J.C.Hildreth (Sm)	2007	14	26	1	109	756	30.24	2	2	12
L.J.Hill (Le)	–	12	21	3	85*	554	30.77	–	2	22/2
A.J.Hodd (Y)	2016	13	20	2	59	436	24.22	–	4	39/1
M.G.Hogan (Gm)	2013	13	17	10	29*	100	14.28	–	–	4
† M.D.E.Holden (M/Nh)	–	11	19	1	153	758	42.11	2	3	5
J.O.Holder (WI)	–	5	7	–	43	110	15.71	–	–	2
I.G.Holland (H)	–	9	13	4	58*	234	26.00	–	2	1
K.A.Hope (WI)	–	6	12	–	105	231	19.25	1	–	5
S.D.Hope (WI)	–	6	12	2	147	642	64.20	3	2	2
P.J.Horton (Le)	–	11	21	–	71	534	25.42	–	2	9
A.J.Hose (Sm)	–	3	6	–	68	194	32.33	–	2	1
H.R.Hosein (De)	–	5	8	2	68	170	28.33	–	1	7
D.Houghton (LBU)	–	1	2	1	29	35	35.00	–	–	–
B.A.C.Howell (Gs)	2012	2	3	–	163	204	68.00	1	–	–
A.L.Hughes (De)	2017	13	22	2	142	800	40.00	2	3	15
† C.F.Hughes (Nh)	–	3	6	–	21	60	10.00	–	–	3
M.S.T.Hughes (OU)	–	1	2	–	41	42	21.00	–	–	–
M.D.Hunn (K)	–	3	1	1	0*	0	–	–	–	1
† R.Hussain (OU)	–	2	4	–	15	34	8.50	–	–	1
J.W.Hutson (Sx)	–	1	1	–	25	25	25.00	–	–	2
B.A.Hutton (Nt)	–	9	13	–	61	210	16.15	–	1	6
Imran Qayyum (K)	–	3	5	1	39	40	10.00	–	–	2
Imran Tahir (De)	–	4	6	1	18*	41	8.20	–	–	2
C.A.Ingram (Gm)	2017	12	20	2	155*	672	37.33	2	1	5
† M.F.Jahanfar (DU)	–	1	1	–	2	2	2.00	–	–	2
K.M.Jarvis (La)	2015	10	12	2	30	106	10.60	–	–	3
A.Javid (Wa)	–	1	2	–	14	22	11.00	–	–	–
J.W.Jenner (Sx)	–	1	1	–	68	68	68.00	–	1	–
† K.K.Jennings (Du/E/EL)	–	17	32	2	102*	784	26.13	1	3	16
R.A.Jones (Le)	–	2	4	2	23*	45	22.50	–	–	1
R.P.Jones (La)	–	3	5	–	35	87	17.40	–	–	3
C.J.Jordan (Sx)	2014	11	17	3	147	438	31.28	1	2	13
A.S.Joseph (WI)	–	3	3	–	31	45	15.00	–	–	1
R.I.Keogh (Nh)	–	12	22	3	105*	408	21.47	1	1	5
S.C.Kerrigan (La/Nh)	2013	6	7	2	62	177	35.40	–	2	3
H.Klaasen (SAA)	–	3	5	–	103	152	30.40	1	–	9
R.K.Kleinveldt (Nh)	2016	12	19	1	86	394	21.88	–	1	8
D.Klein (Le)	–	9	14	3	26	138	12.54	–	–	5
T.Kohler-Cadmore (Wo/Y)	2014	7	11	–	102	393	35.72	1	2	5
H.G.Kuhn (SA/SAA)	–	7	13	1	200*	513	42.75	2	1	4
N.R.Kumar (LU)	–	2	2	–	141	175	87.50	1	–	–
B.I.W.Ladd-Gibbon (LU)	–	2	2	1	6*	10	10.00	–	–	–
† M.B.Lake (OU)	–	2	4	1	48	63	21.00	–	–	–
M.J.Lamb (Wa)	–	7	14	–	71	329	23.50	–	2	3
† T.W.M.Latham (Du)	–	4	7	1	124	382	63.66	2	1	5

	Cap	M	I	NO	HS	Runs	Avge	100	50	Ct/St
J.L.Lawlor (CfU)	–	2	2	1	50*	67	67.00	–	1	1
D.W.Lawrence (EL/Ex)	2017	16	26	4	141*	880	40.00	3	3	11
J.Leach (Wo)	2012	14	19	2	57*	347	20.41	–	2	7
† M.J.Leach (EL/Sm)	2017	15	22	5	52	253	14.88	–	1	4
J.A.Leaning (Y)	2016	11	16	1	118	518	34.53	1	3	6
A.Z.Lees (Y)	2014	15	26	3	102	631	27.43	2	2	8
† K.S.Leverock (CfU)	–	2	1	–	21	21	21.00	–	–	1
R.E.Levi (Nh)	2017	10	19	3	115	734	45.87	2	3	12
J.D.Libby (Nt)		15	22	2	109	565	28.25	1	1	5
C.J.Liddle (Gs)	2017	6	7	3	21	54	13.50	–	–	1
L.S.Livingstone (EL/La)	2017	13	22	3	224	805	42.36	2	3	12
D.L.Lloyd (Gm)		9	16	1	88	282	18.80	–	1	4
† M.J.Lumb (Nt)	2012	8	9	–	117	292	32.44	1	–	2
N.M.Lyon (Wo)	2017	4	5	3	6*	15	7.50	–	–	1
† A.Lyth (Y)	2010	14	24	1	194	749	32.56	2	2	22
B.J.McCarthy (Du)		5	6	2	39	129	32.25	–	–	3
J.A.McCollum (DU)	–	2	2	–	64	71	35.50	–	1	–
P.F.McDermott (LBU)	–	2	4	–	20	46	11.50	–	–	–
C.M.MacDonell (De)		1	2	1	17*	26	26.00	–	–	–
A.H.McGrath (DU)	–	1	1	–	12	12	12.00	–	–	–
J.N.McIver (OU)	–	2	4	.	22	53	13.25	–	–	–
C.J.McKay (Le)	2015	11	18	4	66	347	24.78	–	1	2
C.McKerr (De/Sy)		4	4	1	17	34	11.33	–	–	1
† R.McLaren (La)		15	21	1	107	606	30.30	1	2	7
L.D.McManus (H)		11	16	2	41*	323	23.07	–	–	29/3
W.L.Madsen (De)	2011	13	22	–	121	667	30.31	1	5	14
† S.J.Magoffin (Sx)	2013	2	2	1	5	5	5.00	–	–	–
K.A.Maharaj (SA)	–	5	8	2	24*	83	13.83	–	–	1
S.Mahmood (La)		3	4	3	4*	5	5.00	–	–	1
G.T.Main (Du)		2	3	1	13	13	6.50	–	–	–
† D.J.Malan (E/M)	2010	13	24	2	115	682	31.00	1	4	4
A.K.Markram (SAA)	–	3	6	1	102*	212	42.40	1	1	5
J.Marsden (OU)	–	1	2	1	8*	8	8.00	–	–	1
† S.E.Marsh (Y)		2	3	1	125*	225	112.50	1	1	1
J.D.Marshall (DU)	–	2	3	1	41*	85	42.50	–	–	1
A.T.A.Martin (OU)	–	2	4	–	28	48	12.00	–	–	–
S.C.Meaker (Sy)	2012	10	14	4	49	174	17.40	–	–	3
A.J.Mellor (Wa)		4	8	–	59	118	14.75	–	–	4
† B.M.A.J.Mendis (De)		7	12	1	27	132	12.00	–	–	3
C.A.J.Meschede (Gm)		7	9	–	87	296	32.88	–	1	3
C.N.Miles (Gs)	2011	10	13	1	47	137	11.41	–	–	2
A.F.Milne (K)		5	8	2	51	121	20.16	–	1	1
T.P.Milnes (De)		4	6	–	53	96	16.00	–	1	2
D.K.H.Mitchell (Wo)	2005	14	26	3	161	1266	55.04	7	3	21
Mohammad Amir (Ex)		3	2	1	22*	44	44.00	–	–	1
T.J.Moores (Nt)		1	2	–	1	1	0.50	–	–	–
A.O.Morgan (Gm)		4	7	1	17	33	5.50	–	–	–
† M.Morkel (SA)	–	5	8	3	20*	78	15.60	–	–	2
C.H.Morris (SA)	–	3	5	1	36	100	25.00	–	–	3
† T.H.Moses (CU)	–	3	6	1	80*	145	29.00	–	1	1
P.W.A.Mulder (SAA)	–	2	4	–	42	68	17.00	–	–	–
S.J.Mullaney (Nt)	2013	12	16	–	168	709	44.31	1	5	15
D.Murphy (Nh)	2017	6	8	–	30	81	10.12	–	–	12/3
† J.R.Murphy (Gm)		4	6	–	27	97	16.16	–	–	1
† T.J.Murtagh (M)	2008	12	17	6	27	134	12.18	–	–	2
† P.Mustard (Gs)	2016	15	21	–	72	602	28.66	–	3	22

	Cap	M	I	NO	HS	Runs	Avge	100	50	Ct/St
C.D.Nash (Sx)	2008	12	21	–	118	578	27.52	1	3	12
M.A.Naylor (OU)	–	1	2	–	19	19	9.50	–	–	–
R.I.Newton (Nh)	2017	14	25	–	166	1060	42.40	2	10	2
† A.S.S.Nijjar (CfU/Ex)		3	2	–	30	30	15.00	–	–	–
K.Noema-Barnett (Gs)	2015	11	14	1	59	291	22.38	–	1	6
† M.J.Norris (CfU)	–	2	3	–	20	41	13.66	–	–	1
S.A.Northeast (K)	2012	13	23	3	173*	1017	50.85	3	4	5
L.C.Norwell (Gs)	2011	12	13	5	24	99	12.37	–	–	4
D.Olivier (SA/SAA)	–	4	7	3	15*	29	7.25	–	–	–
G.Onions (Du)		8	10	–	15	58	5.80	–	–	1
F.S.Organ (H)		1	1	–	16	16	16.00	–	–	–
D.O'Sullivan (CfU)	–	1	1	–	2	2	2.00	–	–	–
C.Overton (Sm)	2016	13	21	3	44*	287	15.94	–	–	9
J.Overton (EL/Sm)		6	9	1	37	107	13.37	–	–	2
X.G.Owen (DU)	–	2	2	2	1*	2	–	–	–	–
A.P.Palladino (De)	2012	11	18	2	32	161	10.06	–	–	3
H.J.Palmer (CU)	–	2	4	–	19	29	7.25	–	–	3
G.D.Panayi (Wa)		2	3	–	16	17	5.66	–	–	–
C.F.Parkinson (De)		5	6	4	75	103	51.50	–	1	3
M.W.Parkinson (La)		5	6	3	13	20	6.66	–	–	1
† W.D.Parnell (K)		2	3	1	51*	100	50.00	–	1	–
S.D.Parry (La)	2015	14	18	1	44	307	18.05	–	1	3
J.S.Patel (Wa)	2012	13	24	2	100	608	27.63	1	2	9
† R.Patel (Sy)		4	6	–	81	170	28.33	–	1	2
R.H.Patel (M)		2	4	2	7*	12	6.00	–	–	1
S.R.Patel (Nt)	2008	15	21	2	257*	919	48.36	2	2	7
D.Paterson (SAA)	–	2	2	1	18*	18	18.00	–	–	1
S.A.Patterson (Y)	2012	10	13	4	44*	165	18.33	–	–	5
† J.L.Pattinson (Nt)	2017	5	5	1	89*	197	49.25	–	2	–
D.A.Payne (Gs)	2011	11	12	5	54*	238	34.00	–	1	1
M.L.Pettini (Le)		7	12	1	110*	303	27.54	1	2	1
T.H.S.Pettman (OU)	–	1	2	–	25	34	17.00	–	–	–
V.D.Philander (SA/Sx)		8	13	5	73*	388	48.50	–	4	2
D.L.Piedt (SAA)	–	3	5	–	31	63	12.60	–	–	1
O.L.Pike (CfU)	–	1	–	–	–	–	–	–	–	–
M.W.Pillans (Le)		4	7	–	56	107	15.28	–	1	1
L.E.Plunkett (EL/Y)	2013	3	3	–	39	92	30.66	–	–	–
H.W.Podmore (De/Gm)		6	10	2	66*	154	19.25	–	–	3
† E.J.Pollock (DU)	–	2	3	1	52	123	61.50	–	1	1
O.J.Pope (Sy)		6	10	3	100*	270	38.57	1	1	3
J.A.Porter (EL/Ex)	2015	15	17	8	10*	53	5.88	–	–	4
† W.T.S.Porterfield (Wa)		6	11	–	89	262	23.81	–	1	4
J.T.Potticary (LBU)	–	2	4	–	32	72	18.00	–	–	1
M.J.Potts (Du)		5	6	2	53*	69	17.25	–	1	–
J.E.Poulson (CU)	–	1	2	2	16*	21	–	–	–	–
† K.O.A.Powell (WI)	–	6	12	1	100*	412	37.45	1	1	6
S.W.Poynter (Du)		9	14	1	65	269	20.69	–	1	30
R.D.Pringle (Du)		13	22	4	71	459	25.50	–	3	9
† L.A.Procter (La/Nh)		6	10	–	94	306	30.60	–	3	3
C.A.Pujara (Nt)	2017	8	12	–	112	333	27.75	1	1	7
M.R.Quinn (Ex)		3	3	–	15	19	6.33	–	–	1
A.J.W.Rackow (OU)	–	1	2	–	95	118	59.00	–	1	1
K.Rabada (SA)	–	4	6	–	30	85	14.16	–	–	3
† B.A.Raine (Le)		9	17	4	57	301	23.15	–	2	1
† R.Rampaul (Sy)		2	4	2	3	4	2.00	–	–	–
† W.B.Rankin (Wa)	2013	5	9	4	21*	61	12.20	–	–	1

236

	Cap	M	I	NO	HS	Runs	Avge	100	50	Ct/St
A.U.Rashid (Y)	2008	7	10	1	65	211	23.44	–	1	–
† D.M.W.Rawlins (Sx)		5	9	–	96	217	24.11	–	2	–
O.P.Rayner (M)	2015	11	15	2	52*	274	21.07	–	1	15
C.M.W.Read (Nt)	1999	15	19	2	124	661	38.8	1	3	56/1
† L.M.Reece (De)		12	21	1	168	732	36.60	2	5	4
† R.A.Reifer (WI)		1	1	–	13	13	13.00	–	–	–
G.H.Rhodes (Wo)	2016	8	15	2	52	379	29.15	–	2	5
M.A.Richardson (Nh)		1	–	–	–	–	–	–	–	–
M.J.Richardson (Du)		10	16	1	82	460	30.66	–	4	20
A.E.N.Riley (K)		1	1	–	0	0	0.00	–	–	–
† S.E.Rippington (CU)	–	2	4	2	2*	2	1.00	–	–	–
K.A.J.Roach (WI)	–	5	7	3	40*	78	19.50	–	–	–
O.E.Robinson (Sx)		4	8	1	41*	116	16.57	–	–	2
A.J.Robson (Sx)		4	8	1	72	169	24.14	–	1	3
S.D.Robson (EL/M)	2013	12	21	–	159	832	39.61	2	4	11
G.H.Roderick (Gs)	2013	9	13	1	96	403	33.58	–	4	24/1
T.S.Roland-Jones (E/M)	2012	13	20	4	53	334	20.87	–	1	2
J.E.Root (E/Y)	2012	9	15	1	190	751	53.64	2	5	9
† W.T.Root (Nt)		2	3	–	132	150	50.0	1	–	–
A.M.Rossington (Nh)		9	14	1	117	475	36.53	2	2	19/2
† R.R.Rossouw (H)		8	13	–	99	253	19.46	–	1	7
A.P.Rouse (K)		12	19	2	95*	530	31.17	–	3	35/1
T.D.Rouse (CfU/Sm)		5	8	1	69	125	17.85	–	1	1
J.J.Roy (Sy)	2014	5	7	1	87	257	42.83	–	2	–
† J.A.Rudolph (Gm)	2014	12	21	1	142	634	31.70	2	1	3
C.Rushworth (Du)		13	17	3	57	174	12.42	–	1	5
A.Sakande (Sx)		4	4	2	17	31	15.50	–	–	1
R.A.Sale (CU)	–	1	2	–	28	42	21.00	–	–	2
M.E.T.Salisbury (H)		3	5	2	17*	33	11.00	–	–	–
P.D.Salt (Sx)		3	5	–	72	105	21.00	–	–	2
A.G.Salter (Gm)		13	20	5	88	623	41.53	–	5	6
B.W.Sanderson (Nh)		10	16	5	16*	72	6.54	–	–	3
G.S.Sandhu (De)		1	2	1	46*	55	55.00	–	–	–
† K.C.Sangakkara (Sy)	2015	10	16	2	200	1491	106.50	8	2	6
R.J.Sayer (Le)		4	6	–	31	58	9.66	–	–	2
D.N.C.Scott (OU)	–	2	4	–	18	45	11.25	–	–	1
J.A.L.Scriven (CfU)	–	2	2	1	16	18	18.00	–	–	1
R.S.Second (SAA)	–	2	3	–	31	60	20.00	–	–	2
N.J.Selman (Gm)		15	27	2	142*	902	36.08	4	3	16
N.V.S.Senaratne (CU)	–	2	4	–	33	79	19.75	–	–	2
A.Shahzad (Le/Sx)		2	2	–	5	6	3.00	–	–	1
† J.D.Shantry (Wo)	2009	6	8	4	30*	94	23.50	–	–	3
J.Shaw (Gs/Y)	2016	6	7	–	13	26	3.71	–	–	–
A.Sheikh (Nh)		1	1	–	7	7	7.00	–	–	–
B.J.Shoare (LBU)	–	2	4	–	47	58	14.50	–	–	1
C.E.Shreck (Le)		2	2	–	26	26	13.00	–	–	–
D.P.Sibley (Sy/Wa)		14	26	5	104*	804	38.28	1	8	7
† R.J.Sidebottom (Y)	2000	8	11	8	12*	57	19.00	–	–	2
R.N.Sidebottom (Wa)		6	12	5	13	26	3.71	–	–	–
F.P.A.Simon (DU)	–	1	1	–	1	1	1.00	–	–	–
J.A.Simpson (M)	2011	14	22	2	90	570	28.50	–	3	53/1
† B.T.Slater (De)		9	17	3	74*	556	39.71	–	2	4
D.Smit (De)		8	13	1	41	237	19.75	–	–	18/3
G.P.Smith (Nt)		4	6	2	73	164	41.00	–	2	8
J.F.Smith (SAA)	–	2	3	–	18	35	11.66	–	–	2
L.P.Smith (Sx)		1	1	–	0	0	0.00	–	–	–

	Cap	M	I	NO	HS	Runs	Avge	100	50	Ct/St
R.A.J.Smith (Gm)		3	4	–	38	89	22.25	–	–	–
T.M.J.Smith (Gs)	2013	2	3	1	14*	31	15.50	–	–	–
W.R.Smith (H)	2015	1	2	–	18	20	10.00	–	–	–
M.D.Sonczak (De)		1	1	–	9	9	9.00	–	–	–
N.A.Sowter (M)		1	2	–	37	37	18.50	–	–	–
C.T.Steel (Du)		13	24	2	224	899	40.86	2	4	3
D.I.Stevens (K)	2005	13	21	3	115	822	45.66	2	5	2
R.A.Stevenson (H)		1	2	1	20	39	39.00	–	–	–
G.Stewart (K)		1	2	1	15*	15	15.00	–	–	–
S.K.Stewart-Taylor (DU)	–	1	1	–	8	8	8.00	–	–	–/1
P.R.Stirling (M)	2016	8	13	–	111	454	34.92	1	3	4
† B.A.Stokes (Du/E)		8	13	–	112	527	40.53	2	4	16
O.P.Stone (Wa)		1	2	1	32	39	39.00	–	–	–
† M.D.Stoneman (E/EL/Sy)		17	28	1	197	1481	54.85	4	7	6
† Sukhjit Singh (Wa)		5	8	2	16*	18	3.00	–	–	1
† B.Swanson (OU)	–	1	2	1	0*	0	0.00	–	–	1
W.A.Tavaré (Gs)	2014	11	18	1	110	532	31.29	2	2	7
B.J.Taylor (H)		2	4	2	18	55	27.50	–	–	–
B.R.M.Taylor (Nt)	2015	4	5	–	61	123	24.60	–	1	6
C.J.Taylor (Ex)		1	1	–	13	13	13.00	–	–	–
J.M.R.Taylor (Gs)	2010	15	21	4	143	697	41.00	2	2	10
J.P.A.Taylor (De)		1	1	1	0*	0	–	–	–	–
M.D.Taylor (Gs)	2013	5	7	3	36	55	13.75	–	–	–
N.P.Taylor (OU)	–	1	2	–	4	6	3.00	–	–	–
T.A.I.Taylor (De)		7	11	1	69	192	19.20	–	1	2
R.N.ten Doeschate (Ex)	2006	15	20	2	168*	717	39.83	1	4	8
† J.W.Tetley (CU)		2	4	–	42	65	16.25	–	–	–
S.J.Thakor (De)		6	11	1	132	328	32.80	1	–	1
I.A.A.Thomas (K)		1	–	–	–	–	–	–	–	–
A.T.Thomson (Wa)		2	4	–	26	70	17.50	–	–	1
† G.T.Thornton (Wa)		2	3	1	10	19	9.50	–	–	–
C.O.Thurston (LU)	–	2	2	–	126	128	64.00	1	–	–
P.J.A.Tice (CU)	–	2	4	1	54	95	31.66	–	1	8
A.D.Tillcock (LU)	–	2	2	1	16*	32	32.00	–	–	3
J.C.Tongue (Wo)	2017	14	18	3	41	138	9.20	–	–	2
R.J.W.Topley (H)		2	3	2	16	23	23.00	–	–	–
† J.C.Tredwell (K)	2007	7	10	3	55	184	26.28	–	1	7
P.D.Trego (Sm)	2007	8	12	–	68	257	21.41	–	2	1
† M.E.Trescothick (Sm)	1999	14	27	2	119*	714	28.56	2	1	21
† L.Trevaskis (Du)		1	2	–	9	14	7.00	–	–	–
I.J.L.Trott (Wa)	2005	15	27	–	175	1097	40.62	4	5	10
A.R.I.Umeed (Wa)		8	14	–	113	325	23.21	1	–	9
G.L.van Buuren (Gs)	2016	8	13	1	88*	268	22.33	–	2	3
F.O.E.van den Bergh (Sy)		1	1	–	5	5	5.00	–	–	–
T.van der Gugten (Gm)		5	7	–	21	64	9.14	–	–	–
R.E.van der Merwe (Sm)		3	5	–	24	33	6.60	–	–	2
P.A.van Meekeren (Sm)		1	2	1	1*	1	1.00	–	–	1
† S.van Zyl (Sx)		13	22	1	166*	1023	48.71	2	4	6
D.J.Vilas (La)		15	24	3	244	762	36.28	1	3	14
G.C.Viljoen (De)		5	8	1	19*	36	5.14	–	–	–
J.M.Vince (H)	2013	13	21	–	147	738	35.14	2	3	13
A.Virdi (Sy)		3	4	1	8*	18	6.00	–	–	1
A.C.Voges (M)	2016	9	14	3	92	402	36.54	–	3	12
G.Wade (Nh)		1	–	–	–	–	–	–	–	–
G.G.Wagg (Gm)	2013	3	6	1	33*	93	18.60	–	–	2
† N.Wagner (Ex)		10	13	3	50	242	24.20	–	1	4

238

	Cap	M	I	NO	HS	Runs	Avge	100	50	Ct/St
M.J.Waite (Y)		1	2	–	18	22	11.00	–	–	–
A.G.Wakely (Nh)	2012	14	26	4	112	776	35.27	2	2	14
C.D.Wallace (LBU)	–	2	4	–	35	109	27.25	–	–	–
† P.I.Walter (Ex)		6	6	3	68*	144	48.00	–	1	–
J.J.Weatherley (H/K)		8	12	–	36	235	19.58	–	–	1
† W.J.Weighell (Du)		4	7	3	58	162	40.50	–	2	–
† D.A.C.Wells (OU)	–	2	4	–	33	42	10.50	–	–	–
† L.W.P.Wells (Sx)	2016	12	22	2	258	1292	64.60	4	4	4
T.J.Wells (Le)		3	4	–	46	110	27.50	–	–	1
M.H.Wessels (Nt)	2014	15	20	2	202*	913	50.72	3	3	23
T.Westley (E/EL/Ex)	2013	18	27	4	111	894	38.86	3	3	9
† I.J.Westwood (Wa)	2008	4	7	–	153	253	36.14	1	1	1
B.T.J.Wheal (H)		6	7	2	18	40	8.00	–	–	2
A.J.A.Wheater (Ex)		9	12	–	102	325	27.08	1	2	17/2
G.G.White (Nh)		3	4	–	47	88	22.00	–	–	–
R.G.White (LU)		2	2	–	69	76	38.00	–	–	3
R.A.Whiteley (Wo)	2013	5	9	1	53	170	21.25	–	1	6
S.G.Whittingham (Sx)		5	8	2	22	43	7.16	–	–	1
D.Wiese (Sx)	2016	10	15	–	66	404	26.93	–	2	3
† A.R.Wilkinson (OU)	–	2	2	–	12	12	6.00	–	–	–
D.J.Willey (Y)	2016	2	2	–	19	27	13.50	–	–	–
D.R.Williams (DU)	–	1	1	–	32	32	32.00	–	–	1
G.C.Wilson (Sy)	2014	9	14	1	97	401	30.84	–	3	17
N.J.Winder (CU)	–	1	1	–	1	1	1.00	–	–	–
C.R.Woakes (E/Wa)	2009	3	6	1	61*	184	36.80	–	2	–
C.P.Wood (H)		1	2	–	5	5	2.50	–	–	–
† L.Wood (Nt)		7	10	3	44	235	33.57	–	–	2
M.A.Wood (Du/E)		7	12	2	72*	229	22.90	–	1	1
T.A.Wood (De)		1	1	–	15	15	15.00	–	–	2
C.J.C.Wright (Wa)	2013	9	16	3	41	241	18.53	–	–	2
L.J.Wright (Sx)	2007	12	21	1	118	742	37.10	1	4	6
Yasir Shah (K)		3	4	1	48	131	43.66	–	–	1
† S.A.Zaib (Nh)		1	1	1	20*	20	–	–	–	–
M.S.Zaidi (CU)	–	1	2	–	3	4	2.00	–	–	–
K.Zondo (SAA)	–	3	5	–	95	127	25.40	–	1	–

BOWLING

See BATTING AND FIELDING section for details of matches and caps

	Cat	O	M	R	W	Avge	Best	5wI	10wM
K.J.Abbott (H)	RFM	415.3	131	1092	60	18.20	7-41	4	–
T.B.Abell (Sm)	RM	27	6	96	2	48.00	2-71	–	–
Abhiraj Singh (DU)	SLA	52.4	3	225	5	45.00	3-79	–	–
C.N.Ackermann (Le)	OB	104	9	394	6	65.66	3-45	–	–
J.H.K.Adams (H)	LM	1	1	0	0				
B.M.R.Akram (LU)	RMF	39	5	194	7	27.71	5-54	1	–
A.M.Ali (Le)	OB	6	0	46	1	46.00	1-10	–	–
M.M.Ali (E/Wo)	OB	233	40	805	33	24.39	6-53	2	1
J.Allenby (Sm)	RM	14	6	25	0				
J.M.Anderson (E/La)	RFM	415	125	938	60	15.63	7-42	4	–
Z.S.Ansari (Sy)	SLA	38	10	113	1	113.00	1-22	–	–
J.C.Archer (Sx)	RFM	475.1	91	1543	61	25.29	7-67	4	1
A.T.Arif (CU)	RM	2	0	15	0				
Ashar Zaidi (Ex)	SLA	25	5	43	3	14.33	3-17	–	–
M.A.Ashraf (LBU)	RMF	16.3	5	50	0				
R.Ashwin (Wo)	OB	184.2	29	583	20	29.15	5-68	2	–

	Cat	O	M	R	W	Avge	Best	5wI	10wM
Azeem Rafiq (Y)	OB	127.4	17	459	10	45.90	3- 50	–	–
M.Azharullah (Nh)	RFM	192	36	677	31	21.83	5- 63	2	–
G.J.Bailey (H)	RM	2	0	9	0				
T.E.Bailey (La)	RMF	223.2	52	635	26	24.42	5- 44	2	1
A.J.Ball (K)	LFM	26	7	64	5	12.80	3- 54	–	–
J.T.Ball (Nt)	RFM	183.2	39	675	27	25.00	3- 36	–	–
C.T.Bancroft (Gs)	RM	7	0	67	1	67.00	1- 67	–	–
K.H.D.Barker (Wa)	LMF	315	63	994	29	34.27	3- 21	–	–
E.G.Barnard (Wo)	RMF	321.3	48	1187	47	25.25	4- 23	–	–
A.P.Barton (CU/Sx)	LMF	83	15	280	9	31.11	5- 31	1	–
G.J.Batty (Sy)	OB	312.1	67	859	27	31.81	3- 70	–	–
T.Bavuma (SA/SAA)	RM	5	0	14	0				
A.P.Beard (Ex)	RFM	112	17	404	7	57.71	3- 47	–	–
W.A.T.Beer (Sx)	LB	62.4	5	179	15	11.93	6- 29	2	1
D.J.Bell-Drummond (K)	RMF	1	0	10	0				
G.K.Berg (H)	RMF	391.5	103	987	37	26.67	4- 28	–	–
D.M.Bess (Sm)	OB	265.5	62	8443	36	23.41	7-117	3	1
D.Bishoo (WI)	LB	67	7	220	5	44.00	1- 17	–	–
O.S.Bocking (LBU)	RFM	58	7	223	7	31.85	4- 52	–	–
R.S.Bopara (Ex)	RM	145.2	18	525	13	40.38	2- 10	–	–
S.G.Borthwick (Du)	LBG	78.1	1	352	5	70.40	1- 5	–	–
N.Brand (CfU)	SLA	11.3	3	34	4	8.50	3- 7	–	–
K.C.Brathwaite (WI/Y)	OB	19	5	32	2	16.00	2- 21	–	–
T.T.Bresnan (Y)	RFM	262	56	934	30	31.13	4- 53	–	–
A.D.F.Brewster (CfU)	RFM	46	11	191	3	63.66	2- 87	–	–
D.R.Briggs (Sx)	SLA	264.1	47	788	16	49.25	3- 40	–	–
S.C.J.Broad (E/Nt)	RFM	367.2	88	1038	38	27.31	3- 34	–	–
T.M.J.Brock (OU)	RM	38	3	137	6	22.83	3- 46	–	–
H.C.Brook (Y)	RM	19	4	65	1	65.00	1- 54	–	–
H.J.H.Brookes (Wa)	RMF	11	1	43	0				
J.A.Brooks (Y)	RFM	205	24	865	23	37.60	5-113	1	–
C.R.Brown (CfU/Gm)	OB	4	0	14	0				
P.R.Brown (Wo)	RM	42.4	4	199	6	33.16	2- 15	–	–
N.L.Buck (Nh)	RMF	241.4	40	815	36	22.63	6- 34	3	–
S.F.G.Bullen (LBU)	(WK)	4.3	0	29	0				
J.E.Burke (Le)	RMF	10	0	57	0				
M.A.Carberry (H/Le)	RM	5	2	5	0				
L.J.Carey (Gm)	RFM	279.3	54	1060	35	30.28	4- 85	–	–
B.A.Carse (Du)	RF	58	4	191	3	63.66	2- 61	–	–
A.Carter (Nh)	RM	22	5	90	5	18.00	3- 51	–	–
M.Carter (Nt)	OB	25	3	161	4	40.25	4-106	–	–
K.Carver (Y)	SLA	35.2	4	118	4	29.50	2- 10	–	–
L.J.Chapman (CU)	OB	67	14	258	8	32.25	6- 78	1	–
Z.J.Chappell (Le)	RMF	133.5	17	567	10	56.70	4-108	–	–
R.L.Chase (WI)	OB	89.2	13	314	9	34.88	4-113	–	–
J.Clark (La)	RMF	191.5	26	662	22	30.09	4- 81	–	–
R.Clarke (Sy/Wa)	RFM	378	96	1095	38	28.81	7- 55	1	–
M.E.Claydon (K)	RMF	262.5	48	936	26	36.00	5- 54	1	–
B.O.Coad (Y)	RMF	386.4	108	1081	53	20.39	6- 25	4	1
J.J.Cobb (Nh)	OB	46	2	157	3	52.33	2- 44	–	–
M.T.Coles (K)	RMF	335	60	1313	32	41.03	6- 84	1	–
P.D.Collingwood (Du)	RM	77.2	21	199	4	49.75	2- 29	–	–
T.G.L.Colverd (CU)	OB	2	1	2	0				
N.R.D.Compton (M)	OB	1	0	2	0				
S.C.Cook (Du)	RM	1	0	16	0				
S.J.Cook (Ex/LU)	RFM	186.4	42	533	22	24.22	5- 18	2	–

	Cat	O	M	R	W	Avge	Best	5wI	10wM
W.Cook (LBU)	RFM	35	1	202	2	101.00	1-33	–	–
J.M.Cooke (DU)	RFM	52	6	247	1	247.00	1-61	–	–
G.T.G.Cork (De)	LMF	30	4	128	0				
M.J.Cosgrove (Le)	RM	39	1	163	2	81.50	1-10	–	–
B.D.Cotton (De)	RMF	23	2	123	0				
P.Coughlin (Du)	RM	208.1	31	804	27	29.77	5-49	2	1
M.S.Crane (EL/H)	LB	239.1	34	919	16	57.43	5-40	1	–
R.J.Crichard (CU)	RMF	50.4	11	142	11	12.90	6-68	2	1
M.J.J.Critchley (De)	LB	10.2	0	66	2	33.00	2-21	–	–
S.J.Croft (La)	RMF	24.5	2	58	0				
S.P.Crook (Nh)	RFM	93.4	6	430	4	107.50	2-35	–	–
M.L.Cummins (WI)	RF	61.1	12	188	3	62.66	2-43	–	–
S.M.Curran (EL/Sy)	LMF	388.5	74	1332	31	42.32	3-74	–	–
T.K.Curran (Sy)	RFM	256.3	50	832	24	34.66	4-69	–	–
O.C.Currill (Gs)	RMF	15	2	83	0				
C.J.Dala (SAA)	RFM	61.4	5	265	6	44.16	3-63	–	–
A.D.Dalgleish (CU)	LM	.3	1	6	0				
J.H.Davey (Sm)	RMF	75	17	186	3	62.00	2-33	–	–
W.S.Davis (De)	RFM	103.5	13	410	14	29.28	4-60	–	–
L.A.Dawson (E/H)	SLA	395	102	1004	37	27.13	4-22	–	–
T.B.de Bruyn (SA/SAA)	RMF	28	6	98	4	24.50	2-24	–	–
M.de Lange (Gm)	RF	345.5	47	1315	34	38.67	5-95	1	–
H.E.Dearden (Le)	OB	18.4	0	95	2	47.50	1- 0	–	–
C.S.Delport (Le)	RM	7	1	30	0				
J.L.Denly (K)	LB	70.3	11	253	8	31.62	2-49	–	–
C.D.J.Dent (Gs)	SLA	16.4	0	130	1	130.00	1-61	–	–
J.W.Dernbach (Sy)	RFM	157.3	40	476	12	39.66	3-51	–	–
N.J.Dexter (Le)	RMF	121	23	456	14	32.57	5-71	2	–
M.W.Dixon (Ex)	RF	43	10	138	5	27.60	2-22	–	–
B.L.D'Oliveira (Wo)	LB	60	0	271	0				
G.S.Drissell (Gs)	OB	12	0	58	0				
B.M.Duckett (Nh)	OB	9	0	41	1	41.00	1-21	–	–
J.P.Duminy (SA)	OB	17	2	72	0				
E.J.H.Eckersley (Le)	LB	1	0	2	0				
F.H.Edwards (H)	RFM	221.5	35	794	33	24.06	5-49	2	–
D.Elgar (SA/Sm)	SLA	4	0	32	1	32.00	1- 4	–	–
S.M.Ervine (H)	RM	135.4	31	341	7	48.71	2- 1	–	–
D.A.Escott (OU)	LB	14	1	34	0				
S.T.Evans (Le/LU)		5	0	21	0				
W.N.Fazackerley (Le)	RFM	12	2	83	1	83.00	1-32	–	–
S.A.Feszczur-Hatchett (LBU)	LMF	58	8	220	2	110.00	2-91	–	–
H.Z.Finch (Sx)	RM	1	0	2	0				
S.T.Finn (M)	RFM	287.2	45	1045	34	30.73	8-79	1	–
M.D.Fisher (Y)	RFM	60.3	11	195	8	24.37	5-54	1	–
L.J.Fletcher (Nt)	RMF	268.1	51	843	38	22.18	4-35	–	–
M.H.A.Footitt (Nt/Sy)	LFM	220.5	33	814	31	26.25	6-14	2	–
J.E.C.Franklin (M)	LM	102	21	280	12	23.33	4-40	–	–
S.T.Gabriel (WI)	RFM	76	10	350	9	38.88	4-51	–	–
R.N.Gamble (LU)	RMF	42	9	156	3	52.00	2-16	–	–
G.H.S.Garton (EL/Sx)	LF	98	5	419	12	34.91	3-20	–	–
W.R.S.Gidman (K)	RM	78.2	14	279	10	27.90	3- 0	–	–
R.J.Gleeson (Nh)	RMF	222.2	44	745	40	18.62	5-46	3	–
J.S.D.Gnodde (OU)	SLA	2	0	15	0				
O.J.G.Graham (LBU)	OB	53	6	188	4	47.00	2-60	–	–
B.W.Graves (DU)	SLA	1	0	6	0				
L.Gregory (Sm)	RMF	176.3	49	484	21	23.04	5-74	1	–

	Cat	O	M	R	W	Avge	Best	5wI	10wM
G.T.Griffiths (Le)	RMF	139	24	434	8	54.25	4-101	–	–
T.D.Groenewald (Sm)	RFM	243.4	71	646	26	24.84	5- 65	1	–
J.O.Grundy (OU)	LMF	54	10	186	3	62.00	2- 86	–	–
N.R.T.Gubbins (EL/M)	LB	1	0	4	0			–	–
C.J.Guest (CU)	OB	37	3	143	0			–	–
H.F.Gurney (Nt)	LFM	307.1	56	1032	35	29.48	4- 19	–	–
C.J.Haggett (K)	RMF	133	39	342	9	38.00	3- 40	–	–
S.R.Hain (Wa)	OB	1	0	7	0			–	–
H.Hameed (La)	LB	4	1	9	0			–	–
Hamidullah Qadri (De)	OB	101.3	22	288	10	28.80	5- 60	1	–
G.T.Hankins (Gs)	OB	2.1	0	13	0			–	–
O.J.Hannon-Dalby (Wa)	RMF	108.1	27	316	15	21.06	4- 29	–	–
G.H.I.Harding (Du)	SLA	36	2	186	4	46.50	4-111	–	–
A.Harinath (Le)	OB	1	0	5	0			–	–
S.R.Harmer (Ex)	OB	546.2	128	1429	74	19.31	9- 95	4	2
J.A.R.Harris (K/M)	RFM	269.1	57	890	34	26.17	4- 56	–	–
A.H.J.A.Hart (H)	RM	43.5	8	111	5	22.20	3- 17	–	–
C.F.Hartley (K)	RMF	29.2	6	124	6	20.66	4- 80	–	–
J.W.Hastings (Wo)	RFM	161.1	41	550	16	34.37	3- 44	–	–
T.D.Heathfield (OU)	RMF	54	20	127	3	42.33	1- 26	–	–
T.G.Helm (EL/M)	RMF	211.5	37	739	20	36.95	5- 59	1	–
R.P.Hemmings (De)	RM	24	6	94	0			–	–
B.E.Hendricks (SAA)	LFM	62.5	13	199	10	19.90	5- 20	1	–
R.F.Higgins (M)	OB	98	24	281	12	23.41	4- 75	–	–
M.G.Hogan (Gm)	RFM	383.4	88	1075	52	20.67	6- 43	3	1
M.D.E.Holden (M/Nh)	OB	43	3	203	4	50.75	2- 59	–	–
J.O.Holder (WI)	RMF	128.2	24	428	12	35.66	4- 54	–	–
I.G. Holland (H)	RMF	158	45	416	19	21.89	4- 16	–	–
P.J.Horton (Le)	RM	1.4	0	14	0			–	–
D.Houghton (LBU)	RM	25	2	108	0				
B.A.C.Howell (Gs)	RMF	21	2	82	1	82.00	1- 34	–	–
A.L.Hughes (De)	RM	33	8	121	0				
C.F.Hughes (Nh)	SLA	2	0	16	0				
M.S.T.Hughes (M)	RM	13	0	66	1	66.00	1- 66	–	–
M.D.Hunn (K)	RFM	71.5	15	264	8	33.00	3- 90	–	–
B.A.Hutton (Nt)	RM	289.2	64	995	37	26.89	5- 52	2	1
Imran Qayyum (K)	SLA	50.5	5	198	6	33.00	3- 46	–	–
Imran Tahir (De)	LB	123.1	16	407	13	31.30	5- 76	2	–
C.A.Ingram (Gm)	LB	37.1	0	155	2	77.50	1- 17	–	–
K.M.Jarvis (La)	RFM	274.3	71	804	36	22.33	6- 61	2	–
A.Javid (Wa)	OB	4	0	15	0			–	–
K.K.Jennings (DuE/EL)	RMF	76	11	251	13	19.30	3- 37	–	–
R.A.Jones (L)	RMF	58	5	228	5	45.60	2- 50	–	–
C.J.Jordan (Sx)	RFM	353.5	57	1182	36	32.83	5- 46	1	–
A.S.Joseph (WI)	RFM	56	11	213	5	42.60	4- 72	–	–
R.I.Keogh (Nh)	OB	112.1	17	461	9	51.22	3- 44	–	–
S.C.Kerrigan (La/Nh)	SLA	203.4	38	676	17	39.76	4- 62	–	–
R.K.Kleinveldt (Nh)	RMF	350.1	68	1153	50	23.06	9- 65	2	1
D.Klein (Le)	LMF	206	21	958	28	34.21	6- 80	2	–
N.R.Kumar (LU)	OB	8	0	24	1	24.00	1- 22	–	–
B.I.W.Ladd-Gibbon (LU)	RM	33	3	182	4	45.50	3- 47	–	–
M.B.Lake (OU)	RM	45	9	156	2	78.00	1- 33	–	–
M.J.Lamb (Wa)	RM	20	4	66	3	22.00	1- 19	–	–
J.L.Lawlor (CfU)	OB	32	5	105	3	35.00	1- 26	–	–
D.W.Lawrence (EL/Ex)	LB	29	9	85	4	21.25	1- 0	–	–
J.Leach (Wo)	RMF	397.5	73	1338	69	19.39	5- 32	4	1

	Cat	O	M	R	W	Avge	Best	5wI	10wM
M.J.Leach (EL/Sm)	SLA	540.1	154	1403	53	26.47	6- 78	4	–
J.A.Leaning (Y)	RMF	6	0	26	0			–	–
K.S.Leverock (CfU)	LM	37	2	159	1	159.00	1- 56	–	–
J.D.Libby (Nt)	OB	10	0	41	0			–	–
C.J.Liddle (Gs)	LFM	131.1	26	468	10	46.80	2- 30	–	–
L.S.Livingstone (La)	LB	115	19	353	9	39.22	6- 52	1	–
D.L.Lloyd (Gm)	OB	79	8	341	6	56.83	2- 21	–	–
M.J.Lumb (Nt)	RM	2	0	5	0			–	–
N.M.Lyon (Wo)	OB	131.4	21	403	6	67.16	3- 94	–	–
A.Lyth (Y)	RM	40.3	2	130	3	43.33	2- 45	–	–
B.J.McCarthy (Du)	RMF	164.2	23	653	24	27.20	6- 63	1	–
J.A.McCollum (DU)	RM	3	1	8	0			–	–
C.M.MacDonell (De)	RFM	21	5	60	2	30.00	2- 57	–	–
A.H.McGrath (DU)	LM	29	4	108	4	27.00	4-108	–	–
J.N.McIver (OU)	OB	89	19	254	3	84.66	2- 60	–	–
C.J.McKay (La)	RFM	389.1	91	1150	46	25.00	4- 37	–	–
C.McKerr (De/Sy)	RFM	110.5	20	392	15	26.13	5- 54	2	1
R.McLaren (H)	RMF	387	83	1249	32	39.03	5-104	1	–
W.L.Madsen (De)	OB	60.3	5	260	7	37.14	2- 12	–	–
S.J.Magoffin (Sx)	RMF	27	10	69	5	13.80	5- 51	1	–
K.A.Maharaj (SA)	SLA	180.5	33	562	17	33.05	4- 85	–	–
S.Mahmood (La)	RFM	69.3	10	256	12	21.33	4- 50	–	–
G.T.Main (Du)	RMF	43	3	219	3	73.00	2- 58	–	–
D.J.Malan (E/M)	LB	39	4	132	7	18.85	2- 1	–	–
A.K.Markram (SAA)	OB	1	0	6	0			–	–
J.Marsden (OU)	RFM	43.4	18	103	5	20.60	4- 47	–	–
S.C.Meaker (Sy)	RMF	235.3	38	926	24	38.58	4- 92	–	–
B.M.A.J.Mendis (De)	LB	252	24	908	30	30.26	6-204	1	–
C.A.J.Meschede (Gm)	RMF	138	22	4482	14	34.42	4- 61	–	–
C.N.Miles (Gs)	RMF	245	35	974	27	36.07	5- 99	1	–
A.F.Milne (K)	RMF	184	51	572	13	44.00	4- 68	–	–
T.P.Milnes (De)	RMF	97.4	16	458	5	91.60	2- 58	–	–
D.K.H.Mitchell (Wo)	RM	7.4	0	37	1	37.00	1- 16	–	–
Mohammad Amir (Ex)	LF	76.2	19	189	14	13.50	5- 18	2	1
A.O.Morgan (Gm)	SLA	14	4	22	0			–	–
M.Morkel (SA)	RF	175	37	550	20	27.50	4- 41	–	–
C.H.Morris (SA)	RFM	57.5	10	241	9	26.77	3- 38	–	–
T.H.Moses (CU)	RMF	80	15	238	6	39.66	3- 62	–	–
P.W.A.Mulder (SAA)	RM	34	3	137	4	34.25	3- 71	–	–
S.J.Mullaney (Nt)	RM	177	58	486	25	19.44	5- 32	1	–
T.J.Murtagh (M)	RFM	372	93	995	36	27.63	6- 63	1	–
P.Mustard (Gs)	LBG	20	2	141	0			–	–
C.D.Nash (Sx)	OB	24	6	66	0			–	–
R.I.Newton (Nh)	OB	9	0	82	1	82.00	1- 82	–	–
A.S.S.Nijjar (CfU/Ex)	SLA	48	5	202	3	67.33	1- 37	–	–
K.Noema-Barnett (Gs)	RM	254.4	59	737	23	32.04	4- 31	–	–
L.C.Norwell (Gs)	RMF	332	70	1069	59	18.11	8- 43	5	2
D.Olivier (SA/SAA)	RF	109.2	17	440	13	33.84	3- 38	–	–
G.Onions (Du)	RFM	237	48	725	32	22.65	6- 62	1	–
D.O'Sullivan (CfU)	RFM	26	3	92	4	23.00	3- 29	–	–
C.Overton (Sm)	RFM	373.5	106	1030	46	22.39	5- 47	2	–
J.Overton (EL/Sm)	RFM	126	24	391	17	23.00	3- 30	–	–
X.G.Owen (DU)	RM	61.4	9	197	3	65.66	3- 55	–	–
A.P.Palladino (De)	RMF	274.4	58	889	25	35.56	4- 36	–	–
G.D.Panayi (Wa)	RFM	38.3	7	141	4	35.25	3- 75	–	–
C.F.Parkinson (Le)	SLA	147.2	14	556	17	32.70	8-148	1	1

243

	Cat	O	M	R	W	Avge	Best	5wI	10wM
M.W.Parkinson (La)	LB	76.4	7	308	14	22.00	4- 68	–	–
W.D.Parnell (K)	LFM	57.1	16	162	7	23.14	3- 48	–	–
S.D.Parry (La)	SLA	334.1	75	792	29	27.31	5- 45	1	–
J.S.Patel (Wa)	OB	482	149	1222	41	29.80	6- 50	1	–
R.Patel (Sy)	RMF	42	8	128	2	64.00	1- 11	–	–
R.H.Patel (M)	SLA	70	7	221	12	18.41	7- 81	2	1
S.R.Patel (Nt)	SLA	243	64	732	26	28.15	5- 43	1	–
D.Paterson (SAA)	RFM	41.4	13	128	8	16.00	7- 27	1	–
S.A.Patterson (Y)	RMF	306.2	78	808	27	29.92	4- 46	–	–
J.L.Pattinson (Nt)	RFM	139.3	34	386	32	12.06	5- 29	2	–
D.A.Payne (Gs)	LMF	272.1	50	845	28	30.17	3- 29	–	–
T.H.S.Pettman (OU)	RFM	46	9	184	4	46.00	3- 82	–	–
V.D.Philander (SA/Sx)	RMF	201.3	47	663	26	25.50	4- 39	–	–
D.L.Piedt (SAA)	OB	109.1	20	352	10	35.20	3- 36	–	–
O.L.Pike (CfU)	RFM	19.2	2	82	3	27.33	3- 82	–	–
M.W.Pillans (H)	RF	101.1	9	416	12	34.66	3- 63	–	–
L.E.Plunkett (EL/Y)	RFM	65.3	17	202	7	28.85	4- 73	–	–
H.W.Podmore (De/M)	RM	113.4	15	434	9	48.22	3- 68	–	–
J.A.Porter (EL/Ex)	RFM	459	108	1423	85	16.74	7- 55	5	1
M.J.Potts (Du)	RM	163	37	465	14	33.21	3- 48	–	–
J.E.Poulson (CU)	RM	25.5	11	52	3	17.33	3- 30	–	–
R.D.Pringle (Du)	OB	197.5	41	688	15	45.86	4- 73	–	–
L.A.Procter (La/Nh)	RM	77	9	298	7	42.57	3- 43	–	–
C.A.Pujara (Nt)	LB	5	0	17	0				
M.R.Quinn (Ex)	RMF	61.5	13	221	6	36.83	3- 66	–	–
K.Rabada (SA)	RF	151	30	514	16	32.12	4- 91	–	–
B.A.Raine (Le)	RMF	256.1	54	777	33	23.54	6- 66	2	–
R.Rampaul (Sy)	RMF	62	15	193	3	64.33	1- 47	–	–
W.B.Rankin (Wa)	RFM	114.2	13	423	12	35.25	3- 48	–	–
A.U.Rashid (Y)	LB	108	10	500	10	50.00	3- 94	–	–
D.M.W.Rawlins (Sx)	SLA	40	1	161	1	161.00	1- 46	–	–
O.P.Rayner (M)	OB	265.3	62	778	20	38.90	4- 35	–	–
L.M.Reece (De)	LM	127.3	26	473	8	59.12	3- 38	–	–
R.A.Reifer (WI)	LM	24	3	100	1	100.00	1-100	–	–
G.H.Rhodes (Wo)	OB	38	7	202	3	67.33	1- 12	–	–
M.A.Richardson (Nh)	RMF	28	3	101	0				
A.E.N.Riley (K)	OB	21	5	63	2	31.50	2- 37	–	–
K.A.J.Roach (WI)	RF	128.2	36	402	18	22.33	5- 43	2	–
O.E.Robinson (Sx)	RM	149.3	30	412	19	21.58	5- 69	1	–
T.S.Roland-Jones (E/M)	RFM	366.4	86	1214	45	26.97	5- 57	1	–
J.E.Root (E/Y)	OB	18.4	0	71	1	71.00	1- 22	–	–
W.T.Root (Nt)	OB	7.2	1	29	3	9.66	3- 29	–	–
A.M.Rossington (Nh)	RM	12	1	48	0				
T.D.Rouse (CfU/Sm)	OB	15	1	59	2	29.50	2- 31	–	–
C.Rushworth (Du)	RMF	436.3	96	1217	47	25.89	5- 52	1	–
A.Sakande (Sx)	RFM	76.4	11	299	13	23.00	5- 43	1	–
R.A.Sale (CU)		9	3	21	0				
M.E.T.Salisbury (H)	RMF	74.3	11	271	8	33.87	3- 65	–	–
A.G.Salter (Gm)	OB	170.4	13	676	14	48.28	3- 60	–	–
B.W.Sanderson (Nh)	RMF	334.1	93	860	40	21.50	5- 39	2	–
G.S.Sandhu (Du)	LMF	21.3	2	87	3	29.00	3- 60	–	–
R.J.Sayer (Le)	OB	120	16	410	3	136.66	1- 31	–	–
A.Shahzad (Le/Sx)	RMF	73	7	291	6	48.50	3- 91	–	–
J.D.Shantry (Wo)	LM	100.3	19	310	11	28.18	3- 54	–	–
J.Shaw (Gs/Y)	RMF	143	22	594	14	42.42	5-118	1	–
A.Sheikh (Nh)	LFM	8	1	36	1	36.00	1- 36	–	–

244

	Cat	O	M	R	W	Avge	Best	5wI	10wM
B.J.Shoare (LBU)	OB	8	0	28	1	28.00	1- 28	–	–
C.E.Shreck (Le)	RFM	63	15	183	2	91.50	1- 42	–	–
D.P.Sibley (Sy/Wa)	OB	8.4	0	67	1	67.00	1- 50	–	–
R.J.Sidebottom (Y)	LFM	186.4	43	518	25	20.72	5- 56	1	–
R.N.Sidebottom (Wa)	RMF	129.5	28	510	23	22.17	4- 29	–	–
F.P.A.Simon (DU)	RMF	32	7	128	3	42.66	2- 68	–	–
J.A.Simpson (M)	(WK)	2	0	21	0				
B.T.Slater (De)	OB	2	0	6	0				
D.Smit (De)	LB	10.5	0	57	0				
J.F.Smith (SAA)	RMF	9	2	24	0				
R.A.J.Smith (RM)	RM	69.4	6	302	9	33.55	3- 64	–	–
T.M.J.Smith (Gs)	SLA	70.4	7	263	9	29.22	3- 73	–	–
M.D.Sonczak (De)	SLA	35	5	116	3	38.66	2- 56	–	–
N.A.Sowter (M)	LB	10.1	1	25	1	25.00	1- 23	–	–
C.T.Steel (Du)	LB	65.2	3	275	8	34.37	2- 24	–	–
D.I.Stevens (K)	RM	414.4	109	1157	63	18.36	8- 75	7	–
R.A.Stevenson (H)	RMF	15	2	55	0				
G.Stewart (K)	RMF	20	5	89	2	44.50	2- 52	–	–
P.R.Stirling (M)	OB	57	8	165	4	41.25	2- 70	–	–
B.A.Stokes (Du/E)	RFM	176.3	37	582	16	36.37	6- 22	1	–
O.P.Stone (Wa)	RMF	17	3	70	1	70.00	1- 70	–	–
Sukhjit Singh (Wa)	SLA	152.4	30	452	17	26.58	6-144	2	–
B.Swanson (OU)	SLA	31	13	62	1	62.00	1- 40	–	–
W.A.Tavaré (Gs)	RM	8	1	52	0				
B.J.Taylor (H)	OB	64	3	275	4	68.75	2- 57	–	–
C.J.Taylor (Ex)	RM	19	4	64	4	16.00	2- 20	–	–
J.M.R.Taylor (Gs)	OB	152.2	15	633	14	45.21	3- 50	–	–
J.P.A.Taylor (De)	RM	17	1	77	1	77.00	1- 14	–	–
M.D.Taylor (Gs)	LMF	127	19	492	10	49.20	3- 80	–	–
T.A.I.Taylor (De)	RMF	173	34	688	17	40.47	4- 67	–	–
R.N.ten Doeschate (Ex)	RMF	26.1	4	96	4	24.00	2- 16	–	–
S.J.Thakor (De)	RM	64.3	9	302	6	50.33	4- 45	–	–
I.A.A.Thomas (K)	RMF	22	6	72	2	36.00	1- 28	–	–
A.T.Thomson (Wa)	OB	3	2	1	0				
G.T.Thornton (Wa)	RMF	36.2	4	138	4	34.50	4- 34	–	–
A.D.Tillcock (LU)	SLA	31	4	151	0				
J.C.Tongue (Wo)	RM	333.4	46	1212	47	25.78	6- 97	2	–
R.J.W.Topley (H)	LMF	44.2	6	178	2	89.00	1- 56	–	–
J.C.Tredwell (K)	OB	88	20	273	7	39.00	3- 33	–	–
P.D.Trego (Sm)	RMF	79.5	13	265	7	37.85	5- 67	1	–
L.Trevaskis (Du)	SLA	26	3	126	1	126.00	1- 69	–	–
I.J.L.Trott (Wa)	RM	36	4	111	1	111.00	1- 48	–	–
A.R.I.Umeed (Wa)	LB	14	0	73	2	36.50	1- 19	–	–
G.L.van Buuren (Gs)	SLA	122.1	25	360	9	40.00	4- 18	–	–
F.O.E.van den Bergh (Sy)	SLA	57	13	145	4	36.25	3- 84	–	–
T.van der Gugten (Gm)	RFM	158.2	43	505	22	22.95	5-101	1	–
R.E.van der Merwe (Sm)	SLA	68.4	17	189	11	17.18	4- 22	–	–
P.A.van Meekeren (Sm)	RMF	34	9	132	4	33.00	4- 60	–	–
S.van Zyl (Sx)	RM	116.1	24	368	10	36.80	2- 25	–	–
G.C.Viljoen (De)	RF	139.5	27	517	24	21.54	8- 90	3	1
J.M.Vince (H)	RM	8.5	0	38	1	38.00	1- 13	–	–
A.Virdi (Sy)	OB	88	13	271	6	45.16	3- 82	–	–
A.C.Voges (M)	SLA	17	0	80	1	80.00	1- 15	–	–
G.Wade (Nh)	RMF	18	0	100	1	100.00	1-100	–	–
G.G.Wagg (Gm)	LM	60	10	206	7	29.42	2- 14	–	–
N.Wagner (Ex)	LMF	316.4	54	1095	31	35.32	6- 48	1	–

	Cat	O	M	R	W	Avge	Best	5wI	10wM
M.J.Waite (Y)	RFM	16	0	70	3	23.33	2- 41	–	–
A.G.Wakely (Nh)	RM	9.2	0	75	0				
P.I.Walter (Ex)	LMF	93	20	287	7	41.00	2- 14	–	–
J.J.Weatherley (H/K)	OB	15	3	55	1	55.00	1- 46	–	–
W.J.Weighell (Du)	RMF	94.5	8	438	11	39.81	3- 51	–	–
T.J.Wells (Le)	RMF	26.4	2	166	6	27.66	4- 46	–	–
M.H.Wessels (Nt)	(WK)	5	0	15	0				
T.Westley (E/EL/Ex)	OB	30.3	5	101	3	33.66	1- 6	–	–
B.T.J.Wheal (H)	RMF	120.5	22	476	15	31.73	4- 98	–	–
G.G.White (Nh)	SLA	72	9	305	3	101.66	2- 40	–	–
R.A.Whiteley (Wo)	LM	2	0	20	0				
S.G.Whittingham (Sx)	RFM	105.5	12	494	15	32.93	5- 80	1	–
D.Wiese (Sx)	RMF	248.3	44	834	22	37.90	4- 63	–	–
A.R.Wilkinson (OU)	LFM	62	12	259	7	37.00	3- 35	–	–
D.J.Willey (Y)	LMF	60	15	148	4	37.00	2- 20	–	–
D.R.Williams (DU)	LB	30	1	143	3	47.66	2- 82	–	–
N.J.Winder (CU)	SLA	28	11	71	0				
C.R.Woakes (E/Wa)	RFM	77.2	13	281	9	31.22	3- 38	–	–
C.P.Wood (H)	LM	3	0	12	0				
L.Wood (Nt)	LM	139.2	17	540	19	28.42	4- 31	–	–
M.A.Wood (Du/E)	RF	179	30	586	14	41.85	5- 54	1	–
C.J.C.Wright (Wa)	RFM	221.3	41	757	20	37.85	5-113	1	–
Yasir Shah (K)	LB	155.5	22	533	14	38.07	5-132	1	–
S.A.Zaib (Nh)	SLA	36.3	6	115	6	19.16	6-115	1	–
M.S.Zaidi (CU)	LB	15	0	58	0				

FIRST-CLASS CAREER RECORDS

Compiled by Philip Bailey

The following career records are for all players who appeared in first-class cricket during the 2017 season, and are complete to the end of that season. Some players who did not appear in 2017 but may do so in 2018 are included.

BATTING AND FIELDING

'1000' denotes instances of scoring 1000 runs in a season. Where these have been achieved outside the British Isles they are shown after a plus sign.

	M	I	NO	HS	Runs	Avge	100	50	1000	Ct/St
Abbott, K.J.	85	117	21	97*	1762	18.35	–	6	–	17
Abell, T.B.	45	81	8	135	2172	29.75	3	13	–	33
Ackermann, C.N.	83	146	14	150	5181	39.25	11	32	0+1	65
Adair, M.R.	2	3	2	32	66	66.00	–	–	–	–
Adams, J.H.K.	218	383	28	262*	13370	37.66	23	72	5	174
Akram, B.M.R.	6	7	1	160	348	58.00	2	–	–	2
Ali, A.M.	15	25	1	80	639	26.62	–	3	–	6
Ali, M.M.	172	292	27	250	10194	38.46	19	65	2	100
Allenby, J.	153	240	30	138*	7784	37.06	10	56	1	165
Alsop, T.P.	25	42	–	117	1085	25.83	1	8	–	24
Ambrose, T.R.	224	342	32	251*	10284	33.17	16	62	–	581/40
Amla, H.M.	213	351	29	311*	15966	49.58	47	77	0+2	167
Anderson, C.J.	50	85	10	167	2727	36.36	4	12	–	38
Anderson, J.M.	216	272	105	81	1718	10.28	–	1	–	129
Andersson, M.K.	2	4	–	12	16	4.00	–	–	–	4
Ansari, Z.S.	71	116	15	112	3009	29.79	3	15	1	31
Archer, J.C.	20	28	6	81*	833	37.86	–	6	–	13
Arif, A.T.	7	12	–	49	145	12.08	–	–	–	1
Arshad, U.	17	21	1	84	548	27.40	–	3	–	6
Ashar Zaidi	112	179	13	202	6019	36.25	12	29	0+1	84
Ashraf, M.A.	24	21	6	24	80	5.33	–	–	–	3
Ashwin, R.	91	123	23	124	3419	34.19	6	19	–	37
Azeem Rafiq	38	45	5	100	866	21.65	1	4	–	14
Azharullah	111	149	76	58*	968	13.26	–	1	–	23
Bailey, G.J.	139	246	21	200*	9022	40.09	22	45	–	119
Bailey, T.E.	31	42	9	58	596	18.06	–	2	–	3
Bairstow, J.M.	151	244	31	246	10018	47.03	21	54	3	391/18
Ball, A.J.	31	45	3	69	855	20.35	–	4	–	20
Ball, J.T.	44	66	10	49*	748	13.35	–	–	–	6
Ballance, G.S.	133	215	22	210	9362	48.50	32	44	3+1	111
Bancroft, C.T.	63	115	8	211	3948	36.89	10	15	–	78/1
Banks, L.	2	4	–	29	57	14.25	–	–	–	1
Barker, K.H.D.	102	136	23	125	3336	29.52	6	15	–	32
Barnard, E.G.	33	45	10	75	1083	30.94	–	7	–	15
Bartlett, G.A.	4	8	1	28	100	14.28	–	–	–	3
Barton, A.P.	7	13	3	13*	37	3.70	–	–	–	4
Batty, G.J.	253	374	64	133	7276	23.47	3	30	–	161
Bavuma, T.	113	186	25	162	6032	37.42	12	32	–	55
Beard, A.P.	8	7	5	58*	79	39.50	–	1	–	1
Beer, W.A.T.	14	16	3	39	288	22.15	–	–	–	5
Bell, I.R.	292	492	51	262*	19129	43.37	51	101	4	220
Bell-Drummond, D.J.	82	138	12	206*	4385	34.80	9	23	1	37
Berg, G.K.	112	170	20	130*	4510	30.06	2	25	–	61

247

F-C	M	I	NO	HS	Runs	Avge	100	50	1000	Ct/St
Bess, D.M.	12	19	4	55	298	19.86	–	1	–	10
Billings, S.W.	53	75	7	171	2271	33.39	3	11	–	137/9
Bishoo, D.	89	147	30	47*	1406	12.01	–	–	–	44
Blackwood, J.	71	130	8	147	3945	32.33	4	26	–	65
Blake, A.J.	38	60	6	105*	1343	24.87	1	6	–	23
Bocking, O.S.	2	4	1	1*	1	0.33	–	–	–	–
Bopara, R.S.	196	318	34	229	11475	40.40	27	48	1	100
Borthwick, S.G.	141	238	23	216	7756	36.07	16	41	4	185
Bracewell, D.A.J.	78	120	16	105	2669	25.66	2	13	–	36
Bracey, J.R.	7	10	1	156	463	51.44	1	3	–	6
Bragg, W.D.	111	196	8	161*	5673	30.17	6	35	3	46/1
Brand, N.	5	7	2	46	154	30.80	–	–	–	2
Brathwaite, K.C.	115	203	15	212	7647	40.67	19	38	–	77
Bresnan, T.T.	182	242	38	169*	6071	29.75	6	31	–	92
Brewster, A.D.F.	2	1	1	1*	1	–	–	–	–	–
Briggs, D.R.	89	108	27	120*	1420	17.53	1	1	–	31
Broad, S.C.J.	179	243	37	169	4533	22.00	1	23	–	63
Brock, T.M.J.	1	2	–	2	2	1.00	–	–	–	–
Brodrick, C.A.J.	1	1	–	52	52	52.00	–	1	–	1
Brook, H.C.	5	7	–	38	82	11.71	–	–	–	1
Brookes, H.J.H.	1	2	–	11	15	7.50	–	–	–	–
Brooks, J.A.	106	123	46	109*	1306	16.96	1	3	–	28
Broughton, B.M.	3	5	2	46	86	28.66	–	–	–	3
Brown, B.C.	110	170	26	163	5464	37.94	13	29	1	289/15
Brown, C.R.	4	7	–	35	154	22.00	–	–	–	–
Brown, K.R.	83	136	6	132	3505	26.96	2	22	–	51
Brown, P.R.	4	5	3	5*	12	6.00	–	–	–	1
Browne, N.L.J.	64	104	9	255	4257	44.81	13	17	3	48
Buck, N.L.	74	102	29	43	923	12.64	–	–	–	15
Bullen, S.F.G.	5	8	–	56	196	24.50	–	1	–	–
Burgess, M.G.K.	13	18	2	146	777	48.56	1	4	–	23
Burke, J.E.	13	17	1	79	274	17.12	–	2	–	6
Burnham, J.T.A.	26	44	4	135	1018	25.45	1	6	–	9
Burns, R.J.	92	160	13	219*	6199	42.17	11	35	4	82
Buttler, J.C.	81	126	12	144	3593	31.51	4	20	–	168/2
Byrom, E.J.	8	15	–	56	401	26.73	–	1	–	2
Callis, E.	2	3	1	84	131	65.50	–	1	–	1
Carberry, M.A.	204	357	25	300*	13675	41.18	35	66	4	93
Carey, L.J.	14	19	3	54	231	14.43	–	1	–	4
Carlson, K.S.	13	22	1	191	696	33.14	2	2	–	5
Carse, B.A.	11	11	4	61*	267	38.14	–	1	–	2
Carter, A.	36	41	14	39	307	11.37	–	–	–	8
Carter, M.	5	8	1	33	64	9.14	–	–	–	4
Carver, K.	7	11	4	20	107	15.28	–	–	–	4
Chanderpaul, S.	370	602	108	303*	26925	54.50	76	139	1+1	191
Chapman, L.J.	2	4	–	13	18	4.50	–	–	–	–
Chappell, Z.J.	10	16	2	96	387	27.64	–	2	–	–
Chase, R.L.	54	88	17	137*	3154	44.42	6	19	–	26
Chohan, D.	3	6	–	83	121	20.16	–	1	–	1
Chopra, V.	179	292	20	233*	9776	35.94	20	49	3	213
Christian, D.T.	76	129	17	131*	3446	30.76	5	15	–	83
Clark, G.	18	33	–	109	1004	30.42	1	8	–	12
Clark, J.	4	6	–	32	76	12.66	–	–	–	3
Clark, J.	31	43	4	140	1078	27.64	1	4	–	4
Clarke, J.M.	44	73	7	194	2867	43.43	9	12	1	20
Clarke, R.	225	341	39	214	9926	32.86	16	52	1	337

248

F-C	M	I	NO	HS	Runs	Avge	100	50	1000	Ct/St
Claydon, M.E.	101	128	28	77	1556	15.56	–	4	–	11
Coad, B.O.	15	18	6	28	146	12.16	–	–	–	1
Cobb, J.J.	113	193	22	148*	4503	26.33	3	26	–	50
Cockbain, I.A.	50	85	6	151*	2382	30.15	4	13	–	34
Coles, M.T.	106	140	18	103*	2461	20.17	1	12	–	56
Collingwood, P.D.	294	506	52	206	16594	36.55	35	85	3	340
Colverd, T.G.L.	5	10	–	64	163	16.30	–	1	–	3
Compton, N.R.D.	187	327	37	254*	11679	40.27	26	55	6	93
Cook, A.N.	266	472	35	294	21047	48.16	60	100	7+1	277
Cook, S.C.	199	367	31	390	13651	40.62	41	56	0+4	128
Cook, S.J.	9	8	4	3	4	1.00	–	–	–	–
Cook, W.	2	4	–	42	45	11.25	–	–	–	–
Cooke, C.B.	63	107	15	171	3504	38.08	4	23	–	82/1
Cooke, J.M.	2	2	–	21	28	14.00	–	–	–	6
Cork, G.T.G.	2	3	–	49	53	17.66	–	–	–	1
Cosgrove, M.J.	194	346	19	233	13839	42.32	35	78	4	124
Cotton, B.D.	20	29	9	43	314	15.70	–	–	–	3
Coughlin, P.	29	45	7	85	1035	27.23	–	6	–	13
Cox, O.B.	89	143	21	124	3609	29.58	3	21	–	232/12
Crane, M.S.	27	36	14	29	228	10.36	–	–	–	8
Crawley, Z.	5	7	–	62	137	19.57	–	1	–	4
Crichard, R.J.	5	6	2	27*	97	24.25	–	–	–	3
Critchley, M.J.J.	18	28	4	137*	775	32.29	2	2	–	7
Croft, S.J.	156	244	22	156	7367	33.18	12	42	–	162
Crook, S.P.	100	135	19	145	3682	31.74	5	19	–	33
Cullen, T.N.	6	9	–	42	154	17.11	–	–	–	13/1
Cummins, M.L.	56	66	28	29*	239	6.28	–	–	–	21
Curran, S.M.	34	51	7	96	1277	29.02	–	10	–	10
Curran, T.K.	51	69	9	60	1062	17.70	–	5	–	20
Currill, O.C.	1	–	–	–	–	–	–	–	–	–
Dala, C.J.	44	51	19	79*	346	10.81	–	1	–	14
Dalgleish, A.D.	2	4	–	41	94	23.50	–	–	–	3
Davey, J.H.	15	25	2	72	420	18.26	–	3	–	8
Davies, A.L.	48	71	4	140*	2490	37.16	3	16	1	130/13
Davies, R.C.	20	25	1	86	415	17.29	–	3	–	36/6
Davies, S.M.	196	323	32	200*	11653	40.04	23	53	6	446/27
Davis, W.S.	12	16	4	25	106	8.83	–	–	–	2
Dawson, L.A.	131	215	23	169	6279	32.70	8	34	1	133
de Bruyn, T.B.	42	74	6	202*	3025	44.48	7	16	–	41
de Grandhomme, C.	89	147	19	144*	4514	35.26	10	26	–	90
de Kock, Q.	50	84	8	194	3566	46.92	9	24	–	183/12
de Lange, M.	64	88	10	65	1091	13.98	–	1	–	31
Dearden, H.E.	13	25	–	87	481	19.24	–	2	–	14
Delport, C.S.	61	106	6	163	3206	32.06	3	19	–	36
Denly, J.L.	173	299	21	227	10032	36.08	23	51	4	75
Dent, C.D.J.	114	202	19	268	6991	38.20	13	43	3	137
Dernbach, J.W.	103	126	45	56*	742	9.16	–	–	1	15
Dewhurst, A.C.H.	1	2	–	91	94	47.00	–	1	–	1
Dexter, N.J.	141	237	27	163*	7290	34.71	17	34	–	88
Dickinson, C.M.	4	6	–	99	211	35.16	–	2	–	4
Dickson, S.R.	41	66	6	318	2275	37.91	4	11	–	21
Dixon, M.W.	12	12	3	22	68	7.55	–	–	–	1
D'Oliveira, B.L.	41	72	2	202*	2189	31.27	6	5	–	23
Donald, A.H.T.	35	64	3	234	1989	32.60	2	13	1	29
Dowrich, S.O.	74	110	21	131*	2873	32.28	3	18	–	181/20
Drissell, G.S.	1	1	–	0	0	0.00	–	–	–	–

F-C	M	I	NO	HS	Runs	Avge	100	50	1000	Ct/St
du Plessis, F.	121	196	21	176	7002	40.01	14	43	–	107
Duckett, B.M.	62	104	6	282*	4094	41.77	13	19	2	53/3
Duminy, J.P.	108	174	27	260*	6774	46.08	20	30	–	79
Eckersley, E.J.H.	101	181	12	158	5559	32.89	14	17	1	149/3
Edwards, F.H.	107	153	56	40	682	7.03	–	–	–	19
Elgar, D.	154	269	22	268	10681	43.24	32	40	0+1	118
Elliott, G.D.	83	134	7	196*	3883	30.57	8	20	–	46
Ellis, E.J.	5	8	1	18	54	7.71	–	–	–	11/1
Ervine, S.M.	225	351	42	237*	11256	36.42	22	56	1	193
Escott, D.A.	2	4	–	125	197	49.25	1	–	–	4
Eskinazi, S.S.	25	44	3	179	1472	35.90	4	6	–	16
Evans, L.J.	58	100	6	213*	2974	31.63	5	16	–	48
Evans, S.T.	3	4	–	114	163	40.75	1	–	–	1
Faulkner, J.P.	62	94	12	121	2565	31.28	2	15	–	26
Fazakerley, W.N.	1	2	–	0	0	0.00	–	–	–	–
Fell, T.C.	60	102	5	171	3020	31.13	5	12	1	49
Feszczur-Hatchett, S.A.	2	4	1	24*	35	11.66	–	–	–	–
Finch, A.J.	66	108	5	288*	3767	36.57	6	24	–	61
Finch, H.Z.	24	38	5	135*	926	28.06	2	5	–	25
Finn, S.T.	145	176	59	56	1061	9.06	–	1	–	47
Fisher, M.D.	5	6	1	37	86	17.20	–	–	–	1
Fletcher, L.J.	91	129	26	92	1516	14.71	–	4	–	22
Foakes, B.T.	77	117	24	141*	3892	41.84	8	20	–	136/13
Footitt, M.H.A.	92	117	35	34	640	7.80	–	–	–	24
Foster, J.S.	283	418	52	212	13533	36.97	23	69	1	823/60
Fraine, W.A.R.	2	3	–	23	48	16.00	–	–	–	–
Franklin, J.E.C.	206	321	46	219	9780	35.56	22	44	–	107
Fuller, J.K.	41	48	5	93	859	19.97	–	4	–	17
Gabriel, S.T.	81	107	44	20*	344	5.46	–	–	–	20
Gamble, R.N.	6	6	–	32	51	8.50	–	–	–	2
Garton, G.H.S.	9	10	2	18*	79	9.87	–	–	–	3
Gibson, R.	1	1	–	0	0	0.00	–	–	–	–
Gidman, W.R.S.	78	121	21	143	3646	36.46	5	21	1	36
Gleeson, R.J.	16	17	6	31	160	14.54	–	–	–	4
Gnodde, J.S.D.	3	6	1	54	91	18.20	–	1	–	2
Godleman, B.A.	127	226	11	204	7009	32.60	15	33	1	87
Graham, O.J.G.	2	4	–	41	56	14.00	–	–	–	1
Graves, B.W.M.	1	1	–	0	0	0.00	–	–	–	–
Greenidge, A.D.	2	4	–	22	35	8.75	–	–	–	1
Gregory, L.	59	83	9	137	1531	20.68	1	4	–	23
Griffiths, G.T.	6	8	3	14*	37	7.40	–	–	–	–
Groenewald, T.D.	124	176	58	78	2184	18.50	–	6	–	40
Grundy, J.O.	6	9	2	53	126	18.00	–	1	–	1
Gubbins, N.R.T.	44	76	2	201*	2708	36.59	5	19	1	14
Guest, C.J.	2	4	–	9	21	5.25	–	–	–	2
Gurney, H.F.	92	115	53	42*	351	5.66	–	–	–	11
Haggett, C.J.	38	50	13	80	873	23.59	–	2	–	9
Hain, S.R.	47	74	6	208	2139	31.45	7	7	–	37
Hales, A.D.	107	182	6	236	6655	37.81	13	38	3	84
Hameed, H.	39	67	8	122	2229	37.77	4	14	1	21
Hamidullah Qadri	3	6	4	11*	20	10.00	–	–	–	2
Handscomb, P.S.P.	82	137	11	215	5167	41.00	12	30	–	116/4
Hankins, G.T.	22	35	1	116	862	25.35	1	5	–	26
Hannon-Dalby, O.J.	53	61	23	40	265	6.97	–	–	–	5
Harding, G.H.I.	1	1	–	0	0	0.00	–	–	–	–
Harinath, A.	72	126	6	154	3797	31.64	6	21	–	19

F-C	M	I	NO	HS	Runs	Avge	100	50	1000	Ct/St
Harmer, S.R.	101	154	32	100*	3125	25.61	1	19	–	96
Harris, J.A.R.	121	170	37	87*	2811	21.13	–	12	–	34
Harrison, J.	1	2	–	38	52	26.00	–	–	–	5/1
Hart, A.H.J.A.	2	4	1	36	44	14.66	–	–	–	1
Hartley, C.F.	3	4	–	5	7	1.75	–	–	–	–
Hasan Azad	6	7	1	99	252	42.00	–	2	–	2
Hastings, J.W.	76	108	7	93	2231	22.08	–	11	–	35
Head, T.M.	54	99	3	192	3308	34.45	5	22	–	20
Heathfield, T.D.	2	2	2	12*	12	–	–	–	–	–
Helm, T.G.	17	24	5	28	241	12.68	–	–	–	6
Hemmings, R.P.	2	1	–	19	19	19.00	–	–	–	1
Hendricks, B.E.	67	73	25	27	431	8.97	–	–	–	17
Henriques, M.C.	72	113	12	265	3560	35.24	6	19	–	31
Henry, M.J.	43	53	11	75*	981	23.35	–	3	–	19
Hetmyer, S.O.	22	40	3	107	1198	32.37	1	6	–	23
Hickey, A.J.	4	7	3	36*	92	23.00	–	–	–	1
Higgins, R.F.	4	7	–	45	129	18.42	–	–	–	–
Hildreth, J.C.	234	383	29	303*	15344	43.34	41	68	6	193
Hill, L.J.	24	44	5	126	986	25.28	1	3	–	39/2
Hodd, A.J.	111	157	25	123	3634	27.53	4	21	–	266/23
Hogan, M.G.	131	185	71	57	1852	16.24	–	2	–	68
Holden, M.D.E.	11	19	1	153	758	42.11	2	3	–	5
Holder, J.O.	53	81	8	103*	1663	22.78	1	8	–	33
Holland, I.G.	10	14	4	58*	258	25.80	–	2	–	1
Hope, K.A.	37	68	5	105*	1856	29.46	2	10	–	31
Hope, S.D.	41	70	6	215*	2729	42.64	8	10	–	36
Horton, P.J.	191	324	24	209	10963	36.54	23	59	3	185/1
Hose, A.J.	4	8	–	68	212	26.50	–	2	–	1
Hosein, H.R.	23	36	8	108	883	31.53	1	6	–	63/1
Houghton, D.	1	2	1	29	35	35.00	–	–	–	–
Howell, B.A.C.	62	96	12	163	2316	27.57	2	11	–	31
Hughes, A.L.	44	74	9	142	1962	30.18	4	7	–	32
Hughes, C.F.	80	146	9	270*	4441	32.41	10	19	–	57
Hughes, M.S.T.	3	6	–	116	391	65.16	2	1	–	2
Hunn, M.D.	19	16	11	32*	94	18.80	–	–	–	8
Hussain, R.	2	4	–	15	34	8.50	–	–	–	1
Hutson, J.W.	1	1	–	25	25	25.00	–	–	–	2
Hutton, B.A.	33	51	6	74	970	21.55	–	4	–	16
Imran Qayyum	5	7	2	39	40	8.00	–	–	–	3
Imran Tahir	194	246	62	77*	2617	14.22	–	4	–	81
Ingram, C.A.	111	195	17	190	6641	37.30	14	30	–	75
Jahanfar, M.F.	1	1	–	2	2	2.00	–	–	–	2
Jarvis, K.M.	73	99	32	57	977	14.58	–	1	–	20
Javid, A.	32	51	6	133	1090	24.22	2	3	–	16
Jenner, J.W.	1	1	–	68	68	68.00	–	1	–	–
Jennings, K.K.	93	167	10	221*	5345	34.04	14	20	1	57
Jones, R.A.	58	89	17	62	895	12.43	–	2	–	21
Jones, R.P.	7	12	2	106*	299	29.90	1	–	–	6
Jordan, C.J.	94	129	21	147	2700	25.00	2	12	–	114
Joseph, A.S.	22	37	7	31	186	6.20	–	–	–	8
Junaid Khan	75	101	30	71	740	10.42	–	2	–	12
Keogh, R.I.	59	97	8	221	2704	30.38	7	7	–	15/1
Kerrigan, S.C.	104	122	42	62*	1058	13.22	–	3	–	36
Kettleborough, J.M.	22	39	1	81	950	25.00	–	6	–	12
Klaasen, H.	56	85	13	201	3333	46.29	8	13	–	179/11
Klein, D.	53	76	15	66	1066	17.47	–	4	–	17

F-C	M	I	NO	HS	Runs	Avge	100	50	1000	Ct/St
Kleinveldt, R.K.	143	200	23	115*	3564	20.13	1	16	–	70
Klinger, M.	182	321	33	255	11320	39.30	30	49	1+2	179
Kohler-Cadmore, T.	40	66	4	169	1914	30.87	4	10	–	48
Kuhn, H.G.	138	240	23	244*	9494	43.75	23	44	0+1	330/18
Kumar, N.R.	15	23	1	141	644	29.27	2	2	–	5
Ladd-Gibbon, B.I.W.	2	2	1	6*	10	10.00	–	–	–	–
Lake, M.B.	6	11	1	66	147	14.70	–	1	–	2
Lamb, M.J.	8	16	–	71	331	20.68	–	2	–	3
Latham, T.W.M.	84	148	11	261	5778	42.17	12	37	–	102/1
Lawlor, J.L.	6	8	2	81	261	43.50	–	3	–	3
Lawrence, D.W.	40	62	7	161	2359	42.89	7	10	1	32
Leach, J.	70	102	12	114	2386	26.51	2	16	–	20
Leach, M.J.	51	64	17	52	578	12.29	–	1	–	16
Leaning, J.A.	51	79	8	123	2269	31.95	4	11	–	39
Lees, A.Z.	85	144	12	275*	4785	36.25	12	22	2	62
Leverock, K.S.	4	4	–	25	69	17.25	–	–	–	1
Levi, R.E.	88	144	15	168	5012	38.85	10	29	–	69
Libby, J.D.	36	59	4	144	1723	31.32	4	6	–	10
Liddle, C.J.	31	32	16	53	197	12.31	–	1	–	8
Lilley, A.M.	13	17	5	63	398	33.16	–	2	–	4
Livingstone, L.S.	31	51	11	224	1950	48.75	6	10	–	43
Lloyd, D.L.	45	75	9	107	1797	27.22	3	6	–	15
Lumb, M.J.	210	352	18	221*	11443	34.26	21	58	3	118
Lyon, N.M.	119	151	46	75	1357	12.92	–	2	–	49
Lyth, A.	148	245	11	251	9202	39.32	22	48	3	188
McCarthy, B.J.	14	20	6	51*	360	25.71	–	1	–	7
McCollum, J.A.	6	9	1	119*	303	37.87	1	1	–	–
McCollum, B.B.	150	261	13	302	9210	37.13	17	46	–	308/19
McDermott, P.F.	2	4	–	20	46	11.50	–	–	–	–
Macdonell, C.M.	6	10	3	91	325	46.42	–	2	–	1
McGrath, A.H.	1	1	–	12	12	12.00	–	–	–	–
McIver, J.N.	6	11	1	51	199	19.90	–	1	–	1
McKay, C.J.	85	122	16	66	2097	19.78	–	8	–	18
McKerr, C.	4	4	1	17	34	11.33	–	–	–	–
McLaren, R.	143	212	40	140	5793	33.68	7	29	–	68
McManus, L.D.	24	34	4	132*	936	31.20	1	4	–	54/9
Madsen, W.L.	156	277	22	231*	10031	39.33	26	51	4	137
Magoffin, S.J.	154	207	54	79	2592	16.94	–	5	–	35
Maharaj, K.A.	91	123	25	114*	2185	22.29	2	7	–	32
Mahmood, S.	4	5	4	4*	5	5.00	–	–	–	1
Main, G.T.	4	4	2	13	13	6.50	–	–	–	1
Malan, D.J.	149	253	19	182*	8715	37.24	18	45	2	153
Markram, A.K.	33	55	4	182	2144	42.03	5	10	–	33
Marsden, J.	8	10	5	27*	55	11.00	–	–	–	5
Marsh, M.R.	70	117	10	211	3087	28.85	4	17	–	36
Marsh, S.E.	129	227	25	182	8260	40.89	22	39	–	121
Marshall, J.D.	2	3	1	41*	85	42.50	–	–	–	1
Martin, A.T.	3	6	–	28	52	8.66	–	–	–	1
Meaker, S.C.	84	111	23	94	1404	15.95	–	6	–	16
Mellor, A.J.	9	16	1	59	282	18.80	–	1	–	15
Mendis, B.M.A.J.	145	228	31	206*	6942	35.23	18	31	–	116
Mennie, J.M.	48	78	13	79*	1097	16.87	–	5	–	21
Meschede, C.A.J.	66	93	12	107	2099	25.91	2	11	–	23
Miles, C.N.	54	74	9	62*	1142	17.56	–	5	–	13
Miller, D.A.	57	91	7	177	2987	35.55	5	17	–	66
Mills, T.S.	32	38	15	31*	260	11.30	–	–	–	9

F-C	M	I	NO	HS	Runs	Avge	100	50	1000	Ct/St
Milne, A.F.	23	35	13	97	632	28.72	–	4	–	10
Milnes, T.P.	25	34	4	56	625	20.83	–	3	–	6
Mitchell, D.K.H.	178	321	37	298	11550	40.66	31	47	6	242
Mohammad Abbas	60	88	28	40	423	7.05	–	–	–	19
Mohammad Amir	52	79	12	66	1060	15.82	–	2	–	9
Mohammad Nabi	30	49	4	117	1159	25.75	2	4	–	14
Moores, T.J.	7	12	–	41	202	16.83	–	–	–	7
Morgan, A.O.	14	25	5	103*	467	23.35	1	1	–	4
Morgan, E.J.G.	93	153	16	209*	4791	34.97	11	22	1	71/1
Morkel, M.	116	141	26	82*	1649	14.33	–	4	–	41
Morris, C.H.	52	77	9	154	2096	30.82	3	10	–	47
Moses, T.H.	3	6	1	80*	145	29.00	–	1	–	1
Mulder, P.W.A.	7	13	2	104	309	28.09	1	–	–	6
Mullaney, S.J.	111	184	8	168	6001	34.09	12	32	1	106
Murphy, D.	78	105	22	135*	2205	26.56	1	12	–	207/19
Murphy, J.R.	6	9	–	27	136	15.11	–	–	–	2
Murtagh, T.J.	204	266	78	74*	3695	19.65	–	10	–	59
Mustard, P.	210	322	36	130	8700	30.41	7	52	–	670/19
Myburgh, J.G.	108	190	23	203	6841	40.96	16	39	–	61
Nash, C.D.	184	314	19	184	11424	38.72	23	59	4	114
Naylor, M.A.	1	2	–	19	19	9.50	–	–	–	–
Neesham, J.D.S.	47	81	8	147	2353	32.23	5	10	–	44
Newton, R.I.	82	143	11	202*	4825	36.55	12	23	1	24
Nijjar, A.S.S.	10	12	5	53	185	26.42	–	1	–	1
Noema-Barnett, K.	73	107	13	107	2566	27.29	2	15	–	35
Norris, M.J.	4	6	–	32	104	17.33	–	–	–	2
Northeast, S.A.	136	233	18	191	8528	39.66	19	45	3	69
Norwell, L.C.	67	84	34	102	700	14.00	1	1	–	15
Olivier, D.	66	86	23	72	857	13.60	–	3	–	23
Onions, G.	170	219	81	65	1900	13.76	–	1	–	33
Organ, F.S.	1	1	–	16	16	16.00	–	–	–	–
O'Sullivan, D.	1	1	–	2	2	2.00	–	–	–	–
Overton, C.	60	84	12	138	1645	22.84	1	7	–	36
Overton, J.	45	61	17	56	766	17.40	–	4	–	4
Owen, X.G.	2	2	2	1*	2	–	–	–	–	–
Palladino, A.P.	143	200	41	106	2464	15.49	1	7	–	39
Palmer, H.J.	4	8	–	32	123	15.37	–	–	–	4
Panayi, G.D.	2	3	–	16	17	5.66	–	–	–	–
Parkinson, C.F.	9	13	6	75	183	26.14	–	1	–	3
Parkinson, M.W.	9	11	4	13	36	5.14	–	–	–	2
Parnell, W.D.	61	83	8	111*	2024	26.98	2	11	–	19
Parry, S.D.	23	28	2	44	445	17.11	–	–	–	7
Patel, J.S.	249	328	71	120	5805	22.58	3	25	–	124
Patel, R.	4	6	–	81	170	28.33	–	1	–	2
Patel, R.H.	24	34	17	26*	187	11.00	–	–	–	6
Patel, S.R.	198	319	17	257*	11337	37.53	26	53	4	129
Paterson, D.	83	103	24	59	855	10.82	–	1	–	34
Patterson, S.A.	132	152	39	63*	1839	16.27	–	3	–	23
Pattinson, J.L.	51	60	14	89*	1183	25.71	–	5	–	14
Payne, D.A.	76	91	28	67*	1337	21.22	–	6	–	26
Perera, N.L.T.C.	32	50	6	113*	1389	31.56	1	8	–	23
Pettini, M.L.	178	296	42	209	8933	35.16	15	49	1	120
Pettman, T.H.S.	1	2	–	25	34	17.00	–	–	–	–
Philander, V.D.	146	196	38	168	4107	25.99	2	15	–	38
Piedt, D.L.	85	118	13	92	1683	16.02	–	7	–	48
Pietersen, K.P.	217	358	26	355*	16522	49.76	50	71	3	152

F-C	M	I	NO	HS	Runs	Avge	100	50	1000	Ct/St
Pike, O.L.	1	–	–	–	–	–	–	–	–	–
Pillans, M.W.	39	56	5	56	709	13.90	–	1	–	20
Plunkett, L.E.	155	213	39	126	4376	25.14	3	22	–	86
Podmore, H.W.	12	18	4	66*	209	14.92	–	1	–	4
Pollock, E.J.	5	7	1	52	184	30.66	–	1	–	1
Pope, O.J.D.	6	10	3	100*	270	38.57	1	1	–	3
Porter, J.A.	49	54	22	34	216	6.75	–	–	–	17
Porterfield, W.T.S.	125	208	7	186	6171	30.70	9	33	–	133
Potticary, J.T.	2	4	–	32	72	18.00	–	–	–	–
Potts, M.J.	5	6	2	53*	69	17.25	–	1	–	–
Poulson, J.E.	2	3	2	40	61	61.00	–	–	–	–
Powell, K.O.A.	91	163	7	139	5245	33.62	7	27	–	72
Poynter, S.W.	24	34	1	125	783	23.72	1	2	–	68/2
Poysden, J.E.	10	8	2	47	71	11.83	–	–	–	2
Prasanna, S.	98	155	7	81	3216	21.72	–	18	–	70
Pringle, R.D.	36	56	8	99	1255	26.14	–	8	–	21
Procter, L.A.	68	104	6	137	3105	31.68	3	17	–	17
Pujara, C.A.	156	254	34	352	12490	56.77	41	43	0+3	113/1
Quinn, M.R.	27	34	5	50	298	10.27	–	1	–	5
Rabada, K.	37	45	12	48*	456	13.81	–	–	–	13
Rackow, A.J.W.	1	2	–	95	118	59.00	–	1	–	1
Raine, B.A.	53	88	9	72	1608	20.35	–	7	–	10
Rampaul, R.	69	102	22	64*	1068	13.35	–	2	–	20
Rankin, W.B.	103	121	51	56*	639	9.12	–	1	–	26
Rashid, A.U.	166	236	38	180	6577	33.21	10	37	–	78
Rashid Khan	2	3	1	52	85	42.50	–	1	–	–
Rawlins, D.M.W.	5	9	–	96	217	24.11	–	2	–	–
Rayner, O.P.	129	170	28	143*	3079	21.68	2	13	–	173
Read, C.M.W.	349	526	87	240	16361	37.26	26	92	3	1051/53
Read, J.	1	1	–	14	14	14.00	–	–	–	4
Reece, L.M.	41	72	6	168	2235	33.86	3	17	–	21
Reifer, R.A.	51	86	8	89	1981	25.39	–	10	–	29
Rhodes, G.H.	14	26	4	99	653	29.68	–	4	–	7
Rhodes, W.M.H.	19	28	2	95	693	26.65	–	3	–	9
Richardson, M.A.	1	–	–	–	–	–	–	–	–	–
Richardson, M.J.	92	156	11	148	4439	30.61	5	25	2	178/5
Riley, A.E.N.	52	66	23	34	429	9.97	–	–	–	27
Rippington, S.E.	2	4	2	2*	2	1.00	–	–	–	–
Roach, K.A.J.	92	124	23	53	1189	11.77	–	2	–	31
Robinson, O.E.	27	39	8	110	787	25.38	1	3	–	9
Robson, A.J.	57	105	3	120	3164	31.01	2	28	2	45
Robson, S.D.	128	226	16	231	8082	38.48	19	33	2	127
Roderick, G.H.	69	109	15	171	3562	37.89	5	25	–	175/4
Roland-Jones, T.S.	97	133	26	103*	2383	22.27	1	9	–	30
Ronchi, L.	100	158	15	148	5614	39.25	16	23	–	343/17
Root, J.E.	112	193	21	254	8873	51.58	22	45	3	105
Root, W.T.	8	12	1	133	501	45.54	2	2	–	–
Rossington, A.M.	51	81	9	138*	2549	35.40	6	16	–	99/9
Rossouw, R.R.	87	153	6	319	6193	42.12	18	26	0+1	108
Rouse, A.P.	24	34	2	95*	828	25.87	–	4	–	78/4
Rouse, T.D.	9	13	1	69	205	17.08	–	1	–	5
Roy, J.J.	78	127	11	143	4376	37.72	8	20	1	72
Rudolph, J.A.	294	508	31	228*	19825	41.56	51	93	4+1	244
Rushworth, C.	100	137	36	57	1322	13.08	–	1	–	22
Sakande, A.	9	11	3	33	103	12.87	–	–	–	4
Sale, R.A.	1	2	–	28	42	21.00	–	–	–	2

F-C	M	I	NO	HS	Runs	Avge	100	50	1000	Ct/St
Salisbury, M.E.T.	16	24	5	24	157	8.26	–	–	–	3
Salt, P.D.	7	10	1	72	203	22.55	–	1	–	2
Salter, A.G.	44	67	14	88	1378	26.00	–	7	–	20
Sanderson, B.W.	32	39	11	42	187	6.67	–	–	–	6
Sandhu, G.S.	7	6	3	46*	76	25.33	–	–	–	–
Sangakkara, K.C.	260	430	31	319	20911	52.40	64	86	2+1	372/33
Santner, M.J.	38	55	4	118	1476	28.94	2	8	–	31
Sarfraz Ahmed	134	210	42	213*	7043	41.92	10	49	–	415/47
Sayer, R.J.	11	13	2	34	152	13.81	–	–	–	3
Scott, D.N.C.	2	4	–	18	45	11.25	–	–	–	1
Scott, G.F.B.	4	5	2	16*	37	12.33	–	–	–	2
Scriven, J.A.L.	2	2	1	16	18	18.00	–	–	–	1
Second, R.S.	84	140	13	210	5372	42.29	15	24	0+1	295/13
Selman, N.J.	25	46	4	142*	1372	32.66	6	5	–	23
Senaratne, N.V.S.	8	16	–	82	330	20.62	–	1	–	2
Shahid Afridi	113	185	4	164	5695	31.46	12	31	–	78
Shahzad, A.	97	128	31	88	2237	23.06	–	6	–	16
Shamsi, T.	70	84	24	30*	505	8.41	–	–	–	19
Shantry, J.D.	92	118	32	106	1640	19.06	2	2	–	30
Sharma, I.	108	136	54	31*	676	8.24	–	–	–	24
Shaw, J.	21	26	6	29	194	9.70	–	–	–	5
Sheikh, A.	10	14	4	12	47	4.70	–	–	–	3
Shoare, B.J.	2	4	–	47	58	14.50	–	–	–	1
Shreck, C.E.	175	211	109	56	801	7.85	–	1	–	49
Sibley, D.P.	36	63	7	242	1843	32.91	2	13	–	25
Siddle, P.M.	134	174	32	103*	2491	17.54	1	5	–	45
Sidebottom, R.J.	230	284	91	61	2684	13.90	–	3	–	64
Sidebottom, R.N.	7	14	6	13	26	3.25	–	–	–	–
Simon, F.P.A.	1	1	–	1	1	1.00	–	–	–	–
Simpson, J.A.	130	205	32	143	5471	31.62	5	33	–	403/20
Singh, A.R.	2	2	–	44	44	22.00	–	–	–	2
Slater, B.T.	56	104	5	119	2978	30.08	3	17	–	20
Smit, D.	133	200	35	156*	5948	36.04	9	33	0+1	351/22
Smith, G.P.	105	194	10	158*	4963	26.97	8	22	–	86
Smith, J.F.	30	50	3	121	1230	26.17	3	6	–	17
Smith, L.P.	1	1	–	0	0	0.00	–	–	–	–
Smith, R.A.J.	19	23	4	57*	374	19.68	–	1	–	3
Smith, T.M.J.	43	59	12	80	1055	22.44	–	2	–	12
Smith, W.R.	172	292	21	210	8986	33.15	17	35	1	109
Sodhi, I.S.	55	82	13	82*	1585	22.97	–	8	–	21
Sohail Khan	89	119	30	65	1328	14.92	–	2	–	21
Sole, C.B.	1	–	–	–	–	–	–	–	–	–
Sonczak, M.D.	1	1	–	9	9	9.00	–	–	–	–
Southee, T.G.	92	126	9	156	2016	17.23	1	5	–	44
Sowter, N.A.	1	2	–	37	37	18.50	–	–	–	–
Stanlake, B.	2	2	2	1*	1	–	–	–	–	–
Steel, C.T.	19	33	2	224	1214	39.16	2	7	–	7
Stevens, D.I.	278	437	26	208	14721	35.81	33	75	3	192
Stevenson, R.A.	4	5	1	30	73	18.25	–	–	–	–
Stewart, G.	1	2	1	15*	15	15.00	–	–	–	–
Stewart-Taylor, S.K.	1	1	–	8	8	8.00	–	–	–	0/1
Stirling, P.R.	57	87	4	146	2458	29.61	5	13	–	29
Stoinis, M.P.	43	73	5	170	2386	35.08	4	16	–	12
Stokes, B.A.	113	187	9	258	6207	34.87	14	31	–	77
Stone, O.P.	26	34	8	60	446	17.15	–	1	–	14
Stoneman, M.D.	152	266	7	197	9140	35.28	20	44	5	76

F-C	M	I	NO	HS	Runs	Avge	100	50	1000	Ct/St
Sukhjit Singh	5	8	2	16*	18	3.00	–	–	–	1
Swanson, B.	1	2	1	0*	0	0.00	–	–	–	1
Sykes, J.S.	12	19	4	34	186	12.40	–	–	–	6
Tamim Iqbal	81	150	7	206	6157	43.05	14	37	–	27
Tavaré, W.A.	54	92	6	139	2721	31.63	6	14	1	36
Taylor, B.J.	5	8	3	36	112	22.40	–	–	–	2
Taylor, B.R.M.	121	219	12	217	8331	40.24	28	30	1+1	137/4
Taylor, C.J.	3	4	–	26	62	15.50	–	–	–	1
Taylor, J.E.	98	152	22	106	1538	11.83	1	1	–	23
Taylor, J.M.R.	57	85	8	156	2498	32.44	6	8	–	32
Taylor, J.P.A.	1	1	1	0*	0	–	–	–	–	–
Taylor, L.R.P.L.	146	246	21	290	9812	43.60	23	50	–	185
Taylor, M.D.	28	38	18	36	270	13.50	–	–	–	3
Taylor, N.P.	1	2	–	4	6	3.00	–	–	–	–
Taylor, T.A.I.	25	39	6	80	587	17.78	–	2	–	5
ten Doeschate, R.N.	160	233	35	259*	9581	48.38	26	44	1	97
Tetley, J.W.	6	11	–	42	128	11.63	–	–	–	7/1
Thakor, S.J.	51	80	12	134	2571	37.80	5	12	–	11
Thomas, I.A.A.	20	30	14	13	97	6.06	–	–	–	3
Thomson, A.T.	6	7	–	26	113	16.14	–	–	–	2
Thornton, G.T.	2	3	1	10	19	9.50	–	–	–	–
Thurston, C.O.	4	4	–	126	143	35.75	1	–	–	1
Tice, P.J.A.	4	7	1	54	162	27.00	–	1	–	9/1
Tillcock, A.D.	2	2	1	16*	32	32.00	–	–	–	3
Tongue, J.C.	15	18	3	41	138	9.20	–	–	–	2
Topley, R.J.W.	34	41	19	16	94	4.27	–	–	–	8
Tredwell, J.C.	177	247	31	124	4727	21.88	4	17	–	196
Trego, P.D.	215	318	37	154*	9464	33.67	15	54	1	86
Trescothick, M.E.	375	647	36	284	25598	41.89	65	123	8	534
Trevaskis, L.	1	2	–	9	14	7.00	–	–	–	–
Trott, I.J.L.	266	444	43	226	17616	43.93	43	86	8	212
Umeed, A.R.I.	15	25	1	113	497	20.70	2	–	–	13
van Buuren, G.L.	67	104	17	235	4021	46.21	10	23	–	40
van den Bergh, F.O.E.	7	9	1	34	62	7.75	–	–	–	1
van der Gugten, T.	25	34	6	57	300	10.71	–	1	–	4
van der Merwe, R.E.	61	99	14	205*	2865	33.70	5	18	–	45
van Meekeren, P.A.	7	12	2	34	100	10.00	–	–	–	2
van Zyl, S.	152	254	37	172	9424	43.42	23	42	1+1	92
Vasconcelos, R.S.	4	8	1	79	208	29.71	–	2	–	2
Vilas, D.J.	115	176	20	244	6001	38.46	13	28	–	306/14
Viljoen, G.C.	99	135	17	72	1679	14.22	–	6	–	30
Vince, J.M.	133	219	18	240	7802	38.81	20	30	2	119
Virdi, G.S.	3	4	1	8*	18	6.00	–	–	–	–
Voges, A.C.	211	351	52	269*	13881	46.42	32	72	0+1	283
Wade, G.	1	–	–	–	–	–	–	–	–	–
Wagg, G.G.	147	216	22	200	5284	27.23	4	31	–	49
Wagner, M.	140	184	38	70	2373	16.25	–	7	–	38
Waite, M.J.	1	2	–	18	22	11.00	–	–	–	–
Wakely, A.G.	122	195	14	123	5717	31.58	7	31	–	80
Wallace, C.D.	6	8	–	35	144	18.00	–	–	–	3/1
Waller, M.T.C.	8	9	1	28	91	11.37	–	–	–	5
Walter, P.I.	8	8	3	68*	219	43.80	–	1	–	–
Weatherley, J.J.	10	15	–	83	331	22.06	–	1	–	1
Weighell, W.J.	9	15	4	58	284	25.81	–	2	–	2
Wells, D.A.C.	2	4	–	33	42	10.50	–	–	–	–
Wells, L.W.P.	110	183	11	258	6546	38.05	17	26	2	54

F-C	M	I	NO	HS	Runs	Avge	100	50	1000	Ct/St
Wells, T.J.	17	27	2	87*	522	20.88	–	2	–	8
Wessels, M.H.	185	304	26	202*	10172	36.58	22	51	2	297/16
Westley, T.	149	246	19	254	8326	36.67	18	41	1	102
Westwood, I.J.	159	266	22	196	8077	33.10	16	42	–	83
Wheal, B.T.J.	19	22	7	18	94	6.26	–	–	–	4
Wheater, A.J.A.	117	173	20	204*	5646	36.90	11	31	–	182/10
White, G.G.	39	55	5	65	659	13.18	–	2	–	12
White, R.G.	6	6	–	69	110	18.33	–	1	–	6
Whiteley, R.A.	71	115	12	130*	2788	27.06	3	14	–	47
Whittingham, S.G.	12	13	4	22	63	7.00	–	–	–	2
Wiese, D.	95	151	16	208	4549	33.69	9	24	–	66
Wilkinson, A.R.	2	2	–	12	12	6.00	–	–	–	–
Willey, D.J.	64	89	10	104*	2137	27.05	2	14	–	14
Williams, D.R.	2	1	–	32	32	32.00	–	–	–	2
Williamson, K.S.	123	212	17	284*	9516	48.80	27	48	–	114
Wilson, G.C.	94	143	20	160*	4282	34.81	3	26	–	169/5
Winder, N.J.	1	1	–	1	1	1.00	–	–	–	–
Woakes, C.R.	127	186	46	152*	5083	36.30	9	21	–	55
Wood, C.P.	40	57	5	105*	1270	24.42	1	6	–	12
Wood, L.	23	35	8	100	774	28.66	1	2	–	6
Wood, M.A.	43	70	14	72*	1182	21.10	–	3	–	10
Wood, T.A.	3	5	–	15	47	9.40	–	–	–	3
Worrall, D.J.	27	40	17	26	229	9.95	–	–	–	9
Wright, C.J.C.	131	169	40	77	2357	18.27	–	9	–	22
Wright, L.J.	134	206	23	226*	7273	39.74	17	37	1	57
Yasir Shah	111	152	21	71	2224	16.97	–	6	–	62
Zaib, S.A.	6	8	2	65*	168	28.00	–	1	–	3
Zaidi, M.S.	1	2	–	3	4	2.00	–	–	–	–
Zampa, A.	30	48	5	74	982	22.83	–	5	–	7
Zondo, K.	95	150	8	175	4395	30.95	8	25	–	59

BOWLING

'50wS' denotes instances of taking 50 or more wickets in a season. Where these have been achieved outside the British Isles they are shown after a plus sign.

	Runs	Wkts	Avge	Best	5wI	10wM	50wS
Abbott, K.J.	6911	319	21.66	8- 45	20	2	1+1
Abell, T.B.	129	3	43.00	2- 71	–	–	–
Ackermann, C.N.	1737	39	44.53	3- 45	–	–	–
Adair, M.R.	108	1	108.00	1- 61	–	–	–
Adams, J.H.K.	718	13	55.23	2- 16	–	–	–
Akram, B.M.R.	592	17	34.82	5- 54	1	–	–
Ali, A.M.	86	1	86.00	1- 10	–	–	–
Ali, M.M.	11447	288	39.74	6- 29	9	2	–
Allenby, J.	7902	298	26.51	6- 54	5	1	1
Alsop, T.P.	66	2	33.00	2- 59	–	–	–
Ambrose, T.R.	1	1	1.00	1- 0	–	–	–
Amla, H.M.	277	1	277.00	1- 10	–	–	–
Anderson, C.J.	1663	40	41.57	5- 22	1	–	–
Anderson, J.M.	21494	837	25.67	7- 42	42	6	4
Ansari, Z.S.	4592	128	35.87	6- 30	6	–	–
Archer, J.C.	2321	89	26.07	7- 67	4	1	1
Arif, A.T.	503	7	71.85	2- 29	–	–	–
Arshad, U.	955	36	26.52	4- 78	–	–	–
Ashar Zaidi	2803	94	29.81	4- 50	–	–	–
Ashraf, M.A.	1434	43	33.34	5- 32	1	–	–

F-C	Runs	Wkts	Avge	Best	5wI	10wM	50wS
Ashwin, R.	11729	446	26.29	7- 59	39	10	0+1
Azeem Rafiq	2804	71	39.49	5- 50	1	–	–
Azharullah	10345	362	28.57	7- 74	17	2	0+1
Bailey, G.J.	55	0					
Bailey, T.E.	2758	90	30.64	5- 12	5	1	–
Bairstow, J.M.	1	0					
Ball, A.J.	1498	34	44.05	3- 36	–	–	–
Ball, J.T.	3787	143	26.48	6- 49	4	–	1
Ballance, G.S.	154	0					
Bancroft, C.T.	67	1	67.00	1- 67	–	–	–
Barker, K.H.D.	8440	318	26.54	6- 40	12	1	3
Barnard, E.G.	2955	94	31.43	4- 23	–	–	–
Barton, A.P.	612	11	55.63	5- 31	1	–	–
Batty, G.J.	21678	656	33.04	8- 68	26	3	2
Bavuma, T.	278	7	39.71	2- 34	–	–	–
Beard, A.P.	704	16	44.00	4- 62	–	–	–
Beer, W.A.T.	898	29	30.96	6- 29	2	1	–
Bell, I.R.	1615	47	34.36	4- 4	–	–	–
Bell-Drummond, D.J.	64	0					
Berg, G.K.	7403	239	30.97	6- 56	4	–	–
Bess, D.M.	1107	49	22.59	7-117	5	1	–
Billings, S.W.	4	0					
Bishoo, D.	9864	353	27.94	9- 78	19	4	0+1
Blackwood, J.	392	10	39.20	3- 44	–	–	–
Blake, A.J.	129	3	43.00	2- 9	–	–	–
Bocking, O.S.	223	7	31.85	4- 52	–	–	–
Bopara, R.S.	8803	239	36.83	5- 49	3	–	–
Borthwick, S.G.	7582	200	37.91	6- 70	3	–	–
Bracewell, D.A.J.	8157	239	34.12	7- 35	8	–	–
Bragg, W.D.	459	5	91.80	2- 10	–	–	–
Brand, N.	164	4	41.00	3- 7	–	–	–
Brathwaite, K.C.	883	20	44.15	6- 29	1	–	–
Bresnan, T.T.	15861	511	31.03	5- 36	8	–	–
Brewster, A.D.F.	191	3	63.66	2- 87	–	–	–
Briggs, D.R.	8103	233	34.77	6- 45	8	–	–
Broad, S.C.J.	17665	641	27.55	8- 15	26	3	–
Brock, T.M.J.	137	6	22.83	3- 61	–	–	–
Brook, H.C.	65	1	65.00	1- 54	–	–	–
Brookes, H.J.H.	43	0					
Brooks, J.A.	10439	383	27.25	6- 65	14	–	3
Brown, B.C.	93	1	93.00	1- 48	–	–	–
Brown, C.R.	14	0					
Brown, K.R.	65	2	32.50	2- 30	–	–	–
Brown, P.R.	199	6	33.16	2- 15	–	–	–
Browne, N.L.J.	171	0					
Buck, N.L.	6902	194	35.57	6- 34	7	–	–
Bullen, S.F.G.	29	0					
Burke, J.E.	704	23	30.60	4- 19	–	–	–
Burns, R.J.	127	2	63.50	1- 18	–	–	–
Buttler, J.C.	11	0					
Carberry, M.A.	1074	17	63.17	2- 85	–	–	–
Carey, L.J.	1390	48	28.95	4- 85	–	–	–
Carlson, K.S.	178	6	29.66	5- 28	1	–	–
Carse, B.A.	798	20	39.90	3- 38	–	–	–
Carter, A.	3200	108	29.62	5- 40	2	–	–
Carter, M.	672	17	39.52	7- 56	1	1	–
Carver, K.	543	18	30.16	4-106	–	–	–

258

F-C	Runs	Wkts	Avge	Best	5wI	10wM	50wS
Chanderpaul, S.	2537	60	42.28	4- 48	–	–	–
Chapman, L.J.	258	8	32.25	6- 78	1	–	–
Chappell, Z.J.	771	15	51.40	4-108	–	–	–
Chase, R.L.	2598	89	29.19	7- 22	4	1	–
Chopra, V.	128	0					
Christian, D.T.	5267	155	33.98	5- 24	3	–	–
Clark, J.	1998	52	38.42	4- 81	–	–	–
Clarke, J.M.	22	0					
Clarke, R.	13447	413	32.55	7- 55	4	–	–
Claydon, M.E.	9102	278	32.74	6-104	8	–	2
Coad, B.O.	1246	55	22.65	6- 25	4	1	1
Cobb, J.J.	1449	17	85.23	2- 11	–	–	–
Cockbain, I.A.	44	1	44.00	1- 23	–	–	–
Coles, M.T.	9770	334	29.25	6- 51	11	2	2
Collingwood, P.D.	6269	159	39.42	5- 52	2	–	–
Colverd, T.G.L.	2	0					
Compton, N.R.D.	229	3	76.33	1- 1	–	–	–
Cook, A.N.	211	7	30.14	3- 13	–	–	–
Cook, S.C.	466	11	42.36	3- 42	–	–	–
Cook, S.J.	711	26	27.34	5- 18	2	–	–
Cook, W.	202	2	101.00	1- 33	–	–	–
Cooke, J.M.	247	1	247.00	1- 61	–	–	–
Cork, G.T.G.	198	0					
Cosgrove, M.J.	2349	52	45.17	3- 3	–	–	–
Cotton, B.D.	1640	37	44.32	4- 20	–	–	–
Coughlin, P.	2094	69	30.34	5- 49	2	1	–
Crane, M.S.	3008	70	42.97	5- 35	2	–	–
Crichard, R.J.	514	20	25.70	6- 68	3	1	–
Critchley, M.J.J.	1068	10	106.80	3- 50	–	–	–
Croft, S.J.	2903	71	40.88	6- 41	1	–	–
Crook, S.P.	7976	195	40.90	5- 48	3	–	–
Cummins, M.L.	3904	160	24.40	7- 45	9	1	–
Curran, S.M.	2814	86	32.72	7- 58	4	–	–
Curran, T.K.	4983	171	29.14	7- 20	6	1	1
Currill, O.C.	83	0					
Dala, C.J.	3679	111	33.14	5- 20	5	–	–
Dalgleish, A.D.	118	5	23.60	3- 49	–	–	–
Davey, J.H.	775	25	31.00	4- 53	–	–	–
Davis, W.S.	1224	38	32.21	7-146	1	–	–
Dawson, L.A.	6005	169	35.53	7- 51	3	–	–
de Bruyn, T.B.	281	8	35.12	2- 24	–	–	–
de Grandhomme, C.	4122	139	29.65	6- 24	2	–	–
de Kock, Q.	9	0					
de Lange, M.	7117	243	29.28	7- 23	9	2	–
Dearden, H.E.	95	2	47.50	1- 0	–	–	–
Delport, C.S.	723	14	51.64	2- 10	–	–	–
Denly, J.L.	1869	39	47.92	3- 43	–	–	–
Dent, C.D.J.	793	8	99.12	2- 21	–	–	–
Dernbach, J.W.	9210	279	33.01	6- 47	10	–	1
Dexter, N.J.	4891	148	33.04	6- 63	6	–	–
Dickson, S.R.	44	2	22.00	1- 15	–	–	–
Dixon, M.W.	1124	27	41.62	5-124	1	–	–
D'Oliveira, B.L.	1773	33	53.72	5- 48	1	–	–
Drissell, G.S.	58	0					
du Plessis, F.	1477	41	36.02	4- 39	–	–	–
Duckett, B.M.	49	1	49.00	1- 21	–	–	–
Duminy, J.P.	3162	77	41.06	5-108	1	–	–

F-C	Runs	Wkts	Avge	Best	5wI	10wM	50wS
Eckersley, E.J.H.	67	2	33.50	2- 29	–	–	–
Edwards, F.H.	10955	350	31.30	7- 87	21	2	–
Elgar, D.	2539	50	50.78	4- 22	–	–	–
Elliott, G.D.	3378	92	36.71	5- 33	1	–	–
Ervine, S.M.	11836	280	42.27	6- 82	5	–	–
Escott, D.A.	105	6	17.50	6- 71	1	–	–
Evans, L.J.	259	2	129.50	1- 29	–	–	–
Evans, S.T.	21	0					
Faulkner, J.P.	4737	190	24.93	5- 5	5	–	–
Fazakerley, W.N.	83	1	83.00	1- 32	–	–	–
Fell, T.C.	17	0					
Feszczur-Hatchett, S.A.	220	2	110.00	2- 91	–	–	–
Finch, A.J.	257	4	64.25	1- 0	–	–	–
Finch, H.Z.	109	2	54.50	1- 9	–	–	–
Finn, S.T.	14986	522	28.70	9- 37	13	1	2
Fisher, M.D.	438	13	33.69	5- 54	1	–	–
Fletcher, L.J.	7751	270	28.70	5- 52	3	–	–
Foakes, B.T.	6	0					
Footitt, M.H.A.	8894	345	25.77	7- 62	21	1	2
Foster, J.S.	128	1	128.00	1-122	–	–	–
Franklin, J.E.C.	13504	479	28.19	7- 14	14	1	–
Fuller, J.K.	3817	113	33.77	6- 24	5	1	–
Gabriel, S.T.	6565	215	30.53	5- 11	5	–	–
Gamble, R.N.	684	9	76.00	2- 16	–	–	–
Garton, G.H.S.	839	23	36.47	3- 20	–	–	–
Gibson, R.	42	1	42.00	1- 42	–	–	–
Gidman, W.R.S.	5053	212	23.83	6- 15	9	1	2
Gleeson, R.J.	1420	57	24.91	5- 46	3	–	–
Gnodde, J.S.D.	141	1	141.00	1- 33	–	–	–
Godleman, B.A.	35	0					
Graham, O.J.G.	188	4	47.00	2- 60	–	–	–
Graves, B.W.M.	6	0					
Gregory, L.	4766	167	28.53	6- 47	9	1	–
Griffiths, G.T.	434	8	54.25	4-101	–	–	–
Groenewald, T.D.	10804	362	29.84	6- 50	15	–	–
Grundy, J.O.	433	11	39.36	3- 41	–	–	–
Gubbins, N.R.T.	52	0					
Guest, C.J.	143	0					
Gurney, H.F.	8335	268	31.10	6- 61	6	–	–
Haggett, C.J.	2923	83	35.21	4- 15	–	–	–
Hain, S.R.	31	0					
Hales, A.D.	173	3	57.66	2- 63	–	–	–
Hameed, H.	21	0					
Hamidullah Qadri	288	10	28.80	5- 60	1	–	–
Handscomb, P.S.P.	21	0					
Hankins, G.T.	13	0					
Hannon-Dalby, O.J.	4097	109	37.58	5- 68	2	–	–
Harding, G.H.I.	186	4	46.50	4-111	–	–	–
Harinath, A.	195	5	39.00	2- 1	–	–	–
Harmer, S.R.	11893	391	30.41	9- 95	16	3	1+1
Harris, J.A.R.	11725	401	29.23	9- 34	12	2	2
Hart, A.H.J.A.	111	5	22.20	3- 17	–	–	–
Hartley, C.F.	314	11	28.54	4- 80	–	–	–
Hasan Azad	2	0					
Hastings, J.W.	6506	239	27.22	7- 60	7	–	–
Head, T.M.	1495	26	57.50	3- 42	–	–	–
Heathfield, T.D.	127	3	42.33	1- 26	–	–	–

F-C	Runs	Wkts	Avge	Best	5wI	10wM	50wS
Helm, T.G.	1457	47	31.00	5- 59	1	–	–
Hemmings, R.P.	152	0					
Hendricks, B.E.	5251	228	23.03	6- 26	12	1	0+1
Henriques, M.C.	3169	101	31.37	5- 17	2	–	–
Henry, M.J.	4594	161	28.53	5- 18	7	–	–
Hickey, A.J.	204	6	34.00	2- 19	–	–	–
Higgins, R.F.	281	12	23.41	4- 75	–	–	–
Hildreth, J.C.	492	6	82.00	2- 39	–	–	–
Hill, L.J.	6	0					
Hodd, A.J.	21	0					
Hogan, M.G.	12364	503	24.58	7- 92	20	2	3
Holden, M.D.E.	203	4	50.75	2- 59	–	–	–
Holder, J.O.	3294	119	27.68	5- 30	4	–	–
Holland, I.G.	429	20	21.45	4- 16	–	–	–
Hope, K.A.	3	0					
Hope, S.D.	5	0					
Horton, P.J.	80	2	40.00	2- 6	–	–	–
Houghton, D.	108	0					
Howell, B.A.C.	2838	85	33.38	5- 57	1	–	–
Hughes, A.L.	1241	22	56.40	4- 46	–	–	–
Hughes, C.F.	1297	27	48.03	3- 87	–	–	–
Hughes, M.S.T.	87	2	43.50	1- 16	–	–	–
Hunn, M.D.	1647	46	35.80	5- 99	1	–	–
Hutton, B.A.	3133	106	29.55	5- 29	4	2	–
Imran Qayyum	481	12	40.08	3-158	–	–	–
Imran Tahir	20881	784	26.63	8- 42	53	11	2+2
Ingram, C.A.	2133	50	42.66	4- 16	–	–	–
Jarvis, K.M.	7458	284	26.26	7- 35	16	2	2
Javid, A.	355	3	118.33	1- 1	–	–	–
Jennings, K.K.	750	27	27.77	3- 37	–	–	–
Jones, R.A.	5276	162	32.56	7-115	5	–	–
Jordan, C.J.	9160	284	32.25	7- 43	9	–	1
Joseph, A.S.	1710	60	28.50	7- 46	4	–	–
Junaid Khan	7448	304	24.50	7- 46	20	3	0+1
Keogh, R.I.	2593	65	39.89	9- 52	1	1	–
Kerrigan, S.C.	9844	322	30.57	9- 51	13	3	2
Klaasen, H.	50	2	25.00	1- 12	–	–	–
Klein, D.	5173	191	27.08	8- 72	10	1	–
Kleinveldt, R.K.	12208	436	28.00	9- 65	20	2	2
Klinger, M.	3	0					
Kuhn, H.G.	12	0					
Kumar, N.R.	535	11	48.63	3- 58	–	–	–
Ladd-Gibbon, B.I.W.	182	4	45.50	3- 47	–	–	–
Lake, M.B.	328	7	46.85	2- 41	–	–	–
Lamb, M.J.	66	3	22.00	1- 19	–	–	–
Latham, T.W.M.	18	1	18.00	1- 7	–	–	–
Lawlor, J.L.	154	3	51.33	1- 26	–	–	–
Lawrence, D.W.	214	7	30.57	1- 0	–	–	–
Leach, J.	6472	246	26.30	6- 73	12	1	3
Leach, M.J.	4422	167	26.47	7-106	11	1	2
Leaning, J.A.	270	3	90.00	2- 30	–	–	–
Lees, A.Z.	77	2	38.50	2- 51	–	–	–
Leverock, K.S.	284	2	142.00	1- 56	–	–	–
Libby, J.D.	224	3	74.66	1- 13	–	–	–
Liddle, C.J.	2204	44	50.09	3- 42	–	–	–
Lilley, A.M.	1296	36	36.00	5- 23	2	–	–
Livingstone, L.S.	583	11	53.00	6- 52	1	–	–

F-C	Runs	Wkts	Avge	Best	5wI	10wM	50wS
Lloyd, D.L.	2032	42	48.38	3- 36	–	–	–
Lumb, M.J.	260	6	43.33	2- 10	–	–	–
Lyon, N.M.	14156	393	36.02	8- 50	12	2	–
Lyth, A.	1290	29	44.48	2- 9	–	–	–
McCarthy, B.J.	1439	48	29.97	6- 63	2	–	–
McCollum, J.A.	8	0					
McCullum, B.B.	140	1	140.00	1- 1	–	–	–
Macdonell, C.M.	308	2	154.00	2- 57	–	–	–
McGrath, A.H.	108	4	27.00	4-108	–	–	–
McIver, J.N.	610	6	101.66	3- 64	–	–	–
McKay, C.J.	7787	281	27.71	6- 40	7	–	2
McKerr, C.	392	15	26.13	5- 54	2	1	–
McLaren, R.	11693	426	27.44	8- 38	14	1	1+1
Madsen, W.L.	1368	25	54.72	3- 45	–	–	–
Magoffin, S.J.	13498	581	23:23	8- 20	27	4	5
Maharaj, K.A.	8717	326	26.73	7- 89	16	2	–
Mahmood, S.	377	13	29.00	4- 50	–	–	–
Main, G.T.	319	8	39.87	3- 72	–	–	–
Malan, D.J.	2078	52	39.96	5- 61	1	–	–
Markram, A.K.	161	2	80.50	1- 2	–	–	–
Marsden, J.	698	26	26.84	5- 41	1	–	–
Marsh, M.R.	3259	114	28.58	6- 84	1	–	–
Marsh, S.E.	155	2	77.50	2- 20	–	–	–
Meaker, S.C.	8289	276	30.03	8- 52	11	2	1
Mendis, B.M.A.J.	7758	288	26.93	6- 37	14	–	–
Mennie, J.M.	4781	183	26.12	7- 96	6	–	0+1
Meschede, C.A.J.	4983	133	37.46	5- 84	1	–	–
Miles, C.N.	5592	197	28.38	6- 63	11	1	2
Miller, D.A.	42	0					
Mills, T.S.	2008	55	36.50	4- 25	–	–	–
Milne, A.F.	2072	63	32.88	5- 47	1	–	–
Milnes, T.P.	1986	47	42.25	7- 39	2	–	–
Mitchell, D.K.H.	1016	23	44.17	4- 49	–	–	–
Mohammad Abbas	5669	259	21.88	8- 46	21	7	0+2
Mohammad Amir	4683	205	22.84	7- 61	11	2	0+1
Mohammad Nabi	1815	81	22.40	6- 33	3	–	–
Morgan, A.O.	849	15	56.60	2- 37	–	–	–
Morgan, E.J.G.	90	2	45.00	2- 24	–	–	–
Morkel, M.	11287	411	27.46	6- 23	13	2	–
Morris, C.H.	4191	166	25.24	8- 44	2	1	–
Moses, T.H.	238	6	39.66	3- 62	–	–	–
Mulder, P.W.A.	522	27	19.33	7- 25	1	–	–
Mullaney, S.J.	2862	84	34.07	5- 32	1	–	–
Murphy, D.	43	1	43.00	1- 40	–	–	–
Murphy, J.R.	135	2	67.50	2- 90	–	–	–
Murtagh, T.J.	18566	691	26.86	7- 82	28	4	6
Mustard, P.	150	1	150.00	1- 9	–	–	–
Myburgh, J.G.	2160	45	48.00	4- 56	–	–	–
Nash, C.D.	3205	75	42.73	4- 12	–	–	–
Neesham, J.D.S.	3087	92	33.55	5- 65	2	–	–
Newton, R.I.	107	1	107.00	1- 82	–	–	–
Nijjar, A.S.S.	691	15	46.06	2- 33	–	–	–
Noema-Barnett, K.	4066	120	33.88	4- 20	–	–	–
Northeast, S.A.	147	1	147.00	1- 60	–	–	–
Norwell, L.C.	6670	248	26.89	8- 43	10	3	2
Olivier, D.	5708	267	21.37	6- 60	16	2	0+2
Onions, G.	16427	619	26.53	9- 67	26	3	7

F-C	Runs	Wkts	Avge	Best	5wI	10wM	50wS
O'Sullivan, D.	92	4	23.00	3- 29	–	–	–
Overton, C.	4940	189	26.13	6- 74	4	–	–
Overton, J.	3604	103	34.99	6- 95	2	–	–
Owen, X.G.	197	3	65.66	3- 55	–	–	–
Palladino, A.P.	11563	386	29.95	7- 53	13	–	2
Panayi, G.D.	141	4	35.25	3- 41	–	–	–
Parkinson, C.F.	1087	31	35.06	8-148	1	1	–
Parkinson, M.W.	671	24	27.95	5- 49	1	–	–
Parnell, W.D.	5386	178	30.25	7- 51	6	1	–
Parry, S.D.	1442	47	30.68	5- 23	2	–	–
Patel, J.S.	24729	721	34.29	7- 38	26	2	5
Patel, R.	128	2	64.00	1- 11	–	–	–
Patel, R.H.	2372	75	31.62	7- 81	3	1	–
Patel, S.R.	11662	303	38.48	7- 68	4	1	–
Paterson, D.	6426	279	23.03	7- 20	10	1	0+2
Patterson, S.A.	9765	348	28.06	6- 56	6	–	2
Pattinson, J.L.	4844	220	22.01	6- 32	9	–	–
Payne, D.A.	6528	198	32.96	6- 26	3	–	–
Perera, N.L.T.C.	2212	55	40.21	5- 69	1	–	–
Pettini, M.L.	263	1	263.00	1- 72	–	–	–
Pettman, T.H.S.	184	4	46.00	3- 82	–	–	–
Philander, V.D.	11245	514	21.87	7- 61	22	2	0+2
Piedt, D.L.	9164	301	30.44	7- 92	16	1	0+3
Pietersen, K.P.	3760	73	51.50	4- 31	–	–	–
Pike, O.L.	82	3	27.33	3- 82	–	–	–
Pillans, M.W.	3453	126	27.40	6- 67	3	1	0+1
Plunkett, L.E.	14273	452	31.57	6- 33	11	1	3
Podmore, H.W.	968	31	31.22	4- 54	–	–	–
Porter, J.A.	4779	206	23.19	7- 55	7	1	3
Porterfield, W.T.S.	138	2	69.00	1- 29	–	–	–
Potts, M.J.	465	14	33.21	3- 48	–	–	–
Poulson, J.E.	133	5	26.60	3- 30	–	–	–
Powell, K.O.A.	337	9	37.44	3- 29	–	–	–
Poysden, J.E.	752	21	35.80	5- 53	1	–	–
Prasanna, S.	10500	487	21.56	8- 59	36	8	0+4
Pringle, R.D.	2286	58	39.41	7-107	2	1	–
Procter, L.A.	2686	75	35.81	7- 71	2	–	–
Pujara, C.A.	146	5	29.20	2- 4	–	–	–
Quinn, M.R.	2869	101	28.40	7- 76	1	1	–
Rabada, K.	3772	154	24.49	9- 33	7	3	–
Raine, B.A.	4595	156	29.45	6- 66	5	–	1
Rampaul, R.	6188	206	30.03	7- 51	9	1	–
Rankin, W.B.	8875	334	26.57	6- 55	9	–	1
Rashid, A.U.	17185	490	35.07	7-107	19	1	2
Rashid Khan	265	20	13.25	8- 74	2	1	–
Rawlins, D.M.W.	161	1	161.00	1- 46	–	–	–
Rayner, O.P.	9406	286	32.88	8- 46	10	1	1
Read, C.M.W.	90	0					
Reece, L.M.	1015	22	46.13	4- 28	–	–	–
Reifer, R.A.	2525	100	25.25	6- 74	3	–	–
Rhodes, G.H.	465	6	77.50	2- 83	–	–	–
Rhodes, W.M.H.	829	25	33.16	3- 42	–	–	–
Richardson, M.A.	101	0					
Richardson, M.J.	13	0					
Riley, A.E.N.	4245	117	36.28	7-150	5	–	1
Rippington, S.E.	177	6	29.50	3- 51	–	–	–
Roach, K.A.J.	7803	273	28.58	7- 23	11	1	–

F-C	Runs	Wkts	Avge	Best	5wI	10wM	50wS
Robinson, O.E.	2500	84	29.76	6- 33	2	–	–
Robson, A.J.	127	0					
Robson, S.D.	110	2	55.00	1- 4	–	–	–
Roland-Jones, T.S.	9155	362	25.29	6- 50	16	3	2
Ronchi, L.	12	0					
Root, J.E.	1531	30	51.03	3- 33	–	–	–
Root, W.T.	52	3	17.33	3- 29	–	–	–
Rossington, A.M.	66	0					
Rossouw, R.R.	70	3	23.33	1- 1	–	–	–
Rouse, T.D.	185	5	37.00	2- 31	–	–	–
Roy, J.J.	495	14	35.35	3- 9	–	–	–
Rudolph, J.A.	2696	61	44.19	5- 80	3	–	–
Rushworth, C.	8758	359	24.39	9- 52	18	2	3
Sakande, A.	728	23	31.65	5- 43	1	–	–
Sale, R.A.	21	0					
Salisbury, M.E.T.	1266	27	46.88	4- 50	–	–	–
Salter, A.G.	3268	64	51.06	3- 5	–	–	–
Sanderson, B.W.	2477	112	22.11	8- 73	7	1	1
Sandhu, G.S.	548	14	39.14	4- 49	–	–	–
Sangakkara, K.C.	150	1	150.00	1- 13	–	–	–
Santner, M.J.	2668	56	47.64	3- 51	–	–	–
Sarfraz Ahmed	5	0					
Sayer, R.J.	1123	14	80.21	2- 41	–	–	–
Scott, G.F.B.	121	2	60.50	2- 67	–	–	–
Second, R.S.	187	4	46.75	4-105	–	–	–
Selman, N.J.	8	0					
Shahid Afridi	7098	266	26.68	6-101	8	–	–
Shahzad, A.	8709	249	34.97	5- 46	4	–	–
Shamsi, T.	7083	277	25.57	8- 85	18	5	0+2
Shantry, J.D.	7783	266	29.25	7- 60	12	2	2
Sharma, I.	10680	337	31.69	7- 24	11	2	–
Shaw, J.	2131	55	38.74	5- 79	2	–	–
Sheikh, A.	1011	24	42.12	4- 97	–	–	–
Shoare, B.J.	28	1	28.00	1- 28	–	–	–
Shreck, C.E.	18353	577	31.80	8- 31	23	2	4
Sibley, D.P.	264	4	66.00	2-103	–	–	–
Siddle, P.M.	12562	451	27.85	8- 54	17	–	0+1
Sidebottom, R.J.	18138	762	23.80	7- 37	31	4	4
Sidebottom, R.N.	603	24	25.12	4- 29	–	–	–
Simon, F.P.A.	128	3	42.66	2- 68	–	–	–
Simpson, J.A.	21	0					
Singh, A.R.	225	5	45.00	3- 79	–	–	–
Slater, B.T.	113	0					
Smit, D.	3501	106	33.02	7- 27	3	–	–
Smith, G.P.	73	1	73.00	1- 64	–	–	–
Smith, J.F.	947	42	22.54	6- 49	1	–	–
Smith, R.A.J.	1471	38	38.71	3- 23	–	–	–
Smith, T.M.J.	3641	74	49.20	4- 35	–	–	–
Smith, W.R.	1394	28	49.78	3- 34	–	–	–
Sodhi, I.S.	6486	167	38.83	7- 59	7	1	–
Sohail Khan	9823	381	25.78	9-109	29	6	0+3
Sole, C.B.	44	0					
Sonczak, M.D.	116	3	38.66	2- 56	–	–	–
Southee, T.G.	9568	344	27.81	8- 27	15	1	–
Sowter, N.A.	25	1	25.00	1- 23	–	–	–
Stanlake, B.	151	7	21.57	3- 50	–	–	–
Steel, C.T.	393	9	43.66	2- 24	–	–	–

F-C	Runs	Wkts	Avge	Best	5wI	10wM	50wS
Stevens, D.I.	11284	421	26.80	8- 75	19	1	3
Stevenson, R.A.	270	3	90.00	1- 15	–	–	–
Stewart, G.	89	2	44.50	2- 52	–	–	–
Stirling, P.R.	997	23	43.34	2- 27	–	–	–
Stoinis, M.P.	1593	33	48.27	3- 24	–	–	–
Stokes, B.A.	7771	256	30.35	7- 67	6	1	–
Stone, O.P.	2280	73	31.23	5- 44	2	–	–
Stoneman, M.D.	150	0					
Sukhjit Singh	452	17	26.58	6-144	2	–	–
Swanson, B.	62	1	62.00	1- 40	–	–	–
Sykes, J.S.	1166	21	55.52	4-176	–	–	–
Tamim Iqbal	193	0					
Tavaré, W.A.	82	0					
Taylor, B.J.	494	11	44.90	4- 64	–	–	–
Taylor, B.R.M.	225	4	56.25	2- 36	–	–	–
Taylor, C.J.	70	5	14.00	2- 20	–	–	–
Taylor, J.E.	8081	300	26.93	8- 59	15	2	–
Taylor, J.M.R.	3290	75	43.86	4- 16	–	–	–
Taylor, J.P.A.	77	1	77.00	1- 14	–	–	–
Taylor, L.R.P.L.	378	6	63.00	2- 4	–	–	–
Taylor, M.D.	2788	62	44.96	5- 75	2	–	–
Taylor, T.A.I.	2335	64	36.48	6- 61	2	–	–
ten Doeschate, R.N.	7165	212	33.79	6- 20	7	–	–
Thakor, S.J.	2452	57	43.01	5- 63	1	–	–
Thomas, I.A.A.	1462	45	32.48	4- 48	–	–	–
Thomson, A.T.	326	9	36.22	6-138	1	–	–
Thornton, G.T.	138	4	34.50	4- 34	–	–	–
Tillcock, A.D.	151	0					
Tongue, J.C.	1261	51	24.72	6- 97	2	–	–
Topley, R.J.W.	3401	127	26.77	6- 29	7	2	–
Tredwell, J.C.	15438	426	36.23	8- 66	12	3	1
Trego, P.D.	13827	379	36.48	7- 84	5	1	1
Trescothick, M.E.	1551	36	43.08	4- 36	–	–	–
Trevaskis, L.	126	1	126.00	1- 69	–	–	–
Trott, I.J.L.	3487	70	49.81	7- 39	1	–	–
Umeed, A.R.I.	73	2	36.50	1- 19	–	–	–
van Buuren, G.L.	2223	80	27.78	4- 12	–	–	–
van den Bergh, F.O.E.	667	15	44.46	4- 84	–	–	–
van der Gugten, T.	2463	95	25.92	7- 68	8	1	1
van der Merwe, R.E.	4093	113	36.22	4- 22	–	–	–
van Meekeren, P.A.	718	20	35.90	4- 60	–	–	–
van Zyl, S.	2346	63	37.23	5- 32	1	–	–
Vilas, D.J.	3	0					
Viljoen, G.C.	10330	394	26.21	8- 90	25	5	0+1
Vince, J.M.	983	22	44.68	5- 41	1	–	–
Virdi, G.S.	271	6	45.16	3- 82	–	–	–
Voges, A.C.	2021	56	36.08	4- 92	–	–	–
Wade, G.	100	1	100.00	1-100	–	–	–
Wagg, G.G.	14715	429	34.30	6- 29	12	1	2
Wagner, N.	15617	576	27.11	7- 46	28	2	0+2
Waite, M.J.	70	3	23.33	2- 41	–	–	–
Wakely, A.G.	426	6	71.00	2- 62	–	–	–
Waller, M.T.C.	493	10	49.30	3- 33	–	–	–
Walter, P.I.	501	11	45.54	3- 44	–	–	–
Weatherley, J.J.	96	1	96.00	1- 46	–	–	–
Weighell, W.J.	946	28	33.78	5- 33	1	–	–
Wells, L.W.P.	2202	46	47.86	3- 35	–	–	–

F-C	Runs	Wkts	Avge	Best	5wI	10wM	50wS
Wells, T.J.	858	19	45.15	4- 46	–	–	–
Wessels, M.H.	130	3	43.33	1- 10	–	–	–
Westley, T.	2567	55	46.67	4- 55	–	–	–
Westwood, I.J.	337	7	48.14	2- 39	–	–	–
Wheal, B.T.J.	1618	45	35.95	6- 51	1	–	–
Wheater, A.J.A.	86	1	86.00	1- 86	–	–	–
White, G.G.	2730	65	42.00	6- 44	1	–	–
Whiteley, R.A.	1646	29	56.75	2- 6	–	–	–
Whittingham, S.G.	1179	34	34.67	5- 80	1	–	–
Wiese, D.	7483	271	27.61	6- 58	7	1	–
Wilkinson, A.R.	259	7	37.00	3- 35	–	–	–
Willey, D.J.	4883	161	30.32	5- 29	5	1	–
Williams, D.R.	226	3	75.33	2- 82	–	–	–
Williamson, K.S.	3634	85	42.75	5- 75	1	–	–
Wilson, G.C.	89	0					
Winder, N.J.	71	0					
Woakes, C.R.	10896	433	25.16	9- 36	18	4	3
Wood, C.P.	2906	99	29.35	5- 39	3	–	–
Wood, L.	1977	62	31.88	5- 40	1	–	–
Wood, M.A.	3731	130	28.70	5- 32	6	–	–
Worrall, D.J.	3055	102	29.95	6- 96	4	–	–
Wright, C.J.C.	12316	365	33.74	6- 22	10	–	1
Wright, L.J.	4862	120	40.51	5- 65	3	–	–
Yasir Shah	12848	464	27.68	7- 76	26	3	–
Zaib, S.A.	345	11	31.36	6-115	2	–	–
Zaidi, M.S.	58	0					
Zampa, A.	3840	83	46.26	6- 62	1	1	–
Zondo, K.	1378	38	36.26	6- 52	2	–	–

LIMITED-OVERS CAREER RECORDS

Compiled by Philip Bailey

The following career records, to the end of the 2017 season, include all players currently registered with first-class counties. These records are restricted to performances in limited-overs matches of 'List A' status as defined by the Association of Cricket Statisticians and Historians now incorporated by ICC into their Classification of Cricket. The following matches qualify for List A status and are included in the figures that follow: Limited-Overs Internationals; Other International matches (e.g. Commonwealth Games, 'A' team internationals); Premier domestic limited-overs tournaments in Test status countries; Official tourist matches against the main first-class teams.

The following matches do NOT qualify for inclusion: World Cup warm-up games; Tourist matches against first-class teams outside the major domestic competitions (e.g. Universities, Minor Counties etc.); Festival, pre-season friendly games and Twenty20 Cup matches.

	M	Runs	Avge	HS	100	50	Wkts	Avge	Best	Econ
Abbott, K.J.	94	470	18.07	56	–	1	121	29.97	4-21	5.16
Abell, T.B.	12	343	38.11	106	1	1	–	–	–	–
Ackermann, C.N.	54	1266	31.65	92	–	9	25	39.68	3-35	4.44
Adams, J.H.K.	108	3605	40.05	131	2	27	1	105.00	1-34	7.97
Ali, A.M.	15	308	23.69	88	–	3	1	93.00	1-31	5.47
Ali, M.M.	174	4491	30.14	158	10	20	110	46.44	3-28	5.38
Alsop, T.P.	25	775	33.69	116	2	4	–	–	–	–
Ambrose, T.R.	170	3883	32.63	135	3	22	–	–	–	–
Amla, H.M.	214	8926	45.54	159	28	45	0	–	–	10.50
Anderson, C.J.	81	1933	28.85	131*	1	11	67	24.89	5-26	5.94
Anderson, J.M.	255	373	9.32	28	–	–	352	28.41	5-23	4.83
Archer, J.C.	10	130	21.66	45	–	–	16	29.81	5-42	5.13
Ashar Zaidi	100	2780	33.49	141	4	12	75	31.06	4-39	4.38
Azeem Rafiq	35	252	18.00	52*	–	1	43	29.65	5-30	5.65
Bairstow, J.M.	99	2911	38.81	174	5	15	–	–	–	68/8
Ball, J.T.	77	163	10.18	28	–	–	90	34.65	5-51	5.83
Ballance, G.S.	97	3819	49.59	152*	7	23	–	–	–	–
Bancroft, C.T.	34	959	33.06	176	1	6	–	–	–	–
Barber, T.E.	2	0	0.00	0	–	–	2	25.00	2-22	6.25
Barker, K.H.D.	55	496	17.71	56	–	1	63	31.61	4-33	5.87
Barnard, E.G.	24	280	23.33	51	–	1	28	34.71	3-37	5.92
Batty, G.J.	257	2325	15.50	83*	–	5	241	32.00	5-35	4.61
Beer, W.A.T.	53	349	15.17	45*	–	–	47	40.82	3-27	5.17
Bell, I.R.	310	10904	40.99	158	12	79	33	34.48	5-41	5.29
Bell-Drummond, D.J.	62	2294	41.70	171*	4	16	0	–	–	7.50
Berg, G.K.	75	1133	23.60	75	–	5	58	35.98	4-24	5.49
Billings, S.W.	76	2430	43.39	175	5	17	–	–	–	70/7
Blake, A.J.	77	1435	29.28	116	1	8	3	24.66	2-13	5.28
Bopara, R.S.	306	9265	40.28	201*	14	55	229	28.24	5-63	5.28
Borthwick, S.G.	95	1304	21.73	87	–	7	65	41.38	5-38	6.04
Bracewell, D.A.J.	56	685	20.75	80	–	4	72	29.43	4-43	5.10
Bresnan, T.T.	266	2964	21.17	95*	–	9	302	33.76	5-48	5.21
Briggs, D.R.	82	278	12.63	25	–	–	86	36.39	4-32	5.16
Broad, S.C.J.	151	620	11.92	45*	–	–	216	30.51	5-23	5.27
Brook, H.C.	1	–	–	–	–	–	–	–	–	–
Brooks, J.A.	36	49	4.90	10	–	–	37	34.48	3-30	4.83
Brown, B.C.	58	782	23.69	62	–	5	–	–	–	55/10
Brown, K.R.	76	2331	38.21	129	2	14	0	–	–	17.00
Browne, N.L.J.	21	557	30.94	99	–	3	–	–	–	–
Buck, N.L.	47	92	7.66	21	–	–	53	36.94	4-39	6.27
Burgess, M.G.K.	10	184	18.40	49	–	1	–	–	–	6/0
Burnham, J.T.A.	5	69	17.25	26	–	–	–	–	–	–
Burns, R.J.	41	1254	36.88	95	–	10	–	–	–	–

267

L-O	M	Runs	Avge	HS	100	50	Wkts	Avge	Best	Econ
Buttler, J.C.	168	4670	44.05	129	6	30	–	–	–	177/21
Carberry, M.A.	171	4659	32.35	150*	6	34	11	27.00	3-37	5.53
Carey, L.J.	4	9	–	9*	–	–	3	61.00	1-21	6.10
Carlson, K.S.	9	223	24.77	63	–	1	1	30.00	1-30	6.00
Carver, K.	13	49	–	35*	–	–	12	25.75	3- 5	4.75
Chanderpaul, S.	415	13252	42.33	150	13	97	56	24.78	4-22	4.95
Chappell, Z.J.	8	114	28.50	59*	–	1	5	73.40	2-44	6.13
Chopra, V.	100	3840	42.19	124	8	25	0	–	–	6.00
Christian, D.T.	117	2804	32.98	117	2	14	105	32.88	6-48	5.48
Clark, G.	18	445	26.17	114	1	1	–	–	–	–
Clark, J.	38	686	32.66	79*	–	3	29	36.82	4-34	6.18
Clarke, J.M.	35	855	28.50	131*	1	4	–	–	–	17/2
Clarke, R.	221	4019	25.76	98*	–	21	137	38.91	5-26	5.41
Claydon, M.E.	96	253	7.66	19	–	–	122	31.72	4-39	5.59
Coad, B.O.	11	3	–	2*	–	–	11	43.36	4-63	6.50
Cobb, J.J.	83	2705	37.05	137	6	16	31	49.48	3-34	5.87
Cockbain, I.A.	59	1331	31.69	108*	1	8	–	–	–	–
Coles, M.T.	72	525	14.18	100	1	1	121	22.60	6-32	5.65
Collingwood, P.D.	425	11221	34.52	132	10	65	272	33.47	6-31	4.82
Compton, N.R.D.	118	3098	35.20	131	6	19	1	53.00	1- 0	5.21
Cook, A.N.	159	5840	40.00	137	12	34	0	–	–	3.33
Cooke, C.B.	72	2102	36.87	137*	2	13	–	–	–	37/2
Cosgrove, M.J.	145	4320	32.00	121	4	34	18	63.38	2-21	6.41
Coughlin, P.	23	154	12.83	22	–	–	16	49.25	3-36	5.59
Cox, O.B.	57	737	19.91	82	–	1	–	–	–	51/8
Crane, M.S.	22	38	9.50	16*	–	–	38	29.63	4-30	6.18
Crawley, Z.	1	2	2.00	2	–	–	–	–	–	–
Critchley, M.J.J.	21	203	20.30	49	–	–	15	55.20	4-48	6.73
Croft, S.J.	142	3668	34.93	127	2	28	60	39.16	4-24	5.45
Crook, S.P.	88	1198	21.39	100	1	5	82	34.79	5-36	5.77
Curran, S.M.	37	466	23.30	57	–	1	47	31.72	4-32	5.42
Curran, T.K.	53	412	17.16	44	–	–	79	27.26	5-16	5.46
Davey, J.H.	72	1132	23.10	91	–	5	88	26.29	6-28	5.48
Davies, A.L.	24	591	32.83	73*	–	4	–	–	–	24/5
Davies, S.M.	176	5487	36.33	127*	9	34	–	–	–	137/42
Davis, W.S.	1	–	–	–	–	–	–	–	–	–
Dawson, L.A.	140	3052	32.46	113*	2	16	121	34.20	6-47	4.84
de Grandhomme, C.	108	2197	25.54	151	2	6	59	41.74	4-37	5.27
de Lange, M.	68	372	12.40	29	–	–	129	23.18	5-49	5.28
Delport, C.S.	102	2591	30.12	169*	2	15	37	40.13	4-42	5.95
Denly, J.L.	135	4055	34.36	115	6	20	22	21.95	3-19	4.96
Dent, C.D.J.	55	1334	29.00	151*	3	2	12	34.33	4-43	5.64
Dernbach, J.W.	138	228	7.60	31	–	–	222	26.39	6-35	5.88
Dexter, N.J.	101	1949	29.98	135*	2	8	42	51.33	4-22	5.61
Dickson, S.R.	20	532	28.00	99	–	4	–	–	–	–
Dixon, M.W.	11	17	5.66	12	–	–	7	67.14	3-40	5.73
D'Oliveira, B.L.	45	515	19.80	73*	–	2	31	44.93	3-35	5.19
Donald, A.H.T.	17	178	12.71	53	–	1	–	–	–	–
Duckett, B.M.	53	1916	44.55	220*	3	13	–	–	–	28/3
Eckersley, E.J.H.	38	896	28.00	108	1	4	–	–	–	21/1
Edwards, F.H.	80	131	10.07	21*	–	–	95	31.63	6-22	5.13
Elliott, G.D.	211	5126	33.50	115	7	28	130	33.36	5-34	5.39
Ervine, S.M.	243	5598	30.42	167*	7	26	206	34.24	5-50	5.61
Evans, L.J.	44	1008	33.60	134*	1	2	0	–	–	8.83
Faulkner, J.P.	115	1831	30.51	116	1	10	162	29.71	4-20	5.32
Fell, T.C.	32	1033	38.25	116*	1	9	–	–	–	–
Finch, A.J.	158	5432	36.70	154	11	34	7	39.28	2-44	5.32
Finch, H.Z.	19	655	43.66	92*	–	6	0	–	–	9.00
Finn, S.T.	133	314	10.46	42*	–	–	186	28.86	5-33	5.10
Fisher, M.D.	21	116	38.66	36*	–	–	18	42.83	3-32	5.80
Fletcher, L.J.	59	224	14.00	40*	–	–	55	40.78	4-44	5.67

L-O	M	Runs	Avge	HS	100	50	Wkts	Avge	Best	Econ
Foakes, B.T.	52	1224	33.08	92	–	11	–	–	–	63/6
Footitt, M.H.A.	36	28	4.66	11*	–	–	47	29.51	5-28	6.25
Foster, J.S.	223	3357	28.44	83*	–	16	–	–	–	246/65
Franklin, J.E.C.	283	5633	32.56	133*	4	33	226	34.09	5-42	4.94
Fuller, J.K.	52	597	22.11	45	–	–	70	29.74	6-35	5.78
Garton, G.H.S.	15	20	6.66	7*	–	–	20	34.50	4-43	6.44
Gidman, W.R.S.	57	829	25.90	94	–	4	51	31.70	4-36	4.73
Gleadall, A.F.	1	–	–	–	–	–	0	–	–	7.33
Gleeson, R.J.	15	18	3.60	6*	–	–	18	30.27	5-47	5.84
Godleman, B.A.	52	1517	34.47	109*	1	8	–	–	–	–
Gregory, L.	51	631	21.03	105*	1	2	73	25.93	4-23	6.21
Griffiths, G.T.	11	7	7.00	5*	–	–	14	32.42	3-35	5.17
Groenewald, T.D.	99	701	20.02	57	–	2	107	33.64	4-22	5.55
Gubbins, N.R.T.	26	872	33.53	141	2	4	–	–	–	–
Gurney, H.F.	88	58	5.80	13*	–	–	104	34.30	5-24	5.82
Haggett, C.J.	19	159	13.25	45	–	–	24	34.29	4-59	5.96
Hain, S.R.	23	1166	55.52	109	4	6	–	–	–	–
Hales, A.D.	152	5570	38.95	187*	16	27	0	–	–	15.00
Hameed, H.	8	275	39.28	88	–	2	–	–	–	–
Hamidullah Qadri	1	–	–	–	–	–	0	–	–	6.00
Hankins, G.T.	3	100	33.33	67	–	1	–	–	–	–
Hannon-Dalby, O.J.	35	77	15.40	21*	–	–	51	31.86	5-27	6.22
Harding, G.H.I.	5	20	–	18*	–	–	4	62.75	2-52	5.34
Harinath, A.	7	108	21.60	52	–	1	0	–	–	5.33
Harmer, S.R.	63	763	20.62	44*	–	–	62	40.04	4-42	5.04
Harris, J.A.R.	58	300	11.11	32	–	–	79	28.86	4-38	5.74
Head, T.M.	58	1983	38.88	202	4	10	16	53.93	2- 9	5.74
Helm, T.G.	18	90	15.00	25	–	–	21	26.47	5-33	4.75
Henry, M.J.	73	427	15.25	48*	–	–	123	25.72	6-45	5.48
Hepburn, A.	2	32	32.00	32	–	–	6	13.00	4-34	4.14
Higgins, R.F.	17	241	17.21	48*	–	–	6	32.83	3-32	5.68
Hildreth, J.C.	193	4886	33.46	151	6	21	6	30.83	2-26	7.40
Hill, L.J.	30	583	23.32	86	–	3	–	–	–	15/2
Hodd, A.J.	71	916	22.34	91	–	2	–	–	–	69/16
Hogan, M.G.	64	154	15.40	27	–	–	99	28.12	5-44	5.05
Holden, M.D.E.	3	78	78.00	55	–	1	–	–	–	–
Holland, I.G.	2	11	–	11*	–	–	3	39.00	2-57	6.15
Horton, P.J.	107	2584	30.40	111*	2	13	1	7.00	1- 7	3.50
Hose, A.J.	20	593	34.88	101*	1	3	–	–	–	–
Hosein, H.R.	4	42	42.00	40	–	–	–	–	–	1/1
Howell, B.A.C.	70	1624	36.08	122	1	9	59	33.37	3-37	5.04
Hughes, A.L.	48	581	24.20	96*	–	2	31	44.61	3-31	5.38
Hunn, M.D.	7	7	7.00	5*	–	–	6	43.00	2-31	5.37
Hutton, B.A.	9	66	22.00	33*	–	–	9	48.66	3-72	6.34
Imran Qayyum	6	18	9.00	18	–	–	7	38.71	3-42	5.01
Ingram, C.A.	178	7182	46.94	142	18	45	36	31.22	4-39	5.42
Javid, A.	40	578	28.90	43	–	–	24	47.33	4-42	5.76
Jennings, K.K.	47	1432	40.91	139	3	9	3	144.66	1- 9	6.38
Jones, R.A.	13	49	12.25	26	–	–	5	110.80	1-25	7.33
Jordan, C.J.	72	560	14.73	55	–	1	109	28.84	5-28	5.71
Keogh, R.I.	33	821	30.40	134	1	7	2	301.50	1-49	5.74
Kerrigan, S.C.	35	30	3.33	10	–	–	28	46.50	3-21	5.36
Kettleborough, J.M.	5	84	21.00	26	–	–	–	–	–	–
Klein, D.	24	102	12.75	26	–	–	36	24.66	5-35	4.71
Kleinveldt, R.K.	153	1623	20.28	128	1	3	173	31.90	4-22	4.76
Klinger, M.	170	7114	49.06	166*	16	44	–	–	–	–
Kohler-Cadmore, T.	31	817	27.23	119	2	2	–	–	–	–
Kuhn, H.G.	143	3554	30.37	141*	8	19	–	–	–	165/22
Lamb, D.J.	2	5	–	4*	–	–	4	27.00	2-51	5.40
Lamb, M.J.	2	14	7.00	12	–	–	0	–	–	9.00
Latham, T.W.M.	111	3226	34.68	137	5	17	–	–	–	78/8

L-O	M	Runs	Avge	HS	100	50	Wkts	Avge	Best	Econ
Lawrence, D.W.	11	159	17.66	35	–	–	6	42.50	3-35	5.54
Leach, J.	31	490	27.22	63	–	1	36	39.00	4-30	6.02
Leach, M.J.	16	22	7.33	18	–	–	21	30.52	3- 7	4.66
Leaning, J.A.	40	919	31.68	131*	2	4	9	26.22	5-22	5.55
Lees, A.Z.	46	1172	29.30	102	1	8	–	–	–	–
Levi, R.E.	122	4147	38.39	166	8	26	–	–	–	–
Liddle, C.J.	69	125	6.25	18	–	–	97	26.60	5-18	5.80
Lilley, A.M.	11	20	6.66	10	–	–	15	21.40	4-30	5.17
Livingstone, L.S.	35	928	34.37	129	1	5	17	37.23	3-51	5.28
Lloyd, D.L.	30	469	20.39	65	–	2	15	37.53	5-53	5.91
Lyth, A.	106	3131	34.03	136	3	16	3	86.66	1- 6	6.19
McCarthy, B.J.	13	68	8.50	16*	–	–	25	27.48	4-59	6.46
Macdonell, C.M.	2	19	19.00	19	–	–	–	–	–	–
McManus, L.D.	15	175	21.87	35	–	–	–	–	–	14/6
Madsen, W.L.	88	2638	41.21	138	4	16	11	19.81	3-27	4.80
Magoffin, S.J.	53	228	20.72	24*	–	–	66	31.57	4-58	4.72
Mahmood, S.	11	38	–	27*	–	–	8	57.37	3-55	6.20
Main, G.T.	2	–	–	–	–	–	4	18.50	2-35	4.35
Malan, D.J.	142	4928	42.11	185*	10	24	38	30.26	4-25	5.73
Markram, A.K.	26	1007	41.95	183	4	1	12	24.50	4-45	5.15
Marsh, M.R.	90	2351	33.58	104	2	16	81	30.17	5-33	5.43
Marsh, S.E.	130	4965	41.37	186	12	27	1	31.00	1-14	5.16
Meaker, S.C.	67	97	6.06	21*	–	–	75	34.33	4-37	6.13
Mellor, A.J.	2	–	–	–	–	–	–	–	–	–
Mennie, J.M.	27	180	10.58	33	–	–	27	43.25	4-58	5.19
Meschede, C.A.J.	52	462	14.90	45	–	–	51	34.56	4- 5	5.55
Miles, C.N.	32	76	7.60	16	–	–	37	35.86	4-29	6.09
Mills, T.S.	23	7	1.75	3*	–	–	22	35.77	3-23	5.97
Mitchell, D.K.H.	119	3037	34.12	107	2	20	70	34.85	4-19	5.56
Mohammad Abbas	40	121	8.64	15*	–	–	54	28.40	4-31	4.86
Mohammad Nabi	117	2912	30.65	146	3	12	129	30.96	5-12	4.26
Moores, T.J.	4	22	11.00	10	–	–	–	–	–	2/1
Morgan, A.O.	3	32	16.00	29	–	–	2	40.50	2-49	5.78
Morgan, E.J.G.	309	9169	37.42	161	18	51	0	–	–	7.00
Mullaney, S.J.	95	1585	29.90	111	1	9	86	31.76	4-29	5.20
Murphy, J.R.	1	6	6.00	6	–	–	0	–	–	6.40
Murtagh, T.J.	181	776	10.92	35*	–	–	225	31.04	4-14	5.15
Mustard, P.	205	5484	30.63	143	7	34	–	–	–	214/48
Myburgh, J.G.	110	2731	29.36	112	1	17	25	62.08	2-22	5.09
Nash, C.D.	116	3222	30.98	124*	2	20	43	32.90	4-40	5.52
Newton, R.I.	38	986	29.87	107	1	4	–	–	–	–
Nijjar, A.S.S.	3	21	21.00	21	–	–	1	107.00	1-39	5.09
Noema-Barnett, K.	75	1171	22.51	74	–	6	47	42.91	3-42	5.10
Northeast, S.A.	88	2462	32.82	132	3	13	–	–	–	–
Norwell, L.C.	17	47	5.87	16	–	–	23	31.13	6-52	5.50
Olivier, D.	28	76	8.44	18	–	–	32	26.65	3-12	4.97
Onions, G.	87	130	5.90	19	–	–	99	31.04	4-45	5.09
Overton, C.	51	484	17.28	60*	–	1	58	34.94	3-21	5.28
Overton, J.	24	230	23.00	40*	–	–	37	27.89	4-42	6.49
Palladino, A.P.	56	267	10.68	31	–	–	54	37.00	5-49	5.37
Parkinson, C.F.	1	3	3.00	3	–	–	1	44.00	1-44	4.88
Parry, S.D.	89	318	12.72	31	–	–	108	30.12	5-17	5.03
Patel, J.S.	210	734	9.53	50	–	1	257	30.61	5-43	4.65
Patel, R.H.	17	39	13.00	18	–	–	17	41.00	3-71	5.16
Patel, S.R.	228	5852	35.25	129*	6	33	207	32.63	6-13	5.40
Patterson, S.A.	81	207	14.78	25*	–	–	101	28.23	6-32	5.00
Payne, D.A.	58	102	11.33	23	–	–	101	22.76	7-29	5.65
Pettini, M.L.	188	4811	29.88	159	9	30	–	–	–	–
Pillans, M.W.	12	79	19.75	20*	–	–	16	21.50	3-14	4.91
Plunkett, L.E.	180	1507	20.64	72	–	3	234	30.08	5-52	5.43
Podmore, H.W.	6	1	–	1*	–	–	4	68.00	2-46	6.91

L-O	M	Runs	Avge	HS	100	50	Wkts	Avge	Best	Econ
Pope, O.J.D.	6	138	27.60	55	–	1	–	–	–	–
Porter, J.A.	14	5	–	5*	–	–	15	33.13	4-40	5.25
Poynter, S.W.	27	376	23.50	109	1	–	–	–	–	–
Poysden, J.E.	23	33	4.71	10*	–	–	24	37.91	3-33	5.92
Prasanna, S.	140	1669	15.45	95	–	7	196	24.18	7-26	4.47
Pringle, R.D.	32	415	18.04	125	1	–	10	68.30	2-39	6.12
Procter, L.A.	31	481	30.06	97	–	4	13	44.76	3-29	6.46
Pujara, C.A.	82	3572	54.12	158*	10	23	0	–	–	8.00
Quinn, M.R.	32	124	17.71	36	–	–	44	34.95	4-71	5.74
Raine, B.A.	14	164	16.40	43	–	–	13	50.46	3-62	6.30
Rampaul, R.	170	628	11.62	86*	–	1	255	24.40	5-49	4.80
Rankin, W.B.	105	122	7.17	18*	–	–	129	28.35	4-34	4.97
Rashid, A.U.	160	1454	20.77	71	–	2	205	30.87	5-27	5.32
Rashid Khan	30	386	19.30	60*	–	2	64	15.18	7-18	4.02
Rawlins, D.M.W.	1	41	41.00	41	–	–	0	–	–	7.50
Rayner, O.P.	61	508	22.08	61	–	1	53	38.05	4-35	5.15
Read, J.	1	–	–	–	–	–	–	–	–	–
Reece, L.M.	27	424	22.31	59	–	2	6	81.00	4-35	6.45
Rhodes, G.H.	5	5	5.00	5*	–	–	5	32.40	2-34	5.78
Rhodes, W.M.H.	21	252	16.80	46	–	–	11	33.09	2-22	5.26
Richardson, M.J.	17	697	58.08	100*	1	7	–	–	–	–
Riley, A.E.N.	27	45	11.25	21*	–	–	23	39.26	2-30	5.34
Robinson, O.E.	8	75	25.00	30	–	–	4	64.75	2-61	6.16
Robson, S.D.	16	407	29.07	88	–	2	–	–	–	–
Roderick, G.H.	37	727	29.08	104	1	5	–	–	–	37/4
Roland-Jones, T.S.	71	553	19.06	65	–	1	113	24.29	4-10	5.09
Root, J.E.	133	5105	46.40	133*	11	31	30	47.46	3-52	5.48
Root, W.T.	9	259	64.75	107*	1	1	0	–	–	5.47
Rossington, A.M.	36	926	37.04	97	–	7	–	–	–	20/4
Rossouw, R.R.	133	4864	39.22	156	10	29	1	44.00	1-17	5.86
Rouse, A.P.	17	249	27.66	61*	–	1	–	–	–	15/2
Roy, J.J.	133	4352	35.96	162	10	24	0	–	–	12.00
Rushworth, C.	67	153	11.76	38*	–	–	102	25.12	5-31	5.36
Sakande, A.	2	7	–	7*	–	–	3	36.00	2-62	7.80
Salisbury, M.E.T.	6	5	–	5*	–	–	5	33.60	4-55	6.46
Salt, P.D.	7	186	26.57	81	–	1	–	–	–	–
Salter, A.G.	28	282	23.50	51	–	1	11	72.45	2-41	5.25
Sanderson, B.W.	18	43	21.50	19*	–	–	17	34.11	3-36	6.04
Sayer, R.J.	15	138	12.54	26	–	–	11	60.27	2-65	5.57
Scott, G.F.B.	1	4	4.00	4	–	–	0	–	–	9.33
Selman, N.J.	1	6	6.00	6	–	–	–	–	–	–
Shantry, J.D.	73	188	11.05	31	–	–	92	30.43	4-29	5.60
Sharma, I.	113	153	6.95	31	–	–	167	28.73	5-21	5.34
Sibley, D.P.	12	164	20.50	37	–	–	1	53.00	1-20	6.62
Siddle, P.M.	45	106	7.06	25*	–	–	48	35.43	4-27	4.65
Simpson, J.A.	72	1105	25.69	82*	–	6	–	–	–	58/10
Slater, B.T.	23	873	51.35	148*	3	4	–	–	–	–
Smit, D.	115	2036	32.83	109	1	11	45	38.06	4-39	4.89
Smith, R.A.J.	13	33	6.60	10	–	–	12	38.33	4-76	6.86
Smith, T.M.J.	68	445	23.42	65	–	1	55	39.63	4-26	5.46
Smith, W.R.	110	2516	29.25	120*	2	20	12	35.58	2-19	5.78
Sodhi, I.S.	60	213	9.68	35	–	–	81	30.13	4-10	4.92
Sohail Khan	73	465	11.92	39	–	–	132	24.13	6-44	5.26
Sole, C.B.	9	15	5.00	10*	–	–	14	25.50	4-28	4.95
Sole, T.B.	1	54	54.00	54	–	1	1	69.00	1-69	6.90
Sowter, N.A.	2	0	0.00	0	–	–	0	–	–	7.75
Stanlake, B.	6	2	1.00	1*	–	–	8	30.75	4-37	5.12
Steel, C.T.	7	132	26.40	77	–	1	0	–	–	9.40
Stevens, D.I.	300	7476	30.14	147	7	46	141	32.37	5-32	4.82
Stevenson, R.A.	3	0	0.00	0	–	–	2	71.00	1-28	7.10
Stirling, P.R.	155	4796	33.53	177	10	21	61	39.24	6-55	4.98

L-O	M	Runs	Avge	HS	100	50	Wkts	Avge	Best	Econ
Stoinis, M.P.	40	1028	30.23	146*	2	7	27	33.40	4-43	5.02
Stokes, B.A.	128	3454	35.24	164	7	16	113	29.27	5-61	5.73
Stone, O.P.	17	90	22.50	24*	–	–	11	50.54	3-34	5.26
Stoneman, M.D.	70	2575	41.53	144*	6	16	1	8.00	1- 8	12.00
Tattersall, J.A.	2	0	0.00	0	–	–	–	–	–	–
Tavaré, W.A.	8	221	27.62	77	–	2	–	–	–	–
Taylor, B.J.	2	2	–	2*	–	–	4	18.25	2-23	4.86
Taylor, J.M.R.	36	690	30.00	68	–	5	29	35.20	4-38	5.17
Taylor, L.R.P.L.	242	8465	43.41	132*	21	53	3	81.00	1-13	4.58
Taylor, M.D.	17	37	18.50	16	–	–	14	52.64	3-48	5.90
Taylor, T.A.I.	5	–	–	–	–	–	5	45.00	3-48	6.19
ten Doeschate, R.N.	203	5517	45.97	180	11	28	166	30.46	5-50	5.77
Thomas, I.A.A.	13	12	6.00	5*	–	–	20	30.90	4-51	5.94
Thomason, A.D.	9	105	21.00	28	–	–	4	42.50	4-64	8.50
Tongue, J.C.	4	12	12.00	11*	–	–	4	40.50	2-46	6.89
Topley, R.J.W.	45	41	6.83	19	–	–	78	24.83	4-26	5.60
Tredwell, J.C.	265	1877	17.22	88	–	4	275	32.56	6-27	4.71
Trego, P.D.	179	4197	31.79	147	8	21	164	32.40	5-40	5.59
Trescothick, M.E.	372	12229	37.28	184	28	63	57	28.84	4-50	4.90
Trott, I.J.L.	266	9781	47.94	137	21	66	54	29.29	4-55	5.63
van Buuren, G.L.	62	1309	29.75	119*	1	6	48	30.37	5-35	4.67
van den Bergh, F.O.E.	3	29	–	29*	–	–	0	–	–	4.69
van der Gugten, T.	37	235	18.07	36	–	–	49	30.89	5-24	5.47
van der Merwe, R.E.	155	2327	26.74	165*	1	8	209	26.19	5-26	4.82
van Meekeren, P.A.	30	68	6.80	15*	–	–	30	27.90	3-22	4.81
van Zyl, S.	116	3350	35.63	114*	5	18	20	46.35	4-24	5.26
Vasconcelos, R.S.	8	150	18.75	38	–	–	–	–	–	–
Vilas, D.J.	132	3572	35.01	120	7	16	–	–	–	135/22
Viljoen, G.C.	76	465	15.50	54*	–	2	109	31.02	6-19	5.94
Vince, J.M.	112	3651	37.63	178	6	18	1	84.00	1-18	6.00
Wagg, G.G.	124	1643	18.88	62*	–	3	138	34.07	4-35	5.93
Wagner, N.	92	474	12.15	42	–	–	149	26.53	5-34	5.34
Waite, M.J.	11	246	35.14	71	–	1	13	32.61	4-65	6.18
Wakely, A.G.	73	1911	31.32	109*	2	12	5	26.20	2-14	5.77
Waller, M.T.C.	54	97	16.16	25*	–	–	42	38.04	3-37	5.60
Walter, P.I.	4	15	–	11*	–	–	7	22.14	4-37	5.81
Weatherley, J.J.	2	29	14.50	27	–	–	0	–	–	5.66
Weighell, W.J.	8	22	11.00	14	–	–	18	23.11	5-57	6.30
Wells, L.W.P.	18	110	8.46	23	–	–	6	29.66	3-19	5.11
Wells, T.J.	24	387	25.80	67	–	1	15	44.46	3-44	6.82
Wessels, M.H.	162	4178	30.49	146	4	22	1	48.00	1- 0	5.87
Westley, T.	71	2093	33.75	111*	4	15	20	41.50	4-60	4.95
Wheal, B.T.J.	9	21	10.50	13	–	–	14	25.78	4-38	5.03
Wheater, A.J.A.	71	1323	25.94	135	2	5	–	–	–	29/11
White, G.G.	76	420	14.48	40	–	–	84	27.75	6-37	5.03
Whiteley, R.A.	61	1054	23.95	77	–	6	8	52.87	1-17	6.66
Wiese, D.	125	2874	34.21	108	1	15	112	36.42	5-25	5.37
Willey, D.J.	107	1286	21.79	167	2	3	107	33.37	5-62	5.70
Williamson, K.S.	175	6726	45.75	145*	13	43	63	35.68	5-51	5.27
Wilson, G.C.	180	3358	23.15	113	1	20	–	–	–	130/27
Woakes, C.R.	143	1483	22.81	95*	–	2	167	33.89	6-45	5.52
Wood, C.P.	63	311	12.44	41	–	–	88	25.97	5-22	5.49
Wood, L.	3	56	56.00	52	–	1	3	29.66	2-44	5.56
Wood, M.A.	45	66	7.33	15*	–	–	59	29.81	4-33	5.17
Worrall, D.J.	16	24	12.00	8*	–	–	16	44.00	4-26	5.15
Wright, C.J.C.	99	229	10.90	42	–	–	100	35.68	4-20	5.58
Wright, L.J.	198	4488	31.38	143*	9	16	111	38.11	4-12	5.34
Zaib, S.A.	6	44	14.66	17	–	–	2	26.00	2-22	8.66
Zampa, A.	50	423	16.92	66	–	3	73	31.06	4-18	5.28

FIRST-CLASS CRICKET RECORDS

To the end of the 2017 season

TEAM RECORDS

HIGHEST INNINGS TOTALS

1107	Victoria v New South Wales	Melbourne	1926-27
1059	Victoria v Tasmania	Melbourne	1922-23
952-6d	Sri Lanka v India	Colombo	1997-98
951-7d	Sind v Baluchistan	Karachi	1973-74
944-6d	Hyderabad v Andhra	Secunderabad	1993-94
918	New South Wales v South Australia	Sydney	1900-01
912-8d	Holkar v Mysore	Indore	1945-46
910-6d	Railways v Dera Ismail Khan	Lahore	1964-65
903-7d	England v Australia	The Oval	1938
900-6d	Queensland v Victoria	Brisbane	2005-06
887	Yorkshire v Warwickshire	Birmingham	1896
863	Lancashire v Surrey	The Oval	1990
860-6d	Tamil Nadu v Goa	Panjim	1988-89
850-7d	Somerset v Middlesex	Taunton	2007

Excluding penalty runs in India, there have been 34 innings totals of 800 runs or more in first-class cricket. Tamil Nadu's total of 860-6d was boosted to 912 by 52 penalty runs.

HIGHEST SECOND INNINGS TOTAL

770	New South Wales v South Australia	Adelaide	1920-21

HIGHEST FOURTH INNINGS TOTAL

654-5	England (set 696 to win) v South Africa	Durban	1938-39

HIGHEST MATCH AGGREGATE

2376-37	Maharashtra v Bombay	Poona	1948-49

RECORD MARGIN OF VICTORY

Innings and 851 runs: Railways v Dera Ismail Khan   Lahore   1964-65

MOST RUNS IN A DAY

721	Australians v Essex	Southend	1948

MOST HUNDREDS IN AN INNINGS

6	Holkar v Mysore	Indore	1945-46

LOWEST INNINGS TOTALS

12	†Oxford University v MCC and Ground	Oxford	1877
12	Northamptonshire v Gloucestershire	Gloucester	1907
13	Auckland v Canterbury	Auckland	1877-78
13	Nottinghamshire v Yorkshire	Nottingham	1901
14	Surrey v Essex	Chelmsford	1983
15	MCC v Surrey	Lord's	1839
15	†Victoria v MCC	Melbourne	1903-04
15	†Northamptonshire v Yorkshire	Northampton	1908
15	Hampshire v Warwickshire	Birmingham	1922

† *Batted one man short*

There have been 28 instances of a team being dismissed for under 20.

LOWEST MATCH AGGREGATE BY ONE TEAM

34 (16 and 18)	Border v Natal	East London	1959-60

LOWEST COMPLETED MATCH AGGREGATE BY BOTH TEAMS

105	MCC v Australians	Lord's	1878

FEWEST RUNS IN AN UNINTERRUPTED DAY'S PLAY

Australia (80) v Pakistan (15-2)   Karachi   1956-57

TIED MATCHES

Before 1949 a match was considered to be tied if the scores were level after the fourth innings, even if the side batting last had wickets in hand when play ended. Law 22 was amended in 1948 and since then a match has been tied only when the scores are level after the fourth innings has been completed. There have been 56 tied first-class matches, five of which would not have qualified under the current law. The most recent are:

Warwickshire (446-7d & forfeit) v Essex (66-0d & 380)	Birmingham	2003
Worcestershire (262 & 247) v Zimbabweans (334 & 175)	Worcester	2003
Habib Bank (245 & 178) v WAPDA (233 & 190)	Lahore	2011-12
Border (210 & 210) v Boland (219 & 201)	East London	2012-13

BATTING RECORDS
35,000 RUNS IN A CAREER

	Career	I	NO	HS	Runs	Avge	100
J.B.Hobbs	1905-34	1315	106	316*	61237	50.65	197
F.E.Woolley	1906-38	1532	85	305*	58969	40.75	145
E.H.Hendren	1907-38	1300	166	301*	57611	50.80	170
C.P.Mead	1905-36	1340	185	280*	55061	47.67	153
W.G.Grace	1865-1908	1493	105	344	54896	39.55	126
W.R.Hammond	1920-51	1005	104	336*	50551	56.10	167
H.Sutcliffe	1919-45	1088	123	313	50138	51.95	149
G.Boycott	1962-86	1014	162	261*	48426	56.83	151
T.W.Graveney	1948-71/72	1223	159	258	47793	44.91	122
G.A.Gooch	1973-2000	990	75	333	44846	49.01	128
T.W.Hayward	1893-1914	1138	96	315*	43551	41.79	104
D.L.Amiss	1960-87	1139	126	262*	43423	42.86	102
M.C.Cowdrey	1950-76	1130	134	307	42719	42.89	107
A.Sandham	1911-37/38	1000	79	325	41284	44.82	107
G.A.Hick	1983/84-2008	871	84	405*	41112	52.23	136
L.Hutton	1934-60	814	91	364	40140	55.51	129
M.J.K.Smith	1951-75	1091	139	204	39832	41.84	69
W.Rhodes	1898-1930	1528	237	267*	39802	30.83	58
J.H.Edrich	1956-78	979	104	310*	39790	45.47	103
R.E.S.Wyatt	1923-57	1141	157	232	39405	40.04	85
D.C.S.Compton	1936-64	839	88	300	38942	51.85	123
G.E.Tyldesley	1909-36	961	106	256*	38874	45.46	102
J.T.Tyldesley	1895-1923	994	62	295*	37897	40.60	86
K.W.R.Fletcher	1962-88	1167	170	228*	37665	37.77	63
C.G.Greenidge	1970-92	889	75	273*	37354	45.88	92
J.W.Hearne	1909-36	1025	116	285*	37252	40.98	96
L.E.G.Ames	1926-51	951	95	295	37248	43.51	102
D.Kenyon	1946-67	1159	59	259	37002	33.63	74
W.J.Edrich	1934-58	964	92	267*	36965	42.39	86
J.M.Parks	1949-76	1227	172	205*	36673	34.76	51
M.W.Gatting	1975-98	861	123	258	36549	49.52	94
D.Denton	1894-1920	1163	70	221	36479	33.37	69
G.H.Hirst	1891-1929	1215	151	341	36323	34.13	60
I.V.A.Richards	1971/72-93	796	63	322	36212	49.40	114
A.Jones	1957-83	1168	72	204*	36049	32.89	56
W.G.Quaife	1894-1928	1203	185	255*	36012	35.37	72
R.E.Marshall	1945/46-72	1053	59	228*	35725	35.94	68
M.R.Ramprakash	1987-2012	764	93	301*	35659	53.14	114
G.Gunn	1902-32	1061	82	220	35208	35.96	62

HIGHEST INDIVIDUAL INNINGS

501*	B.C.Lara	Warwickshire v Durham	Birmingham	1994
499	Hanif Mohammed	Karachi v Bahawalpur	Karachi	1958-59
452*	D.G.Bradman	New South Wales v Queensland	Sydney	1929-30
443*	B.B.Nimbalkar	Maharashtra v Kathiawar	Poona	1948-49
437	W.H.Ponsford	Victoria v Queensland	Melbourne	1927-28
429	W.H.Ponsford	Victoria v Tasmania	Melbourne	1922-23
428	Aftab Baloch	Sind v Baluchistan	Karachi	1973-74
424	A.C.MacLaren	Lancashire v Somerset	Taunton	1895
405*	G.A.Hick	Worcestershire v Somerset	Taunton	1988
400*	B.C.Lara	West Indies v England	St John's	2003-04
394	Naved Latif	Sargodha v Gujranwala	Gujranwala	2000-01
390	S.C.Cook	Lions v Warriors	East London	2009-10
385	B.Sutcliffe	Otago v Canterbury	Christchurch	1952-53
383	C.W.Gregory	New South Wales v Queensland	Brisbane	1906-07
380	M.L.Hayden	Australia v Zimbabwe	Perth	2003-04
377	S.V.Manjrekar	Bombay v Hyderabad	Bombay	1990-91
375	B.C.Lara	West Indies v England	St John's	1993-94
374	D.P.M.D.Jayawardena	Sri Lanka v South Africa	Colombo	2006
369	D.G.Bradman	South Australia v Tasmania	Adelaide	1935-36
366	N.H.Fairbrother	Lancashire v Surrey	The Oval	1990
366	M.V.Sridhar	Hyderabad v Andhra	Secunderabad	1993-94
365*	C.Hill	South Australia v NSW	Adelaide	1900-01
365*	G.St A.Sobers	West Indies v Pakistan	Kingston	1957-58
364	L.Hutton	England v Australia	The Oval	1938
359*	V.M.Merchant	Bombay v Maharashtra	Bombay	1943-44
359*	S.B.Gohel	Gujarat v Orissa	Jaipur	2016-17
359	R.B.Simpson	New South Wales v Queensland	Brisbane	1963-64
357*	R.Abel	Surrey v Somerset	The Oval	1899
357	D.G.Bradman	South Australia v Victoria	Melbourne	1935-36
356	B.A.Richards	South Australia v W Australia	Perth	1970-71
355*	G.R.Marsh	W Australia v S Australia	Perth	1989-90
355*	K.P.Pietersen	Surrey v Leicestershire	The Oval	2015
355	B.Sutcliffe	Otago v Auckland	Dunedin	1949-50
353	V.V.S.Laxman	Hyderabad v Karnataka	Bangalore	1999-00
352	W.H.Ponsford	Victoria v New South Wales	Melbourne	1926-27
352	C.A.Pujara	Saurashtra v Karnataka	Rajkot	2012-13
351*	S.M.Gugale	Maharashtra v Delhi	Mumbai	2016-17
351	K.D.K.Vithanage	Tamil Union v SL Air	Katunayake	2014-15
350	Rashid Israr	Habib Bank v National Bank	Lahore	1976-77

There have been 214 triple hundreds in first-class cricket, W.V.Raman (313) and Arjan Kripal Singh (302*) for Tamil Nadu v Goa at Panjim in 1988-89 providing the only instance of two batsmen scoring 300 in the same innings.

MOST HUNDREDS IN SUCCESSIVE INNINGS

6	C.B.Fry	Sussex and Rest of England	1901
6	D.G.Bradman	South Australia and D.G.Bradman's XI	1938-39
6	M.J.Procter	Rhodesia	1970-71

TWO DOUBLE HUNDREDS IN A MATCH

244	202*	A.E.Fagg	Kent v Essex	Colchester	1938

TRIPLE HUNDRED AND HUNDRED IN A MATCH

333	123	G.A.Gooch	England v India	Lord's	1990
319	105	K.C.Sangakkara	Sri Lanka v Bangladesh	Chittagong	2013-14

DOUBLE HUNDRED AND HUNDRED IN A MATCH MOST TIMES

4	Zaheer Abbas	Gloucestershire	1976-81

TWO HUNDREDS IN A MATCH MOST TIMES

8	Zaheer Abbas	Gloucestershire and PIA	1976-82
8	R.T.Ponting	Tasmania, Australia and Australians	1992-2006
7	W.R.Hammond	Gloucestershire, England and MCC	1927-45
7	M.R.Ramprakash	Middlesex, Surrey	1990-2010

MOST HUNDREDS IN A SEASON

18	D.C.S.Compton	1947	16	J.B.Hobbs	1925

100 HUNDREDS IN A CAREER

	Total		100th Hundred	
	Hundreds	Inns	Season	Inns
J.B.Hobbs	197	1315	1923	821
E.H.Hendren	170	1300	1928-29	740
W.R.Hammond	167	1005	1935	679
C.P.Mead	153	1340	1927	892
G.Boycott	151	1014	1977	645
H.Sutcliffe	149	1088	1932	700
F.E.Woolley	145	1532	1929	1031
G.A.Hick	136	871	1998	574
L.Hutton	129	814	1951	619
G.A.Gooch	128	990	1992-93	820
W.G.Grace	126	1493	1895	1113
D.C.S.Compton	123	839	1952	552
T.W.Graveney	122	1223	1964	940
D.G.Bradman	117	338	1947-48	295
I.V.A.Richards	114	796	1988-89	658
M.R.Ramprakash	114	764	2008	676
Zaheer Abbas	108	768	1982-83	658
A.Sandham	107	1000	1935	871
M.C.Cowdrey	107	1130	1973	1035
T.W.Hayward	104	1138	1913	1076
G.M.Turner	103	792	1982	779
J.H.Edrich	103	979	1977	945
L.E.G.Ames	102	951	1950	915
G.E.Tyldesley	102	961	1934	919
D.L.Amiss	102	1139	1986	1081

MOST 400s: 2 – B.C.Lara, W.H.Ponsford

MOST 300s or more: 6 – D.G.Bradman; 4 – W.R.Hammond, W.H.Ponsford

MOST 200s or more: 37 – D.G.Bradman; 36 – W.R.Hammond; 22 – E.H.Hendren

MOST RUNS IN A MONTH

1294 (avge 92.42)	L.Hutton	Yorkshire	June 1949

MOST RUNS IN A SEASON

Runs			I	NO	HS	Avge	100	Season
3816	D.C.S.Compton	Middlesex	50	8	246	90.85	18	1947
3539	W.J.Edrich	Middlesex	52	8	267*	80.43	12	1947
3518	T.W.Hayward	Surrey	61	8	219	66.37	13	1906

The feat of scoring 3000 runs in a season has been achieved 28 times, the most recent instance being by W.E.Alley (3019) in 1961. The highest aggregate in a season since 1969 is 2755 by S.J.Cook in 1991.

1000 RUNS IN A SEASON MOST TIMES

28	W.G.Grace (Gloucestershire), F.E.Woolley (Kent)

HIGHEST BATTING AVERAGE IN A SEASON

(Qualification: 12 innings)

Avge			I	NO	HS	Runs	100	Season
115.66	D.G.Bradman	Australians	26	5	278	2429	13	1938
106.50	K.C.Sangakkara	Surrey	16	2	200	1491	8	2017
104.66	D.R.Martyn	Australians	14	5	176*	942	5	2001
103.54	M.R.Ramprakash	Surrey	24	2	301*	2278	8	2006
102.53	G.Boycott	Yorkshire	20	5	175*	1538	6	1979
102.00	W.A.Johnston	Australians	17	16	28*	102	–	1953
101.70	G.A.Gooch	Essex	30	3	333	2746	12	1990
101.30	M.R.Ramprakash	Surrey	25	5	266*	2026	10	2007
100.12	G.Boycott	Yorkshire	30	5	233	2503	13	1971

FASTEST HUNDRED AGAINST AUTHENTIC BOWLING

35 min	P.G.H.Fender	Surrey v Northamptonshire	Northampton	1920

FASTEST DOUBLE HUNDRED

113 min	R.J.Shastri	Bombay v Baroda	Bombay	1984-85

FASTEST TRIPLE HUNDRED

181 min	D.C.S.Compton	MCC v NE Transvaal	Benoni	1948-49

MOST SIXES IN AN INNINGS

23	C.Munro	Central Districts v Auckland	Napier	2014-15

MOST SIXES IN A MATCH

23	C.Munro	Central Districts v Auckland	Napier	2014-15

MOST SIXES IN A SEASON

80	I.T.Botham	Somerset and England		1985

MOST FOURS IN AN INNINGS

72	B.C.Lara	Warwickshire v Durham	Birmingham	1994

MOST RUNS OFF ONE OVER

36	G.St A.Sobers	Nottinghamshire v Glamorgan	Swansea	1968
36	R.J.Shastri	Bombay v Baroda	Bombay	1984-85

Both batsmen hit for six all six balls of overs bowled by M.A.Nash and Tilak Raj respectively.

MOST RUNS IN A DAY

390*	B.C.Lara	Warwickshire v Durham	Birmingham	1994

There have been 19 instances of a batsman scoring 300 or more runs in a day.

LONGEST INNINGS

1015 min	R.Nayyar (271)	Himachal Pradesh v Jammu & Kashmir	Chamba	1999-00

HIGHEST PARTNERSHIPS FOR EACH WICKET

First Wicket

561	Waheed Mirza/Mansoor Akhtar	Karachi W v Quetta	Karachi	1976-77
555	P.Holmes/H.Sutcliffe	Yorkshire v Essex	Leyton	1932
554	J.T.Brown/J.Tunnicliffe	Yorkshire v Derbys	Chesterfield	1898

Second Wicket

580	Rafatullah Mohmand/Aamer Sajjad	WAPDA v SSGC	Sheikhupura	2009-10
576	S.T.Jayasuriya/R.S.Mahanama	Sri Lanka v India	Colombo	1997-98
480	D.Elgar/R.R.Rossouw	Eagles v Titans	Centurion	2009-10
475	Zahir Alam/L.S.Rajput	Assam v Tripura	Gauhati	1991-92
465*	J.A.Jameson/R.B.Kanhai	Warwickshire v Glos	Birmingham	1974

Third Wicket

624	K.C.Sangakkara/D.P.M.D.Jayawardena	Sri Lanka v South Africa	Colombo	2006
594*	S.M.Gugale/A.R.Bawne	Maharashtra v Delhi	Mumbai	2016-17
539	S.D.Jogiyani/R.A.Jadeja	Saurashtra v Gujarat	Surat	2012-13
523	M.A.Carberry/N.D.McKenzie	Hampshire v Yorkshire	Southampton	2011

Fourth Wicket

577	V.S.Hazare/Gul Mahomed	Baroda v Holkar	Baroda	1946-47
574*	C.L.Walcott/F.M.M.Worrell	Barbados v Trinidad	Port-of-Spain	1945-46
502*	F.M.M.Worrell/J.D.C.Goddard	Barbados v Trinidad	Bridgetown	1943-44
470	A.I.Kallicharran/G.W.Humpage	Warwickshire v Lancs	Southport	1982

Fifth Wicket

520*	C.A.Pujara/R.A.Jadeja	Saurashtra v Orissa	Rajkot	2008-09
494	Marchall Ayub/Mehrab Hossain Jr	Central Zone v East Zone	Bogra	2012-13
479	Misbah-ul-Haq/Usman Arshad	Sui NGP v Lahore Shalimar	Lahore	2009-10
464*	M.E.Waugh/S.R.Waugh	NSW v W Australia	Perth	1990-91
423	Mosaddek Hossain/Al-Amin	Barisal v Rangpur	Savar	2014-15
420	Mohd. Ashraful/Marshall Ayub	Dhaka v Chittagong	Chittagong	2006-07
410*	A.S.Chopra/S.Badrinath	India A v South Africa A	Delhi	2007-08
405	S.G.Barnes/D.G.Bradman	Australia v England	Sydney	1946-47
401	M.B.Loye/D.Ripley	Northants v Glamorgan	Northampton	1998

Sixth Wicket

487*	G.A.Headley/C.C.Passailaigue	Jamaica v Tennyson's	Kingston	1931-32
428	W.W.Armstrong/M.A.Noble	Australians v Sussex	Hove	1902
417	W.P.Saha/L.R.Shukla	Bengal v Assam	Kolkata	2010-11
411	R.M.Poore/E.G.Wynyard	Hampshire v Somerset	Taunton	1899

Seventh Wicket

460	Bhupinder Singh jr/P.Dharmani	Punjab v Delhi	Delhi	1994-95
371	M.R.Marsh/S.M.Whiteman	Australia A v India A	Brisbane	2014
366*	J.M.Bairstow/T.T.Bresnan	Yorkshire v Durham	Chester-le-Street	2015

Eighth Wicket

433	V.T.Trumper/A.Sims	Australians v C'bury	Christchurch	1913-14
392	A.Mishra/J.Yadav	Haryana v Karnataka	Hubli	2012-13
332	I.J.L.Trott/S.C.J.Broad	England v Pakistan	Lord's	2010

Ninth Wicket

283	J.Chapman/A.Warren	Derbys v Warwicks	Blackwell	1910
268	J.B.Commins/N.Boje	SA 'A' v Mashonaland	Harare	1994-95
261	W.L.Madsen/T.Poynton	Derbys v Northants	Northampton	2012
251	J.W.H.T.Douglas/S.N.Hare	Essex v Derbyshire	Leyton	1921

Tenth Wicket

307	A.F.Kippax/J.E.H.Hooker	NSW v Victoria	Melbourne	1928-29
249	C.T.Sarwate/S.N.Banerjee	Indians v Surrey	The Oval	1946
239	Aqil Arshad/Ali Raza	Lahore Whites v Hyderabad	Lahore	2004-05

BOWLING RECORDS – 2000 WICKETS IN A CAREER

	Career	Runs	Wkts	Avge	100w
W.Rhodes	1898-1930	69993	**4187**	16.71	23
A.P.Freeman	1914-36	69577	**3776**	18.42	17
C.W.L.Parker	1903-35	63817	**3278**	19.46	16
J.T.Hearne	1888-1923	54352	**3061**	17.75	15
T.W.J.Goddard	1922-52	59116	**2979**	19.84	16
W.G.Grace	1865-1908	51545	**2876**	17.92	10
A.S.Kennedy	1907-36	61034	**2874**	21.23	15
D.Shackleton	1948-69	53303	**2857**	18.65	20
G.A.R.Lock	1946-70/71	54709	**2844**	19.23	14
F.J.Titmus	1949-82	63313	**2830**	22.37	16
M.W.Tate	1912-37	50571	**2784**	18.16	13+1
G.H.Hirst	1891-1929	51282	**2739**	18.72	15

	Career	Runs	Wkts	Avge	100w
C.Blythe	1899-1914	42136	**2506**	16.81	14
D.L.Underwood	1963-87	49993	**2465**	20.28	10
W.E.Astill	1906-39	57783	**2431**	23.76	9
J.C.White	1909-37	43759	**2356**	18.57	14
W.E.Hollies	1932-57	48656	**2323**	20.94	14
F.S.Trueman	1949-69	42154	**2304**	18.29	12
J.B.Statham	1950-68	36999	**2260**	16.37	13
R.T.D.Perks	1930-55	53771	**2233**	24.07	16
J.Briggs	1879-1900	35431	**2221**	15.95	12
D.J.Shepherd	1950-72	47302	**2218**	21.32	12
E.G.Dennett	1903-26	42571	**2147**	19.82	12
T.Richardson	1892-1905	38794	**2104**	18.43	10
T.E.Bailey	1945-67	48170	**2082**	23.13	9
R.Illingworth	1951-83	42023	**2072**	20.28	10
F.E.Woolley	1906-38	41066	**2068**	19.85	8
N.Gifford	1960-88	48731	**2068**	23.56	4
G.Geary	1912-38	41339	**2063**	20.03	11
D.V.P.Wright	1932-57	49307	**2056**	23.98	10
J.A.Newman	1906-30	51111	**2032**	25.15	9
A.Shaw	1864-97	24580	**2026+1**	12.12	9
S.Haigh	1895-1913	32091	**2012**	15.94	11

ALL TEN WICKETS IN AN INNINGS

This feat has been achieved 81 times in first-class matches (excluding 12-a-side fixtures).

Three Times: A.P.Freeman (1929, 1930, 1931)

Twice: V.E.Walker (1859, 1865); H.Verity (1931, 1932); J.C.Laker (1956)

Instances since 1945:

W.E.Hollies	Warwickshire v Notts	Birmingham	1946
J.M.Sims	East v West	Kingston on Thames	1948
J.K.R.Graveney	Gloucestershire v Derbyshire	Chesterfield	1949
T.E.Bailey	Essex v Lancashire	Clacton	1949
R.Berry	Lancashire v Worcestershire	Blackpool	1953
S.P.Gupte	President's XI v Combined XI	Bombay	1954-55
J.C.Laker	Surrey v Australians	The Oval	1956
K.Smales	Nottinghamshire v Glos	Stroud	1956
G.A.R.Lock	Surrey v Kent	Blackheath	1956
J.C.Laker	England v Australia	Manchester	1956
P.M.Chatterjee	Bengal v Assam	Jorhat	1956-57
J.D.Bannister	Warwicks v Combined Services	Birmingham (M & B)	1959
A.J.G.Pearson	Cambridge U v Leicestershire	Loughborough	1961
N.I.Thomson	Sussex v Warwickshire	Worthing	1964
P.J.Allan	Queensland v Victoria	Melbourne	1965-66
I.J.Brayshaw	Western Australia v Victoria	Perth	1967-68
Shahid Mahmood	Karachi Whites v Khairpur	Karachi	1969-70
E.E.Hemmings	International XI v W Indians	Kingston	1982-83
P.Sunderam	Rajasthan v Vidarbha	Jodhpur	1985-86
S.T.Jefferies	Western Province v OFS	Cape Town	1987-88
Imran Adil	Bahawalpur v Faisalabad	Faisalabad	1989-90
G.P.Wickremasinghe	Sinhalese v Kalutara	Colombo	1991-92
R.L.Johnson	Middlesex v Derbyshire	Derby	1994
Naeem Akhtar	Rawalpindi B v Peshawar	Peshawar	1995-96
A.Kumble	India v Pakistan	Delhi	1998-99
D.S.Mohanty	East Zone v South Zone	Agartala	2000-01
O.D.Gibson	Durham v Hampshire	Chester-le-Street	2007
M.W.Olivier	Warriors v Eagles	Bloemfontein	2007-08
Zulfiqar Babar	Multan v Islamabad	Multan	2009-10

MOST WICKETS IN A MATCH

19   J.C.Laker   England v Australia   Manchester   1956

MOST WICKETS IN A SEASON

Wkts		Season	Matches	Overs	Mdns	Runs	Avge
304	A.P.Freeman	1928	37	1976.1	423	5489	18.05
298	A.P.Freeman	1933	33	2039	651	4549	15.26

The feat of taking 250 wickets in a season has been achieved on 12 occasions, the last instance being by A.P.Freeman in 1933. 200 or more wickets in a season have been taken on 59 occasions, the last being by G.A.R.Lock (212 wickets, average 12.02) in 1957.

The highest aggregates of wickets taken in a season since the reduction of County Championship matches in 1969 are as follows:

Wkts		Season	Matches	Overs	Mdns	Runs	Avge
134	M.D.Marshall	1982	22	822	225	2108	15.73
131	L.R.Gibbs	1971	23	1024.1	295	2475	18.89
125	F.D.Stephenson	1988	22	819.1	196	2289	18.31
121	R.D.Jackman	1980	23	746.2	220	1864	15.40

Since 1969 there have been 50 instances of bowlers taking 100 wickets in a season.

MOST HAT-TRICKS IN A CAREER

7   D.V.P.Wright
6   T.W.J.Goddard, C.W.L.Parker
5   S.Haigh, V.W.C.Jupp, A.E.G.Rhodes, F.A.Tarrant

ALL-ROUND RECORDS
THE 'DOUBLE'

3000 runs and 100 wickets: J.H.Parks (1937)
2000 runs and 200 wickets: G.H.Hirst (1906)
2000 runs and 100 wickets: F.E.Woolley (4), J.W.Hearne (3), W.G.Grace (2), G.H.Hirst (2), W.Rhodes (2), T.E.Bailey, D.E.Davies, G.L.Jessop, V.W.C.Jupp, J.Langridge, F.A.Tarrant, C.L.Townsend, L.F.Townsend
1000 runs and 200 wickets: M.W.Tate (3), A.E.Trott (2), A.S.Kennedy
Most Doubles: 16 – W.Rhodes; 14 – G.H.Hirst; 10 – V.W.C.Jupp
Double in Debut Season: D.B.Close (1949) – aged 18, the youngest to achieve this feat.

The feat of scoring 1000 runs and taking 100 wickets in a season has been achieved on 305 occasions, R.J.Hadlee (1984) and F.D.Stephenson (1988) being the only players to complete the 'double' since the reduction of County Championship matches in 1969.

WICKET-KEEPING RECORDS
1000 DISMISSALS IN A CAREER

	Career	Dismissals	Ct	St
R.W.Taylor	1960-88	**1649**	1473	176
J.T.Murray	1952-75	**1527**	1270	257
H.Strudwick	1902-27	**1497**	1242	255
A.P.E.Knott	1964-85	**1344**	1211	133
R.C.Russell	1981-2004	**1320**	1192	128
F.H.Huish	1895-1914	**1310**	933	377
B.Taylor	1949-73	**1294**	1083	211
S.J.Rhodes	1981-2004	**1263**	1139	124
D.Hunter	1889-1909	**1253**	906	347
H.R.Butt	1890-1912	**1228**	953	275
J.H.Board	1891-1914/15	**1207**	852	355
H.Elliott	1920-47	**1206**	904	302
J.M.Parks	1949-76	**1181**	1088	93
R.Booth	1951-70	**1126**	948	178
L.E.G.Ames	1926-51	**1121**	703	418

	Career	Dismissals	Ct	St
C.M.W.Read	1997-2017	**1104**	1051	53
D.L.Bairstow	1970-90	**1099**	961	138
G.Duckworth	1923-47	**1096**	753	343
H.W.Stephenson	1948-64	**1082**	748	334
J.G.Binks	1955-75	**1071**	895	176
T.G.Evans	1939-69	**1066**	816	250
A.Long	1960-80	**1046**	922	124
G.O.Dawkes	1937-61	**1043**	895	148
R.W.Tolchard	1965-83	**1037**	912	125
W.L.Cornford	1921-47	**1017**	675	342

MOST DISMISSALS IN AN INNINGS

9	(8ct, 1st)	Tahir Rashid	Habib Bank v PACO	Gujranwala	1992-93
9	(7ct, 2st)	W.R.James	Matabeleland v Mashonaland CD	Bulawayo	1995-96
8	(8ct)	A.T.W.Grout	Queensland v W Australia	Brisbane	1959-60
8	(8ct)	D.E.East	Essex v Somerset	Taunton	1985
8	(8ct)	S.A.Marsh	Kent v Middlesex	Lord's	1991
8	(6ct, 2st)	T.J.Zoehrer	Australians v Surrey	The Oval	1993
8	(7ct, 1st)	D.S.Berry	Victoria v South Australia	Melbourne	1996-97
8	(7ct, 1st)	Y.S.S.Mendis	Bloomfield v Kurunegala Youth	Colombo	2000-01
8	(7ct, 1st)	S.Nath	Assam v Tripura (on debut)	Gauhati	2001-02
8	(8ct)	J.N.Batty	Surrey v Kent	The Oval	2004
8	(8ct)	Golam Mabud	Sylhet v Dhaka	Dhaka	2005-06
8	(8ct)	D.C.de Boorder	Otago v Wellington	Wellington	2009-10
8	(8ct)	R.S.Second	Free State v North West	Bloemfontein	2011-12
8	(8ct)	T.L.Tsolekile	South Africa A v Sri Lanka A	Durban	2012

MOST DISMISSALS IN A MATCH

14	(11ct, 3st)	I.Khaleel	Hyderabad v Assam	Guwahati	2011-12
13	(11ct, 2st)	W.R.James	Matabeleland v Mashonaland CD	Bulawayo	1995-96
12	(8ct, 4st)	E.Pooley	Surrey v Sussex	The Oval	1868
12	(9ct, 3st)	D.Tallon	Queensland v NSW	Sydney	1938-39
12	(9ct, 3st)	H.B.Taber	NSW v South Australia	Adelaide	1968-69
12	(12ct)	P.D.McGlashan	Northern Districts v Central Districts	Whangarei	2009-10
12	(11ct, 1st)	T.L.Tsolekile	Lions v Dolphins	Johannesburg	2010-11
12	(12ct)	Kashif Mahmood	Lahore Shalimar v Abbottabad	Abbottabad	2010-11
12	(12ct)	R.S.Second	Free State v North West	Bloemfontein	2011-12

MOST DISMISSALS IN A SEASON

128	(79ct, 49st)	L.E.G.Ames		1929

FIELDING RECORDS
750 CATCHES IN A CAREER

1018	F.E.Woolley	1906-38	784	J.G.Langridge	1928-55
887	W.G.Grace	1865-1908	764	W.Rhodes	1898-1930
830	G.A.R.Lock	1946-70/71	758	C.A.Milton	1948-74
819	W.R.Hammond	1920-51	754	E.H.Hendren	1907-38
813	D.B.Close	1949-86			

MOST CATCHES IN AN INNINGS

7	M.J.Stewart	Surrey v Northamptonshire	Northampton	1957
7	A.S.Brown	Gloucestershire v Nottinghamshire	Nottingham	1966
7	R.Clarke	Warwickshire v Lancashire	Liverpool	2011

MOST CATCHES IN A MATCH

10	W.R.Hammond	Gloucestershire v Surrey	Cheltenham	1928
9	R.Clarke	Warwickshire v Lancashire	Liverpool	2011

MOST CATCHES IN A SEASON

78	W.R.Hammond	1928	77	M.J.Stewart	1957

ENGLAND LIMITED-OVERS INTERNATIONALS 2017

INDIA v ENGLAND

LIMITED-OVERS INTERNATIONALS

Maharashtra CA Stadium, Pune, 15 January. Toss: India. **INDIA** won by three wickets. England 350-7 (50; J.E.Root 78, J.J.Roy 73, B.A.Stokes 62). India 356-7 (48.1; V.Kohli 122, K.M.Jadhav 120, J.T.Ball 3-67). Award: K.M.Jadhav.

Barabati Stadium, Cuttack, 19 January. Toss: England. **INDIA** won by 15 runs. India 381-6 (50; Yuvraj Singh 150, M.S.Dhoni 134, C.R.Woakes 4-60). England 366-8 (50; E.J.G.Morgan 102, J.J.Roy 82, M.M.Ali 55, J.E.Root 54, R.Ashwin 3-65). Award: Yuvraj Singh.
England's highest score in the second innings in all LOIs.

Eden Gardens, Kolkata, 22 January. Toss: India. **ENGLAND** won by 5 runs. England 321-8 (50; J.J.Roy 65, B.A.Stokes 57*, J.M.Bairstow 56, H.H.Pandya 3-49). India 316-9 (50; K.M.Jadhav 90, H.H.Pandya 56, V.Kohli 55, B.A.Stokes 3-63). Award: B.A.Stokes. Series award: K.M.Jadhav.

TWENTY20 INTERNATIONALS

Green Park, Kanpur, 26 January. Toss: England. **ENGLAND** won by seven wickets. India 147-7 (20). England 148-3 (18.1; E.J.G.Morgan 51). Award: M.M.Ali (2-21).

Vidarbha CA Stadium, Nagpur, 29 January. Toss: England. **INDIA** won by 5 runs. India 144-8 (20; K.L.Rahul 71, C.J.Jordan 3-22). England 139-6 (20; A.Nehra 3-28). Award: J.J.Bumrah (2-20).

M.Chinnaswamy Stadium, Bangalore, 1 February. Toss: England. **INDIA** won by 75 runs. India 202-6 (20; S.K.Raina 63, M.S.Dhoni 56). England 127 (16.3; Y.S.Chahal 6-25, J.J.Bumrah 3-14). Award: Y.S.Chahal. Series award: Y.S.Chahal.
Y.S.Chahal became only the third man to take six wickets in an innings in all IT20s.

WEST INDIES v ENGLAND

LIMITED-OVERS INTERNATIONALS

Sir Vivian Richards Stadium, North Sound, Antigua, 3 March. Toss: West Indies. **ENGLAND** won by 45 runs. England 296-6 (50; E.J.G.Morgan 107, B.A.Stokes 55, S.W.Billings 52). West Indies 251 (47.2; J.N.Mohammed 72, J.L.Carter 52, L.E.Plunkett 4-40, C.R.Woakes 4-47). Award: E.J.G.Morgan.

Sir Vivian Richards Stadium, North Sound, Antigua, 3 March. Toss: West Indies. **ENGLAND** won by four wickets. West Indies 225 (47.5; J.N.Mohammed 50, L.E.Plunkett 3-32). England 226-6 (48.2; J.E.Root 90*, C.R.Woakes 68*, J.J.Roy 52, A.R.Nurse 3-34). Award: J.E.Root.

Kensington Oval, Bridgetown, Barbados, 9 March. Toss: West Indies. **ENGLAND** won by 186 runs. England 328 (50; A.D.Hales 110, J.E.Root 101, A.S.Joseph 4-76, J.O.Holder 3-41). West Indies 142 (39.2; C.R.Woakes 3-16, L.E.Plunkett 3-27). Award: A.D.Hales. Series award: C.R.Woakes.
England's biggest victory over West Indies in all LOIs.

ENGLAND v IRELAND
ROYAL LONDON LIMITED-OVERS INTERNATIONALS

County Ground, Bristol, 5 May. Toss: Ireland. **ENGLAND** won by seven wickets. Ireland 126 (33; A.U.Rashid 5-27). England 127-3 (20; A.D.Hales 55). Award: A.U.Rashid.

Lord's, London, 7 May. Toss: Ireland. **ENGLAND** won by 85 runs. England 328-6 (50; E.J.G.Morgan 76, J.E.Root 73, J.M.Bairstow 72*). Ireland 243 (46.1; W.T.S.Porterfield 82, L.E.Plunkett 3-23, J.E.Root 3-52). Award: J.E.Root.

ENGLAND v SOUTH AFRICA
ROYAL LONDON LIMITED-OVERS INTERNATIONALS

Headingley, Leeds, 24 May. Toss: South Africa. **ENGLAND** won by 72 runs. England 339-6 (50; E.J.G.Morgan 107, M.M.Ali 77*, A.D.Hales 61). South Africa 267 (45; H.M.Amla 73, F.du Plessis 67, C.R.Woakes 4-38). Award: M.M.Ali.

Rose Bowl, Southampton, 27 May. Toss: South Africa. **ENGLAND** won by 2 runs. England 330-6 (50; B.A.Stokes 101, J.C.Buttler 65*). South Africa 328-5 (50; Q.de Kock 98, D.A.Miller 71* A.B.de Villiers 52, L.E.Plunkett 3-64). Award: B.A.Stokes.

Lord's, London, 29 May. Toss: South Africa. **SOUTH AFRICA** won by seven wickets. England 153 (31.1; J.M.Bairstow 51, K.Rabada 4-39, K.A.Maharaj 3-25, W.D.Parnell 3-43). South Africa 156-3 (28.5; H.M.Amla 55). Award: K.Rabada. Series award: E.J.G.Morgan. England debut: T.S.Roland-Jones.

ICC CHAMPIONS TROPHY

The Oval, London, 1 June. Toss: England. **ENGLAND** won by eight wickets. Bangladesh 305-6 (50; Tamim Iqbal 128, Mushfiqur Rahim 79, L.E.Plunkett 4-59). England 308-2 (47.2; J.E.Root 133*, A.D.Hales 95, E.J.G.Morgan 75*). Award: J.E.Root.

Sophia Gardens, Cardiff, 6 June. Toss: New Zealand. **ENGLAND** won by 87 runs. England 310 (49.3; J.E.Root 64, J.C.Buttler 61*, A.D.Hales 56, C.J.Anderson 3-55, A.F.Milne 3-79). New Zealand 223 (44.3; K.S.Williamson 87, L.E.Plunkett 4-55). Award: J.T.Ball (2-31).

Edgbaston, Birmingham, 10 June. Toss: England. **ENGLAND** won by 40 runs (D/L method). Australia 277-9 (50; T.M.Head 71*, A.J.Finch 68, S.P.D.Smith 56, M.A.Wood 4-33, A.U.Rashid 4-41). England 240-4 (40.2; B.A.Stokes 102*, E.J.G.Morgan 87). Award: B.A.Stokes.

Semi-final

Sophia Gardens, Cardiff, 14 June. Toss: Pakistan. **PAKISTAN** won by eight wickets. England 211 (49.5; Hasan Ali 3-35). Pakistan 215-2 (37.1; Azhar Ali 76, Fakhar Zaman 57). Award: Hasan Ali.

Final

PAKISTAN beat India by 180 runs. Series award: Hasan Ali.

ENGLAND v SOUTH AFRICA
NATWEST TWENTY20 INTERNATIONALS

Rose Bowl, Southampton, 21 June. Toss: South Africa. **ENGLAND** won by nine wickets. South Africa 142-3 (20; A.B.de Villiers 65*, F.Behardien 64*). England 143-1 (14.3; J.M.Bairstow 60*). Award: J.M.Bairstow. England debut: M.S.Crane.

County Ground, Taunton, 23 June. Toss: England. **SOUTH AFRICA** won by 3 runs. South Africa 174-8 (20; T.K.Curran 3-33). England 171-6 (20; J.J.Roy 67). Award: C.H.Morris (2-18). England debuts: T.K.Curran, L.S.Livingstone.

Sophia Gardens, Cardiff, 25 June. Toss: South Africa. **ENGLAND** won by 19 runs. England 181-8 (20; D.J.Malan 78, D.Paterson 4-32). South Africa 162-7 (20; C.J.Jordan 3-31). Award: D.J.Malan. England debut: D.J.Malan.

ENGLAND v WEST INDIES

NATWEST TWENTY20 INTERNATIONAL

Riverside Ground, Chester-le-Street, 16 September. Toss: England. **WEST INDIES** won by 21 runs. West Indies 176-9 (20; E.Lewis 51, A.U.Rashid 3-25, L.E.Plunkett 3-27). England 155 (19.3; C.R.Brathwaite 3-20, K.O.K.Williams 3-35). Award: S.P.Narine (2-15).

ROYAL LONDON LIMITED-OVERS INTERNATIONALS

Old Trafford, Manchester, 19 September. Toss: West Indies. **ENGLAND** won by seven wickets. West Indies 204-9 (42; B.A.Stokes 3-43). England 210-3 (30.5/42; J.M.Bairstow 100*, J.E.Root 54). Award: J.M.Bairstow.

Trent Bridge, Nottingham, 21 September. Toss: West Indies. **NO RESULT.** England 21-0 (2.2).

County Ground, Bristol, 24 September. Toss: West Indies. **ENGLAND** won by 124 runs. England 369-9 (50; M.M.Ali 102, J.E.Root 84, B.A.Stokes 73, M.L.Cummins 3-82). West Indies 245 (39.1; C.H.Gayle 94, L.E.Plunkett 5-52, A.U.Rashid 3-34). Award: M.M.Ali. *M.M.Ali reached 100 in 53 balls (7 fours, 8 sixes) – the fastest LOI century in England.*

The Oval, London, 27 September. Toss: England. **ENGLAND** won by 6 runs (D/L method). West Indies 356-5 (50; E.Lewis 176*, J.O.Holder 77, C.R.Woakes 3-71). England 258-5 (35.1; J.J.Roy 84, A.S.Joseph 5-56). Award: E.Lewis.

Rose Bowl, Southampton, 29 September. Toss: England. **ENGLAND** won by nine wickets. West Indies 288-6 (50; S.D.Hope 72). England 294-1 (38; J.M.Bairstow 141*, J.J.Roy 96). Award: J.M.Bairstow. Series award: M.M.Ali. England debut: T.K.Curran.

ENGLAND RESULTS IN 2017

	P	W	L	T	NR
Limited Overs	20	15	4	–	1
Twenty20	7	3	4	–	–
Overall	27	18	8	–	1

600 RUNS IN LIMITED-OVERS INTERNATIONALS IN 2017

	M	I	NO	HS	Runs	Avge	100	50	S/Rate
J.E.Root	19	18	4	133*	983	70.21	2	7	92.12
E.J.G.Morgan	20	18	1	107	781	45.94	3	3	98.73
B.A.Stokes	15	13	3	102*	616	61.60	2	4	106.94

20 WICKETS IN LIMITED-OVERS INTERNATIONALS IN 2017

	Pl	O	M	R	W	Avge	Best	4wI	Econ
L.E.Plunkett	18	143.5	5	809	36	22.47	5-52	4	5.62
A.U.Rashid	17	123.2	3	672	26	25.84	5-27	2	5.44
C.R.Woakes	12	88.0	8	454	22	20.63	4-38	3	5.15

LIMITED-OVERS INTERNATIONALS
CAREER RECORDS

These records, complete to 11 March 2018, include all players registered for county cricket for the 2018 season at the time of going to press, plus those who have appeared in LOI matches for ICC full member countries since 1 December 2016.

ENGLAND – BATTING AND FIELDING

	M	I	NO	HS	Runs	Avge	100	50	Ct/St
M.M.Ali	73	62	10	128	1449	27.86	3	5	24
T.R.Ambrose	5	5	1	6	10	2.50	–	–	3
J.M.Anderson	194	79	43	28	273	7.58	–	–	53
J.M.Bairstow	42	38	8	141*	1451	48.36	4	6	20/2
J.T.Ball	17	5	1	28	37	9.25	–	–	4
G.S.Ballance	16	15	1	79	279	21.21	–	2	8
G.J.Batty	10	8	2	17	30	5.00	–	–	4
I.R.Bell	161	157	14	141	5416	37.87	4	35	54
S.W.Billings	13	10	–	62	248	24.80	–	2	10
R.S.Bopara	120	109	21	101*	2695	30.62	1	14	35
S.G.Borthwick	2	2	–	15	18	9.00	–	–	–
T.T.Bresnan	85	64	20	80	871	19.79	–	1	20
D.R.Briggs	1	–	–	–	–	–	–	–	–
S.C.J.Broad	121	68	25	45*	529	12.30	–	–	27
J.C.Buttler	109	92	18	129	2816	38.05	5	15	139/19
M.A.Carberry	6	6	–	63	114	19.00	–	1	2
R.Clarke	20	13	–	39	144	11.07	–	–	11
P.D.Collingwood	197	181	37	120*	5092	35.36	5	26	108
A.N.Cook	92	92	4	137	3204	36.40	5	19	36
T.K.Curran	8	5	4	30	70	70.00	–	–	4
S.M.Davies	8	8	–	87	244	30.50	–	1	8
L.A.Dawson	1	1	–	10	10	10.00	–	–	–
J.L.Denly	9	9	–	67	268	29.77	–	2	5
J.W.Dernbach	24	8	1	5	19	2.71	–	–	5
B.M.Duckett	3	3	–	63	123	41.00	–	2	–
S.T.Finn	69	30	13	35	136	8.00	–	–	15
J.S.Foster	11	6	3	13	41	13.66	–	–	13/7
H.F.Gurney	10	6	4	6*	15	7.50	–	–	1
A.D.Hales	59	57	2	171	2018	36.69	5	12	22
C.J.Jordan	31	21	7	38*	169	12.07	–	–	19
S.C.Meaker	2	2	–	1	2	1.00	–	–	–
E.J.G.Morgan †	177	164	23	124*	5287	37.49	10	30	66
P.Mustard	10	10	–	83	233	23.30	–	1	9/2
G.Onions	4	1	–	1	1	1.00	–	–	–
S.D.Parry	2	–	–	–	–	–	–	–	–
S.R.Patel	36	22	7	70*	482	32.13	–	1	7
L.E.Plunkett	65	38	13	56	516	20.64	–	1	22
W.B.Rankin †	7	2	1	4	5	2.50	–	–	–
A.U.Rashid	64	28	7	69	444	21.14	–	1	20
T.S.Roland-Jones	1	1	1	37*	37	–	–	–	–
J.E.Root	107	101	14	133*	4451	51.16	11	27	50
J.J.Roy	57	56	2	180	2006	37.14	4	11	21
B.A.Stokes	67	59	9	102*	1791	35.82	3	11	34
R.J.W.Topley	10	5	4	6	7	7.00	–	–	2
J.C.Tredwell	45	25	11	30	163	11.64	–	–	14
M.E.Trescothick	123	122	6	137	4335	37.37	12	21	49
I.J.L.Trott	68	65	10	137	2819	51.25	4	22	14

ENGLAND – BATTING AND FIELDING (continued)

	M	I	NO	HS	Runs	Avge	100	50	Ct/St
J.M.Vince	5	4	–	51	104	26.00	–	1	4
D.J.Willey	34	19	10	26	140	15.55	–	–	17
C.R.Woakes	76	55	18	95*	1034	27.94	–	4	32
M.A.Wood	26	9	5	13	43	10.75	–	–	5
L.J.Wright	50	39	4	52	707	20.20	–	2	18

ENGLAND – BOWLING

	O	M	R	W	Avge	Best	4wI	R/Over
M.M.Ali	575.5	9	2914	60	48.56	3-32	–	5.06
J.M.Anderson	1597.2	125	7861	269	29.22	5-23	13	4.92
J.T.Ball	152.5	5	951	21	45.28	5-51	1	6.22
G.J.Batty	73.2	1	366	5	73.20	2-40	–	4.99
I.R.Bell	14.4	0	88	6	14.66	3- 9	–	6.00
R.S.Bopara	310	11	1523	40	38.07	4-38	1	4.91
S.G.Borthwick	9	0	72	0	–	–	–	8.00
T.T.Bresnan	703.3	35	3813	109	34.98	5-48	4	5.42
D.R.Briggs	10	0	39	2	19.50	2-39	–	3.90
S.C.J.Broad	1018.1	56	5364	178	30.13	5-23	10	5.26
M.A.Carberry	1	0	12	0	–	–	–	12.00
R.Clarke	78.1	3	415	11	37.72	2-28	–	5.30
P.D.Collingwood	864.2	14	4294	111	38.68	6-31	4	4.96
T.K.Curran	61.4	2	377	12	31.41	5-35	1	6.11
L.A.Dawson	8	0	70	2	35.00	2-70	–	8.75
J.W.Dernbach	205.4	6	1308	31	42.19	4-45	1	6.35
S.T.Finn	591.4	38	2996	102	29.37	5-33	6	5.06
H.F.Gurney	75.5	4	432	11	39.27	4-55	1	5.69
C.J.Jordan	255.2	5	1521	43	35.37	5-29	1	5.95
S.C.Meaker	19	1	110	2	55.00	1-45	–	5.78
G.Onions	34	1	185	4	46.25	2-58	–	5.44
S.D.Parry	19	2	92	4	23.00	3-32	–	4.84
S.R.Patel	197.5	4	1091	24	45.45	5-41	1	5.51
L.E.Plunkett	520.2	12	3022	100	30.22	5-52	4	5.80
W.B.Rankin	53.1	3	241	10	24.10	4-46	1	4.53
A.U.Rashid	543.4	6	3002	93	32.27	5-27	6	5.52
T.S.Roland-Jones	7	2	34	1	34.00	1-34	–	4.85
J.E.Root	200.4	2	1151	20	57.55	3-52	–	5.73
B.A.Stokes	363.3	6	2205	58	38.01	5-61	2	6.06
R.J.W.Topley	77.1	6	410	16	25.62	4-50	1	5.31
J.C.Tredwell	350.4	18	1666	60	27.76	4-41	3	4.75
M.E.Trescothick	38.4	0	219	4	54.75	2- 7	–	5.66
I.J.L.Trott	30.3	0	166	2	83.00	2-31	–	5.44
D.J.Willey	230.3	15	1300	36	36.11	4-34	1	5.63
C.R.Woakes	609	32	3355	109	30.77	6-45	10	5.50
M.A.Wood	226.1	6	1231	27	45.59	4-33	1	5.44
L.J.Wright	173	2	884	15	58.93	2-34	–	5.10

† *E.J.G.Morgan has also made 23 appearances for Ireland; and W.B.Rankin has also made 39 appearances for Ireland (see below).*

LOI

AUSTRALIA – BATTING AND FIELDING

	M	I	NO	HS	Runs	Avge	100	50	Ct/St
A.C.Agar	4	3	1	9*	14	7.00	–	–	2
G.J.Bailey	90	85	10	156	3044	40.58	3	22	48
A.T.Carey	1	1	–	27	27	27.00	–	–	1
H.W.R.Cartwright	2	2	–	1	2	1.00	–	–	1
D.T.Christian	19	18	5	39	273	21.00	–	–	10
M.J.Cosgrove	3	3	–	74	112	37.33	–	1	–
N.M.Coulter-Nile	21	14	5	16	86	9.55	–	–	7
P.J.Cummins	39	20	8	36	144	12.00	–	–	6
J.P.Faulkner	69	52	22	116	1032	34.40	1	4	21
A.J.Finch	88	84	1	148	3200	38.55	10	18	43
P.S.P.Handscomb	8	7	–	82	149	21.28	–	1	6
J.W.Hastings	29	21	11	51	271	27.10	–	1	5
J.R.Hazlewood	41	10	8	11*	21	10.50	–	–	12
T.M.Head	34	31	2	128	1064	36.68	1	7	11
S.D.Heazlett	1	1	–	4	4	4.00	–	–	–
M.C.Henriques	11	10	1	18	81	9.00	–	–	4
U.T.Khawaja	18	17	2	98	469	31.26	–	4	3
C.A.Lynn	1	1	–	16	16	16.00	–	–	–
N.M.Lyon	13	6	4	30	46	23.00	–	–	2
M.R.Marsh	53	49	9	102*	1428	35.70	1	11	25
S.E.Marsh	53	52	2	151	1896	37.92	3	12	13
G.J.Maxwell	81	72	8	102	2069	32.32	1	15	50
J.M.Mennie	2	2	–	1	1	1.00	–	–	–
T.D.Paine	30	30	3	111	854	31.62	1	5	41/4
J.A.Richardson	1	–	–	–	–	–	–	–	–
K.W.Richardson	15	5	2	19	30	10.00	–	–	2
P.M.Siddle	17	4	2	9*	21	10.50	–	–	1
S.P.D.Smith	108	94	12	164	3431	41.84	8	19	62
B.Stanlake	2	1	1	1*	1	–	–	–	–
M.A.Starc	72	35	16	52*	262	13.78	–	1	19
M.P.Stoinis	13	13	4	146*	566	62.88	1	4	4
A.J.Tye	4	4	2	8	23	11.50	–	–	1
M.S.Wade	94	80	11	100*	1777	25.75	1	10	108/9
D.A.Warner	106	104	4	179	4343	43.43	14	17	49
C.L.White	91	77	16	105	2072	33.96	2	11	37
A.Zampa	31	14	4	12	67	6.70	–	–	7

AUSTRALIA – BOWLING

	O	M	R	W	Avge	Best	4wI	R/Over
A.C.Agar	30	0	182	4	45.50	1-12	–	6.06
D.T.Christian	121.1	4	595	20	29.75	5-31	1	4.91
M.J.Cosgrove	5	0	13	1	13.00	1- 1	–	2.60
N.M.Coulter-Nile	185.2	5	985	37	26.62	4-48	1	5.31
P.J.Cummins	338	15	1821	64	28.45	4-24	4	5.38
J.P.Faulkner	535.1	12	2962	96	30.85	4-32	4	5.53
A.J.Finch	25.2	0	130	2	65.00	1- 2	–	5.13
J.W.Hastings	247.4	7	1256	42	29.90	6-45	2	5.07
J.R.Hazlewood	354.2	22	1675	69	24.27	6-52	4	4.72
T.M.Head	127.3	0	737	12	61.41	2-22	–	5.78
M.C.Henriques	59	1	306	7	43.71	3-32	–	5.18
N.M.Lyon	120	9	592	17	34.82	4-44	1	4.93
M.R.Marsh	283.2	6	1564	44	35.54	5-33	2	5.52
G.J.Maxwell	317.4	7	1765	45	39.22	4-46	2	5.55
J.M.Mennie	20	2	131	3	43.66	3-49	–	6.55
J.A.Richardson	10	1	57	2	28.50	2-57	–	5.70

AUSTRALIA – BOWLING (continued)

	O	M	R	W	Avge	Best	4wI	R/Over
K.W.Richardson	129.5	9	698	21	33.23	5-68	1	5.37
P.M.Siddle	125.1	9	581	15	38.73	3-55	–	4.64
S.P.D.Smith	174.2	1	931	27	34.48	3-16	–	5.34
B.Stanlake	13	1	68	1	68.00	1-55	–	5.23
M.A.Starc	598.5	32	2954	141	20.95	6-28	14	4.93
M.P.Stoinis	75.1	0	437	7	62.42	3-49	–	5.81
A.J.Tye	36.3	0	169	8	21.12	5-46	1	4.63
D.A.Warner	1	0	8	0	–	–	–	8.00
C.L.White	55.1	2	351	12	29.25	3- 5	–	6.36
A.Zampa	256.4	3	1459	42	34.73	3-16	–	5.68

SOUTH AFRICA – BATTING AND FIELDING

	M	I	NO	HS	Runs	Avge	100	50	Ct/St
K.J.Abbott	28	13	4	23	76	8.44	–	–	7
H.M.Amla	164	161	11	159	7535	50.23	26	35	81
T.Bavuma	2	2	–	113	161	80.50	1	–	1
F.Behardien	59	49	14	70	1074	30.68	–	6	27
Q.de Kock	90	90	5	178	3860	45.41	13	15	116/6
M.de Lange	4	–	–	–	–	–	–	–	–
A.B.de Villiers	223	213	39	176	9427	54.17	25	52	171/5
F.du Plessis	117	112	14	185	4379	44.68	9	29	60
J.P.Duminy	184	166	37	150*	4767	36.95	4	25	76
Imran Tahir	85	28	12	29	128	8.00	–	–	17
C.A.Ingram	31	29	3	124	843	32.42	3	3	12
H.Klaasen	4	4	1	43*	110	36.66	–	–	7
R.K.Kleinveldt	10	7	–	43	105	15.00	–	–	4
K.A.Maharaj	2	–	–	–	–	–	–	–	–
A.K.Markram	7	7	–	66	193	27.57	–	1	4
D.A.Miller	105	93	27	138*	2503	37.92	4	10	50
M.Morkel	114	45	17	32*	239	8.53	–	–	29
C.H.Morris	34	23	3	62	393	19.65	–	1	6
P.W.A.Mulder	1	1	–	2	2	2.00	–	–	–
L.T.Ngidi	4	3	2	6	10	10.00	–	–	1
W.D.Parnell	65	38	14	56	508	21.16	–	1	12
D.Paterson	3	–	–	–	–	–	–	–	2
A.L.Phehlukwayo	25	15	8	42*	225	32.14	–	–	5
D.Pretorius	12	5	–	50	86	17.20	–	1	3
K.Rabada	48	20	9	26	177	16.09	–	–	13
R.R.Rossouw	36	35	3	132	1239	38.71	3	7	22
T.Shamsi	7	3	2	0*	0	0.00	–	–	1
R.E.van der Merwe	13	7	3	12	39	9.75	–	–	3
D.Wiese	6	6	1	41*	102	20.40	–	–	–
K.Zondo	3	3	–	54	96	32.00	–	1	1

SOUTH AFRICA – BOWLING

	O	M	R	W	Avge	Best	4wI	R/Over
K.J.Abbott	217.1	13	1051	34	30.91	4-21	1	4.83
F.Behardien	124.4	2	719	14	51.35	3-19	–	5.76
M.de Lange	34.5	0	198	10	19.80	4-46	1	5.68
A.B.de Villiers	32	0	202	7	28.85	2-15	–	6.31
F.du Plessis	32	0	189	2	94.50	1- 8	–	5.90
J.P.Duminy	539.3	8	2891	65	44.47	4-16	1	5.35
Imran Tahir	736.3	30	3449	139	24.81	7-45	8	4.68
C.A.Ingram	1	0	17	0	–	–	–	17.00
R.K.Kleinveldt	85.3	6	448	12	37.33	4-22	1	5.23

	O	M	R	W	Avge	Best	4wI	R/Over
K.A.Maharaj	16.1	0	97	4	24.25	3-25	–	6.00
A.K.Markram	5	0	38	2	19.00	2-18	–	7.60
M.Morkel	930	45	4595	180	25.52	5-21	9	4.94
C.H.Morris	252	5	1415	35	40.42	4-31	2	5.61
P.W.A.Mulder	8	0	32	1	32.00	1-32	–	4.00
L.T.Ngidi	33	2	204	8	25.50	4-51	1	6.18
W.D.Parnell	485.1	20	2738	94	29.12	5-48	5	5.64
D.Paterson	26.5	0	180	4	45.00	3-44	–	6.70
A.L.Phehlukwayo	171.4	8	975	26	37.50	4-40	2	5.67
D.Pretorius	94.2	4	461	17	27.11	3- 5	–	4.88
K.Rabada	404.4	24	2068	75	27.57	6-16	5	5.11
R.R.Rossouw	7.3	0	44	1	44.00	1-17	–	5.86
T.Shamsi	57	4	278	7	39.71	3-36	–	4.87
R.E.van der Merwe	117.3	2	561	17	33.00	3-27	–	4.77
D.Wiese	49	0	316	9	35.11	3-50	–	6.44

WEST INDIES – BATTING AND FIELDING

	M	I	NO	HS	Runs	Avge	100	50	Ct/St
S.A.Ambris	1	1	1	38*	38	–	–	–	1
R.R.Beaton	2	2	1	12*	15	15.00	–	–	–
D.Bishoo	27	17	5	16	90	7.50	–	–	4
C.R.Brathwaite	25	23	2	33*	281	13.38	–	–	9
K.C.Brathwaite	10	10	–	78	278	27.80	–	1	3
J.L.Carter	28	25	2	54	524	22.78	–	3	7
S.Chanderpaul	268	251	40	150	8778	41.60	11	59	73
R.L.Chase	8	6	1	33*	68	13.60	–	–	4
S.S.Cottrell	5	4	2	8	14	7.00	–	–	1
M.L.Cummins	11	3	1	5	10	5.00	–	–	1
F.H.Edwards	50	22	14	13	73	9.12	–	–	4
S.T.Gabriel	18	13	7	12*	21	3.50	–	–	1
C.H.Gayle	274	269	17	215	9502	37.70	23	47	116
S.O.Hetmyer	5	5	–	127	202	40.40	1	–	3
J.O.Holder	73	58	16	99*	1183	28.16	–	6	30
K.A.Hope	7	6	–	46	138	23.00	–	–	1
S.D.Hope	29	26	3	101	878	38.17	1	4	31/3
A.S.Joseph	14	6	3	27	74	24.66	–	–	4
E.Lewis	28	25	1	176*	784	32.66	2	1	10
N.O.Miller	49	27	13	51	284	20.28	–	1	17
J.N.Mohammed	26	22	1	91*	529	25.19	–	4	3
A.R.Nurse	29	22	7	44	249	16.60	–	–	9
V.Permaul	7	4	1	10	19	6.33	–	–	1
K.O.A.Powell	39	37	–	83	897	24.24	–	8	10
R.Powell	19	16	1	101	398	26.53	1	1	8
R.Rampaul	92	40	11	86*	362	12.48	–	1	14
K.A.J.Roach	69	43	27	34	216	13.50	–	–	16
M.N.Samuels	195	184	26	133*	5282	33.43	10	28	50
J.E.Taylor	90	42	9	43*	278	8.42	–	–	20
C.A.K.Walton	9	8	–	19	53	6.62	–	–	9/1
K.O.K.Williams	8	5	4	168	19	19.00	–	–	–

WEST INDIES – BOWLING

	O	M	R	W	Avge	Best	4wI	R/Over
R.R.Beaton	17	1	102	1	102.00	1-60	–	6.00
D.Bishoo	226	6	1051	31	33.90	3-30	–	4.65
C.R.Brathwaite	192	8	1060	26	40.77	5-27	2	5.52

WEST INDIES – BOWLING (continued)

	O	M	R	W	Avge	Best	4wI	R/Over
K.C.Brathwaite	25.2	0	140	1	140.00	1-56	–	5.52
J.L.Carter	20.4	0	141	3	47.00	2-14	–	6.82
S.Chanderpaul	123.2	0	636	14	45.42	3-18	–	5.15
R.L.Chase	6.5	1	48	1	48.00	1-15	–	7.02
S.S.Cottrell	33.4	0	210	7	30.00	3-62	–	6.23
M.L.Cummins	75	3	474	9	52.66	3-82	–	6.32
F.H.Edwards	356.2	23	1812	60	30.20	6-22	2	5.08
S.T.Gabriel	139.5	5	782	23	34.00	3-17	–	5.59
C.H.Gayle	1195.5	38	5705	163	34.85	5-46	4	4.76
J.O.Holder	581.2	37	3166	98	32.30	5-27	5	5.44
A.S.Joseph	110.1	3	706	23	30.69	5-56	2	6.40
N.O.Miller	345.1	16	1619	44	36.79	4-43	2	4.69
J.N.Mohammed	22.2	1	116	0	–	–	–	5.19
A.R.Nurse	224.2	3	1160	30	38.66	4-62	1	5.17
V.Permaul	55.1	0	271	8	33.87	3-40	–	4.91
R.Powell	19.2	0	119	1	119.00	1-38	–	6.15
R.Rampaul	672.1	33	3434	117	29.35	5-49	10	5.10
K.A.J.Roach	578.1	43	2869	104	27.58	6-27	6	4.96
M.N.Samuels	834.5	22	4040	85	47.52	3-25	–	4.83
J.E.Taylor	723.3	31	3780	128	29.53	5-48	4	5.22
K.O.K.Williams	55	0	293	9	32.55	4-43	1	5.32

NEW ZEALAND – BATTING AND FIELDING

	M	I	NO	HS	Runs	Avge	100	50	Ct/St
C.J.Anderson	49	45	5	131*	1109	27.72	1	4	11
T.D.Astle	6	4	2	49	69	34.50	–	–	2
H.K.Bennett	16	7	5	4*	10	5.00	–	–	3
T.A.Boult	66	29	18	21*	121	11.00	–	–	15
D.A.J.Bracewell	16	9	2	30	79	11.28	–	–	3
N.T.Broom	39	39	4	109*	943	26.94	1	5	9
D.G.Brownlie	16	15	1	63	361	25.78	–	1	6
M.S.Chapman	5	5	1	124*	160	40.00	1	–	1
C.de Grandhomme	19	16	5	74*	389	35.36	–	1	4
G.D.Elliott	83	69	11	115	1976	34.06	2	11	17
L.H.Ferguson	16	8	3	19	40	8.00	–	–	4
J.E.C.Franklin	110	80	27	98*	1270	23.96	–	4	26
M.J.Guptill	159	156	17	237*	5976	42.99	13	34	76
M.J.Henry	35	14	5	48*	170	18.88	–	–	11
S.C.Kuggeleijn	2	1	1	11*	11	–	–	–	–
T.W.M.Latham	74	72	8	137	2134	33.34	4	11	49/5
A.F.Milne	40	17	7	36	168	16.80	–	–	21
C.Munro	40	36	1	87	905	25.85	–	6	16
J.D.S.Neesham	41	37	7	74	811	27.03	–	4	17
H.M.Nicholls	27	255	7	83*	595	33.05	–	6	12
J.S.Patel	43	15	8	34	95	13.57	–	–	13
S.H.A.Rance	2	–	–	–	–	–	–	–	3
L.Ronchi †	81	66	9	170*	1321	23.17	1	3	100/10
M.J.Santner	53	42	15	67	771	28.55	–	2	21
I.S.Sodhi	22	7	1	5	13	2.16	–	–	4
T.G.Southee	133	80	29	55	626	12.27	–	1	37
L.R.P.L.Taylor	204	190	33	181*	7267	46.28	19	41	130
B.J.Watling	27	25	2	96*	573	24.91	–	5	20
K.S.Williamson	127	121	11	145*	5156	46.87	11	33	53
G.H.Worker	7	7	1	58	225	37.50	–	3	2

NEW ZEALAND – BOWLING

	O	M	R	W	Avge	Best	4wI	R/Over
C.J.Anderson	247.3	10	1502	60	25.03	5-63	3	6.06
T.D.Astle	28	1	150	7	21.42	3-33	–	5.35
H.K.Bennett	119.4	4	621	27	23.00	4-16	2	5.18
T.A.Boult	590.2	41	3006	122	24.63	7-34	9	5.09
D.A.J.Bracewell	132.2	15	667	22	30.31	4-55	1	5.04
C.de Grandhomme	104	2	562	10	56.20	2-40	–	5.40
G.D.Elliott	217	8	1179	39	30.23	4-31	1	5.43
L.H.Ferguson	128	1	748	21	35.61	3-17	–	5.84
J.E.C.Franklin	641.2	34	3354	81	41.40	5-42	1	5.22
M.J.Guptill	18.1	0	98	4	24.50	2- 6	–	5.39
M.J.Henry	295.5	15	1648	67	24.59	5-30	7	5.57
S.C.Kuggeleijn	14	2	58	5	11.60	3-41	–	4.14
A.F.Milne	300.1	7	1581	41	38.56	3-49	–	5.26
C.Munro	75	1	386	7	55.14	2-10	–	5.14
J.D.S.Neesham	198.2	2	1293	34	38.02	4-42	2	6.51
J.S.Patel	335.4	9	1691	49	34.51	3-11	–	5.03
S.H.A.Rance	17.3	1	110	1	110.00	1-44	–	6.28
M.J.Santner	408.1	6	2001	59	33.91	5-50	1	4.90
I.S.Sodhi	182.2	5	1025	29	35.34	4-58	1	5.62
T.G.Southee	1111.3	70	6669	176	34.14	7-33	6	5.40
L.R.P.L.Taylor	7	0	35	0	–	–	–	5.00
K.S.Williamson	221.3	2	1207	35	34.48	4-22	1	5.44
G.H.Worker	1	0	5	0	–	–	–	5.00

† L.Ronchi has also made 4 appearances for Australia.

INDIA – BATTING AND FIELDING

	M	I	NO	HS	Runs	Avge	100	50	Ct/St
R.Ashwin	111	61	19	65	675	16.07	–	1	30
J.J.Bumrah	37	5	2	10*	11	3.66	–	–	12
Y.S.Chahal	23	2	1	1	1	1.00	–	–	4
S.Dhawan	102	101	6	137	4361	45.90	13	25	46
M.S.Dhoni	315	269	77	183*	9793	51.00	9	67	294/104
S.S.Iyer	6	5	–	88	210	42.00	–	2	3
R.A.Jadeja	136	93	32	87	1914	31.37	–	10	51
K.M.Jadhav	40	27	7	120	798	39.90	2	3	19
K.D.Karthik	79	67	17	79	1496	29.92	–	9	53/7
V.Kohli	208	200	35	183	9588	58.10	35	46	100
Kuldeep Yadav	20	7	5	19	23	11.50	–	–	2
B.Kumar	86	40	14	53*	379	14.57	–	1	23
Mohammed Shami	50	23	12	25	116	10.54	–	–	16
M.K.Pandey	22	17	6	104*	432	39.27	1	2	6
H.H.Pandya	38	25	4	83	628	29.90	–	4	16
A.R.Patel	38	20	6	38	181	12.92	–	–	15
C.A.Pujara	5	5	–	27	51	10.20	–	–	–
A.M.Rahane	90	87	3	111	2962	35.26	3	24	48
K.L.Rahul	10	9	2	100*	248	35.42	1	1	5
I.Sharma	80	28	13	13	72	4.80	–	–	19
R.G.Sharma	180	174	26	264	6594	44.55	17	34	60
S.N.Thakur	3	–	–	–	–	–	–	–	3
Washington Sundar	1	–	–	–	–	–	–	–	1
U.T.Yadav	71	23	14	18*	79	8.77	–	–	20
Yuvraj Singh	301	275	39	150	8609	36.47	14	52	93

LOI   **INDIA – BOWLING**

	O	M	R	W	Avge	Best	4wI	R/Over
R.Ashwin	1003.3	35	4937	150	32.91	4-25	1	4.91
J.J.Bumrah	309.5	19	1440	64	22.50	5-27	4	4.64
Y.S.Chahal	197.1	10	939	43	21.83	5-22	2	4.76
M.S.Dhoni	6	0	31	1	31.00	1-14	–	5.16
S.S.Iyer	1	0	2	0	–	–	–	2.00
R.A.Jadeja	1134.2	45	5561	155	35.87	5-36	6	4.90
K.M.Jadhav	98.5	0	593	16	32.00	3-29	–	5.18
V.Kohli	106.5	1	665	4	166.25	1-15	–	6.22
Kuldeep Yadav	162.4	6	781	39	20.02	4-23	2	4.80
B.Kumar	690.4	57	3448	90	38.31	5-42	3	4.99
Mohammed Shami	420.5	29	2309	91	25.37	4-35	6	5.48
H.H.Pandya	267.2	3	1458	39	37.38	3-31	–	5.45
A.R.Patel	318	13	1409	45	31.31	3-34	–	4.43
I.Sharma	622.1	29	3563	115	30.98	4-34	6	5.72
R.G.Sharma	98.5	2	515	8	64.37	2-27	–	5.21
S.N.Thakur	21.5	0	126	5	25.20	4-52	1	5.77
Washington Sundar	10	0	65	1	65.00	1-65	–	6.50
U.T.Yadav	553.1	23	3290	102	32.25	4-31	4	5.94
Yuvraj Singh	831.2	18	4227	110	38.42	5-31	3	5.08

PAKISTAN – BATTING AND FIELDING

	M	I	NO	HS	Runs	Avge	100	50	Ct/St
Aamer Yamin	4	3	2	62	95	95.00	–	1	–
Ahmed Shehzad	81	81	1	124	2605	32.56	6	14	28
Asad Shafiq	60	58	4	84	1336	24.74	–	9	14
Azhar Ali	53	53	3	102	1845	36.90	3	12	8
Babar Azam	41	40	5	125*	1789	51.11	7	7	22
Faheem Ashraf	8	7	2	23	78	15.60	–	–	3
Fakhar Zaman	13	13	1	114	550	45.83	1	4	8
Haris Sohail	24	23	3	89*	887	44.35	–	9	9
Hasan Ali	30	13	4	51	108	12.00	–	1	8
Imad Wasim	30	21	9	63*	430	35.83	–	3	8
Imam-ul-Haq	4	4	1	100	149	49.66	1	–	–
Junaid Khan	66	26	13	25	60	4.61	–	–	5
Kamran Akmal	157	138	14	124	3236	26.09	5	10	157/31
Mohammad Amir	40	25	8	73*	328	19.29	–	2	6
Mohammad Hafeez	200	199	13	140*	6107	32.83	11	34	76
Mohammad Nawaz[3]	10	9	2	53	166	23.71	–	–	2
Mohammad Rizwan	25	22	6	75*	460	28.75	–	3	24
Rumman Raees	9	4	1	16	27	9.00	–	–	2
Sarfraz Ahmed	85	64	13	105	1729	33.90	2	8	85/22
Shadab Khan	17	7	3	54	206	51.50	–	3	5
Sharjeel Khan	25	25	–	152	812	32.48	1	6	6
Shoaib Malik	261	236	38	143	6975	35.22	9	41	92
Sohail Khan	13	6	1	7	25	5.00	–	–	3
Umar Akmal	116	105	17	102*	3044	34.59	2	20	77/13
Umar Amin	16	16	1	59	271	18.06	–	1	6
Usman Khan	2	–	–	–	–	–	–	–	1
Wahab Riaz	79	56	13	54*	589	13.69	–	2	23

PAKISTAN – BOWLING

	O	M	R	W	Avge	Best	4wI	R/Over
Aamer Yamin	26	1	154	2	77.00	1-38	–	5.92
Ahmed Shehzad	19.1	1	140	2	70.00	1-22	–	7.30
Asad Shafiq	2	0	18	0	–	–	–	9.00

PAKISTAN – BOWLING (continued)

	O	M	R	W	Avge	Best	4wI	R/Over
Azhar Ali	43	0	260	4	65.00	2-26	–	6.04
Faheem Ashraf	50.2	1	258	7	36.85	2-37	–	5.12
Fakhar Zaman	6.3	0	44	1	44.00	1-19	–	6.76
Haris Sohail	82	0	473	10	47.30	3-45	–	5.76
Hasan Ali	250.5	8	1327	62	21.40	5-34	4	5.29
Imad Wasim	210.3	4	945	28	33.75	5-14	1	4.48
Junaid Khan	518.1	28	2747	97	28.31	4-12	3	5.30
Mohammad Amir	339.1	22	1653	57	29.00	4-28	1	4.87
Mohammad Hafeez	1218.5	47	5019	136	36.90	4-41	1	4.11
Mohammad Nawaz[3]	77.3	1	405	11	36.81	4-42	1	5.22
Rumman Raees	77.1	2	464	14	33.14	3-49	–	6.01
Shadab Khan	140	3	690	24	28.75	3-42	–	4.92
Shoaib Malik	1277.5	38	5953	154	38.65	4-19	1	4.65
Sohail Khan	111	4	597	19	31.42	5-55	1	5.37
Umar Amin	7	0	24	0	–	–	–	3.42
Usman Khan	13.3	0	72	6	12.00	5-34	1	5.33
Wahab Riaz	615.5	19	3503	102	34.34	5-46	5	5.68

SRI LANKA – BATTING AND FIELDING

	M	I	NO	HS	Runs	Avge	100	50	Ct/St
M.A.Aponso	6	5	4	2*	6	6.00	–	–	–
P.V.D.Chameera	20	12	6	19*	90	15.00	–	–	4
L.D.Chandimal	139	126	21	111	3433	32.69	4	21	58/7
M.K.P.A.D.Dananjaya	19	14	2	50*	154	12.83	–	1	7
D.M.de Silva	17	16	2	78*	335	23.92	–	3	8
P.C.de Silva	7	7	1	44	94	15.66	–	–	4
P.W.H.de Silva	9	7	1	22	63	10.50	–	–	4
D.P.D.N.Dickwella	36	34	1	116	1074	32.54	2	5	28/6
A.M.Fernando	1	–	–	–	–	–	–	–	–
A.N.P.R.Fernando	28	12	8	7	18	4.50	–	–	6
M.V.T.Fernando	6	6	4	7*	27	13.50	–	–	2
P.L.S.Gamage	9	5	3	3	4	2.00	–	–	2
D.A.S.Gunaratne	29	23	4	114*	558	29.36	1	1	10
M.D.Gunathilleke	33	32	1	116	957	30.87	1	7	12
G.S.N.F.G.Jayasuriya	6	4	1	31	51	17.00	–	–	3
C.K.Kapugedera	102	84	7	95	1624	21.09	–	8	31
K.M.D.N.Kulasekara	184	123	37	73	1327	15.43	–	4	46
C.B.R.L.S.Kumara	4	3	2	5	6	6.00	–	–	1
D.S.M.Kumara	1	1	–	7	7	7.00	–	–	–
R.A.S.Lakmal	75	40	19	26	161	7.66	–	–	14
L.D.Madushanka	4	4	1	7	14	4.66	–	–	–
S.L.Malinga	204	102	31	56	496	6.98	–	1	29
A.D.Mathews	196	166	44	139*	5107	41.86	2	35	48
B.K.G.Mendis	44	42	2	102	1239	30.97	1	11	23
E.M.D.Y.Munaweera	2	2	–	11	15	7.50	–	–	2
S.S.Pathirana	18	14	1	56	332	25.53	–	1	4
M.D.K.Perera	12	11	–	30	123	11.18	–	–	2
M.D.K.J.Perera	73	70	5	135	1856	28.55	3	9	27/2
N.L.T.C.Perera	133	101	14	80*	1586	18.22	–	8	52
S.Prasanna	38	35	3	95	405	12.65	–	2	6
P.M.Pushpakumara	2	2	–	8	11	5.50	–	–	2
W.S.R.Samarawickrama	3	3	–	42	42	14.00	–	–	–
P.A.D.L.R.Sandakan	12	6	2	5	11	2.75	–	–	3
T.A.M.Siriwardana	26	23	1	66	513	23.31	–	3	5
W.U.Tharanga	223	212	17	174*	6780	34.76	15	37	48
H.D.R.L.Thirimanne	117	97	12	139*	2946	34.65	4	20	37

	M	I	NO	HS	Runs	Avge	100	50	Ct/St
J.D.F.Vandersay	11	7	1	25	71	11.83	–	–	1
D.S.Weerakkody	3	3	–	58	73	24.33	–	1	2

SRI LANKA – BOWLING

	O	M	R	W	Avge	Best	4wI	R/Over
M.A.Aponso	52	1	258	7	36.85	4-18	1	4.96
P.V.D.Chameera	125.1	5	678	15	45.20	3-51	–	5.41
M.K.P.A.D.Dananjaya	156.1	4	777	21	37.00	6-54	2	4.97
D.M.de Silva	40	0	212	4	53.00	2-35	–	5.30
P.C.de Silva	52.4	2	256	5	51.20	2-29	–	4.86
P.W.H.de Silva	43.1	0	296	9	32.88	3-15	–	6.05
A.M.Fernando	2	0	22	0	–	–	–	11.00
A.N.P.R.Fernando	216.2	12	1287	33	39.00	3-28	–	5.94
M.V.T.Fernando	39.3	4	247	3	82.33	1-35	–	6.25
P.L.S.Gamage	67	3	392	9	43.55	4-57	1	5.85
D.A.S.Gunaratne	130	3	678	22	30.81	3-10	–	5.21
M.D.Gunathilleke	47	1	268	6	44.66	3-48	–	5.70
G.S.N.F.G.Jayasuriya	16	0	89	1	89.00	1-15	–	5.56
C.K.Kapugedera	44	0	225	2	112.50	1-24	–	5.11
K.M.D.N.Kulasekara	1377.1	106	6751	199	33.92	5-22	5	4.90
C.B.R.L.S.Kumara	30	0	256	4	64.00	2-73	–	8.53
D.S.M.Kumara	6.1	1	26	3	8.66	3-26	–	4.21
R.A.S.Lakmal	573.2	34	3072	98	31.34	4-13	3	5.35
L.D.Madushanka	24	0	172	4	43.00	2-70	–	7.16
S.L.Malinga	1638.2	93	8705	301	28.92	6-38	16	5.31
A.D.Mathews	845.1	54	3901	114	34.21	6-20	2	4.61
B.K.G.Mendis	3.2	0	28	0	–	–	–	8.40
S.S.Pathirana	127.3	2	720	15	48.00	3-37	–	5.64
M.D.K.Perera	73	1	384	13	29.53	3-48	–	5.26
N.L.T.C.Perera	807.1	25	4667	149	31.32	6-44	7	5.78
S.Prasanna	309.1	9	1673	32	52.28	3-32	–	5.41
P.M.Pushpakumara	19	0	105	1	105.00	1-40	–	5.52
P.A.D.L.R.Sandakan	90.2	0	571	15	38.06	4-52	1	6.32
T.A.M.Siriwardana	98.1	2	530	9	58.88	2-27	–	5.39
H.D.R.L.Thirimanne	17.2	0	94	3	31.33	2-36	–	5.42
J.D.F.Vandersay	74.5	2	430	10	43.00	3-50	–	5.74

A.N.P.R.Fernando is also known as N.Pradeep.

ZIMBABWE – BATTING AND FIELDING

	M	I	NO	HS	Runs	Avge	100	50	Ct/St
R.P.Burl	13	11	2	30*	139	15.44	–	–	6
T.L.Chatara	52	34	13	23	148	7.04	–	–	5
T.S.Chisoro	13	10	6	42*	84	21.00	–	–	6
A.G.Cremer	92	67	20	58	732	15.57	–	1	35
C.R.Ervine	76	73	10	130*	2029	32.20	2	11	35
S.M.Ervine	42	34	7	100	698	25.85	1	2	5
K.M.Jarvis	31	21	6	20	91	6.06	–	–	7
H.Masakadza	189	188	4	178*	5307	28.84	5	33	69
S.F.Mire	33	33	–	112	734	22.24	1	3	8
P.J.Moor	30	27	2	52	443	17.72	–	2	18/1
C.B.Mpofu	79	39	19	6	46	2.30	–	–	11
C.T.Mumba	2	2	1	2*	3	3.00	–	–	1
T.K.Musakanda	11	11	1	60	249	24.90	–	1	8
B.Muzarabani	10	8	3	1*	2	0.40	–	–	5
R.Ngarava	6	4	1	10	12	4.00	–	–	1

ZIMBABWE – BATTING AND FIELDING (continued)

	M	I	NO	HS	Runs	Avge	100	50	Ct/St
Sikandar Raza	81	78	12	141	2255	34.16	3	12	30
B.R.M.Taylor	178	177	15	145*	5720	35.30	9	34	103/25
D.T.Tiripano	15	11	3	19	84	10.50	–	–	–
B.V.Vitori	24	14	3	20*	86	7.81	–	–	4
M.N.Waller	79	72	6	99*	1259	19.07	–	5	22
S.C.Williams	112	108	14	102	2957	31.45	1	26	39
C.Zhuwao	3	3	–	45	61	20.30	–	–	–

ZIMBABWE – BOWLING

	O	M	R	W	Avge	Best	4wI	R/Over
R.P.Burl	13.4	0	81	2	40.50	1- 2	–	5.92
T.L.Chatara	429.2	36	2184	70	31.20	4-33	1	5.08
T.S.Chisoro	94	6	398	14	28.42	3-16	–	4.23
A.G.Cremer	741.4	26	3459	111	31.16	6-46	7	4.66
S.M.Ervine	274.5	10	1561	41	38.07	3-29	–	5.67
K.M.Jarvis	250.4	9	1488	36	41.33	3-36	–	5.93
H.Masakadza	300.2	5	1590	38	41.84	3-39	–	5.29
S.F.Mire	69.3	0	433	7	61.85	3-49	–	6.23
C.B.Mpofu	617.5	40	3340	87	38.39	6-52	3	5.40
C.T.Mumba	10.2	0	67	0	–	–	–	6.48
T.K.Musakanda	2	0	11	0	–	–	–	5.50
B.Muzarabani	73	2	402	12	33.50	4-47	1	5.50
R.Ngarava	46	2	274	8	34.25	2-37	–	5.95
Sikandar Raza	355.2	15	1726	44	39.22	3-21	–	4.85
B.R.M.Taylor	66	0	406	9	45.11	3-54	–	6.15
D.T.Tiripano	79.5	6	447	14	31.92	5-63	1	5.39
B.V.Vitori	198.5	4	1149	32	35.90	5-20	2	5.77
M.N.Waller	111	0	566	10	56.60	2-44	–	5.09
S.C.Williams	540.4	19	2646	54	49.00	3-15	–	4.89
C.Zhuwao	3	0	15	0	–	–	–	5.00

BANGLADESH – BATTING AND FIELDING

	M	I	NO	HS	Runs	Avge	100	50	Ct/St
Abul Hasan	7	3	–	7	11	3.66	–	–	1
Anumul Haque	34	31	–	120	1005	32.41	3	3	10
Imrul Kayes	70	70	1	112	1998	28.95	2	14	21
Liton Das	12	12	1	36	165	15.00	–	–	9
Mahmudullah	153	133	35	128*	3327	33.94	3	18	52
Mashrafe Mortaza	185	136	22	51*	1602	14.05	–	1	55
Mehedi Hasan	8	5	–	51	91	18.20	–	1	1
Mohammad Mithun	3	2	–	26	36	18.00	–	–	1
Mohammad Saifuddin	3	3	1	16	30	15.00	–	–	1
Mosaddek Hossain	18	15	6	50*	288	32.00	–	1	8
Mushfiqur Rahim	184	170	27	117	4718	32.99	5	28	146/41
Mustafizur Rahman	27	13	10	18*	36	12.00	–	–	6
Nasir Hossain	65	52	8	100	1281	29.11	1	6	34
Nurul Hasan	2	2	–	44	68	34.00	–	–	2/1
Rubel Hossain	85	43	22	17	116	5.52	–	–	13
Sabbir Rahman	51	45	5	65	1027	25.67	–	5	29
Shakib Al Hasan	185	174	24	134*	5243	34.95	7	37	43
Soumya Sarkar	32	31	3	127*	967	34.53	1	6	15
Subashis Roy	1	1	1	1*	1	–	–	–	1
Sunzamul Islam	3	1	–	19	19	19.00	–	–	–
Tamim Iqbal	179	177	5	154	6018	34.98	9	41	43
Tanbir Hayder	2	2	–	3	5	2.50	–	–	1
Taskin Ahmed	32	16	6	14	41	4.10	–	–	7

LOI   **BANGLADESH – BOWLING**

	O	M	R	W	Avge	Best	4wI	R/Over
Abul Hasan	36	1	244	0	–	–	–	6.77
Mahmudullah	621	14	3197	70	45.67	3- 4	–	5.14
Mashrafe Mortaza	1535.5	114	7313	237	30.85	6-26	7	4.76
Mehedi Hasan	59	1	303	7	43.28	2-43	–	5.13
Mohammad Saifuddin	11	0	75	1	75.00	1-15	–	6.81
Mosaddek Hossain	71.2	1	365	10	36.50	3-13	–	5.11
Mustafizur Rahman	211.1	13	979	51	19.19	6-43	4	4.63
Nasir Hossain	209.2	4	988	24	41.16	3-26	–	4.71
Rubel Hossain	629.4	22	3555	107	33.22	6-26	8	5.64
Sabbir Rahman	35.2	0	244	3	81.33	1-12	–	6.90
Shakib Al Hasan	1557.1	79	6924	235	29.46	5-47	8	4.44
Soumya Sarkar	13	0	70	0	–	–	–	5.38
Subashis Roy	10	1	45	1	45.00	1-45	–	4.50
Sunzamul Islam	25	–	79	5	15.80	2-22	–	3.16
Tamim Iqbal	1	0	13	0	–	–	–	13.00
Tanbir Hayder	10	–	67	0	–	–	–	6.70
Taskin Ahmed	235.3	6	1401	45	31.13	5-28	3	5.94

ASSOCIATES – BATTING AND FIELDING

	M	I	NO	HS	Runs	Avge	100	50	Ct/St
J.H.Davey (Scotland)	29	26	5	64	471	22.42	–	2	9
B.J.McCarthy (Ireland)	19	11	2	16*	75	8.33	–	–	6
Mohammad Nabi (Afghan)	94	84	10	116	2211	29.87	1	11	48
E.J.G.Morgan (Ireland)	23	23	2	115	744	35.42	1	5	9
T.J.Murtagh (Ireland)	37	24	7	23*	148	8.70	–	–	9
S.W.Poynter (Ireland)	16	15	4	36	170	15.45	–	–	17
W.B.Rankin (Ireland)	45	19	13	18*	54	9.00	–	–	11
Rashid Khan (Afghan)	40	31	4	60*	565	20.92	–	2	12
R.A.J.Smith (Scotland)	2	1	–	10	10	10.00	–	–	–
C.B.Sole (Scotland)	8	4	–	4	9	2.25	–	–	3
P.R.Stirling (Ireland)	92	90	2	177	3055	34.71	6	15	35
R.N.ten Doeschate (Neth)	33	32	9	119	1541	67.00	5	9	13
T.van der Gugten (Neth)	4	2	–	2	4	2.00	–	–	–
P.A.van Meekeren (Neth)	2	1	1	15*	15	–	–	–	–
B.T.J.Wheal (Scotland)	7	4	3	2*	2	2.00	–	–	–
S.G.Whittingham (Scotland)	4	3	2	3*	6	6.00	~	~	3
G.C.Wilson (Ireland)	92	86	11	113	1862	24.82	1	12	62/10

ASSOCIATES – BOWLING

	O	M	R	W	Avge	Best	4wI	R/Over
J.H.Davey	199.5	18	1014	47	21.57	6-28	3	5.07
B.J.McCarthy	164.2	6	970	41	23.65	5-46	3	5.90
Mohammad Nabi	730	29	3130	99	31.61	4-30	2	4.28
T.J.Murtagh	314	24	1428	39	36.61	4-32	1	4.54
W.B.Rankin	363.2	27	1762	59	29.86	4-44	1	4.84
Rashid Khan	325.3	19	1286	90	14.28	7-18	7	3.95
R.A.J.Smith	15	0	97	1	97.00	1-34	–	6.46
C.B.Sole	63	4	282	13	21.69	4-28	1	4.47
P.R.Stirling	380.4	3	1819	40	45.47	6-55	2	4.77
R.N.ten Doeschate	263.2	18	1327	55	24.12	4-31	3	5.03
T.van der Gugten	21	3	85	8	10.62	5-24	1	4.04
P.A.van Meekeren	11	0	79	1	79.00	1-54	–	7.18
B.T.J.Wheal	59.5	6	265	10	26.50	3-36	–	4.42
S.G.Whittingham	33.5	2	174	7	24.85	3-58	–	5.14

LIMITED-OVERS INTERNATIONALS RESULTS

1970-71 to 11 March 2018

This chart excludes all matches involving multinational teams.

	Opponents	Matches	E	A	SA	WI	NZ	I	P	SL	Z	B	Ass	Tied	NR
England	Australia	142	56	81	–	–	–	–	–	–	–	–	–	2	3
	South Africa	59	26	–	29	–	–	–	–	–	–	–	–	1	3
	West Indies	96	49	–	–	42	–	–	–	–	–	–	–	–	5
	New Zealand	89	40	–	–	–	43	–	–	–	–	–	–	2	4
	India	96	39	–	–	–	–	52	–	–	–	–	–	2	3
	Pakistan	82	49	–	–	–	–	–	31	–	–	–	–	–	2
	Sri Lanka	69	33	–	–	–	–	–	–	34	–	–	–	1	1
	Zimbabwe	30	21	–	–	–	–	–	–	–	8	–	–	–	1
	Bangladesh	20	16	–	–	–	–	–	–	–	–	4	–	–	–
	Associates	24	21	–	–	–	–	–	–	–	–	–	1	–	2
Australia	South Africa	96	–	47	45	–	–	–	–	–	–	–	–	3	1
	West Indies	139	–	73	–	60	–	–	–	–	–	–	–	3	3
	New Zealand	136	–	90	–	–	39	–	–	–	–	–	–	–	7
	India	128	–	73	–	–	–	45	–	–	–	–	–	–	10
	Pakistan	98	–	62	–	–	–	–	32	–	–	–	–	1	3
	Sri Lanka	96	–	60	–	–	–	–	–	32	–	–	–	–	4
	Zimbabwe	30	–	27	–	–	–	–	–	–	2	–	–	–	1
	Bangladesh	20	–	18	–	–	–	–	–	–	–	1	–	–	1
	Associates	23	–	22	–	–	–	–	–	–	–	–	0	–	1
S Africa	West Indies	61	–	–	44	15	–	–	–	–	–	–	–	1	1
	New Zealand	70	–	–	41	–	24	–	–	–	–	–	–	–	5
	India	83	–	–	46	–	–	34	–	–	–	–	–	–	3
	Pakistan	73	–	–	47	–	–	–	25	–	–	–	–	–	1
	Sri Lanka	66	–	–	35	–	–	–	–	29	–	–	–	1	1
	Zimbabwe	38	–	–	35	–	–	–	–	–	2	–	–	–	1
	Bangladesh	20	–	–	17	–	–	–	–	–	–	3	–	–	–
	Associates	23	–	–	23	–	–	–	–	–	–	–	0	–	–
W Indies	New Zealand	64	–	–	–	30	27	–	–	–	–	–	–	–	7
	India	121	–	–	–	61	–	56	–	–	–	–	–	1	3
	Pakistan	133	–	–	–	70	–	–	60	–	–	–	–	3	–
	Sri Lanka	56	–	–	–	28	–	–	–	25	–	–	–	–	2
	Zimbabwe	47	–	–	–	35	–	–	–	–	10	–	–	1	1
	Bangladesh	28	–	–	–	19	–	–	–	–	–	7	–	–	2
	Associates	28	–	–	–	23	–	–	–	–	–	–	3	–	2
N Zealand	India	101	–	–	–	–	44	51	–	–	–	–	–	1	5
	Pakistan	103	–	–	–	–	47	–	53	–	–	–	–	1	2
	Sri Lanka	95	–	–	–	–	45	–	–	41	–	–	–	1	8
	Zimbabwe	38	–	–	–	–	27	–	–	–	9	–	–	1	1
	Bangladesh	31	–	–	–	–	21	–	–	–	–	10	–	–	–
	Associates	17	–	–	–	–	17	–	–	–	–	–	0	–	–
India	Pakistan	129	–	–	–	–	–	52	73	–	–	–	–	–	4
	Sri Lanka	158	–	–	–	–	–	90	–	56	–	–	–	1	11
	Zimbabwe	63	–	–	–	–	–	51	–	–	10	–	–	2	–
	Bangladesh	33	–	–	–	–	–	27	–	–	–	5	–	–	1
	Associates	27	–	–	–	–	–	25	–	–	–	–	2	–	–
Pakistan	Sri Lanka	153	–	–	–	–	–	–	90	58	–	–	–	1	4
	Zimbabwe	54	–	–	–	–	–	–	47	–	4	–	–	1	2
	Bangladesh	35	–	–	–	–	–	–	31	–	–	4	–	–	–
	Associates	29	–	–	–	–	–	–	27	–	–	–	1	–	1
Sri Lanka	Zimbabwe	57	–	–	–	–	–	–	–	44	11	–	–	–	2
	Bangladesh	44	–	–	–	–	–	–	–	36	–	6	–	–	2
	Associates	22	–	–	–	–	–	–	–	21	–	–	1	–	–
Zimbabwe	Bangladesh	69	–	–	–	–	–	–	–	–	28	41	–	–	–
	Associates	76	–	–	–	–	–	–	–	–	49	–	24	1	2
Bangladesh	Associates	40	–	–	–	–	–	–	–	–	–	27	12	1	1
Associates	Associates	225	–	–	–	–	–	–	–	–	–	–	215	1	9
		3984	350	553	362	383	334	483	469	376	133	108	260	34	139

MERIT TABLE OF ALL L-O INTERNATIONALS

	Matches	Won	Lost	Tied	No Result	% Won (exc NR)
Australia	908	553	312	9	34	63.27
South Africa	589	362	205	6	16	63.17
Pakistan	889	469	394	8	18	53.84
India	939	483	409	7	40	53.72
West Indies	773	383	354	9	27	51.34
England	707	350	325	8	24	51.24
Sri Lanka	816	376	399	5	36	48.20
New Zealand	744	334	365	6	39	47.37
Bangladesh	340	108	225	–	7	32.42
Zimbabwe	502	133	354	6	11	27.08
Associate Members (v Full*)	309	45	255	1	8	14.95

* Results of games between two Associate Members and those involving multi-national sides are excluded from this list; Associate Members have participated in 486 LOIs, 225 LOIs being between Associate Members.

TEAM RECORDS

HIGHEST TOTALS

† Batting Second

444-3	(50 overs)	England v Pakistan	Nottingham	2016
443-9	(50 overs)	Sri Lanka v Netherlands	Amstelveen	2006
439-2	(50 overs)	South Africa v West Indies	Johannesburg	2014-15
438-9†	(49.5 overs)	South Africa v Australia	Johannesburg	2005-06
438-4	(50 overs)	South Africa v India	Mumbai	2015-16
434-4	(50 overs)	Australia v South Africa	Johannesburg	2005-06
418-5	(50 overs)	South Africa v Zimbabwe	Potchefstroom	2006-07
418-5	(50 overs)	India v West Indies	Indore	2011-12
417-6	(50 overs)	Australia v Afghanistan	Perth	2014-15
414-7	(50 overs)	India v Sri Lanka	Rajkot	2009-10
413-5	(50 overs)	India v Bermuda	Port of Spain	2006-07
411-8†	(50 overs)	Sri Lanka v India	Rajkot	2009-10
411-4	(50 overs)	South Africa v Ireland	Canberra	2014-15
408-5	(50 overs)	South Africa v West Indies	Sydney	2014-15
408-9	(50 overs)	England v New Zealand	Birmingham	2015
404-5	(50 overs)	India v Sri Lanka	Kolkata	2014-15
402-2	(50 overs)	New Zealand v Ireland	Aberdeen	2008
401-3	(50 overs)	India v South Africa	Gwalior	2009-10
399-6	(50 overs)	South Africa v Zimbabwe	Benoni	2010-11
399-9	(50 overs)	England v South Africa	Bloemfontein	2015-16
398-5	(50 overs)	Sri Lanka v Kenya	Kandy	1995-96
398-5	(50 overs)	New Zealand v England	The Oval	2015
397-5	(44 overs)	New Zealand v Zimbabwe	Bulawayo	2005
393-6	(50 overs)	New Zealand v West Indies	Wellington	2014-15
392-6	(50 overs)	South Africa v Pakistan	Pretoria	2006-07
392-4	(50 overs)	India v New Zealand	Christchurch	2008-09
392-4	(50 overs)	India v Sri Lanka	Mohali	2017-18
391-4	(50 overs)	England v Bangladesh	Nottingham	2005
387-5	(50 overs)	India v England	Rajkot	2008-09
385-7	(50 overs)	Pakistan v Bangladesh	Dambulla	2010
384-6	(50 overs)	South Africa v Sri Lanka	Centurion	2016-17
383-6	(50 overs)	India v Australia	Bangalore	2013-14
381-6	(50 overs)	India v England	Cuttack	2016-17
378-5	(50 overs)	Australia v New Zealand	Canberra	2016-17
377-6	(50 overs)	Australia v South Africa	Basseterre	2006-07
377-8	(50 overs)	Sri Lanka v Ireland	Dublin	2016
376-2	(50 overs)	India v New Zealand	Hyderabad, India	1999-00
376-9	(50 overs)	Australia v Sri Lanka	Sydney	2014-15
375-3	(50 overs)	Pakistan v Zimbabwe	Lahore	2015

375-5	(50 overs)	India v Sri Lanka	Colombo (RPS)	2017
374-4	(50 overs)	India v Hong Kong	Karachi	2008
373-6	(50 overs)	India v Sri Lanka	Taunton	1999
373-8	(50 overs)	New Zealand v Zimbabwe	Napier	2011-12
372-6	(50 overs)	New Zealand v Zimbabwe	Whangarei	2011-12
372-2	(50 overs)	West Indies v Zimbabwe	Canberra	2014-15
372-6†	(49.2 overs)	South Africa v Australia	Durban	2016-17
371-9	(50 overs)	Pakistan v Sri Lanka	Nairobi	1996-97
371-6	(50 overs)	Australia v South Africa	Durban	2016-17
370-4	(50 overs)	India v Bangladesh	Dhaka	2010-11

The highest score for Zimbabwe is 351-7 (v Kenya, Mombasa, 2008-09), and for Bangladesh 329-6 (v Pakistan, Dhaka, 2014-15).

HIGHEST MATCH AGGREGATES

| 872-13 | (99.5 overs) | South Africa v Australia | Johannesburg | 2005-06 |
| 825-15 | (100 overs) | India v Sri Lanka | Rajkot | 2009-10 |

LARGEST RUNS MARGINS OF VICTORY

290 runs	New Zealand beat Ireland	Aberdeen	2008
275 runs	Australia beat Afghanistan	Perth	2014-15
272 runs	South Africa beat Zimbabwe	Benoni	2010-11
258 runs	South Africa beat Sri Lanka	Paarl	2011-12
257 runs	India beat Bermuda	Port of Spain	2006-07
257 runs	South Africa beat West Indies	Sydney	2014-15
256 runs	Australia beat Namibia	Potschefstroom	2002-03
256 runs	India beat Hong Kong	Karachi	2008
255 runs	Pakistan beat Ireland	Dublin	2016
245 runs	Sri Lanka beat India	Sharjah	2000-01
243 runs	Sri Lanka beat Bermuda	Port of Spain	2006-07
234 runs	Sri Lanka beat Pakistan	Lahore	2008-09
233 runs	Pakistan beat Bangladesh	Dhaka	1999-00
232 runs	Australia beat Sri Lanka	Adelaide	1984-85
231 runs	South Africa beat Netherlands	Mohali	2010-11
229 runs	Australia beat Netherlands	Basseterre	2006-07
224 runs	Australia beat Pakistan	Nairobi	2002
221 runs	South Africa beat Netherlands	Basseterre	2006-07
217 runs	Pakistan beat Sri Lanka	Sharjah	2001-02
215 runs	Australia beat New Zealand	St George's	2006-07
215 runs	West Indies beat Netherlands	Delhi	2010-11
214 runs	South Africa Beat India	Mumbai	2015-16
212 runs	South Africa beat Zimbabwe	Centurion	2009-10
210 runs	New Zealand beat USA	The Oval	2004
210 runs	Sri Lanka beat Canada	Hambantota	2010-11
210 runs	England beat New Zealand	Birmingham	2015
209 runs	South Africa beat West Indies	Cape Town	2003-04
208 runs	South Africa beat Kenya	Cape Town	2001-02
208 runs	Australia beat India	Sydney	2003-04
208 runs	West Indies beat Canada	Kingston	2009-10
206 runs	New Zealand beat Australia	Adelaide	1985-86
206 runs	Sri Lanka beat Netherlands	Colombo (RPS)	2002-03
206 runs	South Africa beat Bangladesh	Dhaka	2010-11
206 runs	South Africa beat Ireland	Benoni	2016-17
205 runs	Pakistan beat Kenya	Hambantota	2010-11
204 runs	New Zealand beat West Indies	Christchurch	2017-18
203 runs	Australia beat Scotland	Basseterre	2006-07
203 runs	West Indies beat New Zealand	Hamilton	2013-14
202 runs	England beat India	Lord's	1975
202 runs	South Africa beat Kenya	Nairobi	1996-97
202 runs	Zimbabwe beat Kenya	Dhaka	1998-99
202 runs	New Zealand beat Zimbabwe	Napier	2011-12
201 runs	South Africa beat Ireland	Canberra	2014-15

200 runs		India beat Bangladesh	Dhaka	2002-03
200 runs		New Zealand beat India	Dambulla	2010
200 runs		Australia beat Scotland	Edinburgh	2013
200 runs		South Africa beat Bangladesh	East London	2017-18

LOWEST TOTALS (Excluding reduced innings)

35	(18.0 overs)	Zimbabwe v Sri Lanka	Harare	2003-04
36	(18.4 overs)	Canada v Sri Lanka	Paarl	2002-03
38	(15.4 overs)	Zimbabwe v Sri Lanka	Colombo (SSC)	2001-02
43	(19.5 overs)	Pakistan v West Indies	Cape Town	1992-93
43	(20.1 overs)	Sri Lanka v South Africa	Paarl	2011-12
44	(24.5 overs)	Zimbabwe v Bangladesh	Chittagong	2009-10
45	(40.3 overs)	Canada v England	Manchester	1979
45	(14.0 overs)	Namibia v Australia	Potchefstroom	2002-03
54	(26.3 overs)	India v Sri Lanka	Sharjah	2000-01
54	(23.2 overs)	West Indies v South Africa	Cape Town	2003-04
54	(13.5 overs)	Zimbabwe v Afghanistan	Harare	2016-17
55	(28.3 overs)	Sri Lanka v West Indies	Sharjah	1986-87
58	(18.5 overs)	Bangladesh v West Indies	Dhaka	2010-11
58	(17.4 overs)	Bangladesh v India	Dhaka	2014
58	(16.1 overs)	Afghanistan v Zimbabwe	Sharjah	2015-16
61	(22.0 overs)	West Indies v Bangladesh	Chittagong	2011-12
63	(25.5 overs)	India v Australia	Sydney	1980-81
63	(18.3 overs)	Afghanistan v Scotland	Abu Dhabi	2014-15
64	(35.5 overs)	New Zealand v Pakistan	Sharjah	1985-86
65	(24.0 overs)	USA v Australia	Southampton	2004
65	(24.3 overs)	Zimbabwe v India	Harare	2005
67	(31.0 overs)	Zimbabwe v Sri Lanka	Harare	2008-09
67	(24.4 overs)	Canada v Netherlands	King City	2013
67	(24.0 overs)	Sri Lanka v England	Manchester	2014
68	(31.3 overs)	Scotland v West Indies	Leicester	1999
69	(28.0 overs)	South Africa v Australia	Sydney	1993-94
69	(22.5 overs)	Zimbabwe v Kenya	Harare	2005-06
69	(23.5 overs)	Kenya v New Zealand	Chennai	2010-11
70	(25.2 overs)	Australia v England	Birmingham	1977
70	(26.3 overs)	Australia v New Zealand	Adelaide	1985-86
70	(23.5 overs)	West Indies v Australia	Perth	2012-13
70	(24.4 overs)	Bangladesh v West Indies	St George's	2014

The lowest for England is 86 (v A, Manchester, 2001).

LOWEST MATCH AGGREGATES

73-11	(23.2 overs)	Canada (36) v Sri Lanka (37-1)	Paarl	2002-03
75-11	(27.2 overs)	Zimbabwe (35) v Sri Lanka (40-1)	Harare	2003-04
78-11	(20.0 overs)	Zimbabwe (38) v Sri Lanka (40-1)	Colombo (SSC)	2001-02

BATTING RECORDS

5000 RUNS IN A CAREER

		LOI	I	NO	HS	Runs	Avge	100	50
S.R.Tendulkar	I	463	452	41	200*	18426	44.83	49	96
K.C.Sangakkara	SL/Asia/ICC	404	380	41	169	14234	41.98	25	93
R.T.Ponting	A/ICC	375	365	39	164	13704	42.03	30	82
S.T.Jayasuriya	SL/Asia	445	433	18	189	13430	32.36	28	68
D.P.M.D.Jayawardena	SL/Asia	448	418	39	144	12650	33.37	19	77
Inzamam-ul-Haq	P/Asia	378	350	53	137*	11739	39.52	10	83
J.H.Kallis	SA/Afr/ICC	328	314	53	139	11579	44.36	17	86
S.C.Ganguly	I/Asia	311	300	23	183	11363	41.02	22	72
R.S.Dravid	I/Asia/ICC	344	318	40	153	10889	39.16	12	83
B.C.Lara	WI/ICC	299	289	32	169	10405	40.48	19	63
T.M.Dilshan	SL	330	303	41	161*	10290	39.27	22	47
M.S.Dhoni	I/Asia	318	272	78	183*	9967	51.37	10	67

		LOI	I	NO	HS	Runs	Avge	100	50
Mohammad Yousuf	P/Asia	288	272	40	141*	9720	41.71	15	64
A.C.Gilchrist	A/ICC	287	279	11	172	9619	35.89	16	55
V.Kohli	I	208	200	35	183	9588	58.10	35	46
A.B.de Villiers	SA/Afr	228	218	39	176	9577	53.50	25	53
C.H.Gayle	WI/ICC	277	272	17	215	9557	37.47	23	48
M.Azharuddin	I	334	308	54	153*	9378	36.92	7	58
P.A.de Silva	SL	308	296	30	145	9284	34.90	11	64
Saeed Anwar	P	247	244	19	194	8824	39.21	20	43
S.Chanderpaul	WI	268	251	40	150	8778	41.60	11	59
Yuvraj Singh	I/Asia	304	278	40	150	8701	36.55	14	52
D.L.Haynes	WI	238	237	28	152*	8648	41.37	17	57
M.S.Atapattu	SL	268	259	32	132*	8529	37.57	11	59
M.E.Waugh	A	244	236	20	173	8500	39.35	18	50
V.Sehwag	I/Asia/ICC	251	245	9	219	8273	35.05	15	38
H.H.Gibbs	SA	248	240	16	175	8094	36.13	21	37
Shahid Afridi	P/Asia/ICC	398	369	27	124	8064	23.57	6	39
S.P.Fleming	NZ/ICC	280	269	21	134*	8037	32.40	8	49
M.J.Clarke	A	245	223	44	130	7981	44.58	8	58
S.R.Waugh	A	325	288	58	120*	7569	32.90	3	45
H.M.Amla	SA	164	161	11	159	7535	50.23	26	35
A.Ranatunga	SL	269	255	47	131*	7456	35.84	4	49
Javed Miandad	P	233	218	41	119*	7381	41.70	8	50
L.R.P.L.Taylor	NZ	204	190	33	181*	7267	46.28	19	41
Younus Khan	P	265	255	23	144	7249	31.24	7	48
Salim Malik	P	283	256	38	102	7170	32.88	5	47
N.J.Astle	NZ	223	217	14	145*	7090	34.92	16	41
G.C.Smith	SA/Afr	197	194	10	141	6989	37.98	10	47
Shoaib Malik	P	261	236	38	143	6975	35.22	9	41
M.G.Bevan	A	232	196	67	108*	6912	53.58	6	46
G.Kirsten	SA	185	185	19	188*	6798	40.95	13	45
A.Flower	Z	213	208	16	145	6786	35.34	4	55
W.U.Tharanga	SL/Asia	223	212	17	174*	6780	34.76	15	37
I.V.A.Richards	WI	187	167	24	189*	6721	47.00	11	45
R.G.Sharma	I	180	174	26	264	6594	44.55	17	34
G.W.Flower	Z	221	214	18	142*	6571	33.52	6	40
Ijaz Ahmed	P	250	232	29	139*	6564	32.33	10	37
A.R.Border	A	273	252	39	127*	6524	30.62	3	39
R.B.Richardson	WI	224	217	30	122	6248	33.41	5	44
M.L.Hayden	A/ICC	161	155	15	181*	6133	43.80	10	36
Mohammad Hafeez	P	200	199	13	140*	6107	32.83	11	34
B.B.McCullum	NZ	260	228	28	166	6083	30.41	5	32
D.M.Jones	A	164	161	25	145	6068	44.61	7	46
E.J.G.Morgan	E/Ire	200	187	25	124*	6031	37.22	11	35
Tamim Iqbal	B	179	177	5	154	6018	34.98	9	41
M.J.Guptill	NZ	159	156	17	237*	5976	42.99	13	34
D.C.Boon	A	181	177	16	122	5964	37.04	5	37
J.N.Rhodes	SA	245	220	51	121	5935	35.11	2	33
Ramiz Raja	P	198	197	15	119*	5841	32.09	9	31
R.R.Sarwan	WI	181	169	33	120*	5804	42.67	5	38
C.L.Hooper	WI	227	206	43	113*	5761	35.34	7	29
S.R.Watson	A	190	169	27	185*	5757	40.54	9	33
B.R.M.Taylor	Z	178	177	15	145*	5720	35.30	9	34
S.K.Raina	I	223	192	35	116*	5568	35.46	5	36
W.J.Cronje	SA	188	175	31	112	5565	38.64	2	39
M.E.K.Hussey	A	185	157	44	109*	5442	48.15	3	39
I.R.Bell	E	161	157	14	141	5416	37.87	4	35
A.Jadeja	I	196	179	36	119	5359	37.47	6	30
D.R.Martyn	A	208	182	51	144*	5346	40.80	5	37
H.Masakadza	Z	189	188	4	178*	5307	28.84	5	33
M.N.Samuels	WI	195	184	26	133*	5282	33.43	10	28
Shakib Al Hasan	B	185	174	24	134*	5243	34.95	7	37

301

		LOI	I	NO	HS	Runs	Avge	100	50
G.Gambhir	I	147	143	11	150*	**5238**	39.68	11	34
A.D.R.Campbell	Z	188	184	14	131*	**5185**	30.50	7	30
R.S.Mahanama	SL	213	198	23	119*	**5162**	29.49	4	35
K.S.Williamson	NZ	127	121	11	145*	**5156**	46.87	11	33
C.G.Greenidge	WI	128	127	13	133*	**5134**	45.03	11	31
Misbah-ul-Haq	P	162	149	31	96*	**5122**	43.40	–	42
A.D.Mathews	SL	196	166	44	139*	**5107**	41.86	2	35
P.D.Collingwood	E	197	181	37	120*	**5092**	35.36	5	26
A.Symonds	A	198	161	33	156	**5088**	39.75	6	30
Abdul Razzaq	P/Asia	265	228	57	112	**5080**	29.70	3	23

HIGHEST INDIVIDUAL INNINGS

264	R.G.Sharma	India v Sri Lanka	Kolkata	2014-15
237*	M.J.Guptill	New Zealand v West Indies	Wellington	2014-15
219	V.Sehwag	India v West Indies	Indore	2011-12
215	C.H.Gayle	West Indies v Zimbabwe	Canberra	2014-15
209	R.G.Sharma	India v Australia	Bangalore	2013-14
208*	R.G.Sharma	India v Sri Lanka	Mohali	2017-18
200*	S.R.Tendulkar	India v South Africa	Gwalior	2009-10
194*	C.K.Coventry	Zimbabwe v Bangladesh	Bulawayo	2009
194	Saeed Anwar	Pakistan v India	Madras	1996-97
189*	I.V.A.Richards	West Indies v England	Manchester	1984
189*	M.J.Guptill	New Zealand v England	Southampton	2013
189	S.T.Jayasuriya	Sri Lanka v India	Sharjah	2000-01
188*	G.Kirsten	South Africa v UAE	Rawalpindi	1995-96
186*	S.R.Tendulkar	India v New Zealand	Hyderabad	1999-00
185*	S.R.Watson	Australia v Bangladesh	Dhaka	2010-11
185	F.du Plessis	South Africa v Sri Lanka	Cape Town	2016-17
183*	M.S.Dhoni	India v Sri Lanka	Jaipur	2005-06
183	S.C.Ganguly	India v Sri Lanka	Taunton	1999
183	V.Kohli	India v Pakistan	Dhaka	2011-12
181*	M.L.Hayden	Australia v New Zealand	Hamilton	2006-07
181*	L.R.P.L.Taylor	New Zealand v England	Dunedin	2017-18
181	I.V.A.Richards	West Indies v Sri Lanka	Karachi	1987-88
180*	M.J.Guptill	New Zealand v South Africa	Hamilton	2016-17
180	J.J.Roy	England v Australia	Melbourne	2017-18
179	D.A.Warner	Australia v Pakistan	Adelaide	2016-17
178*	H.Masakadza	Zimbabwe v Kenya	Harare	2009-10
178	D.A.Warner	Australia v Afghanistan	Perth	2014-15
178	Q.de Kock	South Africa v Australia	Centurion	2016-17
177	P.R.Stirling	Ireland v Canada	Toronto	2010
176*	E.Lewis	West Indies v England	The Oval	2017
176	A.B.de Villiers	South Africa v Bangladesh	Paarl	2017-18
175*	Kapil Dev	India v Zimbabwe	Tunbridge Wells	1983
175	H.H.Gibbs	South Africa v Australia	Johannesburg	2005-06
175	S.R.Tendulkar	India v Australia	Hyderabad, India	2009-10
175	V.Sehwag	India v Bangladesh	Dhaka	2010-11
175	C.S.MacLeod	Scotland v Canada	Christchurch	2013-14
174*	W.U.Tharanga	Sri Lanka v India	Kingston	2013
173	M.E.Waugh	Australia v West Indies	Melbourne	2000-01
173	D.A.Warner	Australia v South Africa	Cape Town	2016-17
172*	C.B.Wishart	Zimbabwe v Namibia	Harare	2002-03
172	A.C.Gilchrist	Australia v Zimbabwe	Hobart	2003-04
172	L.Vincent	New Zealand v Zimbabwe	Bulawayo	2005
171*	G.M.Turner	New Zealand v East Africa	Birmingham	1975
171*	R.G.Sharma	India v Australia	Perth	2015-16
171	A.D.Hales	England v Pakistan	Nottingham	2016
170*	L.Ronchi	New Zealand v Sri Lanka	Dunedin	2014-15
169*	D.J.Callaghan	South Africa v New Zealand	Pretoria	1994-95
169	B.C.Lara	West Indies v Sri Lanka	Sharjah	1995-96
169	K.C.Sangakkara	Sri Lanka v South Africa	Colombo (RPS)	2013

169	D.Ramdin	West Indies v Bangladesh	Basseterre	2014
168*	Q.de Kock	South Africa v Bangladesh	Kimberley	2017-18
167*	R.A.Smith	England v Australia	Birmingham	1993
166	B.B.McCullum	New Zealand v Ireland	Aberdeen	2008

The highest for Bangladesh is 154 by Tamim Iqbal (v Zimbabwe, Bulawayo, 2009).

HUNDRED ON DEBUT

D.L.Amiss	103	England v Australia	Manchester	1972
D.L.Haynes	148	West Indies v Australia	St John's	1977-78
A.Flower	115*	Zimbabwe v Sri Lanka	New Plymouth	1991-92
Salim Elahi	102*	Pakistan v Sri Lanka	Gujranwala	1995-96
M.J.Guptill	122*	New Zealand v West Indies	Auckland	2008-09
C.A.Ingram	124	South Africa v Zimbabwe	Bloemfontein	2010-11
R.J.Nicol	108*	New Zealand v Zimbabwe	Harare	2011-12
P.J.Hughes	112	Australia v Sri Lanka	Melbourne	2012-13
M.J.Lumb	106	England v West Indies	North Sound	2013-14
M.S.Chapman	124*	Hong Kong v UAE	Dubai	2015-16
K.L.Rahul	100*	India v Zimbabwe	Harare	2016
T.Bavuma	113	South Africa v Ireland	Benoni	2016-17
Imam-ul-Haq	100	Pakistan v Sri Lanka	Abu Dhabi	2017-18

Shahid Afridi scored 102 for P v SL, Nairobi, 1996-97, in his second match having not batted in his first.

| **Fastest 100** | 31 balls | A.B.de Villiers (149) | SA v WI | Johannesburg | 2014-15 |
| **Fastest 50** | 16 balls | A.B.de Villiers (149) | SA v WI | Johannesburg | 2014-15 |

15 HUNDREDS

		Inns	100	E	A	SA	WI	NZ	I	P	SL	Z	B	Ass
S.R.Tendulkar	I	452	49	2	9	5	4	5	–	5	8	5	1	5
V.Kohli	I	200	35	3	5	4	4	5	–	2	8	1	3	–
R.T.Ponting	A	365	30*	5	–	2	2	6	6	1	4	1	1	2
S.T.Jayasuriya	SL	433	28	4	2	–	1	5	7	3	–	1	4	1
H.M.Amla	SA	161	26	2	1	–	5	2	2	5	3	2	2	
A.B.de Villiers	SA	218	25	2	1	–	5	1	6	3	2	3	1	1
K.C.Sangakkara	SL	380	25	1	1	–	2	2	6	2	–	–	5	2
C.H.Gayle	WI	272	23	2	–	3	–	2	4	3	1	3	1	4
S.C.Ganguly	I	300	22	1	1	3	–	3	–	2	4	3	1	4
T.M.Dilshan	SL	303	22	2	1	2	–	3	4	2	–	2	4	2
H.H.Gibbs	SA	240	21	2	3	–	5	2	2	1	2	1	1	
Saeed Anwar	P	244	20	–	1	–	2	4	4	–	7	2	–	
L.R.P.L.Taylor	NZ	190	19	5	2	1	1	–	2	3	1	2	2	–
B.C.Lara	WI	289	19	1	3	3	–	2	–	5	2	1	1	1
D.P.M.D.Jayawardena	SL	418	19*	5	–	1	3	4	2	–	–	1	2	
M.E.Waugh	A	236	18	1	–	2	3	3	3	1	1	3	–	1
R.G.Sharma	I	174	17	–	6	2	–	1	–	–	5	1	2	–
D.L.Haynes	WI	237	17	2	6	–	2	2	4	1	–	–		
J.H.Kallis	SA	314	17	1	1	–	4	3	2	1	3	1	–	1
N.J.Astle	NZ	217	16	2	1	1	1	–	5	2	–	3	–	1
A.C.Gilchrist	A	279	16*	2	–	2	–	2	1	1	6	1	–	–
W.U.Tharanga	SL	212	15	3	1	1	1	1	2	1	–	2	3	–
V.Sehwag	I	245	15	1	–	2	6	–	2	2	–	1	1	
Mohammad Yousuf	P	273	15	1	1	2	2	1	1	2	2	3	1	

* = Includes hundred scored against multi-national side. The most for England is 12 by M.E.Trescothick (in 122 innings), for Zimbabwe 9 by B.R.M.Taylor (177), and for Bangladesh 9 by Tamim Iqbal (177).

HIGHEST PARTNERSHIP FOR EACH WICKET

1st	286	W.U.Tharanga/S.T.Jayasuriya	Sri Lanka v England	Leeds	2006
2nd	372	C.H.Gayle/M.N.Samuels	West Indies v Zimbabwe	Canberra	2014-15
3rd	258	D.M.Bravo/D.Ramdin	West Indies v Bangladesh	Basseterre	2014
4th	275*	M.Azharuddin/A.Jadeja	India v Zimbabwe	Cuttack	1997-98
5th	256*	D.A.Miller/J.P.Duminy	South Africa v Zimbabwe	Hamilton	2014-15
6th	267*	G.D.Elliott/L.Ronchi	New Zealand v Sri Lanka	Dunedin	2014-15
7th	177	J.C.Buttler/A.U.Rashid	England v New Zealand	Birmingham	2015
8th	138*	J.M.Kemp/A.J.Hall	South Africa v India	Cape Town	2006-07
9th	132	A.D.Mathews/S.L.Malinga	Sri Lanka v Australia	Melbourne	2010-11
10th	106*	I.V.A.Richards/M.A.Holding	West Indies v England	Manchester	1984

BOWLING RECORDS

200 WICKETS IN A CAREER

		LOI	Balls	R	W	Avge	Best	5w	R/Over
M.Muralitharan	SL/Asia/ICC	350	18811	12326	534	23.08	7-30	10	3.93
Wasim Akram	P	356	18186	11812	502	23.52	5-15	6	3.89
Waqar Younis	P	262	12698	9919	416	23.84	7-36	13	4.68
W.P.J.U.C.Vaas	SL/Asia	322	15775	11014	400	27.53	8-19	4	4.18
Shahid Afridi	P/Asia/ICC	398	17620	13632	395	34.51	7-12	9	4.62
S.M.Pollock	SA/Afr/ICC	303	15712	9631	393	24.50	6-35	5	3.67
G.D.McGrath	A/ICC	250	12970	8391	381	22.02	7-15	7	3.88
B.Lee	A	221	11185	8877	380	23.36	5-22	9	4.76
A.Kumble	I/Asia	271	14496	10412	337	30.89	6-12	2	4.30
S.T.Jayasuriya	SL	445	14874	11871	323	36.75	6-29	4	4.78
J.Srinath	I	229	11935	8847	315	28.08	5-23	3	4.44
D.L.Vettori	NZ/ICC	295	14060	9674	305	31.71	5- 7	2	4.12
S.L.Malinga	SL	204	9830	8705	301	28.92	6-38	7	5.31
S.K.Warne	A/ICC	194	10642	7541	293	25.73	5-33	1	4.25
Saqlain Mushtaq	P	169	8770	6275	288	21.78	5-20	6	4.29
A.B.Agarkar	I	191	9484	8021	288	27.85	6-42	2	5.07
Z.Khan	I/Asia	200	10097	8301	282	29.43	5-42	1	4.93
J.H.Kallis	SA/Afr/ICC	328	10750	8680	273	31.79	5-30	2	4.84
A.A.Donald	SA	164	8561	5926	272	21.78	6-23	2	4.15
J.M.Anderson	E	194	9584	7861	269	29.22	5-23	2	4.92
Abdul Razzaq	P/Asia	265	10941	8564	269	31.83	6-35	3	4.69
Harbhajan Singh	I/Asia	236	12479	8973	269	33.35	5-31	3	4.31
M.Ntini	SA/ICC	173	8687	6559	266	24.65	6-22	4	4.53
Kapil Dev	I	225	11202	6945	253	27.45	5-43	1	3.72
Shoaib Akhtar	P/Asia/ICC	163	7764	6169	247	24.97	6-16	4	4.76
K.D.Mills	NZ	170	8230	6485	240	27.02	5-25	1	4.72
M.G.Johnson	A	153	7489	6038	239	25.26	6-31	3	4.83
H.H.Streak	Z/Afr	189	9468	7129	239	29.82	5-32	1	4.51
Mashrafe Mortaza	B/Asia	187	9310	7421	238	31.18	6-26	1	4.78
D.Gough	E/ICC	159	8470	6209	235	26.42	5-44	2	4.39
Shakib Al Hasan	B	185	9343	6924	235	29.46	5-47	1	4.78
C.A.Walsh	WI	205	10822	6918	227	30.47	5- 1	1	3.83
C.E.L.Ambrose	WI	176	9353	5429	225	24.12	5-17	4	3.48
Abdur Razzaq	B	153	7965	6065	207	29.29	5-29	4	4.56
C.J.McDermott	A	138	7460	5018	203	24.71	5-44	1	4.03
C.Z.Harris	NZ	250	10667	7613	203	37.50	5-42	1	4.28
C.L.Cairns	NZ/ICC	215	8168	6594	201	32.80	5-42	1	4.84

BEST FIGURES IN AN INNINGS

8-19	W.P.J.U.C.Vaas	Sri Lanka v Zimbabwe	Colombo (SSC)	2001-02
7-12	Shahid Afridi	Pakistan v West Indies	Providence	2013
7-15	G.D.McGrath	Australia v Namibia	Potchefstroom	2002-03
7-18	Rashid Khan	Afghanistan v West Indies	Gros Islet	2017
7-20	A.J.Bichel	Australia v England	Port Elizabeth	2002-03
7-30	M.Muralitharan	Sri Lanka v India	Sharjah	2000-01
7-33	T.G.Southee	New Zealand v England	Wellington	2014-15
7-34	T.A.Boult	New Zealand v West Indies	Christchurch	2017-18

7-36	Waqar Younis	Pakistan v England	Leeds	2001
7-37	Aqib Javed	Pakistan v India	Sharjah	1991-92
7-45	Imran Tahir	South Africa v West Indies	Basseterre	2016
7-51	W.W.Davis	West Indies v Australia	Leeds	1983
6- 4	S.T.R.Binny	India v Bangladesh	Dhaka	2014
6-12	A.Kumble	India v West Indies	Calcutta	1993-94
6-13	B.A.W.Mendis	Sri Lanka v India	Karachi	2008
6-14	G.J.Gilmour	Australia v England	Leeds	1975
6-14	Imran Khan	Pakistan v India	Sharjah	1984-85
6-14	M.F.Maharoof	Sri Lanka v West Indies	Mumbai	2006-07
6-15	C.E.H.Croft	West Indies v England	Kingstown	1980-81
6-16	Shoaib Akhtar	Pakistan v New Zealand	Karachi	2001-02
6-16	K.Rabada	South Africa v Bangladesh	Dhaka	2015
6-18	Azhar Mahmood	Pakistan v West Indies	Sharjah	1999-00
6-19	H.K.Olonga	Zimbabwe v England	Cape Town	1999-00
6-19	S.E.Bond	New Zealand v Zimbabwe	Harare	2005
6-20	B.C.Strang	Zimbabwe v Bangladesh	Nairobi	1997-98
6-20	A.D.Mathews	Sri Lanka v India	Colombo (RPS)	2009-10
6-22	F.H.Edwards	West Indies v Zimbabwe	Harare	2003-04
6-22	M.Ntini	South Africa v Australia	Cape Town	2005-06
6-23	A.A.Donald	South Africa v Kenya	Nairobi	1996-97
6-23	A.Nehra	India v England	Durban	2002-03
6-23	S.E.Bond	New Zealand v Australia	Port Elizabeth	2002-03
6-25	S.B.Styris	New Zealand v West Indies	Port of Spain	2002
6-25	W.P.J.U.C.Vaas	Sri Lanka v Bangladesh	Pietermaritzburg	2002-03
6-26	Waqar Younis	Pakistan v Sri Lanka	Sharjah	1989-90
6-26	Mashrafe Mortaza	Bangladesh v Kenya	Nairobi	2006
6-26	Rubel Hossain	Bangladesh v New Zealand	Dhaka	2013-14
6-26	Yasir Shah	Pakistan v Zimbabwe	Harare	2015-16
6-27	Naved-ul-Hasan	Pakistan v India	Jamshedpur	2004-05
6-27	C.R.D.Fernando	Sri Lanka v England	Colombo (RPS)	2007-08
6-27	M.Kartik	India v Australia	Mumbai	2007-08
6-27	K.A.J.Roach	West Indies v Netherlands	Delhi	2010-11
6-27	S.P.Narine	West Indies v South Africa	Providence	2016
6-28	H.K.Olonga	Zimbabwe v Kenya	Bulawayo	2002-03
6-28	J.H.Davey	Scotland v Afghanistan	Abu Dhabi	2014-15
6-28	M.A.Starc	Australia v New Zealand	Auckland	2014-15
6-29	B.P.Patterson	West Indies v India	Nagpur	1987-88
6-29	S.T.Jayasuriya	Sri Lanka v England	Moratuwa	1992-93
6-29	B.A.W.Mendis	Sri Lanka v Zimbabwe	Harare	2008-09
6-30	Waqar Younis	Pakistan v New Zealand	Auckland	1993-94
6-31	P.D.Collingwood	England v Bangladesh	Nottingham	2005
6-31	M.G.Johnson	Australia v Sri Lanka	Pallekele	2011
6-33	T.A.Boult	New Zealand v Australia	Hamilton	2016-17
6-34	Zahoor Khan	UAE v Ireland	Dubai (ICCA)	2016-17
6-35	S.M.Pollock	South Africa v West Indies	East London	1998-99
6-35	Abdul Razzaq	Pakistan v Bangladesh	Dhaka	2001-02
6-38	Shahid Afridi	Pakistan v Australia	Dubai	2009
6-38	S.L.Malinga	Sri Lanka v Kenya	Colombo (RPS)	2010-11
6-39	K.H.MacLeay	Australia v India	Nottingham	1983
6-39	D.W.Steyn	South Africa v Pakistan	Port Elizabeth	2013-14

The best figures for Ireland are 6-55 by P.R.Stirling v Afghanistan, Greater Noida, 2016-17).

HAT-TRICKS

Jalaluddin	Pakistan v Australia	Hyderabad	1982-83
B.A.Reid	Australia v New Zealand	Sydney	1985-86
C.Sharma	India v New Zealand	Nagpur	1987-88
Wasim Akram	Pakistan v West Indies	Sharjah	1989-90
Wasim Akram	Pakistan v Australia	Sharjah	1989-90
Kapil Dev	India v Sri Lanka	Calcutta	1990-91
Aqib Javed	Pakistan v India	Sharjah	1991-92
D.K.Morrison	New Zealand v India	Napier	1993-94
Waqar Younis	Pakistan v New Zealand	East London	1994-95

Saqlain Mushtaq	Pakistan v Zimbabwe	Peshawar	1996-97
E.A.Brandes	Zimbabwe v England	Harare	1996-97
A.M.Stuart	Australia v Pakistan	Melbourne	1996-97
Saqlain Mushtaq	Pakistan v Zimbabwe	The Oval	1999
W.P.J.U.C.Vaas	Sri Lanka v Zimbabwe	Colombo (SSC)	2001-02
Mohammad Sami	Pakistan v West Indies	Sharjah	2001-02
W.P.J.U.C.Vaas[1]	Sri Lanka v Bangladesh	Pietermaritzburg	2002-03
B.Lee	Australia v Kenya	Durban	2002-03
J.M.Anderson	England v Pakistan	The Oval	2003
S.J.Harmison	England v India	Nottingham	2004
C.K.Langeveldt	South Africa v West Indies	Bridgetown	2004-05
Shahadat Hossain	Bangladesh v Zimbabwe	Harare	2006
J.E.Taylor	West Indies v Australia	Mumbai	2006-07
S.E.Bond	New Zealand v Australia	Hobart	2006-07
S.L.Malinga[2]	Sri Lanka v South Africa	Providence	2006-07
A.Flintoff	England v West Indies	St Lucia	2008-09
M.F.Maharoof	Sri Lanka v India	Dambulla	2010
Abdur Razzak	Bangladesh v Zimbabwe	Dhaka	2010-11
K.A.J.Roach	West Indies v Netherlands	Delhi	2010-11
S.L.Malinga	Sri Lanka v Kenya	Colombo (RPS)	2010-11
S.L.Malinga	Sri Lanka v Australia	Colombo (RPS)	2011
D.T.Christian	Australia v Sri Lanka	Melbourne	2011-12
N.L.T.C.Perera	Sri Lanka v Pakistan	Colombo (RPS)	2012
C.J.McKay	Australia v England	Cardiff	2013
Rubel Hossain	Bangladesh v New Zealand	Dhaka	2013-14
P.Utseya	Zimbabwe v South Africa	Harare	2014
Taijul Islam	Bangladesh v Zimbabwe	Dhaka	2014-15
S.T.Finn	England v Australia	Melbourne	2014-15
J.P.Duminy	South Africa v Sri Lanka	Sydney	2014-15
K.Rabada	South Africa v Bangladesh	Mirpur	2015
J.P.Faulkner	Australia v Sri Lanka	Colombo (RPS)	2016
Taskin Ahmed	Bangladesh v Sri Lanka	Dambulla	2016-17
P.W.H.de Silva	Sri Lanka v Zimbabwe	Galle	2017
Kuldeep Yadav	India v Australia	Kolkata	2017-18
D.S.K.Madushanka	Sri Lanka v Bangladesh	Dhaka	2017-18

[1] The first three balls of the match. Took four wickets in opening over (W W W 4 wide W 0).
[2] Four wickets in four balls.

WICKET-KEEPING RECORDS

100 DISMISSALS IN A CAREER

Total			LOI	Ct	St
482†‡	K.C.Sangakkara	Sri Lanka/Asia/ICC	360	384	98
472‡	A.C.Gilchrist	Australia/ICC	287	417	55
424	M.V.Boucher	South Africa/Africa	295	402	22
404	M.S.Dhoni	India/Asia	318	297	107
287‡	Moin Khan	Pakistan	219	214	73
242†‡	B.B.McCullum	New Zealand	185	227	15
233	I.A.Healy	Australia	168	194	39
220‡	Rashid Latif	Pakistan	166	182	38
206‡	R.S.Kaluwitharana	Sri Lanka	187	131	75
204‡	P.J.L.Dujon	West Indies	169	183	21
189	R.D.Jacobs	West Indies	147	160	29
188	D.Ramdin	West Indies	139	181	7
187	Kamran Akmal	Pakistan	154	156	31
185	Mushfiqur Rahim	Bangladesh	184	144	41
181	B.J.Haddin	Australia	126	170	11
165	D.J.Richardson	South Africa	122	148	17
165†‡	A.Flower	Zimbabwe	213	133	32
163†‡	A.J.Stewart	England	170	148	15
158	J.C.Buttler	England	109	139	19
154‡	N.R.Mongia	India	140	110	44

Total				Ct	St
145	T.Taibu	Zimbabwe/Africa	150	112	33
136†‡	A.C.Parore	New Zealand	179	111	25
126	Khaled Masud	Bangladesh	126	91	35
124	R.W.Marsh	Australia	92	120	4
122	Q.de Kock	South Africa	90	116	6
117	L. Ronchi	New Zealand/Aus	85	105	12
117	M.S.Wade	Australia	94	108	9
107	Sarfraz Ahmed	Pakistan	85	85	22
103	Salim Yousuf	Pakistan	86	81	22

† Excluding catches taken in the field. ‡ Excluding matches when not wicket-keeper.

SIX DISMISSALS IN AN INNINGS

6	(6ct)	A.C.Gilchrist	Australia v South Africa	Cape Town	1999-00
6	(6ct)	A.J.Stewart	England v Zimbabwe	Manchester	2000
6	(5ct/1st)	R.D.Jacobs	West Indies v Sri Lanka	Colombo (RPS)	2001-02
6	(5ct/1st)	A.C.Gilchrist	Australia v England	Sydney	2002-03
6	(6ct)	A.C.Gilchrist	Australia v Namibia	Potchefstroom	2002-03
6	(6ct)	A.C.Gilchrist	Australia v Sri Lanka	Colombo (RPS)	2003-04
6	(6ct)	M.V.Boucher	South Africa v Pakistan	Cape Town	2006-07
6	(5ct/1st)	M.S.Dhoni	India v England	Leeds	2007
6	(6ct)	A.C.Gilchrist	Australia v India	Baroda	2007-08
6	(5ct/1st)	A.C.Gilchrist	Australia v India	Sydney	2007-08
6	(6ct)	M.J.Prior	England v South Africa	Nottingham	2008
6	(6ct)	J.C.Buttler	England v South Africa	The Oval	2013
6	(6ct)	M.H.Cross	Scotland v Canada	Christchurch	2013-14
6	(5ct/1st)	Q.de Kock	South Africa v New Zealand	Mt Maunganui	2014-15
6	(6ct)	Sarfraz Ahmed	Pakistan v South Africa	Auckland	2014-15

FIELDING RECORDS

100 CATCHES IN A CAREER

Total			LOI	Total			LOI
218	D.P.M.D.Jayawardena	Sri Lanka/Asia	448	117	C.H.Gayle	West Indies/ICC	277
160	R.T.Ponting	Australia/ICC	375	113	Inzamam-ul-Haq	Pakistan/Asia	378
156	M.Azharuddin	India	334	111	S.R.Waugh	Australia	325
140	S.R.Tendulkar	India	463	109	R.S.Mahanama	Sri Lanka	213
133	S.P.Fleming	New Zealand/ICC	280	108	P.D.Collingwood	England	197
131	J.H.Kallis	South Africa/Africa/ICC	328	108	M.E.Waugh	Australia	244
130	L.R.P.L.Taylor	New Zealand	204	108	H.H.Gibbs	South Africa	248
130	Younus Khan	Pakistan	265	108	S.M.Pollock	South Africa/Africa/ICC	303
130	M.Muralitharan	Sri Lanka/Asia/ICC	350	106	M.J.Clarke	Australia	245
127	A.R.Border	Australia	273	105	M.E.K.Hussey	Australia	185
127	Shahid Afridi	Pakistan/Asia/ICC	398	105	G.C.Smith	South Africa/Africa	197
124	R.S.Dravid	India/Asia/ICC	344	105	J.N.Rhodes	South Africa	245
123	S.T.Jayasuriya	Sri Lanka	445	104	I.V.A.Richards	West Indies	187
120	C.L.Hooper	West Indies	227	100	V.Kohli	India	208
120	B.C.Lara	West Indies/ICC	299	100	S.K.Raina	India	223
118	T.M.Dilshan	Sri Lanka	330	100	S.C.Ganguly	India/Asia	311

The most for Zimbabwe is 86 by G.W.Flower (221), and for Bangladesh 55 by Mashrafe Mortaza (185).

FIVE CATCHES IN AN INNINGS

5	J.N.Rhodes	South Africa v West Indies	Bombay (BS)	1993-94

APPEARANCE RECORDS

250 MATCHES

463	S.R.Tendulkar	India	404	K.C.Sangakkara	Sri Lanka/Asia/ICC
448	D.P.M.D.Jayawardena	Sri Lanka/Asia	398	Shahid Afridi	Pakistan/Asia/ICC
445	S.T.Jayasuriya	Sri Lanka/Asia	378	Inzamam-ul-Haq	Pakistan/Asia

375	R.T.Ponting	Australia/ICC		287	A.C.Gilchrist	Australia/ICC
356	Wasim Akram	Pakistan		283	Salim Malik	Pakistan
350	M.Muralitharan	Sri Lanka/Asia/ICC		280	S.P.Fleming	New Zealand/ICC
344	R.S.Dravid	India/Asia/ICC		277	C.H.Gayle	West Indies/ICC
334	M.Azharuddin	India		273	A.R.Border	Australia
330	T.M.Dilshan	Sri Lanka/Asia/ICC		271	A.Kumble	India/Asia
328	J.H.Kallis	South Africa/Africa/ICC		269	A.Ranatunga	Sri Lanka
325	S.R.Waugh	Australia		268	M.S.Atapattu	Sri Lanka
322	W.P.J.U.C.Vaas	Sri Lanka/Asia		268	S.Chanderpaul	West Indies
318	M.S.Dhoni	India/Asia		265	Abdul Razzaq	Pakistan/Asia
311	S.C.Ganguly	India/Asia		265	Younus Khan	Pakistan
308	P.A.de Silva	Sri Lanka		262	Waqar Younis	Pakistan
304	Yuvraj Singh	India/Asia		261	Shoaib Malik	Pakistan
303	S.M.Pollock	South Africa/Africa/ICC		260	B.B.McCullum	New Zealand
299	B.C.Lara	West Indies/ICC		251	V.Sehwag	India/Asia/ICC
295	M.V.Boucher	South Africa/Africa		250	C.Z.Harris	New Zealand
295	D.L.Vettori	New Zealand/ICC		250	Ijaz Ahmed	Pakistan
288	Mohammad Yousuf	Pakistan/Asia		250	G.D.McGrath	Australia/ICC

The most for England is 197 by P.D.Collingwood, for Zimbabwe 221 by G.W.Flower, and for Bangladesh 185 by Mohammad Ashraful and Shakib Al Hasan.

The most consecutive appearances is 185 by S.R.Tendulkar for India (Apr 1990-Apr 1998).

100 MATCHES AS CAPTAIN

LOI			W	L	T	NR	% Won (exc NR)
230	R.T.Ponting	Australia/ICC	165	51	2	12	75.68
218	S.P.Fleming	New Zealand	98	106	1	13	47.80
199	M.S.Dhoni	India	110	74	4	11	58.51
193	A.Ranatunga	Sri Lanka	89	95	1	8	48.10
178	A.R.Border	Australia	107	67	1	3	61.14
174	M.Azharuddin	India	90	76	2	6	53.57
150	G.C.Smith	South Africa/Africa	92	51	1	6	63.88
147	S.C.Ganguly	India/Asia	76	66	—	5	53.52
139	Imran Khan	Pakistan	75	59	1	4	55.55
138	W.J.Cronje	South Africa	99	35	1	3	73.33
129	D.P.M.D.Jayawardena	Sri Lanka	71	49	1	8	58.67
125	B.C.Lara	West Indies	59	59	—	7	50.42
118	S.T.Jayasuriya	Sri Lanka	66	47	2	3	57.39
109	Wasim Akram	Pakistan	66	41	2	—	60.55
106	S.R.Waugh	Australia	67	35	3	1	63.80
105	I.V.A.Richards	West Indies	67	36	—	2	65.04
103	A.B.de Villers	South Africa	59	39	1	4	59.59

The most for England is 78 by A.N.Cook, for Zimbabwe 86 by A.D.R.Campbell, and for Bangladesh 69 by Habibul Bashar.

100 LOI UMPIRING APPEARANCES

209	R.E.Koertzen	South Africa	09.12.1992	to	09.06.2010
200	B.F.Bowden	New Zealand	23.03.1995	to	06.02.2016
190	Alim Dar	Pakistan	16.02.2000	to	16.02.2018
181	S.A.Bucknor	West Indies	18.03.1989	to	29.03.2009
174	D.J.Harper	Australia	14.01.1994	to	19.03.2011
174	S.J.A.Taufel	Australia	13.01.1999	to	02.09.2012
172	D.R.Shepherd	England	09.06.1983	to	12.07.2005
152	R.B.Tiffin	Zimbabwe	25.10.1992	to	19.02.2017
139	D.B.Hair	Australia	14.12.1991	to	24.08.2008
137	S.J.Davis	Australia	12.12.1992	to	17.06.2015
125	I.J.Gould	England	20.06.2006	to	13.02.2018
122	E.A.R.de Silva	Sri Lanka	22.08.1999	to	13.06.2012
107	D.L.Orchard	South Africa	02.12.1994	to	07.12.2003
100	R.S.Dunne	New Zealand	06.02.1989	to	26.02.2002

ENGLAND TWENTY20 INTERNATIONALS CAREER RECORDS

These records, complete to 5 April 2018, include all players registered for county cricket for the 2018 season at the time of going to press.

BATTING AND FIELDING

	M	I	NO	HS	Runs	Avge	100	50	Ct/St
M.M.Ali	22	19	5	72*	202	14.42	–	1	6
T.R.Ambrose	1	–	–	–	–	–	–	–	1/1
J.M.Anderson	19	4	3	1*	1	1.00	–	–	3
J.M.Bairstow	23	18	5	60*	329	25.30	–	2	23
G.J.Batty	1	1	–	4	4	4.00	–	–	–
I.R.Bell	8	8	1	60*	188	26.85	–	1	4
S.W.Billings	17	15	–	53	205	13.66	–	1	11/1
R.S.Bopara	38	35	10	65*	711	28.44	–	3	7
S.G.Borthwick	1	1	–	14	14	14.00	–	–	1
T.T.Bresnan	34	22	9	47*	216	16.61	–	–	10
D.R.Briggs	7	1	1	0*	0	–	–	–	1
S.C.J.Broad	56	26	10	18*	118	7.37	–	–	21
J.C.Buttler	61	53	11	73*	1069	25.45	–	5	22/3
M.A.Carberry	1	1	–	7	7	7.00	–	–	1
P.D.Collingwood	36	33	2	79	583	18.80	–	3	15
A.N.Cook	4	4	–	26	61	15.25	–	–	1
M.S.Crane	2	–	–	–	–	–	–	–	–
T.K.Curran	6	3	2	6	8	8.00	–	–	1
S.M.Davies	5	5	–	33	102	20.40	–	–	2/1
L.A.Dawson	6	2	1	10	17	17.00	–	–	2
J.L.Denly	5	5	–	14	20	4.00	–	–	1
J.W.Dernbach	34	7	2	12	24	4.80	–	–	8
S.T.Finn	21	3	3	8*	14	–	–	–	6
J.S.Foster	5	5	2	14*	37	12.33	–	–	3/3
H.F.Gurney	2	–	–	–	–	–	–	–	–
A.D.Hales	52	52	6	116*	1456	31.65	1	7	27
C.J.Jordan	30	20	9	27*	163	14.81	–	–	13
L.S.Livingstone	2	2	–	16	16	8.00	–	–	1
D.J.Malan	5	5	–	78	250	50.00	–	4	1
S.C.Meaker	2	–	–	–	–	–	–	–	1
T.S.Mills	4	1	–	0	0	0.00	–	–	1
E.J.G.Morgan	72	70	14	85*	1678	29.96	–	9	32
P.Mustard	2	2	–	40	60	30.00	–	–	2
S.D.Parry	5	1	–	1	1	1.00	–	–	2
S.R.Patel	18	14	2	67	189	15.75	–	1	3
L.E.Plunkett	15	8	2	18	23	3.83	–	–	5
W.B.Rankin †	2	–	–	–	–	–	–	–	–
A.U.Rashid	28	12	7	9*	38	7.60	–	–	9
J.E.Root	25	23	4	90*	743	39.10	–	4	14
J.J.Roy	27	27	–	78	518	19.18	–	2	3
B.A.Stokes	21	18	5	38	192	14.76	–	–	8
R.J.W.Topley	6	1	1	1*	1	–	–	–	1
J.C.Tredwell	17	6	3	22	32	10.66	–	–	2
M.E.Trescothick	3	3	–	72	166	55.33	–	2	2
I.J.L.Trott	7	7.	1	51	138	23.00	–	1	–
J.M.Vince	7	7	–	46	194	27.71	–	–	4
D.J.Willey	20	14	3	21	119	10.81	–	–	9
C.R.Woakes	8	7	4	37	91	30.33	–	–	1
M.A.Wood	4	2	2	5*	10	–	–	–	–
L.J.Wright	51	45	5	99*	759	18.97	–	4	14

BOWLING

	O	M	R	W	Avge	Best	4wI	R/Over
M.M.Ali	52	0	400	14	28.57	2-21	–	7.69
J.M.Anderson	70.2	1	552	18	30.66	3-23	–	7.84
G.J.Batty	3	0	17	0	–	–	–	5.66
R.S.Bopara	53.4	1	387	16	24.18	4-10	1	7.21
S.G.Borthwick	4	0	15	1	15.00	1-15	–	3.75
T.T.Bresnan	110.3	1	887	24	36.95	3-10	–	8.02
D.R.Briggs	18	0	199	5	39.80	2-25	–	11.05
S.C.J.Broad	195.3	2	1491	65	22.93	4-24	1	7.62
P.D.Collingwood	39	0	347	16	21.68	4-22	1	8.89
M.S.Crane	8	0	62	1	62.00	1-38	–	7.75
T.K.Curran	21	0	195	7	27.85	3-33	–	9.28
L.A.Dawson	20	0	152	5	30.40	3-27	–	7.60
J.L.Denly	1	0	9	1	9.00	1- 9	–	9.00
J.W.Dernbach	117	1	1020	39	26.15	4-22	1	8.71
S.T.Finn	80	0	583	27	21.59	2-16	–	7.28
H.F.Gurney	8	0	55	3	18.33	2-26	–	6.87
C.J.Jordan	108	0	948	34	27.88	4-28	1	8.77
D.J.Malan	2	0	27	1	27.00	1-27	–	13.50
S.C.Meaker	7.5	0	70	2	35.00	1-28	–	8.93
T.S.Mills	16	0	116	3	38.66	1-27	–	7.25
S.D.Parry	16	0	138	3	46.00	2-33	–	8.62
S.R.Patel	42	0	321	7	45.85	2- 6	–	7.64
L.E.Plunkett	55.5	1	416	19	21.89	3-21	–	7.45
W.B.Rankin†	4	0	24	1	24.00	1-24	–	6.00
A.U.Rashid	89	1	694	23	30.17	3-25	–	7.79
J.E.Root	14	0	139	6	23.16	2- 9	–	9.92
B.A.Stokes	53.4	1	485	10	48.50	3-26	–	9.03
R.J.W.Topley	17.1	0	173	5	34.60	3-24	–	10.07
J.C.Tredwell	52.5	0	416	7	59.42	1-16	–	7.87
D.J.Willey	66.5	0	575	24	23.95	3-20	–	8.60
C.R.Woakes	27	0	253	7	36.14	2-40	–	9.37
M.A.Wood	14.3	0	139	8	17.37	3-26	–	9.58
L.J.Wright	55	0	465	18	25.83	2-24	–	8.45

† *W.B.Rankin has also made 24 appearances for Ireland.*

INTERNATIONAL TWENTY20 RECORDS

MATCH RESULTS
2004-05 to 5 March 2018

Opponents		Matches	Won											Tied	NR
			E	A	SA	WI	NZ	I	P	SL	Z	B	Ass		
England	Australia	15	5	9	–	–	–	–	–	–	–	–	–	–	1
	South Africa	15	6	–	8	–	–	–	–	–	–	–	–	–	1
	West Indies	15	4	–	–	11	–	–	–	–	–	–	–	–	–
	New Zealand	16	10	–	–	–	5	–	–	–	–	–	–	–	1
	India	11	6	–	–	–	–	5	–	–	–	–	–	–	–
	Pakistan	14	9	–	–	–	–	–	4	–	–	–	–	1	–
	Sri Lanka	8	4	–	–	–	–	–	–	4	–	–	–	–	–
	Zimbabwe	1	1	–	–	–	–	–	–	–	0	–	–	–	–
	Bangladesh	0	–	–	–	–	–	–	–	–	–	0	–	–	–
	Associates	5	2	–	–	–	–	–	–	–	–	–	2	–	1
Australia	South Africa	17	–	11	6	–	–	–	–	–	–	–	–	–	–
	West Indies	11	–	5	–	6	–	–	–	–	–	–	–	–	–
	New Zealand	9	–	7	–	–	1	–	–	–	–	–	–	1	–
	India	15	–	5	–	–	–	10	–	–	–	–	–	–	–
	Pakistan	14	–	6	–	–	–	–	7	–	–	–	–	1	–
	Sri Lanka	13	–	5	–	–	–	–	–	8	–	–	–	–	–
	Zimbabwe	1	–	0	–	–	–	–	–	–	1	–	–	–	–
	Bangladesh	4	–	4	–	–	–	–	–	–	–	0	–	–	–
	Associates	1	–	1	–	–	–	–	–	–	–	–	0	–	–
S Africa	West Indies	10	–	–	6	4	–	–	–	–	–	–	–	–	–
	New Zealand	15	–	–	11	–	4	–	–	–	–	–	–	–	–
	India	13	–	–	5	–	–	8	–	–	–	–	–	–	–
	Pakistan	11	–	–	6	–	–	–	5	–	–	–	–	–	–
	Sri Lanka	9	–	–	5	–	–	–	–	4	–	–	–	–	–
	Zimbabwe	3	–	–	3	–	–	–	–	–	0	–	–	–	–
	Bangladesh	6	–	–	6	–	–	–	–	–	–	0	–	–	–
	Associates	4	–	–	4	–	–	–	–	–	–	–	0	–	–
W Indies	New Zealand	13	–	–	–	3	6	–	–	–	–	–	–	3	1
	India	8	–	–	–	5	–	2	–	–	–	–	–	–	1
	Pakistan	11	–	–	–	3	–	–	8	–	–	–	–	–	–
	Sri Lanka	9	–	–	–	3	–	–	–	6	–	–	–	–	–
	Zimbabwe	3	–	–	–	2	–	–	–	–	1	–	–	–	–
	Bangladesh	6	–	–	–	3	–	–	–	–	–	2	–	–	1
	Associates	8	–	–	–	5	–	–	–	–	–	–	2	–	1
N Zealand	India	8	–	–	–	–	6	2	–	–	–	–	–	–	–
	Pakistan	18	–	–	–	–	8	–	10	–	–	–	–	–	–
	Sri Lanka	15	–	–	–	–	7	–	–	6	–	–	–	1	1
	Zimbabwe	6	–	–	–	–	6	–	–	–	0	–	–	–	–
	Bangladesh	7	–	–	–	–	7	–	–	–	–	0	–	–	–
	Associates	4	–	–	–	–	4	–	–	–	–	–	0	–	–
India	Pakistan	8	–	–	–	–	–	6	1	–	–	–	–	1	–
	Sri Lanka	14	–	–	–	–	–	10	–	4	–	–	–	–	–
	Zimbabwe	7	–	–	–	–	–	5	–	–	2	–	–	–	–
	Bangladesh	5	–	–	–	–	–	5	–	–	–	0	–	–	–
	Associates	5	–	–	–	–	–	4	–	–	–	–	0	–	1
Pakistan	Sri Lanka	18	–	–	–	–	–	–	13	5	–	–	–	–	–
	Zimbabwe	9	–	–	–	–	–	–	9	–	0	–	–	–	–
	Bangladesh	10	–	–	–	–	–	–	8	–	–	2	–	–	–
	Associates	7	–	–	–	–	–	–	7	–	–	–	0	–	–
Sri Lanka	Zimbabwe	3	–	–	–	–	–	–	–	3	0	–	–	–	–
	Bangladesh	9	–	–	–	–	–	–	–	7	–	2	–	–	–
	Associates	6	–	–	–	–	–	–	–	6	–	–	0	–	–
Zimbabwe	Bangladesh	9	–	–	–	–	–	–	–	–	4	5	–	–	–
	Associates	14	–	–	–	–	–	–	–	–	5	–	8	1	–
Bangladesh	Associates	15	–	–	–	–	–	–	–	–	–	10	4	–	1
Associates	Associates	141	–	–	–	–	–	–	–	–	–	–	137	4	–
		652	47	53	60	45	54	57	72	53	13	21	153	9	15

MATCH RESULTS SUMMARY

	Matches	Won	Lost	Tied	NR	Win %
Afghanistan	63	41	22	0	0	65.07
India	94	57	34	1	2	61.95
Pakistan	120	72	45	3	0	60.00
South Africa	103	60	42	0	1	58.82
Netherlands	45	24	19	0	2	55.81
Australia	100	53	44	2	1	53.53
Sri Lanka	104	53	49	1	1	51.45
New Zealand	111	54	49	5	3	50.00
West Indies	94	45	42	3	4	50.00
England	100	47	48	1	4	48.95
Ireland	61	26	29	0	6	47.27
Scotland	44	18	23	0	3	43.90
Hong Kong	24	10	14	0	0	41.66
United Arab Emirates	26	9	17	0	0	34.61
Kenya	29	10	19	0	0	34.48
Papua New Guinea	9	3	6	0	0	33.33
Oman	17	5	11	0	1	31.25
Bangladesh	71	21	48	0	2	30.43
Nepal	11	3	8	0	0	27.27
Zimbabwe	56	13	42	1	0	23.21
Canada	19	4	14	0	1	21.05
Bermuda	3	0	3	0	0	0.00

Pakistan's three IT20s v a World XI in 2017 (W2, L1) are excluded from these figures.

INTERNATIONAL TWENTY20 RECORDS
(To 5 March 2018)

TEAM RECORDS
HIGHEST INNINGS TOTALS
† Batting Second

263-3	Australia v Sri Lanka	Pallekele	2016
260-6	Sri Lanka v Kenya	Johannesburg	2007-08
260-5	India v Sri Lanka	Indore	2017-18
248-6	Australia v England	Southampton	2013
245-6	West Indies v India	Lauderhill	2016
245-5†	Australia v New Zealand	Auckland	2017-18
244-4†	India v West Indies	Lauderhill	2016
243-5	New Zealand v West Indies	Mt Maunganui	2017-18
243-6	New Zealand v Australia	Auckland	2017-18
241-6	South Africa v England	Centurion	2009-10
236-6†	West Indies v South Africa	Johannesburg	2014-15
231-7	South Africa v West Indies	Johannesburg	2014-15
230-8†	England v South Africa	Mumbai	2015-16
229-4	South Africa v England	Mumbai	2015-16
225-7	Ireland v Afghanistan	Abu Dhabi	2013-14
224-4	South Africa v Bangladesh	Potchefstroom	2017-18
221-5	Australia v England	Sydney	2006-07
219-4	South Africa v India	Johannesburg	2011-12
218-4	India v England	Durban	2007-08
215-5	Sri Lanka v India	Nagpur	2009-10
215-3	Sri Lanka v West Indies	Pallekele	2015-16
215-6	Afghanistan v Zimbabwe	Sharjah	2015-16

The highest total for Pakistan is 203-5 (v Bangladesh, Karachi, 2008), for Zimbabwe 200-2 (v New Zealand, Hamilton, 2011-12) and for Bangladesh is 193-5 (v Sri Lanka, Dhaka, 2017-18).

LOWEST COMPLETED INNINGS TOTALS
† Batting Second

39 (10.3)	Netherlands v Sri Lanka	Chittagong	2013-14
53 (14.3)	Nepal v Ireland	Belfast	2015
56† (18.4)	Kenya v Afghanistan	Sharjah	2013-14
60† (15.3)	New Zealand v Sri Lanka	Chittagong	2013-14
67 (17.2)	Kenya v Ireland	Belfast	2008
68† (16.4)	Ireland v West Indies	Providence	2009-10
69† (17.0)	Hong Kong v Nepal	Chittagong	2013-14
69† (17.4)	Nepal v Netherlands	Amstelveen	2015
70	Bermuda v Canada	Belfast	2008
70† (15.4)	Bangladesh v New Zealand	Kolkata	2015-16
71 (19.0)	Kenya v Ireland	Dubai	2011-12
71 (13.2)	Ireland v Afghanistan	Dubai	2016-17
72 (17.1)	Afghanistan v Bangladesh	Dhaka	2013-14
72	Nepal v Hong Kong	Colombo (PSS)	2014-15
73 (16.5)	Kenya v New Zealand	Durban	2007-08
73† (16.4)	UAE v Netherlands	Dubai	2015-16
74 (17.3)	India v Australia	Melbourne	2007-08
74† (19.1)	Pakistan v Australia	Dubai	2012
75† (19.2)	Canada v Zimbabwe	King City (NW)	2008-09
78 (17.3)	Bangladesh v New Zealand	Hamilton	2009-10
78† (18.5)	Kenya v Scotland	Aberdeen	2013
79† (14.3)	Australia v England	Southampton	2005
79-7†	West Indies v Zimbabwe	Port-of-Spain	2009-10
79† (18.1)	India v New Zealand	Nagpur	2015-16
80† (16.0)	Afghanistan v South Africa	Bridgetown	2009-10
80† (15.5)	New Zealand v Pakistan	Christchurch	2010-11
80† (17.2)	Afghanistan v England	Colombo (RPS)	2012-13
80† (14.4)	England v India	Colombo (RPS)	2012-13

The lowest total for South Africa is 100 (v Pakistan, Centurion, 2012-13), for Sri Lanka 82 (v India, Visakhapatnam, 2015-16), and for Zimbabwe 84 (v New Zealand, Providence, 2009-10).

LARGEST RUNS MARGIN OF VICTORY

172 runs	Sri Lanka beat Kenya	Johannesburg	2007
130 runs	South Africa beat Scotland	The Oval	2009
119 runs	New Zealand beat West Indies	Mt Maunganui	2017-18
116 runs	England beat Afghanistan	Colombo (RPS)	2012-13

BATTING RECORDS
1200 RUNS IN A CAREER

Runs			M	I	NO	HS	Avge	50	R/100B
2271	M.J.Guptill	NZ	75	73	7	105	34.40	16	132.8
2140	B.B.McCullum	NZ	71	70	10	123	35.66	15	136.2
1983	V.Kohli	I	57	53	14	90*	50.84	18	137.3
1889	T.M.Dilshan	SL	80	79	12	104*	28.19	14	120.5
1822	J.P.Duminy	SA	76	70	22	96*	37.95	11	124.7
1821	Shoaib Malik	P	92	86	24	75	29.37	6	117.6
1816	Mohammad Shahzad	Af	60	60	3	118*	31.85	13	136.2
1792	D.A.Warner	A	70	70	3	90*	26.74	13	140.1
1690	Umar Akmal	P	82	77	14	94	26.82	8	122.9
1679	R.G.Sharma	I	74	67	12	118	30.52	14	135.7
1678	E.J.G.Morgan	E	72	70	14	85*	29.96	9	132.3
1672	A.B.de Villiers	SA	78	75	11	79*	26.12	10	135.1

Runs		M	I	NO	HS	Avge	50	R/100B
1658	Mohammad Hafeez	P	81	78	5	86	22.71	9	113.7
1589	C.H.Gayle	WI	55	51	4	117	33.80	15	145.1
1493	D.P.M.D.Jayawardena	SL	55	55	8	100	31.76	10	133.1
1469	M.N.Samuels	WI	60	58	10	89*	30.60	10	115.2
1462	S.R.Watson	A	58	56	6	124*	29.24	11	145.3
1460	H.Masakadza	Z	52	52	2	93*	29.20	10	118.4
1456	A.D.Hales	E	52	52	6	116*	31.65	8	136.2
1444	M.S.Dhoni	I	89	78	39	56	37.02	2	126.5
1416	Ahmed Shehzad	P	55	55	2	111*	26.71	8	115.7
1415	L.R.P.L.Taylor	NZ	81	73	17	63	25.26	5	121.0
1405	Shahid Afridi	P	98	90	12	54*	18.01	4	150.7
1396	S.K.Raina	I	68	58	11	101	29.70	5	134.1
1382	K.C.Sangakkara	SL	56	53	9	78	31.40	8	119.5
1316	K.S.Williamson	NZ	51	49	7	73*	31.33	8	120.9
1286	Tamim Iqbal	B/Wd	60	60	5	103*	23.38	5	115.4
1277	H.M.Amla	SA/Wd	43	43	6	97*	34.51	8	132.6
1223	Shakib Al Hasan	B	61	61	8	84	23.07	6	121.2
1206	A.J.Finch	A	36	36	6	156	40.20	8	151.6

The most for Ireland is 1002 by W.T.S.Porterfield (54 innings).

HIGHEST INDIVIDUAL INNINGS

Score	Balls				
156	63	A.J.Finch	A v E	Southampton	2013
145*	65	G.J.Maxwell	A v SL	Pallekele	2016
125*	62	E.Lewis	WI v I	Kingston	2017
124*	71	S.R.Watson	A v I	Sydney	2015-16
123	58	B.B.McCullum	NZ v B	Pallekele	2012-13
122	60	Babar Hayat	HK v Oman	Fatullah	2015-16
119	56	F.du Plessis	SA v WI	Johannesburg	2014-15
118*	67	Mohammad Shahzad	Af v Z	Sharjah	2015-16
118	43	R.G.Sharma	I v SL	Indore	2017-18
117*	51	R.E.Levi	SA v NZ	Hamilton	2011-12
117*	68	Shaiman Anwar	UAE v PNG	Abu Dhabi	2017
117	57	C.H.Gayle	WI v SA	Johannesburg	2007-08
116*	56	B.B.McCullum	NZ v A	Christchurch	2009-10
116*	64	A.D.Hales	E v SL	Chittagong	2013-14
114*	70	M.van Wyk	SA v WI	Durban	2014-15
111*	62	Ahmed Shehzad	P v B	Dhaka	2013-14
110*	51	K.L.Rahul	I v WI	Lauderhill	2016
109*	58	C.Munro	NZ v I	Rajkot	2017-18
106	66	R.G.Sharma	I v SA	Dharamsala	2015-16
105	54	M.J.Guptill	NZ v A	Auckland	2017-18
104*	57	T.M.Dilshan	SL v A	Pallekele	2011
104	53	C.Munro	NZ v WI	Mt Maunganui	2017-18
103*	63	Tamim Iqbal	B v Oman	Dharmasala	2015-16
103*	58	G.J.Maxwell	A v E	Hobart	2017-18
101*	69	M.J.Guptill	NZ v SA	East London	2012-13
101*	69	D.A.Miller	SA v B	Potchefstroom	2017-18
101	60	S.K.Raina	I v SA	Gros Islet	2009-10
101	54	C.Munro	NZ v B	Mt Maunganui	2016-17
100*	48	C.H.Gayle	WI v E	Mumbai	2015-16
100	64	D.P.M.D.Jayawardena	SL v Z	Providence	2009-10
100	58	R.D.Berrington	Sc v B	The Hague	2012
100	49	E.Lewis	WI v I	Lauderhill	2016

The highest score for Zimbabwe is 93* by H.Masakadza (v B, Khulna, 2015-16) and for Ireland 79 by P.R.Stirling (v Af, Dubai DSC, 2011-12).

MOST SIXES IN AN INNINGS

14	A.J.Finch (156)	A v E	Southampton	2013
13	R.E.Levi (117*)	SA v NZ	Hamilton	2011-12
12	E.Lewis (125*)	WI v I	Kingston	2017

HIGHEST PARTNERSHIP FOR EACH WICKET

1st	171*	M.J.Guptill/K.S.Williamson	NZ v P	Hamilton	2015-16
2nd	166	D.P.M.D.Jayawardena/K.C.Sangakkara	SL v WI	Bridgetown	2009-10
3rd	152	A.D.Hales/E.J.G.Morgan	E v SL	Chittagong	2013-14
4th	161	D.A.Warner/G.J.Maxwell	A v SA	Johannesburg	2015-16
5th	119*	Shoaib Malik/Misbah-ul-Haq	P v A	Johannesburg	2007-08
6th	101*	C.L.White/M.E.K.Hussey	A v SL	Bridgetown	2009-10
7th	91	P.D.Collingwood/M.H.Yardy	E v WI	The Oval	2007
8th	80	P.L.Mommsen/S.M.Sharif	Sc v Ne	Edinburgh	2015
9th	66	D.J.Bravo/J.E.Taylor	WI v P	Dubai	2016-17
10th	31*	Wahab Riaz/Shoaib Akhtar	P v NZ	Auckland	2010-11

BOWLING RECORDS
50 WICKETS IN A CAREER

Wkts			Matches	Overs	Mdns	Runs	Avge	Best	R/Over
97	Shahid Afridi	P	98	357.2	4	2362	24.35	4-11	6.61
90	S.L.Malinga	SL	68	241.5	–	1780	19.77	5-31	7.36
85	Umar Gul	P	60	200.3	2	1443	16.97	5-6	7.19
85	Saeed Ajmal	P	64	238.2	2	1516	17.83	4-19	6.36
73	Shakib Al Hasan	B	61	221.5	1	1509	20.67	4-15	6.80
66	B.A.W.Mendis	SL	39	147.3	5	952	14.42	6-8	6.45
66	K.M.D.N.Kulasekara	SL	58	205.1	6	1530	23.18	4-31	7.45
65	S.C.J.Broad	E	56	195.3	2	1491	22.93	4-24	7.62
62	T.G.Southee	NZ	51	178.0	2	1543	24.88	5-18	8.66
61	Mohammad Nabi	Af	60	209.4	5	1513	24.80	4-10	7.21
58	D.W.Steyn	SA	42	150.1	2	1009	17.39	4-9	6.71
58	N.L.McCullum	NZ	63	187.1	–	1278	22.03	4-16	6.82
57	Imran Tahir	SA/Wd	36	132.5	–	904	15.85	5-24	6.80
54	K.J.O'Brien	Ire	59	139.3	–	998	18.48	4-45	7.15
54	S.Badree	WI/Wd	45	169.0	3	1011	18.72	4-15	5.98
54	Sohail Tanvir	P	57	202.2	3	1454	26.92	3-12	7.18
52	G.H.Dockrell	Ire	46	142.4	1	927	17.82	4-20	6.49
52	R.Ashwin	I	46	171.0	2	1193	22.94	4-8	6.97
52	D.J.Bravo	WI	66	173.4	–	1470	28.26	4-28	8.46
51	G.P.Swann	E	39	135.0	4	859	16.84	3-13	6.36
50	S.P.Narine	WI	48	171.4	1	1034	20.68	4-12	6.02

The most wickets for Australia is 48 by S.R.Watson (58 matches), and for Zimbabwe 35 by A.G.Cremer (29 matches).

BEST FIGURES IN AN INNINGS

6- 8	B.A.W.Mendis	SL v Z	Hambantota	2012-13
6-16	B.A.W.Mendis	SL v A	Pallekele	2011
6-25	Y.S.Chahal	I v E	Bangalore	2016-17
5- 3	H.M.R.K.B.Herath	SL v NZ	Chittagong	2013-14
5- 3	Rashid Khan	Af v Ire	Greater Noida	2016-17
5- 6	Umar Gul	P v NZ	The Oval	2009
5- 6	Umar Gul	P v SA	Centurion	2012-13
5-13	Elias Sunny	B v Ire	Belfast	2012
5-13	Samiullah Shenwari	Af v K	Sharjah	2013-14
5-14	Imad Wasim	P v WI	Dubai	2016-17
5-18	T.G.Southee	NZ v P	Auckland	2010-11

5-19	R.McLaren	SA v WI	North Sound	2009-10
5-19	Ahsan Malik	Neth v SA	Chittagong	2013-14
5-20	N.Odhiambo	K v Sc	Nairobi (Gym)	2009-10
5-22	Mustafizur Rahman	B v NZ	Kolkata	2015-16
5-23	D.Wiese	SA v WI	Durban	2014-15
5-24	A.C.Evans	Sc v Neth	Edinburgh	2015
5-24	Imran Tahir	SA v NZ	Auckland	2016-17
5-24	B.Kumar	I v SA	Johannesburg	2017-18
5-26	D.J.G.Sammy	WI v Z	Port of Spain	2009-10
5-27	M.R.J.Watt	Sc v Neth	Dubai	2015-16
5-27	J.P.Faulkner	A v P	Mohali	2015-16
5-31	S.L.Malinga	SL v E	Pallekele	2012-13

The best figures for England are 4-10 by R.S.Bopara (v WI, The Oval, 2011), for Zimbabwe 4-28 by W.P.Masakadza (v Sc, Nagpur, 2015-16), and for Ireland 4-11 by A.R.Cusack (v WI, Kingston, 2013-14).

HAT-TRICKS

B.Lee	Australia v Bangladesh	Melbourne	2007-08
J.D.P.Oram	New Zealand v Sri Lanka	Colombo (RPS)	2009
T.G.Southee	New Zealand v Pakistan	Auckland	2010-11
N.L.T.C.Perera	Sri Lanka v India	Ranchi	2015-16
S.L.Malinga	Sri Lanka v Bangladesh	Colombo (RPS)	2016-17
Faheem Ashraf	Pakistan v Sri Lanka	Abu Dhabi	2017-18

WICKET-KEEPING RECORDS
25 DISMISSALS IN A CAREER

Dis			Matches	Ct	St
78	M.S.Dhoni	India	89	49	29
60	Kamran Akmal	Pakistan	54	28	32
52	Mohammad Shahzad	Afghanistan	60	25	27
51	D.Ramdin	West Indies	58	32	19
47	Mushfiqur Rahim	Bangladesh	63	22	25
45	K.C.Sangakkara	Sri Lanka	56	25	20
39	Q.de Kock	South Africa	31	30	9
32†	B.B.McCullum	New Zealand	71	24	8
29‡	L.Ronchi	Aus/New Zealand	32	24	5
28†	A.B.de Villiers	South Africa	78	21	7
27	W.Barresi	Netherlands	35	26	1
26	Sarfraz Ahmed	Pakistan	38	19	7
25	N.J.O'Brien	Ireland	30	15	10

† *Excluding catches taken in the field.* ‡ *L.Ronchi played 3 matches for Australia.*

The most for England is 24 (21 ct, 3 st) by J.C.Buttler, for Australia 23 (17 ct, 6 st) by B.J.Haddin, and for Zimbabwe 14 (12 ct, 2 st) by B.R.M.Taylor.

MOST DISMISSALS IN AN INNINGS

5 (3 ct, 2 st) Mohammad Shahzad Afghanistan v Oman   Abu Dhabi   2015-16

FIELDING RECORDS
25 CATCHES IN A CAREER

Total			Matches	Total			Matches
44†	A.B.de Villiers	South Africa	78	37	Shoaib Malik	Pakistan	92
44	L.R.P.L.Taylor	New Zealand	81	36	S.K.Raina	India	68
41	D.A.Warner	Australia	70	35	D.J.Bravo	West Indies	66
39	D.A.Miller	South Africa	60	34	J.P.Duminy	South Africa	76
39	M.J.Guptill	New Zealand	74	32	Mohammad Nabi	Afghanistan	60
38	Umar Akmal	Pakistan	82	32	E.J.G.Morgan	England	72

Total			Matches	Total			Matches
31	D.J.G.Sammy	West Indies/World	68	27	V.Kohli	India	57
30	Shahid Afridi	Pakistan	98	26	N.L.McCullum	New Zealand	63
28	P.W.Borren	Netherlands	43	26	T.M.Dilshan	Sri Lanka	80
28	R.G.Sharma	India	74	25	K.A.Pollard	West Indies	56
27	A.D.Hales	England	52				

† *Excluding catches taken as a wicket-keeper.*

The most for Zimbabwe is 18 by E.Chigumbura (47 matches), for Bangladesh 23 by Mahmudullah (62 matches), and for Ireland 24 by G.H.Dockrell (46 matches).

MOST CATCHES IN AN INNINGS

4	D.J.G.Sammy	West Indies v Ireland	Providence	2009-10
4	P.W.Borren	Netherlands v Bangladesh	The Hague	2012
4	C.J.Anderson	New Zealand v South Africa	Port Elizabeth	2012-13
4	L.D.Chandimal	Sri Lanka v Bangladesh	Chittagong	2013-14
4	A.M.Rahane	India v England	Birmingham	2014
4	Babar Hayat	Hong Kong v Afghanistan	Dhaka	2015-16

APPEARANCE RECORDS – 60 APPEARANCES

98	*Shahid Afridi*	*Pakistan*	68	N.L.T.C.Perera	Sri Lanka/World
92	Shoaib Malik	Pakistan	68	S.K.Raina	India
89	M.S.Dhoni	India	68	D.J.G.Sammy	West Indies/World
82	Umar Akmal	Pakistan	66	D.J.Bravo	West Indies
81	Mohammad Hafeez	Pakistan	64	Saeed Ajmal	Pakistan
81	L.R.P.L.Taylor	New Zealand	63	N.L.McCullum	New Zealand
80	T.M.Dilshan	Sri Lanka	63	Mushfiqur Rahim	Bangladesh
78	A.B.de Villiers	South Africa	62	Mahmudullah	Bangladesh
76	J.P.Duminy	South Africa	61	J.C.Buttler	England
75	M.J.Guptill	New Zealand	61	Shakib Al Hasan	Bangladesh
74	R.G.Sharma	India	60	D.A.Miller	South Africa/World
72	E.J.G.Morgan	England	60	Mohammad Nabi	Afghanistan
71	B.B.McCullum	New Zealand	60	Mohammad Shahzad	Afghanistan
71	A.D.Mathews	Sri Lanka	60	M.N.Samuels	West Indies
70	D.A.Warner	Australia	60	Tamim Iqbal	Bangladesh/World
68	S.L.Malinga	Sri Lanka	60	Umar Gul	Pakistan

The most for Zimbabwe is 52 by H.Masakadza, and for Ireland 59 by K.J.O'Brien.

25 MATCHES AS CAPTAIN

			W	L	T	NR	%age wins
72	M.S.Dhoni	India	41	28	1	2	58.57
56	W.T.S.Porterfield	Ireland	26	26	–	4	50.00
47	D.J.G.Sammy	West Indies	27	17	1	2	60.00
43	Shahid Afridi	Pakistan	19	23	1	–	44.18
38	Asghar Stanikzai	Afghanistan	29	9	–	–	76.31
37	P.W.Borren	Netherlands	21	15	–	1	58.33
35	F.du Plessis	South Africa	20	15	–	–	57.14
33	K.S.Williamson	New Zealand	17	15	–	1	53.12
30	P.D.Collingwood	England	17	11	–	2	60.71
29	Mohammad Hafeez	Pakistan	17	11	1	–	58.62
29	E.J.G.Morgan	England	14	14	1	–	48.27
28	G.J.Bailey	Australia	14	13	1	–	50.00
28	B.B.McCullum	New Zealand	13	14	–	1	48.14
28	Mashrafe Mortaza	Bangladesh	10	17	–	1	37.03
28	D.L.Vettori	New Zealand	13	13	2	–	46.42
27	G.C.Smith	South Africa	18	9	–	–	66.66
27	S.C.J.Broad	England	11	15	–	1	42.30

INDIAN PREMIER LEAGUE 2017

The tenth IPL tournament was held in India between 5 April and 21 May.

Team	P	W	L	T	NR	Pts	Net RR
1 Mumbai Indians (5)	14	10	4	–	–	20	+0.78
2 Rising Pune Supergiant (7)	14	9	5	–	–	18	+0.17
3 Sunrisers Hyderabad (3)	14	8	5	–	1	17	+0.59
4 Kolkata Knight Riders (4)	14	8	6	–	–	16	+0.64
5 Kings XI Punjab (8)	14	7	7	–	–	14	–0.01
6 Delhi Daredevils (6)	14	6	8	–	–	12	–0.51
7 Gujarat Lions (1)	14	4	10	–	–	8	–0.41
8 Royal Challengers Bangalore (2)	14	3	10	–	1	7	–1.29

1st Qualifying Match: At Wankhede Stadium, Mumbai, 16 May (floodlit). Toss: Mumbai Indians. **RISING PUNE SUPERGIANT** won by 20 runs. Rising Pune Supergiant 162-4 (20; M.K.Tiwary 58, A.M.Rahane 56). Mumbai Indians 142-9 (20; P.A.Patel 52, Washington Sundar 3-16; S.N.Thakur 3-37). Award: Washington Sundar.

Eliminator: At M.Chinnaswamy Stadium, Bangalore, 17 May (floodlit). Toss: Kolkata Knight Riders. **KOLKATA KNIGHT RIDERS** won by seven wickets (D/L method). Sunrisers Hyderabad 128-7 (20; N.M.Coulter-Nile 3-20). Kolkata Knight Riders 48-3 (5.2/6). Award: N.M.Coulter-Nile.

2nd Qualifying Match: At M.Chinnaswamy Stadium, Bangalore, 19 May (floodlit). Toss: Mumbai Indians. **MUMBAI INDIANS** won by six wickets. Kolkata Knight Riders 107 (18.5; K.V.Sharma 4-16; J.J.Bumrah 3-7). Mumbai Indians 111-4 (14.3). Award: K.V.Sharma.

FINAL: At Rajiv Gandhi International Stadium, Hyderabad, 21 May (floodlit). Toss: Mumbai Indians. **MUMBAI INDIANS** won by 1 run. Mumbai Indians 129-8 (20). Rising Pune Supergiant 128-6 (20; S.P.D.Smith 51; M.G.Johnson 3-26). Award: K.H.Pandya (Mumbai Indians 47). Series award: B.A.Stokes (Rising Pune Supergiant).

IPL winners:	2008	Rajasthan Royals	2009	Deccan Chargers
	2010	Chennai Super Kings	2011	Chennai Super Kings
	2012	Kolkata Knight Riders	2013	Mumbai Indians
	2014	Kolkata Knight Riders	2015	Mumbai Indians
	2016	Sunrisers Hyderabad		

TEAM RECORDS
HIGHEST TOTALS

263-5 (20)	Bangalore v Pune	Bangalore	2013
248-3 (20)	Bangalore v Gujarat	Bangalore	2016

LOWEST TOTALS

49 (9.4)	Bangalore v Kolkata	Kolkata	2017
58 (15.1)	Rajasthan v Bangalore	Cape Town	2009

LARGEST MARGINS OF VICTORY

146 runs	Mumbai (212-3) v Delhi (66)	Delhi	2017

There have been ten victories in IPL history by ten wickets, the most recent being:

10 wickets	Gujarat (183-4) v Kolkata (184-0)	Rajkot	2017
10 wickets	Delhi (67) v Punjab (68-0)	Chandigarh	2017

See *Playfair Cricket Annual 2017* for a list of the other ten-wicket victories. Delhi beat Punjab by ten wickets in a reduced game in 2009.

BATTING RECORDS
MOST RUNS IN IPL

4540	S.K.Raina	Chennai, Gujarat	2008-17
4418	V.Kohli	Bangalore	2008-17

800 RUNS IN A SEASON

Runs			Year	M	I	NO	HS	Ave	100	50	6s	4s	R/100B
973	V.Kohli	Bangalore	2016	16	16	4	113	81.08	4	7	38	83	152.0
848	D.A.Warner	Hyderabad	2016	17	17	3	93*	60.57	–	9	31	88	151.4

HIGHEST SCORES

Score	Balls				
175*	66	C.H.Gayle	Bangalore v Pune	Bangalore	2013
158*	73	B.B.McCullum	Kolkata v Bangalore	Bangalore	2008
133*	59	A.B.de Villiers	Bangalore v Mumbai	Mumbai	2015
129*	52	A.B.de Villiers	Bangalore v Mumbai	Bangalore	2016
128*	62	C.H.Gayle	Bangalore v Delhi	Delhi	2012
127	56	M.Vijay	Chennai v Rajasthan	Chennai	2010

K.P.Pietersen 103* (Delhi v Deccan at Delhi, 2012) and B.A.Stokes 103* (Pune v Gujarat at Pune, 2017) are the only England-qualified centurions in the IPL.

FASTEST HUNDRED

30 balls	C.H.Gayle (175*)	Bangalore v Pune	Bangalore	2013

MOST SIXES IN AN INNINGS

17	C.H.Gayle	Bangalore v Pune	Bangalore	2013

HIGHEST STRIKE RATE IN A SEASON (Qualification: 100 runs or more)

R/100B	Score	Balls		
204.34	188	92	B.B.McCullum	Kolkata	2008

HIGHEST STRIKE RATE IN AN INNINGS (Qualification: 25 runs, 350+ strike rate)

R/100B	Score	Balls			
422.2	38*	9	C.H.Morris	Delhi v Pune	Pune	2017
400.0	28	7	J.A.Morkel	Chennai v Bangalore	Chennai	2012
387.5	31	8	A.B.de Villiers	Bangalore v Pune	Bangalore	2013
385.7	27*	7	B.Akhil	Bangalore v Deccan	Hyderabad	2008
372.7	41	11	A.B.de Villiers	Bangalore v Mumbai	Bangalore	2015
350.0	35	10	C.H.Gayle	Bangalore v Hyderabad	Hyderabad	2015
350.0	35*	10	S.N.Khan	Bangalore v Hyderabad	Bangalore	2016

BOWLING RECORDS
MOST WICKETS IN IPL

154	S.L.Malinga	Mumbai	2008-17
134	A.Mishra	Deccan, Delhi, Hyderabad	2008-17

25 WICKETS IN A SEASON

Wkts			Year	P	O	M	Runs	Avge	Best	4w	R/Over
32	D.J.Bravo	Chennai	2013	18	62.3	–	497	15.53	4-42	1	7.95
28	S.L.Malinga	Mumbai	2011	16	63.0	2	375	13.39	5-13	1	5.95
28	J.P.Faulkner	Rajasthan	2013	16	63.1	2	427	15.25	5-16	2	6.75
26	D.J.Bravo	Chennai	2015	17	52.2	–	426	16.38	3-22	–	8.14
26	B.Kumar	Hyderabad	2017	14	52.2	–	369	14.19	5-19	1	7.05
25	M.Morkel	Delhi	2012	16	63.0	1	453	18.12	4-20	1	7.19

BEST BOWLING FIGURES IN AN INNINGS

6-14	Sohail Tanvir	Rajasthan v Chennai	Jaipur	2008
6-19	A.Zampa	Pune v Hyderabad	Visakhapatnam	2016
5- 5	A.Kumble	Bangalore v Rajasthan	Cape Town	2009
5-12	I.Sharma	Deccan v Kochi	Kochi	2011
5-13	S.L.Malinga	Mumbai v Delhi	Delhi	2011

MOST ECONOMICAL BOWLING ANALYSIS

O	M	R	W				
4	1	6	0	F.H.Edwards	Deccan v Kolkata	Cape Town	2009
4	1	6	1	A.Nehra	Delhi v Punjab	Bloemfontein	2009

MOST EXPENSIVE BOWLING ANALYSIS

O	M	R	W				
4	0	66	0	I.Sharma	Hyderabad v Chennai	Hyderabad	2013
4	0	65	0	U.T.Yadav	Delhi v Bangalore	Delhi	2013
4	0	65	1	Sandeep Sharma	Punjab v Hyderabad	Hyderabad	2014

BIG BASH 2017-18

The seventh Big Bash tournament was held in Australia between 19 December and 4 February.

Team	P	W	L	T	NR	Pts	Net RR
1 Perth Scorchers (1)	10	8	2	–	–	16	+0.15
2 Adelaide Strikers (6)	10	7	3	–	–	14	+0.80
3 Melbourne Renegades (5)	10	6	4	–	–	12	+0.29
4 Hobart Hurricanes (7)	10	5	5	–	–	10	–0.29
5 Sydney Sixers (3)	10	4	6	–	–	8	+0.33
6 Sydney Thunder (8)	10	4	6	–	–	8	–0.03
7 Brisbane Heat (2)	10	4	6	–	–	8	–0.43
8 Melbourne Stars (4)	10	2	8	–	–	4	–0.92

1st Semi-final: At Perth Stadium, 1 February (floodlit). Toss: Perth Scorchers. **HOBART HURRICANES** won by 71 runs. Hobart Hurricanes 210-4 (20; M.S.Wade 71, B.R.McDermott 67*). Perth Scorchers 139 (17.5; D.T.Christian 4-17, T.S.Rogers 3-31). Award: M.S.Wade.

2nd Semi-final: At Adelaide Oval, 2 February (floodlit). Toss: Adelaide Strikers. **ADELAIDE STRIKERS** won by 1 run. Adelaide Strikers 178-5 (20; T.M.Head 85*, J.Weatherald 57). Melbourne Renegades 177-4 (20). Award: T.M.Head.

FINAL: At Adelaide Oval, 4 February (floodlit). Toss: Adelaide Strikers. **ADELAIDE STRIKERS** won by 25 runs. Adelaide Strikers 202-2 (20; J.Weatherald 115). Hobart Hurricanes 177-5 (20; D.J.M.Short 68, P.M.Siddle 3-17). Award: J.Weatherald. Series award: D.J.M.Short (Hobart Hurricanes).

Big Bash winners:

2011-12	Sydney Sixers	2012-13	Brisbane Heat
2013-14	Perth Scorchers	2014-15	Perth Scorchers
2015-16	Sydney Thunder	2016-17	Perth Scorchers

TEAM RECORDS
HIGHEST TOTALS

223-8 (20)	Hobart v Melbourne Renegades	Melbourne (Dock)	2016-17
222-4 (20)	Melbourne Renegades v Hobart	Melbourne (Dock)	2016-17

LOWEST TOTALS

57 (12.4)	Melbourne Renegades v Melbourne Stars	Melbourne (Dock)	2014-15
69 (15.2)	Perth v Melbourne Stars	Perth	2012-13

LARGEST MARGINS OF VICTORY

112 runs	Melbourne Ren (57) v Melbourne Stars (169-6)	Melbourne (Dock)	2014-15
10 wickets	Perth (171-0) v Melbourne Renegades (171-4)	Melbourne (Dock)	2015-16

BATTING RECORDS
MOST RUNS IN BIG BASH

1802	M.Klinger	Adelaide Strikers, Perth Scorchers	2011-18
1669	A.J.Finch	Melbourne Renegades	2011-18

500 RUNS IN A SEASON

Runs			Year	M	I	NO	HS	Ave	100	50	6s	4s	R/100B
572	D.J.M.Short	Hobart	2017-18	11	11	1	122*	57.20	1	4	26	53	148.5

HIGHEST SCORES

Score	Balls				
122*	69	D.J.M.Short	Hobart v Brisbane	Brisbane	2017-18
117	60	L.J.Wright	Melbourne S v Hobart	Hobart	2011-12
115	70	J.Weatherald	Adelaide v Hobart	Adelaide	2017-18

FASTEST HUNDRED

39 balls | C.J.Simmons (102) | Perth v Adelaide | Perth | 2013-14

MOST SIXES IN AN INNINGS

11	C.H.Gayle (100*)	Sydney T v Adelaide	Sydney (SA)	2011-12
11	C.J.Simmons (112)	Perth v Sydney Sixers	Sydney	2013-14
11	C.A.Lynn (98*)	Brisbane v Perth	Perth	2016-17

HIGHEST STRIKE RATE IN AN INNINGS (Qualification: 25 runs, 325+ strike rate)

R/100B	Score	Balls				
377.7	34	9	D.T.Christian	Brisbane v Hobart	Hobart	2014-15
329.4	56	17	C.H.Gayle	Melbourne R v Adelaide	Melbourne (Dk)	2015-16
327.2	36*	11	B.J.Rohrer	Melbourne R v Brisbane	Melbourne (Dk)	2013-14

HIGHEST PARTNERSHIPS

172	R.J.Quiney/L.J.Wright	Melbourne S v Hobart	Hobart	2011-12
171*	S.E.Marsh/M.Klinger	Perth v Melbourne R	Melbourne (Dk)	2015-16
171	A.T.Carey/J.Weatherald	Adelaide v Hobart	Adelaide	2017-18

BOWLING RECORDS
MOST WICKETS IN BIG BASH

| 85 | B.Laughlin | Adelaide Strikers, Hobart Hurricanes | 2011-18 |
| 63 | S.A.Abbott | Sydney Sixers, Sydney Thunder | 2011-18 |

20 WICKETS IN A SEASON

Wkts			Year	P	O	M	Runs	Avge	Best	4w	R/Over
20	S.A.Abbott	Sydney Sixers	2016-17	10	37.0	–	323	16.15	5-16	2	8.72

BEST BOWLING FIGURES IN AN INNINGS

6- 7	S.L.Malinga	Melbourne S v Perth	Perth	2012-13
6-11	I.S.Sodhi	Adelaide v Sydney T	Sydney (Show)	2016-17
5-14	D.T.Christian	Hobart v Adelaide	Hobart	2016-17
5-16	S.A.Abbott	Sydney S v Adelaide	Adelaide	2016-17

MOST ECONOMICAL BOWLING ANALYSIS

O	M	R	W				
4	2	3	3	M.G.Johnson	Perth v Melbourne S	Perth	2016-17
4	1	7	6	S.L.Malinga	Melbourne S v Perth	Perth	2012-13
4	1	7	1	Fawad Ahmed	Melbourne R v Brisbane	Melbourne (Dk)	2014-15

MOST EXPENSIVE BOWLING ANALYSIS

O	M	R	W				
4	0	60	0	D.J.Worrall	Melbourne S v Hobart	Melbourne	2014-15
4	0	59	0	N.L.T.C.Perera	Melbourne R v Hobart	Melbourne (Dk)	2016-17
3.3	0	57	1	S.A.Abbott	Sydney S v Adelaide	Adelaide	2015-16

WICKET-KEEPING RECORDS
MOST DISMISSALS IN BIG BASH

| 33 | T.P.Ludeman | Adelaide Strikers, Melbourne Renegades | 2012-18 |

MOST DISMISSALS IN A SERIES

| 14 | A.T.Carey | Adelaide Strikers | 2017-18 |

MOST DISMISSALS IN AN INNINGS

| 5 | T.J.F.Triffitt | Perth v Melbourne R | Perth | 2012-13 |

IRELAND INTERNATIONALS

The following players have played for Ireland since 1 September 2016. Details correct to 3 March 2018.

ANDERSON, John, b Durban, South Africa 6 Oct 1982. Brother-in-law of E.C.Joyce (*see below*). RHB, LB. KwaZulu-Natal 2002-03. Ireland debut 2012. Leinster 2017. **LOI**: 8 (2014 to 2016-17); HS 39 v A (Benoni) 2016-17; BB – . **IT20**: 4 (2015); HS 9 v Scot (Bready) 2015; BB – . HS 127 Ire v Neth (Deventer) 2013. BB 2-92 Ire v Afghan (Greater Noida) 2016-17. LO HS 45 Ire A v B A (Cox's Bazar) 2017-18. LO BB – . T20 HS 41* . T20 BB – .

BALBIRNIE, Andrew (St Andrew's C, Dublin; UWIC), b Dublin 28 Dec 1990. 6'2". RHB, OB. Cardiff MCCU 2012-13. Ireland debut 2012. Middlesex 2012-15. Leinster 2017. Ireland Wolves 2017-18. **LOI**: 41 (2010 to 2017-18); HS 102 v UAE (Dubai, ICCA) 2017-18; BB 1-26 v Afghan (Dubai, DSC) 2014-15. **IT20**: 10 (2015 to 2015-16); HS 31 v Scot (Bready) 2015 and 31 v Neth (Dublin) 2015. HS 205* Ire v Neth (Dublin) 2017. BB 4-23 Lein v North-West (Bready) 2017. LO HS 129 Ire v NZ A (Dubai, CA) 2014-15. LO BB 1-26 (*see LOI*). T20 HS 71* .

CHASE, Peter Karl David (Malahide Community S), b Dublin 9 Oct 1993. 6'4". RHB, RMF. Durham 2014, taking 5-64 v Notts (Chester-le-St) on debut. Ireland debut 2016. Leinster 2017. **LOI**: 22 (2014-15 to 2017-18); HS 14 v NZ (Dublin) 2017; BB 3-33 v B (Dublin) 2017. HS 16 Ire v Afghan (Greater Noida) 2016-17. BB 5-64 (*see above*). LO HS 22* Ire v SL A (Belfast) 2014. LO BB 3-33 (*see LOI*). T20 HS 2* . T20 BB 4-11.

DOCKRELL, George Henry (Gonzaga C, Dublin), b Dublin 22 Jul 1992. 6'3". RHB, SLA. Ireland 2010 to date. Somerset 2011-14. Sussex 2015. Leinster 2017. Ireland Wolves 2017-18. **LOI**: 75 (2009-10 to 2017-18); HS 62* v Afghan (Sharjah) 2017-18; BB 4-24 v Scot (Belfast) 2013. **IT20**: 46 (2009-10 to 2016-17); HS 13* v Afghan (Abu Dhabi) 2016-17; BB 4-20 v Neth (Dubai) 2009-10. HS 53 Ire v Namibia (Belfast) 2011. BB 6-27 Sm v Middx (Taunton) 2012. LO HS 62* (*see LOI*). LO BB 4-24 (*see LOI*). T20 HS 29* . T20 BB 4-20.

JOYCE, Edmund Christopher (Presentation C, Bray, Co Wicklow; Trinity C, Dublin), b Dublin 22 Sep 1978. Brother of four Ireland cricketers: Augustine (2000), Dominick (2004-06), Cecilia (2001-07) and Isobel, her twin (1999-2007). 5'11". LHB, RM. Ireland 1997-98 to date. Middlesex 1999-2008; cap 2002. Sussex 2009-16; cap 2009; captain 2013-15. Leinster 2017. MCC 2006, 2008. **LOI** (E/Ire): 74 (17 for E 2006 to 2006-07; 57 for Ire 2010-11 to 2017-18); HS 160* Ire v Afghan (Belfast) 2016. **IT20** (E/Ire): 18 (2 for E 2006 to 2006-07; 16 for Ire 2011-12 to 2013-14); HS 78* Ire v Scot (Dubai, DSC) 2011-12. F-c Tour (Eng A): WI 2005-06. 1000 runs (9); most – 1668 (2005). HS 250 Sx v Derbys (Derby) 2016. BB M 2-34 v Cambridge U (Cambridge) 2004. LO HS 160* (*see LOI*). LO BB 2-10 M v Notts (Nottingham) 2003 (NL). T20 HS 78* .

LITTLE, Joshua B., b Dublin 1 Nov 1999. RHB, LFM. Awaiting f-c and List-A debut. **IT20**: 2 (2016 to 2016-17); HS 0; BB – . T20 HS 0. T20 BB 3-17.

McBRINE, Andrew Robert, b Londonderry 30 Apr 1993. Son of A.McBrine (Ireland 1985-92), nephew of J.McBrine (Ireland 1986). LHB, OB. Ireland debut 2013. North-West 2017. Ireland Wolves 2017-18. **LOI**: 24 (2014 to 2017-18); HS 79 v SL (Dublin) 2016; BB 3-42 v UAE (Dubai, ICCA) 2016-17. **IT20**: 19 (2013-14 to 2016-17); HS 14* v UAE (Dubai, DSC) 2016-17; BB 2-7 v PNG (Townsville) 2015-16. HS 67 NW v Leinster (Oak Hill) 2017. BB 4-63 Ire A v B A (Sylhet) 2017-18. LO HS 79 (*see LOI*). LO BB 3-32 NW v Northern (Waringstown) 2017. T20 HS 52* . T20 BB 3-19.

McCARTHY, B.J. – *see DURHAM*.

MULDER, Jacob Isaac, b Perth, Western Australia 11 Aug 1995. RHB, LB. Ireland debut 2017. Northern 2017. **LOI:** 4 (2016-17); HS 15* v Afghan (Greater Noida) 2016-17; BB 3-57 v Afghan (Greater Noida) 2016-17 – different matches. **IT20:** 8 (2016 to 2016-17); HS 5* v Afghan (Greater Noida) 2016-17; BB 4-16 v Scot (Dubai, DSC) 2016-17. HS 38* Ire v Neth (Dublin) 2017. BB 2-33 Northern v North-West (Comber) 2017. LO HS 17* and LO BB 3-42 Ire A v B A (Cox's Bazar) 2017-18. T20 HS 5*. T20 BB 4-16.

MURTAGH, T.J. – see *MIDDLESEX*.

O'BRIEN, Kevin Joseph (Marian C, Dublin; Tallaght I of Tech), b Dublin 4 Mar 1984. RHB, RM. Son of B.A.O'Brien (Ireland 1966-81) and younger brother of N.J.O'Brien (see *below*). Ireland debut 2006-07. Nottinghamshire 2009. Surrey 2014. Leicestershire 2015-16 (l-o and T20 only). Leinster 2017. **LOI:** 119 (2006 to 2017-18, 4 as captain); HS 142 v Kenya (Nairobi) 2006-07; BB 4-13 v Neth (Amstelveen) 2013. **IT20:** 59 (2008 to 2016-17, 4 as captain); HS 42* v Neth (Sylhet) 2013-14; BB 4-45 v Afghan (Greater Noida) 2016-17. HS 171* Ire v Kenya (Nairobi) 2008-09. BB 5-39 Ire v Canada (Toronto) 2010. LO HS 142 (*see LOI*). LO BB 4-13 (*see LOI*). T20 HS 119. T20 BB 4-22.

O'BRIEN, Niall John (Marian C, Dublin), b Dublin 8 Nov 1981. Son of B.A.O'Brien (Ireland 1966-81); elder brother of K.J.O'Brien (*see above*). 5'6''. LHB, WK. Kent 2004-06. Ireland debut 2005-06. Northamptonshire 2007-12; cap 2011. Leicestershire 2013-16. North-West 2017. MCC 2012. **LOI:** 94 (2006 to 2017-18); HS 109 v NZ (Dublin) 2017. **IT20:** 30 (2008 to 2015-16); HS 50 v Canada (Colombo, SSC) 2009-10. HS 182 Nh v Glamorgan (Cardiff) 2012. BB 1-4 K v Cambridge UCCE (Cambridge) 2006. LO HS 121 Nh v Hants (Southampton) 2011 (CB40). T20 HS 84.

PORTERFIELD, W.T.S. – see *WARWICKSHIRE*.

POYNTER, S.W. – see *DURHAM*.

RANKIN, W.B. – see *WARWICKSHIRE*.

SINGH, Simranjit ('**Simi**'), b Bathlana, Punjab, India 4 Feb 1988. RHB, OB. Leinster 2017. Ireland Wolves 2017-18. **LOI:** 4 (2017 to 2017-18); HS 45 v Scot (Dubai, ICCA) 2017-18; BB – . HS 121 Ire A v B A (Sylhet) 2017-18. BB 3-59 Leinster v North-West (Oak Hill) 2017. LO HS 70* Leinster v North-West (Dublin, Vineyard) 2017. LO BB 2-25 Leinster v Northern (Dublin, Rathmines) 2017. T20 HS 109. T20 BB 3-19.

STIRLING, P.R. – see *MIDDLESEX*.

TERRY, Sean Paul (Aquinas C, Perth; Notre Dame U, Perth, Australia), b Southampton, Hants 1 Aug 1991. Son of V.P.Terry (Hampshire and England 1978-96). 5'11''. RHB, OB. Hampshire 2012-15. Northamptonshire 2016. Leinster 2017. Ireland Wolves 2017-18. **LOI:** 5 (2016 to 2016-17); HS 16 v SA (Benoni) 2016-17. **IT20:** 1 (2016); HS 4 v Hong Kong (Bready) 2016. HS 73 Leinster v Northern (Dublin, Castle Ave) 2017. LO HS 65 Ire A v B A (Cox's Bazar) 2017-18. T20 HS 26.

THOMPSON, Greg James (Friends' S, Lisburn; Durham U), b Lisburn, Co Antrim 17 Sep 1987. 6'0''. RHB, LB. Ireland debut 2004. Durham UCCE 2007-08. Northern 2017. **LOI:** 3 (2007-08); HS 2 v B (Dhaka) 2007-08; BB 1-35 v B (Dhaka) 2007-08 – different matches. **IT20:** 8 (2016 to 2016-17); HS 44 v Hong Kong (Bready) 2016. HS 38 DU v Durham (Durham) 2007. BB 3-76 Ire v Scot (Belfast) 2007. LO HS 23 Northern v North-West (Waringstown) 2017. LO BB 1-2 La v B A (Liverpool) 2005. T20 HS 56.

THOMPSON, Stuart Robert (Limavady GS; U of Northumbria), b Eglinton, Londonderry 15 Aug 1991. LHB, RM. Ireland debut 2012. North-West 2017. Ireland Wolves 2017-18. **LOI**: 20 (2013 to 2017); HS 39 v Scot (Dublin) 2014; BB 2-17 v WI (Kingston) 2013-14. **IT20**: 20 (2013-14 to 2016-17); HS 56 v Afghan (Greater Noida) 2016-17; BB 3-10 v Nepal (Belfast) 2015. HS 46 NW v Northern (Comber) 2017. BB 3-32 NW v Northern (Eglinton) 2017. LO HS 51 Ire v SL A (Belfast) 2014. LO BB 3-51 Ire v SA A (Belfast) 2012. T20 HS 56. T20 BB 3-10.

TUCKER, Lorcan J., b Dublin 10 Sep 1996. RHB, WK. Leinster 2017. **IT20**: 4 (2016 to 2016-17); HS 16 v Afghan (Greater Noida) 2016-17. HS 56 Leinster v NW (Oak Hill) 2017. LO HS 30 Leinster v Northern (Dublin, Rathmines) 2017. T20 HS 44.

WILSON, G.C. – *see* DERBYSHIRE.

YOUNG, Craig Alexander (Strabane HS; North West IHE, Belfast), b Londonderry 4 Apr 1990. RHB, RM. Ireland debut 2013. North-West 2017. **LOI**: 13 (2014 to 2017); HS 11 v Scot (Dublin) 2014; BB 5-46 v Scot (Dublin) 2014 – different matches. **IT20**: 15 (2015 to 2016-17); HS 2* v Hong Kong (Bready) 2016; BB 2-15 v PNG (Townsville) 2015-16. HS 23 and BB 5-37 NW v Northern (Eglinton) 2017. LO HS 26 Ire v SL A (Belfast) 2014. LO BB 5-46 (*see LOI*). T20 HS 4. T20 BB 5-15.

PRINCIPAL FIXTURES

Tue 1 – Thu 3 May		
IPC	Oak Hill	Leinster v North-West
Fri 11 – Tue 15 May		
TM	**Dublin**	**IRELAND v PAKISTAN**
Fri 18 May		
T20[F]	Carrickfergus	Northern v North-West
T20[F]	Cork	Munster v Leinster
Fri 25 May		
T20[F]	Belfast	Northern v Leinster
T20[F]	Eglinton	North-West v Munster
Mon 28 May		
LO	Stormont	Northern v North-West
Tue 29 – Thu 31 May		
IPC	Comber	Northern v Leinster
Mon 4 June		
LO	Dublin, Vine	Leinster v Northern
Fri 8 June		
T20[F]	Bready	North-West v Leinster
T20[F]	Cork	Munster v Northern
Tue 19 June		
LO	Eglinton	North-West v Leinster
Wed 20 – Fri 22 June		
IPC	Bready	North-West v Leinster

Wed 27 June		
IT20	**Dublin**	**Ireland v India**
Fri 29 June		
IT20	**Dublin**	**Ireland v India**
Sun 1 July		
LO	Stormont	Northern v Leinster
Mon 2 – Wed 4 July		
IPC	Comber	Northern v North-West
Fri 6 July		
T20	Sandymount	Munster v North-West
T20[F]	Sandymount	Leinster v Northern
Sat 7 July		
T20	Sandymount	Munster v Northern
T20[F]	Sandymount	Leinster v North-West
Sun 8 July		
T20	Sandymount	North-West v Northern
T20[F]	Sandymount	Leinster v Munster
Mon 16 July		
LO	Eglinton	North-West v Northern
Tue 17 – Thu 19 July		
IPC	Bready	North-West v Northern
Tue 4 – Thu 6 September		
IPC	Dublin	Leinster v North-West
Sun 9 September		
LO	Leinster CC	Leinster v North-West

ENGLAND WOMEN INTERNATIONALS

The following players have played for England since 1 September 2016, and include all those who joined the tour to India from 22 March to 12 April. Details correct to 21 March 2018.

BEAUMONT, Tamsin (**'Tammy'**) Tilley, b Dover, Kent 11 Mar 1991. RHB, WK. MBE 2018. Kent 2007 to date. Diamonds 2007-12. Sapphires 2008. Emeralds 2011-13. Surrey Stars 2016 to date. **Tests**: 3 (2013 to 2017-18); HS 70 v A (Sydney) 2017-18. **LOI**: 47 (2009-10 to 2017-18); HS 168* v P (Taunton) 2016. **IT20**: 47 (2009-10 to 2017-18); HS 82 v P (Bristol) 2016.

BRUNT, Katherine Helen, b Barnsley, Yorks 2 Jul 1985. RHB, RMF. Yorkshire 2004 to date. Sapphires 2006-08. Diamonds 2011-12. Yorkshire Diamonds 2016 to date. **Tests**: 11 (2004 to 2017-18); HS 52 v A (Worcester) 2009; BB 6-69 v A (Worcester) 2009. **LOI**: 106 (2004-05 to 2017-18); HS 52 v A (Coffs Harbour) 2017-18; BB 5-18 v A (Wormsley) 2011. **IT20**: 60 (2005 to 2017-18); HS 35 v WI (Arundel) 2012; BB 3-6 v NZ (Lord's) 2009.

CROSS, Kathryn (**'Kate'**) Laura, b Manchester, Lancs 3 Oct 1991. RHB, RMF. Lancashire 2005 to date. Sapphires 2007-08. Emeralds 2012. W Australia 2017-18. Lancashire Thunder 2016 to date. **Tests**: 3 (2013-14 to 2015); HS 4* v A (Canterbury) 2015; BB 3-29 v I (Wormsley) 2014. **LOI**: 14 (2013-14 to 2016); HS 4* v I (Scarborough) 2014; BB 5-24 v NZ (Lincoln) 2014-15. **IT20**: 4 (2013-14 to 2014-15); HS – ; BB 2-27 v NZ (Whangarei) 2014-15.

DAVIDSON-RICHARDS, Alice Natica, b Tunbridge Wells, Kent 29 May 1994. RHB, RFM. Kent 2010 to date. Sapphires 2011-12. Emeralds 2013. Yorkshire Diamonds 2016 to date. Awaiting international debut.

ECCLESTONE, Sophie (Helsby HS), b Chester 6 May 1999. RHB, SLA. Cheshire 2013-14. Lancashire 2015 to date. Lancashire Thunder 2016 to date. **Tests**: 1 (2017-18); HS 8* and BB 3-107 v A (Sydney) 2017-18. **LOI**: 2 (2016-17 to 2017-18); HS 3 v WI (Florence Hall) 2016-17 and 3 v A (Coffs Harbour) 2017-18; BB 2-28 v WI (Florence Hall) 2016-17. **IT20**: 5 (2016 to 2017-18); HS 6 v A (Sydney) 2017-18; BB 2-24 v A (Canberra) 2017-18.

ELWISS, Georgia Amanda, b Wolverhampton, Staffs 31 May 1991. RHB, RMF. Staffordshire 2004-10. Sapphires 2006-12. Diamonds 2008. Australia CT 2009-10 to 2010-11. Emeralds 2011. Sussex 2011 to date. Rubies 2013. Loughborough Lightning 2016 to date. **Tests**: 2 (2015 to 2017-18); HS 46 v A (Canterbury) 2015; BB 1-40 v A (Sydney) 2017-18. **LOI**: 25 (2011-12 to 2016-17); HS 77 v P (Taunton) 2016; BB 3-17 v I (Wormsley) 2012. **IT20**: 13 (2011-12 to 2016); HS 18 v SA (Paarl) 2015-16; BB 2-9 v P (Chennai) 2015-16.

FARRANT, Natasha (**'Tash'**) Eleni (Sevenoaks S), b Athens, Greece 29 May 1996. LHB, LM. Kent 2012 to date. Sapphires 2013. W Australia 2016-17. Southern Vipers 2016 to date. **LOI**: 1 (2013-14); HS 1* and BB 1-14 v WI (Port of Spain) 2013-14. **IT20**: 9 (2013 to 2016); HS 1* and BB 2-15 v P (Loughborough) 2013.

GEORGE, Katie Louise, b Haywards Heath, Sussex 7 Apr 1999. LHB, LM. Hampshire 2013 to date. Southern Vipers 2016 to date. Awaiting international debut.

GUNN, Jennifer (**'Jenny'**) Louise, b Nottingham 9 May 1986. RHB, RMF. MBE 2014. Nottinghamshire 2001-15. Emeralds 2006-08. S Australia 2006-07 to 2007-08. Diamonds 2007. W Australia 2008-09. Yorkshire 2011. Rubies 2012-13. Warwickshire 2016 to date. Yorkshire Diamonds 2016 to date. **Tests**: 11 (2004 to 2014); HS 62* and 59 v I (Wormsley) 2014. **LOI**: 142 (2003-04 to 2017-18); HS 73 v NZ (Taunton) 2007; BB 5-22 v P (Louth) 2013. **IT20**: 98 (2004 to 2017-18, 3 as captain); HS 69 v SL (Colombo, NCC) 2010-11; BB 5-18 v NZ (Bridgetown) 2013-14.

HARTLEY, Alexandra, b Blackburn, Lancs 26 Sep 1993. RHB, SLA. Lancashire 2008 to date. Emeralds 2011-13. Rubies 2012. Middlesex 2013-16. Surrey Stars 2016 to date. **LOI**: 20 (2016 to 2017-18); HS 2* v WI (Florence Hall) 2016-17 and 2* v A (Brisbane) 2017-18; BB 4-24 v WI (Kingston) 2016-17. **IT20**: 2 (2016 to 2017-18); BB 2-19 v P (Chelmsford) 2016.

HAZELL, Danielle ('**Danni**'), b Durham 13 May 1988. RHB, OB. Durham 2002-04. Sapphires 2006-13. Emeralds 2007. Yorkshire 2008 to date. Diamonds 2011-12. Yorkshire Diamonds 2016. Lancashire Thunder 2017. **Tests**: 3 (2010-11 to 2013-14); HS 15 v A (Perth) 2013-14; BB 2-32 v A (Sydney) 2010-11. **LOI**: 50 (2009-10 to 2017); HS 45 and BB 3-21 v SL (Colombo, RPS) 2016-17. **IT20**: 73 (2009-10 to 2017-18); HS 18* v WI (Arundel) 2012; BB 4-12 v WI (Hove) 2012.

JONES, Amy Ellen, b Solihull, Warwicks 13 Jun 1993. RHB, WK. Warwickshire 2008 to date. Diamonds 2011. Emeralds 2012. Rubies 2013. W Australia 2017-18. Loughborough Lightning 2016 to date. **LOI**: 20 (2012-13 to 2016-17); HS 41 v SL (Mumbai, BS) 2012-13. **IT20**: 15 (2013 to 2016); HS 14 v A (Melbourne) 2013-14 and 14 v SA (Johannesburg) 2015-16.

KNIGHT, Heather Clare, b Rochdale, Lancs 26 Dec 1990. RHB, OB. OBE 2018. Devon 2008-09. Emeralds 2008-13. Berkshire 2010-16. Sapphires 2011-12. Tasmania 2014-15 to 2015-16. Western Storm 2016 to date. **Tests**: 6 (2010-11 to 2017-18, 1 as captain); HS 157 v A (Wormsley) 2013; BB 1-7 v I (Wormsley) 2014. **LOI**: 78 (2009-10 to 2017-18, 23 as captain); HS 106 v P (Leicester) 2017; BB 5-26 v P (Leicester) 2016. **IT20**: 39 (2010-11 to 2017-18, 6 as captain); HS 51 v A (Canberra) 2017-18; BB 3-10 v NZ (Whangarei) 2014-15 – separate matches.

LANGSTON, Bethany Alicia, b Harold Wood, Essex 6 Sep 1992. RHB, RM. Essex 2009-15. Diamonds 2011-12. Emeralds 2013. Yorkshire 2016 to date. Otago 2016-17 to date. Loughborough Lightning 2016 to date. **LOI**: 4 (2016-17); HS 21 v SL (Colombo, RPS) 2016-17; BB 1-23 v SL (Colombo, SSC) 2016-17. **IT20**: 2 (2013-14); HS – ; BB 1-16 v WI (Bridgetown) 2013-14.

MARSH, Laura Alexandra, b Pembury, Kent 5 Dec 1986. RHB, RMF/OB. Sussex 2003-10. Rubies 2006-07. Emeralds 2008. Sapphires 2011. Kent 2011 to date. New South Wales 2015-16. Otago 2015-16. Surrey Stars 2016 to date. **Tests**: 8 (2006 to 2017-18); HS 55 v A (Wormsley) 2013; BB 3-44 v I (Leicester) 2014. **LOI**: 89 (2006 to 2017-18); HS 67 v Ire (Kibworth) 2010; BB 5-15 v P (Sydney) 2008-09. **IT20**: 60 (2007 to 2015-16); HS 54 v P (Galle) 2012-13; BB 3-12 v P (Chennai) 2015-16.

SCIVER, Natalie Ruth, b Tokyo, Japan 20 Aug 1992. RHB, RM. Surrey 2010 to date. Rubies 2011. Emeralds 2012-13. Surrey Stars 2016 to date. **Tests**: 4 (2013-14 to 2016-17); HS 49 and BB 1-30 v A (Perth) 2013-14. **LOI**: 44 (2013 to 2017-18); HS 137 v P (Leicester) 2017; BB 3-3 v WI (Bristol) 2017. **IT20**: 40 (2013 to 2017-18); HS 47 and BB 4-15 v A (Cardiff) 2015.

SHRUBSOLE, Anya, b Bath, Somerset 7 Dec 1991. RHB, RMF. MBE 2018. Somerset 2004 to date. Rubies 2006-12. Emeralds 2006-13. Western Storm 2016 to date. **Tests**: 5 (2013 to 2017-18); HS 20 v A (Sydney) 2017-18; BB 4-51 v A (Perth) 2013-14. **LOI**: 49 (2008 to 2017-18); HS 29 v NZ (Mt Maunganui) 2014-15; BB 6-46 v I (Lord's) 2017, in World Cup final. **IT20**: 49 (2008 to 2017-18); HS 10* v SA (Paarl) 2015-16; BB 5-11 v NZ (Wellington) 2011-12.

SMITH, Bryony Frances, b Sutton, Surrey 12 Dec 1997. RHB, OB. Surrey 2014 to date. Surrey Stars 2016 to date. Awaiting international debut.

TAYLOR, Sarah Jane (Bede's S, Upper Dicker), b Whitechapel, London 20 May 1989. RHB, WK. Sussex 2004 to date. Rubies 2006-12. Emeralds 2008-13. Wellington 2010-11 to 2011-12. S Australia 2014-15 to 2015-16. Lancashire Thunder 2017. **Tests**: 9 (2006 to 2017-18); HS 40 v I (Wormsley) 2014. **LOI**: 113 (2006 to 2017-18); HS 147 v SA (Bristol) 2017. **IT20**: 84 (2006 to 2017-18); HS 77 v A (Chelmsford) 2013.

WILSON, Frances Claire, b Aldershot, Hants 7 Nov 1991. RHB, OB. Somerset 2006-14. Diamonds 2011. Emeralds 2012. Rubies 2013. Middlesex 2015 to date. Wellington 2016-17 to date. Western Storm 2016 to date. **Tests**: 1 (2017-18); HS 13 v A Sydney) 2017-18. **LOI**: 17 (2010-11 to 2017-18); HS 81 v I (Derby) 2017. **IT20**: 10 (2010-11 to 2017-18); HS 43* v P (Southampton) 2016.

WINFIELD, Lauren, b York 16 Aug 1990. RHB, WK. Yorkshire 2007 to date. Diamonds 2011. Sapphires 2012. Rubies 2013. Yorkshire Diamonds 2016 to date. **Tests**: 3 (2014 to 2017-18); HS 35 v I (Wormsley) 2014. **LOI**: 35 (2013 to 2017-18); HS 123 v P (Worcester) 2016. **IT20**: 18 (2013 to 2016); HS 74 v SA (Birmingham) 2014 and 74 v P (Bristol) 2016.

WYATT, Danielle ('Danni') Nicole, b Stoke-on-Trent, Staffs 22 Apr 1991. RHB, OB/RM. Staffordshire 2005-12. Emeralds 2006-08. Sapphires 2011-13. Victoria 2011-12 to 2015-16. Nottinghamshire 2013-15. Sussex 2016 to date. Lancashire Thunder 2016. Southern Vipers 2017. **LOI**: 53 (2009-10 to 2017); HS 44 v WI (Florence Hall) 2016-17; BB 3-7 v SA (Cuttack) 2012-13. **IT20**: 73 (2009-10 to 2017-18); HS 100 v A (Canberra) 2017-18; BB 4-11 v SA (Basseterre) 2010. **IT20**: 73 (2009-10 to 2017-18); HS 100 v A (Canberra) 2017-18; BB 4-11 v SA (Basseterre) 2010.

WOMEN'S TEST CRICKET RECORDS

1934-35 to 5 April 2018

RESULTS SUMMARY

	Opponents	Tests	Won by										Drawn
			E	A	NZ	SA	WI	I	P	SL	Ire	H	
England	Australia	49	9	12	–	–	–	–	–	–	–	–	28
	New Zealand	23	6	–	0	–	–	–	–	–	–	–	17
	South Africa	6	2	–	–	0	–	–	–	–	–	–	4
	West Indies	3	2	–	–	–	0	–	–	–	–	–	1
	India	13	1	–	–	–	–	2	–	–	–	–	10
Australia	New Zealand	13	–	4	1	–	–	–	–	–	–	–	8
	West Indies	2	–	0	–	–	0	–	–	–	–	–	2
	India	9	–	4	–	–	–	0	–	–	–	–	5
New Zealand	South Africa	3	–	–	1	0	–	–	–	–	–	–	2
	India	6	–	–	0	–	–	0	–	–	–	–	6
South Africa	India	2	–	–	–	0	–	2	–	–	–	–	–
	Netherlands	1	–	–	–	1	–	–	–	–	–	0	–
West Indies	India	6	–	–	–	–	1	1	–	–	–	–	4
	Pakistan	1	–	–	–	–	0	–	0	–	–	–	1
Pakistan	Sri Lanka	1	–	–	–	–	–	–	0	1	–	–	–
	Ireland	1	–	–	–	–	–	–	0	–	1	–	–
		139	20	20	2	1	1	5	0	1	1	0	88

	Tests	Won	Lost	Drawn	Toss Won
England	94	20	14	59	55
Australia	73	20	10	43	25
New Zealand	45	2	10	33	21
South Africa	12	1	5	6	6
West Indies	12	1	3	8	6†
India	36	5	6	25	18†
Pakistan	3	–	2	1	1
Sri Lanka	1	1	–	–	1
Ireland	1	1	–	–	1
Netherlands	1	–	1	–	1

† Results of tosses in five of the six India v West Indies Tests in 1976-77 are not known

TEAM RECORDS
HIGHEST INNINGS TOTALS

569-6d	Australia v England	Guildford	1998
525	Australia v India	Ahmedabad	1983-84
517-8	New Zealand v England	Scarborough	1996
503-5d	England v New Zealand	Christchurch	1934-35
497	England v South Africa	Shenley	2003
467	India v England	Taunton	2002
455	England v South Africa	Taunton	2003
448-9d	Australia v England	Sydney	2017-18
440	West Indies v Pakistan	Karachi	2003-04
427-4d	Australia v England	Worcester	1998
426-7d	Pakistan v West Indies	Karachi	2003-04
426-9d	India v England	Blackpool	1986
414	England v New Zealand	Scarborough	1996
414	England v Australia	Guildford	1998
404-9d	India v South Africa	Paarl	2001-02
403-8d	New Zealand v India	Nelson	1994-95

| 400-6d | India v South Africa | | | | Mysore | | | 2014-15 |

The highest totals for countries not included above are:

316	South Africa v England				Shenley			2003
193-3d	Ireland v Pakistan				Dublin			2000
108	Netherlands v South Africa				Rotterdam			2007

LOWEST INNINGS TOTALS

35	England v Australia	Melbourne	1957-58
38	Australia v England	Melbourne	1957-58
44	New Zealand v England	Christchurch	1934-35
47	Australia v England	Brisbane	1934-35
50	Netherlands v South Africa	Rotterdam	2007
53	Pakistan v Ireland	Dublin	2000

The lowest innings totals for countries not included above are:

65	India v West Indies	Jammu	1976-77
67	West Indies v England	Canterbury	1979
89	South Africa v New Zealand	Durban	1971-72

BATTING RECORDS
1000 RUNS IN TESTS

		Career	M	I	NO	HS	Avge	100	50
1935	J.A.Brittin (E)	1979-98	27	44	5	167	49.61	5	11
1645	C.M.Edwards (E)	1996-2014	22	41	5	117	45.69	4	9
1594	R.Heyhoe-Flint (E)	1960-79	22	38	3	179	45.54	3	10
1301	D.A.Hockley (NZ)	1979-96	19	29	4	126*	52.04	4	7
1164	C.A.Hodges (E)	1984-92	18	31	2	158*	40.13	2	6
1110	S.Agarwal (I)	1984-95	13	23	1	190	50.45	4	4
1078	E.Bakewell (E)	1968-79	12	22	4	124	59.88	4	7
1030	S.C.Taylor (E)	1999-2009	15	27	2	177	41.20	4	2
1007	M.E.Maclagan (E)	1934-51	14	25	1	119	41.95	2	6
1002	K.L.Rolton (A)	1995-2009	14	22	4	209*	55.66	2	5

HIGHEST INDIVIDUAL INNINGS

242	Kiran Baluch	P v WI	Karachi	2003-04
214	M.Raj	I v E	Taunton	2002
213*	E.A.Perry	A v E	Sydney	2017-18
209*	K.L.Rolton	A v E	Leeds	2001
204	K.E.Flavell	NZ v E	Scarborough	1996
204‡	M.A.J.Goszko	A v E	Shenley	2001
200	J.Broadbent	A v E	Guildford	1998
193	D.A.Annetts	A v E	Collingham	1987
192	M.D.T.Kamini	I v SA	Mysore	2014-15
190	S.Agarwal	I v E	Worcester	1986
189	E.A.Snowball	E v NZ	Christchurch	1934-35
179	R.Heyhoe-Flint	E v A	The Oval	1976
177	S.C.Taylor	E v SA	Shenley	2003
176*	K.L.Rolton	A v E	Worcester	1998
167	J.A.Brittin	E v A	Harrogate	1998
161*	E.C.Drumm	E v A	Christchurch	1994-95
160	B.A.Daniels	E v NZ	Scarborough	1996
158*	C.A.Hodges	E v NZ	Canterbury	1984
157	H.C.Knight	E v A	Wormsley	2013
155*	P.F.McKelvey	NZ v E	Wellington	1968-69

‡ *On debut*

FIVE HUNDREDS

		M	I	E	A	NZ	SA	WI	IND	P	SL	IRE
							Opponents					
5	J.A.Brittin (E)	27	44	–	3	1	–	–	1	–	–	–

HIGHEST PARTNERSHIP FOR EACH WICKET

1st	241	Kiran Baluch/Sajjida Shah	P v WI	Karachi	2003-04
2nd	275	M.D.T.Kamini/P.G.Raut	I v SA	Mysore	2014-15
3rd	309	L.A.Reeler/D.A.Annetts	A v E	Collingham	1987
4th	253	K.L.Rolton/L.C.Broadfoot	A v E	Leeds	2001
5th	138	J.Logtenberg/C.van der Westhuizen	SA v E	Shenley	2003
6th	229	J.M.Fields/R.L.Haynes	A v E	Worcester	2009
7th	157	M.Raj/J.Goswami	I v E	Taunton	2002
8th	181	S.J.Griffiths/D.L.Wilson	A v NZ	Auckland	1989-90
9th	107	B.Botha/M.Payne	SA v NZ	Cape Town	1971-72
10th	119	S.Nitschke/C.R.Smith	A v E	Hove	2005

BOWLING RECORDS

50 WICKETS IN TESTS

Wkts		Career	M	Balls	Runs	Avge	Best	5wI	10wM
77	M.B.Duggan (E)	1949-63	17	3734	1039	13.49	7- 6	5	–
68	E.R.Wilson (A)	1948-58	11	2885	803	11.80	7- 7	4	2
63	D.F.Edulji (I)	1976-91	20	5098†	1624	25.77	6- 64	1	–
60	M.E.Maclagan (E)	1934-51	14	3432	935	15.58	7- 10	3	–
60	C.L.Fitzpatrick (A)	1991-2006	23	3603	1147	19.11	5- 29	2	–
60	S.Kulkarni (I)	1976-91	19	3320†	1647	27.45	6- 99	5	–
57	R.H.Thompson (A)	1972-85	16	4304	1040	18.24	5- 33	1	–
55	J.Lord (NZ)	1966-79	15	3108	1049	19.07	6-119	4	1
50	E.Bakewell (E)	1968-79	12	2697	831	16.62	7- 61	3	1

† *Excludes balls bowled in Sixth Test v West Indies 1976-77*

TEN WICKETS IN A TEST

13-226	Shaiza Khan	P v WI	Karachi	2003-04
11- 16	E.R.Wilson	A v E	Melbourne	1957-58
11- 63	J.M.Greenwood	E v WI	Canterbury	1979
11-107	L.C.Pearson	E v A	Sydney	2002-03
10- 65	E.R.Wilson	A v NZ	Wellington	1947-48
10- 75	E.Bakewell	E v WI	Birmingham	1979
10- 78	J.Goswami	I v E	Taunton	2006
10-107	K.Price	A v I	Lucknow	1983-84
10-118	D.A.Gordon	A v E	Melbourne	1968-69
10-137	J.Lord	NZ v A	Melbourne	1978-79

SEVEN WICKETS IN AN INNINGS

8-53	N.David	I v E	Jamshedpur	1995-96
7- 6	M.B.Duggan	E v A	Melbourne	1957-58
7- 7	E.R.Wilson	A v E	Melbourne	1957-58
7-10	M.E.Maclagan	E v A	Brisbane	1934-35
7-18	A.Palmer	A v E	Brisbane	1934-35
7-24	L.Johnston	A v NZ	Melbourne	1971-72
7-34	G.E.McConway	E v I	Worcester	1986
7-41	J.A.Burley	NZ v E	The Oval	1966
7-51	L.C.Pearson	E v A	Sydney	2002-03
7-59	Shaiza Khan	P v WI	Karachi	2003-04
7-61	E.Bakewell	E v WI	Birmingham	1979

HAT-TRICKS

E.R.Wilson	Australia v England	Melbourne	1957-58
Shaiza Khan	Pakistan v West Indies	Karachi	2003-04
R.M.Farrell	Australia v England	Sydney	2010-11

WICKET-KEEPING AND FIELDING RECORDS
25 DISMISSALS IN TESTS

Total			Tests	Ct	St	
58	C.Matthews	Australia	20	46	12	1984-95
43	J.Smit	England	21	39	4	1992-2006
36	S.A.Hodges	England	11	19	17	1969-79
28	B.A.Brentnall	New Zealand	10	16	12	1966-72

EIGHT DISMISSALS IN A TEST

9 (8ct, 1st)	C.Matthews	A v I	Adelaide	1990-91
8 (6ct, 2st)	L.Nye	E v NZ	New Plymouth	1991-92

SIX DISMISSALS IN AN INNINGS

8 (6ct, 2st)	L.Nye	E v NZ	New Plymouth	1991-92
6 (2ct, 4st)	B.A.Brentnall	NZ v SA	Johannesburg	1971-72

20 CATCHES IN THE FIELD IN TESTS

Total			Tests	
25	C.A.Hodges	England	18	1984-92
21	S.Shah	India	20	1976-91
20	L.A.Fullston	Australia	12	1984-87

APPEARANCE RECORDS
25 TEST MATCH APPEARANCES

27	J.A.Brittin	England	1979-98

12 MATCHES AS CAPTAIN

			Won	Lost	Drawn	
14	P.F.McKelvey	New Zealand	2	3	9	1966-79
12	R.Heyhoe-Flint	England	2	–	10	1966-76
12	S.Rangaswamy	India	1	2	9	1976-84

ENGLAND TEST RESULT IN 2017

At North Sydney Oval, on 9, 10, 11, 12 November (day/night). Toss: England. Result: **MATCH DRAWN**. England 280 (T.T.Beaumont 70, H.C.Knight 62) and 206-2 (H.C.Knight 79*). Australia 448-9d (E.A.Perry 213*). Award: E.A.Perry. England debuts: S.Ecclestone and F.C.Wilson.

WOMEN'S LIMITED-OVERS RECORDS

1973 to 9 March 2018
RESULTS SUMMARY

	Matches	Won	Lost	Tied	No Result	% Won (exc NR)
Australia	311	240	63	2	6	78.68
England	324	190	+22	2	10	60.50
India	251	138	108	1	4	55.87
New Zealand	322	164	150	2	6	51.89
South Africa	173	83	81	2	7	50.00
West Indies	161	77	79	1	4	49.04
Sri Lanka	152	55	92	–	5	37.41
Trinidad & Tobago	6	2	4	–	–	33.33
Pakistan	147	41	104	–	2	28.27
Ireland	145	39	100	–	6	28.05
Bangladesh	30	7	21	–	2	25.00
Jamaica	5	1	4	–	–	20.00
Netherlands	101	19	81	–	1	19.00
Denmark	33	6	27	–	–	18.18
International XI	18	3	14	–	1	17.64
Young England	6	1	5	–	–	16.66
Scotland	8	1	7	–	–	12.50
Japan	5	–	5	–	–	0.00

TEAM RECORDS
HIGHEST INNINGS TOTALS

455-5 (50 overs)	New Zealand v Pakistan	Christchurch	1996-97
412-3 (50 overs)	Australia v Denmark	Mumbai	1997-98
397-4 (50 overs)	Australia v Pakistan	Melbourne	1996-97
378-5 (50 overs)	England v Pakistan	Worcester	2016
377-7 (50 overs)	England v Pakistan	Leicester	2017

LARGEST RUNS MARGIN OF VICTORY

408 runs	New Zealand beat Pakistan	Christchurch	1996-97
374 runs	Australia beat Pakistan	Melbourne	1996-97

LOWEST INNINGS TOTALS

22 (23.4 overs)	Netherlands v West Indies	Deventer	2008
23 (24.1 overs)	Pakistan v Australia	Melbourne	1996-97
24 (21.3 overs)	Scotland v England	Reading	2001

BATTING RECORDS
2100 RUNS IN A CAREER

Runs		Career	M	I	NO	HS	Avge	100	50
6259	M.Raj (I)	1999-2018	189	170	47	114*	50.88	6	49
5992	C.M.Edwards (E)	1997-2016	191	180	23	173*	38.16	9	46
4844	B.J.Clark (A)	1991-2005	118	114	12	229*	47.49	5	30
4814	K.L.Rolton (A)	1995-2009	141	132	32	154*	48.14	8	33
4204	S.R.Taylor (WI)	2008-2018	110	109	14	171	44.25	5	31
4101	S.C.Taylor (E)	1998-2011	126	120	18	156*	40.20	8	23
4064	D.A.Hockley (NZ)	1982-2000	118	115	18	117	41.89	4	34
3952	S.W.Bates (NZ)	2006-2018	109	104	12	168	42.95	9	23
3786	S.J.Taylor (E)	2006-2017	113	106	13	147	40.70	6	19
3492	A.J.Blackwell (A)	2003-2017	144	124	27	114	36.00	3	25
3248	A.E.Satterthwaite (NZ)	2007-2018	106	100	14	137*	37.76	6	16
2999	M.M.Lanning (A)	2011-2017	63	63	8	152*	54.52	11	11
2919	H.M.Tiffen (NZ)	1999-2009	117	111	16	100	30.72	1	18
2857	M.du Preez (SA)	2007-2018	108	102	17	116*	33.61	2	13
2856	A.Chopra (I)	1995-2012	127	112	21	100	31.38	1	18
2844	E.C.Drumm (NZ)	1992-2006	101	94	13	116	35.11	2	19
2728	L.C.Sthalekar (A)	2001-2013	125	111	22	104*	30.65	2	16
2630	L.M.Keightley (A)	1995-2005	82	78	12	156*	39.84	4	21
2611	D.J.S.Dottin (WI)	2008-2018	110	105	11	112*	27.77	1	17
2554	L.S.Greenway (E)	2003-2016	126	111	26	125*	30.04	1	12

Runs		Career	M	I	NO	HS	Avge	100	50
2438	S.J.McGlashan (NZ)	2002-2016	134	125	16	97*	22.36	–	14
2419	T.Chetty (SA)	2007-2018	100	91	12	95	30.62	–	16
2413	E.A.Perry (A)	2007-2017	94	72	24	95*	50.27	–	24
2201	R.J.Rolls (NZ)	1997-2007	104	91	3	114	25.01	2	13
2195	Bismah Maroof (P)	2006-2017	95	92	11	99	27.09	–	11
2180	Javeria Khan (P)	2008-2017	85	82	10	133*	30.27	1	14
2121	J.A.Brittin (E)	1979-1998	63	59	9	138*	42.42	5	8
2121	H.Kaur (I)	2009-2018	81	69	12	171*	37.21	3	11

HIGHEST INDIVIDUAL INNINGS

229*	B.J.Clark	Australia v Denmark	Mumbai	1997-98
188	D.B.Sharma	India v Ireland	Potchefstroom	2017
178*	A.C.Jayangani	Sri Lanka v Australia	Bristol	2017
173*	C.M.Edwards	England v Ireland	Pune	1997-98
171*	H.Kaur	India v Australia	Derby	2017
171	S.R.Taylor	West Indies v Sri Lanka	Mumbai	2012-13
168*	T.T.Beaumont	England v Pakistan	Taunton	2016
168	S.W.Bates	New Zealand v Pakistan	Sydney	2008-09
157	R.H.Priest	New Zealand v Sri Lanka	Lincoln	2015-16
156*	L.M.Keightley	Australia v Pakistan	Melbourne	1996-97
156*	S.C.Taylor	England v India	Lord's	2006
154*	K.L.Rolton	Australia v Sri Lanka	Christchurch	2000-01
153*	J.Logtenberg	South Africa v Netherlands	Deventer	2007
152*	M.M.Lanning	Australia v Sri Lanka	Bristol	2017
151	K.L.Rolton	Australia v Ireland	Dublin	2005

HIGHEST PARTNERSHIP FOR EACH WICKET

1st	320	D.B.Sharma/P.G.Raut	India v Ireland	Potchefstroom	2017
2nd	275	T.T.Beaumont/S.J.Taylor	England v South Africa	Bristol	2017
3rd	244	K.L.Rolton/L.C.Sthalekar	Australia v Ireland	Dublin	2005
4th	224*	J.Logtenberg/M.du Preez	South Africa v Netherlands	Deventer	2007
5th	188*	S.C.Taylor/J.Cassar	England v Sri Lanka	Lincoln	2000-01
6th	142	S.Luus/C.L.Tryon	South Africa v India	Dublin	2016
7th	104*	S.J.Tsukigawa/N.J.Browne	New Zealand v England	Chennai	2006-07
8th	85*	S.L.Clarke/N.J.Shaw	England v Scotland	Reading	2001
9th	73	L.R.F.Askew/I.T.Guha	England v New Zealand	Chennai	2006-07
10th	76	A.J.Blackwell/K.M.Beams	Australia v India	Derby	2017

BOWLING RECORDS
100 WICKETS IN A CAREER

		LOI	Balls	R	W	Avge	Best	4w	R/Over
J.Goswami (I)	2002-2018	166	8023	4335	**200**	21.67	6-31	7	3.24
C.L.Fitzpatrick (A)	1993-2007	109	6017	3023	**180**	16.79	5-14	11	3.01
L.C.Sthalekar (A)	2001-2013	125	5964	3646	**146**	24.97	5-35	2	3.66
A.Mohammed (WI)	2003-2017	111	4984	2766	**145**	19.07	7-14	11	3.32
N.David (I)	1995-2008	97	4892	2305	**141**	16.34	5-20	6	2.82
J.L.Gunn (E)	2004-2017	142	5828	3749	**135**	27.77	5-22	6	3.85
S.R.Taylor (WI)	2008-2018	110	4661	2497	**130**	19.20	4-17	5	3.21
K.H.Brunt (E)	2005-2017	106	5231	3023	**127**	23.80	5-18	6	3.46
E.A.Perry (A)	2007-2017	94	4382	3204	**126**	25.42	5-19	3	4.38
D.van Niekerk (SA)	2009-2018	88	3756	2216	**121**	18.31	5-17	8	3.53
Sana Mir (P)	2005-2017	105	5117	3179	**117**	27.17	5-32	5	3.72
S.Ismail (SA)	2007-2018	79	3845	2319	**115**	20.16	6-10	5	3.61
H.A.S.D.Siriwardene (SL)	2003-2017	103	4681	2973	**112**	26.54	4-11	6	3.81
L.A.Marsh (E)	2006-2017	89	4618	2936	**109**	26.93	5-15	4	3.81
C.E.Taylor (E)	1988-2005	105	5140	2443	**102**	23.95	4-13	2	2.85
I.T.Guha (E)	2001-2011	83	3767	2345	**101**	23.21	5-14	4	3.73
N.Al Khadeer (I)	2002-2012	78	4036	2402	**100**	24.02	5-14	5	3.57

SIX OR MORE WICKETS IN AN INNINGS

7- 4	Sajjida Shah	Pakistan v Japan	Amsterdam	2003
7- 8	J.M.Chamberlain	England v Denmark	Haarlem	1991

7-14	A.Mohammed	West Indies v Pakistan	Dhaka	2011-12
7-24	S.Nitschke	Australia v England	Kidderminster	2005
6-10	J.Lord	New Zealand v India	Auckland	1981-82
6-10	M.Maben	India v Sri Lanka	Kandy	2003-04
6-10	S.Ismail	South Africa v Netherlands	Savar	2011-12
6-20	G.L.Page	New Zealand v Trinidad & T	St Albans	1973
6-20	D.B.Sharma	India v Sri Lanka	Ranchi	2015-16
6-31	J.Goswami	India v New Zealand	Southgate	2011
6-32	B.H.McNeill	New Zealand v England	Lincoln, NZ	2007-08
6-36	S.Luus	South Africa v Ireland	Dublin	2016
6-46	A.Shrubsole	England v India	Lord's	2017

WICKET-KEEPING AND FIELDING RECORDS
100 DISMISSALS IN A CAREER

Total			LOI	Ct	St
137	T.Chetty	South Africa	100	95	42
133	R.J.Rolls	New Zealand	104	89	44
123	S.J.Taylor	England	113	78	45
114	J.Smit	England	109	69	45

SIX DISMISSALS IN AN INNINGS

6 (4ct, 2st)	S.L.Illingworth	New Zealand v Australia	Beckenham	1993
6 (1ct, 5st)	V.Kalpana	India v Denmark	Slough	1993
6 (2ct, 4st)	Batool Fatima	Pakistan v West Indies	Karachi	2003-04
6 (4ct, 2st)	Batool Fatima	Pakistan v Sri Lanka	Colombo (PSS)	2011

50 CATCHES IN THE FIELD IN A CAREER

Total			LOI	Career
60	J.Goswani	India	166	2002-2018
57	S.W.Bates	New Zealand	109	2006-2018
55	A.J.Blackwell	Australia	144	2003-2017
54	S.R.Taylor	West Indies	110	2008-2018
52	L.S.Greenway	England	126	2003-2016
52	C.M.Edwards	England	191	1997-2016

FOUR CATCHES IN THE FIELD IN AN INNINGS

4	Z.J.Goss	Australia v New Zealand	Adelaide	1995-96
4	J.L.Gunn	England v New Zealand	Lincoln, NZ	2014-15

APPEARANCE RECORDS
125 APPEARANCES

191	C.M.Edwards	England	1997-2016
189	M.Raj	India	1999-2018
166	J.Goswami	India	2002-2018
144	A.J.Blackwell	Australia	2003-2017
142	J.L.Gunn	England	2004-2017
141	K.L.Rolton	Australia	1995-2009
134	S.J.McGlashan	New Zealand	2002-2016
127	A.Chopra	India	1995-2012
126	L.S.Greenway	England	2003-2016
126	S.C.Taylor	England	1998-2011
125	N.J.Browne	New Zealand	2002-2014
125	L.C.Sthalekar	Australia	2001-2013

100 CONSECUTIVE APPEARANCES

109	M.Raj	India	17.04.2004 to 07.02.2013
101	M.du Preez	South Africa	08.03.2009 to 05.02.2018

100 MATCHES AS CAPTAIN

			Won	Lost	No Result	
117	C.M.Edwards	England	72	38	7	2005-2016
112	M.Raj	India	69	40	3	2004-2018
101	B.J.Clark	Australia	83	17	1	1994-2005

WOMEN'S INTERNATIONAL TWENTY20 RECORDS

2004 to 21 March 2018

MATCH RESULTS SUMMARY

	Matches	Won	Lost	Tied	NR	Win %
England	105	75	27	2	1	72.11
West Indies	99	59	34	4	2	60.82
New Zealand	96	57	36	2	1	60.00
Australia	101	60	39	2	–	59.40
India	78	40	37	–	1	51.94
South Africa	76	30	44	–	2	40.54
Pakistan	81	31	47	2	1	38.75
Sri Lanka	71	19	49	–	3	27.94
Ireland	44	10	34	–	–	22.72
Bangladesh	34	5	29	–	–	14.70
Netherlands	11	–	10	–	1	0.00

WOMEN'S INTERNATIONAL TWENTY20 RECORDS
(To 21 March 2018)

TEAM RECORDS – HIGHEST INNINGS TOTALS † Batting Second

205-1	South Africa v Netherlands	Potchefstroom	2010-11
191-4	West Indies v Netherlands	Potchefstroom	2010-11
191-4	Australia v Ireland	Sylhet	2013-14
188-3	New Zealand v Sri Lanka	Christchurch	2015-16
187-5	England v Pakistan	Bristol	2016
186-7	New Zealand v South Africa	Taunton	2007
186-1	Australia v Ireland	Dublin	2015
185-2	Australia v Pakistan	Sylhet	2013-14
184-4	West Indies v Ireland	Dublin	2008
181-6†	England v Australia	Canberra	2017-18
180-5	England v South Africa	Taunton	2007
180-5	New Zealand v West Indies	Gros Islet	2010

LOWEST COMPLETED INNINGS TOTALS † Batting Second

44 (15.3)	Bangladesh v Pakistan	Bangkok	2016-17
54† (18.2)	Bangladesh v India	Bangkok	2016-17
57† (19.4)	Sri Lanka v Bangladesh	Guangzhou	2012-13
58-9†	Bangladesh v England	Sylhet	2013-14
59-8	Sri Lanka v Australia	Colombo (SSC)	2016-17
60† (16.5)	Pakistan v England	Taunton	2009
60 (19.4)	New Zealand v England	Whangarei	2014-15

BATTING RECORDS – 1300 RUNS IN A CAREER

Runs			M	I	NO	HS	Avge	50	R/100B
2605	C.M.Edwards	E	95	93	14	92*	32.97	12	106.9
2474	S.R.Taylor	WI	80	79	13	90	37.48	19	102.2†
2337	S.W.Bates	NZ	91	89	4	94*	27.49	15	106.6
2091	S.J.Taylor	E	84	82	11	77	29.45	15	109.7
1959	D.J.S.Dottin	WI	94	93	18	112*	26.12	11	125.5†
1930	M.M.Lanning	A	70	69	8	126	31.63	11	115.8
1900	M.Raj	I	68	65	18	76*	40.42	13	95.7†
1401	Bismah Maroof	P	78	72	16	65*	25.01	4	84.9
1329	S.F.M.Devine	NZ	64	61	9	70	25.55	4	118.8

Runs			M	I	NO	HS	Avge	50	R/100B
1314	A.J.Blackwell	A	95	81	19	61	21.19	1	92.9
1305	H.Kaur	I	73	64	13	77	25.58	4	95.7†

† *No information on balls faced for games at Roseau on 22 and 23 February 2012.*

HIGHEST INDIVIDUAL INNINGS

Score	Balls				
126	65	M.M.Lanning	A v Ire	Sylhet	2013-14
117*	70	B.L.Mooney	A v E	Canberra	2017-18
116*	71	S.A.Fritz	SA v Neth	Potchefstroom	2010-11
112*	45	D.J.S.Dottin	WI v SA	Basseterre	2010
112	67	D.J.S.Dottin	WI v SL	Coolidge	2017-18
100	57	D.N.Wyatt	A v A	Canberra	2017-18

HIGHEST PARTNERSHIP FOR EACH WICKET

1st	170	S.A.Fritz/T.Chetty	SA v Neth	Potchefstroom	2010-11
2nd	121	H.K.Matthews/D.J.S.Dottin	WI v SL	Coolidge	2017-18
3rd	124	T.D.Smartt/S.A.C.A.King	WI v Neth	Potchefstroom	2010-11
4th	147*	K.L.Rolton/K.A.Blackwell	A v E	Taunton	2005
5th	118	S.F.Daley/D.J.S.Dottin	WI v SA	Basseterre	2010
6th	68	K.L.Rolton/A.J.Blackwell	A v SA	Taunton	2009
7th	51	S.R.Taylor/M.R.Aguilleira	WI v SL	Cayon	2010
8th	39	L.E.Kaushalya/K.A.D.A.Kanchana	SL v I	Ranchi	2015-16
9th	33*	D.Hazell/H.L.Colvin	E v WI	Bridgetown	2013-14
10th	23*	L.N.McCarthy/E.J.Tice	Ire v SL	Dublin	2013

BOWLING RECORDS – 60 WICKETS IN A CAREER

Wkts			Matches	Overs	Mdns	Runs	Avge	Best	R/Over
106	A.Mohammed	WI	92	314.3	6	1675	15.80	5-10	5.32
80	E.A.Perry	A	85	273.5	4	1571	19.63	4-12	5.73
75	D.Hazell	E	73	276.0	6	1453	19.37	4-12	5.26
72	S.F.Daley	WI	68	227.1	8	1113	15.45	5-15	4.89
70	J.L.Gunn	E	98	210.5	1	1304	18.62	5-18	6.18
68	A.Shrubsole	E	49	165.3	5	929	13.66	5-11	5.61
68	S.R.Taylor	WI	80	206.1	4	1117	16.42	3-10	5.41
67	Sana Mir	P	79	278.2	7	1473	21.98	4-13	5.29
64	S.Ismail	SA	63	213.4	7	1268	19.81	5-30	5.93
63	H.L.Colvin	E	50	186.5	4	971	15.41	4- 9	5.19
60	Nida Dar	P	70	209.4	6	1074	17.90	3-12	5.12
60	L.C.Sthalekar	A	54	199.2	1	1161	19.35	4-18	5.82
60	L.A.Marsh	E	60	224.3	4	1169	19.48	3-12	5.20

FIVE OR MORE WICKETS IN AN INNINGS

6-17	A.E.Satterthwaite	NZ v E	Taunton	2007
5- 8	S.Luus	SA v Ire	Chennai	2015-16
5-10	A.Mohammed	WI v SA	Cape Town	2009-10
5-10	M.Strano	A v NZ	Geelong	2016-17
5-11	A.Shrubsole	E v NZ	Wellington	2011-12
5-11	J.Goswami	I v A	Visakhapatnam	2011-12
5-12	A.Mohammed	WI v NZ	Bridgetown	2013-14
5-13	A.S.S.Fletcher	WI v SL	Coolidge	2017-18
5-15	S.F.Daley	WI v SL	Colombo (RPS)	2012-13
5-16	P.Roy	I v P	Taunton	2009
5-16	S.L.Quintyne	WI v E	Bridgetown	2013-14
5-18	J.L.Gunn	E v NZ	Bridgetown	2013-14

| 5-22 | J.L.Hunter | A v WI | Colombo (RPS) | 2012-13 |
| 5-30 | S.Ismail | SA v I | Johannesburg | 2017-18 |

HAT-TRICKS

Asmavia Iqbal	Pakistan v England	Loughborough	2012
Ekta Bisht	Sri Lanka v India	Colombo (NCC)	2012-13
M.Kapp	South Africa v Bangladesh	Potchefstroom	2013-14
N.R.Sciver	England v New Zealand	Bridgetown	2013-14
Sana Mir	Pakistan v Sri Lanka	Sharjah	2014-15
A.M.Peterson	New Zealand v Australia	Geelong	2016-17

WICKET-KEEPING RECORDS – 30 DISMISSALS IN A CAREER

Dis			Matches	Ct	St
69	S.J.Taylor	England	84	22	47
68	R.H.Priest	New Zealand	68	38	30
57	T.Chetty	South Africa	68	34	23
55	M.R.Aguilleira	West Indies	84	27	28
50	Batool Fatima	Pakistan	45	11	39
47	A.J.Healy	Australia	75	18	29
40	J.M.Fields	Australia	37	25	15
31	S.Naik	India	31	10	21

FIVE DISMISSALS IN AN INNINGS

5 (1ct, 4st)	Kycia A.Knight	West Indies v Sri Lanka	Colombo (RPS)	2012-13
5 (1ct, 4st)	Batool Fatima	Pakistan v Ireland	Dublin	2013
5 (1ct, 4st)	Batool Fatima	Pakistan v Ireland	Dublin	2013

FIELDING RECORDS – 30 CATCHES IN A CAREER

Total			Matches	Total			Matches
55	J.L.Gunn	England	98	33	A.J.Blackwell	Australia	95
54	L.S.Greenway	England	85	32	S.A.C.A.King	West Indies	76
41	S.W.Bates	New Zealand	91	30	H.Kaur	India	73
33	J.E.Cameron	Australia	64				

FOUR CATCHES IN AN INNINGS

| 4 | L.S.Greenway | England v New Zealand | Chelmsford | 2010 |

APPEARANCE RECORDS – 75 APPEARANCES

98	J.L.Gunn	England	84	S.J.Taylor	England
95	A.J.Blackwell	Australia	80	S.R.Taylor	West Indies
95	C.M.Edwards	England	79	S.A.Campbelle	West Indies
94	D.J.S.Dottin	West Indies	79	Sana Mir	Pakistan
92	A.Mohammed	West Indies	79	A.E.Satterthwaite	New Zealand
91	S.W.Bates	New Zealand	78	Bismah Maroof	Pakistan
85	L.S.Greenway	England	76	S.A.C.A.King	West Indies
85	E.A.Perry	Australia	76	S.J.McGlashan	New Zealand
84	M.R.Aguilleira	West Indies	75	A.J.Healy	Australia

50 MATCHES AS CAPTAIN

			W	L	T	NR	%age wins
93	C.M.Edwards	England	68	23	1	1	73.91
70	M.R.Aguilleira	West Indies	38	28	2	2	55.88
65	Sana Mir	Pakistan	26	36	2	1	40.62
54	S.W.Bates	New Zealand	32	21	1	–	59.25
50	M.du Preez	South Africa	24	25	–	1	48.97

KIA SUPER LEAGUE 2017

The second Kia Super League tournament was held between 10 August and 1 September.

Team	P	W	L	T	NR	Pts	Net RR
1 Southern Vipers (1)	5	4	1	–	–	8	+2.00
2 Surrey Stars (4)	5	4	1	–	–	8	+0.29
3 Western Storm (2)	5	3	2	–	–	6	–0.88
4 Loughborough Lightning (3)	5	2	3	–	–	4	+0.66
5 Yorkshire Diamonds (5)	5	2	3	–	–	4	–0.31
6 Lancashire Thunder (6)	5	–	5	–	–	0	–1.69

Semi-final: At County Ground, Hove, 1 September. Toss: Surrey Stars. **WESTERN STORM** won by three wickets. Surrey Stars 100-7 (20; S.I.R.Dunkley-Brown 30, A.Shrubsole 3-22). Western Storm 101-7 (18.5; S.R.Taylor 37*, M.Kapp 3-11). Award: S.R.Taylor.

FINAL: County Ground, Hove, 1 September (floodlit). Toss: Western Storm. **WESTERN STORM** won by seven wickets. Southern Vipers 145-5 (20; H.K.Matthews 31, M.du Preez 31, S.R.Taylor 3-28). Western Storm 151-3 (18; R.H.Priest 72, S.R.Taylor 30*, S.N.Luff 30*). Award: R.H.Priest.

Previous winner: 2016   Southern Vipers

TEAM RECORDS – HIGHEST TOTALS

180-2 (20)	Vipers v Lightning	Derby	2017
171-3 (20)	Lightning v Stars	The Oval	2017

LOWEST TOTALS

64 (16.3)	Diamonds v Vipers	Southampton	2016
70 (18.5)	Storm v Vipers	Southampton	2017

LARGEST MARGINS OF VICTORY

95 runs	Diamonds (166-6) v Thunder (71)	Manchester	2016
10 wickets	Diamonds (160-7) v Storm (161-0)	York	2017

BATTING RECORDS – MOST RUNS IN A SEASON

289 (ave 57.80)	S.R.Taylor	Western Storm	2016
261 (ave 43.50)	R.H.Priest	Western Storm	2017

HIGHEST SCORES

Score	Balls				
119*	72	S.W.Bates	Vipers v Lightning	Derby	2017
106*	65	R.H.Priest	Storm v Diamonds	York	2017
91	64	D.van Niekerk	Lightning v Stars	Loughborough	2016

MOST SIXES IN AN INNINGS

6	L.Lee (72)	Stars v Storm	The Oval	2017

HIGHEST STRIKE RATE IN AN INNINGS (Qualification: 30 runs, 200+ strike rate)

R/100B	Score	Balls				
200.0	90*	45	N.R.Sciver	Stars v Storm	Bristol	2016
200.0	72	36	R.H.Priest	Storm v Vipers	Hove	2017
200.0	52	26	R.H.Priest	Storm v Thunder	Bristol	2017

BOWLING RECORDS – 10 WICKETS IN A SEASON

Wkts			Year	P	O	M	Runs	Avge	Best	4w	R/Over
12	N.R.Sciver	Stars	2017	6	21.5	1	141	11.75	3-11	–	6.45
11	S.R.Taylor	Storm	2016	7	26.0	–	177	16.09	4-14	1	6.80

BEST BOWLING FIGURES IN AN INNINGS

5-23	A.Shrubsole	Storm v Diamonds	Leeds	2016
5-26	R.M.Farrell	Stars v Thunder	Manchester	2017

MOST ECONOMICAL BOWLING ANALYSIS

O	M	R	W				
4	1	5	4	S.R.Taylor	Storm v Lightning	Taunton	2017

MOST EXPENSIVE BOWLING ANALYSIS

O	M	R	W				
4	0	47	1	N.R.Sciver	Stars v Lightning	Loughborough	2016
4	0	47	0	N.R.Sciver	Stars v Lightning	The Oval	2017

KIA SUPER LEAGUE FIXTURES 2018

Sun 22 July
Southport — Lancashire Thunder v Loughborough Lightning
Guildford — Surrey Stars v Southern Vipers
Taunton — Western Storm v Yorkshire Diamonds

Wed 25 July
Southampton — Southern Vipers v Loughborough Lightning

Thu 26 July
Cheltenham — Western Storm v Surrey Stars

Fri 27 July
Leeds — Yorkshire Diamonds v Lancashire Thunder

Sun 29 July
Liverpool — Lancashire Thunder v Southern Vipers
Guildford — Surrey Stars v Yorkshire Diamonds
Taunton — Western Storm v Loughborough Lightning

Tue 31 July
Loughborough — Loughborough Lightning v Yorkshire Diamonds
Arundel — Southern Vipers v Western Storm
The Oval — Surrey Stars v Lancashire Thunder

Thu 2 August
Loughborough — Loughborough Lightning v Surrey Stars
York — Yorkshire Diamonds v Southern Vipers

Fri 3 August
Manchester — Lancashire Thunder v Western Storm

Sat 4 August
Loughborough — Loughborough Lightning v Southern Vipers

Sun 5 August
Scarborough — Yorkshire Diamonds v Western Storm

Tue 7 August
Manchester — Lancashire Thunder v Surrey Stars

Wed 8 August
Southampton — Southern Vipers v Yorkshire Diamonds

Thu 9 August
Guildford — Surrey Stars v Loughborough Lightning
Taunton — Western Storm v Lancashire Thunder

Sat 11 August
Loughborough — Loughborough Lightning v Lancashire Thunder
Bristol — Western Storm v Southern Vipers

Sun 12 August
York — Yorkshire Diamonds v Surrey Stars

Tue 14 August
Blackpool — Lancashire Thunder v Yorkshire Diamonds
Hove — Southern Vipers v Surrey Stars

Wed 15 August
Birmingham — Loughborough Lightning v Western Storm

Sat 18 August
Southampton — Southern Vipers v Lancashire Thunder
The Oval — Surrey Stars v Western Storm
Leeds — Yorkshire Diamonds v Loughborough Lightning

Mon 27 August
Hove — Semi-final and FINAL

MCCA FIXTURES 2018

Sun 29 April

	KNOCK-OUT TROPHY
High Wycombe	Buckinghamshire v Cambridgeshire
North Perrott	Dorset v Cornwall
Whitchurch	Shropshire v Herefordshire
Swindon	Wiltshire v Wales MC

Sun 6 May

	TWENTY20 COMPETITION
Toft	Cheshire v Cumberland (1)
Jesmond	Northumberland v Lincolnshire (1)
Wargrave	Berkshire v Shropshire (2)
Bicester & N Oxford	Oxfordshire v Herefordshire (2)
Bishop's Stortford	Hertfordshire v Cambridgeshire (3)
Woolpit	Suffolk v Norfolk (3)
Truro	Cornwall v Devon (4)
Bashley	Dorset v Wiltshire (4)

Mon 7 May

	TWENTY20 COMPETITION
Knypersley	Staffordshire v Cheshire (1)
Amersham	Buckinghamshire v Berkshire (2)
Shrewsbury	Shropshire v Oxfordshire (2)
Ampthill	Bedfordshire v Hertfordshire (3)
Peterborough	Cambridgeshire v Suffolk (3)
Sidmouth	Devon v Dorset (4)
Newport	Wales MC v Cornwall (4)

Sun 20 May

	KNOCK-OUT TROPHY
1.Manor Park	Norfolk v Bedfordshire
2.Ipswich School	Suffolk v Bucks/Cambs
3.Himley	Staffordshire v Shrops/Herefords
4.Oxton	Cheshire v Cumberland
5.Sidmouth	Devon v Wiltshire/Wales MC
6.Bracebridge	Lincolnshire v Northumberland
7.Oratory School	Berkshire v Dorset/Cornwall
8.Welwyn Gdn City	Hertfordshire v Oxfordshire

Sun 27 May

	TWENTY20 COMPETITION
Jesmond	Northumberland v Staffordshire (1)
Scunthorpe	Lincolnshire v Cumberland (1)
Colwall	Herefordshire v Shropshire (2)
Banbury	Oxfordshire v Buckinghamshire (2)
Manor Park	Norfolk v Cambridgeshire (3)
Bury St Edmunds	Suffolk v Bedfordshire (3)
Wimborne	Dorset v Wales MC (4)
South Wilts	Wiltshire v Devon (4)

Sun 3 June

	TWENTY20 COMPETITION
Marple	Cheshire v Northumberland (1)
Rolleston	Staffordshire v Lincolnshire (1)
Falkland	Berkshire v Oxfordshire (2)
High Wycombe	Buckinghamshire v Herefordshire (2)
Dunstable	Bedfordshire v Norfolk (3)
Harpenden	Hertfordshire v Suffolk (3)
St Austell	Cornwall v Dorset (4)
Newport	Wales MC v Wiltshire (4)

Sun 10 June	**KNOCK-OUT TROPHY = Quarter-finals**
Match W	Winner Match 4 v Winner Match 6
Match X	Winner Match 5 v Winner Match 7
Match Y	Winner Match 1 v Winner Match 3
Match Z	Winner Match 8 v Winner Match 2

Sun 17 June	**TWENTY20 COMPETITION**
Penrith	Cumberland v Staffordshire (1)
Bourne	Lincolnshire v Cheshire (1)
Eastnor	Herefordshire v Berkshire (2)
Whitchurch	Shropshire v Buckinghamshire (2)
Manor Park	Norfolk v Hertfordshire (3)
March	Cambridgeshire v Bedfordshire (3)
North Devon	Devon v Wales MC (4)
Calne	Wiltshire v Cornwall (4)

Sun 24 – Tue 26 June	**MCCA CHAMPIONSHIP**
Wargrave	Berkshire v Oxfordshire
Tring Park	Buckinghamshire v Bedfordshire
Wisbech	Cambridgeshire v Cumberland
Sandford	Devon v Wales MC
Sherborne School	Dorset v Wiltshire
Colwall	Herefordshire v Cornwall
Bishop's Stortford	Hertfordshire v Northumberland
Sleaford	Lincolnshire v Norfolk
Shifnal	Shropshire v Cheshire
West Brom Dartmth	Staffordshire v Suffolk

Sun 1 July	**KNOCK-OUT TROPHY – Semi-finals**
tbc	Winner Match Y v Winner Match W
tbc	Winner Match X v Winner Match Z

Sun 8 – Tue 10 July	**MCCA CHAMPIONSHIP**
Werrington	Cornwall v Devon
Netherfield	Cumberland v Staffordshire
Eastnor	Herefordshire v Shropshire
Cleethorpes	Lincolnshire v Cambridgeshire
Jesmond	Northumberland v Buckinghamshire
Banbury	Oxfordshire v Dorset
Bury St Edmunds	Suffolk v Bedfordshire
Abergavenny	Wales MC v Cheshire
Corsham	Wiltshire v Berkshire

Sun 15 July	**TWENTY20 COMPETITION**
Workington	Cumberland v Northumberland (1)

Sun 22 – Tue 24 July	**MCCA CHAMPIONSHIP**
Bedford School	Bedfordshire v Northumberland
Finchampstead	Berkshire v Shropshire
Chesham	Buckinghamshire v Lincolnshire
Nantwich	Cheshire v Dorset
St Austell	Cornwall v Wiltshire
Furness	Cumberland v Hertfordshire
Plymouth	Devon v Herefordshire
St Edward's School	Oxfordshire v Wales MC
Checkley	Staffordshire v Cambridgeshire
Copdock	Suffolk v Norfolk

Sun 5 – Tue 7 August
Flitwick
Falkland
Fenner's
Truro
Bournemouth
Brockhampton
North Mymms
Grantham
Manor Park
Pontarddulais

MCCA CHAMPIONSHIP
Bedfordshire v Cumberland
Berkshire v Devon
Cambridgeshire v Buckinghamshire
Cornwall v Cheshire
Dorset v Shropshire
Herefordshire v Oxfordshire
Hertfordshire v Suffolk
Lincolnshire v Northumberland
Norfolk v Staffordshire
Wales MC v Wiltshire

Sun 12 – Tue 14 August
Manor Park

MCCA CHAMPIONSHIP
Norfolk v Hertfordshire

Sun 19 – Tue 23 August
Chester, Br Hall
Sidmouth
Hertford
Manor Park
Jesmond
Banbury
Oswestry
Longton
Ipswich School
South Wilts

MCCA CHAMPIONSHIP
Cheshire v Berkshire
Devon v Dorset
Hertfordshire v Bedfordshire
Norfolk v Cambridgeshire
Northumberland v Cumberland
Oxfordshire v Cornwall
Shropshire v Wales MC
Staffordshire v Buckinghamshire
Suffolk v Lincolnshire
Wiltshire v Herefordshire

Sun 26 August
Wormsley

TWENTY20 COMPETITION
FINALS DAY (Reserve day 27 Aug)

Tue 28 August
Wormsley

MCCA v MCC

Wed 29 August
Wormsley

KNOCKOUT TROPHY
FINAL (Reserve day 30 Aug)

Sun 2 – Tue 4 September
Luton Town & I
Tring Park
Saffron Walden
Alderley Edge
Carlisle
North Perrott
S Northumberland
Bridgnorth
Usk
Marlborough

MCCA CHAMPIONSHIP
Bedfordshire v Norfolk
Buckinghamshire v Hertfordshire
Cambridgeshire v Suffolk
Cheshire v Herefordshire
Cumberland v Lincolnshire
Dorset v Berkshire
Northumberland v Staffordshire
Shropshire v Devon
Wales MC v Cornwall
Wiltshire v Oxfordshire

Sun 16 – Wed 19 September
Banbury

MCCA CHAMPIONSHIP
FINAL

MCCA TWENTY20 COMPETITION GROUPS

Group 1	*Group 2*	*Group 3*	*Group 4*
Cheshire	Berkshire	Bedfordshire	Cornwall
Cumberland	Buckinghamshire	Cambridgeshire	Devon
Lincolnshire	Herefordshire	Hertfordshire	Dorset
Northumberland	Oxfordshire	Norfolk	Wales MC
Staffordshire	Shropshire	Suffolk	Wiltshire

SECOND XI CHAMPIONSHIP FIXTURES 2018

THREE-DAY MATCHES

APRIL

Mon 16	Kibworth	Leics v MCC YC
	Notts SC	Notts v Derbyshire
Tue 17	Hove	Sussex v Essex
Mon 23	Liverpool	Lancashire v Derbyshire
	H Wycombe	MCC YC v Northants
Tue 24	Polo Farm Cant	Kent v Somerset
	EFSG, Birm	Warwicks v Worcs

MAY

Tue 1	Uxbridge	Middlesex v Glos
	Taunton Vale	Somerset v Surrey
Mon 7	Hem Heath	Derbyshire v Warwicks
Wed 9	Beckenham	Kent v Middlesex
	H Wycombe	MCC YC v Worcs
	Milton Keynes	Northants v Lancashire
	Leeds	Yorkshire v Durham
Tue 15	Newport	Glamorgan v Sussex
	Southampton	Hampshire v Kent
Tue 22	Chester-le-St	Durham v Northants
	Billericay	Essex v Hampshire
	Newport	Glamorgan v Somerset
	Kibworth	Leics v Notts
	EFSG, Birm	Warwicks v Yorkshire
	Barnt Green	Worcs v Lancashire
Mon 28	Southgate	Middlesex v Surrey
	Notts SC	Notts v Durham
Tue 29	Northampton	Northants v Derbyshire
Wed 30	Neath	Glamorgan v Hampshire
	Hove	Sussex v Kent

JUNE

Tue 5	Chester-le-St	Durham v Lancashire
	B Stortford	Essex v Somerset
	Beckenham	Kent v Glamorgan
	Stourbridge	Worcs v Notts
Wed 6	Blackstone	Sussex v Middlesex
	York	Yorkshire v MCC YC
Mon 11	Rockhampton	Glos v Surrey
	Barnt Green	Warwicks v MCC YC
Tue 12	Billericay	Essex v Glamorgan
	Southport	Lancashire v Yorkshire
	Kidderminster	Worcs v Durham
Mon 18	Polo Farm Cant	Kent v Glos
	Radlett	Middlesex v Hampshire
	LSE, N Malden	Surrey v Sussex

Mon 25	Notts SC	Notts v MCC YC
Tue 26	Burnopfield	Durham v Derbyshire
	Chester BH	Lancashire v Warwicks
	Kidderminster	Worcs v Northants
	York	Yorkshire v Leics

JULY

Tue 3	Neath	Glamorgan v Middlesex
	tbc	Leics v Wotcs
	H Wycombe	MCC YC v Derbyshire
	EFSG, Birm	Warwicks v Durham
Mon 9	Glossop	Derbyshire v Yorkshire
Tue 10	S N'berland	Durham v MCC YC
	tbc	Leics v Warwicks
	Uxbridge	Middlesex v Essex
	LSE, N Malden	Surrey v Hampshire
Wed 11	Taunton Vale	Somerset v Sussex
Tue 17	Bristol CC	Glos v Essex
	Southampton	Hampshire v Somerset
Tue 24	Bath	Glos v Sussex
	H Wycombe	MCC YC v Lancashire
	Desborough T	Northants v Yorkshire
	Taunton Vale	Somerset v Middlesex
	LSE, N Malden	Surrey v Glamorgan
	EFSG, Birm	Warwicks v Notts
Wed 25	Kibworth	Leics v Durham
Tue 31	Coggeshall	Essex v Kent
	Southampton	Hampshire v Glos
	Liverpool	Lancashire v Notts
	Desborough T	Northants v Leics
	Harrogate	Yorkshire v Worcs

AUGUST

Mon 6	Belper Mead	Derbyshire v Worcs
	Notts SC	Notts v Northants
	LSE, N Malden	Surrey v Kent
Mon 13	Notts SC	Notts v Yorkshire
	LSE, N Malden	Surrey v Essex
Tue 14	Taunton Vale	Somerset v Glos
Wed 15	Blackpool	Lancashire v Leics
Mon 20	Chesterfield	Derbyshire v Leics
	Preston Nth	Sussex v Northants
Tue 21	Bristol CC	Glos v Glamorgan
Wed 22	Holcot	Northants v Warwicks

SEPTEMBER

Tue 4	tbc	FINAL (Four days)

SECOND XI TROPHY FIXTURES 2018

ONE-DAY MATCHES

APRIL
Mon 16	Hove	Sussex v Essex	
Mon 23	Polo Farm Cant	Kent v Somerset	
Thu 26	Northwood	MCC YC v Northants	
Mon 30	Saffron Walden	Unicorns v Hampshire	
	Ampthill (tbc)	Northants v Derbyshire	

MAY
Tue 1	Saffron Walden	Unicorns v Essex
	Barnt Green	Worcs v Warwicks
Wed 2	Leicester	Leics v Northants
Thu 3	Alvaston & B	Derbyshire v Worcs
	Notts SC	Notts v Warwicks
Fri 4	Stamford Brg	Yorkshire v Leics
Mon 7	Rockhampton	Glos v Surrey
Tue 8	Southampton	Hampshire v Sussex
	Beckenham	Kent v Middlesex
	Northwood	MCC YC v Worcs
	Northampton	Northants v Lancashire
	Taunton Vale	Somerset v Surrey
	Leeds	Yorkshire v Durham
Wed 9	Rockhampton	Glos v Glamorgan
Thu 10	Hem Heath	Derbyshire v Warwicks
	Taunton Vale	Somerset v Glamorgan
Sun 13	Uxbridge	Middlesex v Unicorns
Mon 14	Newport	Glamorgan v Sussex
	Southampton	Hampshire v Kent
	Dunstable	Northants v Notts
	LSE, N Malden	Surrey v Essex
	Newbury	Unicorns v Somerset
Tue 15	Liverpool	Lancashire v Yorkshire
	Northwood	MCC YC v Durham
	Southgate	Middlesex v Glos
	Barnt Green	Warwicks v Leics

	Kidderminster	Worcs v Notts
Wed 16	Repton S	Derbyshire v Yorkshire
	Bath	Somerset v Glos
Thu 17	Hartlepool	Durham v Worcs
	Southend	Essex v Middlesex
	Crosby	Lancashire v Derbyshire
	Lutterworth	Leics v MCC YC
Mon 21	Chester-le-St	Durham v Northants
	Billericay	Essex v Hampshire
	Bristol CC	Glos v Kent
	Lutterworth	Leics v Notts
	Birmingham	Warwicks v Yorkshire
	Barnt Green	Worcs v Lancashire
Tue 22	Sunbury	Middlesex v Surrey
Thu 24	LSE, N Malden	Surrey v Sussex
	Bristol CC	Unicorns v Glos
Fri 25	Cardiff	Glamorgan v Unicorns
Tue 29	Neath	Glamorgan v Hampshire
	Crosby	Lancashire v Leics
	Hove	Sussex v Kent
Thu 31	Grantham	Notts v Durham

JUNE
Fri 1	Birmingham	Warwicks v MCC YC
Mon 4	Chester-le-St	Durham v Lancashire
	B Stortford	Essex v Somerset
	Bromley	Kent v Glamorgan
	Long Eaton	Notts v Derbyshire
Tue 5	Blackstone	Sussex v Middlesex
	York	Yorkshire v MCC YC
Fri 8	LSE, N Malden	Surrey v Hampshire
Fri 15	tbc	Semi-finals
Thu 21	tbc	FINAL

SECOND XI TWENTY20 CUP FIXTURES 2018

ONE-DAY MATCHES

MAY

Mon 14	Moseley	Warwicks v Durham

JUNE

Mon 11	Derby	Derbyshire v Notts
	Chelmsford	Essex v Glamorgan
	Worcester	Worcs v Durham
Wed 13	Eastbourne	Sussex v Unicorns
Thu 14	Newclose, IoW	Hampshire v Unicorns
Mon 18	Northwood	MCC YC v Leics
Tue 19	Derby	Derbyshire v Lancashire
	Brandon CC	Durham v Yorkshire
Thu 21	Polo Farm Cant	Kent v Glos
Mon 25	Burnopfield	Durham v Derbyshire
	Westhoughton	Lancashire v Warwicks
	LSE, N Malden	Surrey v Middlesex
	Worcester	Worcs v Northants
Tue 26	Bristol CC	Glos v Somerset
	Uxbridge	Middlesex v Kent
	Horsham	Sussex v Hampshire
Wed 27	LSE, N Malden	Surrey v Kent
Thu 28	Port Talbot	Glamorgan v Somerset
	Beckenham	Kent v Sussex
	Richmond	Middlesex v Hampshire
	Grantham	Notts v MCC YC

JULY

Mon 2	Newport	Glamorgan v Middlesex
	Leicester	Leics v Worcs
	Northwood	MCC YC v Derbyshire
	Northampton	Northants v Warwicks
Tue 3	East Grinstead	Sussex v Surrey
Wed 4	Taunton Vale	Somerset v Essex
	Harrogate	Yorkshire v Lancashire
Thu 5	Billericay	Essex v Unicorns

	Southampton	Hampshire v Surrey
	Worksop Col	Notts v Northants
Fri 6	Folkestone	Kent v Unicorns
Mon 9	S N'berland	Durham v MCC YC
	Newport	Glamorgan v Glos
	Manchester	Lancashire v Northants
	tbc	Leics v Warwicks
	Radlett	Middlesex v Essex
Tue 10	Taunton Vale	Somerset v Sussex
Thu 12	Barnsley	Yorkshire v Derbyshire
Mon 16	Bedminster	Glos v Essex
	Southampton	Hampshire v Somerset
	Birmingham	Warwicks v Worcs
Wed 18	Worksop Col	Notts v Yorkshire
	Wolverhampton	Worcs v MCC YC
Thu 19	Denby	Derbyshire v Leics
Mon 23	Bath	Glos v Sussex
	Slough	MCC YC v Lancashire
	Finedon	Northants v Yorkshire
	Taunton Vale	Somerset v Middlesex
	LSE, N Malden	Surrey v Glamorgan
	Barnt Green	Warwicks v Notts
Tue 24	Leicester	Leics v Durham
Mon 30	Southampton	Hampshire v Glos
	Liverpool	Lancashire v Notts
	Desborough T	Northants v Leics
	Marske	Yorkshire v Worcs

AUGUST

Wed 1	Knypersley	Unicorns v Surrey
Thu 2	Manor Pk, Nor	Unicorns v Glamorgan
Fri 3	Coggeshall	Essex v Kent
Thu 9	Arundel	FINALS DAY

PRINCIPAL FIXTURES 2018

CC1   Specsavers County Championship Division 1
CC2   Specsavers County Championship Division 2
F   Floodlit
FCF   First-Class Friendly
LOI   Royal London Limited-Overs International

50L   Royal London One-Day Cup
T20   Vitality T20 Blast
[T20]   Other Twenty20 match
IT20   Vitality Twenty20 International
TM   Investec Test Match
MCCU   MCC University
Uni   University match

Tue 27 – Fri 30 March
FCF[F]   Barbados   MCC v Essex

Sun 1 – Tue 3 April
Uni	Cambridge	Cambridge MCCU v Notts
Uni	Bristol	Glos v Cardiff MCCU
Uni	Canterbury	Kent v Oxford MCCU
Uni	Hove	Sussex v Loughboro MCCU
Uni	Birmingham	Warwicks v Durham MCCU
Uni	Worcs, RGS	Worcs v Leeds/Brad MCCU

Sat 7 – Tue 9 April
Uni	Cambridge	Cambridge MCCU v Essex
Uni	Southampton	Hampshire v Cardiff MCCU
Uni	Loughborough	Loughboro MCCU v Lancashire
Uni	Northwood	Middlesex v Durham MCCU
Uni	Oxford	Oxford MCCU v Northants
Uni	Leeds	Yorkshire v Leeds/Brad MCCU

Fri 13 – Mon 16 April
CC1	Southampton	Hampshire v Worcs
CC1	Manchester	Lancashire v Notts
CC1	Leeds	Yorkshire v Essex
CC2	Canterbury	Kent v Glos
CC2	Lord's	Middlesex v Northants
CC2	Birmingham	Warwicks v Sussex

Fri 13 – Sun 15 April
Uni	Chester-le-St	Durham v Durham MCCU
Uni	Cardiff	Glamorgan v Cardiff MCCU
Uni	Leeds, W'wd	Leeds/Brad MCCU v Derbyshire
Uni	Leicester	Leics v Loughboro MCCU
Uni	Taunton V	Somerset v Oxford MCCU
Uni	The Oval	Surrey v Cambridge MCCU

Fri 20 – Mon 23 April
CC1	Chelmsford	Essex v Lancashire
CC1	Taunton	Somerset v Worcs
CC1	The Oval	Surrey v Hampshire
CC1	Leeds	Yorkshire v Notts
CC2	Derby	Derbyshire v Middlesex
CC2	Chester-le-St	Durham v Kent
CC2	Bristol	Glos v Glamorgan
CC2	Leicester	Leics v Sussex
CC2	Northampton	Northants v Warwicks

Fri 27 – Mon 30 April
CC1	Southampton	Hampshire v Essex
CC1	Manchester	Lancashire v Surrey
CC1	Taunton	Somerset v Yorkshire
CC1	Worcester	Worcs v Notts
CC2	Leicester	Leics v Derbyshire
CC2	Lord's	Middlesex v Glamorgan
CC2	Northampton	Northants v Durham
CC2	Hove	Sussex v Glos

Sat 28 April – Tue 1 May
FCF   Canterbury   Kent v Pakistanis

Thu 3 – Sun 6 May
CC2   Birmingham   Warwicks v Derbyshire

Fri 4 – Mon 7 May
CC1	Chelmsford	Essex v Yorkshire
CC1	Manchester	Lancashire v Somerset
CC1	Nottingham	Notts v Hampshire
CC1	The Oval	Surrey v Worcs
CC2	Chester-le-St	Durham v Leics
CC2	Cardiff	Glamorgan v Kent
CC2	Hove	Sussex v Middlesex
FCF	Northampton	Northants v Pakistanis

Fri 11 – Mon 14 May
CC1	Nottingham	Notts v Lancashire
CC1	Taunton	Somerset v Hampshire
CC1	The Oval	Surrey v Yorkshire
CC1	Worcester	Worcs v Essex
CC2	Derby	Derbyshire v Durham
CC2	Canterbury	Kent v Sussex
CC2	Leicester	Leics v Glamorgan
CC2	Lord's	Middlesex v Glos
CC2	Birmingham	Warwicks v Northants

Thu 17 May
50L[F]	Manchester	Lancashire v Notts
50L	Radlett	Middlesex v Essex
50L	Northampton	Northants v Leics
50L	Hove	Sussex v Kent
50L	Birmingham	Warwicks v Derbyshire

Fri 18 May

50L^F	Chester-le-St	Durham v Yorkshire
50L	Cardiff	Glamorgan v Glos
50L	The Oval	Surrey v Somerset

Sat 19 – Sun 20 May

| | Leicester | Leics v Pakistanis |

Sat 19 May

| 50L | Hove | Sussex v Hampshire |
| 50L | Worcester | Worcs v Derbyshire |

Sun 20 May

50L	Bristol	Glos v Essex
50L	Manchester	Lancashire v Durham
50L	Radlett	Middlesex v Kent
50L	Welbeck	Notts v Northants
50L	Taunton	Somerset v Glamorgan
50L	Leeds	Yorkshire v Warwicks

Mon 21 May

| 50L^F | Southampton | Hampshire v Surrey |

Tue 22 May

| 50L | Taunton | Somerset v Sussex |

Wed 23 May

50L	Derby	Derbyshire v Durham
50L^F	Cardiff	Glamorgan v Middlesex
50L	Southampton	Hampshire v Essex
50L	Leicester	Leics v Notts
50L	Northampton	Northants v Lancashire
50L	The Oval	Surrey v Glos
50L	Leeds	Yorkshire v Worcs

Thu 24 – Mon 28 May

| TM1 | Lord's | ENGLAND v PAKISTAN |

Fri 25 May

50L	Derby	Derbyshire v Leics
50L	Gosforth	Durham v Worcs
50L^F	Chelmsford	Essex v Somerset
50L^F	Bristol	Glos v Hampshire
50L	Canterbury	Kent v Glamorgan
50L	Blackpool	Lancashire v Warwicks
50L	Hove	Sussex v Middlesex
50L	Leeds	Yorkshire v Notts

Sun 27 May

50L	Chelmsford	Essex v Surrey
50L	Bristol	Glos v Sussex
50L	Southampton	Hampshire v Kent
50L	Leicester	Leics v Yorkshire
50L	Northampton	Northants v Durham
50L	Nottingham	Notts v Warwicks
50L	Taunton	Somerset v Middlesex
50L	Worcester	Worcs v Lancashire

Tue 29 May

50L^F	Canterbury	Kent v Somerset
50L	The Oval	Surrey v Sussex
50L	Worcester	Worcs v Leics

Wed 30 May

50L	Derby	Derbyshire v Yorkshire
50L	Chelmsford	Essex v Glamorgan
50L	Northwood	Middlesex v Hampshire
50L^F	Birmingham	Warwicks v Northants

Thu 31 May

| 50L | tbc | Leics v Lancashire |
| ^{F} | Lord's | West Indies v World XI |

Fri 1 – Tue 5 June

| TM2 | Leeds | ENGLAND v PAKISTAN |

Fri 1 June

50L^F	Chester-le-St	Durham v Warwicks
50L	Cardiff	Glamorgan v Sussex
50L	Beckenham	Kent v Surrey
50L^F	Northampton	Northants v Derbyshire
50L	Nottingham	Notts v Worcs
50L	Taunton	Somerset v Glos

Sun 3 June

50L	Derby	Derbyshire v Lancashire
50L	Chester-le-St	Durham v Notts
50L	Swansea	Glamorgan v Hampshire
50L	Beckenham	Kent v Glos
50L	Lord's	Middlesex v Surrey
50L	Eastbourne	Sussex v Essex
50L	Birmingham	Warwicks v Leics
50L	Worcester	Worcs v Northants

Tue 5 June

| 50L | Manchester | Lancashire v Yorkshire |

Wed 6 June

50L^F	Chelmsford	Essex v Kent
50L^F	Bristol	Glos v Middlesex
50L^F	Southampton	Hampshire v Somerset
50L^F	The Oval	Surrey v Glamorgan

Thu 7 June

50L^F	Leicester	Leics v Durham
50L^F	Nottingham	Notts v Derbyshire
50L^F	Birmingham	Warwicks v Worcs
50L^F	Leeds	Yorkshire v Northants
^{F}	Hove	Sussex v Australians

Sat 9 – Tue 12 June

CC1	Southampton	Hampshire v Surrey
CC1	Manchester	Lancashire v Essex
CC1	Taunton	Somerset v Notts
CC2	Chester-le-St	Durham v Derbyshire
CC2	Bristol	Glos v Kent

CC2	Northampton	Northants v Leics
CC2	Birmingham	Warwicks v Glamorgan

Sat 9 June
	Lord's	Middlesex v Australians

Sun 10 June
LOI	Edinburgh	**Scotland v England**

Wed 13 June
LOI[F]	The Oval	**England v Australia**

Thu 14 June
50L[F]	tbc	Quarter-final 1 & 2

Sat 16 June
LOI	Cardiff	**England v Australia**

Sun 17 June
50L	tbc	Semi-final 1
	Birmingham	Warwicks v West Indies A
	Leeds	Yorkshire v India A

Mon 18 June
50L[F]	tbc	Semi-final 2

Tue 19 June
LOI[F]	Nottingham	**England v Australia**
	Leicester	Leics v India A
	Worcester	Worcs v West Indies A

Wed 20 – Sat 23 June
CC1	Chelmsford	Essex v Notts
CC1[F]	Southampton	Hampshire v Yorkshire
CC1	Guildford	Surrey v Somerset
CC1	Worcester	Worcs v Lancashire
CC2	Swansea	Glamorgan v Derbyshire
CC2	Tunbridge W	Kent v Warwicks
CC2	Leicester	Leics v Middlesex
CC2[F]	Northampton	Northants v Glos
CC2	Arundel	Sussex v Durham

Thu 21 June
LOI[F]	Chester-le-St	**England v Australia**

Fri 22 June
	Derby	England Lions v India A
	Lord's	Oxford U v Cambridge U

Sat 23 June
	Derby	England Lions v West Indies A

Sun 24 June
LOI	Manchester	**England v Australia**

Mon 25 – Thu 28 June
CC1[F]	Chelmsford	Essex v Somerset
CC1	Manchester	Lancashire v Hampshire
CC1[F]	Nottingham	Notts v Worcs
CC1	Scarborough	Yorkshire v Surrey
CC2[F]	Derby	Derbyshire v Leics

CC2[F]	Chester-le-St	Durham v Warwicks
CC2	Cardiff	Glamorgan v Northants
CC2[F]	Canterbury	Kent v Middlesex

Mon 25 June
	Leicester	India A v West Indies A

Tue 26 June
	Leicester	England Lions v India A

Wed 27 June
IT20[F]	Birmingham	**England v Australia**

Thu 28 June
	Northampton	England Lions v West Indies A

Fri 29 June
	Northampton	India A v West Indies A

Sat 30 June
50L	Lord's	FINAL

Mon 2 – Thu 5 July
FCF	Oxford	Oxford U v Cambridge U

Mon 2 July
	The Oval	Lions/A team final

Tue 3 July
IT20	Manchester	**England v India**

Wed 4 – Sat 7 July
FCF	Beckenham	India A v West Indies A

Wed 4 July
T20[F]	Chelmsford	Essex v Sussex
T20[F]	Northampton	Northants v Leics
T20[F]	Nottingham	Notts v Warwicks

Thu 5 July
T20[F]	Manchester	Lancashire v Worcs
T20[F]	Lord's	Middlesex v Surrey
T20[F]	Leeds	Yorkshire v Durham

Fri 6 July
IT20	Cardiff	**England v India**
T20[F]	Derby	Derbyshire v Lancashire
T20[F]	Chelmsford	Essex v Middlesex
T20[F]	Southampton	Hampshire v Glamorgan
T20[F]	Leicester	Leics v Durham
T20[F]	Northampton	Northants v Notts
T20	Taunton	Somerset v Glos
T20[F]	The Oval	Surrey v Kent
T20	Worcester	Worcs v Warwicks

Sun 8 July
IT20	Bristol	**England v India**
T20	Derby	Derbyshire v Worcs
T20	Cardiff	Glamorgan v Sussex
T20	Manchester	Lancashire v Northants
T20	Leicester	Leics v Notts

T20	Uxbridge	Middlesex v Glos
T20	Taunton	Somerset v Kent
T20	Birmingham	Warwicks v Yorkshire

Tue 10 – Fri 13 July
FCF	Taunton	India A v West Indies A

Wed 11 July
T20^F	Bristol	Glos v Kent
T20^F	Leeds	Yorkshire v Derbyshire

Thu 12 July
LOI	Nottingham	**England v India**
T20^F	Southampton	Hampshire v Sussex
T20^F	The Oval	Surrey v Essex

Fri 13 July
T20^F	Derby	Derbyshire v Notts
T20^F	Chester-le-St	Durham v Yorkshire
T20^F	Chelmsford	Essex v Glamorgan
T20^F	Bristol	Glos v Somerset
T20	Beckenham	Kent v Hampshire
T20^F	Hove	Sussex v Surrey
T20^F	Birmingham	Warwicks v Leics
T20	Worcester	Worcs v Northants

Sat 14 July
LOI	Lord's	**England v India**
T20	Manchester	Lancashire v Derbyshire

Sun 15 July
T20	Birmingham	Warwicks v Durham
T20	Worcester	Worcs v Yorkshire

Mon 16 – Thu 19 July
CC2	Cheltenham	Glos v Sussex
FCF	Worcester	England Lions v India A

Mon 16 – Wed 18 July
FCF	The Oval	Surrey v West Indies A

Tue 17 July
LOI	Leeds	**England v India**
T20^F	Nottingham	Notts v Durham

Wed 18 July
T20^F	Leicester	Leics v Lancashire

Thu 19 July
T20^F	Lord's	Middlesex v Somerset
T20^F	Northampton	Northants v Derbyshire

Fri 20 July
T20^F	Chester-le-St	Durham v Worcs
T20^F	Cardiff	Glamorgan v Somerset
T20	Cheltenham	Glos v Essex
T20^F	Southampton	Hampshire v Middlesex
T20^F	Canterbury	Kent v Surrey
T20^F	Manchester	Lancashire v Yorkshire

T20^F	Nottingham	Notts v Leics
T20^F	Birmingham	Warwicks v Northants

Sat 21 July
T20^F	Chelmsford	Essex v Hampshire

Sun 22 – Wed 25 July
CC1	Manchester	Lancashire v Yorkshire
CC1	Nottingham	Notts v Surrey
CC1	Worcester	Worcs v Somerset
CC2	Chesterfield	Derbyshire v Northants
CC2	Cheltenham	Glos v Durham
CC2	Canterbury	Kent v Leics
CC2	Lord's	Middlesex v Warwicks
CC2^F	Hove	Sussex v Glamorgan

Wed 25 – Sat 28 July
FCF	Chelmsford	Essex v Indians

Thu 26 July
T20^F	Lord's	Middlesex v Hampshire
T20^F	The Oval	Surrey v Somerset

Fri 27 July
T20	Cheltenham	Glos v Glamorgan
T20^F	Canterbury	Kent v Sussex
T20^F	Leicester	Leics v Derbyshire
T20^F	Northampton	Northants v Worcs
T20^F	Nottingham	Notts v Lancashire
T20^F	Leeds	Yorkshire v Warwicks

Sat 28 July
T20	Chesterfield	Derbyshire v Yorkshire
T20	Chester-le-St	Durham v Notts

Sun 29 July
T20	Cardiff	Glamorgan v Kent
T20	Taunton	Somerset v Middlesex
T20	Hove	Sussex v Hampshire
T20	Worcester	Worcs v Lancashire

Tue 31 July
T20^F	The Oval	Surrey v Glamorgan
T20^F	Leeds	Yorkshire v Leics

Wed 1 – Sun 5 August
TM1	Birmingham	**ENGLAND v INDIA**

Wed 1 August
T20	Taunton	Somerset v Hampshire
T20^F	Hove	Sussex v Glos

Thu 2 August
T20^F	Chester-le-St	Durham v Northants
T20^F	Canterbury	Kent v Essex
T20^F	Leicester	Leics v Warwicks
T20^F	Lord's	Middlesex v Sussex
T20^F	Nottingham	Notts v Derbyshire

Fri 3 August

T20^F	Derby	Derbyshire v Warwicks
T20^F	Cardiff	Glamorgan v Glos
T20^F	Southampton	Hampshire v Kent
T20^F	Manchester	Lancashire v Leics
T20	Taunton	Somerset v Essex
T20^F	The Oval	Surrey v Middlesex
T20	Worcester	Worcs v Durham
T20^F	Leeds	Yorkshire v Northants

Sat 4 August

T20^F	Nottingham	Notts v Worcs

Sun 5 August

T20	Chelmsford	Essex v Surrey
T20	Canterbury	Kent v Glos
T20	Richmond	Middlesex v Glamorgan
T20	Northampton	Northants v Warwicks
T20	Hove	Sussex v Somerset

Tue 7 August

T20^F	Cardiff	Glamorgan v Essex
T20^F	Manchester	Lancashire v Durham

Wed 8 August

T20^F	Derby	Derbyshire v Northants
T20^F	Chester-le-St	Durham v Leics
T20^F	Southampton	Hampshire v Somerset

Thu 9 – Mon 13 August

TM2	Lord's	ENGLAND v INDIA

Thu 9 August

T20^F	Bristol	Glos v Middlesex
T20^F	The Oval	Surrey v Sussex
T20^F	Birmingham	Warwicks v Notts
T20	Worcester	Worcs v Derbyshire
T20^F	Leeds	Yorkshire v Lancashire

Fri 10 August

T20^F	Chelmsford	Essex v Glos
T20^F	Cardiff	Glamorgan v Hampshire
T20^F	Manchester	Lancashire v Warwicks
T20^F	Leicester	Leics v Worcs
T20^F	Northampton	Northants v Durham
T20^F	Nottingham	Notts v Yorkshire
T20	Taunton	Somerset v Surrey
T20^F	Hove	Sussex v Kent

Sat 11 August

T20^F	Derby	Derbyshire v Leics

Sun 12 August

T20	Chester-le-St	Durham v Lancashire
T20	Bristol	Glos v Surrey
T20	Southampton	Hampshire v Essex
T20	Beckenham	Kent v Middlesex
T20	Taunton	Somerset v Glamorgan
T20	Worcester	Worcs v Notts

Tue 14 August

T20^F	Hove	Sussex v Glamorgan

Wed 15 August

T20^F	The Oval	Surrey v Hampshire
T20^F	Birmingham	Warwicks v Lancashire

Thu 16 August

T20^F	Bristol	Glos v Sussex
T20^F	Canterbury	Kent v Somerset
T20^F	Lord's	Middlesex v Essex
T20^F	Northampton	Northants v Yorkshire

Fri 17 August

T20^F	Chester-le-St	Durham v Derbyshire
T20^F	Chelmsford	Essex v Kent
T20^F	Cardiff	Glamorgan v Surrey
T20^F	Southampton	Hampshire v Glos
T20^F	Leicester	Leics v Northants
T20^F	Hove	Sussex v Middlesex
T20^F	Birmingham	Warwicks v Worcs
T20^F	Leeds	Yorkshire v Notts

Sat 18 – Wed 22 August

TM3	Nottingham	ENGLAND v INDIA

Sun 19 – Wed 22 August

CC1	Southampton	Hampshire v Notts
CC1	Taunton	Somerset v Essex
CC1^F	The Oval	Surrey v Lancashire
CC1	Scarborough	Yorkshire v Worcs
CC2	Cardiff	Glamorgan v Durham
CC2	Leicester	Leics v Kent
CC2	Northampton	Northants v Middlesex
CC2	Hove	Sussex v Derbyshire
CC2	Birmingham	Warwicks v Glos

Thu 23 August

T20^F	tbc	Quarter-final 1

Fri 24 August

T20^F	tbc	Quarter-final 2

Sat 25 August

T20^F	tbc	Quarter-final 3

Sun 26 August

T20	tbc	Quarter-final 4

Wed 29 August – Sat 1 September

CC1	Chelmsford	Essex v Hampshire
CC1	Southport	Lancashire v Worcs
CC1	The Oval	Surrey v Notts
CC1	Leeds	Yorkshire v Somerset
CC2	Derby	Derbyshire v Kent
CC2	Chester-le-St	Durham v Northants
CC2	Colwyn Bay	Glamorgan v Warwicks
CC2	Bristol	Glos v Leics
CC2	Lord's	Middlesex v Sussex

Thu 30 August – Mon 3 September		
TM4	Southampton	**ENGLAND v INDIA**
Tue 4 – Fri 7 September		
CC1	Chelmsford	Essex v Surrey
CC1	Nottingham	Notts v Yorkshire
CC1	Taunton	Somerset v Lancashire
CC1	Worcester	Worcs v Hampshire
CC2	Derby	Derbyshire v Glamorgan
CC2	Bristol	Glos v Middlesex
CC2	Canterbury	Kent v Northants
CC2	Hove	Sussex v Leics
CC2	Birmingham	Warwicks v Durham
Fri 7 – Tue 11 September		
TM5	The Oval	**ENGLAND v INDIA**
Mon 10 – Thu 13 September		
CC1	Southampton	Hampshire v Somerset
CC1	Nottingham	Notts v Essex
CC1	Worcester	Worcs v Surrey
CC1	Leeds	Yorkshire v Lancashire
CC2	Chester-le-St	Durham v Sussex
CC2	Cardiff	Glamorgan v Glos
CC2	Leicester	Leics v Warwicks

CC2	Lord's	Middlesex v Kent
CC2	Northampton	Northants v Derbyshire
Sat 15 September		
T20F	Birmingham	Semi-finals and FINAL
Tue 18 – Fri 21 September		
CC1	Chelmsford	Essex v Worcs
CC1	Taunton	Somerset v Surrey
CC1	Leeds	Yorkshire v Hampshire
CC2	Bristol	Glos v Northants
CC2	Canterbury	Kent v Glamorgan
CC2	Leicester	Leics v Durham
CC2	Lord's	Middlesex v Derbyshire
CC2	Hove	Sussex v Warwicks
Mon 24 – Thu 27 September		
CC1	Southampton	Hampshire v Lancashire
CC1	Nottingham	Notts v Somerset
CC1	The Oval	Surrey v Essex
CC1	Worcester	Worcs v Yorkshire
CC2	Derby	Derbyshire v Glos
CC2	Chester-le-St	Durham v Middlesex
CC2	Cardiff	Glamorgan v Leics
CC2	Northampton	Northants v Sussex
CC2	Birmingham	Warwicks v Kent

TEST MATCH CHAMPIONSHIP SCHEDULE

Months indicate the start of a series. Number of Tests in brackets. All series, especially those involving Pakistan and Zimbabwe, are subject to confirmation. Other Tests involving Ireland and Afghanistan, after their matches in Dublin on 11-15 May and in Bangalore on 14-18 June, respectively, my still be arranged.

2018	May	**England hosts Pakistan (2)**		Nov	Pakistan hosts New Zealand (3)
	May	Ireland hosts Pakistan (1)		Nov	Bangladesh hosts West Indies (2)
	Jun	Zimbabwe hosts Australia (1)		Dec	Australia hosts India (4)
	Jun	India hosts Afghanistan (1)		Dec	New Zealand hosts Sri Lanka (2)
	July	West Indies hosts Sri Lanka (3)		Dec	South Africa hosts Pakistan (3)
	Aug	**England hosts India (5)**	2019	Jan	Australia hosts Sri Lanka (2)
	Aug	Zimbabwe hosts Pakistan (2)		Jan	Bangladesh hosts Zimbabwe (3)
	Aug	Sri Lanka hosts South Africa (3)		**Feb**	**West Indies hosts England (3)**
	Aug	Zimbabwe hosts Pakistan (2)		Feb	New Zealand hosts Bangladesh (3)
	Aug	Australia hosts Bangladesh (2)		Feb	South Africa hosts Sri Lanka (3)
	Oct	**Sri Lanka hosts England (3)**		Mar	India hosts Zimbabwe (1)
	Oct	India hosts West Indies (3)		Mar	Pakistan hosts Australia (3)
	Oct	South Africa hosts Zimbabwe (1)			**30 May – 15 July World Cup in England**

Copyright © 2018 Headline Publishing Group

The right of Ian Marshall to be identified as the Author of
the Work has been asserted by him in accordance with the
Copyright, Designs and Patents Act 1988.

First published in 2018

by HEADLINE PUBLISHING GROUP

Front cover photograph James Anderson
(England and Lancashire)
© Michael Dodge/Getty Images

Back cover photograph Heather Knight
(England and Berkshire)
© Mark Kerton/Action Plus via Getty Images

1

Apart from any use permitted under UK copyright law, this publication
may only be reproduced, stored, or transmitted, in any form, or by any
means, with prior permission in writing of the publishers or, in the
case of reprographic production, in accordance with the terms
of licences issued by the Copyright Licensing Agency.

Every effort has been made to fulfil requirements with regard to
reproducing copyright material. The author and publisher will
be glad to rectify any omissions at the earliest opportunity.

Cataloguing in Publication Data is available from the British Library

ISBN: 978 1 4722 4982 1

Typeset in Times by
Letterpart Limited, Caterham on the Hill, Surrey

Printed and bound in Great Britain by
Clays Ltd St Ives plc

Headline's policy is to use papers that are natural, renewable and
recyclable products and made from wood grown in sustainable forests.
The logging and manufacturing processes are expected to conform
to the environmental regulations of the country of origin.

HEADLINE PUBLISHING GROUP

An Hachette UK Company
Carmelite House
50 Victoria Embankment
London EC4Y 0DZ

www.headline.co.uk
www.hachette.co.uk